3RD EDITION

INDUSTRY MATTERS

ENGLISCH FÜR INDUSTRIEKAUFLEUTE

von
Michael Benford
Isobel Williams

sowie
Sandra Haberkorn und Sabine Steeg-Hintermeier

unter Mitarbeit der Verlagsredaktion

Cornelsen

INDUSTRY MATTERS

Verfasser/in:	Michael Benford, Bochum Isobel Williams, Berlin
Verfasserinnen KMK-Seiten:	Sandra Haberkorn und Sabine Steeg-Hintermeier, Wiesbaden
Berater/innen:	Marc Engels, Erkelenz; Sandra Haberkorn, Wiesbaden; Alexandra Köpf, Ulm; Freya Preuss, Bochum; Bianca Sonnenschein, Erkelenz
Projektleitung:	Andreas Goebel
Verlagsredaktion:	Kari-ann Warnakulasuriya
Außenredaktion:	James Abram
Redaktionelle Mitarbeit:	Verena Groß, Katarina Hlavata, Christine House, Oliver Busch (Wörterverzeichnisse)
Bildredaktion:	Gertha Maly, Christina Scheuerer
Layoutkonzept:	finedesign, Berlin
Gesamtgestaltung und technische Umsetzung:	vitaledesign, Berlin
Umschlaggestaltung:	vitaledesign, Berlin
Coverfoto:	Shutterstock / Valerii Iavtushenko (Fabrik); Shutterstock / Undrey (Innenbüro)
Illustrationen:	Oxford Designers & Illustrators

Erhältlich sind auch:
Handreichungen für den Unterricht mit MP3-CD und Online-Zusatzmaterialien
ISBN 978-3-06-451642-7

www.cornelsen.de

1. Auflage, 1. Druck 2018

Alle Drucke dieser Auflage sind inhaltlich unverändert und können im Unterricht nebeneinander verwendet werden.

Druck: Mohn Media Mohndruck, Gütersloh

ISBN 978-3-06-451640-3
ISBN 978-3-06-451641-0 (E-Book)

PEFC
PEFC/04-31-1033

PEFC zertifiziert
Dieses Produkt stammt aus nachhaltig bewirtschafteten Wäldern und kontrollierten Quellen.
www.pefc.de

Vorwort

Industry Matters 3rd edition ist eine Neubearbeitung des bewährten Englisch-Lehrwerks für Industriekaufleute und wurde für die Ausbildung in Berufsschulen sowie die innerbetriebliche Aus- und Weiterbildung konzipiert.

Das Lehrwerk setzt Englischkenntnisse voraus, die dem Niveau B1 des Europäischen Referenzrahmens *(Common European Framework of Reference)* entsprechen. Es deckt die Themen der aktuellen Lehrpläne der Bundesländer für Englisch in der Berufsschule konsequent ab.

Industry Matters 3rd edition besteht aus zwölf Units, die flexibel einsetzbar sind. Jede Unit umfasst vier abgeschlossene Lernsituationen, die jeweils in einer Doppelstunde bearbeitet werden können. Eine Unit ist wie folgt aufgebaut:

Foundation: Diese Doppelseite bietet Ihnen mit Grundwissen und elementarem Themenvokabular einen Einstieg in das Thema der Unit.

Part A/B: Diese stark berufsbezogenen ausgerichteten Module können je nach Umfang der Inputmaterialien jeweils zwei bis vier Seiten umfassen. Hier werden fachspezifische Schwerpunkte der Unit mithilfe authentischer und aktueller Materialien behandelt.

Communication: Berufliche Kommunikation steht im Fokus des abschließenden *Communication*-Teils. Ein „Das kann ich"-Kästchen – eine Checkliste zur Selbstevaluation – rundet die Unit ab und ermöglicht es den Lernenden, über ihren persönlichen Lernerfolg zu reflektieren.

Alle Lernsituationen sind so konzipiert, dass sie ausgelassen oder zu einem anderen Zeitpunkt behandelt werden können. Somit berücksichtigt die Modulstruktur einer jeden Unit die organisatorische Vielfalt des Englischunterrichts und schafft größtmögliche Flexibilität im Unterricht.

Besonderer Wert wird in diesem Lehrwerk auf **Handlungsorientierung** und direkten Berufsbezug gelegt: Jedes Modul beginnt mit einer branchenspezifischen *Situation* und führt über handlungs- und kompetenzorientierte Lernschritte zu einem Handlungsprodukt. Dieses Lernziel ist jeweils zu Beginn des Moduls mit einem Pfeil gekennzeichnet und ermöglicht so eine schnelle Orientierung.

Unterschiedliche Aktions- und Sozialformen ermöglichen zudem den Einsatz von kooperativen Lernformen und fördern **eigenverantwortliches Lernen**.

Um der Heterogenität der Auszubildenden gerecht zu werden, finden sich zahlreiche Aufgaben zur **Binnendifferenzierung** in den Units. Diese sind mit einem Strich unter der Aufgabenziffer gekennzeichnet und verweisen auf editierbare Kopiervorlagen in den Handreichungen, die alternative Bearbeitungsmöglichkeiten für die jeweilige Aufgabe zur Verfügung stellen.

Zur Vorbereitung auf die **KMK-Prüfung** Stufen II und III werden anhand von sechs Unterrichtseinheiten und einer kompletten Musterprüfung prüfungsrelevante Materialien und Aufgaben angeboten und so eine systematische Prüfungsvorbereitung ermöglicht.

Grundlegende grammatikalische Strukturen werden durchweg im **situativen Kontext** vermittelt, ergänzt durch eine systematische Grammatikübersicht im Anhang und Übungsmaterialien in den Handreichungen. Zur Erweiterung des berufsrelevanten Wortschatzes werden Themenwortschätze im Anhang angeboten sowie eine umfangreiche *Unit word list* mit allen neuen Wörtern in chronologischer Reihenfolge wie auch eine *A–Z word list* mit allen neuen Wörtern in alphabetischer Reihenfolge. Außerdem im Anhang finden Sie berufsbezogene *Useful phrases*, die eine effektive berufliche Kommunikation erleichtern plus eine Aufstellung der Incoterms.

Sämtliche Audiomaterialien finden Sie in den Handreichungen für den Unterricht und darüber hinaus geben kurze **Videos** passend zu den Themen kurze Einblicke in das spätere Berufsleben und vermitteln Fachwissen in motivierender Form. Diese Materialien und die dazugehörigen Arbeitsblätter stehen den Lehrkräften online zur Verfügung.

Der Verlag, die Autoren sowie die Berater und Beraterinnen wünschen Ihnen viel Erfolg und Freude mit *Industry Matters 3rd edition*.

Table of contents

1 Working conditions

FOUNDATION: My apprenticeship

Situation: You are an apprentice at Orbit Group AG, a specialist steel company whose working language is English. The company is looking for new international trainees.
→ **You write a description of your apprenticeship for the trainee section of the website.**

1 Describing two apprenticeships

Your line manager asks you to write an English description of your apprenticeship for the website, so you look online for some examples.

A 2)) **Read and listen to what Sophie says, then copy and complete the chart.**

Hello. My name is Sophie, I'm 19 years old. I'm from Bremen. I left school last year with A levels in English, German and Mathematics. I work at ABC Manufacturing where I'm training to be an industrial management assistant. My apprenticeship lasts for three years. I'm doing a work-based apprenticeship. I work in the office from 9 to 5 and do block release at vocational school every three months. I get a small salary from the company. It's not much, but I still live with my parents, so I don't have expenses like rent or food. My colleagues are great and help me a lot. I'd like to work in one of the company's foreign branches one day.

1 school qualifications		
2 training company		
3 name of apprenticeship		
4 details of apprenticeship	– length	
	– type	
	– hours in company	
	– time at vocational school	
5 who pays her living expenses		
6 hopes for the future		

B 3)) **Listen to Robert describing his training and answer these questions.**

1 What are Robert's school qualifications?
2 Where does he work?
3 What will Robert be when he qualifies?
4 How long does his apprenticeship last?
5 What type of training course is he doing?
6 How is his training divided between the office and vocational school?
7 Who pays for Robert's course?
8 What does Robert hope for the future?

2 Talking about your apprenticeship

You talk about your apprenticeship with your colleagues.

Work with a partner from a different training company. Ask and answer questions about your apprenticeship. Use ideas from exercise 1 to structure your conversation.

› *Useful phrases: Describing apprenticeships, page 187*

Asking for information

Who do you work for?
What is the name of your company?
Where is the company located?
How many employees does your company have?

› *Grammar: Questions and short answers, page 154*

3 Reading about the dual education system

You also read online about Germany's dual system of vocational training.

Read the text then answer the FAQs below it.

Most students in Germany complete their school education between the ages of 15 and 18. After that, some of them enter a dual training scheme at a vocational college. With this scheme, an apprentice gets job experience at work and theoretical knowledge of their profession at school.

An apprenticeship usually lasts between 24 and 36 months, depending on the profession. Apprentices spend 50 to 70 per cent of their time working in companies and the rest of the time in the classroom. Depending on the profession, an apprentice may do day release or block release.

The employer is responsible for the apprentice's training and education. They give the apprentices a special apprenticeship contract. The contract protects the apprentice from being fired during the training programme.

Gaining a vocational college qualification gives young workers good chances in their future lives. The qualification standards are the same throughout the whole of Germany, which means that the qualification is recognized by every company. Even though the German qualification is not recognized in some countries, the fact that someone has trained in Germany is often enough to get them a good position abroad.

FAQs

1. I would like to work in commerce. How can a dual training scheme help me?
2. Why do some apprenticeships last longer than others?
3. How will my time be split between in-company training and vocational school?
4. My friend is doing block release and I am doing day release. Why aren't we doing the same thing?
5. Who is responsible for my training?
6. Can my employer stop my training before I've finished my apprenticeship?
7. I might have to move to a different town after I qualify. How will my qualification help me find a new employer?
8. I would like to work abroad. How will my qualification help me get a job?

4 Writing about your apprenticeship

It is time to write about your apprenticeship for the trainee information page on your company website.

Write a short description of your training. Give your name, age and say where you are from. Then structure the rest of your description as below. Write about 150 words.

- your school qualification
- where you work
- what you are training to be
- a short explanation of the dual system
- a short description of your apprenticeship (block/day release; hours in the office / at school)

› *Thematic vocabulary, Training and apprenticeships, page 201*
› *Useful phrases: Describing apprenticeships, page 187*

PART A: Working conditions at my company

Situation: Orbit Group AG, a specialist steel company, encourages its employees to work at its branches all over the world. You attend a seminar in the UK about working conditions.
→ **You make a poster about working conditions at your training company in Germany.**

1 Describing ideal working conditions

The trainer first tells you to brainstorm some ideas about your ideal working conditions.

A **Choose the ten most import factors from the word cloud and add ideas of your own.**

medium-sized company · subsidized travel · hot-desking · smart clothes · small company · quiet office · overtime · open-plan office · canteen · big company · flexitime · customer contact · shift work · business English · company smartphone · company car · dress code · busy office · home office · job-sharing

B **Discuss your list with a partner. What points do you agree and disagree on? Give reasons.**

C **Conduct a class survey and find the five most important points. Explain why they are important to you.**

Agreeing and disagreeing

In my opinion, / I think a busy office is really important.
– I agree with you. / Yes, I think you're right.
– I disagree / don't agree. I think … is more important.

2 Comparing conditions

You listen to two other seminar participants, Lisa and Lukas, answering interview questions about their individual working conditions.

A 4 **Listen to the two interviews and make notes on the following points:**

- the size of the company
- current department
- total number of apprentices
- working hours, breaks, overtime
- dress code
- business trips
- employees' availability outside working hours
- facilities and benefits offered by the company
- job prospects at the company

B **Find an apprentice in your class from another company or department and interview each other about your working conditions. Use the list of points above.**

› *Grammar: Questions and short answers, page 154*
› *Thematic vocabulary: Training and apprenticeships, page 201*

3 Looking the part

Like most companies, Orbit Group AG has a dress code for its office staff regarding clothes, shoes, make-up and employees' general appearance.

A Copy the table below and complete it with words from the list to show what is and isn't appropriate for office staff to wear at your training company. Add more information if necessary.

a dress • black shoes • brown shoes • denim • earrings • flat shoes • flip-flops • heavy make-up • jacket • jacket and trousers • loud colours • low-cut tops • low-heeled shoes • shirt and tie • short skirts • shorts • skirt and blouse • suit • trainers • trouser suit • visible body piercings • visible tattoos

Dress code	appropriate		not appropriate	
	male	female	male	female
clothes				
shoes				
piercings, tattoos, jewellery, etc.				

B Read the article about a dress code dispute and then answer the questions below.

#myheelsmychoice

The following is an extract from an interview with Nicola Thorp, a young woman who broke her employer's dress code rules. She was sent by an agency to work as a receptionist at a management consultancy in London.

"That day I was wearing flat black shoes, and they gave me a dress and a jacket to wear which I put on and the supervisor said, 'Well, you're not going to wear those (pointing at my flat shoes). We only have women in heels in reception', and I said, 'Well, I think that's ridiculous.' I pointed to a male colleague and said, 'Well, he's wearing flat shoes. Why can't I?' and of course that's laughed at. I understand because that's a much bigger issue for people to get their heads round. Then she said to me, 'You can go out and buy a pair of heels if you like. We'll let you work.' I refused and was sent home [...] without pay."

The agency that employed her, Portico, said that personal appearance guidelines are in line with standard industry practice. After this incident, Nicola Thorp started a petition to change the law and used her Twitter account to get support online.

1 What clothes was Nicola expected to wear?
2 How did Nicola respond when she was asked to change her shoes?
3 What did her supervisor suggest and what happened when Nicola did not accept the suggestion?
4 What was the legal situation regarding high heels in the workplace?

C Was Nicola Thorp right or wrong? Her discussion on Twitter using the hashtag #myheelsmychoice attracted a lot of media attention. Divide your class into two groups, employees and employers, prepare arguments from your group's point of view and have a class discussion about what an employer can and can't expect an employee to wear in the workplace. Include the following points:

- the type of work (e.g. office, factory, hospital, hotel, commerce, banking, ...)
- customer-facing jobs versus back-office jobs
- company image/uniform

4 Describing your working conditions

Now it is time to describe the working conditions in your training company.

Working in groups, create a poster about the working conditions (in your department/company) and present it to the class. Use your answers in exercise 2B and add ideas of your own.

PART B: Working conditions abroad

Situation: Orbit Group AG, a specialist steel company, sends you to an international seminar about training and working conditions in different countries.
→ You discuss the advantages and disadvantages of the dual system of vocational training in Germany with other apprentices.

1 Comparing working conditions

You attend the seminar and the trainer gives you a diagram about how much paid free time to expect when working in different countries.

A **With a partner, use the list below to guess the names of the countries, giving reasons for your answers.**

Austria · Germany · Greece · Japan · UK · USA

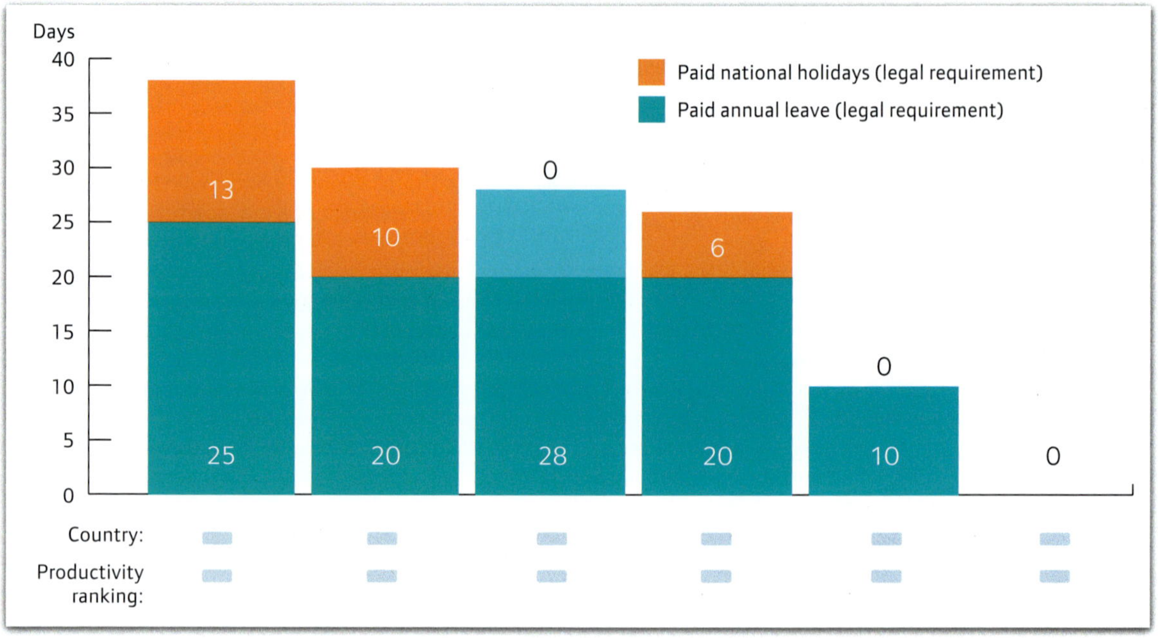

B **5))) Check your answers by listening to what the trainer says about the countries. Put them in order of productivity (1–6).**

C **5))) Listen again and complete the phrases from the dialogue with the words you hear.**

1 … the only country in which employers ___ pay their employees for national holidays and annual leave.
2 … they are ___ to last in our diagram …
3 Germany has the second ___ number of paid days off work …
4 Which of these two ___ pay its employees for 28 days' annual leave …?
5 Sorry, it's the UK in ___ place followed by …
6 … Greece, which has the ___ productivity.

D **Does anything surprise you about the data? Discuss it with your partner and the class.**

Expressing obligation

A German company **has to** give its employees paid annual leave.
German employers **have to** pay their employees on national holidays.
An American company **doesn't have to** give its employees paid annual leave.
American employers **don't have to** pay their employees on national holidays.

› *Grammar: Modals and their substitutes, page 158*

2 Describing your training

Two seminar participants, Selina from the US and Daniel from the UK, tell your group how they are preparing for a career in commerce.

Hi, I'm Selina Gonzales, I'm 19 and I've always wanted to work in commerce. I left school at 18 with a High School Diploma, I speak Spanish and I'm doing a 2-year associate's degree course in business administration at Rockland Community College in New York State. My final grade will be based on my coursework.
In my fourth semester, I'll do an internship at a company. Studying at a 2-year college from home is a lot cheaper than going to a 4-year college in a different city. I live at home for free and get help from my folks with the tuition fees, too. I also have time to work part-time in a convenience store, so I won't be in debt when I graduate. With my associate's degree I can either get a good job or do a bachelor's degree. My career goal is to be a buyer in the clothing industry.

I'm Daniel Chandler, I'm 19 and I left school last year with two A-levels. I wanted to learn about commerce and I didn't like the idea of going to uni and getting into debt, so I'm earning money by doing a work-based intermediate apprenticeship in business administration at Southampton Trading Ltd. I have an assessor from Eastleigh College, and she regularly visits me at my workplace. She talks to my line manager and gives me homework, which I upload to my electronic portfolio. My employer pays my college fees. There's no time limit or final examination because my grades are based on my assessor's reports and my coursework. I hope to complete the apprenticeship next year and then do an advanced apprenticeship with day release at Eastleigh College. This will take me another year and improve my chances of a better job, but my long-term goal is to have my own business one day.

Infobox

Nach Abschluss der Sekundarstufe II (evtl. mit *High School Diploma* [gleicht dem dt. Abitur]) besuchen viele nordamerikanische Schüler/innen ein *community college*, eine zweijährige Bildungseinrichtung zur Berufsausbildung und Vorbereitung auf ein Hochschulstudium dar. Der durch den Besuch eines *community college* erworbene Abschluss nennt sich *associate's degree*, und kann zum Erwerb eines *bachelor's degree* (Bachelorabschluss) angerechnet werden. Letzteres wird i. d. R. nach einem vierjährigen Studium an einer Hochschule erlangt. In Nordamerika ist eine Lehre (*apprenticeship*) im europäischen Sinne fast ausschließlich nur in technischen Berufen möglich.

Work with a partner and use the two texts and the notes below to role-play a conversation with Selina (US) and then with Daniel (UK) in which you both talk about your training.

- introductions
- academic qualifications
- current course/job
- finance
- assessment/grades
- future plans

Talking about the future

I**'ll do** an internship.
I **won't be** in debt
Will you **study**?

› *Grammar: Future with will and going to, page 155*

3 Comparing different training systems

The vocational training systems in industrialized countries vary greatly.

A **Take a few minutes to list the pros and cons of the German dual system. Think about:**

- how you get theoretical/practical training
- your experience at your company/college
- vocational training in other countries (e.g. UK, USA or a country you know about)

B **Make a list of pros and cons on the board and have a discussion about the dual system.**

COMMUNICATION: Introductions and small talk

Situation: You work in the Export department in the German branch of Orbit Group AG, a specialist steel company.
→ **You look after a visitor from England until your supervisor, Ms Müller, is ready to meet him.**

1 Introducing yourself and others to colleagues

The Human Resources department at Orbit Group AG stores information about its employees on computerized personnel files.

A 6 **Listen to the people introducing themselves. Copy and complete the entries in your notebook.**

Name: Martyna Nowak
Age: ___[1]
Place of birth: Poland
Job description: ___[2]

Name: Halil Özdemir
Age: ___[3]
Place of birth: ___[4]
Job description: training supervisor

Name: Deema Mansour
Age: ___[5]
Place of birth: Syria
Job description: ___[6]

Name: Robert Klein
Age: 21
Place of birth: ___[7]
Job description: ___[8]

Name: Canan Tolon
Age: ___[9]
Place of birth: Turkey
Job description: ___[10]

Name: Alexei Melnyk
Age: 29
Place of birth: ___[11]
Job description: ___[12]

B **You have three minutes to introduce yourself to the other people in the class.**

My name is …

I'm … years old.

I was born in …

I'm a/an …

Introducing yourself

I'm Sophie. I'm **from** Berlin. (NOT: I'm ~~coming~~ from Berlin.)
I work **at** ABC Import/Export. (NOT: I work ~~by~~ ABC Import/Export.)
I'm **an** office manager. / I'm **a** management assistant. (NOT: ~~My job is …~~)

C **Introduce one of the people you met to the rest of the class.**

This is …

He's/She's … years old.

He/She was born in …

He's/She's a/an …

2 Making formal introductions

A **Work with a partner. Introduce yourself in a formal way to your partner (a visitor).**

B **Now formally introduce your partner to another pair.** › *Useful phrases: Making introductions, page 187*

3 Making small talk

A **In groups, choose suitable topics for small talk in business. Say which topics you should avoid.**

holidays | your city/town | religion | the journey to the meeting place | illnesses | sport | politics | the weather | pay | where someone works

B **Match the questions (1–6) to the possible responses (a–f).**

1 Is this your first time in Berlin?
2 How is your hotel?
3 It's lovely weather, isn't it?
4 How was your journey?
5 Where are you based?

a Yes. It's fantastic. We've been very lucky this year.
b Very nice. I travelled by train this time.
c Yes. I've heard that it's a very interesting city.
d Fine. I have a good view from the window in my room.
e In Scotland. In Edinburgh, in fact.

4 Meeting and greeting the visitor

Now it is time to meet the visitor. You know that the person Ms Müller is expecting is called Mr Brown.

A **Work in groups of three. Complete the dialogue. Then close your books and practise the dialogue.**

You	*Excuse*[1] me. *Are you*[2] Mr Brown?
Visitor	Yes, I am.
You	I'm (own name). ___[3] do you do? ___[4] to Orbit Group.
Visitor	Thank you. It's ___ ___ ___ ___[5].
You	I'm afraid Ms Müller has been held up, but she'll be here in a few minutes. ___ ___ ___[6] your coat?
Visitor	Yes, thank you. Here you are.
You	___[7] you like something to drink?
Visitor	Yes, please. I'd like a cup of coffee with milk and sugar.
You	Here you are. Is this your ___ ___[8] in Germany?
Visitor	No. I've been here before, but only on holiday.
You	Oh. Here's Ms Müller now. Mr Brown, ___ ___[9] Ms Müller.
Ms Müller	___[10] morning, Mr Brown. Sorry to keep you waiting.
Visitor	No problem. Your assistant has been looking after me very well.

Offering help/refreshments

Can I take your coat?
Would you like something to drink?
Would you like some tea or coffee?

› *Useful phrases: Showing visitors around the company, page 189*

B **Write your own dialogue and practise it in your group.**

DAS KANN ICH (Unit 1)

- Eine kurze Beschreibung meiner dualen Ausbildung auf Englisch erstellen. (Foundation)
- Ein englisches Plakat über die Arbeitsbedingungen im Ausbildungsbetrieb gestalten. (Part A)
- Die Vor- und Nachteile des dualen Ausbildungssystems auf Englisch diskutieren. (Part B)
- Eine/n englischsprachige/n Besucher/in empfangen und jemandem vorstellen. (Communication)

2 My workplace

FOUNDATION: In the office

Situation: You are doing a work placement in the Administration department of a British manufacturing company. The office environment and cybersecurity are important aspects of your work.
→ **You summarize the cybersecurity procedures at your training company.**

1 Thinking about office activities

Before you start your inventory, you think about some of the things you have to do in the office.

A **Study the photos (1–6). What are the people doing?**

1

2

3

4

5

6

B **What equipment do you work with regularly?**
What do you (not) enjoy doing?

I use the computer every day. I have to key in data. I enjoy doing that.

Talking about likes and dislikes

I **like to make / making** photocopies.
I **prefer to work / working** at the computer.
I **enjoy meeting** customers. (NOT: I enjoy ~~to meet~~ ...)
I don't **enjoy writing** emails. (NOT: I don't enjoy ~~to write~~ ...)

› *Grammar: Verb + infinitive or -ing form, page 156*

2 Comparing types of offices

On your way to work, you listen to a podcast from Alisha Warner, an office consultant.

A 7)) **Listen and answer the questions.**

1 What is the main purpose of an office environment?
2 What is the benefit of working in a small office?
3 How are the workspaces divided in a lot of open-plan administration offices?
4 Why do some employees dislike this kind of office?
5 What are the two advantages of working at a shared table?
6 What are the pros and cons of hot-desking?

VIDEO 1

Watch the video for more information about different types of office.

B **What type of office do you prefer to work in? Give reasons.**

3 Cybersecurity

Are you and your employer up to date with cybersecurity?

A **Work with a partner and explain to each other what 'phishing' and 'a Trojan' mean.**

B **Match the words in the list with the definitions (1–6).**

botnet • DoS • pharming • ransomware • social engineering • spoofing

1 blocking access to a computer system until a sum of money is paid
2 flooding a computer with so many requests that it cannot operate normally or crashes
3 a network of compromised computers, a 'zombie' network
4 psychological tricks to make people give away sensitive information and/or do things
5 re-directing visitors from a popular website to an identical but fake website
6 sending emails that appear to come from someone else's email address

4 An infamous cyberattack

On average, there are at least 4,000 cyberattacks per day worldwide.

A **Read the text about an attack and answer the questions below.**

The *WannaCry* ransomware attack on 12 May 2017 infected 230,000 computers in over 150 countries. One of the largest organizations hit was the UK's National Health Service, with 70,000 devices such as computers, MRI scanners and blood-storage refrigerators affected. Some hospitals paid the ransom. Other targets were the Nissan and Renault car companies, Deutsche Bahn and FedEx. Experts say that these organizations were using outdated computer systems (e.g. Windows XP and Windows Server 2003) with no security updates.
Security experts now advise companies to …

- use cloud storage offered by a major provider with up-to-date cybersecurity to store all data,
- train their staff to understand the basic principles of cybersecurity,
- install cybersecurity software locally on all company computers and networks.

1 Why do you think some hospitals paid the ransom?
2 What did the organizations targeted have in common?
3 Why do experts now recommend using cloud storage?

B **Work with a partner from the same training company. Answer these questions, then report to the class.**

1 How and where is data stored at your training company?
2 When did you last receive cybersecurity training and what did you learn?
3 What guidelines are there at your company regarding passwords, email attachments and data security?

PART A: An organization chart

Situation: You work at Cantec GmbH, a canning machinery manufacturer in Essen. You are expecting some English-speaking visitors to the company, so you study the organization chart.
→ **You draw an organization chart of your training company.**

1 Understanding an organization chart

The chart shows the management, the heads of department and the numbers of staff and apprentices.

Cantec GmbH

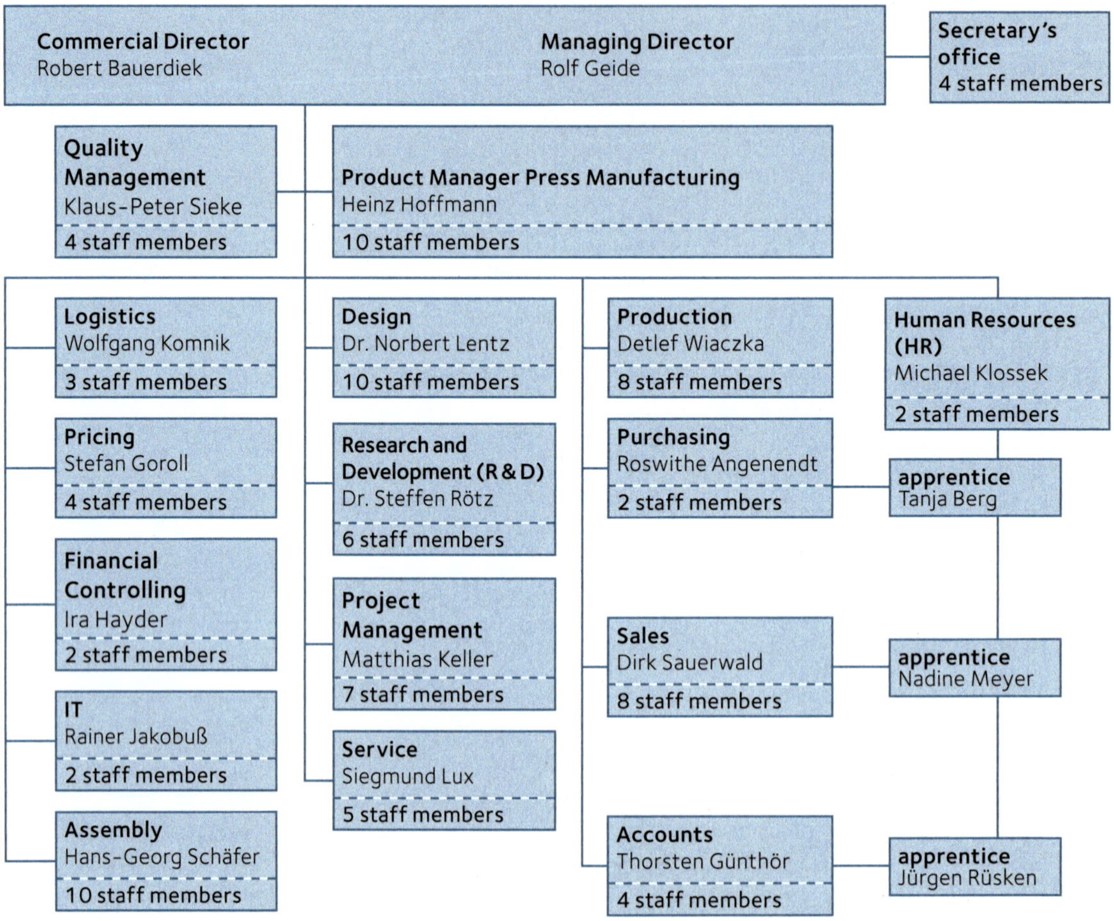

A Find a department in the chart for each of the descriptions below.

1 We work out how much the customer's order will cost.

2 We monitor how much money the company makes and spends.

3 We put the machines together here.

4 We buy the components needed for an order.

5 We find new products and improve existing ones.

6 We're responsible for employing and training people.

B **Decide whether the following statements about the organization chart are true or false. Correct the false statements.**

1 Michael Klossek buys in parts for customer orders.
2 Robert Bauerdiek und Rolf Geide are in charge of the company.
3 Dr Steffen Rötz coordinates people, materials and equipment.
4 Thorsten Günthör deals with invoices.
5 Heinz Hoffmann visits potential customers and makes them offers.
6 Rainer Jakobuß is responsible for computer hardware and software.

C **Who reports to whom? Use the organization chart to complete the statements.**

The designers report to ___[1] and the production engineers report to ___[2]. All the heads of department report to two people - ___[3], the ___[4] Director and ___[5], the ___[6] Director. The apprentices all report to ___[7] because he's the Head of ___[8] . They also report to their heads of department. Tanja Berg, for example, also reports to ___[9] because she's the Head of ___[10].

2 Talking about your company

Four Cantec employees are talking about their jobs.

A 8 **Use the information you hear and the organization chart to find out their names, positions and tasks.**

B 8 **Listen again and complete the sentences with the words you hear.**

1 The people in my department are ___ for a whole contract.
2 Our responsibilities ___ supervising work at customers' sites.
3 My job also ___ going to trade fairs.
4 I'm in ___ of planning.
5 This ___ analysing our sales figures.
6 I really ___ doing my job.
7 My work ___ understanding what materials are needed.

C **Use your answers to exercise 2B to complete the following description.**

I'm in the Logistics department and I ___[1] working there because my work is different every day. Logistics basically ___[2] arranging for goods to be transported to the customer and often ___[3] speaking English. My boss is ___[4] for running the whole department, but I'm in ___[5] of arranging shipments to Scandinavia.

3 Creating your company's organization chart

Now it is time to create an organization chart of your training company.

Work in small groups and draw an organization chart of your company, either as a poster or with suitable software, and present it to the class. Explain who you and the other apprentices in your company report to.

› *Thematic vocabulary: Job titles, page 201; Company departments, page 201*

Describing your company

The management is responsible for **running** the company.
I'm in charge of **arranging** shipments.
My work includes/involves/entails **speaking** English.

› *Grammar: Gerunds, page 157*

PART B: Job profiles

Situation: You work for Möbeltech GmbH in Igelsberg. Peggy Murphy, an Irish work experience student, asks you for help with an assignment.
→ **You create profiles of departments and jobs at your training company.**

1 Describing departments

Peggy has to write job profiles for the apprentice file. She first visits eight of the company's departments and makes notes on them.

A Match four of the names in the box to the departments in the photos.

Accounting • Human Resources (HR) • Export • Marketing • Production • Purchasing • Quality Assurance • Sales

1

2

3

4

B Translate Peggy's notes about six of the departments she visits into German.

1 choose the best suppliers
2 determine salaries and benefits
3 handle all payments and receipts
4 keep to standards and norms
5 maintain and repair equipment
6 monitor products and performance
7 plan the use of manpower and machinery
8 produce financial reports
9 obtain shipping documents
10 recruit, train and promote staff
11 arrange for goods to be shipped abroad
12 visit suppliers' plants

C Match her notes (1–12) with six of the departments from the list in exercise 1A above.

D With a partner, discuss the work of the remaining two departments and write a description of what they do. Compare your ideas with those of other pairs. Do you agree?

› *Thematic vocabulary: Job titles, page 201; Company departments, page 201*
› *Useful phrases: Describing jobs and responsibilities, page 187*

2 Describing jobs

Peggy now interviews some employees and writes down what they say about their jobs.

A 9 **Guess the missing words in the extracts from six of Peggy's interviews then listen to the recording and check your answers. Which departments do the employees work in?**

1. Most of our work ___ negotiating the best possible terms with suppliers.
2. I'm basically ___ for finding the best person for the job.
3. I'm in ___ of public relations.
4. Working in my department ___ understanding customs regulations.
5. It's my ___ to make sure that we sell as many of our products as possible.
6. We ___ the whole manufacturing and delivery process from beginning to end.

B 9 **Listen again, write down more facts about the work of the six departments, then expand your notes into whole sentences. Compare them with your neighbour's. Have you missed anything?**

C **Study the project manager's description of her job and use some of the words to complete what the accounting manager says. Make any necessary changes.**

Project manager

My job means taking responsibility for a whole project. A few months ago, I was in charge of an order from a Norwegian hotel chain and I was responsible for supplying the furniture for six new hotels in Oslo. The project involved working closely with the production manager and meeting the customer's deadlines. I personally oversaw the design of the furniture to the customer's specifications, and the production manager co-ordinated the manpower and machinery needed for the job.

Accounting manager

I'm in ___[1] of the whole accounting department, so I'm personally ___[2] for everything that happens there. I ___[3] its daily operations, and my work often ___[4] working closely with project managers. I also have overall ___[5] for ___[6] deadlines for financial reports, which ___[7] getting the data ready in good time and ___[8] the manpower needed to do the job.

3 Creating a job profile

Now it's your turn to describe your department and the work you do there.

A **Working in small groups, make notes on your department's work and responsibilities, e.g. as a mind map or flow chart, and then write a short text about it, but without naming the department.**

B **Put the texts on the blackboard / walls of your classroom and read what they say. Guess which department each text describes.**

› *Thematic vocabulary: Job titles, page 201; Company departments, page 201*

› *Useful phrases: Describing jobs and responsibilities, page 187*

Describing how often something happens

I **often** go to Scandinavia.
My department **sometimes** organizes training courses.
We **always** make sure our standards are kept to.

› *Grammar: Adverbs of frequency, page 158*

COMMUNICATION: Telephoning

Situation: You are doing a work placement at the UK subsidiary of Hamm Maschinenbau GmbH.
→ **You call a customer and leave a message.**

1 Leaving a voicemail message

Your line manager, Niklas Hartmann, has left you a note asking you to call a customer, Mr Dalton at Esher Engineering, or to leave him a message if he isn't in the office.

A First read the telephone phrases (a–i) and put them in the right order for a phone call or voicemail message.

a Could you ask … (*name*) to call me back / call … ?
b Good morning/afternoon.
c I'd like to speak to/leave a message for … (*name*).
d I'm calling on behalf of … (*name*).
e It's about the …
f My/His/Her number is …
g Thank you. Goodbye.
h The details are as follows: …
i This is … (*name*) from Hamm Engineering UK.

· Phone Esher Engineering to confirm the service checks on their lathes.
· Say that you're calling on my behalf.
· Ask to speak to Roger Dalton. He's the factory manager.
· Tell him that two maintenance technicians will be at the factory at 8.30 on Tuesday, 7 June.
· All checks should be completed by 12.30 at the latest.
· If you only get voicemail, ask Mr Dalton to call me back to confirm the date and time.
· Give him my mobile number (07261 299510). Thanks.

B Work with a partner. Use the phrases (a–i) and the notes above to leave a voicemail message for Mr Dalton. Record your message on your smartphone and play it back to your partner.

2 Understanding voicemail

Mr Dalton was out when you called yesterday and this morning, when you come into the office, you find he has left a message. You pass it on to your line manager, but make three mistakes.

10)) Listen to the recording and find the mistakes in your version of Mr Dalton's message.

While you were out

Caller: Mr Roger Dalton, Esher Engineering

Mr Dalton says that our technicians can't check the lathes on Tuesday, 7 June but they can come on Wednesday, 8 June from 7–12 or on Friday, 10 June after 1 o'clock. Please call his secretary on 0044 1372 454022 to confirm one of the dates.

3 Taking phone calls

Before phoning some clients, you check that you know some frequently-used telephone expressions.

A Work with a partner and decide how you would say the German phrases (a–j) in English.

a Bleiben Sie bitte dran.
b Der Anschluss ist besetzt.
c Ich stelle Sie durch.
d Das habe ich nicht verstanden. Könnten Sie es bitte wiederholen?
e Buchstabieren Sie bitte Ihren Namen.
f Möchten Sie mit jemand anderem sprechen?
g Ich versuche, Sie zu verbinden.
h Möchten Sie eine Nachricht hinterlassen?
i … (Name) ist im Moment nicht da.
j Wie ist Ihr Name bitte?

B 11)) Listen to Niklas Hartmann's phone call to Esher Engineering and check your answers.

C What extra elements are in the English phrases that are missing in the German?

4 Making a phone call

You are back in Germany now and your line manager asks you to phone an English-speaking client.

Giving telephone numbers

Say each digit separately, except for double digits, e.g. 01233455 = "oh (*AE*: zero) one two double-three four double-five".

A **Work with a partner and use the instructions to make a phone call in English.**

Partner A: Ferdinand/Megan Pretorius
Bloemfontein Steel Ltd, South Africa

Nehmen Sie das Telefongespräch auf Englisch entgegen (Begrüßung, Firmenname, Ihr Name).

Partner B: You (own name)
Hamm Maschinenbau GmbH, Germany

Stellen Sie sich vor und sagen Sie, dass Sie mit Dr Botha sprechen möchten.

Der Anschluss von Dr Botha ist besetzt. Ob der/die Anrufer/in jemand anders sprechen möchte?

Äußern Sie die Bitte, mit Hannah Smit verbunden zu werden.

Sie versuchen, den/die Anrufer/in mit Frau Smit zu verbinden und erklären, dass diese im Moment nicht erreichbar ist. Fragen Sie, ob der/die Anrufer/in eine Nachricht hinterlassen möchte?

Ja, Dr Botha möchte Sie auf Ihrem Handy anrufen. Es ist wichtig.

Bitten Sie den/die Anrufer/in, seinen/ihren Namen zu buchstabieren.

Buchstabieren Sie Ihren Vor- und Nachnamen.

Fragen Sie nach der Handynummer.

Geben Sie Ihre Handynummer mit Ländervorwahl (+49 ...) an.

Notieren Sie die Nummer und machen Sie einen Fehler beim Wiederholen.

Korrigieren Sie den Fehler.

Schließen Sie das Gespräch höflich ab.

Schließen Sie das Gespräch höflich ab.

B **Now improvise a typical telephone dialogue with an English-speaking client who calls the company where you are doing your apprenticeship and wishes to speak to somebody who is not available. Include a message, a telephone number and a name to be spelt.**

› *Useful phrases: Telephoning, page 188; Taking telephone calls, page 188*

DAS KANN ICH (Unit 2)

- Die Maßnahmen zur Cybersicherheit in meiner Ausbildungsfirma auf Englisch zusammenfassen. (Foundation)
- Die Struktur meines Ausbildungsbetriebes auf Englisch beschreiben. (Part A)
- Meine Arbeit und meine Abteilung auf Englisch beschreiben. (Part B)
- Eine/n englischsprachige/n Kunden/Kundin anrufen; eine Nachricht hinterlassen. (Communication)

KMK Exam practice 1

1 Produktion: Stufe II

Situation: Der Blog *Worldwide Apprenticeships* sammelt Ausbildungsberichte von jungen Auszubildenden aus aller Welt. Ihr Unternehmen unterstützt diese Initiative, da es für Sie während Ihrer Ausbildung auch die Möglichkeit gibt, an einem Austauschprogramm mit anderen Auszubildenden aus dem Ausland teilzunehmen. Sie werden gebeten, einen persönlichen Bericht zu schreiben.

Aufgabe: Schreiben Sie einen Bericht, der folgende Punkte beinhaltet:

- Fakten über die Firma (Standort(e), Produkte/Dienstleistungen, Mitarbeiter/innen, Abteilungen und Tätigkeiten)
- Ausbildung im Dualen System (Ausbildungsfirma/Berufsschule/Prüfungen)
- Arbeitsbedingungen (Arbeitszeiten, Urlaub, Möglichkeiten der Fortbildung, Verdienstmöglichkeiten, besondere Angebote der Firma)

2 Hörverstehen: Stufe I

Situation: One of your tasks every morning is to listen to the voicemail messages customers have left on your department's answering machine.

12)) **Task: Listen to the telephone messages and write memos for your colleagues including the following information:**

- date and time of call
- who the message is for
- who the message is from, including the company
- message for colleague
- caller's contact details

3 Interaktion: Stufe II

Work with a partner. Partner A: Look here. Partner B: Look at File 1 on page 134.

Situation: Sie arbeiten für die Schmitt & Otte GmbH in Fulda. Ihre Firma produziert hochwertige Sportartikel, die sie weltweit exportiert. Sie befinden sich in der Ausbildung und wurden von Ihrem Chef gebeten, einen englischen Praktikanten / eine englische Praktikantin zu begrüßen. Sie lernen Steve/Sue Mosley kennen, der/die für sechs Monate in Ihrer Firma arbeiten und Sie in den ersten beiden Wochen in der Exportabteilung begleiten wird.

Aufgabe: Gestalten Sie in Partnerarbeit einen Dialog mit Hilfe der folgenden Punkte:

- Begrüßen Sie Ihr Gegenüber. Betreiben Sie Small Talk.
- Fragen Sie nach der Firma Ihres Gesprächspartners / Ihrer Gesprächspartnerin.
- Geben Sie Auskunft über Arbeitsabläufe (Arbeitszeiten, Pausen usw.) und über alles was Ihr/e Gesprächspartner/in wissen möchte.
- Geben Sie Auskunft über das deutsche Ausbildungssystem.
- Geben Sie Tipps zur Freizeitgestaltung und zu Wochenendaktivitäten.
- Beraten Sie Steve/Sue bezüglich der Unterkunft (Nachfrage Personalbüro, eventuell Unterbringung in Wohngemeinschaft mit anderen Azubis, Fahrgemeinschaft).

4 Mediation: Stufe II

Situation: Sie arbeiten für Wenzel und Gabler GmbH, eine Firma, die Bremsscheiben für die Automobilindustrie produziert und weltweit exportiert. Ihr Vorgesetzter, Herr Becker, ist zu einem Firmenevent bei einem neuen Kooperationspartner, Millerman Industries Ltd in Colchester, UK, eingeladen. Er gibt Ihnen eine Übersicht, die er im Internet gefunden hat und bittet Sie, ihm bei der Vorbereitung auf diesen Besuch zu helfen. Er möchte bezüglich der Teammitglieder und ihrer Aufgaben vorbereitet sein.

Aufgabe: Kopieren und vervollständigen Sie die Tabelle für Herrn Becker, indem Sie die wichtigsten Informationen eintragen.

Responsibilities at Millerman Industries Ltd

CEO: Ms Emily Rosenberg
The CEO is responsible for all the company's internal and external activities. In cooperation with the Board of Directors, the CEO establishes and maintains the framework standards for the company. The CEO monitors the directors and establishes instruments of successful management.

Production Manager: Mrs Laura Hunt
The production manager is responsible for the management, supervision and monitoring of all aspects of industrial production. The manufacturing processes must run as reliably and as efficiently as possible. This includes the precise planning of production schedules and resource management, as well as the necessity to meet quality standards and fulfil obligatory safety regulations.

Research and Development Manager: Mr Cliff Hedgebond
The R&D manager conducts thorough studies before a new product is developed. The R&D team carries out extensive market research, evaluates the need for a new product, and develops and plans the complete project with all its specifications. At Millerman Industries Ltd, the R&D manager has to ensure that existing products fulfill customer requirements at all times, which may mean potential changes and updates, especially when problems or malfunctions make it necessary to find new solutions in the manufacturing process.

Financial Director: Mr Robert Hunt
The FD is licensed to give detailed advice on all financial product lines of the company and he supervises the financial transactions. FDs are responsible for all overseas transactions. They are also in charge of tax and revenues.

Customer Care Manager: Mr Ben Miller
The manager of this section controls and trains the employees in the call centre and sets up and evaluates the written correspondence concerning the customers. He is also responsible for identifying the training needs of call centre agents to ensure that all staff have the skills and knowledge to deal with the customers effectively.

Human Resources Director: Mr Regis Colen
The HR Director deals with all questions of recruitment, redundancies, pension schemes and apprenticeships. He initiates the annual evaluation that is obligatory for all members of staff and reports the results to the CEO.

Position:	Englische Anrede, Vor- und Nachname:	Hauptaufgaben / Verantwortlich für: (in Stichworten)
CEO/Geschäftsführerin	*Ms Emily Rosenberg*	– *interner/externer Auftritt der Firma* ...
...	...	...
...	...	

3 My company

FOUNDATION: Types of companies

Situation: The company where you are doing your apprenticeship now has many international business partners, so it decides to add more information in English to its website.
→ **You create a timeline of your company for its English website.**

1 Analysing a timeline

You surf the internet and find an article about Richard Branson, a famous British businessman.

Read the text and complete the timeline (1–8) on page 25.

In 2018, Richard Branson, the inventor of the Virgin brand, was worth $5 billion and his empire included around 400 companies all over the world. His first business venture was in 1959 at the age of nine when he planted Christmas trees on some land near his home in London. He planned to sell them at the age of 18 and move to Bali with the profits. Technically speaking, he was a sole trader because he did not intend to share the profits with anybody, he was his own boss and he had unlimited liability, meaning he bore all the risk. Rabbits ate his Christmas trees and he lost everything.

In 1968, he started again as a sole trader selling records by mail order under the brand name Virgin. He took business away from conventional record stores by offering much lower prices. In 1972, he set up a record company with unknown bands such as the Sex Pistols and Boy George. Such artists were more of a risk, so he made it into a private limited company (Virgin Records Ltd), because its members were only liable to the extent of their investment and did not risk losing their personal wealth, e.g. when fighting broke out at the Sex Pistols' concerts.

Branson added more private limited companies to the Virgin Group and also founded an airline, Virgin Atlantic, in 1984. Later, when he needed a large amount of money to finance his airline, he formed a public limited company called The Virgin Group plc and sold its shares on the stock exchange. However, as the chairman of a public limited company, he disliked the obligation to tell his shareholders what he was doing and to show a short-term profit, so he later bought back all the shares for £200 million and made his company into a private limited company again. In 1993, he entered the railway business and won franchises for major routes by undercutting British Rail. Two years later he founded Virgin Money offering financial services in the UK, Australia and South Africa. In 1999, he launched a new, cheaper mobile phone service in the UK called Virgin Mobile, which now operates in 15 countries.

Richard Branson is also famous for spectacular adventures, including space travel with Virgin Galactic, founded in 2004. However, before tourists can book a voyage for $250,000 per person, there are still many barriers to overcome, as was clearly shown when one of his spacecraft crashed on a test flight killing the pilot. After that, Branson's next business ventures were less spectacular: a chain of healthcare clinics opened in the UK in 2008, and Virgin Hotels was launched two years later in Florida. Branson still hits the headlines with activities such as motor racing, gas balloon racing, drones, robotics and TV shows.

Richard Branson timeline

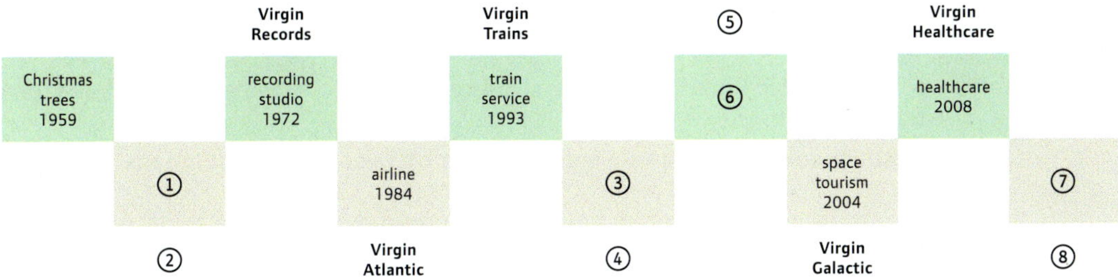

2 Describing your company

You research the different types of company that Richard Branson founded and find these explanations.

Three ways to do business		
Sole trader	**UK: Private limited company (Ltd)* US: Limited liability company (LLC)**	**UK: Public limited company (plc) US: Corporation (Corp/Inc)**
– The company belongs to the sole trader. – The sole trader takes decisions alone. – He/She gets all the profit. – He/She could lose everything.	– The company belongs to a closed circle of members. – The members decide what is best for the company. – The members share the profits. – The members can only lose the money they have invested.	– The company belongs to the shareholders (members of the public). – The directors decide what is best for the company and the shareholders. – The shareholders share the profits. – The shareholders can only lose the money they paid for the shares.

* In South Africa, Australia and New Zealand: Proprietary limited company (Pty Ltd)

Study the explanations of the three different ways to do business and complete the sentences with the correct information.

1 The person who bears most risk is ___.
2 A private limited company is owned by ___.
3 A sole trader has ___ freedom to make decisions.
4 A shareholder in a plc gets ___ of the profit.
5 Members of the public can buy shares in ___.
6 Bankruptcy is a serious risk for ___.

Describing types of company

A public limited company belongs to the shareholders, **who** share the profits. Shareholders can only lose the money **that/which** they paid for the shares if the company goes bankrupt.

› *Grammar: Relative clauses, page 156*

3 Creating a timeline

Your line manager asks you to prepare a timeline for your company's English website.

A **Work in small groups, if possible with people from the same company. Search your company's website for data and visual elements. Find out who bears the risk at your company and include this in your timeline. (If your company is not suitable, choose another local company.)**

B **When you have collected enough material, sketch out your timeline on a large sheet of paper. Add suitable images and graphics to make it visually appealing.**

C **Complete your timeline and hang it on the wall. Do a gallery walk and give each other points for design, clarity and information. Choose the timeline that gets its message across best.**

› *Thematic vocabulary: Company organization, page 202*

PART A: Showing visitors around

Situation: You work at Cantec GmbH, a medium-sized engineering company in Essen that exports canning technology all over the world
→ **You take English-speaking visitors on a guided tour of your training company.**

1 Preparing for visitors

As Cantec GmbH often has visitors from abroad, your line manager asks you to prepare an English version of the layout of the company.

Study the diagram and use the words in the box to complete the labelling.

accounting • assembly • design • finance • human resources • managing director • material delivery • pricing • production • project management • purchasing • quality assurance • research and development • sales • showroom

Third floor **Ground floor**

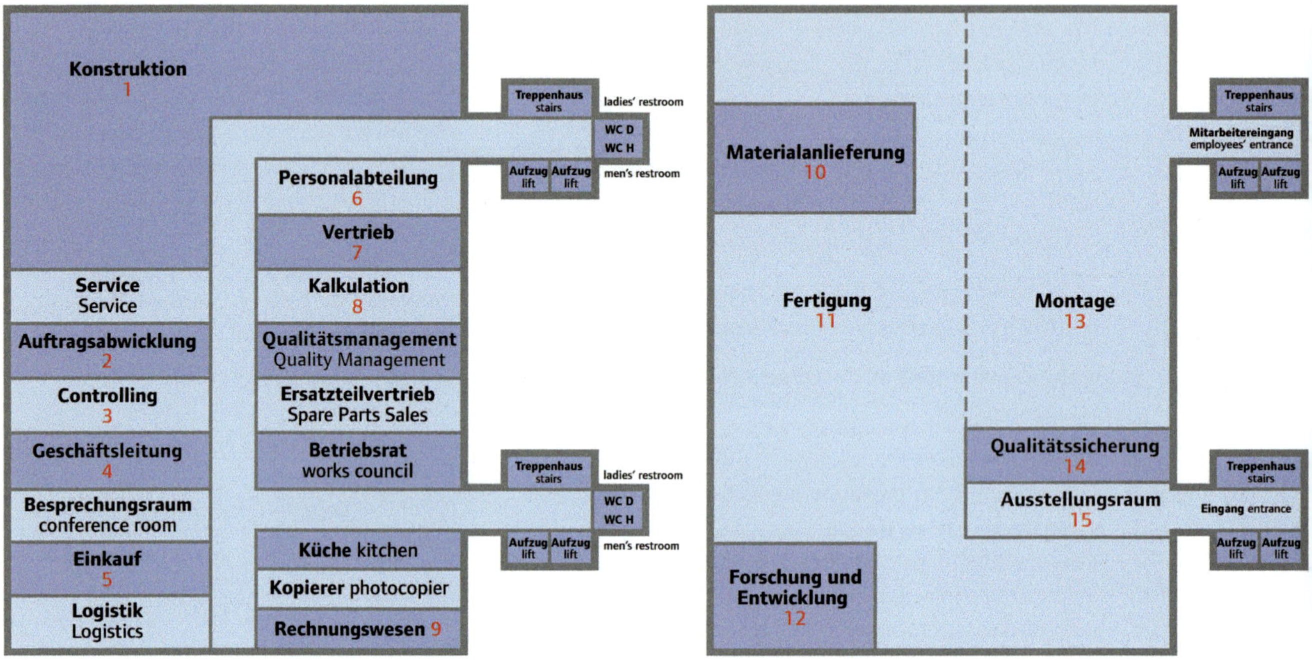

2 Following a tour around a company

To make sure you know suitable English phrases for giving a guided tour, you join two tours around Cantec for visitors from abroad.

A 13)) **Listen to the two tours and write down the following information:**

- who the visitors are
- the starting point of the tour
- the departments visited
- the finishing point

Infobox

BE: lift	*AE:* elevator	*Aufzug*
second floor	third floor	*2. OG*
first floor	second floor	*1. OG*
ground floor	first floor	*Erdgeschoss*

B 13)) **Read the extracts from the first tour below and guess the missing words. Then listen to the recording again to check your answers.**

1 We are ___ to welcome you to our company.
2 We very much hope you ___ your stay here.
3 Are there any ___ before we begin?
4 In that case, we'll ___ here in the conference room.
5 I'll now ___ you down the corridor to the Design department.
6 The gentleman ___ the left of the window is Dr Lenz.
7 Our next ___ is the Quality Management department.
8 It's ___ to go downstairs to the factory to see how our machines are built.
9 Here you can ___ how our production lines are put together.
10 Well, that ___ our tour.

Giving directions

to the left/right of …
between (the) … and (the) …
next to (the) …
opposite (the) …
upstairs/downstairs
to take the lift/elevator/escalator/stairs to the … floor

C **With a partner, practise taking (a) visitor(s) on two or three tours of Cantec's offices and factory. Include the following points in your tour:**

- choose a starting point, two departments on each floor and a finishing point
- greet the visitor(s) politely
- introduce yourself (full name and position)
- offer to answer questions
- add your own ideas
- finish the tour politely

VIDEO 2

Watch the video to see another company tour.

Begin like this: *Good morning and welcome to … . My name is … . I'm … . If you have any questions …*

3 Writing a website post

The Managing Director asks you to write a short article about the Chinese delegation's visit to Cantec for the company website.

13)) **Listen to the first tour again and write a short text including the following information:**

Chinese company: China Tomato, Xinjiang, north-west China
Representatives: Managing director Wang Wei and three colleagues
Details of visit: Importance of canning technology for farmers in China / presentation / tour of company (names of German colleagues and their departments / machines seen in factory) / tour of Essen

Talking about the past

A delegation from China **visited** our company last week.
First of all, we **took** them on a tour of our offices.

› *Grammar: Simple past, page 154*

Begin like this: *Last week we were delighted to welcome a delegation from …*

4 Taking visitors on a tour of your company

Now it's time for you to take some English-speaking visitors on a tour of your own training company.

A **Work in small groups from the same training company. Prepare a plan of your company and label the departments in English.**

B **Find people in your class from another company and use your plan to show them around. Make sure you cover the same points in your tour as in exercise 2C.**

› *Useful phrases: Showing visitors around the company, page 189*
› *Thematic vocabulary: Company departments, page 201*

PART B: A company profile

Situation: You work at Cantec GmbH, a canning machinery manufacturer in Essen. A delegation from China is visiting the company.
→ **You give a presentation in English about your company to visitors from abroad.**

1 Preparing presentation slides

The Sales Director asks you to find suitable slides to use in a presentation for the visitors.

A **You create six slides (A–F). Match them with the headings in the list below.**

can manufacturing process • company data • factory interior • final slide • parent company • world market

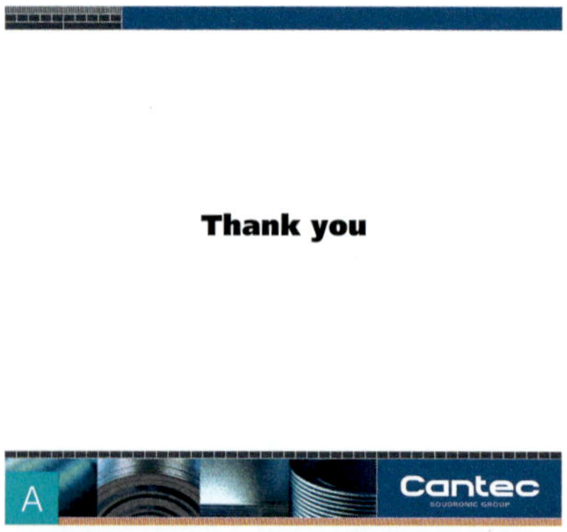

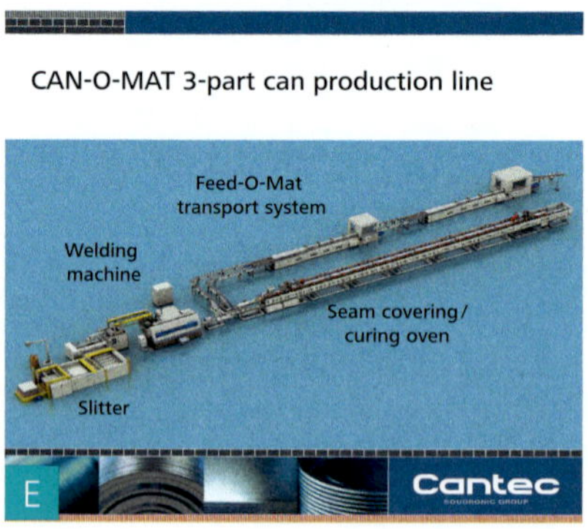

B **With a partner, decide in what order the slides should be shown.**

C 14 **Listen and write down the order in which the Sales Director describes the slides. Is it the same?**

Describing repeated actions

We **export** 98% of our products.
We **transport** all the components to our customers.
We **assemble** them on site.

› *Grammar: Simple present, page 154*

2 Writing a handout

Each visitor from abroad will receive a handout including a profile of Cantec GmbH.

A 14)) **Listen again and make notes on the company and its products under the following headings:**

- name, location, company statistics, parent company
- products/services, customers
- factory, machinery

B **Now write a profile of the company to add to the handout.**

› *Useful phrases: Describing companies, page 189*

VIDEO 3

Watch the video to see another company presentation.

3 Structuring a presentation

The Cantec Sales Director uses a number of expressions that can be used in any presentation.

14)) **Listen again and write the expressions she uses under the headings below.**

Welcoming the audience	Introducing your topic	Structuring your talk	Moving on	Describing visuals	Dealing with questions	Conclusion
Good morning, …	*I'd like to …*	*I'll …*				

4 Optimizing your presentation

Your presentation will be a success if you study the tips below.

Divide the tips into *Before/During/After the presentation*.

Tips for a great presentation

A Always face your audience!
B Decide what visual aids are best for your topic (objects, transparencies, posters, etc.)
C Decide when it is best to give out handouts (before, during or after the presentation).
D Do not overload transparencies or slides with information.
E Do not speak for too long before handing over to your partner.
F Find out about any cultural differences (e.g. attire, gestures and body language).
G Give your contact details (e.g. email, website, business card) if appropriate.
H Make eye contact and do not turn your back on the audience to point to the screen.
I Offer to answer any questions the audience may have.
J Practise with a partner before giving the presentation to your audience.
K Prepare hand-held prompt cards with key words.
L Speak slowly and freely only using your prompt cards.
M Start by explaining what the presentation is about.
N Welcome the audience and introduce yourself/yourselves.

5 Preparing a presentation

Now it is time to prepare a short presentation about your own training company.

Work with a partner and prepare the presentation. Follow the steps in Communication (pages 30–31) to help you. Use posters, slides or your company's products as presentation aids.

› *Useful phrases: Giving presentations, page 189* › *Thematic vocabulary: Company organization, page 202*

COMMUNICATION: A short presentation

Situation: Some trainees from the UK are soon going to start work at your company.
→ **You give a short presentation to the new trainees about your work.**

1 Thinking about the contents of a presentation

Your line manager gives you a list of points you should include in your talk.

what the company does · your department · what you do

A **Work with a partner. Read the list and decide together what you would like to add to your line manager's list above. Make notes.**

B **Compare your notes with another pair and decide on the final points you will cover. Make a mind map.**

C **Agree on the order you will present the contents. Make a numbered list. Write the name and date of your talk at the top of the list.**

Presentation to new trainees: 08.09.20..
1 *Introduction (self/the company)*
2
3

2 Writing the presentation

A **Use your mind map and the list from exercise 1 to write your text. Follow this structure.**

Introduction	– Say in a few words what you are going to talk about.
Main part	– Use one paragraph for each topic. – Use signposts to move from one subject to the next.
Conclusion	– Summarize the main ideas. – Invite questions from the audience.

B **Check the text together for clarity and correctness as follows.**

- Is the information in the text correct? If not, correct it.
- Is the spelling and grammar correct? Use your dictionary and the list of phrases on page 29.

3 Making a prompt card

A presentation comes across best when the presenter looks at the audience and speaks naturally. As it is difficult to do either of these things if you read from a text, you should make yourself a prompt card.

A **Follow the steps below.**

- Highlight important words and phrases in your text.
- Copy the words and phrases onto an index card.
- Include signposts to structure the ideas.

- manufacturing company
- workshop
- apprentices ...

B **Practise your presentation in your group, using only your prompt card.**

4 Listening to presentations

Before you give your own presentation, you listen to some examples.

15 **Copy the feedback sheet below three times then listen to the presentations and evaluate them. Award points from 0 to 3.**

Feedback sheet		
Title of presentation: …		**Points**
Content	You …	
	– covered all the important points.	
Structure	– supported your points with examples.	
	– had an introduction, a main part and a conclusion.	
	– made the presentation easy to follow using *useful phrases*.	
	– summarized the main ideas in the conclusion.	
Delivery	– were friendly, confident and well organized.	
	– spoke clearly and without reading out a prepared text.	
	– looked at the audience when you spoke.	
	– took equal turns with your partner(s).	
Handling questions	– dealt with questions in a friendly manner.	
	– answered all the questions clearly.	
	Overall score	
Comments …		

5 Giving your presentation

Take it in turns to give presentations about your training companies while the class evaluates them using the feedback sheet.

A **Choose two presenters from your group. While presenting, make sure you look directly at the audience, smile and speak slowly and clearly using your prompt cards. Take equal turns to speak, and ask for questions at the end. Make a video of the presentation if possible.**

B **The rest of the class should use the feedback sheet to evaluate the presentations, making sure that all comments are constructive and helpful.**

› *Useful phrases: Giving presentations, page 189*

DAS KANN ICH (Unit 3)

- Einen informativen Zeitstrahl über meine Firma auf Englisch erstellen. (Foundation)
- Englischsprachige Besucher/Besucherinnen durch meinen Ausbildungsbetrieb führen. (Part A)
- Meinen Ausbildungsbetrieb englischsprachigen Besuchern/Besucherinnen präsentieren. (Part B)
- Eine kurze Präsentation über meine Arbeit für neue Auszubildende halten. (Communication)

4 Adding value

FOUNDATION: The supply chain

Situation: Your company imports raw materials from a number of Asian countries. It is reviewing its sourcing policy and so has formed a team to examine the supply chains of some of its products.
→ **You create a fact sheet describing your training company's supply chain.**

1 Looking at the global supply chain

You find an article on the internet describing the supply chain of a pair of jeans.

A **First guess what percentage of the total retail price is spent on each stage of the supply chain (A–H). Then read the article to check your answers.**

Making the most of a pair of jeans

Most consumers assume that retailers makes a huge profit on a pair of cheap jeans made in low-wage countries. We decided to find out what the costs are, stage by stage, from the manufacturer to the retailer, and we got a few surprises along the way.

We chose jeans retailing at £14 per pair at a budget supermarket chain in the UK. They are made in Bangladesh using cotton grown and spun in India, and shipped by a Hong Kong-based middleman. We discovered that a quarter of the £14 (£3.50) goes on materials, such as denim, buttons, studs, zips and special washes. The factory costs are low, as expected, only amounting to 4% (56p), but our first real surprise was that the factory's profit is only 14p per garment, i.e. only 1% of the retail price. Our next shock came when we looked at the logistics of shipping goods from a low-wage country to the UK. The shipping costs for the Hong Kong middleman amount to 3% (42p per pair), but his profit is a massive £1.82, i.e. 13 times more than the factory's profit! The distribution costs to branches of the UK supermarket chain make up another £3.78 or 27% of the price, as well as £2.00 in VAT (20% in the UK). But our final surprise was to discover that the retail price tag of £14 only gives the retailer a profit of 98p, which is seven times more than the factory earns but only about half of the middleman's profit.

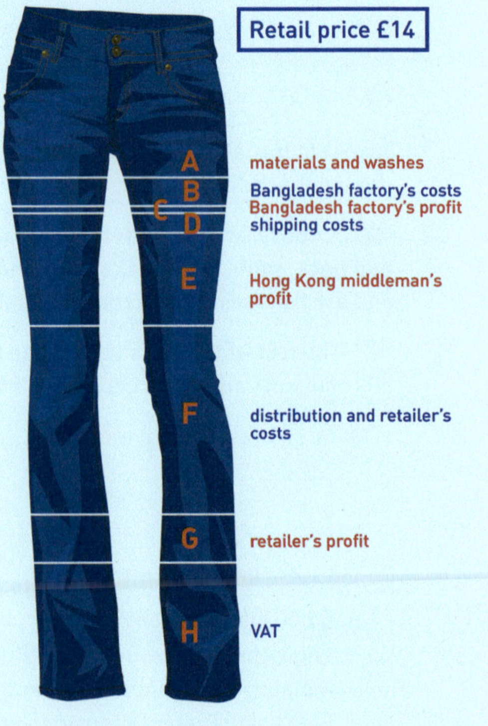

B **Do the following tasks.**

1 Explain what surprises you most about the costs.
2 Calculate the percentage of the price that is profit.
3 Explain why the UK budget supermarket sells jeans made by a factory in Bangladesh.
4 Use the percentages in the text to calculate the factory's and middleman's profits on the last pair of jeans you bought yourself.

2 Understanding the traditional supply chain

Next you examine the traditional supply chain for consumer goods.

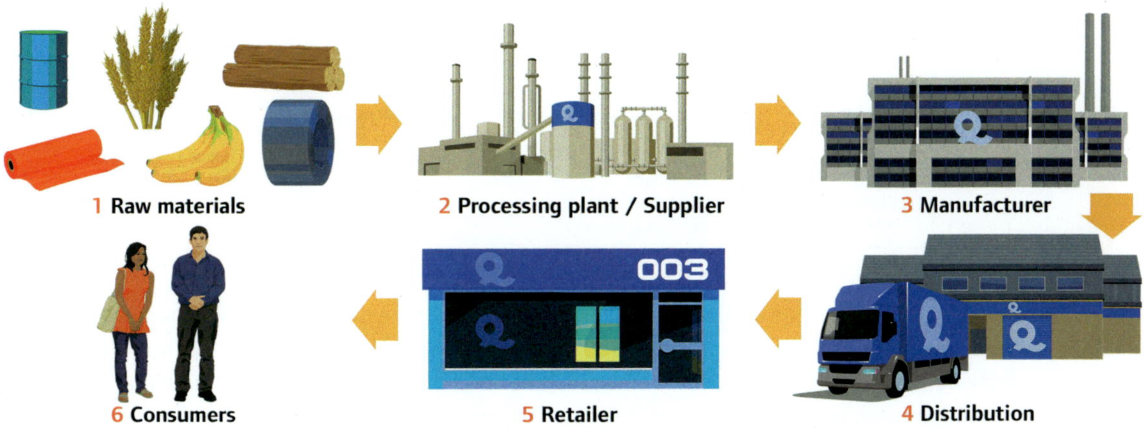

A **Match the words in the list to numbers 1, 2, 3, 5, and 6 of the diagram above. (Number 4 is distribution in each case.) The words in the list make up the supply chains for four separate products.**

blast furnace (*Hochofen*) • car manufacturer • car showroom • child • crude oil • dairy • driver • forest • furniture store • furniture-maker • home-owner • iron ore (*Eisenerz*) • milk • oil refinery • pasteurization plant • plastic toy manufacturer • saw mill (*Sägewerk*) • shopper • supermarket • toy shop

First supply chain: 1 crude oil, 2 oil refinery, 3 ...

B **Examine the text on jeans again and find the locations of each part of the supply chain (1–6).**

3 Describing your company's supply chain

Use information on your own company's products to create a fact sheet describing the supply chain.

A **Form groups from the same training company and make notes on the following points:**

- the source of (raw) materials (conflict zones / minerals?)
- how and where processing/refining takes place (low-wage countries / working conditions?)
- how and where manufacturing takes place (low-wage countries / working conditions?)
- distribution channels (e.g. East to West; road, rail, air or sea; warehousing and storage; CO_2 footprint?)
- retail outlets (e.g. shops, supermarkets and/or online?)

B **Present the information to the class in one of the following ways:**

- (a) wall poster(s) with illustrations/diagrams, captions and explanations
- a PowerPoint presentation
- a short video made with a smartphone/camcorder
- your own idea

› *Useful phrases: Giving presentations, page 189*
› *Thematic vocabulary: The supply chain, page 202*

PART A: Supply chain management

Situation: Your company, Spacemaker GmbH, manufactures a successful line of compact furniture. However, as the business grows, the factory is unable to keep up with demand. Business consultants are called in to analyse the problem and suggest improvements.
→ **You analyse your training company's supply chain and suggest improvements.**

1 Analysing the problem

The team of consultants observes the production process at Spacemaker GmbH, then writes a report.

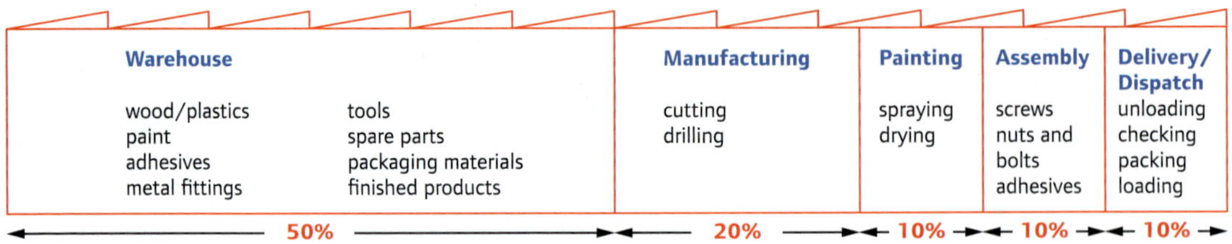

... Less than half of the available factory space is used for the main activities of manufacturing, painting and assembly. Workers currently spend more time looking for materials and parts in the warehouse than making furniture. Large quantities of wood, plastics and packaging materials are stored on the floor of the warehouse, with the result that the metal fittings, paints and adhesives used in every finished product are stored overhead in high bays and only accessible by ladder.

Sometimes the paint shop cannot handle the quantity of parts produced by the manufacturing section, meaning that production stops. In this case, the assembly section has no work and its workers stand idle. At other times, the output of the paint shop exceeds the capacity of the assembly section, leading to delays in delivery to customers.

Read the extract from the report above and match the sentence halves.

1 The manufacturing process ...
2 A lot of time is wasted ...
3 Warehousing accounts for ...
4 Some of the components needed every day ...
5 The output of one section is ...
6 Assembly workers have nothing to do ...
7 When the assembly section is overloaded, ...

A not coordinated with the next.
B are hard to access.
C looking for materials and parts.
D when the paint shop is overloaded.
E deliveries to customers are delayed.
F is extremely inefficient.
G half of the available space.

2 Tackling the problem

An emergency meeting is called to discuss the consultants' report.

A **With a partner use the words in the list to complete eight steps towards solving the problem.**

Standardize · Set · Implement · Evaluate · Develop · Clarify · Break down · Analyse

Step 1: ___ the problem
Step 2: ___ the problem
Step 3: ___ a target that can be achieved
Step 4: ___ the root cause
Step 5: ___ countermeasures
Step 6: ___ countermeasures
Step 7: ___ both results and process
Step 8: ___ success and learn from failures

B 16)) **Listen to the meeting and check your answers to 2A.**

C 16)) **Listen to the recording again and answer the questions.**

1 Why has Spacemaker GmbH asked the business consultants for help?
2 What are the two main causes of the problem according to Sharon Jackson?
3 What is the result of the lack of communication between manufacturing, painting and assembly?
4 Where does the *kanban* system come from?
5 What does it prevent?
6 What must there be before any part is made or moved?
7 Where does the consultant suggest as regards storing smaller and bigger items?
8 How should the countermeasures be implemented?
9 What question must be asked after each countermeasure?
10 What should the company's overall goal be?

D **The consultant suggests changing what is stored on site. Work with a partner and list the items in the diagram of the warehouse that are best stored on site and which should be delivered just in time. Present your ideas to the class and explain your choices.**

3 Lean manufacturing

Sharon Jackson, the consultant, gives the workforce some background literature to understand the basic principles of lean manufacturing as introduced by the Toyota Motor Corporation.

Push system

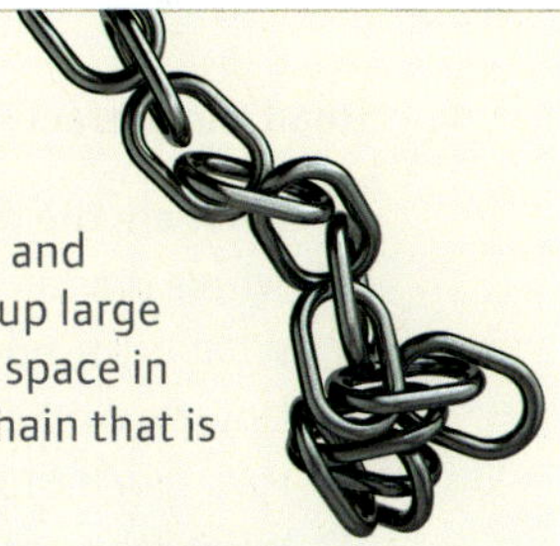

Traditional manufacturing uses a push system to control production. Demand is forecast on the basis of market trends, seasonal fluctuations, experience and/or guesswork. Materials are bought in bulk to take advantage of quantity discounts, and products are mass-produced and stored in anticipation of sales. This method ties up large amounts of capital in work in progress (WIP) and inventory, and large amounts of space in storage. It is inexact, unreliable and wasteful. It can be likened to a heavy metal chain that is uneven, loose and unmanageable when pushed.

Pull system

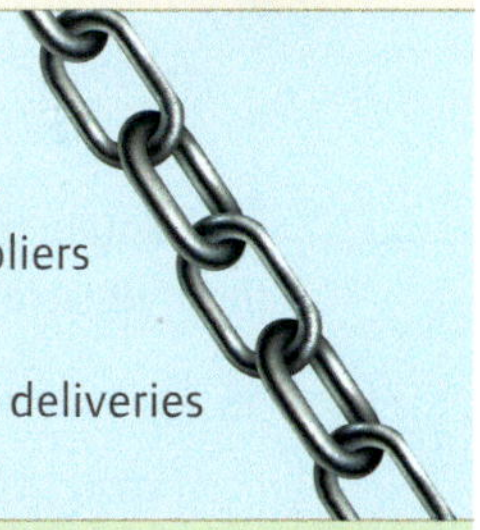

When Taiichi Ohno re-organized the Toyota Motor Corporation in the early 1950s, he was inspired by how American supermarkets managed their inventory. Customers only bought what they needed; the supermarkets only ordered what they needed; the suppliers only delivered the quantities needed. The supermarkets used a pull system.

Taiichi Ohno introduced a pull system at Toyota. He changed over to just-in-time (JIT) deliveries of materials and transformed the work process by introducing the *kanban* system.

Kanban

Kanban means "signboard" in Japanese and in its simplest form a *kanban* is a visual instruction, e.g. an empty bin for parts with a *kanban* telling workers to refill it (1-bin system). In some cases there are two bins with *kanban* cards, one in front of the other. When the front bin is empty, the back bin is pulled forward and the empty bin is refilled (2-bin system). In a 3-bin system, there is one bin with a *kanban* at the factory, one in the storeroom and one with the supplier. When the factory bin is empty, it is sent to the storeroom where it is refilled. The storeroom then sends an empty bin to the supplier and the supplier sends a full bin to the storeroom. Many companies use electronic *kanban* with barcodes or RFID chips.

All items in the work process must have a *kanban*. Any item without one is an error.

Kanban board

A *kanban* board visualizes work as it passes through the production process. Orders can be tracked easily, capacity identified, and overload avoided, e.g. by seeing that there is too much WIP to start another order or that orders are ready for shipment.

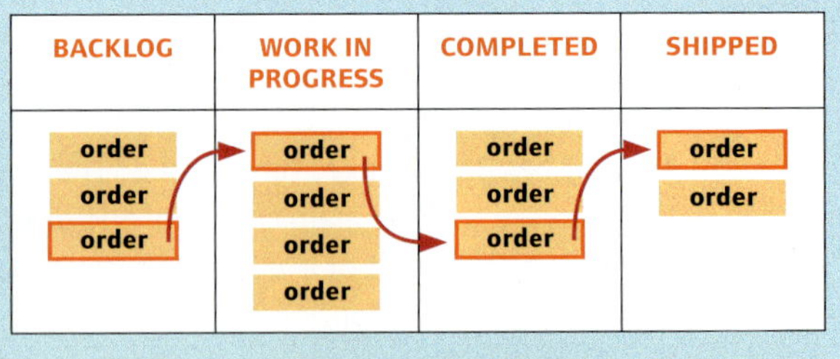

Continuous improvement

Lean production only allows time to be spent on things that add value and is based on the culture of *kaizen*, meaning continuous improvement. This includes the constant fight against *muda*, *mura* and *muri*.

- *muda* – waste. Toyota's "7 wastes" are overproduction, excess inventory, waiting, unnecessary physical movement, unnecessary transportation, correcting defects, and processing to a higher standard than needed.
- *mura* – unevenness, e.g. stopping and starting production
- *muri* – overburden, e.g. overworking employees and/or machines until they break down

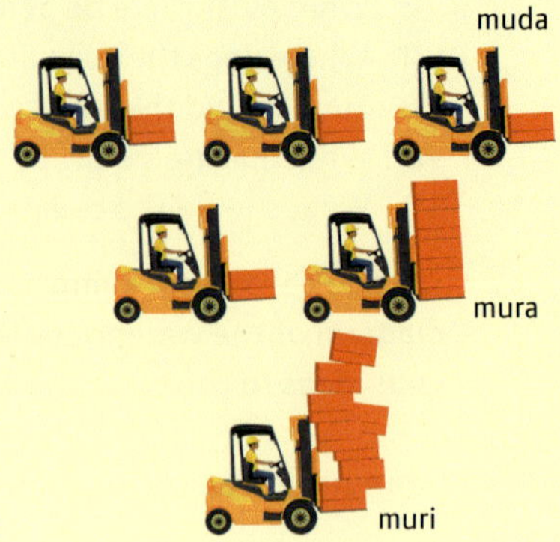

Lean production optimizes the work process and empowers workers to produce or move items without needing permission from their supervisors. It can be likened to a metal chain that becomes tight and is easy to handle when pulled.

A Read the extract from a handout above and answer the questions.

1. What are the disadvantages of a push system?
2. Where did Taiichi Ohno get his ideas about company organization from?
3. What is the advantage of JIT delivery?
4. How do workers know what to do when a *kanban* system is used?
5. How much capacity is there to start work on a new order according to the *kanban* board shown?
6. What other information is shown on the *kanban* board?
7. Why is *kaizen* best described as a culture and not as a project?
8. How does lean production empower workers?

B Explain to a partner what is happening or what is meant in the *muda*, *mura*, *muri*, *loose chain* and *tight chain* illustrations.

C Discuss with a partner whether the following problems are *muda*, *mura* or *muri*.

components are stored on high shelves • there is only one IT specialist • all the machine operators have their break at the same time • faulty goods are reworked by an experienced employee • only the best materials are used for all customers • lorries are unloaded faster on Mondays than on Fridays • the metal-cutting machine is repaired regularly

4 Presenting solutions

In groups from the same training company, analyse the company's supply chain and suggest improvements.

In your group, prepare and give a presentation on one of these topics:

- The lean manufacturing culture at your company.
- How lean manufacturing (e.g. a pull system, JIT, *kanban* or *kaizen*) could be implemented where you work.

› *Useful phrases: Giving presentations, page 189*

PART B: Industry 4.0

Situation: You work at Hoffmann Möbelbau GmbH, a traditional furniture manufacturing company that is part of an international group. The group's business consultants have suggested changing over to Industry 4.0 and making one of the Hoffmann Möbelbau's factories into a smart factory. You join a team to prepare the workforce for the changeover.

→ **You produce a short report explaining how the smart factory will operate.**

1 Understanding the changing face of production

You surf the internet and find a blog with illustrations and descriptions of production methods over the last 300 years.

A **First, put the illustrations in chronological order.**

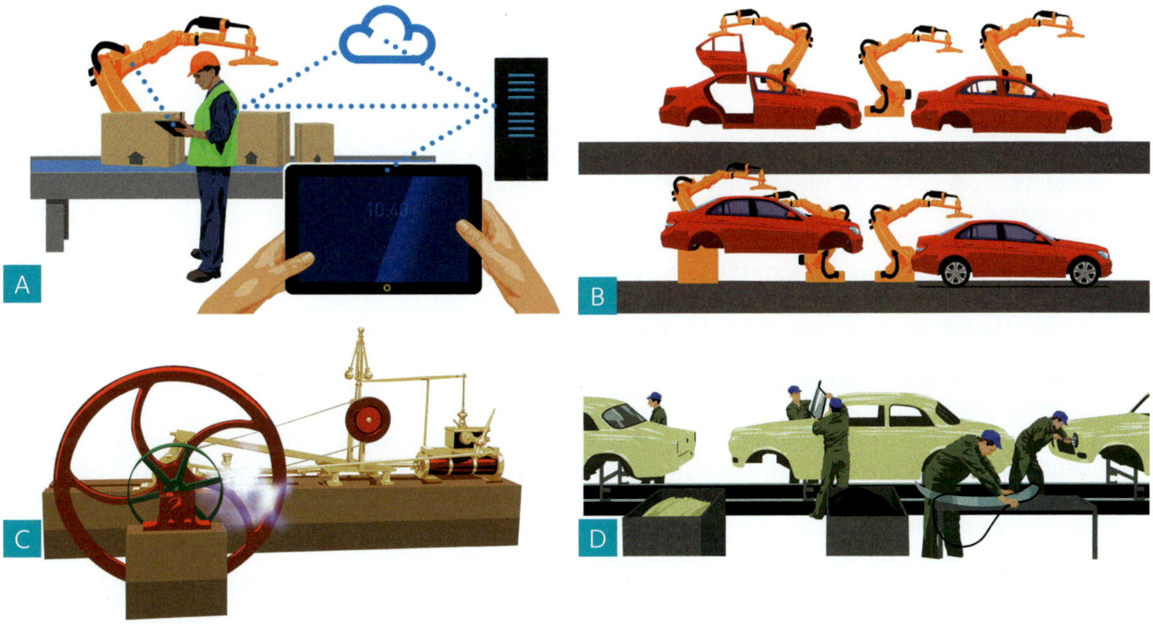

B **Now match the descriptions below to the illustrations (A–D).**

Automated production	digitization with electronic robots and IT systems
Mass production	assembly lines using manual labour and electrical energy
Mechanical production	equipment powered by steam and water
Intelligent production	cyber-physical systems with cloud technology, AI, IoT and big data

2 Reading about intelligent production

You also find the following blog entry on the internet.

TechBloggerPlus: **Mass customization**

We all know that feeling when you try to order a special part for something and are told it's no longer available. Well, I recently went to a TED talk about Industry 4.0, and can now tell you that those days are over because mass customization is here to stay.

The speaker had tried to order a blue piece of wood to repair her wooden fence only to be told by the company she had to wait for two months until they had enough orders to make a new batch. She then reflected on how industry had changed over the centuries.

Before the Industrial Revolution, a fence was made from local wood, painted by hand and left to dry in the sun. The arrival of mechanical production meant it could be painted more quickly with a steam-driven painting machine. The next step was mass production of standardized goods using an assembly line powered by an electric motor and an electric oven to speed up the drying process. Inspectors were also employed to check the quality of the products and to correct errors. Later, when production was automated, the unskilled workers on the assembly line were replaced by robots, and the inspectors by a computer-operated inspection tool. However, if there was a problem, for example the paint not drying fast enough, no one knew exactly the cause was. Perhaps it was the wood, or the brush, the assembly line, the paint, or maybe the oven. There was not enough computing power to link up and analyse all the data at the different stages of production. The problem was therefore solved by trial and error, or not at all.

Now, with intelligent production, such problems are a thing of the past. Wherever Industry 4.0 is implemented, goods are made in smart factories using cyber-physical systems. Big data provides information on every tiny detail of the manufacturing process. Every component has a tag and is identified and processed by machines using sensors and actuators. Machines communicate with each other autonomously by Ethernet, and without any human intervention. Production lines can be programmed to make any quantity of any product in any shape, size or colour, and they order materials as they are required. Faults are detected and compensated for automatically. Downtime is a thing of the past. The wood for the fence would be ready in two hours, not two months. Welcome to the world of mass customization.

A **With a partner, study the pictures on page 37 and the text above and answer the questions.**

1 What is the difference between standardized and customized products?
2 What energy sources and technologies have been used in manufacturing since the 18th century?
3 At what point were unskilled workers no longer needed?
4 Why could problems with automated production sometimes only be solved by trial and error?
5 What is the role of Ethernet in Industry 4.0?
6 Why is downtime a thing of the past in Industry 4.0?

B **Research one or more of the following ideas in the context of mass customization and present your findings to the class, e.g. as a poster, OHP or PowerPoint presentation.**

- 3D printing
- a configurator, e.g. for cars, clothing, food
- your own idea

3 Preparing for the future

You find a podcast on the internet in which a business consultant explains how production methods change when Industry 4.0 is introduced.

A 17)) Listen to the first part of the podcast and use the two diagrams below to summarize the differences between shoe-manufacturing in a conventional and in a smart factory.

B Explain what an RFID tag is and how it is used in a smart factory.

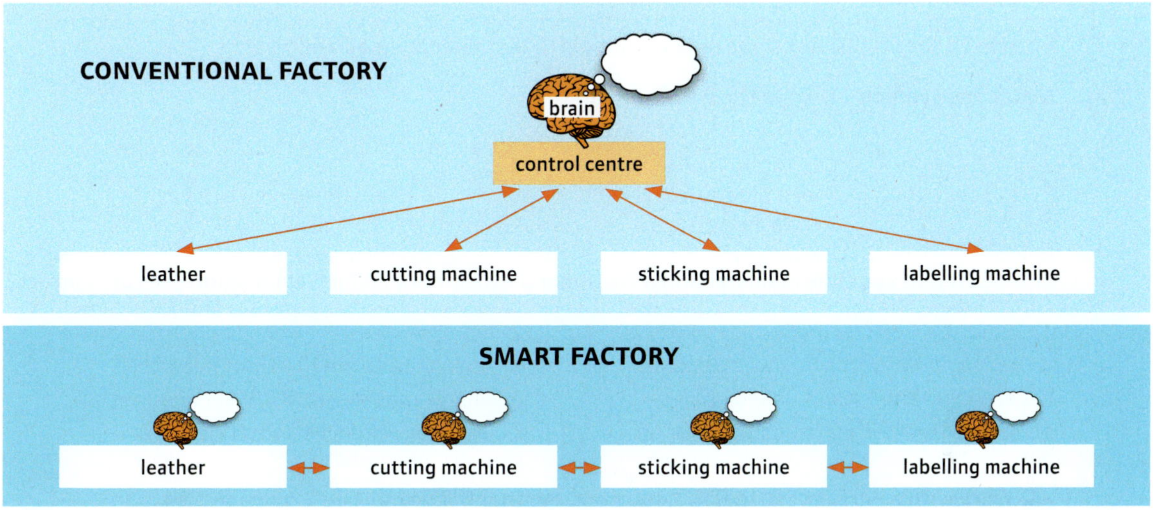

C 18)) Listen to the second part of the podcast and then use the diagram to describe how dairy farming can be adapted to Industry 4.0.

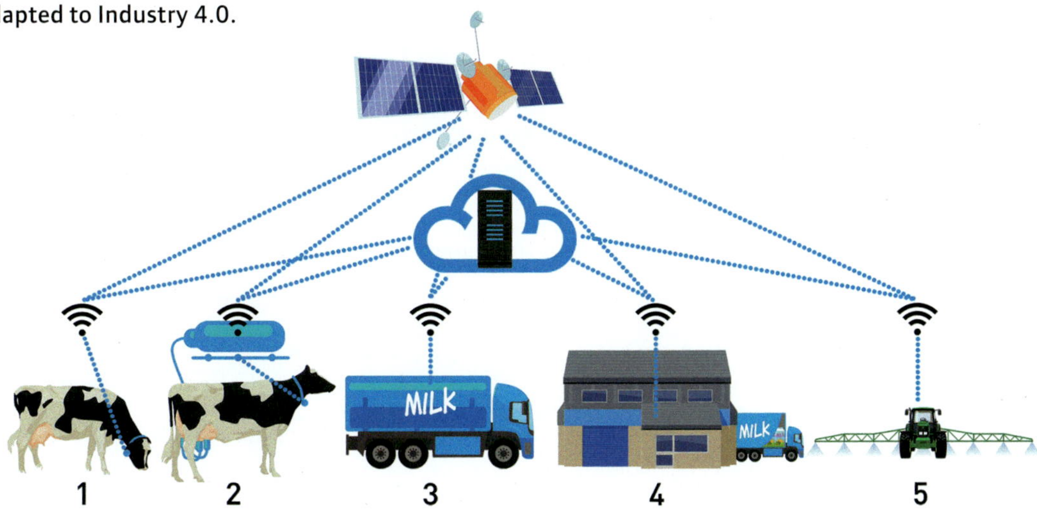

4 Changing over to Industry 4.0

Work in groups from the same training company and look at the situation in your company.

A Draw a diagram showing how goods are manufactured or services are provided at the moment. If your company has already changed over to Industry 4.0, describe the old system.

B Brainstorm the changes that (would) come with the introduction of Industry 4.0 and then draw a second diagram to show how a smart factory/system operates.

C Present the two diagrams to your class.

› *Useful phrases: Giving presentations, page 189*

COMMUNICATION: Emails

Situation: You work in the Sales department at Hoffmann Möbelbau GmbH, a furniture manufacturer. The Sales Manager, Marita Maffay, asks you to reply to an enquiry from a potential customer.
→ **You write an email in reply to a customer enquiry.**

1 Giving email addresses over the phone

You check the English for some of the symbols that appear in email addresses.

A Match the symbols (1–6) to the words (a–f).

1 +	**4** -	**a** at	**e** plus
2 _	**5** .	**b** dot	**e** number
3 @	**6** 3	**c** hyphen	**f** underscore

B 19)) **Listen to your line manager and a customer on the phone. Which email addresses are correct?**

1
- **a** m.maffay@hoffmann-moebelbau.de
- **b** mmaffay@hoffmann_moebelbau.de
- **c** m.maffay@hoffmann_moebelbau.de

2
- **a** maryannbrown@5+5_services.net
- **b** mary-anne-brown@5+5services.net
- **c** maryann-brown@5+5services.net

C Work with a partner. Partner A: Look here. Partner B: Look at File 2 on page 134.

Dictate these email addresses to Partner B. Check B's answers.

1 DavidMcCarthy+list@net.us
2 sergei-nikitin@com.ru
3 your own email address
4 the email address of your firm or another email address you often write to

Can you spell that, please?

Could you repeat that, please?

2 Writing a subject line

The first indication of what is in an email is the subject line. This must state clearly what the email is about.

A Work with a partner. Study the subject lines (a–f) below and find an email which …

1 is a request for information.
2 gives information about a meeting.
3 asks for assistance.
4 contains new information.
5 announces a change of plan.
6 is a covering letter for a brochure.

- **a** **Subject:** Need your help with English
- **b** **Subject:** New venue for event on Saturday
- **c** **Subject:** Flyer (attached)
- **d** **Subject:** Meeting 25.03. Starting time?
- **e** **Subject:** Update on project
- **f** **Subject:** Agenda

B With your partner, write suitable subject lines for the following emails (1–6).

1 Sorry, I would like to change the date of the meeting to Friday 12 July.
2 Could you send me information about the presentation, please?
3 I am on holiday from 21.03 till 04.04 inclusive and will answer emails when I return.
4 I am writing to confirm your application for a stand at the Technical Trades Fair. The stand number is C208.
5 As promised, here is the link to the website www.tipsformails.com.
6 This is just to let you know that I am interviewing a new export clerk at 12.30.

3 Writing a reply to an email enquiry

The Sales Manager gives you the enquiry below and asks you to reply by email in her name.

From i.johansen@svendsen-design.no
To: m.maffay@hoffmann_moebelbau.de
Subject: **Enquiry for customized furniture**

Dear Ms Maffay

Your company has been recommended to us by the Oslo Chamber of Commerce as a supplier of customized furniture.

We equip and furnish hotels and restaurants all over Norway and are looking for a manufacturer of fitted furniture made to our specifications from a variety of different materials at short notice.

Please let us know if you are able to supply such items.

Yours sincerely
Ingrid Johansen
Purchasing Director
Svendsen Design AS

Use a suitable greeting and subject line and reply to Ms Johansen. Include the following points:

- Thanks for enquiry (yesterday's date)
- Smart factory in Bielefeld: customized goods, any quantity or design
- Initial customer consultation: design expert on Skype
- Customer's specifications: digitized and uploaded to Hoffmann's server
- Design: CAD software with 3D visualization
- Cutting technology: laser
- Delivery: 10 days after order

Using polite language in emails

Could and *would like* are more polite than phrases with *can*, *need* or *want*.
~~Can~~ you let me know by Monday? → **Could** you let …
I ~~need~~ the information today. → I **would like** the …
We ~~want~~ to have a meeting. → We **would like** to …

› *Useful phrases: Writing emails, page 190*

Salutation and complimentary close in emails

If you do not know the name of the person you are writing to, begin your email with *Dear Sir or Madam*.
If you do not know your business partner well, use a formal salutation and complimentary close.

	Salutation	Complimentary close	
Formal (to unknown person)	Dear Sir or Madam	Yours faithfully	
Formal (to person whose name you know)	Dear Mr/Ms Smith	Yours sincerely Best regards	Best wishes Regards
Less formal	Dear Paul / Hi Paula Good morning, Paul	Regards Best regards	Best wishes All the best

DAS KANN ICH (Unit 4)

- Ein Informationsblatt über die Lieferkette meiner Firma schreiben. (Foundation)
- Die Lieferkette meiner Firma analysieren und Verbesserungen vorschlagen. (Part A)
- Einen Bericht über intelligente Fabriken auf Englisch schreiben (Part B)
- Eine Kundenanfrage auf Englisch per E-Mail beantworten. (Communication)

Exam practice 2

1 Hörverstehen: Stufe II

Situation: The American-based Car Plus Company, a manufacturer of car components, is about to open a new production plant in Liverpool. For the big opening party and presentation of the plant a lot of things have to be organized.

You work for Spiritz Ltd, a producer of wines, sparkling wines and spirits, which has received an enquiry from Car Plus Company. Your boss has arranged a telephone call with the Purchasing Manager of Car Plus and asks you to make notes during the conversation.

20)) **Task: Listen to the telephone call and make notes about what action needs to be taken.**

2 Leseverstehen: Stufe II

Situation: Sie arbeiten in einem Textilunternehmen in Kassel. Ihre Firma möchte sich auf dem britischen Markt weiter etablieren und sucht dafür einen Logistikpartner vor Ort. Für ein Meeting sollen mehrere infrage kommende Unternehmen zunächst vorgestellt werden. Um einen ersten Überblick zu erhalten, arbeiten alle Teammitglieder mit Übersichten. Sie bearbeiten die Firma Logotech International.

Aufgabe: Lesen Sie den Text und füllen Sie die Tabelle unten stichwortartig auf Deutsch aus.

Logotech International

Logotech International is a privately-owned international distribution and trading company. The company has been highly successful in international trade for over 15 years. The company's main activities are sourcing, distributing and selling fashion articles from overseas markets.

Logotech started out as a family business in 2003 when its core business was suppling fashion stores around the Midlands in the UK. Since then, the company has grown rapidly and now employs over 200 people. The head office is situated in Chorley (UK) with an overseas subsidiary in Mumbai, India and two large warehouses in Manchester and Liverpool. The locations are easily accessible via major motorways, two nearby airports (Liverpool, Manchester) and a port in Liverpool.

The company is well established and has highly-professional sales, marketing, warehousing and distribution operations. Consequently, Logotech International's retail customers now range from outlet centres to major supermarkets and department stores all over Great Britain. TKMix, H-store, G&N and Darlington are just some of their customers.

At the moment, the company is building a large logistics centre at the port of Liverpool which is due to open in about three months. A further milestone was the purchase last year of a freight forwarding company with an impressive fleet of over 30 trucks and lorries. With its experience, knowledge and capital, the company intends to grow further and ensure the success of its suppliers and customers.

Name der Firma	▬	Verkehrstechnische Anbindung	▬
Hauptsitz	▬	Lagerhaltungsmöglichkeiten	▬
Zweigstellen	▬	Kunden	▬
Unternehmensform	▬	Lieferkapazitäten	▬
Gründungsjahr	▬	Aktuelle Aktivitäten	▬
Anzahl der Angestellten	▬		

3 Mediation: Stufe II

Situation: Sie bereiten sich auf ein Auslandspraktikum bei einem Unternehmen für Sanitärbedarf in Bath (UK) vor. Sie fertigen sich eine Übersicht an, die Ihnen helfen soll, einen ersten Überblick über die Handelspartner des Praktikumsbetriebs zu gewinnen.

Aufgabe: Führen Sie die Tabelle fort, indem Sie die wesentlichen Informationen aus dem Text stichwortartig auf Deutsch in die Tabelle einfügen.

Types of traders

Getting a product to the market requires an effective marketing channel for companies that manufacture durable goods and other products. A supply chain typically features various middlemen between the manufacturer and the consumer. The most common links in the supply chain are distributors, wholesalers and retailers.

Distributors

Distributors have a business relationship with the manufacturers that they represent. Many distributors maintain exclusive buying agreements that limit the number of participants or enable distributors to cover a certain territory. The distributor becomes the manufacturer's direct point of contact for prospective buyers of certain products. However, distributors rarely sell a manufacturer's goods directly to consumers. Due to the very large amount of each product they have on hand or are able to acquire from manufacturers, distributors tend to work with wholesale representatives that will buy large quantities of one product. Depending on the product, they can also help in providing product information, technical support and after-sales service to their customers.

Wholesalers

Wholesalers buy a large quantity of products directly from distributors. High-volume purchase orders typically improve a wholesaler's buying power. Many distributors provide discounts for a certain number of items purchased or the total amount spent on merchandise. Wholesalers acquire all types of merchandise, ranging from phones, televisions and computers to bicycles, clothing, furniture and food. Wholesalers have a very strong interest in selling the goods as fast as possible, as storage space is a very costly factor.

Retailers

Retailers consist of small and large businesses that sell products directly to consumers. To realize a profit, retailers search for products that coincide with their business objectives, and find suppliers with the most competitive pricing. In a supply chain, retailers often have the largest profit margin. This profit margin can be reduced due to the costs of store rental or the number of employees. Online retailers are obviously less affected by these factors. Generally, a retailer can buy small quantities of an item from a wholesaler.

Vertragshändler/Distributoren	Großhändler	Einzelhändler
- *repräsentieren Hersteller, zu denen sie eine Geschäftsbeziehung unterhalten*	- *kaufen große Produktmengen direkt von Vertriebshändlern*	- *kleine und große Unternehmen, die direkt an Endverbraucher verkaufen*
-	-	-
-	-	-
-	-	-
-	-	

5 Marketing strategies

FOUNDATION: Market research tools

Situation: You work in the office of Doyle's Sports Gear Ltd, a manufacturer of sports equipment and accessories based in Dublin, Ireland. The company specializes in exercise equipment and sportswear for women. Doyle's Sports Gear is thinking about its options for collecting customer data.

→ **You write a memo with your recommendation for collecting customer data.**

1 Collecting customer data

You talk to your Irish colleagues about different ways of finding out information about your customers.

1

2

3

4

Work in groups and discuss the following questions. Make lists and report back to the class.

1 How do companies collect information about customers?
2 What information does a customer disclose when taking part in any of the activities?
3 What benefits or privileges does a customer have when they take part in the activities above?

2 Reading about market research

Before you write your recommendations, you check what you know about market research.

Why do market research?

Market research helps companies to find out about customer satisfaction and to predict how customers might react to a new product on the market.

Desk or field research?

Field research, which is gathering data directly from the customer, is one way to collect information. The other type of research is done by analysing data that has already been collected and published, for example, statistics or studies. This is called desk research.

Tools for field research

Companies use things like loyalty cards or online questionnaires for field research. Every time a cashier swipes a loyalty card across the scanner at the checkout, every time somebody answers a questionnaire in the street or does an online survey, a company somewhere is gathering data about its customers.

Two types of information the company asks for

Companies are interested in two types of data. The first is personal data, e.g. name, age, address, etc.; the second is purchasing history, e.g. the items or services that a customer buys.

Customer Relationship Management (CRM)

CRM is a strategy for managing all a company's relationships and interactions with current, future and potential customers and for storing all this data in one place, normally a powerful database in the cloud. Cloud-based data systems can be accessed anywhere and at any time, making it possible for all sales personnel to receive updated information instantly, e.g. by smartphone, laptop or desktop computer. In this way, sales teams can work more efficiently and boost overall productivity by improving customer satisfaction and customer loyalty.

Targeting specific customers

Using data collected in the CRM system, a company's sales team can customize its marketing strategies and advertising for a particular type of customer. Rather than waste money on a one-size-fits-all advertising campaign for a particular product or service, the sales team can break down the market into segments and target each one individually, using e.g. social media to reach younger people, and flyers and digital signage for trade fair visitors.

Read the text above and make notes in German on the following:

1 die Gründe, weshalb Firmen Marktforschung betreiben
2 den Unterschied zwischen Desk- und Field-Research
3 die Datenarten, die Firmen interessieren
4 die Vorteile von Customer Relationship Management
5 die Vorteile von Marktsegmentierung

3 Writing a memo with a recommendation

Now you write your recommendation for a good method for collecting customer data.

Work with a partner from the same training company. Discuss the methods for collecting customer data, then decide on a good option for your firm and your specific target group. Write a memo with your recommendation to your line manager.

- Summarize the most important information from the text.
- Make a recommendation: *Our recommendation is as follows: ...*
- Give reasons for your recommendation: *The reasons we believe ... are as follows: ...*

› *Thematic vocabulary: Sales and marketing, page 202*

PART A: A marketing strategy for a new product line

Situation: Your company, Textil-Manufaktur Mahler GmbH, wants to add a line of environmentally-friendly clothing to its product range. The company calls in an international marketing consultant for advice.

→ **You make suggestions to improve your company's marketing strategy.**

1 Discussing the product

You take part in a meeting with the marketing consultant to discuss the first of the new products, an environmentally-friendly unisex jacket.

Study the product brief below and describe the jacket to a partner. Suggest a suitable name for the product.

Product brief

Product	Unisex jacket
Product name	??
USPs (unique selling propositions)	made of – recycled water bottles (PET) – Fair Trade organic cotton
Target group	socially-responsible consumers
Market	Europe and beyond
Distribution	– online – stationary trade?
Sizes	XS, S, M, L, XL, XXL
Price(s)	??

2 Discussing the product

The consultant, Mary Garcia, is talking about the factors to consider before launching the product.

A 21 **Listen to her presentation and write down the four Ps of the marketing mix.**

B 21 **Listen again. Copy the table and make notes on what Mary Garcia says about each of the four Ps.**

First P:	1 2 3
Second P:	1 2
Third P:	1 2
Fourth P:	1 2

3 Reading about YouTube marketing

Mary Garcia mentions marketing your new line on YouTube. You do some research and find an infographic on search engine optimization (SEO).

Keywords

Nothing is more important than choosing the right keywords to describe your video. Good keywords get you more internet traffic and increase your viewer conversion rate, so choose them carefully! If you're marketing wooden furniture, a generic keyword like "furniture" will put you up against big players like IKEA. Instead, use long-tail (specific) keywords like "fitted pine kitchen furniture" to guide potential customers to your video.

Video description

You have a maximum of 800 words in your video description and only the first 25–30 will be visible in your YouTube search results, so place your most important keywords, your site's URL, your blog, your social media and your YouTube channel at the beginning.

Video title

Use the most relevant keywords in your video title, as close to the beginning as possible. Keep it under 66 characters because that's how much you see on the search engine's results page (SERP), e.g. of Google. Include the word "video" to direct traffic to YouTube.

Tags

These help your video to rank higher on the SERP. YouTube's tag box has space for a maximum of 500 characters, and experts recommend that you use three types of tag: **specific tags**, which are one-word keywords closely linked to your video, e.g. *cupboard, pine, fitted*; **compound tags**, which are two or more words describing your video (but without "grammatical" words like *is, that, when*, etc.), e.g. *Scandinavian design, custom-made*; **generic tags**, i.e. non-specific words describing general categories, e.g. *furniture, wooden, modern*.

A Choose two or three of the following generic terms and think of specific examples in each case.

clothing • energy • entertainment • food • housing • music • sport • transport • vehicle

Generic	Specific
clothing	*jeans, T-shirts, ...*

B The production company makes a video showing the new jacket and how it is made. Working in small groups, think of the following items for the video:

- 2 or 3 long-tail keywords
- a video title (max. 66 characters)
- a video description (25–30 words)
- 6 tags (2x specific, 2x compound, 2x generic)

C Compare your results with those of other groups and discuss them in class.

4 Discussing market research results

PRICE

Before the product launch, you interview people in the street to decide on the price of the new jacket. Here is what some of them said.

A €200 is my limit, but for that it has to look great and last more than a couple of years.

B €30 for a jacket? Is it made with slave labour?

C €50? It can't be any good at that price and how much of that is helping the environment?

D €250 for a jacket? You must be kidding! Or is it a designer jacket?

E €150 is a reasonable price for a good jacket and it will help the environment at the same time.

> **Explaining consequences**
>
> **If** we **ask** for €30, people **will think** it's poor quality.
> **If** we **don't ask** for at least €100, people **won't believe** it's a good product.

› *Grammar: Conditional sentences, page 156*

A **Use their answers (A–E) to make at least five sentences about different prices.**

B **Mary Garcia gives you some background literature on pricing. Read the text and then choose a suitable pricing strategy for the jacket with a partner.**

Nice price?

How many people would buy a perfume if it only cost €2 a bottle? And why does a soft drink cost 50 cents at a supermarket but €5.00 at a festival? The price is not just production costs plus profit. Pricing is a strategy. The following is an overview of frequently used pricing strategies.

Penetration pricing: When a company tries to break into an existing market, it sets its prices low at the beginning to attract customers and establish itself. Later the prices are raised. New mobile phone providers often use this strategy.

Premium pricing: Premium prices are artificially high. This is because some consumers believe that a product must be better if it costs more. Luxury goods, such as jewellery or cars, fall into this category.

Psychological pricing: Surveys show that prices ending in 9 sell better than others. A product for €4.99 therefore sells better than for €5.00. This is because the brain concentrates on the left digit of the price (4 in this example) and disregards the rest. €4.99 is therefore perceived to be €4.00 and not almost €5.00.

Value-based pricing: In this case the price is based on the benefits the customer believes they will have from the product and not the cost of producing it. It is basically how much the customer is willing to pay. Fashionwear, pharmaceutical products and goods for which there is a shortage come under this category.

Cost-plus pricing: The cost-plus or cost-based price of a product is its break-even point plus profit. This strategy is often used when there is extreme competition, e.g. budget airlines and discounters, or no competition, e.g. government contracts and public utilities.

C **Present your ideas to the class and give reasons for your choice of pricing strategy.**

5 Distribution channels

PLACE

There are several ways of selling goods to the final consumer and each has its pros and cons. Sometimes a combination of distribution channels is used.

1 **Direct:** There is no intermediary between the producer and the consumer. The final consumer must come to the production site or contact the producer directly. Large aircraft/vessels/vehicles and pick-your-own fruit and vegetables fall into this category. The producer has maximum profit and total control over the product, its promotion and price.

2 **Retailer:** There is one intermediary between the producer and the consumer. High-volume, mass-market products, such as toothpaste and washing powder, are sold to one major retailer, often under the retailer's label, through the retailer's sales network. Profits are shared with the retailer, who also controls the price and promotion of the product.

3 **Wholesaler:** There are two intermediaries between the producer and the consumer. Mass-market products are sold to the wholesaler in bulk and then sold in smaller quantities to multiple retail sites, such as small supermarkets and convenience stores. Profits are shared with two parties, and the manufacturer has little control over the price and promotion of the product.

4 **Agent/Broker:** There are one or more intermediaries between the producer and the consumer. Agents and brokers do not own the product. They use their knowledge of the local market and/or language to arrange for the sale of goods between producers, wholesalers and retailers and work on a commission basis. Non-competing related products, such as sports equipment, are often sold in this way. The producer has greater control over the price and promotion of the product but shares the profits with several parties.

5 **Distributor:** There are one or more intermediaries between the producer and the consumer. Distributors buy goods from the producer and use their retail network to sell them to consumers, wholesalers or retailers. Digital devices and musical instruments are often sold in this way. Distributors control the price and promotion of the product; their profit margin is greater than that of an agent and they often stock competing products.

A **Read the text and summarize the information about each channel in a table with the following headings.**

Channel	Product	Point of sale	Profit-sharing	Control of price and promotion
1 Direct				
2 Retailer				
3 Wholesaler				
4 Agent/Broker				
5 Distributor				

B **Discuss with a partner which distribution channel(s) should be used to sell the jacket. Present your ideas to the class and give reasons for your choice.**

6 Marketing your company's products

The company where you are doing your apprenticeship decides to review its marketing strategies.

A **Work in small groups from the same training company. Choose one or more of your company's products and make notes on the following tasks:**

- analyse the current marketing mix (the four Ps)
- consider ways of optimizing sales by changing the marketing mix

B **Present your ideas to the class.**

› *Thematic vocabulary: Sales and marketing, page 202*

PART B: An advertising strategy

Situation: Your company, Textil-Manufaktur Mahler GmbH, is using an international marketing consultant to help launch a new type of eco-friendly jacket. The jacket is made from recycled plastic bottles and fair-trade organic cotton.

→ **You help to devise an advertising strategy for a new product/line for your company.**

1 Reviewing advertising strategies

The consultant sends your company some literature about the different ways of advertising a product.

A Match the different ways of advertising (A–L) to the definitions (1–12) in the diagram.

- **A** branding
- **B** celebrity endorsement
- **C** guerrilla advertising
- **D** niche advertising
- **E** old media
- **F** online advertising
- **G** pop-up shop
- **H** public relations (PR)
- **I** social media
- **J** stealth advertising
- **K** testimonials
- **L** YouTube

Possible advertising strategies

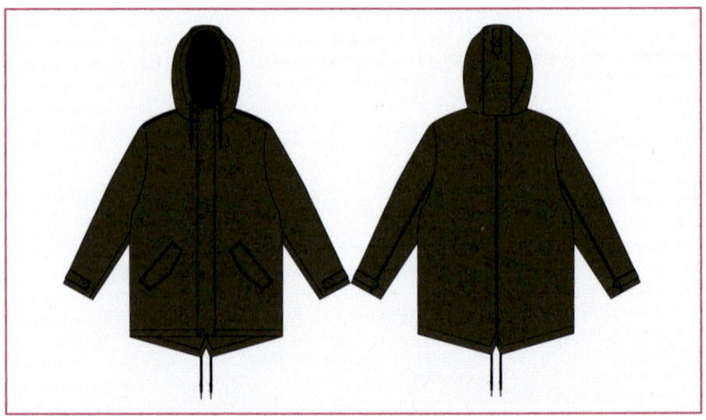

for the *Honesty* line?

1. Facebook, Twitter, Instagram, etc.
2. creating a unique name and image of a product
3. interactive video channel
4. internet, apps and QR codes
5. TV, radio, cinema, newspapers, magazines, etc.
6. reports from satisfied customers
7. secretly paying people to promote products
8. giving money to a good cause
9. support from a famous person
10. targeted advertising
11. temporary retail outlet
12. unconventional activities in public

B With a partner discuss which four ways you would use to advertise the new eco-friendly jacket.

C When you have finished, discuss your ideas in class. Can you agree on the four best ways to advertise the new product?

› *Thematic vocabulary: Advertising strategies, page 202*

2 Launching the campaign

The advertising campaign for the new unisex jacket has been agreed on and starts with an event in the city centre. A BBC radio reporter is covering the event and interviewing your boss.

A 22))) **Listen to the broadcast. Which forms of advertising from exercise 1A are used or are mentioned by Ben Kaiser?**

old media – radio report, ...

B **Use words from the broadcast to complete the reporter's article on the BBC's website.**

How many of us realize that ___[1] of plastic bottles are thrown into the world's oceans every year? Textil-Manufaktur Mahler, a German clothing wholesaler in Dusseldorf, plans to do something about the problem of plastic water bottle ___[2], and that's why they have a new jacket on the market made from 25 ___[3] plastic bottles. The ___[4] price is 150 euros, but when the product was ___[5] at Dusseldorf's busy central station last week, people could pay for it by recycling 25 plastic bottles.
When I arrived, a long queue had formed outside their ___[6] shop and they were joined by Germany's top surfer, Timo von Struck. He plans to paddle down the Rhine, which is over 1,200 km long, on a ___[7] made of plastic bottles and collect plastic ___[8] all the way to help stop the destruction of our oceans and waterways.

3 Creating a brand

Mary Garcia gives you and Ben Kaiser a list of five key points to consider when creating a brand.

Study the table and the extract from Ben's email reply to Mary Garcia. Find the information in his email that corresponds to each of the five points.

1 Image	2 Customers	3 Slogan	4 Logo	5 Colours
Find the words that describe your company best.	Describe the people you are selling to.	Find a catchphrase that says it all.	Design a logo with a clear message.	Choose the colours that suit your products.

Thanks for the information on branding. We've had a think about it and have come up with the following ideas:
We think that a simple drawing of a handshake in pale green and blue tones with the caption "Clothes with a conscience" best shows our priorities.
The many likes that we have received on Facebook recently show that our clientele have a sense of social responsibility and understand that we are an environmentally-conscious, honest and transparent company.

4 Devising an advertising campaign

The company where you are doing your apprenticeship plans to bring out a new product/line and forms a team to choose the best advertising strategy.

A **Work in groups from the same training company. Use the list in exercise 1A (page 50) to review your company's current advertising strategies. How successful are they?**

B **Devise an advertising campaign to launch the new product. How will you attract the public's attention?**

C **Present your ideas to the class. Would they work? Have a class discussion about them.**

› *Useful phrases: Giving presentations, page 189; Thematic vocabulary: Advertising strategies, page 202*

COMMUNICATION: Graphs and charts

Situation: Your union representative is speaking at an international conference next week.
→ **You prepare notes on some graphic information that he can use in his talk.**

1 Describing graphs

You refresh your knowledge of the English expressions for describing graphs.

A Match the names in the list to the diagrams (a–c). There is one name more than you need.

bar chart · line graph · pie chart · table

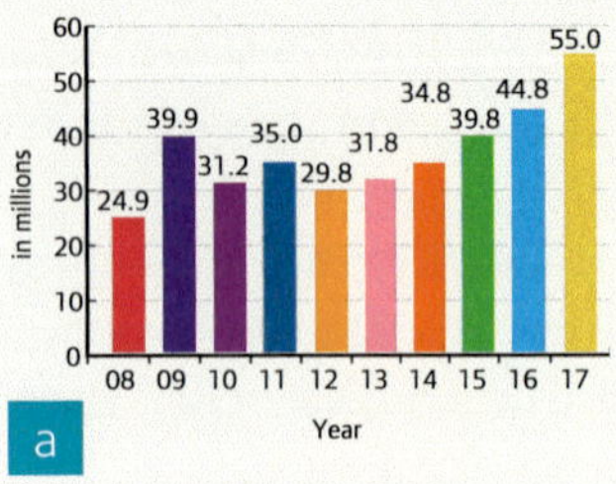

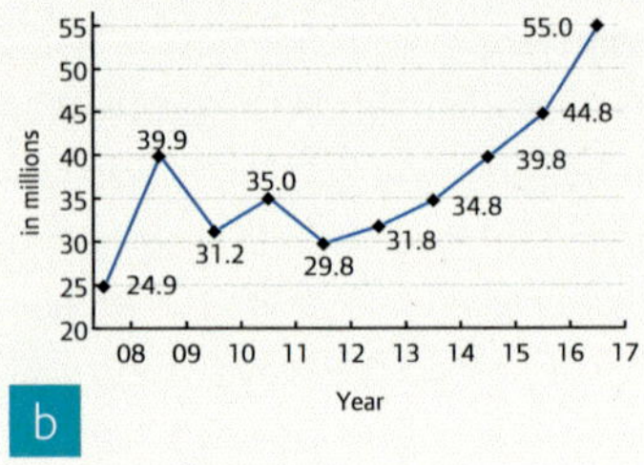

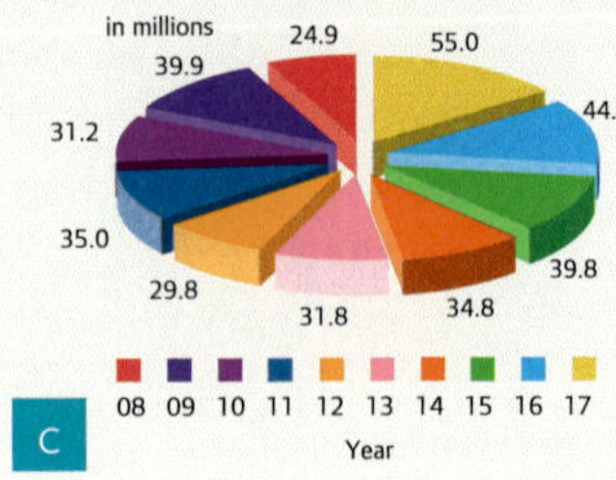

B Match the words/phrases (1–12) to the graphs (a–h). For some graphs, several expressions can be used.

1 to remain constant / stay the same
2 to go up / down
3 to increase / the increase
4 to hit a maximum / minimum
5 to flatten out / level off
6 to decrease / the decrease
7 to drop / the drop
8 to rise / the rise
9 to fluctuate / the fluctuation
10 to fall / the fall
11 to climb / the climb
12 to peak / the peak

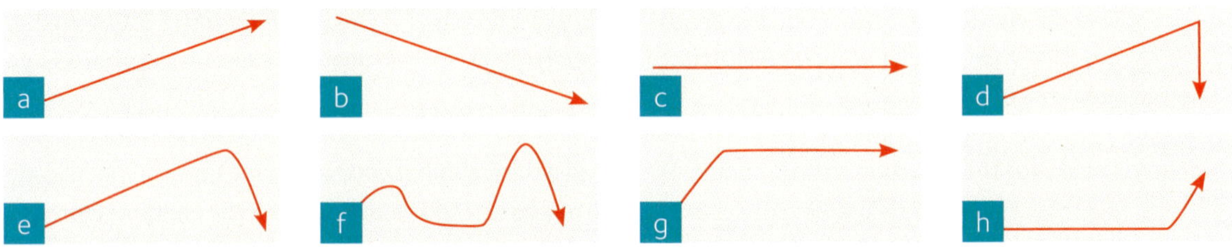

C Work with a partner. Partner A: Look here. Partner B: Look at File 12 on page 140.

Describe this line graph to Partner B. Partner B will draw it. Check Partner B's graph when you have finished. › *Useful phrases: Describing graphs, page 190; Thematic vocabulary: Describing graphs, page 203*

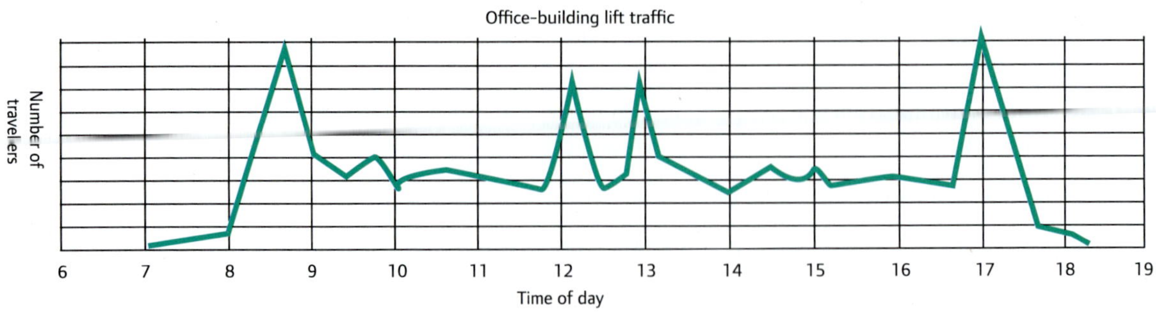

2 Talking about figures

At the conference, your union representative uses a table to describe sales of technical products worldwide in the last financial year.

A 23 **Listen and decide which of the tables is being presented.**

A

Quarterly sales (millions of euros)				
Area	Q. I	Q. II	Q. III	Q. IV
UK	10.3	11.4	8.2	10.5
Germany	8.9	9.3	8.6	7.1
E. Europe	0.2	0.8	1.7	3.6

B

Quarterly sales (€ m)			
Q. I	Q. II	Q. III	Q. IV
10.3	11.4	8.2	10.3
8.0	8.3	8.1	6.2
0.3	0.9	3.8	4.5

C

Quarterly sales (€ m)			
Q. I	Q. II	Q. III	Q. IV
10.3	11.4	8.2	10.7
8.2	7.4	8.0	9.5
0.5	1.6	2.3	2.3

B **Work with a partner. Choose one of the tables and describe the sales figures for Germany or Eastern Europe. Your partner should say which table you are describing.**

3 Describing a table

Your union representative would like to compare and contrast average working hours in Germany with conditions in other countries. You have found the following table.

	Working hours per week	Working day*	Lunch break
Germany	41.1	07.30/08.30–16.00/17.30	30–45 mins (12.00–13.30)
France	37.9	08.00–18.00	60 mins (12.00–14.00)
GB	41.4	08.00/09.00–17.00/18.00	60 mins (12.00–14.00)
Scandinavia	39.1	08.00–16.00	30 mins (11.30–12.00)
USA	40+	08.00–17.00+	30 mins (12.00–13.00)

* The working day: Blue-collar workers in some countries begin work one hour earlier than white-collar workers.

A **Work with a partner. Study the table and write notes, using the following headings:**

Introduction

The table shows information about …

- **Working hours per week**
  The shortest working hours per week are to be found in …
- **Working day**
  In Germany, most people begin work between 7.30 and 8.30 and finish …
- **Lunch breaks**
  People in France and Great Britain have the longest …

B **Work in groups. Discuss what type of graph(s) you could use to present the data on working hours.**

DAS KANN ICH (Unit 5)

- Eine Empfehlung für eine neue Marktforschungsstrategie auf Englisch schreiben. (Foundation)
- Verbesserungen zur Vertriebsstrategie der eigenen Firma auf Englisch erarbeiten. (Part A)
- Eine Werbekampagne für ein neues Produkt auf Englisch vorstellen. (Part B)
- Notizen anhand einer Grafik auf Englisch erstellen. (Communication)

6 Meetings and negotiations

FOUNDATION: Preparations for a meeting

Situation: You work in the Hamburg branch of a British company, Fleming Chocolates Ltd. The company is interested in buying cocoa beans from Grano de Cacao, a farmers' co-operative in Bolivia. After a first video conference, two representatives are coming to Hamburg to negotiate a contract.
→ You send out the agenda to the people who are going to attend the meeting.

1 Preparing for a meeting

First of all, you think about what you have to do to prepare for the meeting that is coming up.

Copy the mind map below and add more ideas of your own.

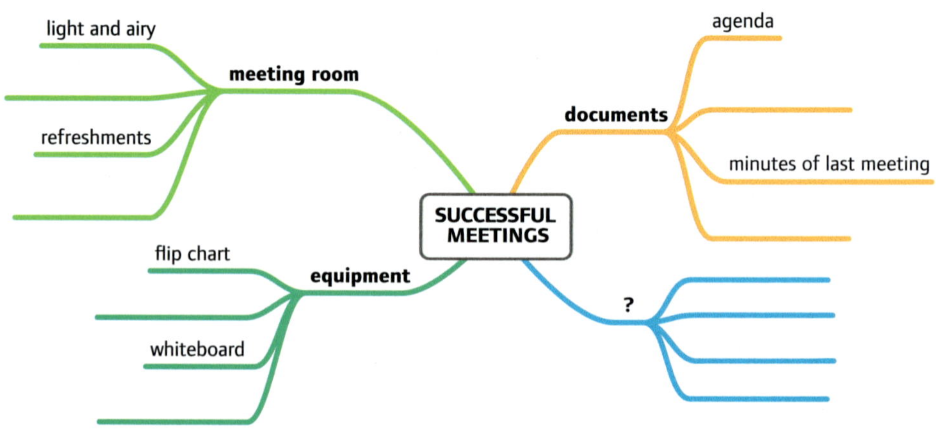

2 Making a to-do list

Your colleagues Penny Jones and Niklas Behringer have received a memo from Mary Brown, the CEO's personal assistant, asking them to prepare for the meeting with the representatives of Grano de Cacao.

Fleming Chocolates Ltd, Hamburg branch **Memo**

To	Penny Jones, Niklas Behringer	**Date**	20 December 20..
From	Mary Brown, PA to CEO	**Ref.**	MB/OAs

Subject Meeting with representatives from Grano de Cacao, Bolivia on 20 January 20..

Please make all the necessary arrangements in good time for the meeting.

24)) Listen to them discussing the details of the meeting, and make a list of what needs to be done.

Before the meeting
▬ the number of participants
▬ a suitable room and equipment (data projector, flipchart, etc.)
▬
On the day of the meeting
▬
After the meeting
▬

➔ Making a to-do list

Anything else we **should do** before the day of the meeting?
We **need to make** a name tag for each participant.
We **have to make sure** each place in the conference room has everything the participants need.

› *Grammar: Modals and their substitutes, page 158*

3 Writing an agenda

You and Niklas discuss the agenda for the meeting with Mary Brown, the CEO's PA.

25)) Listen and write down what is planned for each time listed on the agenda.

Fleming Chocolates Ltd, Hamburg Branch

Meeting with Grano de Cacao representatives **Date:** 20 January 20..

Participants:

Fleming Chocolates Ltd
Jenny Fleming, CEO
Mary Brown, PA to CEO
Helen Clark, Warehouse Manager
Tom Baker, Purchasing Manager

Grano de Cacao
Carmen de Luña, Director
Miguel Reyes, Legal Adviser

Agenda

Start: ▬[1]
Jenny Fleming: ▬[2]
▬[3] of the last meeting and any questions about them
10 a.m. – 12 noon: ▬[4] negotiations on the contract
12.00 – 12.30 p.m.: ▬[5] of the warehouse (Helen Clark)
12.45 – 1.45 p.m.: ▬[6]
2.00 – 4.30 p.m.: ▬[7] the contract
4.30 – 5.00 p.m.: ▬[8], date of next meeting

4 Writing an email

After you and Niklas talk to the CEO's PA, you email the agenda and documents to all the participants.

Write the email to all the participants, including the following points:

- the date, time and place of the meeting
- the agenda
- the tour of the warehouse
- a car to take the visitors from the airport to their hotel
- an invitation for the guests to an evening meal when they arrive
- attachments: all the documents needed for the meeting

› *Useful phrases: Writing emails, page 190* › *Thematic vocabulary: Meetings and presentations, page 203*

PART A: An international meeting

Situation: Your company, Brewery-2-Brewery GmbH in Gelsenkirchen, exports brewing equipment all over the world. You are in the export sales team and attend the next international sales meeting.
→ **You take part in a works council meeting about flexitime.**

1 Preparing for a sales meeting

The Export Sales Director, Sarah Bonrath, has emailed details of the meeting to the participants in advance.

Find the words in her email that match the definitions below.

From: Sarah Bonrath <sarah.bonrath@btwob.com>
Subject: Agenda for sales meeting on 26 June 20..
Attachment(s): Presentation

Dear all

I hope you are all well.

I'm sure you will remember that our last meeting was postponed because some of the participants were unable to attend, so I have scheduled our meeting for 9 a.m. on 26 June.

The items on the agenda are as follows:
1 Presentation (Rajiv Mittal, Mumbai, India)
2 Current order situation
3 Deliveries
4 Installing and operating equipment
5 AOB

As always, the minutes of the meeting will be emailed to you one day later.

Best regards

Sarah Bonrath
Export Sales Director

1 extra points discussed at the end of a meeting
2 the points to be discussed at a meeting
3 a record of all the things said or decided at a meeting
4 to go to (a meeting)
5 to change to a later date
6 to choose a date

2 Attending a meeting

The meeting takes place as planned, but some changes have been made to the agenda.

A 26)) **Listen to the meeting and write down the new items on the agenda in the correct order. Which point is not discussed?**

B 26 **In preparation for taking part in meetings yourself, you make a list of useful phrases. Listen again and fill in the missing words.**

Taking part in meetings

Starting the meeting
Good morning everybody and welcome to …
The first item on today's ___[1] is …

Introducing yourself
I'm … / My name is …

Asking someone to speak
Would you go ___[2], please?
Can you give us a brief update?

Asking for reactions
Would anyone like to ___[3] or ask a question?
Are there any issues?

Starting a new topic
Let's ___[4] on to the next topic, which is …
The next point is …

Asking to speak
Could I just say that …?
Can I ___[5] in on that?

Agreeing and disagreeing
I ___[6] agree with … (name).
Yes, I agree.
(I'm afraid) I don't agree with … (name).
I agree up to a point, but …

Promising action
I'll ___[7] that on to …
We'll get back to you.

Finishing the meeting
Let's ___[8] up the meeting with …
Well, that would seem to be it.

3 Checking the minutes of a meeting

The next day you receive the minutes of the meeting. You check the facts against your own notes and notice that there are five mistakes.

Study the minutes, find the mistakes and correct them. Listen to the recording again, if necessary.

Brewery-2-Brewery GmbH

Minutes of sales meeting on 26 June 20..

Attendees: Sarah Bonrath (Germany), Wen Fang (Singapore), Donald Masters (UK), Rajiv Mittal (India)

1: New agent
Ms Wen Fang from Singapore Trading joined Brewery-2-Brewery as an agent six months ago.

2: Presentation
Rajiv Mittal gave a presentation called "Beer in Mumbai" and said that the figures were not positive.

3: Current order situation
Donald Masters described how his orders were up 10% on last year.
Wen Fang was unable to give any information about sales figures.
Rajiv Mittal stated that his orders were up 5% on last year.

4: Deliveries
Donald Masters reported that deliveries were punctual 95% of the time, which was better than last year (75%).

5: Complaints
Donald Masters complained that some of the equipment had arrived dirty due to poor packing.

AOB
The finance department will contact Rajiv Mittal about travel expenses next week.

4 Taking part in a meeting

Now you take part in a works council meeting and write the minutes of the meeting.

Work in groups of six. Partners A and B: Look here. Partners C and D: Look at File 4 on page 135. Partners E and F: Look at File 5 on page 136.

Situation:
Brewery-2-Brewery is an American-owned company and has 20 employees in the office and 15 in the warehouse. At the last works council meeting, many employees were in favour of introducing flexitime. Today, there is a meeting between the American General Manager and the employees to discuss it. Attending the meeting are:

- the General Manager (Partner A)
- the Human Resources Manager (Partner B)
- the Works Council Representative (Partner C)
- an office worker (Partner D)
- a warehouse employee (Partner E)
- an apprentice wholesaler (Partner F)

VIDEO 4

Watch the video to see more about meetings.

	Office	Warehouse
Working hours	7.30 a.m. – 3.30 p.m.	Early shift: 6.00 a.m. – 2.00 p.m. Day shift: 10.00 a.m. – 6.00 p.m.
Break	9.30 a.m. – 9.45 a.m.	15 minutes taken flexibly
Lunch break	12.00 noon – 12.45 p.m.	

A Use your role card below and the expressions in exercise 2B to conduct a meeting and come to a decision.

Partner A: General Manager

Your opinion on flexitime is neutral and you will decide on the basis of the arguments you hear.

- start the meeting, introduce yourself and ask the participants to introduce themselves
- explain that the meeting is about introducing flexitime
- ask the Works Council Representative to explain why some people want it
- ask if there are any questions
- consult with the HR Manager and come to a decision

Partner B: Human Resources Manager

You are against flexitime because there must always be at least two employees in the warehouse to load and unload lorries early in the morning and late in the afternoon. You would also like to introduce shift work in the office to guarantee the necessary paperwork for the lorries all day.

- introduce yourself
- explain your position
- answer the questions
- consult with the General Manager and come to a decision

› *Useful phrases: Taking part in meetings, page 191*

B When you have finished, write the minutes of the meeting.

› *Thematic vocabulary: Meetings and presentations, page 203*

Talking about the past

Donald Masters **described** his sales figures.
Rajiv Mittal **gave** a presentation.
He **stated** that his orders **were** up.

› *Grammar: Simple past, page 154; Reported speech, page 157*

PART B: Hosting foreign suppliers

Situation: You work in the Purchasing Department of TextilKaiser GmbH, a German fashion manufacturer with suppliers throughout Europe. Your company's annual suppliers' meeting is now taking place in Munich.
→ **You meet a supplier to negotiate new terms of business.**

1 Negotiating using the direct approach

Before the meeting, TextilKaiser's Purchasing Director sends an email to a Romanian clothing manufacturer explaining that new terms will need to be negotiated.

Dear Mr Popescu

I enclose an invitation to our annual suppliers' meeting next month and look forward to speaking to you again in person.

In view of the stiff competition in the global denim and jeans market, we are reviewing all suppliers' contracts in order to reduce costs and remain competitive. We would therefore welcome your suggestions as to how your prices can be reduced significantly.

At the same time the market for low-priced denim is rapidly expanding, so we wish to consider how you can increase production to keep up with this trend and to discuss your suggestions at our meeting.

Please let me know, should you be unable to attend.

Best wishes
Annika Wenzel

Purchasing Director

TextilKaiser GmbH

A **Read the email and answer the questions.**

1 How do we know that Annika Wenzel and the supplier have met before?
2 How many suppliers' contracts are going to be discussed?
3 What suggestions is Mr Popescu expected to make at the meeting?
4 What are the current trends in the denim market?
5 What is the worst-case scenario for Mr Popescu?

B 27)) **Listen to the first version of the dialogue in which the Purchasing Director uses the direct approach to negotiating. Answer the questions.**

1 What three important changes does Annika Wenzel want?
2 How much time does the supplier get to consider the new terms?
3 How do you think the supplier feels after this discussion?

C 27)) **Listen again and write down the exact wording of the questions Annika Wenzel asks Mr Popescu about the three important changes.**

- *Can you …?*
- *Will your company …?*
- *Will you …?*

2 Negotiating using the indirect approach

Annika Wenzel also uses the indirect approach to negotiating.

A 28 **Listen to a second version of her conversation with Mr Popescu and complete the sentences.**

1 Our ___ are 10% ___ than us. Do you see what I mean?
2 We are thinking of ___ 20% more from your ___.
3 We can ___ you with more machines if you can find more ___.
4 We need a ___ delivery period of 30 ___.
5 I ___ that you use Road Train GmbH. Here's their ___.
6 Would you like some time to ___ about the new ___?

How do you think the supplier feels after this discussion?

B **Work with a partner and practise asking for better terms using the direct and the indirect approach.**

Goods or services	Acceptable range
packing charge per (machine)	€20–25
extra guarantee (computer)	12–24 months
quantity discount on 100 units (T-shirts)	3–5%
sale or return agreement (books)	3–6 months

Can you provide … at … per machine?

We can pay a little more for … if you can …

3 Negotiating better conditions

The Croatian company Kolar Leather is a supplier for TextilKaiser GmbH. Today you are going to negotiate with one of the directors of Kolar Leather to obtain better conditions for your company.

Role-play the conversation, using the language box below and the prompts on page 61.

Small talk	
I hope you're well. … is such a beautiful city!	The weather is so good today! Did you have a good trip/flight?
Main negotiating points	
Direct approach Are you prepared to …? Can you reduce the price by … (e.g. €20)? Will you increase … (e.g. production) by …? Are you able to guarantee … (e.g. delivery)? Do you accept these terms?	**Indirect approach** We need to talk about … … is a problem for us. … (e.g. our competitors) are …% cheaper. We're thinking of ordering more/less … We need a maximum/minimum of … How much/many more … can you produce?
Time factor	
Direct approach Let's get down to business. I have a lot of meetings/appointments today. I need an answer now. The next supplier is waiting.	**Indirect approach** Please take your time. Shall we take a break (for coffee/lunch)? Have you had enough time to think about …?
Offering help	
We can help you with … We can give you … if you can …	I suggest that you …

› *Useful phrases: Negotiating, page 192*

Partner A:
Sie (eigener Name), TextilKaiser

Betreiben Sie Small Talk.

Sie müssen über die Preise sprechen, denn die Konkurrenz ist 5 % billiger.

Einer Ihrer Lieferanten in Split schließt gerade seine Firma und verkauft sein gesamtes Inventar. Vielleicht hat er ein Stromaggregat. Sie schlagen vor, dass Herr/Frau Horvat dort anruft und geben ihm/ihr die Telefonnummer des Besitzers.

Sie schlagen vor, eine Kaffeepause zu machen.

Pause

Sie freuen sich und fragen, ob er/sie die Preise reduzieren kann.

Sie freuen sich über diese Lösung und beenden höflich das Gespräch.

Partner B:
Ivan/Nina Horvat, Kolar Leather

Betreiben Sie Small Talk.

Sie haben technische Probleme in Ihrer Werkstatt. Sie könnten Ihre Kosten um 5 % reduzieren, wenn Sie ein neues Stromaggregat (*electricity generator*) hätten. Aber das können Sie sich nicht leisten, denn Stromaggregate sind sehr teuer.

Sie bitten um Zeit, die Firma anzurufen.

Pause

Sie haben den Besitzer angerufen und kaufen ihm ein fast neues Stromaggregat günstig ab.

Wenn die Maschine gut ist, können Sie Ihre Preise in drei Monaten um 5 % reduzieren.

Sie beenden höflich das Gespräch.

4 Role-play: A negotiation competition

You are going to role-play a situation in which a manufacturer negotiates with a supplier. You will get points for the results of your negotiations and will find out who is the better negotiator!

Work with a partner.
Partner A (manufacturer): **Look at File 6 on page 137.**
Partner B (supplier): **Look at File 7 on page 138.**

› *Useful phrases: Negotiating, page 192*

COMMUNICATION: Arrangements for meetings

Situation: You work in the Sales department at Top Mode GmbH, a fashion manufacturer in Dusseldorf. The company is exhibiting at a trade fair in Glasgow next week.
→ **You rearrange the date and time of a meeting for your Sales Director.**

1 Setting up a meeting with a client

Paul Schmidt, the Sales Director, asks you to arrange a meeting with a client for him and leaves you the following instructions.

- Frau Mary Doyle bei InFashion Ltd in Dublin kontaktieren
- Termin für Präsentation unserer Jeansjacken und Besprechung der Einzelheiten ihres Auftrags vereinbaren
- Treffen von ca. 2 Stunden auf der FunFashion Messe in Glasgow vorschlagen
- mögliche Termine: 26. April zwischen 8.00 und 12.00 Uhr oder 27. April zwischen 13.00 und 18.00 Uhr
- Bitte um Angabe des Termins bis morgen zwecks rechtzeitiger Reservierung eines Besprechungsraums

Telling the time in English-speaking countries

When telling the time in English, use the short forms, *a.m.* and *p.m.*

a.m. *(ante meridiem)* = between midnight and midday
p.m. *(post meridiem)* = after 12.00 noon

In English-speaking countries the twenty-four hour clock is generally only used for timetables and diaries.

Write the email to the customer in your name explaining that you are writing on behalf of the Sales Director, Mr Paul Schmidt.

From: Ihr_vorname.Ihr_nachname@topmode.de
To: m.doyle@infashionltd.ie
Subject: Meeting with …

Dear …

2 Rearranging a meeting

Two days before the meeting, Mary Doyle phones to rearrange it. Paul Schmidt answers the phone.

A **Before you listen, discuss with a partner how you would say the phrases at the top of page 63 in English.**

B 29 **Listen to the call. Why is Mary rearranging the meeting? What are the new arrangements?**

C 29 **Listen again. Which English equivalents of the German sentences did you hear?**

› *Useful phrases: Making arrangements, page 192*

Giving dates, days and times

at 6 p.m., **at** lunchtime, **at** the weekend
on Monday, **on** 21 June
in the morning/afternoon/evening,
in January, **in** 2017

1 a Entschuldigen Sie, dass ich so kurzfristig anrufe.
b Es tut mir leid, dass ich Sie damit belästigen muss.
2 a Ich muss unsere Besprechung leider absagen.
b Ich muss unsere Besprechung leider verschieben.
3 a Es ist etwas dazwischen gekommen, das ich leider nicht verschieben kann.
b Entschuldigen Sie, aber ich habe zu diesem Zeitpunkt einen anderen Termin.
4 a Könnten Sie etwas später am selben Tag kommen?
b Schwebt Ihnen ein anderer Termin vor?
5 a Könnten wir das Treffen auf Freitag zur gleichen Zeit verschieben?
b Würde die gleiche Uhrzeit am Freitag für Sie passen?
6 a Ich entschuldige mich für die Umstände.
b Danke für Ihr Verständnis.

3 Confirming the details of a rearranged meeting

Paul asks you to send an email on his behalf to Mary Doyle, confirming the new details of their meeting.

Write the email, stating the new date and time of the meeting. Start and end the email with a suitable salutation and complimentary close.

› *Useful phrases: Writing emails, page 190*

4 Role-play: Changing arrangements

Because Paul is now meeting Mary Doyle on Friday, he has to postpone his breakfast meeting with another business associate, Jane Duncan, on that day. He asks you to arrange a new meeting with her.

Work with a partner. Partner A: Look here. Partner B: Look at File 8 on page 139.

Role-play a phone call with Jane Duncan. Explain Paul's situation and use details from his itinerary below to suggest a new date and time for a meeting with Jane Duncan, e.g. for lunch or dinner.

ITINERARY – **Wed 25th – Sat 28th**			
Wed 25	Flight LH 134 07.20 → Glasgow (arr. 08.40)		Dinner: Hans Treder 19.00 (Wallace Restaurant)
Thur 26	~~Meeting: Mary Doyle 9.30–12.30~~	Meeting: Martin O'Leary, Irish Wool Ltd 14.00–16.00	
Fri 27	~~Working breakfast: Jane Duncan 7.00–9:30~~ *Meeting: Mary Doyle 9.30–12.30*	Meeting: Karin Wood, KW-Shoes Ltd 14.00–18.00	Buffet: Glasgow Retail Trade Association 19.00–22.30
Sat 28	Golf: Harry Jones 11.00		Flight LH 918 19.15 → Dusseldorf (arr. 22.25)

› *Useful phrases: Making arrangements, page 192*

DAS KANN ICH (Unit 6)

- Die Tagesordnungspunkte für ein Meeting erstellen und per E-Mail verteilen. (Foundation)
- An einer Betriebsratssitzung zum Thema gleitende Arbeitszeit teilnehmen. (Part A)
- Neue Lieferbedingungen mit einem Lieferanten auf Englisch aushandeln. (Part B)
- Einen neuen Termin für ein Meeting mit einer Geschäftspartnerin finden. (Communication)

Exam practice 3

1 Produktion: Stufe III

Situation: Your company plans to hold a conference on the digital transformation of the manufacturing sector in a conference centre and hotel near your headquarters. One possible location is the Black Forest Convention Centre, which your company has used for similar events in the past. The new City Seminar Hotel near to your headquarters is also being considered this year.
You have visited the City Seminar Hotel with a team and have received an attractive offer, including accommodation and complete conference services. In addition, you have also requested a customer satisfaction evaluation from an independent review website.
You have been asked to present the City Seminar Hotel and compare it with the Black Forest Convention Centre at the next team meeting.

Task: Write a script for your presentation. Start with a suitable introduction, explain why the meeting is taking place, compare the two locations using the information in the table and charts, and end the presentation appropriately.

Black Forest Convention Centre

Location	Black Forest, beautiful surroundings; 50 km from company; hotel 5 km from convention centre
Meeting rooms	meeting rooms ranging in size from single meeting room to combined meeting rooms of 10,000 square feet
Equipment	state-of-the-art conference facilities and equipment
Specialties	spa with indoor pool, sauna, gym
Ratings/Reviews	awarded "European leading conference hotel star": we were very satisfied in the past 5 years

City Seminar Hotel

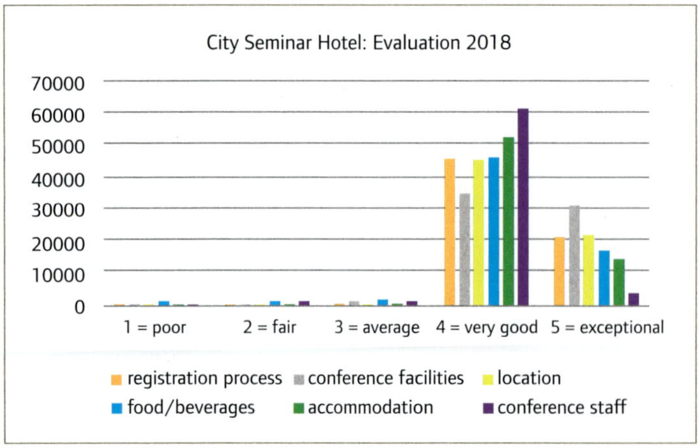

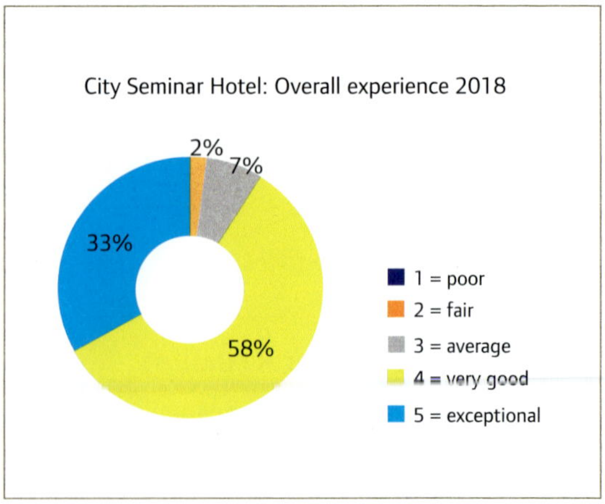

2 Produktion: Stufe II

Situation: You have given your presentation and have now been asked to write a recommendation for the Managing Director.

Task: Write an email to the Managing Director recommending where to hold the conference. Give reasons for your decision.

3 Hörverstehen: Stufe II

Situation: Sie hören ein *brainstorming meeting* bei der Firma BeFair Ltd, die vegane Smoothies produziert. Drei Mitarbeiter/innen der Marketingabteilung (Mr Warden, Leiter der Abteilung, Claudine, seine Assistentin, und Stephanie, eine Praktikantin aus Deutschland) besprechen den neuen Internetauftritt.

30)) **Aufgabe: Hören Sie sich die Diskussion an und füllen Sie die Tabelle aus.**

Datum der Einladung	
Ziel der Besprechung	
Höhe des Budgets	
Wen/Was möchten sie erreichen?	
Vorgeschlagene Lösungen	
Was beinhaltet Pressewerbung?	
Was umfasst ihre Datenbank?	
Aktuelle Aktivitäten	

4 Produktion: Stufe II

Situation: Sie arbeiten für die Firma Zweirad Zatopek, einen Dortmunder Hersteller von Fahrrädern, Fahrradbekleidung und -zubehör. Die Firma unterhält auch eine Niederlassung in Reading, UK. Kurz vor ihrem Urlaub schickt Ihre Chefin Ihnen eine E-Mail.

Aufgabe: Verfassen Sie eine E-Mail an die englischen Kollegen und Kolleginnen, wie von Ihrer Chefin unten gebeten.

Hallo

Bitte kümmern Sie sich während meines Urlaubs um die äußerst wichtige Besprechung am 6. Oktober hier in Dortmund.

- Einladung an alle Abteilungsleiter/innen
- Themen: neuer Firmenname, Verkaufsbericht, schlechter Auftritt auf der diesjährigen Pariser Fahrradmesse
- Dauer: mindestens 5–6 Stunden!

Bieten Sie den Kollegen/Kolleginnen Hilfe bei der Reiseorganisation an, da wir etwas spät mit der Einladung zum Treffen dran sind. Seien Sie höflich aber bestimmt – alle Abteilungsleiter/innen müssen dabei sein!

Vielen Dank
Emilia

7 International trade fairs

FOUNDATION: Preparations for a trade fair

Situation: You work in the Marketing department of BS Electronics GmbH, a German subsidiary of an international company. You are preparing for the ElectroTech trade fair in Dublin.
→ **You discuss promotional giveaways and choose two for your stand.**

1 Planning your exhibition stand

There is a lot to be decided before you can book a stand, so your line manager calls a planning meeting.

Work in groups. Brainstorm ideas about what you need for your stand under the headings below.

Interaction with visitors to the stand
- *up-to-date business cards*

...

Marketing materials
- *brochures and flyers*

...

Refreshments for staff and visitors

...

Other ideas

...

2 Choosing the location of your stand

Your team also has to decide on the location of the stand in the exhibition hall. You listen to the audio descriptions on the information page of the trade fair website.

A 31 **Listen to the audio descriptions of the stands on page 67 and make notes to complete the chart.**

Type of stand	Location	Benefit	Rental fees
Row stands	*open onto the aisle*	*visitors walk past each stand as they go along the aisle*	*the cheapest stands to rent*
Corner stands	*at the end of a row; open onto* ...	*both aisles* ...	*higher than* ...
End of block stands	...	...	...
Island stands	...	...	...
Outdoor stands	...	...	...

B **Compare and contrast the stands on page 67 with a partner. Which one might your own training company rent at a trade fair? Give reasons.**

› *Grammar: Comparatives and superlatives, page 157*

The type of stand you choose will depend on its position to neighbouring stands or how they open onto the aisles. Click for audio description.

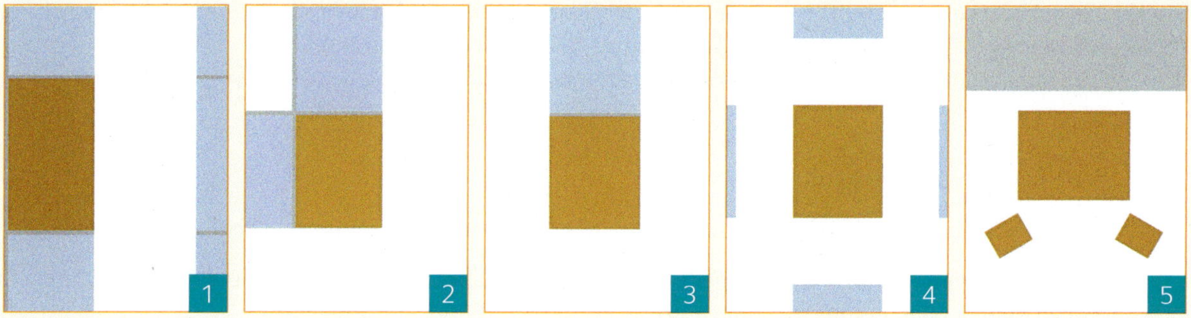

Row stands | Corner stands | End of block stands | Island stands | Outdoor stands

3 Deciding on promotional giveaways

Your line manager would like you to think about the type of giveaways to have on the stand.

A Read the text below and make notes on the following aspects:

- the benefits of giveaways
- the qualities giveaways should have

Why promotional giveaways are important

What are the most important things on your stand at a trade fair? Surprising as it may seem, it's not your sales literature or your business cards but your giveaways.

Promotional items are a major key to attracting people to your stand – and they improve your corporate image. Giveaways help people to see your company in a positive way and they make them more likely to consider your products or services.

For this reason, it's important to hand out top-quality products that have a practical use. Think of giveaways that will be immediately useful to visitors to the fair: tote bags, pens, hand sanitizers, water bottles or coffee in reusable to-go beakers. Some of the most useful trade fair giveaways are ones that will be used every day, such as LED keychain flashlights, phone chargers and sticky notes.

Make sure your giveaway shows your company logo. Remember: it won't help you if users can't immediately link the giveaway to your brand.

B Using information from the text above, or your own ideas, put your top five giveaways in order of priority.

			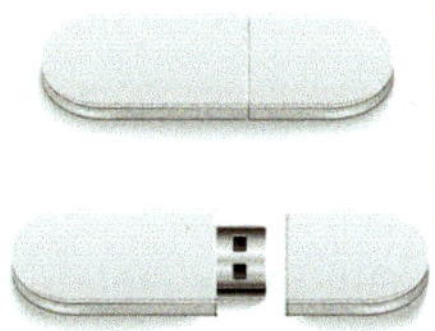	?
anti-stress ball	chocolate drops	USB charger	memory stick	your ideas

C Discuss your choice of giveaways with a partner and then with the class. Choose two giveaways to have on your stand at the trade fair.

› *Thematic vocabulary: Trade fairs, page 203*

PART A: Commissioning a stand

Situation: You work for the trade fair team at Ökobau Müller GmbH in Freiburg. Your company will be exhibiting its products at the next Architecture and Building Expo in Dublin.
→ **You commission a suitable stand and arrange catering for an on-stand event.**

1 Identifying types of stand

You look at a number of exhibition stand companies online, in particular Booth-Tech Ltd from Dublin.

Read the descriptions of the three types of stand and think about which one(s) would be most suitable for Ökobau Müller. Give reasons for your choice.

Exhibit with Booth-Tech Ltd

About to launch a new product? Trying to raise brand awareness? Need a space to demonstrate and discuss your products with a video loop in the background? Whatever the purpose of your stand, Booth-Tech will find the perfect solution with all the features you need. Visit us at www.booth-tech.ie or call +353 1416 6614.

Choose from three types of stand:

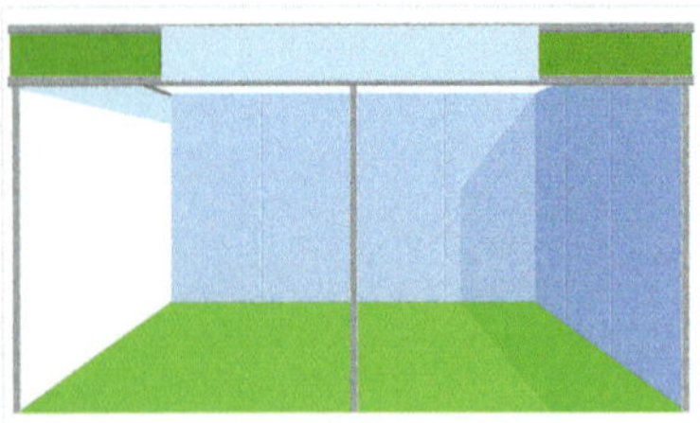

1 Shell scheme
- box-shaped aluminium frame-work with posts at each corner
- assembled in minutes
- suitable for multiple use
- can be made to fit into your vehicle

2 Modular
- simple combination of 1, 2 or 3 wall panels and a floor
- assembled in minutes
- suitable for multiple use
- can be made to fit into your vehicle

3 Bespoke
- any shape, size, style
- unique to your company
- made to your specifications
- planned with 3D visualization

2 Discussing the requirements

Your line manager, Lena Richter, calls Dermot Kennedy at Booth-Tech Ltd to discuss the stand.

A 32)) **Listen to their conversation and make notes on the points below.**

1 purpose of stand
2 size of stand
3 features on stand
4 division of space
5 single/multiple use
6 type of stand

B 32)) **Listen again and complete the sentences with the words you hear.**

1 In that case, I would ___ having a larger stand.
2 And I would also ___ having some literature racks.
3 I would strongly recommend ___ one, so you can store your valuables.
4 I suggest that you ___ the other 25 square metres 50/50.
5 I would recommend that you have an ___ stand.
6 We always recommend ___ a shell scheme stand if you're exhibiting at different locations.

VIDEO 5
Watch the video to see more about designing a stand.

3 Designing the stand

Booth-Tech Ltd sends Lena Richter some suggestions for the layout of the stand.

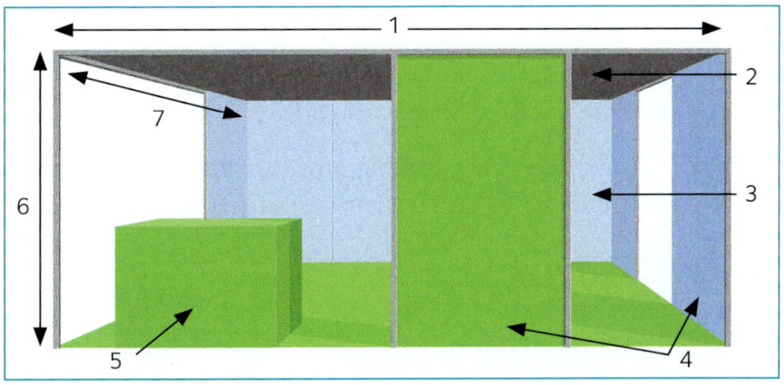

A Read the email and use the highlighted words from it to label the diagram of a stand.

To: lena.richter@oekobau-mueller.de
From: d.kennedy@booth-tech.ie
Subject: Stand layout

Dear Ms Richter

With reference to our phone call yesterday regarding a display stand, I am sending you some examples to help you with your decision.

We make stands with closed, semi-closed or open sides, with or without a roof and counter. Using infill panels along the sides and a backdrop will give you more space for advertising, but open sides will make your stand more accessible to visitors. The dimensions of the stands shown are 4m x 10m x 5m (height/width/depth). The video screen can be placed anywhere you choose.

Please send us a sketch of what you require and details of the vehicle you will use to transport the stand. We will then create a 3D visualization, adapt it as necessary and make you a firm offer.

We look forward to hearing from you soon.

Best regards
Dermot Kennedy

B Summarize the most important points in the email in German for your line manager.

C Use the language box to describe one of the two layouts to a partner. Guess the stand described.

1 (prices starting at €2,500)

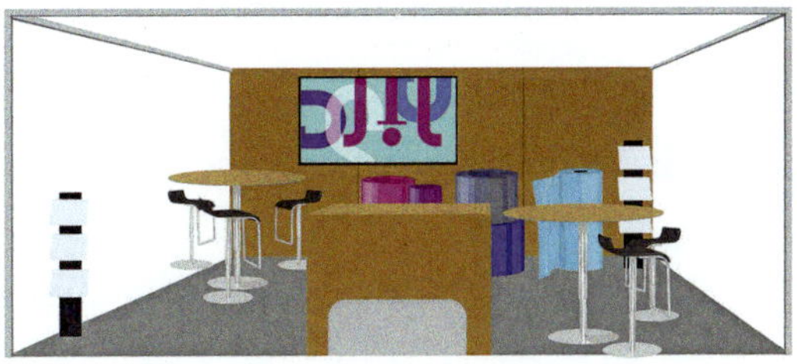

2 (prices starting at €3,000)

Describing a trade fair stand

on the left/right
on the left/right-hand side/panel/wall
at the top/bottom / in the middle
at the back/front
in the (left/right-hand) corner

between / next to / behind / in front of
with/without a roof
open/closed/semi-closed side(s)
an infill panel / a backdrop with (photos/ descriptions/diagrams/data)

4 Planning an on-stand event

Your team plans an on-stand networking event with drinks and snacks at 4 p.m. on both days of the exhibition. 50 visitors have confirmed by email that they will attend over the two days.

A **With a partner, use the brochure below to put together a menu for 25 visitors. You have a budget of €1,200 for a 3-hour event on the first day of the trade fair.**

O'Reilly's Catering Ltd

Let us cater for your event, so you can sit back and enjoy it! Here's just a small selection from our hospitality pack. Bespoke menus available on request. Call us on +353 1419 8000.

Please note:
Minimum 20 covers.
All menus include waiting staff for a maximum 2-hour period.
Any service required in addition to this time is chargeable at €20 per hour.

BEVERAGES

Freshly brewed tea and coffee	€1.80
Fruit and herbal teas and decaffeinated coffee	€1.80
Still and sparkling water (500 ml)	€1.85
Selection of fruit juices (1 litre)	€4.50
Fruit smoothies (200 ml)	€2.20
Smithwick's red ale (500 ml)	€4.50
Guinness (330 ml)	€3.50

Full wine list available on request.

savoury bites
€4.75 p.p.

canapés
€9.95 p.p.

finger buffet
€17.75 p.p.

fork buffet
€19.95 p.p.

B **Now you phone through your order to O'Reilly's Catering.**

Partner A: **Look at File 9 on page 139.** Partner B: **Look at File 10 on page 140.**

5 Commissioning a stand for your company

Your training company requires a stand for trade fairs/exhibitions in English-speaking countries.

Work in groups and do the following tasks:

Either:
1 Discuss and then draw a sketch of a suitable stand to show your company's goods/services.
2 Role-play a phone call to an exhibition stand company in which you ask questions about the six points listed in exercise 2A (page 68).

Or:
1 Put together a menu for an on-stand event at a trade fair.
2 Role-play a phone call to a catering company in which you order food and drinks for the event.

Making suggestions/recommendations

I (would) **suggest having** a larger stand.
I (would) **recommend having** some literature racks.
I (would) **suggest** (that) **you split** the other 25 square metres 50/50.
I (would) **recommend** (that) **you have** an island stand.
Why don't you order a finger buffet?
Have you considered having savoury bites?

› *Grammar: Gerunds, page 157*

› *Useful phrases: Advising customers, page 193*

PART B: Promoting your company

Situation: Your company, Compact Living GmbH, manufactures space-saving furniture. You are going to be on your stand at the 100% Design Show in London, where visitors are expected from all over the world.

→ **You practise how to present your company and its products to visitors from different cultural backgrounds.**

1 Understanding different cultures

As you are expecting visitors to your stand from all over the world, you do some research into business etiquette in different countries.

A **Do this cultural awareness quiz. Complete the sentences with the most suitable answer (a, b or c).**

1 When meeting French business people, it is best to avoid … .
- a personal questions
- b eye contact
- c humour

2 During negotiations with an Italian delegation, one of the team keeps taking phone calls. This is because they … .
- a are not interested in your offer
- b want to make you feel uncomfortable
- c are probably talking to their boss and it would be rude not to answer

3 The best way to be successful with Brazilian business partners is to … .
- a show anger
- b build relationships
- c stress deadlines

4 In Finland people are respected for their … .
- a modesty
- b patience
- c intelligence

5 If you are invited to a meal in a Russian's home, you should … .
- a eat everything on your plate
- b leave a little food on your plate
- c take your plate to the kitchen

6 Which part of a person's body should you not touch in Thailand?
- a head
- b hand
- c shoulder

7 You know an Egyptian businessman but not his wife. When you meet her for the first time, you should … .
- a greet her and offer her your hand
- b wait for her to introduce herself to you
- c wait for the businessman to introduce her to you

8 What is the most commonly-spoken language in the UK after English?
- a Urdu
- b Polish
- c Portuguese

9 If there is a period of silence at a meeting with a Japanese business person, you should … .
- a ask what is wrong
- b break the silence
- c wait

10 Who makes decisions in Chinese companies?
- a the team
- b the managing director
- c a manager

B Work with a partner. Look at the Illustrations by Yang Liu, a Chinese businesswoman living and working in Berlin, about the cultural differences between Germany (blue) and China (red).

Punctuality

View of superiors

Approaching new things

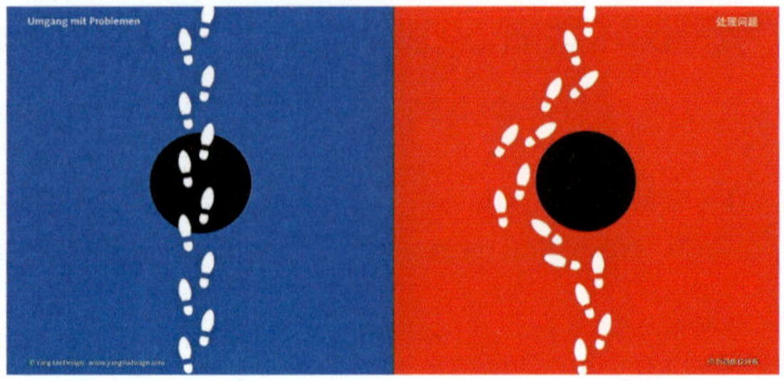

Problem-solving

Source: Yang Liu Design, Berlin

Write at least two sentences to describe each contrast. Compare your results with those of other members of the class and find more examples.

C Discuss any experience you have had of trading partners from different cultures with a partner and then with the class.

VIDEO 6

Watch the video to see more about dealing with different cultures.

2 Adapting to different cultures

Several business people from different countries visit your stand on the first day of the fair and make appointments to come back later. They are interested in your folding tables.

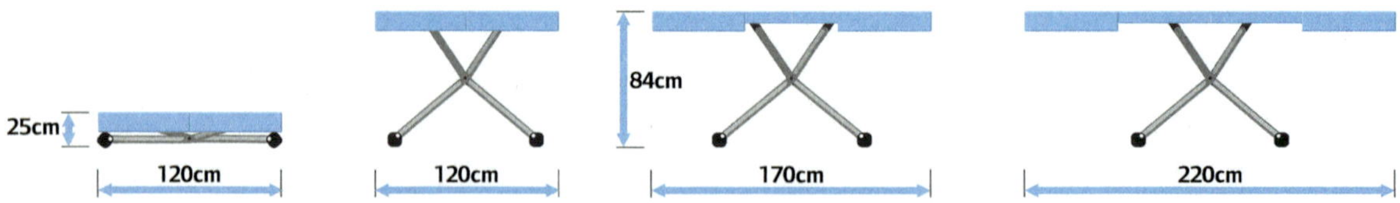

A 33 Listen to the conversations with a Japanese, an Italian and an American business person and make notes on the following points:

- small talk (and topics)
- the focus of the conversation
- the time needed to make a decision
- interruptions during the meeting
- who makes decisions
- any other differences

B Work in small groups. Use the points listed above and ideas of your own to discuss how negotiations are conducted between German business partners. Discuss your ideas with the class.

3 Dealing with foreign customers

Your company, Compact Living GmbH, has a stand at the Heim+Handwerk trade fair in Munich.

A Role-play a conversation with a Japanese business partner using the following prompts.

Partner A: Mitarbeiter/in bei Compact Living GmbH	Partner B: Kunde/Kundin, Nagoya Trading, Japan
Begrüßen Sie den Kunden / die Kundin freundlich. Sie freuen sich, ihn/sie wiederzusehen.	Reagieren Sie freundlich.
Betreiben Sie Small Talk. Bieten Sie etwas zu trinken an.	Sie möchten nur ein Glas Mineralwasser.
Fragen Sie, ob er/sie mehr über den Tisch wissen möchte.	Fragen Sie, aus welchen Materialien der Tisch gemacht werden kann und bitten Sie, die technischen Zeichnungen zu sehen.
Erklären Sie, dass die Tische aus Birkenholz (*birchwood*), Mahagoni (*mahogany*) oder Faserplatten (*fibreboard*) gemacht werden und geben Sie ihm/ihr die technischen Zeichnungen.	Schauen Sie sich die Zeichnungen kommentarlos für mehrere Minuten an. Fragen Sie anschließend, wie schwer der Tisch aus Mahagoni ist.
Er wiegt 15 kg. Fragen Sie, ob er/sie andere platzsparende Möbel aus Mahagoni ansehen möchte.	Sagen Sie, dass Sie die anderen Möbel vielleicht später ansehen werden.
Fragen Sie, ob er/sie weitere Informationen benötigt.	Sie möchten wissen, ob die Tische auch mit höhenverstellbaren Beinen (*height-adjustable legs*) lieferbar sind.
Dies wäre gegen Aufpreis (*at an extra charge*) möglich. Fragen Sie, ob Sie ihm/ihr ein Angebot zuschicken sollen.	Das könnte er/sie vielleicht später machen. Bedanken Sie sich für die Informationen.
Sie haben zu danken. Sagen Sie, dass er/sie vor Ende der Messe gerne wieder vorbeischauen kann.	Sie werden evtl. wieder vorbeischauen und sagen „auf Wiedersehen" auf Deutsch.
Schließen Sie das Gespräch freundlich ab.	

› *Useful phrases: Advising customers, page 193*

B Adapt the instructions in exercise 3A to create similar conversations with customers from Italy and the USA, or any other countries you know. Perform your conversations in front of the class.

COMMUNICATION: Business trips

Situation: You work in the Export Sales department of GlasKlar GmbH in Berlin. The company manufactures glass bottles and jars for the food industry. You and your line manager, Maria Weber, are going to attend a conference in London.
→ **You hire a car at a hotel reception.**

1 Booking the flights

Maria Weber has a friend who works at British Airways. She calls her to find out about flights to and from London.

34 **Listen to their conversation and complete the details of the flights.**

Flight	Date	Departure	Arrival	Details
BA ___[1]	April ___[2]	Berlin Tegel ___[3]	London Heathrow ___[4]	___[5] flight ___[6] class 2 aisle seats
BA ___[7]	April 23	London Heathrow ___[8]	Berlin Tegel ___[9]	___[10] flight ___[11] class 2 seats same row; one ___[12] seat

2 Finding hotel accommodation

The conference centre is 20 minutes away from the airport. Maria asks you to find a hotel online which might be suitable.

Read the text and explain the main features of the hotel to Maria in German.

Crown Palace 4-star hotel

Welcome to the Crown Palace Hotel.

Our modern hotel offers first-class accommodation and business facilities. The spacious, air-conditioned rooms have internet access and a desk. All rooms feature a flat screen TV. The rooms are fitted with minibars, and tea and coffee-making equipment.

The 4-star Crown Palace has a gym with an indoor pool and sauna.

Our breakfast buffet includes a wide range of vegan options.

Our stylish restaurant is open daily from 7 till 10.30 p.m.

Our well-stocked bar is open from 11 till 11 and our lounge serves non-alcoholic drinks and snacks 24 hours a day.

24-hour front desk
Free Wi-Fi available throughout the hotel
100% smoke-free

Our shuttle bus to Heathrow Airport runs every 20 minutes.

The Crown Palace is less than a 30-minute drive away from Thorpe Park, Windsor Castle and the Chiltern Hills Nature Reserve. The university town of Cambridge is only 1.5 hours away.

3 Checking in at a hotel

When you arrive at the hotel, there are three guests in front of you at reception. You listen to the receptionist talking to them.

1 Giovanni Rossi

2 Mary McGregor

3 Yusuf Zuabi

A 35 **Copy the table. Listen to the guests as they check in and fill in the missing information.**

	What questions do the guests ask?	What information does the receptionist give?
Giovanni Rossi	1	2
Mary McGregor	3	4
Yusuf Zuabi	5	6

B **Work with a partner. Role-play a short conversation at the reception. Ask and answer questions about some of the following, or use your own ideas:**

air conditioning • meeting room • taxi to the airport • Wi-Fi

4 Role-play: Hiring a car

Your return flight is in the early evening, so you and Maria decide to take a look at the countryside outside London before you travel back to Berlin.

Work with a partner. Partner A: Look here. Partner B: Look at File 3 on page 134.

Partner A
You are the guest at the hotel. Ask the receptionist for information about hiring a car for the day. Ask about the following:
- where you can hire a car
- the cost of a hire car
- the mileage (included? car returned full or empty?)
- the type of insurance cover; excess in case of accident/damage
- where to pick up / return the car

You decide to book a car for Monday 23 April, 8 a.m. You will pay for it with your Visa card.

› *Thematic vocabulary: Business trips, page 203*

DAS KANN ICH (Unit 7)
- Die passenden Werbegeschenke für einen Messeauftritt suchen. (Foundation)
- Einen Messestand in Auftrag geben und das Catering für ein Event organisieren. (Part A)
- Ein Beratungsgespräch mit einem Kunden / einer Kundin auf Englisch führen. (Part B)
- Ein Mietauto an einer Hotelrezeption in England buchen. (Communication)

8 Enquiries, terms of delivery and payment

FOUNDATION: Finding a new supplier

Situation: You work for AllesMöbel GmbH, a German furniture manufacturer. The company has decided to expand its range of office furniture. Your line manager asks you to look for prospective suppliers at home and abroad.

→ **You collect information for your line manager from an English text.**

1 Finding new suppliers

You think about different sources for getting information about suppliers.

A **Work in small groups. Talk about how to find out about prospective suppliers and their goods.**

B **In your group, collect reasons why your company might need a new supplier. Exchange your findings in class.**

2 Choosing a supplier

Your line manager sends you a link to a podcast describing what to look for in a good supplier.

A **Before you listen, match the German translations (1–8) to the English expressions (a–h).**

1 Anbieter	a a good deal
2 Bonitätsprüfung	b value for money
3 ein gutes Angebot	c defect
4 Fehler	d open-account terms
5 offenes Zahlungsziel	e payment in advance
6 Preis-Leistungs-Verhältnis	f solvency
7 Vorauszahlung	g vendor
8 Zahlungsfähigkeit	h credit check

B 36 Now listen to the podcast and complete the notes with the missing words or phrases.

Points to consider	Choosing a supplier
1 Prices	a the lowest price is not always ▭ b don't jump at an offer just because ▭ c check the whole ▭ before you choose
2 Quality of the goods	a find out if a new supplier can consistently provide ▭ b ▭ from other clients might be useful c be careful with ▭ recommendations on the internet
3 Warranties	a the most common deals with the product being free from ▭ when it leaves the supplier b the buyer has to make a claim within ▭
4 Terms and conditions	a it's important that you know your ▭ b how are the responsibilites and ▭ for transport of the goods shared? c a new supplier might ask for ▭ until your relationship is established
5 Reliability of supplier	a it's important to find out about the ▭ of the supplier b if you don't do this, you might put your business ▭ c search the internet for a company that will do a ▭ for you

C **Work in groups. Rank the points the speaker suggests in order of importance. Compare and discuss your rankings in class.**

3 Collecting information about ethical and environmental aspects

A link from the podcast leads you to the following text. You think your line manager will also want to consider the aspects mentioned in the text before she decides on a new supplier.

List the most important information in the text in German for your line manager.

Choosing a new supplier?

Don't forget to look into the ethical and environmental aspects

Two very important questions you should always ask before you decide on a supplier are: "Is this company ethical in the way they treat their employees?" and "How much do we know about this supplier's attitudes to the environment?"

Regarding the first question, it makes sense to look into the physical environment in which employees work. Do these meet health and safety regulations of the country where the goods are produced? Are employees free to form trade unions, and do they have the right to collective wage bargaining? What is the reputation of the country of origin of the goods as far as human rights are concerned? Is there sexual discrimination? Is there any suspicion that your prospective supplier uses forced labour or child labour?

As far as environmental issues are concerned, are your supplier's production methods sustainable? Are their processes environmentally friendly? Do they comply to standards and regulations? Don't forget. You can always do your bit for the environment if you buy from a domestic supplier. That way, you will avoid long shipping distances and keep your carbon footprint down.

PART A: Enquiries

Situation: You work in the Logistics department of AgriTrade South Africa Pty Ltd, a company that exports fruit and vegetables all over the world.
→ **You send enquiries to a number of suppliers.**

1 Contacting suppliers

As sweet corn goes rotten after a short time, the company decides to set up its own canning facility near Cape Town and to look for a source of canning equipment. One enquiry is to Cantec GmbH, an engineering company in Essen.

To: Dirk Sauerwald, Sales Director <dirk.sauerwald@cantec.com>
From: luke.booysen@agritrade.co.za
Subject: Enquiry about canning technology

Dear Mr Sauerwald

We note from your company's website that you sell fully-integrated can body production lines and we are most interested in your CAN-O-MAT system for three-piece cans.

We are a leading producer and exporter of sweetcorn in South Africa with excellent business contacts all over the country and beyond. Until now we have bought empty cans from Europe, but in order to cut costs for transportation and storage we are looking for a supplier of canning technology, so we can set up our own can-making facility. Initially, we will require approx. 250 million cans per year, diameter 99–119 mm.

Please send us a favourable quotation for a CAN-O-MAT production line, including details of your terms of delivery and payment.

How soon can you deliver?

References are available on request.

We look forward to hearing from you soon.

Yours sincerely

Luke Booysen
Logistics Director

AgriTrade South Africa Pty Ltd, 150 Main Rd, Paarl, 7646, South Africa
Tel. +27 (0) 21 860 1800 Fax. +27 (0) 86 528 0473
Email: info@agritrade.co.za www.agritrade.co.za

Study the email and match the sentence halves.

1 AgriTrade is a South African …
2 Dirk Sauerwald works for a German …
3 The South African company plans …
4 The CAN-O-MAT production line will …
5 Luke Booysen wants Cantec to send him …
6 AgriTrade asks for details of …

a Cantec's terms of delivery and payment.
b a quotation for a CAN-O-MAT system.
c need to produce about 250 million cans per year.
d producer of sweetcorn.
e to make its own cans instead of buying them.
f engineering company called Cantec.

2 Structuring an enquiry

Before you write further enquiries, you check the standard structure used.

A Use the words from the list on the right to translate the enquiries checklist (1–6) into German.

Enquiries checklist

1 source of address
2 description of your company
3 reason for your enquiry
4 your requirements:
- quotation
- sales material
- price list
- discounts
- samples
- terms of delivery and payment
- delivery
- representative's visit

5 references
6 polite ending

(Preis)angebot · Beschreibung Ihrer Gesellschaft · Grund für Ihre Anfrage · höfliche Schlussformel · Ihr Bedarf · Liefer- und Zahlungsbedingungen · Lieferung · Muster/Probe(n) · Preisliste · Quelle der Anschrift · Rabatte · Referenzen · Verkaufsmaterial · Vertreterbesuch

› *Useful phrases: Writing enquiries, page 193*

B Study the email from AgriTrade (on page 78) and make a list of the points on the checklist that it includes.

C Match the phrases below with headings from the checklist and then translate them into German.

1 We would be grateful if a representative could call on us.
2 If your products meet our requirements, we will place a substantial order.
3 Please also let us know if you are able to provide samples.
4 You have been recommended to us by …
5 We would welcome a favourable quotation for these items, including all discounts granted.

3 Enquiring on the phone

Dirk Sauerwald at Cantec in Essen sends an initial proposal for a CAN-O-MAT production line to AgriTrade. Your boss, Luke Booysen, then phones him to discuss further details of the proposal.

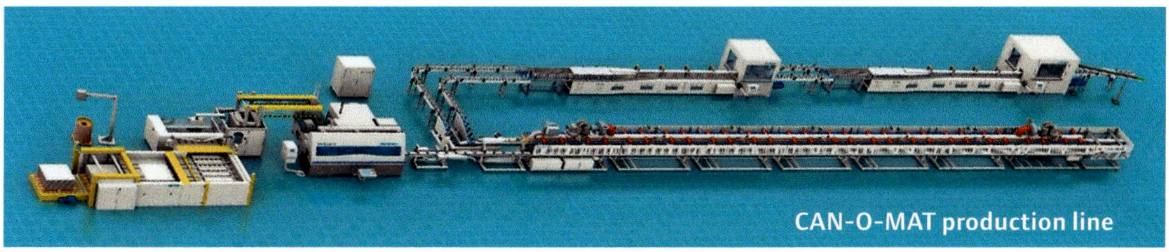
CAN-O-MAT production line

37 **Listen to their telephone conversation and make notes on the following points.**

- delivery period
- training
- price
- payment
- after-sales service

4 Role-play: Telephoning foreign suppliers

Before he makes a decision on the canning facility, Luke Booysen asks you to contact another canning equipment manufacturer.

Work with a partner. Partner A and Partner B: **Look at File 13 on page 141.**

PART B: Understanding terms of delivery and payment

Situation: You have just started work in the Purchasing department of MegaKauf GmbH, which imports goods from all over the world. You are attending a seminar about international trade as part of your training.
→ **You consider terms of delivery, payment and insurance in transit for individual suppliers.**

1 Looking at terms of delivery

The seminar starts by looking at five of the eleven International Commercial Terms (Incoterms®) used by buyers and sellers all over the world.

A **Find the German equivalent in the list for each Incoterm (1–5) in the diagram.**

geliefert Zoll bezahlt (benannter Bestimmungsort) • frei an Bord (benannter Verschiffungshafen) • frachtfrei versichert bis (benannter Bestimmungsort) • frachtfrei bis (benannter Bestimmungsort) • ab Werk (benannter Lieferort)

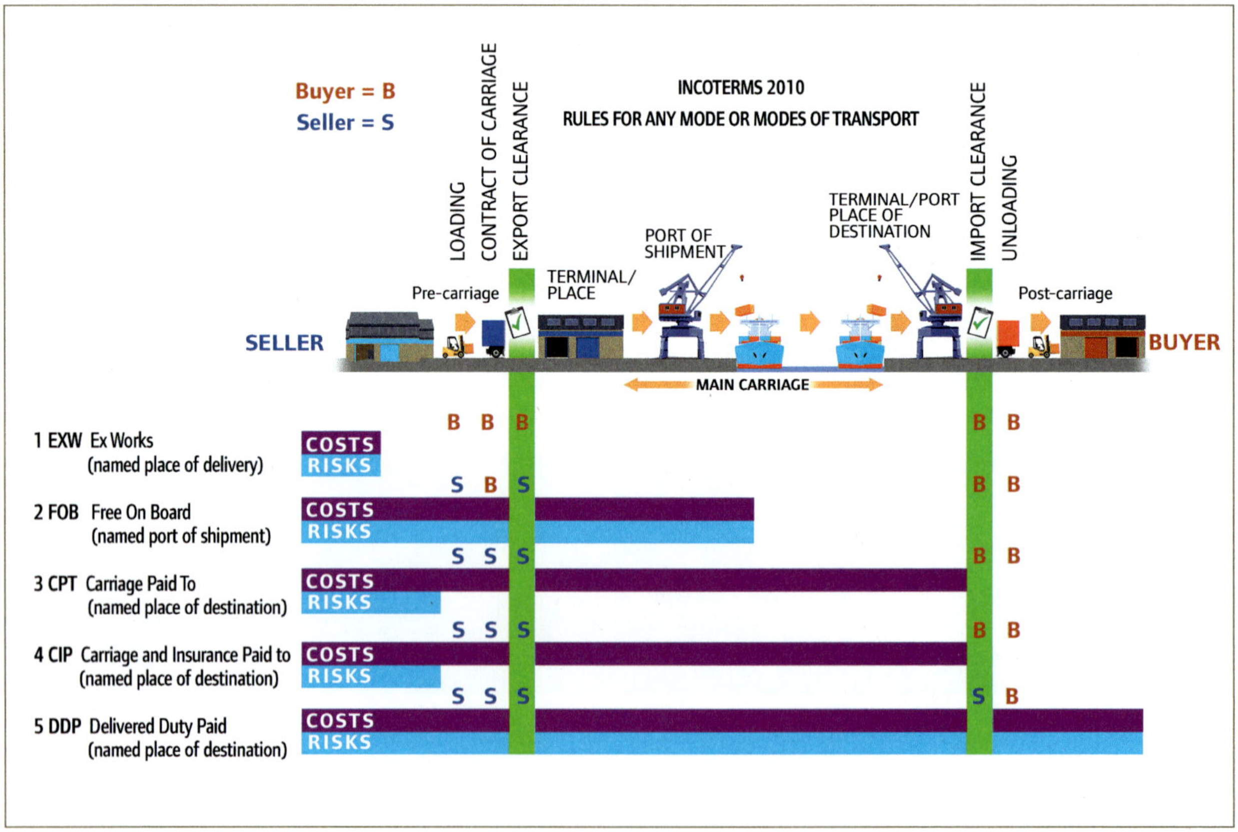

B **With a partner, study the seminar handout (on page 81) about the five Incoterms and then explain who is responsible for the highlighted factors in the following situations (1–5).**

1 **EXW** A German importer in Frankfurt buys a consignment of fruit from a Spanish exporter in Valencia. (loading, export clearance, main carriage)
2 **FOB** A Chinese exporter in Nanjing near the port of Shanghai sells a consignment of clothing to a German importer in Bielefeld. (export clearance, cost of main carriage)

3 **CPT** A German exporter in Cologne sells a consignment of farming machinery to a Portuguese importer in Lisbon. (loading, risk during main carriage)
4 **CIP** A German importer buys a consignment of floor tiles from an Italian exporter. (risk during main carriage, unloading)
5 **DDP** A New Zealand exporter in Wellington sells a consignment of seafood to a German customer in Berlin. (import clearance, unloading)

Incoterms: information sheet

Transport (carriage) costs
When a seller supplies goods using an Incoterm beginning with the letter E or F, this means that they do not pay for the main carriage. In the case of EXW, the seller only makes the goods available at their premises (e.g. factory, warehouse, etc.).

With F terms, the seller only pays for transport of the goods to a convenient location, e.g. a port, an airport or a train station not too far away. In the case of FOB, the seller has the goods loaded on a ship at the port of shipment.

For the seller, C terms include loading and the cost of the main carriage to the destination but not unloading at the destination.

D terms cover all transport costs until the goods have reached their destination.

Risk
E and F terms mean less risk for the seller. In the case of EXW, the seller bears no risk outside their premises. With an F term, the seller bears the risk until the goods have been handed over to the first carrier, e.g. are on board a ship at the port of shipment. With CPT and CIP, the risk to the seller is the same because it passes to the buyer when the goods have been collected by the first carrier. With CIP, the seller also insures the goods for the main carriage but no longer bears any risk when they have been handed over to the first carrier.

D terms cover all risks until the goods have reached their destination.

Import and export clearance
With ten of the eleven Incoterms, export clearance (e.g. export licences, documentation) is arranged and paid for by the seller. The exception is EXW. With ten of the eleven Incoterms, import clearance (e.g. customs duty, import licences and documentation) is arranged and paid for by the buyer. The exception is DDP.

C **Copy the table into your book and complete it for the Incoterms FCA, DAP, DAT, FAS, CFR and CIF. Refer to the full list of Incoterms on page 184.**

	Main carriage		**Seller bears risk**	
	paid	unpaid	including main carriage	excluding main carriage
FCA		✓		
DAP				

2 Choosing the right Incoterm

As part of the seminar, you listen in to some phone calls to foreign suppliers.

A 38 **Listen to three of the calls and identify the Incoterm and the place agreed in each case.**

1 electricity generators
2 garden furniture
3 LED displays

› *Incoterms, page 184*

B 38 **Listen again and note which Incoterm was discussed but not chosen in each case.**

3 Looking at terms of payment

The next topic discussed at the seminar is terms of payment. Payment can be made with or without the help of shipping documents.

A First use the words in the list on the right to find the German equivalents of the terms of payment (a–f). Then put the terms of payment in order of preference for the seller.

Payment without shipping documents

- a 10 days 2%, 30 days net
- b 30% with order, 70% on completion
- c cash on delivery
- d cash with order (CWO)
- e open account terms with monthly/quarterly settlement
- f payment in advance (TT)

Barzahlung bei Auftragserteilung · gegen Nachnahme · offenes Zahlungsziel mit monatlicher/vierteljährlicher Abrechnung · Vorauszahlung/Vorkasse (telegrafische Überweisung) · Zahlung innerhalb 10 Tagen abzüglich 2 % Skonto oder innerhalb 30 Tagen netto · 30 % bei Auftragserteilung, 70 % bei Fertigstellung

› *Terms of payment, page 186*

B Study the text and put the stages of the transaction (A–J) in the diagram in the order in which they take place (1–10).

Payment with shipping documents

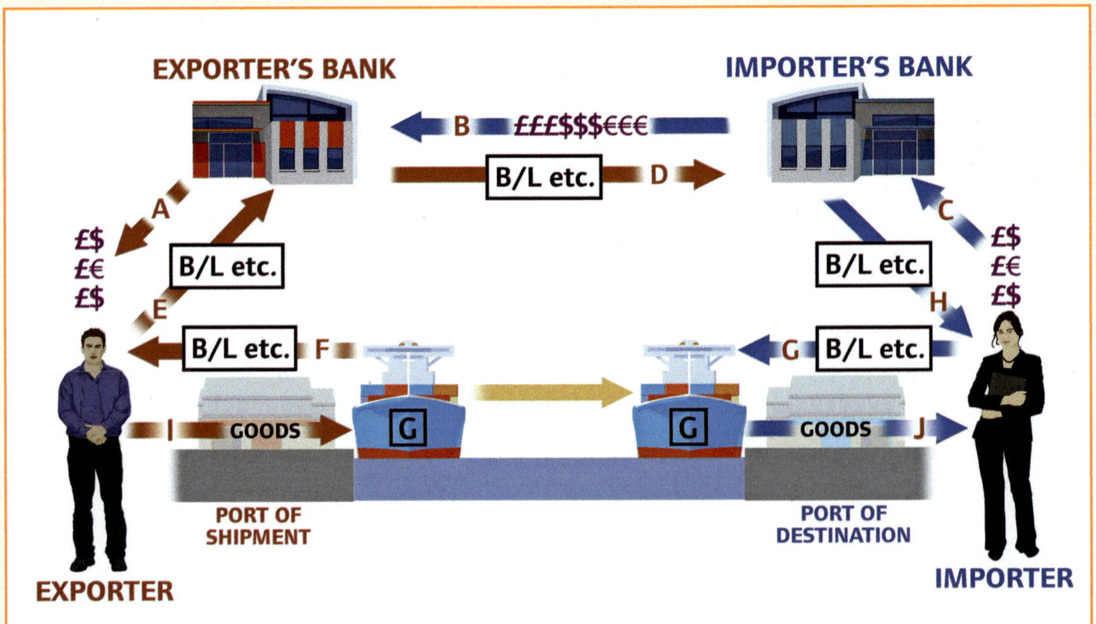

Payment by irrevocable and confirmed documentary letter of credit (simplified)

Payments using shipping documents are based on the principle that the holder of the shipping documents can take possession of the goods. The shipping documents include the commercial invoice, the insurance certificate and either the bill of lading (sea), air waybill (air) or consignment note (road or rail). In international trade, payment is very often made by letter of credit (L/C).
With payment by irrevocable and confirmed documentary letter of credit, the exporter's bank guarantees to buy the documents from the exporter if they are exactly as agreed. It then sells them to the importer's bank, which sells them to the importer.

The following (simplified) example is for sea transport (see diagram). It uses a bill of lading, which is both a document of title (ownership), a contract of carriage and a receipt for the goods.

1 The exporter gives the goods to the shipping company and they are loaded onto a ship.
2 The exporter receives a bill of lading (B/L), showing he has title to the goods.
3 He gives the B/L, the commercial invoice and the insurance certificate to his bank.
4 The bank inspects the documents and, if they are in order, pays the exporter.
5 The exporter's bank now has title to the goods and sells them to the importer's bank.
6 The importer's bank pays the exporter's bank and now has title to the goods.
7 The importer's bank sells the documents to the importer.
8 The importer pays the importer's bank and now has title to the goods.
9 The importer gives the documents to the shipping company at the port of destination.
10 The shipping company gives the importer the goods.

Payment by documentary credit is safe but expensive because both banks charge fees for their services.

› *Terms of payment, page 186; Thematic vocabulary: Shipping documents, page 204*

4 Looking at case studies

The seminar trainer gives you some examples of previous transactions and asks you to suggest suitable terms in each case.

A Choose a suitable Incoterm + place in the following situations.

1 A Spanish company in Valencia buys some heavy road construction machinery from a German company in Duisburg. The buyer requires the exporter to bear all the costs and risks for the goods to their destination, including unloading the machinery at the terminal in Valencia.
2 A German manufacturer near Bielefeld receives an order for 200 tractors from a buyer in Nairobi, Kenya. The goods are to be sent by sea to the Port of Mombasa. The German manufacturer is only prepared to transport the goods to Hamburg and load them on board a ship.
3 An Argentinian beef exporter in Buenos Aires, Argentina sends a consignment of meat by ship from the Port of Buenos Aires to the Port of Rotterdam. The exporter bears the transport costs to the port of destination and also pays for the meat to be insured while it is on board the ship.
4 A German exporter in Dresden is only prepared to load the goods on board the carrier's vehicle at his premises and provide any documents needed.

Infobox

Incoterms including insurance
The Incoterms CIF and CIP require the seller to insure the goods for the main carriage for 110% of their value.

› *Incoterms, page 184*

B Choose a suitable term of payment in these situations.

1 A supplier normally gives the buyer a month to pay but offers a two per cent discount for payment within ten days.
2 A manufacturer will only sell the goods to the buyer if the manufacturer is guaranteed payment by a bank in his country.
3 A reliable customer placing regular orders is allowed to pay every three months.
4 A manufacturer requires almost a third of the sum agreed when the order is placed and the rest when the goods have been manufactured.

› *Terms of payment, page 186*

COMMUNICATION: The layout of business letters

Situation: You work at MedEquip GmbH, a Berlin-based manufacturer of medical supplies and equipment for hospitals and clinics. This week you are helping out in the Sales department.
→ **You write an offer to a new customer in the UK.**

1 Reading an English business letter

Your line manager gives you a letter of enquiry from a new customer.

A **Study the layout and match the parts (1–12) of the letter on page 85 to the labels below (a–l).**

a	address/letterhead	**d**	copies	**g**	inside address	**j**	signature block
b	body of the letter	**e**	date	**h**	reference initials	**k**	subject line
c	complimentary close	**f**	enclosure	**i**	salutation	**l**	attention line

B **Make notes (in German) about all the information that Linda Lambert asks for.**

2 Writing an English business letter

Your line manager asks you to write an offer to Ms Lambert at the Dryden Medical Clinic.

Write the complete offer according to your line manager's notes below. Use the correct layout for a business letter, a suitable salutation and complimentary close, and today's date.

- *Dank für Anfrage nach Bildschirmen für OP-Saale*
- *unterbreiten gerne folgendes Angebot:*
  - *132-Zoll OT-HD Bildschirm zum Preis von € 2.700,–*
  - *Lieferung innerhalb von 2 Wochen nach Auftragserteilung*
  - *Lieferbedingung: DAP London*
- *Gültigkeit des Angebots: 2 Wochen*
- *bei Auftragserteilung innerhalb einer Woche Gewährung von 2 % Rabatt möglich*
- *Versicherung, dass der Auftrag schnell und sorgfältig ausgeführt wird*
- *Verpackung zum Transport in Alucontainer*
- *aktueller Katalog und Preisliste liegen bei*
- *Freude über weitere Aufträge ausdrücken*

› *Useful phrases: Writing business letters, page 193*
› *Thematic vocabulary: Commercial correspondence, page 204*

Salutation and complimentary closes in letters

	Salutation	Complimentary close
to a firm	Dear Sir or Madam	Yours faithfully *(BE)*
		Yours very truly / Cordially yours *(AE)*
to a person	Dear Mr/Ms Brown Dear Sharon/Martin	Yours sincerely *(BE)*
		Sincerely yours / Best personal regards *(AE)*

1 Dryden Medical Clinic
17 Dryden Street
London SE9 2BS
+44 (0)20 129546783
info@drydenclinic.com

2 29 April 20..

3 Our ref: LL/DC

4 MedEquip GmbH
Rudower Straße 250
12489 Berlin
GERMANY

5 For the attention of the Sales Manager

6 Dear Sir or Madam

7 **Enquiry about operating theatre monitors**

8 We have seen your advertisement in this month's editon of the trade magazine "Medical Business". We see that your company sells medical hardware.

We are a large outpatient clinic in London. We are planning to update our operating theatres and are interested in high-definition operating theatre monitors. We would like to place a trial order for one 32" OT-HD monitor. If the product is suitable, we may place further orders.

Please let us have details of your terms of delivery and payment. We would also like to know what type of packaging you use to protect the monitor during transport.

Many thanks for your attention to our enquiry. We look forward to hearing from you soon.

9 Yours faithfully

10 Dryden Medical Clinic

Linda Lambert

Linda Lambert
Clinic Manager

11 cc Dr Alice Black

12 Enc: Information pack "Dryden Medical Clinic"

DAS KANN ICH (Unit 8)

- Eine begründete Lieferantenauswahl treffen. (Foundation)
- Schriftliche und telefonische Anfragen auf Englisch erledigen. (Part A)
- Die passenden Zahlungs- und Lieferbedingungen für internationale Geschäfte aussuchen. (Part B)
- Ein schriftliches Angebot für eine englische Firma erstellen. (Communication)

KMK Exam practice 4

1 Leseverstehen: Stufe II

Situation: Ihre Firma ist als internationaler Hersteller von Büroprodukten oft auf Fachmessen vertreten, um neue Kunden zu akquirieren. Sie haben eine Einladung von Farook International Stationery (FIS) zur Paperworld Middle East erhalten. Ihr Chef bittet Sie, als Entscheidungsgrundlage für eine mögliche Teilnahme die wichtigsten Informationen über die Messe und FIS zusammenzutragen.

Aufgabe: Lesen Sie den Text und fassen Sie die wichtigsten Informationen auf Deutsch tabellenartig zusammen.

Paperworld Middle East

Farook International Stationery (FIS) has been there from the beginning. As the United Arab Emirates' (UAE) biggest manufacturer of stationery and office supplies, the company was naturally one of the first companies to exhibit at the Paperworld Middle East trade fair when it started in 2011 and is now one of its official launch partners. The annual trade fair for industries dealing in stationery, paper and other office supplies, aims to stimulate business opportunities throughout Africa and the Middle East and will be welcoming over 300 exhibitors at this year's fair, which takes place from 27 February to 1 March. The fair is a platform for firms to present an array of different products and services ranging from traditional supplies for schools and offices, arts and crafts materials and writing implements to environmentally-friendly paper-based products, toys, gifts and games.

The trade fair has proven a great success, becoming increasingly popular with international players – the first year attracted 4,420 buyers yet in 2017 this had already risen to 6,443 buyers from over 93 different countries. This achievement can be attributed to the Paperworld brand, which is well received all over the globe, but also to its Dubai location which makes it easily accessible for international markets and a great way to access the emerging markets in the nearby regions.

Farook International Stationery's continued support of the trade fair has of course also been a big factor in the success of the event. FIS started out back in 1980 as a retailer and wholesaler of stationery, but had moved into the manufacturing side of the business by 1990. Since then it has gone a long way towards making customers think of high-quality goods when they see the stamp 'Made in the UAE', building up a good product range and customer base and now exporting 10 product lines to over 90 countries worldwide. These are displayed in their 14 showrooms, 13 of which are in the United Arab Emirates, with the last one in Oman, along with 12 stationery brands from other international companies.

PAPERWORLD

Art der Messe	
Standort	
Anzahl der Aussteller	
Gründungsjahr der Messe	
Termin/Dauer der Messe	
Beispiele für angebotene Produkte	
Enwicklung der Anzahl internationaler Käufer	

Farook International Stationery

Art der Firma	
Weitere Daten und Fakten über die Firma	
Aktuelle Aktivitäten	

2 Interaktion: Stufe II

Work with a partner. Partner A: **Look here.** Partner B: **Look at File 11 on page 140.**

Situation: Your company has a stand at an international trade fair, and you are responsible for welcoming the customers and guests. Some customers have been given appointments but, due to some delays, they have to wait for a short time. You entertain the customers while they are waiting and help out with any problems that may occur.

Aufgabe: Role-play a conversation at the trade fair stand with Partner B. Be prepared to ask and answer questions. You may have to use your imagination and make up possible answers. Use the ideas below to help you.

- Introduce yourself and explain the situation.
- Offer refreshments and engage in small talk (three topics) with the guest.
- Reassure the guest if he/she gets annoyed about waiting.
- Try to find a solution for the customer (possible offers: internet access, information material, voucher for lunch?).

3 Mediation: Stufe III

Situation: Im Rahmen eines Auszubildendenaustauschs zwischen internationalen Standorten Ihrer Firma erwarten Sie im kommenden Monat einen Auszubildenden aus Kanada, der vier Wochen im Einkauf mitarbeiten soll. Ihr Ausbilder bittet Sie daher, aus folgendem Artikel eine Checkliste auf Englisch zu erstellen, welche Aspekte bei der Lieferantenauswahl grundsätzlich zu berücksichtigen sind.

Aufgabe: Lesen Sie den Text und erstellen Sie eine Checkliste auf Englisch.

Lieferantenauswahl

In einer globalen Welt werden die Auswahlmöglichkeiten bei Lieferanten immer größer, der Preisdruck aber auch. Worauf sollte man also bei der Lieferantenauswahl achten?

Natürlich ist der Preis immer noch häufig das entscheidende Kriterium. Günstige Produktpreise und Rabatte oder lange Zahlungsziele tragen dazu bei, die Kosten zu senken. Ein wesentlicher Aspekt ist aber auch, dass die Produkte von guter Qualität und makellos sein sollten. Falls es dennoch einmal zu Problemen wegen eines falschen, kaputten oder fehlerhaften Produkts kommen sollte, sollte der Lieferant eine Entschädigung oder Ersatzlieferung anbieten.

Grundsätzlich ist es wichtig, dass Liefertermine eingehalten werden und der Lieferant immer lieferbereit ist. Vorteilhaft ist hier sicher, wenn ein Lieferant in Standortnähe seinen Sitz hat und keine langen Lieferwege zurückzulegen sind.

Nicht alle Kriterien sind für alle Unternehmen wichtig oder gleichwertig. Der Lieferant sollte flexibel auf Kundenwünsche eingehen und diese gegebenenfalls auch schnell umsetzen. Besonders bei anspruchsvolleren Produkten sind Beratung, Service und Freundlichkeit der Mitarbeiter/innen Aspekte, die berücksichtigt werden sollten. In der heutigen Zeit beschäftigen sich immer mehr Betriebe mit Umweltaspekten, wie z. B. umweltfreundliche und nachhaltige Produkte und Entsorgungs- und Recyclingangebote.

9 Submitting an offer

FOUNDATION: Replies to customer enquiries

Situation: You work in the Sales department of a hiking and outdoor equipment manufacturer. Your company uses templates for making offers in different languages.
→ **You write an offer to a prospective customer.**

1 Looking at different types of offers

Your line manager gives you a list of types of offers in German and asks you to key in the English translations.

A Translate the English expressions (1–8) using the German expressions from the list on the right.

Types of offer

1 firm offer
2 legally binding
3 quotation
4 solicited offer
5 subject to confirmation
6 unsolicited offer
7 valid while stocks last
8 without obligation

(Preis-)Angebot • gültig solange der Vorrat reicht • bindend/verbindlich • unverbindlich • unverlangtes Angebot • verbindliches Angebot • verlangtes Angebot • vorbehaltlich einer Bestätigung

B Translate the German sentences below into English using the expressions from 1A.

1 Alle Preisangaben sind unverbindlich.
2 Ein anderes Unternehmen konnte einen niedrigeren Kostenvoranschlag für die Arbeitskosten anbieten.
3 Verträge sind rechtsverbindliche Vereinbarungen zwischen zwei oder mehr Parteien.
4 Offenbar will die Gesellschaft ABC keine Geschäfte mit uns machen. Sie haben auf das unverlangte Angebot, das wir ihnen letzten Monat schickten, nicht geantwortet.
5 Unser Angebot ist unverbindlich und freibleibend.
6 Unser Festangebot ist freibleibend, solange der Vorrat reicht.
7 Diese Sonderbedingungen sind gültig, solange der Vorrat reicht.
8 Sie schicken ein verlangtes Angebot als Reaktion auf eine Kundenanfrage.

2 Understanding an offer

Your company needs windproof and waterproof material for a new range of retro-look tents. You have received an offer from a Scottish manufacturer, Charles McAdam Ltd, of Dundee.

Summarize the offer below in German for your line manager.

Enquiry about windproof/waterproof tent canvas

We refer to your enquiry of 25 June 20... We are a major manufacturer of quality textiles for the outdoor equipment trade. We are delighted to hear that you are interested in our materials and are planning to use them in the manufacture of your products.

As requested, we enclose our latest catalogue and price list. We are pleased to inform you that everything shown in the catalogue is currently in stock and immediate delivery is guaranteed.

We would like to draw your attention in particular to our Highlander range of windproof and waterproof (2000 mm) material, made of 100% cotton canvas fabric. This material is available in 60" rolls, beige or green. For orders of 100 yards or more, we are pleased to offer a 10% bulk discount.

Our prices are quoted CIF Hamburg, and our terms of payment 30 days, with 2% cash discount for payment within 10 days.

We would like to point out that all our textiles are made with environmentally-friendly materials.

We feel sure that a trial order will convince you of the quality of our goods.

Please contact us if we can be of any further assistance. We look forward to hearing from you soon.

Yours sincerely

Carolanne Adam

Carolanne Adam
Sales Manager
Enc.

› *Thematic vocabulary: Business transactions, page 204*

3 Writing an offer

Your company has received an enquiry from Mike Baird, a retailer of trekking equipment in the UK. Your line manager asks you to complete the reply to the enquiry.

Write the offer using your line manager's notes below.

- *Bezugnahme auf Anfrage über Rucksäcke vom 12. Dezember*
- *Freude ausdrücken über Interesse an Produkten*
- *Fügen aktuellen Katalog bei; derzeit alle Produkte auf Lager*
- *Neues Produkt vorstellen: Ultra-Light 50-Liter Rucksack (wiegt weniger als 1 kg)*
- *Preise verstehen sich ab Werk*
- *Zahlungsbedingungen: 2,5 % Skonto bei Barzahlung innerhalb von 10 Tagen*
- *Stellen Sie sofortige Erledigung der Aufträge in Aussicht und garantieren Sie zuverlässigen Service*
- *Schlagen Sie einen Probeauftrag vor, der von der Qualität unserer Ware zeugt*
- *Stehen jederzeit für weitere Fragen zur Verfügung*
- *geeigneter Schlusssatz*

› *Useful phrases: Writing offers, page 195*

PART A: Offers

Situation: You work in the Sales department at Cantec GmbH, a canning machinery manufacturer in Essen. Your company receives an enquiry from Luke Booysen at AgriTrade Pty Ltd in South Africa (see Unit 8).

→ **You write an email to confirm the details of an offer to the customer.**

1 Making an offer

Your line manager, Dirk Sauerwald, replies to Luke Booysen at AgriTrade.

To:	Luke Booysen, Logistics Director <luke.booysen@agritrade.co.za>
From:	Dirk Sauerwald, Sales Director <dirk.sauerwald@cantec.com>
Subject:	Your enquiry dated 20 October 20.., about a CAN-O-MAT production line
Attachment(s)	canomat.pdf

Dear Mr Booysen

Many thanks for the above-mentioned enquiry.

Our company manufactures high-quality engineering products and has an excellent reputation throughout Europe and South-East Asia. A brochure on our CAN-O-MAT production line is attached for your information. To download details of our entire range together with our export price list, please visit our website at www.cantec.com.

As agreed in our telephone conversation this morning, we will be pleased to supply you with machinery and equipment for the production of round three-piece cans. Our price of €800,000 is quoted FOB European North Sea port, incl. seaworthy packing. Our terms of payment are 1/3 with order, 2/3 by irrevocable and confirmed documentary letter of credit on presentation of the shipping documents. Delivery will be made approx. 6 months after receipt of order.

Please do not hesitate to contact us if you require further details.

We look forward to receiving your order.

Best regards
Dirk Sauerwald
Sales Director

Cantec GmbH & Co. KG, Helenenstraße 149, D-45143 Essen

› *Incoterms, page 184; Terms of payment, page 186*

Read the email and answer the questions.

1 Why does Dirk Sauerwald write to AgriTrade Pty Ltd?
2 Where, outside Europe, is Cantec also well known for its products?
3 Which of Cantec's products does Dirk Sauerwald send AgriTrade more detailed information about?
4 Where will the equipment be loaded on board a ship if AgriTrade accepts Cantec's offer?
5 How much of the price of the machinery will AgriTrade need to pay before Cantec starts work on the order?
6 How long will AgriTrade need to wait before they receive their order?

2 Structuring an offer

When you write offers, you can usually follow a simple structure.

Use the words from the list on the right to translate the offers checklist (1–8) into German.

Offers checklist

1 reference to enquiry
2 description of your company/goods/services
3 sales material
4 price
5 terms and discounts
6 delivery
7 polite ending
8 enclosure(s) (*letter*) / attachment(s) (*email*)

Anlage(n) • Beschreibung Ihrer Firma/Waren/Dienstleistungen • Bezug auf Anfrage • Geschäftsbedingungen und Rabatte • höfliche Schlussformel • Lieferung • Preis • Verkaufsmaterial

› *Useful phrases: Writing offers, page 195*

3 Making an offer on the phone

After the production line has been installed, AgriTrade finds that the noise level is very high. They need to make the line quieter so Luke Booysen contacts Dirk Sauerwald at Cantec to discuss a possible solution.

A 39 **Listen to the dialogue and say if the statements are true or false. Correct the false statements.**

1 AgriTrade is using the production line two or three times a week.
2 Luke Booysen has ordered a noise protection hood.
3 The hood will be sent by sea.
4 Paarl is near Cape Town.
5 Dirk Sauerwald promises to send Luke Booysen another offer with different terms.

B 39 **Listen again and make notes on points 1–6 in the offers checklist above.**

Reference to enquiry – email *Description of goods/services – ...* *...*

4 Evaluating an offer

During his conversation with Luke Booysen, Dirk Sauerwald mentions three Incoterms

A **Look at pages 184–186 and answer the questions below for each of the three Incoterms: FCA, CIF and DAP.**

1 Who pays for the main carriage?
2 Who packs the goods?
3 Who chooses the freight forwarder / vessel?
4 When does the risk pass from the seller to the buyer?
5 Who pays for damage to the goods during the main carriage?
6 Who pays for unloading the goods at their destination?

B **Explain which Incoterm Luke Booysen accepts and why.** › *Incoterms, page 184*

5 Confirming the offer

Dirk Sauerwald asks you to write to Luke Booysen to confirm the details of the offer.

A 39 **Listen again or use your notes from exercise 3B to make a checklist of Cantec's offer.**

B **Use your notes to write an email from Cantec to AgriTrade with all the details of the offer**

› *Useful phrases: Writing offers, page 195; Thematic vocabulary: Business transactions, page 204*

PART B: Comparing offers from different suppliers

Situation: You work in the Purchasing department at Möbelbau Konrad GmbH, a manufacturing company in Dusseldorf specializing in outdoor furniture. The Purchasing Director asks you and your colleagues to contact four suppliers of expanded metal whose products she saw at the EuroBlech trade fair in Hanover.

→ **You compare the offers and recommend a supplier.**

1 Contacting a supplier via chat

The Purchasing Director wants offers for 20 rolls of expanded metal, and she gives you a checklist to fill in for each supplier. First you use the chat function of Alibaba.com to contact TopTech Metals in Shenzhen, China.

A **Read through the chat, copy the checklist on page 95 and fill in the details.**

Möbelbau: Hello, this is MegaKauf in Dusseldorf, Germany.

Anna He: Hello. This is TopTech Metals. My name is Anna. How can I help you?

Möbelbau: Good morning, Anna. We saw your booth at the EuroBlech trade fair in Hanover and need more information about your expanded metal type GF50.

Anna He: Yes, it is very popular. What would you like to know?

Möbelbau: Is the price of €480 per roll an FOB price?

Anna He: Yes, FOB Shenzhen.

Möbelbau: Is there a minimum order quantity?

Anna He: Yes, 5 rolls.

Möbelbau: Thank you. What is the transit time from the Port of Shenzhen to Dusseldorf Central Station?

Anna He: 35 days from the Port of Shenzhen to Bremen then one more day to Dusseldorf.

Möbelbau: Thanks. And the charge for Shenzhen to Dusseldorf?

Anna He: One moment please (*pause*) Using our shipping agent, it is €1,200 for a *20' GP container to Dusseldorf Central Station. One container holds a maximum of 20 rolls. Do you want 20 rolls ?

Möbelbau: Perhaps. How much are 20?

Anna He: 20 rolls cost €9,600.

Möbelbau: Plus €1,200 for transport to Dusseldorf. The import tax and customs duty on €10,800 is about 26% so that comes to (*pause*) €2,808. The total cost would be €13,608.

Anna He: Yes, and that's a very good price.

Möbelbau: OK, but what are your terms of payment?

Anna He: TT – 30% with order, 70% before loading.

Möbelbau: Thanks. How long is your guarantee?

Anna He: 2 years.

Möbelbau: Do you offer a quantity discount?

Anna He: We have a good price and nobody is cheaper than us.

Möbelbau: Thanks. I'll be in touch again soon.

Anna He: Thank you. I will send you photos of all our products via Alibaba. Have a nice day.

Möbelbau: Thanks, you too.

*20' GP – 20-foot general purpose container

B Read through the chat again and answer the questions.

1 How did Möbelbau Konrad find out about TopTech Metals' products?
2 Who will pay for the main carriage if Möbelbau Konrad accepts the price of €480 per roll FOB Shenzhen?
3 How will the expanded metal be transported to Bremen?
4 How much more than the basic price of €9,600 will the expanded metal cost if Möbelbau Konrad decides to buy 20 rolls?
5 How much of the total price will Möbelbau Konrad have to pay before the goods are shipped?
6 What does Anna promise to do after the chat?

C You contact several companies to get the best shipping rates for the rolls of expanded metal. Use words from the chat to complete the email below. Make any necessary changes.

Dear Elaine

I would like to know your ___ [1] for shipping a 20' ___ [2] container of rolls of expanded metal from the ___ [3] of Shenzhen to Dusseldorf Central Station, Germany. Our supplier's terms of delivery are ___ [4], so we require sea transport for the main carriage. Can you offer a ___ [5] time of less than 35 days?

Would you also handle payment of customs ___ [6] and import ___ [7] on our behalf? We have contacted a number of shipping ___ [8] with the same request and hope to hear from you in the very near future.

Best regards

2 Reading an email offer

Your colleague Emil Partmann receives an email from a Finnish supplier, FinMetal Oy, in Oulu, Finland. He then collects additional information on transport costs in a chat with a freight forwarder.

A Study the offer and add the details to your checklist.

To:	emil.partmann@moebelbau-konrad.com
From:	miika.virtanen@finmetal.fi
Subject:	Your enquiry about expanded metal, type EM28
Attachment(s)	finmetal_expanded.pdf

Dear Mr Partmann

Many thanks for the above-mentioned enquiry, which we received this morning.

We are a major manufacturer of metal products with many satisfied customers throughout Europe and beyond. Our current catalogue is attached for your information.

As regards the goods requested, we are pleased to submit the following quotation:

Product:	EM28 expanded metal
Unit price:	€650 per roll
Terms of delivery:	FCA Oulu Station
Terms of payment:	CWO or L/C
Guarantee:	4 years
Quantity discount:	2% as from 50 sets

If regular orders are placed with our company, open account terms may be granted.

We feel sure that a trial order will convince you of the quality of our products and look forward to doing business with you. Please do not hesitate to contact us if you require further details.

Yours sincerely

Miika Virtanen

B Read through the chat and add details of the transport charges to your checklist.

FREIGHT RATE QUOTES • FREIGHT RATE QUOTES • FREIGHT RATE QUOTES •

Emil Partmann 24-May-20.. 7:10

Please let us have quotes for transporting the following from Oulu Train Station, Finland to Dusseldorf Central Station, Germany:
- 20 rolls of expanded metal; 1,750 kg; approx. 30 m^3
- 1 roll of expanded metal; 87.50 kg; approx. 1.50 m^3

24-May-20.. 7:11 Raj Pragasam

Understand. Thank you. Our rate for 1,750 kg in closed wagon is €1,200. For 87.50 kg in shared container it is €400. Delivery period 4 days. Local charges applicable at both ends.

Emil Partmann 24-May-20.. 7:12

Thanks. Will be in touch.

24-May-20.. 7:13 Raj Pragasam

My pleasure!

3 Contacting suppliers by phone

Finally, your colleague phones Officine Mariani SPA in Milan, Italy and Tôlerie Industrielle in Metz, France.

40 **Listen to the two dialogues and add the details for both companies to your checklist.**

Manufacturer / 20 rolls	TopTech Metals, Shenzhen, China	FinMetal Oy, Oulu, Finland	Officine Mariani SPA, Milan, Italy	Tôlerie Industrielle, Metz, France
Unit price				
Minimum order quantity				
Incoterm				
Transit time				
Extra transport costs				
Sub-total				
Import taxes				
Total				
Terms of payment				
Guarantee				
Quantity discount				

4 Comparing the offers

Your company, Möbelbau Konrad GmbH, has its own fleet of lorries and vans. You and your colleagues review the offers.

A **Work in groups of four. Use the data from your checklist and first compare the four Incoterms. Discuss the following points:**

- Who pays for the main carriage in each case?
- What extra transport costs are there for the buyer?
- Where is the risk transferred from the seller to the buyer?

B **Next compare the terms of payment and any discounts. Check the terms offered for …**

- an initial order
- regular orders

C **Now compare the prices and work out the total cost (i.e. price, minimum order quantity, transport costs, taxes, discounts) for each of the four suppliers. Each team member chooses one of the four suppliers and works out the price for …**

1 the smallest possible order
2 20 rolls of expanded metal
3 1,000 rolls of expanded metal

D **What other factors are important when making your final choice of supplier? Discuss your ideas in your team and report back to the class.**

E **Now write a report for your Purchasing Director. Use all the data to recommend the best supplier and give reasons for your choice.**

COMMUNICATION: Clarifying information on the phone

Situation: You work in the Sales department of Marx Kitchens plc, a manufacturer of kitchen equipment and furniture in Birmingham. You sometimes have to clarify details of offers and orders.
→ **You telephone a supplier to sort out a misunderstanding.**

1 Completing a reply to an enquiry

Due to an error, some details are missing from an offer to a prospective customer, John Jamieson. He phones your department and discusses the problems with your line manager, Mary Hamilton.

A **Work with a partner. Decide together who says what, your line manager or the customer.**

1. I'm sorry to hear that.
2. Shall we go through the details together?
3. I would like to have everything sorted out as soon as possible.
4. The most important information is missing.
5. How much is the discount?
6. I think I have all the information I need now.
7. I really must apologize for the problems.
8. I'm so sorry that you've had to go to all this trouble.

B 41 **Listen and check your answers.**

C 41 **Listen to the call again and complete the missing details with numbers and expressions from the list. There are three more items than you need.**

3 · 6 · 10 · 15 · 50 · cash with order · CIF · DDP · delivered from stock · do not include · include

Dear Mr Jamieson

Thank you for your enquiry of 24 April. We are pleased to note that you are interested in our products.

Our terms of delivery are within ___ [1] weeks , ___ [2] Liverpool.
Orders of fewer than ___ [3] items can usually be ___ [4].

Please note that on bulk orders of more than ___ [5] items, we grant a quantity discount of ___ [6] %.

For new customers, we prefer ___ [7] .

As requested, we attach our latest catalogue. Please note that prices ___ [8] VAT (see our terms and conditions, page 6).

We look forward to doing business with you.

Yours sincerely
Mary Hamilton
Sales Department

2 Correcting the details of an order

A few days later, Mr Jamieson sends an order. As there are some errors in the order form, Mary Hamilton phones Mr Jamieson.

A 42 **Listen to the call. What two important details has Mr Jamieson omitted on the order form (page 97)? What mistake has he made in his final calculation?**

B **Re-write the order form, including the missing details and the new total price.**

Dear Ms Hamilton

I refer to our recent telephone conversation. I would like to order the following items:

10 microwave ovens and 25 electric kettles

I attach your order form as requested and look forward to receiving the goods.

Yours sincerely
John Jamieson

Quantity	Item number, description and colour	Unit price	Total
10	Microwave oven	£180	£1,800.00
25	Electric kettle	£27	£675.00
			£2,475.00
		3% discount on bulk order	£74.25 -
		Total price	£2,400.75

3 Role-play: Checking details before placing an order

Last month, while visiting a trade fair, the Purchasing Manager attended a presentation on stainless steel extractor hoods. Before deciding whether to add the hoods to the company's range of products, she asks you to check some details with the supplier, ExHoods Ltd.

Work with a partner. Partner A: **Look here.** Partner B: **Look at File 21 on page 146.**

You work for Marx Kitchens. Call ExHoods to check the details of the product and the terms of delivery. Use the Purchasing Manager's notes on the right.

ExHoods Ltd, presentation, 22 Feb.

stainless steel extractor hoods
Size Large – 45mm x 60mm x 50mm
Price €99.00, EXW
Terms of payment: 1/3 with order, 2/3 30 days after delivery
Customer discount: 5%
Delivery to be made immediately on receipt of order

› *Useful phrases: Clarifying details on the phone, page 196*

Checking information on the phone

A: We can deliver everything by Thursday.
B: Thursday. **Right**.
A: My address is 23 Fairfield Gardens.
B: **Sorry. Did you say** 23 or 33?
A: My number is 0171 452869. (Can you just read that back to me?)
B: **I'll just read that back to you.** 0171 452869.

DAS KANN ICH (Unit 9)

- Ein Kaufangebot an einen Kunden / eine Kundin auf Englisch schreiben. (Foundation)
- Die Details eines Angebots per E-Mail auf Englisch bestätigen. (Part A)
- Verschiedene Angebote vergleichen und eine Kaufempfehlung schreiben. (Part B)
- Die Details einer Bestellung mit einem Kunden / einer Kundin auf Englisch klären. (Communication)

10 An order

FOUNDATION: Introduction to a contract of sale

Situation: You work in the Sales department of Michelsen GmbH, a producer of sugar-free ice teas in Bremen. One of your duties is preparing contracts of sale in English using a template.
→ **You check a standard English contract for a new customer.**

1 Understanding a contract of sale

Your line manager asks you to put together a contract of sale for a new customer in Ireland.

A **Match the German paragraph headings from the list on the right with their English equivalents (1–10) in the checklist below.**

Contract of sale checklist

1 Sale of goods
2 Purchase price
3 Terms of payment
4 Seller's representations
5 Delivery of goods / Shipping
6 Refund and cancellation policy
7 Force majeure
8 Representations
9 General
10 Termination of contract

Allgemeine Bedingungen • Angaben des Verkäufers • Darstellungen • Einkaufspreis • höhere Gewalt • Lieferbedingungen/Versand • Rückvergütung und Stornierungsbedingungen • Vertragsbeendigung • Warenverkauf • Zahlungsbedingungen

B **Look at page 99 and read the extracts (a–j) from an English contract. Find the English equivalents of the following German words and phrases (1–12). They are in the same order.**

1 Vertragspartei
2 Verpflichtungen
3 vor
4 (für etw) verantwortlich sein
5 angefallene Kosten
6 vorbehaltlos
7 fehler-/mangelhaft
8 Umstände
9 übernehmen
10 schriftlich
11 unterzeichnen
12 fällig sein

a Each Party promises the other Party that it has the authority to enter into this Contract and to perform all of its obligations under this Contract.

b If one of the Parties chooses to end the Agreement prior to product delivery, the Buyer is responsible for paying for all work and costs incurred up until that date.

c ... the Buyer shall pay for and accept from the Seller the "Goods" listed at such prices as agreed by the Parties in this Agreement.

d ... the Buyer shall pay to the Seller the purchase price of €... .

e The Buyer will be assumed to have accepted the Goods unconditionally unless a claim that a Good is defective is made within ... days from the date of delivery.

f The Party whose performance has been interrupted by such circumstances shall use every reasonable means to resume full performance of this Agreement as promptly as possible.

g The Seller assumes responsibility for the Goods, and all risk of damage, loss, or delay of the Goods, until the Goods are delivered to or collected by the Buyer.

h The Seller has full right, power, and authority to sell the Goods.

i To change anything in this Contract, the Buyer and the Seller must agree to the change in writing and sign a document showing their Contract.

j Unless otherwise stated, payment for the Goods is due within ... days of the date of the Seller's invoice.

C **Now match the extracts (a–j) to the paragraph headings in the contract of sale checklist (page 98).**

2 A contract for a new customer

Michelsen GmbH has prepared a contract for a new customer, Barney's Café Ltd, in Dublin. Your line manager asks you to check it.

Say if the following statements are true or false according to the extracts from the contract above. Correct the statements that are wrong.

1 Michelsen and Barney's Café have to swear that they have the right to make the contract and to do everything they have to do according to the terms of the contract.
2 If the contract is cancelled before the goods are delivered, Michelsen has to pay for everything that has been done up to the date of cancellation.
3 Barney's Café has to accept the goods and pay the price for them that Michelsen has decided.
4 Barney's Café has to pay Michelsen a specific amount of money for the goods.
5 As soon as the goods have been delivered, Barney's Café must send a written statement to Michelsen saying that it has accepted the goods. If Barney's Café does not do this, Michelsen will believe that Barney's Café has rejected the consignment.
6 If Michelsen has to postpone delivery of the goods for any reason, it must do its best to restart the delivery process as soon as it can.
7 Michelsen has to bear all risks until Barney's Café has the goods in its possession.
8 Michelsen is not allowed to sell the products Barney's Café would like to buy.
9 Michelsen and Barney's Café both have to show in writing that they consent to any alterations to the contract.
10 The contract states that Barney's Café must pay cash in advance for the goods.

PART A: Placing and acknowledging orders

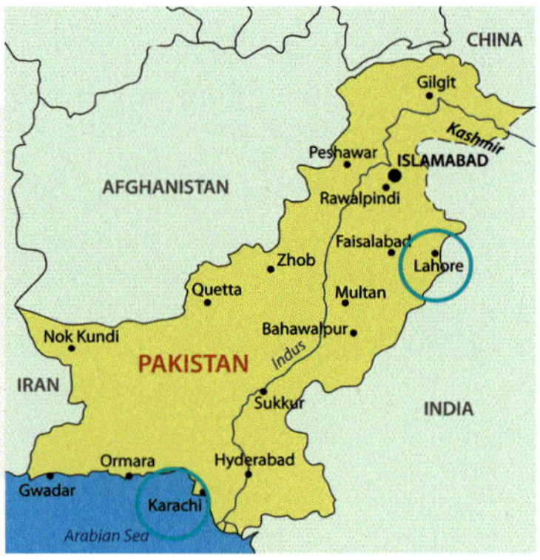

Situation: You work in the Purchasing department at Brinkmeyer Lederwarenmanufaktur GmbH in Dusseldorf. Your company buys its leather from suppliers in Pakistan and, as your products are selling well, you now want to place large orders regularly.

→ You negotiate terms with a supplier, then place an order for goods.

1 Reviewing current terms

Study the last order that your colleague, Sven Maier, placed with A.P. Leather International in Lahore, Pakistan.

To: nasir.mahmood@ap-leather.com.pk
From: sven.maier@blm.de
Subject: Order for hides and nappa leather
16 December 20..
Attachment(s):

Dear Mr Mahmood

Having seen your offer on the internet and spoken to you on the telephone, we now wish to place an order for the following goods:

Quantity	Description	Article no.	Unit price	Total
200	Cow hide	CH42	US$10.00	US$2,000.00
100	Buffalo hide	BH98	US$30.00	US$3,000.00
1,000 sq ft	Brown nappa leather	BNL36	US$3.00	US$3,000.00
500 sq ft	Green nappa leather	GNL35	US$4.00	US$2,000.00
			Total price	**US$10,000.00**

Terms of delivery: EXW Lahore, Pakistan within 30 days after receipt of order
Terms of payment: 25% with order, 75% before loading by transfer to your a/c at Allied Bank Limited
Packing: Container, *LCL, palletized

Transport and insurance of the goods from Lahore to Dusseldorf via the ports of Karachi and Bremen will be arranged by us.

We look forward to receiving your confirmation of order and advice of dispatch in the near future and trust the goods will arrive punctually and in good condition.

Yours sincerely

Sven Maier
Purchasing Department

Brinkmeyer Lederwarenmanufaktur GmbH
Oberkasseler Str. 200, 40545 Düsseldorf, Germany

*LCL = less than a container load. See diagram page 101.

Work with a partner and discuss how the terms of delivery and payment could be improved and any other changes that could be made in Brinkmeyer's favour. Discuss your ideas with the class.

2 Negotiating better terms

Your colleague, Sven Maier, phones Nasir Mahmood at A.P. Leather International to negotiate better terms and to place an order.

A 43)) **Listen to the dialogue and note down the following information:**

- the terms of the last order
- the terms that Brinkmeyer wants
- the terms agreed
- the validity of the new agreement

B **Has Sven Maier negotiated the new terms you expected?**

Symbols and abbreviations			
'	foot (*pl* feet)	m³	cubic metre(s)
"	inch(es)	ft³	cubic foot (*pl* feet)
kg	kilo(s)	lb(s)	pound(s)

› *Conversion tables, page 205*

3 Acknowledging an order

The Pakistani supplier confirms the new terms, but in the email acknowledging Brinkmeyer's next order, some of the details are wrong.

Study the email and compare it with your notes from exercise 2A. Find the three errors in the email.

To: sven.maier@mkg.de

From: nasir.mahmood@ap-leather.com.pk

Subject: Confirmation of your order no. FWL 68D for hides and nappa leather dated 02 January 20..

Dear Mr Maier

We are pleased to confirm the above-mentioned order for delivery FCA Lahore, (FCL or LCL) 30 days after receipt of order, payment of USD150,000.00 to be made 1/3 with order, 1/3 on delivery and 1/3 30 days after delivery.

We look forward to doing further business with you.

Yours sincerely

Nasir Mahmood
Export Sales Director
A.P. Leather International

4 Structuring an order

An order usually covers some or all of the points in the checklist.

A **Use words from the list below to translate the orders checklist (1–8) into German.**

Angaben über die bestellten Waren / Dienstleistungen • Anlage(n)/Anhang/Anhänge • Bestätigung / Versandanzeige • Bezug auf Angebot • höfliche Schlussformel • Internationale Handelsklausel • Liefertermin/-zeit • Lieferung • Preis(e) und Rabatt(e) • Verpackung • Versand • Versicherung • Zahlung

› *Useful phrases: Writing orders, page 196*

Orders checklist

1. reference to offer
2. details of goods/services ordered
3. price(s) and discount(s)
4. delivery
   - Incoterm
   - delivery date/period
   - transport
   - packing
   - insurance
5. payment
6. acknowledgement / advice of dispatch
7. polite ending
8. enclosure(s) (*letter*) / attachment(s) (*email*)

B **Choose 12 of the 16 headings in the list to complete the order below.**

article no. • cash discount • delivery • description • insurance • packing • payment • quantity • quantity discount • size • subtotal • total • total price • trade discount • transport • unit price

___1	___2	___3	___4	___5
100	HQ printer	HQ3000	€60.00	€6,000.00
250	Quickchip laptop	QC99	€100.00	€25,000.00
			– 30% ___6	– €9,300.00
			___7	€21,700.00
			+ 20% *VAT	€4,340.00
			___8	**€26,040.00**

___9: DAP buyer's premises by 30 June 20..
___10: Sturdy cartons
___11: 2% 10 days, 30 days net after receipt of invoice
___12: By road

*value added tax = *Mehrwertsteuer*

Infobox

Structuring an order or acknowledgement
If you are writing about **two or more** items, use a table with headings (see exercise 4B) to make your order easy to understand. If you are only writing about **one** item, just use headings:

Article:	Ladies' fashion jacket
Article no.:	GPS3000
Quantity:	100
List price:	€25.00

Writing prices

Currency symbol first
No space
Comma where there is a point in German
Point where there is a comma in German

€10,500.50

5 Placing an order

Your line manager in the Purchasing department asks you to place an order for industrial sewing machines with Digitex s.r.l., a manufacturer in Perugia, Italy. You phone them, then send a written order.

A **Work with a partner.** Partner A: **Look at File 17 on page 144.** Partner B: **Look at File 15 on page 142.**

B **Now place your order (see exercise 5A) in writing. Include the following points in your order:**

- heutiges Datum
- Ansprechpartner/in: Herr Antonio / Frau Arianna Rossetti (a.rossetti@digitex.it), in der Verkaufsabteilung
- Bezug auf Telefongespräch
- Bestellung unsererseits mit Auftrags-Nr. INM76 von 20 Industrienähmaschinen vom Typ HD500, Stückpreis € 1.500,00 und 10 vom Typ HD1000, Stückpreis € 2.000,00.
- Lieferbedingungen: CPT Düsseldorf auf Paletten, volle Containerladung, per Lkw innerhalb von 30 Tagen nach Auftragseingang
- Versicherung von Perugia nach Düsseldorf wird von uns übernommen
- Zahlungsbedingungen: Barzahlung bei Auftragserteilung
- Bitte um Auftragsbestätigung und Versandanzeige
- Hoffnung auf pünktliche Lieferung der Ware in gutem Zustand
- Aussicht auf weitere Aufträge, wenn die Ware sich gut verkauft
- höfliche Schlussformel

› *Useful phrases: Writing orders, page 196*

PART B: Shipping an order

Situation: You work in the Export Sales department of Brewery-2-Brewery GmbH in Gelsenkirchen. Your company has received an order for microbrewing equipment from Harpoon Brew Supply Inc. in Bedford, Massachusetts, USA.

→ **You fill in an application form for a documentary letter of credit.**

1 Reviewing shipping documents

First you look at an overview of the documents typically needed for an international transaction.

Document	German	Features
1 Bill of lading (B/L) – sea transport	Konnossement	– document of title (negotiable – ownership is transferable) – receipt for the goods – contract of carriage – 'clean' if the goods are in apparent good order and condition – 'foul' if the goods are not in apparent good order and condition
2 Air waybill – air transport	Luftfrachtbrief	– not a document of title (non-negotiable – ownership is not transferable) – receipt for the goods – contract of carriage
3 Consignment note – rail or road transport	Frachtbrief	– not a document of title (non-negotiable – ownership is not transferable) – receipt for the goods – contract of carriage
4 CMR document / truck waybill	Lastwagen-frachtbrief	– not a document of title (non-negotiable – ownership is not transferable) – receipt for the goods – contract of carriage – printed in three languages
5 Multi-modal B/L – sea, air, rail or road transport	multimodales Konnossement	– can be a document of title (negotiable or non-negotiable) – receipt for the goods – contract of carriage
6 Insurance certificate	Versicherungs-schein	– proves that the goods are insured – used in a documentary credit transaction
7 Certificate of origin	Ursprungs-zeugnis	– shows where the goods are from – issued by a chamber of commerce in the exporter's country – used to assess customs duties
8 Commercial invoice	Handels-rechnung	– request for payment – shows the price the buyer has to pay for the goods
9 Pro-forma invoice	Proforma-Rechnung	– not a request for payment – shows how much the buyer will have to pay for the goods
10 Packing list	Packliste	– contains details of the goods (number of packages, weights, dimensions)
11 Bill of exchange (draft)	Wechsel (Tratte)	– the buyer can pay by accepting or paying a bill of exchange

Study the list of documents on page 103 and complete the following sentences with the correct answer.

1 If the bill of lading is 'clean', the goods … .
  a are not dirty b show no sign of damage c are perfect in every way

2 Ownership of the goods can be transferred by selling … .
  a the bill of lading b the air waybill c the consignment note

3 An air waybill, a consignment note, a CMR document and a bill of lading have … .
  a one feature in common b two features in common c three features in common

4 When several modes of transport are combined, goods are sent using … .
  a one transport document b separate transport documents c a consignment note

5 The amount of customs duty to be paid when goods are imported is calculated using … .
  a the insurance certificate b the packing list c the certificate of origin

6 The pro-forma invoice shows how much a product … .
  a cost b costs c will cost

7 The packing list shows … of the goods.
  a the price and value b the size and weight c the quality

8 A bill of exchange is … .
  a a contract of carriage b a receipt for the goods c an instrument of payment

2 Presenting the right documents

Harpoon Brew Supply Inc. agrees to pay by irrevocable and confirmed documentary letter of credit (L/C) opened by the buyer at their bank in the US, payable to the seller at their bank in Germany.

A Read the application form on page 105 and answer the questions.

1 What is the name of the buyer?
2 What is the name of the seller?
3 What is the name of the buyer's bank?
4 What is the name of the seller's bank?
5 When is the deadline for presentation of the shipping documents to the seller's bank?
6 What currency is the price stated in?
7 How do we know that the load cannot be split into parts or loaded from one ship to another?
8 What are the ports of shipment and destination?
9 What is the Incoterm and the port of destination for this shipment?
10 What documents must Brewery-2-Brewery GmbH present to their bank in order to receive payment?

B Find the English equivalents of the following German words and expressions in parts 1–10 of the letter of credit application form. They are in the same order.

1 Auftraggeber/in
2 eröffnen
3 unwiderruflich
4 avisierende Bank
5 zugunsten
6 Begünstigte/r
7 gültig bis
8 eine Tratte ziehen
9 Teillieferung
10 Umladung

Bank of Massachusetts

Application and Agreement for Commercial Letter of Credit

TO: Bank of Massachusetts, N.A. ("Bank of Massachusetts")

A. Application — File No. FGBGT 98

1. Applicant Name & Address (guarantor for Letter of Credit) requests Bank of Massachusetts to issue an irrevocable letter of credit as follows ☑ Full text teletransmission ☐ Courier

Harpoon Brew Supply Inc., 44 Crosby Drive
Bedford, MA 01730, USA

2. Advising Bank Name & Address: (if left blank, the Bank of Massachusetts Banking Center will be used)

Deutsche Bank, Von-Oven-Strasse 12–16,
45879 Gelsenkirchen, Germany

3. For Account of Party / Named Applicant on the Letter of Credit (Name & Address, if different from Applicant):

4. In favor of (Beneficiary Name & Address):

Brewery-2-Brewery GmbH
Karl-Meyer-Strasse 100, 45884 Gelsenkirchen, Germany

5. Expiration Date. Drafts to be drawn on and presented to the negotiating or paying bank on or before:

March 31, 20..

6. Amount: (EUR72,000.00) seventy-two thousand and 00/00

Put in figures and words. For example: ($10,000) Ten thousand and 00/00

Currency: EUR ▾ ______________ (if left blank, U.S. dollars) **Tolerance** 0% ▾

7. Covering: 100 **% of invoice value.** (Full invoice value unless otherwise specified.)

8. Available by drafts: ☑ Sight ☐ ____ Days Sight ☐ ____ Days Date (being the date of the transport document)
Drafts to be drawn on Bank of Massachusetts or Bank of Massachusetts' correspondent, at Bank of Massachusetts' option.

9. Partial Shipment:
☐ Permitted ☑ Not Permitted

10. Transshipment: (Not applicable to Air Shipments or Multimodal Transport Shipments.)
☐ Permitted ☑ Not Permitted

11. Transferable Letter of Credit? ☐ Yes ☑ No

12. Shipment/Dispatch/Taking in Charge From/At	Latest Shipment Date	For Transportation To	Final Destination
North Sea port	March 31, 20..	Port of Boston, MA	Bedford MA, USA

13. Merchandise to be described in invoice as (omit unnecessary details and specify price basis below):
Complete Microbrewery 1000 liters per brew 2-vessel brewhouse in stainless steel

14. Shipping Terms / Price Basis (check one): ☐ FCA ☐ FOB ☑ CFR ☐ CIF ☐ Other: BLANK ▾

15. Documents Required (check applicable boxes below):
☑ Commercial Invoice in 3 original(s) and 3 copies.
☑ Packing List in 3 original(s) and 3 copies.
☑ Certificate of Origin in 3 original(s) and 3 copies.
☑ Negotiable Marine/Air Insurance Policy or Certificate for at least 110% invoice value in duplicate, effected by ☑ Buyer ☐ Seller
Including coverage for: ☐ War Risk ☑ All Risks ☐ Other Risks (specify): ____
☑ Transport Documents: ☑ Marine B/L ☐ Multimodal B/L ☐ Air Waybill ☐ Truck B/L ____ Other
Presented in: ☑ Full Set ☐ 2/3 ☐ 1/3 ____ Copy
Consigned to / the order of ____ (if left blank, consigned to applicant)
Marked Notify Applicant
Marked Freight: ☐ collect ☑ prepaid
☐ Other documents:

16. Special Instructions to be included in the Letter of Credit (unless otherwise stated):
All bank charges (other than those of Bank of Massachusetts) are for the account of the Beneficiary. Discount charges, if any, are for the account of the Beneficiary. All documents are to be sent by the negotiating/paying bank to Bank of Massachusetts in one cover by courier or registered mail.
☐ Other instructions:

17. Special Instructions to Bank of Massachusetts:

18. Documents must be presented to the negotiating or paying bank no later than: 21 days after date of transport document (on board validation applicable for ocean shipment) but within the validity of the Letter of Credit. (Will be 21 days if left blank.)

☑ If this box is marked, Applicant authorizes Bank of Massachusetts to effect payment of any sums due under this Application and Agreement by means of debiting Applicant's account with Bank of Massachusetts set forth below. This authorization does not affect the obligation of Applicant to pay such sums when due, if there are insufficient funds in such account to make such payment when due, or if Bank of Massachusetts fails to debit the account, and this authorization does not affect any setoff rights of Bank of Massachusetts at law or in equity. Applicant's account number with Bank of Massachusetts is 7340001524.

3 Understanding the terms of an L/C

Harpoon Brew Supply Inc. now has a problem with the order and contacts Brewery-2-Brewery GmbH to request a change of plan.

A 44 **Listen to the telephone dialogue between your colleague, Louisa Schneider, in Gelsenkirchen and Kevin King of Harpoon Brew Supply Inc. Note down the following information:**

- the buyer's problem
- what the buyer wishes Brewery-2-Brewery to do to solve the problem
- the changes that Brewery-2-Brewery can make under the terms of the L/C
- the financial consequences of the buyer's problem for Brewery-2-Brewery
- the solution suggested by Brewery-2-Brewery

B **Louisa Schneider expects that Kevin King will need help transferring the microbrewery to its new destination, so she asks you to write an email to Nancy Kline, Brewery-2-Brewery GmbH's agent in New York, to explain the situation. Describe the buyer's problem and explain what can and can't be done to help him.**

To: n.kline@brewery-2-brewery-usa.com
From: name.surname@brewery-2-brewery-de.com
Subject: Harpoon Brew Supply Inc.

Hi Nancy

Thanks for your email. This is the background to Kevin King's request …

› *Useful phrases: Writing emails, page 190*

4 Shipping goods

Kevin King asks Nancy Kline in New York to help him ship the microbrewery to its new destination, so she contacts Lopez Catering in Philadelphia to discuss arrangements. She then calls Kevin King back and explains the details to him.

A 45 **Listen to their telephone conversation and decide if the following statements are true or false. Correct the false statements.**

1. Lopez Catering has agreed to buy the microbrewery.
2. The microbrewery is now at the port of Boston.
3. All the financial formalities have been dealt with.
4. The microbrewery will finally be unloaded at the port of Philadelphia.
5. Nancy Kline suggests sending the goods by road.
6. The microbrewery is packed in six containers.
7. It would take about a week to transport the goods from Boston to Pennsylvania by sea.
8. Nancy Kline will send Kevin King a contract for him to sign.

B 45)) **Listen again and complete the sentences with the words you hear.**

1 Kevin: You mean you can ___ it?
2 Nancy: You now need to get on to your bank and transfer ___ to Lopez Catering.
3 Nancy: The buyer pays for ___ at the port of destination.
4 Nancy: Then the goods will have to be ___ at the port of Boston.
5 Kevin: Would it not be easiest just to send the ___ from Boston to Philadelphia by ship?
6 Nancy: ___ is not allowed.
7 Nancy: But that's without ___ and you would still need to have the containers picked up.
8 Kevin: Well, as Lopez Catering wants ___ delivery, that sounds like the best option.
9 Nancy: It would cost $2,160 for delivery ___.
10 Kevin: What's the delivery time ___ ?
11 Nancy: That's the freight ___ I would recommend.
12 Nancy: They will send you a contract of ___.

C **List the terms of delivery (Incoterms) mentioned in the recording then explain why the term chosen is most suitable in this case.**

› *Incoterms, page 184*

VIDEO 7

Watch the video to see more about orders and shipment.

5 Applying for a letter of credit

Brewery-2-Brewery GmbH has received an order for a microbrewery from a new Irish chain of restaurants called The Dining Experience with its headquarters in Cork. Payment has been agreed by irrevocable and confirmed documentary letter of credit, to be opened through an Irish bank. Today you receive a phone call from Megan Connolly in Cork. She asks you to help her fill in the application form because she has never done this before and does not want to make any mistakes. She emails you the form from the Commercial Credit Bank and you enter the necessary data for her.

Use the following information to complete the application form for the letter of credit (see File 16 on page 143).

Auftraggeber ist The Dining Experience, 22 Shandon Street, Clarke's Bridge, Cork T23 V2TO, Irland (Sachbearbeiter/in: Ms Megan Connolly, Tel. +353 21 429 5555, Fax +353 21 429 6666). Begünstigter ist Brewery-2-Brewery GmbH, Karl-Meyer-Straße 100, 45884 Gelsenkirchen, Deutschland (Sachbearbeiterin: Ms Louisa Schneider, Tel. +49 209 177 8253, Fax +49 209 177 8254).

Das Akkreditiv lautet über 55.000,00 EUR +/– 0 % und ist bis 31. März 20.. gültig. Das Akkreditiv soll durch die avisierende Bank bestätigt werden, wobei sämtliche Gebühren zu Lasten des Auftraggebers gehen.

Die Sendung wird in Gelsenkirchen übernommen und zum Hafen Cork gebracht. Teillieferungen und Umladungen sind nicht erlaubt. Letztes Verladedatum ist 10. März 20.. und die Lieferbedingungen sind CIF Cork.
Bei den einzureichenden Dokumenten handelt es sich um die Handelsrechnung und drei Kopien; Packliste und drei Kopien; Ursprungszeugnis, das den deutschen Ursprung der Ware bestätigt; voller Satz reiner Bordkonnossemente mit dem Vermerk „Fracht bezahlt"; Versicherungszertifikat für den vollen CIF-Wert der Sendung zzgl. 10 %.
Die Sendung besteht aus sechs Holzkisten (*wooden crates*) mit Brauereiausrüstung.

› *Incoterms, page 184; Terms of payment, page 186*
› *Thematic vocabulary: Shipping documents, page 204*

COMMUNICATION: Enquiries, offers and orders

Situation: You work at MedEquip GmbH, a Berlin-based manufacturer of medical supplies and equipment for hospitals and clinics.
→ You write an enquiry and an order to a supplier; you send an offer to a customer.

1 Checking language for enquiries

You check that you know suitable English phrases for writing a letter of enquiry.

TIP

You will find similar phrases in the model letter on page 85.

How would you say these phrases and sentences from a German letter of enquiry in English?

1 Wir haben Ihre Anzeige … gesehen.
2 Wir sind ein/eine … in Deutschland.
3 Wir haben vor, …
4 Wir interessieren uns …
5 Wir möchten eine Probebestellung für … aufgeben.
6 Wenn die Dienstleistungen Ihrer Firma unsere Voraussetzungen erfüllen, …
7 Bitte nennen Sie uns Einzelheiten zu …
8 Die … Bank wird Ihnen gerne Referenzen zukommen lassen.
9 Wir freuen uns, bald von Ihnen zu hören.

2 Writing an enquiry for medical monitors

MedEquip GmbH is looking for a new supplier of computer monitors for its R&D department. Jan Dube, the Purchasing Manager, asks you to write a letter of enquiry to a manufacturer in Scotland.

Write a letter of enquiry to McScreen Ltd using the notes below. Add today's date and your own reference numbers. Remember to use the correct salutation, subject line and complimentary close.

› *Useful phrases: Writing enquiries, page 193*
› *Thematic vocabulary: Business transactions, page 204*

TIP

The letter on page 85 will help you with the layout and address.

Anfrage an McScreen Ltd, Unit 5, Silverbank Industrial Estate, Ferry Road, Edinburgh EH4 2EF, Großbritannien – Details von ihrer Webseite

- *Vorstellung unserer Firma; Geschäftstätigkeit*
- *Bedarf an neuen Computerbildschirmen für Forschungs- und Entwicklungsabteilung*
- *Probeauftrag für einen 32-Zoll hochauflösenden CAD/CAM-Bildschirm (high-definition CAD/CAM computer monitor)*
- *Aussicht auf zusätzliche Aufträge falls Probeauftrag zufriedenstellend*
- *Liefer- und Zahlungsbedingungen?*
- *Referenz: Triodod Bank, Berlin*
- *höfliche Schlussformel*

CC: Jan Dube

3 Writing an offer for wheelchairs

The Sales Manager took a call from a customer in Ireland today. She gives you her notes and asks you to write an offer in reply.

Anruf: Ms Helen O'Meara, Administrator, Toll Road Hospital, Dublin 4J, Irland
Anfrage: ASB35K Sterile Behälter (sterile containers); 350 x 120 x 80 mm
Menge: 100
Lieferbedingungen: DAP Dublin
Zahlungsbedingung: 1/3 bei Bestellung, 2/3 bei Lieferung
Lieferzeit: 2 Wochen nach Bestellung
Preis: € 199,–/Behälter
Neukundenrabatt: 5,0 %
Katalog und aktuelle Preisliste

Read the notes then write the offer using the prompts below.

- Dank für die Anfrage vom … (heutiges Datum)
- Dank für das Interesse an unseren Produkten
- Bestätigung der Produktinformationen und des Preises
- Bestätigung der Liefer- und Zahlungsbedingungen
- Preisliste und Katalog beifügen
- höfliche Schlussformel

› *Useful phrases: Writing offers, page 195*

4 Writing an order for an operating theatre monitor

Neil McCain, the Sales Manager of McScreen Ltd in Edinburgh, replies to your enquiry (see exercise 2). Jan Dube, your Purchasing Manager, is happy with the offer and asks you to write the order.

Use Jan Dube's notes to write the complete order. Don't forget a suitable complimentary close.

› *Useful phrases: Writing orders, page 196*

- Mr McCain für Angebot danken
- Bestellung: ein 32-Zoll HD CAD/CAM-Bildschirm
- Bestätigung des Preises: £ 700,00
- Bestätigung der Lieferbedingungen: DAP Berlin
- Zahlungsbedingung: CWO
- Aussicht auf weitere Bestellungen
- höfliche Schlussformel

DAS KANN ICH (Unit 10)

- Einen englischen Kundenvertrag verstehen und überprüfen. (Foundation)
- Verbesserte Bedingungen aushandeln und eine Bestellung aufgeben. (Part A)
- Ein Antragsformular für ein Akkreditiv auf Englisch ausfüllen. (Part B)
- Eine Anfrage, ein Angebot und eine Bestellung auf Englisch verfassen. (Communication)

Exam practice 5

1 **Leseverstehen: Stufe II**

Situation: Sie arbeiten für eine internationale Firma in Frankfurt, die auch eine Niederlassung in York, UK hat. Die Geschäftsleitung plant Weiterbildungskurse für die englischen Mitarbeiter/innen und hat bereits eine Schulungsakademie vor Ort ausgewählt. Die Frage, wie man die Kurse anbieten will, ist noch nicht geklärt. Ihr Abteilungsleiter hat Sie nun beauftragt, die zwei Kursarten zu vergleichen.

Aufgabe: Lesen Sie die Kursbeschreibungen. Kopieren und vervollständigen Sie anschließend die Tabelle soweit wie möglich.

Individual training

No matter what level you are at, our courses will give you the skills and expertise you need to gain a competitive advantage in the challenging and complex world of export, import and international trade. We evaluate your personal level and start from there, thus guaranteeing the best progress.

- Courses cover a wide range of international trade topics
- Three levels of learning: Introductory, Operational, Management
- One-to-one teaching
- Small classes of no more than 5 people possible – but not from the same company
- Taught in evening classes by quality-assured experts in the subject matter
- Individual work pace
- Focus on yourself, your needs and your goals, work with maximum concentration
- Costs: £75 per 90-minute session
- Costs may be partially tax-deductible

In-house training

Companies are increasingly seeking in-house training because of its flexibility, convenience and cost-effectiveness. Choosing the right training provider is the key to helping your employees and organization achieve their goals and to receiving a strong return on your investment.

- Convenience – as courses are timed to suit your required dates
- Less disruption to work schedules, adaptable to work shifts
- Tailor-made for company needs
- Recognized as tax-deductible
- All skill levels possible, heterogeneous groups are given customized solutions
- Value for money – charges are per event rather than per person (30–35 people in a course), approx. £650
- Time savings – all the work involved in designing the training activity
- Comfortable and relaxed atmosphere among familiar colleagues
- Strengthens teams within company

Aspekt	Einzelschulung	Inhouse-Training
Inhalte/Themen?		
Größe der Lerngruppen?		
Lernniveaus?		
Kosten?		
Wann finden die Kurse statt?		
Qualifikation der Trainer/innen?		
Wie werden die Kurse zusammengestellt?		
Gibt es steuerliche Abschreibungsmöglichkeiten?		
Vorteile in sozialer Hinsicht?		

2 Produktion: Stufe II

Situation: Ihre Firma entschließt sich für ein Inhouse-Training. Dabei sollen die nachfolgenden Aspekte geklärt werden.

Aufgabe: Verfassen Sie eine E-Mail-Anfrage unter Berücksichtigung der folgenden Punkte:

- Zeitraum: Oktober oder November nächsten Jahres
- Themen müssen noch genau mit Geschäftsleitung abgesprochen werden, zwecks Terminabsprache bitte Herrn Fischer telefonisch kontaktieren (0353-1-477184)
- Etwa 60 Teilnehmer/innen in zwei Gruppen
- Einstufungstest vorab möglich? Dann Gruppen eventuell nach Leistungsstand aufteilen
- Kurse sollen nachmittags liegen, allerdings nicht montags und freitags
- Samstag möglich? Extrakosten?
- Welche räumliche Ausstattung muss die Firma bereitstellen?

3 Hörverstehen: Stufe II

Situation: Sie machen ein Praktikum bei einem englischen Hersteller von Zubehör von Motorrädern und Fahrrädern. Für die einzulagernden Waren ist das firmeneigene Außenlager an seine Kapazitätsgrenzen gestoßen. Sie sind dem Lagerleiter zugeteilt und sollen Lösungsmöglichkeiten erarbeiten. In diesem Zusammenhang stellt Ihnen ihr Kollege Tom telefonisch seine Rechercheergebnisse dar.

46 **Aufgabe: Hören Sie sich das Gespräch an, kopieren Sie das Formular und machen Sie sich Notizen.**

	Lager 1	Lager 2
Lage		
Platz/Kapazität		
Kosten		
Verfügbarkeit		
Zusätzliche Informationen		
Kontaktdaten		

11 Problems and complaints

FOUNDATION: Making and dealing with complaints

Situation: You work for Kelvin Kitchen Appliances Ltd, a UK manufacturer of kitchen appliances. The company has had a lot of complaints recently and has lost some customers as a result.
→ **You explain to a new German trainee how to handle complaints properly.**

1 Different ways to complain

You talk to other apprentices about different reasons for complaining.

Work in groups. Describe the last time you made a complaint to a company. What was the problem? How did you make your complaint? What did you do? How did the company react?

2 Making suggestions to improve service

Your line manager has put together a diagram showing the types of complaints the company has received in the last three months. She sends round a memo asking for suggestions about how to make improvements.

In the last three months, we have had a lot of complaints about our deliveries (see pie chart).

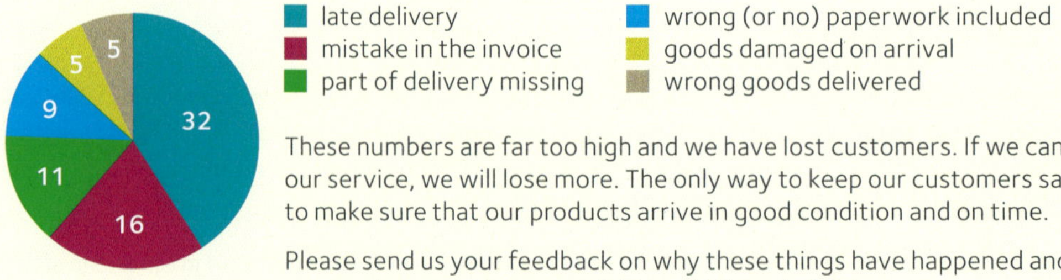

These numbers are far too high and we have lost customers. If we can't improve our service, we will lose more. The only way to keep our customers satisfied is to make sure that our products arrive in good condition and on time.

Please send us your feedback on why these things have happened and your suggestions as to how we might avoid them in future.

A **Talk in groups about what the pie chart shows. Compare and contrast the findings.**

B **Discuss who or what might be responsible for each of the problems. Say how things might be improved. Use your ideas to write a short memo for your supervisor.**

Comparing figures

The majority of complaints were (about) ...
... made up ...% of the complaints.
There were **fewer** complaints about ...
The **fewest** complaints related to ...
... is/was **the same as** ... / **higher/lower than** ...

› *Grammar: Comparatives and superlatives, page 157*

3 Making a complaint

Sometimes Kelvin Kitchen Appliances have problems with consignments from their suppliers. Your line manager describes two ways to make complaints.

47 **Listen and complete the notes your line manager has made for her talk.**

Making a telephone complaint

1 *Before you make the call:*
2 *The start of the call:*
3 *During the call:*
4 *Follow up:*

Making a complaint in writing

5 *Start:*
6 *Body of the letter:*
7 *Suggestions:*
8 *Conclusion:*

4 Mediation: Complaint management

Your line manager wants to make sure that a new trainee from Germany knows the company's policy on dealing with complaints.

Read the text and make a German summary of the most important points for the new trainee.

Taking customer complaints seriously

In a recent study on customer satisfaction carried out by *Business Matters* magazine, people were asked to say what they had expected and what they experienced when making complaints. The results might give some companies a lot to think about.

At the top of the list of expectations, with 93% of the interviewees stating that these things were important to them, were:
1) an acknowledgement of the complaint, and
2) the wish to be taken seriously.

As far as the first expectation was concerned, 81% of the people who took part in the survey said that they had received an acknowledgement. As for being taken seriously, however, only 5% felt that the person who took their complaint listened to them and showed them respect. Similarly, over 67% of complainants expected someone to get back to them, but only 5% were contacted as promised.

65% of the customers who completed the survey expected an apology for the inconvenience they had been caused, but only 35% actually received one. Thanks for bringing the problem to the attention of the company was given in only 25% of the cases.

Saying thank you is cheap. Reimbursement, which was expected by 17.5% of the customers who complained, was given in only 10% of the cases, while other forms of compensation were only given in 2.5% of the cases. 40% of the complainants registered no satisfactory response.

What should companies learn from this survey? Customers who complain expect to be acknowledged and taken seriously; they would like an apology for their inconvenience and a thank you for pointing out the problem. Reimbursement or compensation of some sort came low on the list of complainants' expectations and, not every complainant was reimbursed. In 40% of the cases, there was no satisfactory response. Is it any wonder that companies lose customers?

Make sure that you don't disappoint your customers and drive them away. Take complaints seriously, apologize for the mistake and make sure that you do what you promise to do.

› *Thematic vocabulary, Complaints, page 205*

PART A: A complaint about faulty goods

Situation: You work in the Purchasing department of Kältetechnik Lohmann GmbH in Stuttgart. Last week you ordered a consignment of smoke alarms for your factory from Safety First Ltd, an Irish manufacturer of alarm systems. However, when the alarms arrive you discover that they are sub-standard.
→ **You complain to a manufacturer and respond to a customer's complaint.**

1 Writing a complaint

Your colleague, Tamara Beck, has written to the Sales Director of Safety First Ltd in Dublin.

To: fiona.murphy@safety-first-ltd.ie <Fiona Murphy, Sales Director>
From: tamara.beck@ktl.de
Subject: Order no. VBF900 for 5,000 EW1 smoke alarms dated 12 May 20..
Attachment(s): photos_smoke_alarm.gif

Dear Ms Murphy

The above-mentioned smoke alarms were delivered on 20 May 20...

When we opened the boxes, we discovered that some were without batteries and mounting screws and others did not work when tested and were discoloured.

We enclose photographs of these items for your information.

Please explain why our order was so poorly executed.

Whatever the case may be, you will appreciate that we cannot install the alarms in our factory and must therefore ask you to replace the entire consignment, as these goods are needed urgently.

We feel sure you will understand that our future business relationship will depend on how this matter is dealt with.

We expect to hear from you in the very near future.

Yours sincerely
Tamara Beck

Purchasing Department
Kältetechnik Lohmann GmbH
Vaihinger Straße 52, 70186 Stuttgart, Germany

Read Kältetechnik Lohmann's complaint and match the sentence halves.

1 Kältetechnik Lohmann bought the smoke alarms from ...
2 Kältetechnik Lohmann need smoke alarms for ...
3 When checking the consignment it was discovered that ...
4 The colour of some of the alarms ...
5 Tamara Beck wants ...
6 Kältetechnik Lohmann want the manufacturer to ...
7 Kältetechnik Lohmann will only place further orders ...
8 Tamara Beck expects the manufacturer ...

a had also changed.
b an explanation from the manufacturer.
c their factory in Germany.
d if a satisfactory solution is found.
e some alarms were incomplete and/or faulty.
f to deal with the matter immediately.
g replace all the smoke alarms.
h an Irish manufacturer called Safey First Ltd.

2 Structuring a complaint

Most complaints have a similar structure.

Use words from the list on the right to translate the complaints checklist (1–7) into German.

Complaints checklist

1 Reference to goods
2 Description of problem
3 Request for explanation
4 Consequences for the buyer and seller
5 Request for action
6 Polite ending
7 Enclosure(s) (*letter*) / Attachment(s) (*email*)

Anlage(n)/Anhang/Anhänge • Bezug auf Waren • Bitte um Ergreifung geeigneter Maßnahmen • Bitte um Erklärung • Darstellung des Problems • Folgen für Käufer und Verkäufer • höfliche Schlussformel

› *Useful phrases: Making complaints, page 197*

3 Dealing with a telephone complaint

Hannah Schmidt in the Export Sales department receives a phone call from Gunner Kristoffersen from a Danish DIY chain that bought a consignment of air conditioners from Kältetechnik Lohmann.

A 48 **Listen to the dialogue and note down the following information.**

1 warranty
2 guarantee
3 terms of payment
4 what the retailer wants
5 possible consequences for Kältetechnik Lohmann
6 deadline set by the retailer for a solution

Infobox

Warranty and guarantee

German law distinguishes between **warranty** (*Gewährleistung*) and **guarantee** (*Garantie*). Goods bought in Germany come with a statutory warranty period of 24 months, during which the seller must rectify any defects. If a defect is noticed during the first six months, it is assumed that the goods were faulty at the time of purchase unless the seller can prove otherwise. If a defect is noticed later, the buyer must prove that the goods were faulty at the time of purchase. Under German law, a guarantee is an additional, voluntary promise made by the seller or manufacturer, e.g. to replace or repair a machine during and/or after the warranty period. A guarantee cannot replace the 24-month warranty period, which is usually offered by the manufacturer.

B 48 **Listen to the dialogue again and complete the sentences with the words you hear.**

1 Gunner: We're extremely ___ with the portable air conditioners.
2 Gunner: Some of them are ___, meaning that they cut out after a short time.
3 Gunner: Others are ___, and some of them are ___.
4 Gunner: And let me point out that the air conditioners are still ___ warranty …
5 Hannah: We're ___ sorry to hear that, Mr Kristoffersen.
6 Hannah: I ___ you we'll find a solution as soon as possible.
7 Hannah: I ___ understand, Mr Kristoffersen.
8 Gunner: We expect you to replace the whole consignment free of ___.
9 Gunner: If we don't get replacements, we'll return the whole consignment carriage ___ and ___ all future orders.

C **Find the phrases in exercise 3B to match the German expressions below.**

1 in der Gewährleistungszeit
2 Ich versichere Ihnen
3 Ich habe volles Verständnis dafür
4 unfrei
5 äußerst unzufrieden
6 verfärbt
7 kostenlos
8 fehlerhaft

VIDEO 8

Watch the video to see more about complaints.

4 Replying to a written complaint

Your boss, Hannah Schmidt, responds to the Danish DIY chain's complaint by email.

A **Arrange the parts of her email (A–I) in the correct order.**

A Yours sincerely

B We look forward to doing further business with you.

C Since hearing from you, we have investigated the matter and discovered that there was an error in our Quality Control department.

D Replacements for the faulty appliances will be delivered to you carriage paid within 48 hours.

E I hope this solution will find your approval and would ask you to accept our apologies for the inconvenience caused.

F I have just been informed of your phone call regarding the above-mentioned consignment of air conditioners and am dismayed to hear that the goods are unsatisfactory.

G Hannah Schmidt
Export Sales Manager
Kältetechnik Lohmann GmbH

H Dear Mr Kristoffersen

I Your complaint regarding order no. SA450 for portable ACU2 air conditioners dated 12 July 20..

B **Find two ways of saying sorry or expressing regret (*Bedauern*) in the email.**

› *Useful phrases: Responding to complaints, page 198*

5 Complaining and responding to a complaint

Kältetechnik Lohmann GmbH recently supplied chest freezers to a Swedish company called Scantech AB, Stortorget 95, 25114 Helsingborg, Sweden, and they were installed in supermarkets and butcher's shops all over Sweden. However, there are now complaints from the Swedish customers about their high electricity consumption and noise levels.

A **Write a letter or an email on behalf of the Purchasing Director at Scantech AB, Mr Patrik Berglund (p.berglund@scantech-ab.se) to Ms Hannah Schmidt, the Export Sales Manager at Kältetechnik Lohmann GmbH. Include the following points.**

- heutiges Datum
- Bezug auf Auftrag Nr. GBST12 über 100 Tiefkühltruhen Typ CF99 von vor drei Monaten
- Ware vor zwei Monaten erhalten und in Supermärkten und Metzgereien überall in Schweden installiert
- inzwischen mehr als ein Dutzend Beschwerden von unzufriedenen Kunden eingegangen (siehe Anlagen)
- extrem hoher Stromverbrauch und Geräuschpegel
- Bitte um Erklärung
- unfreie Rücksendung der Geräte an den Hersteller
- nachdrücklicher Hinweis auf umgehenden kostenlosen Ersatz, da Geräte noch in der Gewährleistungszeit
- unverzügliche Bearbeitung der Angelegenheit erwartet
- Fortsetzung der Geschäftsbeziehung von der Regelung der Beschwerde abhängig
- höfliche Schlussformel

› *Useful phrases: Making complaints, page 197*

B **Work with a partner. Partner A and Partner B: Look at File 19 on page 145.**

PART B: A complaint about a quarterly statement

Situation: You work in the Accounting department at Porzellanmanufaktur Querenburg GmbH. Your company's terms of payment with Sligo Supplies Ltd, an Irish supplier of pottery materials, are open account terms with quarterly settlement.

→ You clarify some discrepancies in a quarterly statement with the supplier and ask for the statement to be corrected.

1 Checking terms and prices

On 20 March, Porzellanmanufaktur Querenburg notices a special offer on the Irish supplier's website for pottery materials and immediately places an order for 10 square moulds, 20 deep round moulds and 20 sacks of porcelain clay.

A **Study the special offer and work out the total price of the moulds and clay ordered.**

B **At the beginning of April Porzellanmanufaktur Querenburg receives the following statement for the first quarter. Check the statement and find the four errors.**

Sligo Supplies Ltd — 200 Jinks Ave, Abbeyquarter North, Sligo, F91 X5EH, Ireland

Statement no. PMK9037 — **Date** 31 March 20..

Date	Quantity	Description	Article no.	Unit price (€)	Total (€)
20 Mar 20..	10	Square mould 285 mm	SM28	35.00	350.00
20 Mar 20..	20	Deep round mould 480 mm	RM48	45.00	900.00
20 Mar 20..	20	Porcelain clay 10 kg	PC10	25.00	500.00
				Total	**1,750.00**

C **How much has Porzellanmanufaktur Querenburg been overcharged by?**

2 Writing about payment

Most emails and letters about payment have a similar structure.

Payments checklist (buyer)

1 Reference to invoice/statement
2 Reference to payment of invoice/statement, as appropriate
3 Reference to discrepancies/errors/amendments, as appropriate
4 Polite ending
5 Enclosure(s) (*letter*) / Attachment(s) (*email*)

Anlagen(n)/Anhang/Anhänge · Bezug auf Begleichung der Rechnung/Abrechnung · Bezug auf Rechnung/Abrechnung · höfliche Schlussformel · Bezug auf Unstimmigkeiten/Irrtümer/Änderungen

Use words from the list to translate the payments checklist (1–5) into German.

3 Querying a statement

Your colleague, Rita Ronstadt, in the Accounting department at Porzellanmanufaktur Querenburg contacts the supplier about the statement.

To: rory.kelly@sligo-supplies.ie <Sales Director>
From: rita.ronstadt@pmq.de
Subject: Your statement no. PM9037_Q1 dated 31 March 20.. **Attachment(s)** PM9037_Q1.pdf

Dear Mr Kelly

Thank you for the above-mentioned statement for goods received last quarter.

Having checked it against our own records, we must point out that you have not included our credit note for €498 dated 15 January 20.. . In addition, the square and deep round moulds and the clay in your clearance sale have been incorrectly charged, and you have also omitted to include the special discount of 25% granted on orders for 20 items or more.

You have therefore overcharged us by a total of €1,123.00.

We are returning your statement and would request you to amend it. As soon as we have received the new statement we will remit the sum owing.

Please do not hesitate to contact us should you have any queries.

Best regards
Rita Ronstadt

Accounting Department
Porzellanmanufaktur Querenburg GmbH

A Find the English equivalents of the following German terms in the email.

1 berichtigen
2 Aufzeichnungen
3 belastet
4 Fragen
5 gewährt
6 Gutschrift
7 (mit etw) abgeglichen
8 überweisen
9 versäumt
10 zu viel berechnet

B Use information in the email to answer the following questions.

1 What period of time does the statement cover?
2 How many errors are there in the statement?
3 Which company is owed €498?
4 What must a customer do to qualify for a clearance sale quantity discount?
5 What action does Porzellanmanufaktur Querenburg want Sligo Supplies to take after receiving this email?
6 How much less does Porzellanmanufaktur Querenburg expect to pay?

4 Clarifying a statement

Sligo Supplies contact Porzellanmanufaktur Querenburg to explain the statement.

A 49 **Listen to the telephone conversation between Rory Kelly and Rita Ronstadt and write notes to explain the following:**

- the procedure for including a credit note with an order
- why the moulds and clay were wrongly charged
- the solution suggested by the Irish supplier

B Use your notes to explain what went wrong to a partner.

› *Grammar: Simple past, page 154; Reported speech, page 157*

C 49 **Listen again and note down the English equivalents of these German sentences.**

1 Bitte entschuldigen Sie das Durcheinander mit den Preisen.
2 Wir haben Ihnen eine Gutschrift in Form eines Codes zukommen lassen.
3 Deshalb wurde er bei Ihrer letzten Abrechnung nicht berücksichtigt.
4 Das habe ich auch untersucht.
5 Ich habe wie gewohnt per E-Mail bestellt.
6 Wie geht's jetzt weiter?
7 Wann kann ich mit Ihrer E-Mail rechnen?
8 Bitte setzen Sie sich mit uns in Verbindung, falls Sie weitere Fragen haben.

5 Responding to a query

Rory Kelly emails Rita Ronstadt straight away.

Use words from the list to complete his email.

account · deduct · grant · immediately · investigated · mix-up · omitted · place · returned · sorted

Dear Ms Ronstadt

As explained in our phone call just now about our statement for the last quarter, I have ____[1] the matter and ____[2] out the ____[3]. A credit note for goods that you ____[4] to us last year was ____[5] and some items were also wrongly charged, meaning that all in all you were overcharged by a total of €1,023.00.

Please therefore use the following link to access your ____[6] and ____[7] your order for discounted moulds and clay again, including the code for the credit note that you received from us last year.

http://www.sligo-supplies/ie/account_amend?token=8e4a666

Our accounting system will then automatically ____[8] you a 25% discount on the clearance sale items and ____[9] €498 from the total amount of the statement for the last quarter.

An amended statement will then be sent to you ____[10] for payment.

We apologize for the inconvenience and look forward to doing further business with you.

Best regards

6 Dealing with discrepancies

When checking recent invoices and statements, you find some discrepancies and then deal with them.

A **Work with a partner.** Partner A: **Look at File 20 on page 146.** Partner B: **Look at File 23 on page 148.**

B **When checking the statement for the last quarter sent to Schleuter Sport GmbH (Werstener Feld 398, 01067 Dresden) by an English supplier of goose down (Down Supplies Ltd, 22 Walker Road, Blackburn, BB1 2QE, England), you notice some discrepancies. Write a letter or an email to the supplier to query the statement.**

- Datum: 5. April 20..
- Ansprechpartnerin: Ms Sheena Murray (E-Mail: s.murray@down-supplies.org), Accounts Director
- Bezug auf Abrechnung Nr. GBST/375 vom 2. April 20.. über €31.550,00
- falscher Nachlass bei Positionen 1 und 2 für Gänsedaune, nur 15 % statt der versprochenen 50 % gewährt
- Gutschrift Nr. RBM/6 vom ... (15. des vergangenen Monats) über €185,00 nicht berücksichtigt
- falsch berechnete Abrechnung liegt bei
- Bitte um berichtigte Abrechnung über €25.065,00
- Überweisung des entsprechenden Betrags nach Erhalt der korrigierten Abrechnung
- höfliche Schlussformel

› *Useful phrases: Making complaints, page 197*

COMMUNICATION: A telephone complaint

Situation: You work at MedEquip GmbH, a manufacturer of medical supplies and equipment in Berlin.
→ **You deal with a telephone complaint.**

1 Dealing with complaints on the telephone

Your line manager gives you a list of English phrases for dealing with complaints and tells you to keep it by the phone in case English-speaking customers call.

Match the headings (1–5) to the phrases (a–j). There are at least two phrases for every heading. Some phrases match more than one heading.

1 Apologizing
2 Asking for information
3 Reacting to information
4 Action
5 Ending the call

› *Useful phrases: Responding to complaints, page 198*

a Can I just check with you that I've understood everything?
b Could you tell me what it's about, please?
c Could you give me the order number, please?
d I'll have a replacement sent out as soon as possible.
e I'm sorry to hear that.
f Is there anything else I can do for you today?
g Just a moment while I write that down.
h Oh, no. That doesn't sound at all good.
i Thank you for your call. Once again, I'm sorry that there was a problem.
j We're prepared to replace the goods at our expense.

2 Dealing politely with customers

A new customer, Jerzy Adamczyk, calls to complain about a trial order of operating theatre monitors. Your colleague, Melissa Wolf, takes the call. She is not very polite.

A 50)) **Listen to the phone call and decide how you would improve it. Make a list.**

B 51)) **Now listen to how Melissa should have dealt with the phone call with Jerzy Adamczyk. Which (if any) of your improvements does she make?**

TIP

Making / Dealing with complaints on the phone
Give your name clearly at the start of the call and write down the name of the person you are speaking to immediately. If necessary, check the spelling of the name.

3 Complaining to a supplier

MedEquip GmbH ships many orders in special containers made by Sheffield Metal, a company in England. The latest consignment has not arrived, so your line manager phones to complain about the delay in delivery. Jeanette Hogg answers the phone.

A **Look at the phrases (a–h) below and decide who says what – the caller or the person taking the call. (There are four phrases for each speaker.)**

a delivery was promised
b How can I help you?
c I will do my best
d it's an order for
e the exact details
f the order number?
g to enquire about my order
h We can't fulfil our orders

B When you have finished, match the phrases (a–h) with the gaps (1–8) in the text to complete the transcript of the phone call.

Jeanette	Good morning. Sheffield Metal, Sales Department. Jeannette Hogg speaking.
Max	Good morning. This is Max Jahn from MedEquip in Germany.
Jeanette	Good morning, Mr Jahn. ___[1]
Max	I'm calling ___[2] for containers for medical equipment. The order was sent almost one month ago, on 18 April, and ___[3] by 3 May but, so far, nothing has arrived.
Jeanette	Oh. I'm sorry to hear that. Could you give me ___[4]
Max	Yes. It's DF54736.
Jeanette	DF54736. Just a moment, please. I'll check. I'm sorry, Mr Jahn. I don't seem to have any record of your order. Can I just check that I've understood everything? The order number is DF54736 and you ordered the containers on 18 April. Could you give me ___[5] of the order, please?
Max	Yes, ___[6] your aluminium containers for medical equipment.
Jeanette	Aluminium containers for medical equipment. Mr Jahn, I'll have to speak to my colleague to find out what the problem is. Can I get back to you later?
Max	Well, yes. But I hope it won't take long. ___[7] until we have your containers.
Jeanette	Yes. I realize that, Mr Jahn. I'm very sorry about this and ___[8] to get back to you as soon as possible.
Max	Many thanks for your help, Ms Hogg.

C 52)) **Now listen and check your answers.**

4 Role-play: Dealing with a telephone complaint

Now you make and deal with a telephone complaint.

A Work with a partner. Partner A: Look here. Partner B: Look at File 18 on page 144.

Partner A
You work for MedEquip GmbH in Berlin. You take a call from a customer in the UK who makes a complaint. Before you begin, prepare a sheet for taking notes as follows:

- Date
- Name of customer, company
- Order number of goods
- Date of delivery
- Nature of the complaint
- What you agree with the caller

While you are waiting for Partner B to call, check that you know how to deal with complaints in English (exercises 1 and 2).

› *Useful phrases: Telephoning, page 188; Responding to complaints, page 198*

B When you have finished the phone call, change roles and do it again using different details.

C When you have played both parts, write up the notes you made as Partner A as a memo for your supervisor.

DAS KANN ICH (Unit 11)

- Einem Kollegen / Einer Kollegin die wichtigsten Punkte eines englischen Textes auf Deutsch erklären. (Foundation)
- Sich bei einem Hersteller beschweren; auf eine Beschwerde auf Englisch antworten. (Part A)
- Ungereimtheiten bei einer Abrechnung auf Englisch aufklären. (Part B)
- Mit telefonischen Beschwerden auf Englisch richtig umgehen. (Communication)

12 A job application

FOUNDATION: Where do I go from here?

Situation: You are nearing the end of your course and are thinking about applying for a work placement abroad. You start to think about what you have learned in your apprenticeship and where you might work when you have qualified.
→ **You write a description of your apprenticeship for a European job agency.**

1 Listening to newly-qualified trainees

You listen to an interview with three newly-qualified trainees. They are talking about the jobs they do and where they would like to find a permanent position.

1 Maren

Customer services specialist

2 Garry

Marketing assistant

3 Delon

Industrial management assistant

A 53)) **Listen and say what the speakers liked best about their apprenticeship.**

1 Who enjoyed learning from experienced people?
2 Who liked the mixture of going to vocational college and doing practical work?
3 Who enjoyed going to meetings?

B 53)) **Listen again and complete the table with the missing information.**

Name	What I do at work	I'd like to …
Maren	*respond to customers'* ___[1] *and guide them through the* ___[2]	___[3]
Garry	*analyse* ___[4] *and write* ___[5], *help with* ___[6]	___[7] *and become* ___[8]
Delon	*purchase goods or* ___[9], *make sure that* ___[10] *are up to date,* ___[11] *costs for orders*	___[12] *where I can* ___[13]

2 Thinking about your skills

You think about the skills you have learned during your apprenticeship.

A What do you enjoy most about your apprenticeship? What skills are you learning? How do you learn and develop these skills. First make notes on your own.

B Now talk to a partner about the skills you are learning.

C Now compare your ideas with another pair and make a list of the skills you are all learning, for example, working with spreadsheets, keying in data, etc. (Keep this list; you will need it for Part A).

> **Talking about skills; thinking about possibilities**
>
> I **can** analyse customer feedback and sales data.
> I**'m able to** work on my own.
> They **might be able to** get a job in the UK.
> You **could** look for work in the financial sector.

› *Grammar: Modals and their substitutes, page 158*

D Report your ideas to the class. Then, make a list in English of the different job titles in your field, e.g. industrial management assistant. How can you use the skills you are learning in your preferred area of work?

3 Doing internet research

You search the internet for job opportunities in Europe.

A Work with a partner. Do internet research to find suitable career prospects in Europe. Make a poster, webpage or PowerPoint presentation showing job offers and companies in your sector. Present your ideas to the class.

B If you make posters, pin them to the wall and do a gallery walk. Rank the posters using the categories below. Give points from 1–5 for each category.

headline · design · photos/pictures · content · overall effect

4 Reading about the Europass

While you are doing your research online, you come across the European Skills Passport (Europass). You decide to use it to collect your own personal details for applications and your CV.

Download the Europass and start to complete it with your details. (Your teacher has the correct URL.)

> **INFO**
>
> **The European Skills Passport (Europass)**
>
> This is a standardized CV and language document that can be created online or on your own computer. Potential employers throughout Europe can clearly see your skills and qualifications.
>
> The following sections might be of particular interest to you:
> – **Language Passport** – a self-assessment tool for language skills and qualifications;
> – **Europass Mobility** – a record of skills acquired during a learning experience in a European country;
> – **Certificate Supplement** – a description of skills acquired by holders of vocational training certificates.

5 Describing your apprenticeship

You have contacted an EU job agency asking for help in looking for work experience in Europe. The agent for Germany asks you to write a short description of your apprenticeship in English for the agency file.

Write a short description of your apprenticeship. Before you begin, think about the aspects you should include, e.g. type of training, skills you learned, qualifications you gained, and make notes.

PART A: Applying for a job abroad

Situation: The company you work for is interested in taking on trainees from other countries.
→ **You write a job advertisement in English for the position you are leaving.**

1 Finding a job

Before you write the advertisement, you think about how you got started in your current position.

Work in groups. Talk to colleagues about how you got started in your job. Make notes and report back to the class.

Where did you find out about your job?

How did you apply for the job?

What qualifications did you have when you applied?

2 Two interesting jobs

Your line manager would like to place an advertisement for your position on an international recruitment agency website. You check the website to get ideas for your advertisement.

Study the two advertisements on page 125. What details in them can you use when you write the advertisement for your job? Think about the following aspects:

- the type of employer
- what the company is looking for
- what the requirements are
- what the company offers
- how to apply

www.international-recruitment.com/training/office

Trainee Export Clerk

International freight forwarding company, Hamburg, Germany

As an export clerk, you will prepare airline waybills, complete export customs entries and classify goods. You will also deal with general administrative work, including invoicing and correspondence.

Requirements:
- min. school leaving certificate
- basic knowledge of MS Office, Excel and Outlook
- fluent German and English and one other language

You should have good written skills and good communication skills.
You should also be a quick learner.

Training period: 3 years, dual system, day release at vocational college 2 days a week

Possibility of being taken on full-time after completing your training.

Please submit your application with Ref. number TExCl_14387 here.

www.international-recruitment.com/training/office

Trainee Customer Services Specialist in Industry

Manufacturing company, Essen, Germany

Your training in the workplace includes dealing with enquiries, offers and orders, advising customers and doing market research. You will also prepare and take part in visits to trade fairs and exhibitions.

Requirements:
- a recognized school leaving certificate
- good mathematical skills
- fluent German and English

You should be an accurate worker and be able to work without supervision.
Training takes place over 36 months, including six weeks' block release twice a year.
In the workplace, you will receive continuous support from experienced employees.
Opportunities for follow-up education and promotion within the company.

Please submit your application with Ref. number TCsSp_10732 here.

3 Writing an advertisement for the recruitment agency website

Now you write the advertisement for your current position for the recruitment website.

A **Begin with the job title and the training location, then include information about what the successful candidate will do, etc.**

B **When you have finished, pin your advertisement on the wall and do a gallery walk. Which advert describes your apprenticeship most accurately? Which one sounds like an interesting option for prospective trainees?**

› *Useful phrases: Describing jobs and responsibilities, page 187*

PART B: Interviews

Situation: You have been shortlisted for a position as a German-speaking customer sales representative with a British company.
→ **You prepare for and practise a telephone interview and a face-to-face interview.**

1 Choosing the right candidate

Jennifer Winters, the Recruitment Manager at the British company Energy International plc, carries out telephone interviews with candidates who have applied for the job of customer sales representative.

A 54)) **Listen to the interviews and copy and complete the table below.**

	Interview 1	Interview 2	Interview 3
Name			
Present employer			
Strengths			
Weaknesses			
Why this job?			
Future plans			
Own questions			

B **Discuss the interviews and say which of them were good or bad examples. What did the candidates do right/wrong? Which of the three candidates is the best role model for your own telephone interview?**

2 Preparing for a telephone interview

To further prepare yourself for your telephone interview, you read these tips.

Read the text and note down in German the most important tips for your telephone interview.

TIPS FOR YOUR TELEPHONE OR SKYPE INTERVIEW

Be prepared!
- Before the interview you should gather a copy of the job description along with a copy of your letter of application, your CV and your references, and write a list of questions you want to ask the interviewer and a list of your strengths.
- Pin these documents to the wall so that you can check them during the call without having to flick through piles of paper.

On the day of the call
- Place a notebook and a couple of pens beside the phone so you can take notes during the interview.
- Make sure the room you are in is quiet.
- If it is a telephone interview, use a landline where possible. If you have to use your mobile phone, make sure it is fully charged and that you take the call in a place where reception is good.
- If it is a Skype interview, dress as you would for a face-to-face interview so that you make a good impression. Remember to check that the microphone and video camera on your computer are working before the interview.

During the call
- Concentrate and stay focused. Listen carefully and reply to the interviewer appropriately.
- Be professional and polite. At the end of the call, you can ask, "Do my qualifications meet the company's needs?" However the interview goes, always end with "Thank you for your call." The last few words of a conversation are often the ones that people remember, so always leave a good impression at the end.

3 Role-play: Practising a telephone interview

You and a colleague decide to practise a telephone interview together.

Asking for clarification on the telephone

I'm sorry, could you say that again?
So, if I understand you correctly, …
I don't quite understand what you mean by …

› *Useful phrases: Telephoning, page 188*

A **Work with a partner.**

Partner A: You are the interviewer. Look at File 24 on page 148.
Partner B: You are an applicant for the position. Look at File 14 on page 142.

B **With your partner, prepare a dialogue and role-play a telephone interview.**

4 Preparing for a face-to-face interview

You listen to a podcast in which an expert gives tips on how to handle face-to-face job interviews.

A **What is the expert likely to say? With a partner, brainstorm a list of expressions you might hear and make notes under the headings below.**

VIDEO 9

Watch the video to see more about interviews.

Here are a few expressions from the podcast to start you off.

Stage 1: Greetings and introductions
arrive at the interview on time

Stage 2: Small talk
talk about the weather

Stage 3: The main part of the interview
talk about yourself

Stage 4: Questions from the candidate
do background research into the company before the interview

Stage 5: Further arrangements and the end of the interview
ask when you can expect to hear from the company again

B 55 **Now listen and check. How many of your expressions did you hear?**

5 Practising for an interview

You and your colleague decide to practise the main part of an interview together.

A **First of all, study the list of common interview questions (File 22 on page 147) and how to answer them.**

B **Work with a partner.**

Partner A: Choose one of the job advertisements you read in Part A (page 125) and tell your partner which one you have chosen. Think about the questions the interviewer might ask and how you might answer. Make notes.

Partner B: Study the job advertisement your partner has chosen. Make a list of questions you might ask.

C **When you are both ready, role-play the job interview. When you have finished, change roles if you wish.**

COMMUNICATION: A CV and a covering letter

Situation: You find out online about the documents which you will need for job applications.
→ **You study an English CV and covering letter and write a job application.**

1 Reading a website about CVs

You find an interesting website with tips, but the headings have got mixed up.

Work with a partner. Read the tips (1–9) and match them to the headings (a–i).

a Education and training	**d** Personal details	**g** Work experience
b Hobbies and interests	**e** References	**h** Contact details
c Personal statement	**f** Key skills	**i** Further skills

www.internationalCVs_Technical

TIPS for writing your CV

International CVs

Your CV is a summary of your abilities, work experience, education and qualifications. There is no set format for a British CV but you should keep it short, using clear headings to guide the reader.

1 Give your name and address, telephone number(s) (home/mobile) and email address.

2 This should be a short message that grabs the attention of the reader. Use note form. This helps to keep your CV focused and direct, for example: *Motivated (wholesale) management assistant with experience in German trade industry.*

3 Here you can summarize your skills and experience which are relevant to the job you are applying for.

4 As a general rule, CVs should be in reverse chronological order, listing the most recent position first. For each position, you should provide the dates of the start and end of employment, the employer's name and address, the job title, the main duties and responsibilities and achievements.

5 Give a brief description of qualifications (school, academic and/or professional). Give the names of schools or colleges in reverse chronological order.

6 Here you should write about common skills gained throughout your education and work experience, such as languages, IT skills, good maths skills or a full, clean driving licence. These skills are of interest to any employer.

7 This feature is optional, but could provide something more personal to discuss at an interview. Be careful about what you write; a dangerous sport or *socializing with friends* may not be what an employer wants to hear!

8 Write your date of birth and nationality under this heading.

9 Due to data protection laws, candidates should not provide referees' names, addresses or any other contact details on CVs, but should state that details are available on request. Always ask your referees' permission before you give someone their contact details.

2 Analysing a CV

You also find an example of a British-style CV online.

Study the CV below. What differences can you find between this CV and a German CV?

MARTIN BIENEK
Am Kattenkamp 236, 33611 Bielefeld, Germany
Landline: (+49) 521 394677
Mobile: (+49) 176 3628419
Email: martin.bienek43@gmx.com

PERSONAL STATEMENT
Mobile and flexible industrial management assistant, in final year of 3-year course, seeking position abroad.

KEY SKILLS
Accountancy, Economics
Microsoft Word, Excel
Native speaker of German
Excellent spoken and written English
Good spoken and written Polish

WORK EXPERIENCE

June 20..	Assistant in information office, London Tourist Board Became skilled at dealing with enquiries and interacting with visitors from all over the world.
July 20..	4-week work placement at MöbelTech GmbH, Bielefeld, doing general office work

EDUCATION AND TRAINING

Since 20..	3-year apprenticeship at Vocational College, Bielefeld, Germany
June 20..	*Abitur* (Final examination similar to A-Levels) Main subjects: English, Computer Studies
20..–20..	Primary and secondary education in Bielefeld

FURTHER SKILLS
Full driving licence
First aid certificate

HOBBIES AND INTERESTS
Athletics, football
Training local junior football team

PERSONAL DETAILS
Date of birth: 06 April 20..
Nationality: German

REFERENCES
Available on request

3 Analysing a covering letter

Martin has applied for a job as an industrial management assistant at a food wholesaler in Ireland.

Read Martin's covering letter on the opposite page and match the parts (1–5) with explanations from the list.

- **a** asking the employer to invite you for an interview
- **b** reference to details on your CV
- **c** reference to the position
- **d** saying why the applicant is applying for the position
- **e** stating why the applicant is the best person for the job

4 Writing: An application for a job abroad

You find the following advertisement in a trade magazine and decide to apply for the position.

Prepare your CV and write your application.

German-speaking

Junior Management Assistant

in Export

Location: Dublin, Republic of Ireland
Salary: 21,000 euros to 23,000 euros depending on experience

- **Job description:** duties include
  - frequent contact with customers both face-to-face and on the phone
  - taking orders, making offers and controlling dispatch of goods
- **We are looking for:**
  - relevant vocational school leaving certificate
  - basic knowledge of MS Office
  - fluent German and English
- **You should be:**
  - confident and personable
  - keen to learn
  - flexible
- **What we offer:**
  - an excellent working atmosphere
  - optional language training courses
  - good chances of promotion

Please submit your CV together with a covering letter to:
Ms O'Brien, Human Resources, 22 Grand Canal Harbour, Dublin 2, D02 A342

› *Useful phrases: Writing covering letters, page 200*

Am Kattenkamp 236, 33611 Bielefeld, Germany
Phone: (+49) 521 394677, Mobile: (+49) 176 3628419
Email: martin.bienek43@gmx.com

20 April 20..

Scott Technology Ltd
Silverbank Industrial Estate
DUBLIN
D11 D4E2
IRELAND

Attn. Mr Haig, Human Resources Director

Dear Mr Haig

Industrial management assistant

1 With reference to your advertisement Ref. No. 17673 on the internet, I would like to apply for the post described.

2 I am very interested in the job you are offering as I feel sure it will give me the opportunity to develop both personally and professionally. I am particularly keen to work in a position which allows me to apply my skills on a daily basis.

3 As you can see from the enclosed CV, by June of this year I will have completed the final year of a three-year apprenticeship at a Vocational Training College in Bielefeld, Germany. I will then be a fully-qualified industrial management assistant.

4 As I have practical skills and experience, am flexible and mobile and speak fluent English, German and Polish, I believe I will be a strong member of any team I join and will benefit your company.

5 My CV is enclosed and I am available for an interview at short notice.

I would very much appreciate it if you would consider my application and hope that you will grant me an interview.

I look forward to hearing from you soon.

Yours sincerely

M. Bienek

Martin Bienek

Encl.

DAS KANN ICH (Unit 12)

- Eine Beschreibung meiner Ausbildung auf Englisch verfassen. (Foundation)
- Eine Stellenanzeige auf Englisch schreiben. (Part A)
- Mich auf ein Bewerbungsgespräch auf Englisch gut vorbereiten. (Part B)
- Bewerbungsunterlagen auf Englisch richtig verfassen und gestalten. (Communication)

KMK Exam practice 6

1 Interaktion: Stufe III

Task: Work with partner. Use the role cards to role-play a telephone call between a manufacturer (Partner A) and a wholesaler (Partner B).

Partner A

Situation: You work for Miller Workwear, a manufacturer who specializes in the design and production of high quality workwear. You receive a call from a new customer who you really want to keep as a customer. Work & Business is a wholesaler for workwear and might order large quantities in the future. Unfortunately, there were some problems with the delivery. With the help of the order confirmation and the report from the shipping department below, you try to clarify things and to find a solution. Offer compensation if necessary.

Order confirmation

Order No. 245-9876-A34		
QTY	Product	price/unit
100	Overall 7010 green	38.14
500	Overall 9870 black	34.45
800	Overall EXTRA XD	47.89

Report from shipping department

Order No. 245-9876-A34
Delivery # FG78-II89

100 Overall 7020 green
Article No. has changed, identical with 7010
400 Overall 9870 black
Couldn't send all, not enough in stock, additional delivery maybe in 3 days.
800 Overall EXTRA XD
Everything OK

Notes:
Got a call from forwarding agent, one parcel was accidentally damaged by driver. We should send invoice to the forwarding agent for damages.

Partner B

Situation: You work in the Purchasing department of Work & Business, a wholesaler for workwear. Last month you ordered overalls from a new supplier which were due last week but only arrived today. The warehouse has sent you a report saying that the delivery is not up to standard. Since you need the delivery for customer orders, the matter is quite urgent and you are not satisfied. With the help of the report and the order confirmation, you call the supplier to make a complaint and to find out what can be done.

Order confirmation: Miller Workwear

Order No. 245-9876-A34		
QTY	Product	price/unit
100	Overall 7010 green	38.14
500	Overall 9870 black	34.45
800	Overall EXTRA XD	47.89

Report from warehouse: Work & Business

Order No. 245-9876-A34 from Miller Workwear

100	Overall 7020 green	*wrong article!*
400	Overall 9870 black	*100 items missing!*
800	Overall EXTRA XD	*see below*

Notes:
One box with the overalls arrived crushed, at least 50 overalls are therefore stained.

2 Produktion: Stufe III

Situation: You work for Car Parts International Ltd in Reading, UK. Your company has received a consignment of oil pumps from Rosewater Ltd in Manchester, UK. You receive a standard form from your Logistics department (see below). As the oil pumps are needed urgently for products for an important customer, you need a quick solution.

Task: Write a letter of complaint to Rosewater Ltd.

Your address: 32 Industry Road, Reading RG2 7PS
Contact address for Rosewater Ltd: Mr John Rochester, Sales Manager, Rosewater Ltd, 11 Lower High St, Manchester M3 3ER

Order No: *45672*		Date of Order: *11.01.20..*	Delivery Note: *657/34*
Consignment received on: *13.03.20..*		Freight Forwarder: –	Delivery provider: *UPS*
Visual inspection: *Parcel damaged on outside, dirty and wet*		Possible reasons for outside damage: *rough handling, incorrect storage*	Inspected by: *A.H.*
Missing Items: –	Surplus Items: –	False Items: –	Broken Items: *8*
Short description: *Unpacking showed that pumps in parcel 2 (marked OILPUMP2/3) are all wet and dirty, all 8 pumps have scratches, parts are damaged*			

3 Produktion: Stufe III

Situation: Sie absolvieren Ihre Ausbildung in der Daimler Niederlassung in Hofheim und sind daran interessiert, ein Praktikum in der Zweigstelle in Abu Dhabi zu machen. Der Leiter der Exportabteilung unterstützt Ihr Vorhaben. Er bittet Sie, ein Bewerbungsschreiben anzufertigen, welches er an die Personalleiterin International, Frau Julie McArthur, weiterleiten will. Nach Ihrem Gespräch mit ihm finden Sie am nächsten Tag eine Notiz auf Ihrem Schreibtisch.

Aufgabe: Fertigen Sie ein Bewerbungsanschreiben an.

Hallo,
nach unserem gestrigen Gespräch habe ich ein paar Tipps für Sie bezüglich Ihres Bewerbungsschreibens. Ihr Brief sollte Folgendes enthalten:

- *Bezug auf mich*
- *Gründe, warum Sie nach Abu Dhabi möchten*
  - *a) beruflich: große Niederlassung; Möglichkeit, sich weiterzuentwickeln*
  - *b) persönlich: Interesse an arabischen Ländern; Vater Bauingenieur / Familie hat einige Jahren im Oman gelebt*
- *Gründe, warum Sie für die Stelle geeignet sind (nennen Sie mindestens zwei „soft skills", Frau McArthur legt darauf sehr großen Wert)*

Vergessen Sie nicht, Ihr Schreiben angemessen und höflich zu beginnen und zu beenden!

Viel Glück!

P Partner files

FILE 1: Exam practice 1, exercise 3, Interaktion

Partner B

Sie sind Steve/Sue Mosley, ein englischer Praktikant / eine englische Praktikantin aus Manchester. Dort arbeiten Sie für ein Handelsunternehmen (Wesley Sports Wholesale Ltd), das sich auf Sportartikel spezialisiert hat. Ihre Firma plant auch in Deutschland und Frankreich Niederlassungen aufzubauen. Sie absolvieren ein sechsmonatiges Praktikum in Fulda bei der Firma Schmitt & Otte GmbH, die hochwertige Sportartikel produziert. Heute ist Ihr erster Tag.

Gestalten Sie in Partnerarbeit einen Dialog mithilfe der folgenden Punkte:

- Machen Sie sich bekannt. Betreiben Sie Small Talk.
- Geben Sie Auskunft über Ihre Firma und nennen Sie Gründe, warum Sie nach Deutschland gekommen sind.
- Fragen Sie nach einer Kantine und wo Sie zuerst eingesetzt werden.
- Sie möchten wissen, wie das deutsche Ausbildungssystem funktioniert.
- Informieren Sie sich über Freizeitgestaltung und Aktivitäten am Wochenende.
- Schildern Sie Ihre derzeitige Unterbringung (weit außerhalb von Fulda, sehr einsam, schlechte Anbindung an Nahverkehr). Erkundigen Sie sich nach anderen Unterbringungsmöglichkeiten.

FILE 2: Unit 4, Communication, exercise 1C

Partner B

Dictate these email addresses to Partner A. Check A's answers.

1 beatrice-kuhn@berlin_tools.de
2 Hamish.MacPherson@net.uk
3 your own email address
4 the email address of your firm or another email address you often write to

FILE 3: Unit 7, Communication, exercise 4

Partner B

You are the hotel receptionist.

You begin the conversation. Greet the guest by name and ask how you can help.

You have the following information about hire cars:
- Hire car available through hotel. Hotel has 5% discount with Hertz. Small car, £50 a day, unlimited mileage.
- Insurance included, customer pays 15% ("excess") in case of accident.
- Pick up at hotel; return at Hertz counter, Heathrow.
- Payment is by credit card.

You need to know what time the guest needs the car and when it will be returned. Offer a receipt and wish the guest a pleasant day with the car.

FILE 4: Unit 6, Part A, exercise 4A

Partners C and D

Situation:
Brewery-2-Brewery is an American-owned company and has 20 employees in the office and 15 in the warehouse. At the last works council meeting, many employees were in favour of introducing flexitime. Today, there is a meeting between the American General Manager and the employees to discuss it. Attending the meeting are:

- the General Manager (Partner A)
- the Human Resources Manager (Partner B)
- the Works Council Representative (Partner C)
- an office worker (Partner D)
- a warehouse employee (Partner E)
- an apprentice wholesaler (Partner F)

	Office	Warehouse
Working hours	7.30 a.m. – 3.30 p.m.	Early shift: 6.00 a.m. – 2.00 p.m. Day shift: 10.00 a.m. – 6.00 p.m.
Break	9.30 a.m. – 9.45 a.m.	15 minutes taken flexibly
Lunch break	12.00 noon – 12.45 p.m.	

A **Use your role card below and the expressions in exercise 2B to conduct a meeting and come to a decision.**

Partner C: Works Council Representative

You are in favour of flexitime for the office staff because a lot of the employees need time, e.g. for their children, older relatives, visits to doctors, etc. You would like core time from 9.00 a.m. to 3.00 p.m. with flexible breaks. You don't think that flexitime is a good idea for the warehouse.

- introduce yourself
- explain that flexitime was suggested at the last works council meeting
- ask the other employees to explain their position and then explain yours
- ask the HR manager a question (invent)

Partner D: office worker

You are married with two children (7 and 9). You would like to start work in the office after 8.00 a.m. after you have taken the children to school. Your husband is a lorry driver and leaves home at 5 a.m., so he can't help. When your children are ill, you also need to take them to the doctor's in the morning. You would be happy to make up for a late start by working later in the afternoons when your mother can help out with the children.

- introduce yourself
- explain your position
- ask the HR manager a question (invent)

FILE 5: Unit 6, Part A, exercise 4A

Partners E and F

Situation:
Brewery-2-Brewery is an American-owned company and has 20 employees in the office and 15 in the warehouse. At the last works council meeting, many employees were in favour of introducing flexitime. Today, there is a meeting between the American General Manager and the employees to discuss it. Attending the meeting are:

- the General Manager (Partner A)
- the Human Resources Manager (Partner B)
- the Works Council Representative (Partner C)
- an office worker (Partner D)
- a warehouse employee (Partner E)
- an apprentice wholesaler (Partner F)

	Office	Warehouse
Working hours	7.30 a.m. – 3.30 p.m.	Early shift: 6.00 a.m. – 2.00 p.m. Day shift: 10.00 a.m. – 6.00 p.m.
Break	9.30 a.m. – 9.45 a.m.	15 minutes taken flexibly
Lunch break	12.00 noon – 12.45 p.m.	

A **Use your role card below and the expressions in exercise 2B to conduct a meeting and come to a decision.**

Partner E: warehouse employee

Your priority is not to be on early shift (6.00 a.m. – 2.00 p.m.) for more than two weeks in a row. If flexitime can guarantee this, you will be in favour of it. You don't mind starting early or finishing late.

introduce yourself
- explain your position
- ask the HR manager a question (invent)

Partner F: apprentice wholesaler

You and a lot of other apprentices would like to have flexitime because if you stay out late one night, you can start later the next morning without getting into trouble. You don't like starting work at 6 a.m. but you don't mind working until 6.00 p.m.

- introduce yourself
- explain your position
- ask the HR manager a question (invent)

FILE 6: Unit 6, Part B, exercise 4

Partner A: Manufacturer (own name)

The company where you are doing your apprenticeship has heard of a new supplier of your best-selling product[1]. You have arranged a meeting with the supplier (Partner B) to discuss placing a small initial order.

[1]Choose from: copper (kg) • Euro-pallets • plastic sheeting (square metres / m^2) • stainless steel (tons) • timber (cubic metres / m^3) • wood and metal screws (minimum 1000 pieces) • your own idea.
Agree with Partner B what the product is.

Use the table below to negotiate an order covering the following points:

- **quantity:** you only wish to test a few customers' reactions to the product at the moment
- **discount:** try to get a discount, e.g. an initial order discount or an introductory discount
- **terms of payment:** you want the maximum time to pay
- **delivery period:** you would like the goods as soon as possible

Try to get as many points as possible, but do not show your partner your scoring system.

At the end of the negotiation, use the table to work out your score.

Manufacturer's score sheet			
Quantity[2]	**Discount**	**Terms of payment**	**Delivery period**
10 Score: 25 points	5% Score: 25 points	90 days Score: 25 points	2 days Score: 25 points
20 Score: 20 points	4% Score: 20 points	60 days Score: 20 points	7 days Score: 20 points
30 Score: 15 points	3% Score: 15 points	30 days Score: 15 points	30 days Score: 15 points
50 Score: 10 points	2% Score: 10 points	30% with order, 70% on delivery Score: 10 points	60 days Score: 10 points
100+ Score: 5 points	1% Score: 5 points	in advance Score: 5 points	90 days Score: 5 points

[2]Adapt the quantity to your product as appropriate, e.g. 100 Euro-pallets, 1,000 metal screws, etc.

Questions and negatives

Can you reduce the price? Yes, we **can**. / No, we **can't**.
Will you give a guarantee? Yes, we **will**. / No, we **won't**.
Do you accept the terms? Yes, we **do**. / No, we **don't**.

› *Grammar: Questions and short answers, page 154*

FILE 7: Unit 6, Part B, exercise 4

Partner B: Supplier (John/Joanne Taylor)

You are a salesman/woman for a company in Ireland that has been exporting its products[1] very successfully to a large number of customers for more than 20 years. You meet a new manufacturer (Partner A) to discuss the terms of a first order.

[1]Choose from: copper (kg) · Euro-pallets · plastic sheeting (square metres / m^2) · stainless steel (tons) · timber (cubic metres / m^3) · wood and metal screws (minimum 1000 pieces) · your own idea.
Agree with Partner A what the product is.

Use the table below to negotiate an order covering the following points:

- **quantity:** try to sell as many as possible
- **discount:** your prices are already very competitive
- **terms of payment:** new customers normally pay CWO (cash with order)
- **delivery period:** the product is in great demand and your regular customers have priority

Try to get as many points as possible, but do not show your partner your scoring system.

At the end of the negotiation, use the table to work out your score.

Supplier's score sheet			
Quantity[2]	**Discount**	**Terms of payment**	**Delivery period**
100+ Score: 25 points	1% Score: 25 points	in advance Score: 25 points	90 days Score: 25 points
50 Score: 20 points	2% Score: 20 points	30% with order, 70% on delivery Score: 20 points	60 days Score: 20 points
30 Score: 15 points	3% Score: 15 points	30 days Score: 15 points	30 days Score: 15 points
20 Score: 10 points	4% Score: 10 points	60 days Score: 10 points	7 days Score: 10 points
10 Score: 5 points	5% Score: 5 points	90 days Score: 5 points	2 days Score: 5 points

[2]Adapt the quantity to your product as appropriate, e.g. 100 Europallets, 1,000 metal screws, etc.

Questions and negatives

Can you reduce the price? Yes, we **can**. / No, we **can't**.
Will you give a guarantee? Yes, we **will**. / No, we **won't**.
Do you accept the terms? Yes, we **do**. / No, we **don't**.

› *Grammar: Questions and short answers, page 154*

FILE 8: Unit 6, Communication, exercise 4

Partner B

You are Jane Duncan, a business associate of Paul Schmidt.

Role-play a phone call with Paul Schmidt's assistant (Partner A). Use your itinerary to arrange a new time for a meeting with Paul.

ITINERARY – **Wed 25th – Sat 28th**			
Wed 25	Flight BA 8954 → Glasgow (arr. 13.40)	14.00 – 17.00 Fashion show	
Thur 26	9.15 – 12.45 Meet Gerry Maddox to discuss contract	14.00 – 16.00 Meeting: Kirstie Adam, Fashion Futures	
Fri 27	~~7.00 – 9.30 Working breakfast: Paul Schmidt~~ 10.00 – 12.30 Presentation: New Styles	Meeting: John King, 14.00 – 18.00	Buffet: Glasgow Retail Trade Association 19.00 – 22.30
Sat 28	Shopping	Flight BA 3627 13.15 → London	

› *Useful phrases: Making arrangements, page 192*

FILE 9: Unit 7, Part A, exercise 4B

Partner A

You work for Ökobau Müller GmbH.

Call O'Reilly's Catering Ltd (Partner B) and place an order for the on-stand event using the information on your role card.

- Stellen Sie sich vor (Vor- und Nachname, Firma) und beschreiben Sie kurz Ihr Anliegen (Ort, Uhrzeit).
- Geben Sie Ihre Wünsche für das Buffet an.
- Sie gehen von drei Stunden aus.
- Sie brauchen das Buffet nur einmal am 6. Oktober.
- Fragen Sie, wie viel das Buffet in etwa kosten wird.
- Das Buffet kostet mehr als erwartet. Fragen Sie, warum.
- Entscheiden Sie, ob Sie das Angebot annehmen oder nicht.
- Bitten Sie ggf. um ein schriftliches Angebot per E-Mail (Vorname.Nachname@oekobau-mueller.de).
- Schließen Sie das Gespräch höflich ab.

FILE 10: Unit 7, Part A, exercise 4B

Partner B

You are Liam/Lauren Kelly of O'Reilly's Catering Ltd.

Partner A will call you to discuss an order for an event at a trade fair. Deal with Partner A's requests using the information on the role card.

- Answer the phone (company, first name).
- Ask for details: number of guests; snacks; drinks.
- Recommend the fork buffet (very popular, etc.).
- Ask how long the buffet is expected to last.
- Explain that there will be a service charge for the third hour.
- Ask how often the client wants the buffet.
- Work out the total price and add 5%.
- If Partner A queries the price, explain that food and labour prices have risen by 5%.
- Send a written offer if requested.
- Finish the conversation politely.

FILE 11: KMK Exam practice 4, exercise 2, Interaktion

Partner B

You are the Sales Manager for a large foundry (= *Gießerei*) in Hungary. You have an appointment with a manager from Billing & Sons at an international trade fair. You arrive at their stand on time.

Role-play a conversation at the trade fair stand with Partner A. Be prepared to ask and answer questions. You have to use your imagination and make up possible answers. Use the ideas below to help you.

- Introduce yourself and say that you are expected, show understanding if you have to wait.
- Ask for a different refreshment and engage in small talk with the company representative.
- Show annoyance that nothing is happening.
- Accept one of the offers that the representative makes.

FILE 12: Unit 5, Communication, exercise 1C

Partner B

Describe this line graph to Partner A. Partner A will draw it. Check Partner A's graph when you have finished.

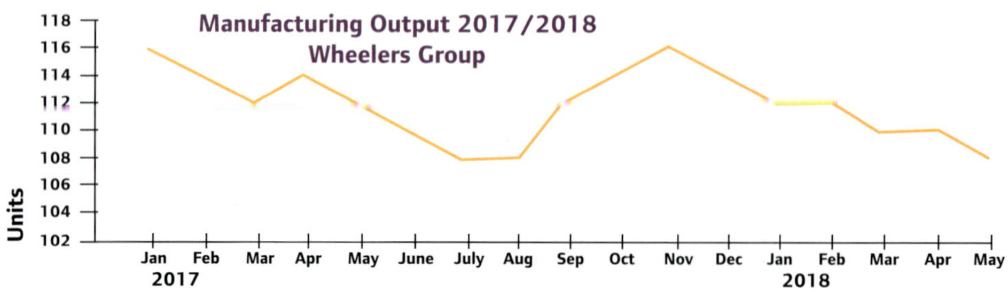

FILE 13: Unit 8, Part A, exercise 4

Partners A and Partner B

Role-play a telephone conversation between AgriTrade South Africa Pty Ltd and an American supplier, using the following prompts.

Partner A: Hersteller
Glen/Glenda Jackson, CanLine Inc., Atlanta, Georgia

Partner B: Kunde/Kundin
Sie (eigener Name), AgriTrade, Südafrika

A: Nehmen Sie den Anruf freundlich entgegen.

B: Stellen Sie sich und Ihr Unternehmen vor. Die amerikanische Firma ist Ihnen von Stellenbosch Trading, SA empfohlen worden.

A: Sie freuen sich und fragen, für welches Produkt er/sie sich interessiert.

B: Laut Website stellt die amerikanische Firma Dosenfertigungslinien her. Fragen Sie, ob auch eine Lieferung nach Südafrika möglich wäre.

A: Erklären Sie, dass Sie normalerweise den amerikanischen Markt mit Fertigungslinien beliefern und ausländische Kunden mit leeren Dosen versorgen, aber es wäre sicherlich möglich, eine ganze Fertigungslinie zu exportieren.

B: Fragen Sie nach den Lieferbedingungen für eine solche Linie.

A: Sie liefern Linien immer ab Werk.

B: Fragen Sie, ob er/sie auch Verpackung für den Seetransport zur Verfügung stellen kann.

A: Danach ist nie gefragt worden, aber Sie finden sicherlich eine Lösung.

B: Fragen Sie, ob er/sie Ihnen behilflich sein könnte, einen geeigneten Spediteur für den Transport der Anlage nach Südafrika zu finden.

A: Sie werden sich erkundigen.

B: Fragen Sie nach den Zahlungsbedingungen.

A: 30 % im Voraus und 70 % bei Fertigstellung.

B: Fragen Sie nach dem Kundendienst.

A: Sie liefern Ersatzteile und bei Problemen schicken Sie eine/n Techniker/in. Dies wäre sicherlich für Südafrika möglich. Fragen Sie, ober er/sie weitere Fragen hat.

B: Sie haben keine weiteren Fragen und schließen das Gespräch höflich ab.

A: Schließen Sie das Gespräch höflich ab.

FILE 14: Unit 12, Part B, exercise 3A

Partner B

There is a job vacancy at Trade International plc. Jennifer/John Stone, Head of Human Resources, calls an applicant for a telephone interview.

You are the applicant. Work with Partner A and role-play the telephone interview. You begin by answering the phone.

- Introduce yourself.
- Say that this is a suitable time for phone call.
- Talk about your CV.
- Describe yourself from your own point of view and from that of your colleagues.
- Give examples of how you are a team player.
- Describe your hobbies.
- Describe your strengths and weaknesses.
- Give reasons for choosing this career.
- Describe what you expect from the job.
- Justify why you should be chosen for the job.
- Ask any questions you may have.

Swap roles when you have finished.

FILE 15: Unit 10, Part A, exercise 5A

Partner B

You work in the Export Sales department of Digitex s.r.l. in Perugia, Italy.

Role-play a telephone call with a customer (Brinkmeyer Lederwarenmanufaktur GmbH) in Dusseldorf, using the information on the role card.

Antonio / Arianna Rossetti, Digitex s.r.l., Perugia, Italien

- Nehmen Sie den Telefonanruf auf Englisch entgegen (Begrüßung, Firmenname, Ihr voller Name).
- Reagieren Sie sehr positiv und fragen Sie, welche Maschinen der Kunde / die Kundin möchte.
- Erklären Sie, dass 15 Maschinen keiner vollen Containerladung entsprechen. 30 wären eine volle Containerladung und viel günstiger.
- Die Preise sind nicht mehr aktuell, denn die Maschinen sind momentan im Angebot und kosten je Maschine € 500,00 weniger. Es sind FCA Preise einschl. Verpackung auf Paletten.
- Sie sind gerne bereit, dem Kunden / der Kundin mit dem Transport der Ware zu helfen. Fragen Sie, ob er/sie die Ware lieber mit der Bahn oder per LKW geliefert haben möchte.
- Sie können den Spediteur (*forwarder*) Sardelli Logistics empfehlen.
- Eine halbe Containerladung mit Lieferung CPT Düsseldorf per LKW kostet € 1.300. Eine volle Containerladung kostet € 1.650. Der Kunde / Die Kundin muss die Ware selbst versichern.
- Zahlungsbedingungen: Barzahlung bei Auftragserteilung
- Lieferung 30 Tage nach Auftragseingang
- Danken Sie für den Auftrag, erklären Sie, dass Sie ihn jetzt schriftlich (*in writing*) brauchen und fragen Sie nach dem Namen und der E-Mail-Adresse des Kunden / der Kundin.
- Erkundigen Sie sich, ob noch weitere Fragen bestehen.
- Danken Sie für die Bestellung und verabschieden Sie sich.

FILE 16: Unit 10, Part B, exercise 5

Application for Irrevocable Documentary Credit

To: COMMERCIAL CREDIT BANK

*Indicates mandatory information to be provided

Applicant Full Name & Address*: (Importer)

Contact Person:

Tel: Fax:

Beneficiary Full Name & Address*: (Exporter)

Contact Person:

Tel: Fax:

Debit Account No.*: 6 9 2 - 2 7 4 - 8 5 1 - 3

Amount of Letter of Credit*

Amount and Currency (in words)

Currency and Amount (in figures) / . Tolerance +/- %

Expiry Date*: / /
D D M M Y Y Y Y
(LC will expire in Beneficiary's country)

☐ LC To Be Confirmed By Advising Bank

Confirmation Charge To Be Paid By: ☐ Beneficiary ☐ Applicant

All Other Bank Charges Including Reimbursement If Any For Account Of*: ☐ Beneficiary ☐ Applicant

Shipment From: Shipment To:

Partial Shipment Allowed ☐ Yes ☐ No

Transhipment Allowed ☐ Yes ☐ No

Latest Shipment Date: / /
D D M M Y Y Y Y

Incoterm Place

Documents Required

Commercial Invoice ☐ plus ☐ copies.

Packing List ☐ plus ☐ copies.

Certificate of Origin ☐ evidencing goods of ________ origin.

☐ For shipment by sea, full set of original clean "on board" bills of lading / ☐ multimodal or combined transport documents. marked ☐ freight prepaid ☐ freight collect and notify ________

☐ Air waybill, marked ☐ freight prepaid ☐ freight collect and notify ________

☐ Original CMR/Truck waybill marked ☐ freight prepaid ☐ freight collect ________

☐ Other transport documents (please specify) ________

☐ If CIF/CIP: Insurance policy/certificate for full CIF/CIP value plus ☐ 10 %

☐ If FOB etc: Insurance covered by applicant/buyer

Goods (brief description including quantity without excessive detail)

FILE 17: Unit 10, Part A, exercise 5A

Partner A

You work in the Purchasing department of Brinkmeyer Lederwarenmanufaktur GmbH in Dusseldorf.

Role-play a telephone call with a supplier (Digitex s.r.l.) in Perugia, Italy, using the information in the role card.

Sie (eigener Name), Einkauf, Brinkmeyer Lederwarenmanufaktur GmbH, Düsseldorf

- Stellen Sie sich vor (Ihr voller Name, Firmenname, Ort) und sagen Sie, dass Sie Industrienähmaschinen bestellen möchten.
- 10 vom Typ HD500 und 5 vom Typ HD1000, evtl. mehr
- Danken Sie für die Auskunft und sagen Sie, dass laut Webseite der Firma die Großhandelspreise € 2.000,00 für Typ HD500 und € 2.500,00 for Typ HD1000 betragen. Sind die Preise aktuell und sind sie ab Werk oder FCA?
- Danken Sie für die Informationen und sagen Sie, dass Sie die Maschinen nach Düsseldorf transportieren lassen möchten. Kann der/die Verkäufer/in Ihnen damit helfen?
- Sie möchten die Ware per LKW bekommen. Kann der/die Verkäufer/in einen Spediteur (*forwarder*) empfehlen?
- Danken Sie dem/der Verkäufer/in und fragen Sie nach den Frachtsätzen (*freight rates*).
- Danken Sie für die Information und fragen Sie nach den Zahlungsbedingungen.
- Lieferzeit?
- Sie möchten 20 Nähmaschinen vom Typ HD500 und 10 vom Typ HD1000 bestellen.
- Geben Sie Ihren vollen Namen und E-Mail-Adresse an (E-Mail: vorname.nachname@blm.de)
- Sie haben keine weiteren Fragen. Sie werden Ihre Bestellung gleich per E-Mail abschicken.
- Bedanken Sie sich und verabschieden Sie sich.

FILE 18: Unit 11, Communication, exercise 4A

Partner B

Role-play a telephone complaint using the prompts below.

You are the customer. Before you begin, make some notes as follows:

- the name of your firm (e.g. London City Clinic)
- the order number
- the date of delivery (e.g. yesterday)
- the problem (e.g. damaged/wrong goods, delay in delivery)
- what you hope from Partner A (e.g. rebate; immediate delivery by express carrier at no charge to your company/hospital)

When you are ready, call Partner A and begin the call.

FILE 19: Unit 11, Part A, exercise 5B

Partners A and B

The Purchasing Director at Murphy's Meats Ltd in Dublin, Ireland, phones Kältetechnik Lohmann to complain about the CF99 chest freezers supplied.

Work with a partner and role-play the phone call using the instructions below.

Partner A: Eigener Name, Verkauf, Kältetechnik Lohmann GmbH, Stuttgart

Partner B: Liam/Lena O'Brien, Einkaufsleiter/in, Murphy's Meats Ltd, Dublin Irland

A: Nehmen Sie den Anruf auf Deutsch entgegen.

B: Stellen Sie sich auf Englisch vor und fragen Sie, ob Sie das Gespräch auf Englisch führen können.

A: Schalten Sie auf Englisch um und fragen Sie freundlich, wie Sie dem/der Anrufer/in helfen können.

B: Es handelt sich um die fünf Tiefkühltruhen vom Typ CF99, die Kältzetechnik Lohmann geliefert hat. Der Stromverbrauch und Geräuschpegel sind extrem hoch.

A: Drücken Sie Ihr Bedauern aus und fragen Sie nach der Auftrags-Nr. und dem Datum.

B: Auftrags-Nr. VBIB94 vom … (vor einem Monat)

A: Sie finden den Auftrag im System. Bitten Sie den/die Anrufer/in, das Problem genauer zu beschreiben.

B: Der Stromverbrauch der Tiefkühltruhen ist 2 kWh pro Liter. Er sollte ca. 0,5 kWh pro Liter sein. Die Geräte sind auch ziemlich laut.

A: Erklären Sie, dass der Fehler inzwischen bekannt ist.

B: Wie dem auch sei, Sie brauchen dringend Ersatz. Fragen Sie, wann Sie damit rechnen können.

A: Ersatz wird umgehend geschickt ohne zusätzliche Kosten für den Kunden / die Kundin.

B: Danken Sie Ihrem/Ihrer Gesprächspartner/in für die schnelle Lösung.

A: Entschuldigen Sie sich für die Unannehmlichkeiten und fragen Sie, ob Sie sonst noch etwas für den Kunden / die Kundin tun können.

B: Es handelte sich nur um das eine Problem.

A: Schließen Sie das Gespräch freundlich ab.

B: Schließen Sie das Gespräch freundlich ab.

› *Useful phrases: Telephoning, page 188*

FILE 20: Unit 11, Part B, exercise 6A

Partner A

Schleuter Sport GmbH, Dresden receives an incorrect invoice for materials from a supplier in the UK.

You work for Cumbria Textiles Ltd, UK. Role-play a telephone conversation with Schleuter Sport GmbH (Partner B), using the following prompts.

Partner A (seller)
Bill/Jill Knightley, Director of Accounting, Cumbria Textiles Ltd, UK

- Nehmen Sie den Telefonanruf auf Englisch entgegen (Firmenname, Begrüßung, Ihr voller Name).
- Sie finden die Rechnung im System und fragen, um was es geht.
- Bitten Sie den/die Anrufer/in um einen Moment Zeit, während Sie nachschauen.
- Erklären Sie, dass nur der pinkfarbene Stoff im Angebot war, nicht aber der gelbe. Entschuldigen Sie sich dafür, dass der pinkfarbene Stoff falsch in Rechnung gestellt wurde. Sie haben dem Kunden / der Kundin € 250,00 zu viel berechnet.
- Fragen Sie, ob der Kunde / die Kundin damit einverstanden ist, eine Gutschrift über € 250,00 zu akzeptieren.
- Bedanken Sie sich und schließen Sie das Gespräch freundlich ab.

FILE 21: Unit 9, Communication, exercise 3

Partner B

You work in the Sales department at ExHoods Ltd. You take a call from an assistant in the Purchasing department at Marx Kitchens and clarify the details of a new product.

Answer the call with your own name. Before you begin, read the details below.

Product: Stainless steel extractor hoods

Sizes: medium 45mm x 60mm x 50mm
large 55mm x 70mm x 60mm

Prices: medium €99.00
large €120.00

Quoted: DDP London

New customer terms of payment: COD

New customer discount: 3%

Delivery: up to 30 days after receipt of order.

› *Useful phrases: Clarifying details on the phone, page 196*

FILE 22: Unit 12, Part B, exercise 5

Common interview questions	Tips
... about yourself – Tell us about yourself. – How would you describe yourself? – What are your hobbies? – What are your strengths and weaknesses?	– Be honest. Show that you are able to use your strengths and indicate that you are working on your "weaknesses".
– Tell us about a mistake you made in the past and how you handled it.	– Be positive. Even if a mistake was made, remember to say that you learned from it.
– What question would you not like us to ask you?	– Say that you hope they do not ask you about a particular department/task as you do not yet have much experience in that department/area. Keep it simple and say something positive.
... about your education, work experience and skills – Why did you choose to train at vocational college? – What responsibilities did you have / do you have during the work placement? / at work? – Please tell me about your present job. – What have you learned in your present job that you think will help you in the position you're applying for with us?	– Talk about the aspects of your education, work experience and skills that are relevant for the job in question. – Talk about a particular project or task which you did successfully.
... about what you know – What languages do you speak? – What computer software are you familiar with?	– Answer honestly. – Be honest. Don't say you know MS Office if you only learned Word, PowerPoint and Excel.
... about your motivation – Why did you apply for this job? – Why do you want to work for this company? – Why do you think you would be a good candidate for this job? – What would you like to achieve in the next five/ten years?	– Show that you have researched the company and know what the job is about. – Stress the positive aspects of the company and the job. – Talk about realistic goals and describe how you would like to progress with your career.
Questions you can ask the interviewer	
– I would like to continue improving my skills. What courses does the company offer? – What kind of training is given to new employees? – Who would I report to? – What are the prospects for promotion? – What are the next stages of the selection process? – When could I start?	

FILE 23: Unit 11, Part B, exercise 6A

Partner B

Schleuter Sport GmbH, Dresden receives an incorrect invoice for materials from a supplier in the UK.

You work for Schleuter Sport GmbH, Dresden. Role-play a telephone conversation with Cumbria Textiles Ltd (Partner A), using the following prompts.

Partner B (buyer)
Sie (eigener Name), Rechnungswesen, Schleuter Sport GmbH, Dresden, Deutschland

- Stellen Sie sich vor (Ihr voller Name, Firmenname, Ort) und sagen Sie, dass Sie wegen Rechnung Nr. RS4230 vom … (*Datum vom 28. des vergangenen Monats*) über € 11.000,00 anrufen.
- Der Preis für die Posten (*items*) 2 und 5 ist falsch. Es handelt sich um eine Bestellung für gelben und pinkfarbenen Stoff (*material*) vom Typ PT27, der im Angebot war, aber es ist der normale Preis von € 55,00 statt € 50,00 berechnet worden. Man hat Ihnen € 500,00 zu viel berechnet.
- Sie sind gerne bereit, ein paar Minuten zu warten.
- Reagieren Sie höflich und bitten Sie um eine berichtigte Rechnung.
- Akzeptieren Sie die vorgeschlagene Lösung und schließen Sie das Gespräch freundlich ab.

FILE 24: Unit 12, Part B, exercise 3A

Partner A

There is a job vacancy at Trade International plc. Jennifer/John Stone, Head of Human Resources, calls an applicant for a telephone interview.

You are Jennifer/John Stone. Work with Partner B and role-play the telephone interview. Partner B answers the phone and begins.

- Introduce yourself.
- Suitable time for phone call?
- Ask the candidate to talk about his/her CV.
- How would the candidate describe himself/herself?
- How would the candidate's colleagues describe him/her?
- Is the candidate a team player? Examples?
- Hobbies?
- Strengths and weaknesses?
- Reason for deciding to train as …
- Expectations of the job?
- Why should this particular candidate be chosen?
- Questions?

Swap roles when you have finished

Mock exam: Stufe II

Schriftliche Prüfung

Zeit:	120 Minuten
Hilfsmittel:	allgemeines zweisprachiges Wörterbuch
Maximale Punktzahl:	100 Punkte

Im Rahmen der schriftlichen Prüfung werden die Aufgabenanteile für die drei Kompetenzbereiche wie folgt gewichtet:

Rezeption	**40 %**
Produktion	**30 %**
Mediation	**30 %**

Im Folgenden werden vier Aufgaben vorgelegt, die Sie bearbeiten sollen. Die erste und die zweite Aufgabe beziehen sich auf Ihre Fähigkeit, englische Texte (gesprochene und geschriebene) zu verstehen = **Rezeption**. Bei der dritten Aufgabe wird von Ihnen erwartet, dass Sie ein Schriftstück erstellen = **Produktion** eines englischen Textes. In der vierten Aufgabe sollen Sie Texte von der deutschen oder englischen in die jeweils andere Sprache übertragen = **Mediation**.

Die Prüfung beginnt mit der Hörverständnisaufgabe. Alle weiteren Aufgaben können in beliebiger Reihenfolge bearbeitet werden.

Rezeption I: Hörverstehen — 20 Punkte

Situation: Sie arbeiten in der Verkaufsabteilung der Firma GreatSpirits Ltd, einem Getränkehersteller in London, der sich auf Spirituosen, Weine und Biere spezialisiert hat. Die meisten Telefonanrufe, die Sie bekommen, erfordern Maßnahmen, daher machen Sie sich auch Notizen, während Sie telefonieren. Auf diese Art und Weise können Sie die Notizen an andere Kollegen und Kolleginnen oder Abteilungen, die Bestellungen durchführen oder sich um Probleme kümmern, weiterreichen.

56 **Aufgabe: Verwenden Sie die untenstehende Darstellung, um sich Notizen zu machen, während Sie sich das Telefongespräch anhören.**

Complaint form

Date:	
From:	
Company:	
Reason for call:	
Product(s) ordered:	
Problem(s):	
Reason for problem(s):	
Action taken / Follow-up action:	
Call received by:	

Situation: Als Auszubildende/r der Firma GreatSpirits Ltd sind Sie in der Marketingabteilung auch dafür zuständig, das jährliche Treffen der Verkaufsleiter/innen aus aller Welt zu planen. Das Treffen soll dieses Jahr in Dublin stattfinden.

Aufgabe: Sie Informieren sich im Internet (siehe unten). Stellen Sie die wichtigsten Aspekte der möglichen Hotels für das Treffen tabellenartig auf Deutsch dar.

	The Duke's Head	Comfort Dublin Airport	The Jerome Hotel
Hotel allgemein			
Kategorie			
Zimmeranzahl			
Lage			
Besonderheit			
Konferenzräume			
Raumanzahl/Kapazitäten			
Ausstattung/Service			

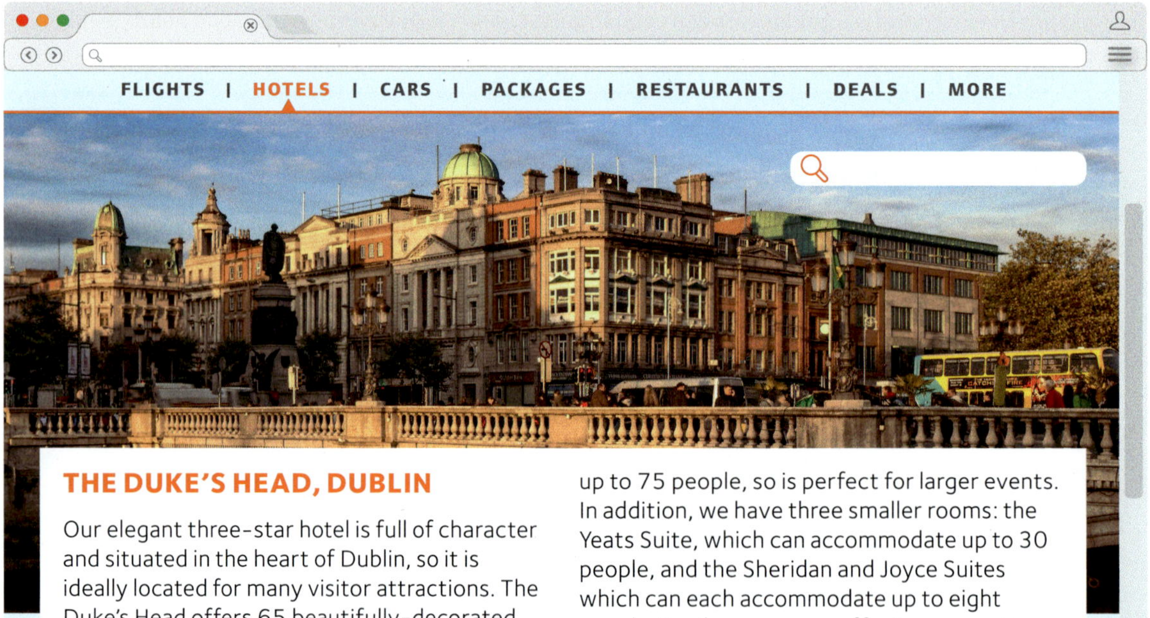

THE DUKE'S HEAD, DUBLIN

Our elegant three-star hotel is full of character and situated in the heart of Dublin, so it is ideally located for many visitor attractions. The Duke's Head offers 65 beautifully-decorated rooms in a collection of five charming Georgian townhouses. We are therefore one of the oldest hotels in the city, having been in operation since 1877. The Duke's Head has been a focal point in Dublin ever since.

We offer a wide-range of conference services to suit every need, whether it be a small intimate meeting or a larger international conference. The Beckett Suite accommodates up to 75 people, so is perfect for larger events. In addition, we have three smaller rooms: the Yeats Suite, which can accommodate up to 30 people, and the Sheridan and Joyce Suites which can each accommodate up to eight people. Furthermore, we offer two executive boardrooms which can seat up to 18 people, and provide the use of a private lounge and air conditioning as well as covering all your technological needs. All our meeting rooms have free Wi-Fi and bottled water.

If you are interested in using our facilities, please contact our sales team who will be more than happy to help organize your successful event.

COMFORT DUBLIN AIRPORT

Our four-star hotel is located close to Dublin Airport and boasts a long-serving, very experienced team, some of whom have been with us for over 25 years. Our 24-hour shuttle service to and from the terminal building is much-appreciated and is completely free of charge. We have a large base of regular customers who enjoy our light and relaxed atmosphere, and who trust us to always make their event a success.

What better place could there be to hold a meeting than in one of our meeting or board rooms directly adjacent to the airport? Our four compact board rooms are ideal for small meetings of up to ten participants. We also have three larger spaces which can generously seat up to 30 guests. Our Executive Suite is our most flexible room: It can host up to 200 people or be divided into four sections to create a variety of rooms suitable for your special event. All our rooms offer natural daylight, complimentary Wi-Fi and an in-built presentation system with state-of-the-art projectors.

Participants can stay in one of our 280 comfort or executive rooms, and our experienced events team is on hand to deal with every aspect of planning your event so that you do not have to worry about a thing. Please contact us to discuss your requirements.

THE JEROME HOTEL, DUBLIN

The Jerome Hotel has long been one of the world's leading hotels, but it's recent renovation has completely updated all our facilities making your five-star experience even more luxurious.

There is no better location for a meeting in Dublin. The Jerome Hotel offers 350 stylish rooms in the very centre of the retail and cultural district, and is just a stone's throw from many historic sights. You just have to step out of the door to find great pubs and restaurants, and there is no shortage of nightlife and theatres nearby.

You can choose from seven elegant boardrooms suitable for 20 guests, or our deluxe suite which holds up to 250 guests. It goes without saying that all these luxurious, elegantly-decorated meeting rooms are fully equipped with the latest technology for your conference and are easily adapted to suit your individual needs.

We at The Jerome Hotel believe that we have a responsibility to our environment and work hard to make our hotel sustainable. Therefore, we only offer locally-sourced food and serve tap water instead of bottled water. Furthermore, all meeting rooms have waste-paper baskets for recycling, lights are turned off once the room is not in use, and we only use recycled paper for photocopying and correspondence.

Produktion — 30 Punkte

Situation: Sie arbeiten für einen der drei in Deutschland führenden Büromaterialhersteller, der sich auf nachhaltige und umweltfreundliche Produkte spezialisiert hat. Auf der internationalen Fachmesse Paperworld in Frankfurt hat Ihre Firma unter anderem die Produkte einer interessanten niederländischen Firma kennengelernt und einige Muster zugesandt bekommen, die zu Ihrem Angebot an Büromaterialprodukten passen.

Aufgabe: Ihr Chef ist von der Qualität überzeugt und bittet Sie, eine Anfrage zu schreiben.

Einkauf:
- *Anfrage an NePaMa NV (info@nepama.nl) schicken mit Bezug auf Messebesuch und Dankeschön für das Musterpaket.*
- *Produkte: 5000 Blatt A0 90g/m² Kunstdruckpapier (art paper); 1000 Blatt A0 150g/m² Postkartenpapier (postcard cardboard); 500 Blatt 300g/m² Umschlagkarton (cover board)*
- *Nachhaltige und umweltfreundliche Materialien wichtig! Zertifikate/Nachweise vorhanden?*
- *Erfragen Sie Liefer- und Zahlungsbedingungen und mögliche Preisnachlässe.*

Mediation **30 Punkte**

Situation: Nach Ihrer Ausbildung arbeiten Sie für die Zweigstelle Ihrer Firma in England. Die Firma bietet Praktika für internationale Auszubildende, Studenten und Studentinnen an.

Aufgabe: Fassen Sie auf Deutsch die wichtigsten Aspekte der Jobbeschreibung für Ihre Personalabteilung in Deutschland zusammen. Benutzen Sie dafür die nebenstehende Tabelle.

Infos über die Firma	
Ort des Praktikums	
Arbeitszeit	
Dauer des Praktikums	
Bezahlung	
Anforderungen an die Bewerber/Bewerberinnen	
Was bietet die Firma / Welche Inhalte lernt man?	
Verlangte Bewerbungsunterlagen und Art der Bewerbung	

PR INTERNSHIP

ECOWORLD is a different kind of furniture manufacturer.

We sell beautiful furniture from sustainable wood production that is a living blueprint for our values: people and the planet are central to everything we do.

We are looking for an enthusiastic and motivated candidate full of creative ideas who can work two to four full days a week at our York office. A positive attitude is a must!

You will gain a deep insight into public relations. When the internship is completed, you will be ready to enter any PR department or firm.

Responsibilities:

- Monitoring the PR inbox for press enquiries
- Building relationships with the media
- Drafting press releases
- Updating the mailing list
- Posting on the *ECOWORLD* blog and social media
- Assisting with event management such as furniture fairs and press days
- Assisting with administrative duties
- Performing market research and analysis activities

This is an unpaid 3-month placement with the possibility to extend if required, but interns will receive *ECOWORLD* vouchers so that they can buy *ECOWORLD* products.

Further requirements:

- a solid understanding of the different social networks
- excellent verbal and written communication skills
- good knowledge of MS Office

Candidates must be currently studying at university or doing an apprenticeship.

To apply: Please submit a covering letter and CV by email with the subject line 'PR Internship' to hr@ecoworld.co.uk.

Mündliche Prüfung

Die mündliche Prüfung ist eine Tandem- oder Gruppenprüfung, bei der Sie Gespräche persönlichen und fachlichen Inhalts in der Fremdsprache führen sollen. Sie dauert pro Kandidat/in ca. 25 min. Zur Vorbereitung haben Sie 20 Minuten Zeit.

Phase I: Sie werden gebeten, sich zu persönlichen oder beruflichen Themen (z.B. Vorstellung des eigenen Werdegangs, der Firma und des Aufgabengebietes) zu äußern. Die Kandidaten/Kandidatinnen werden im Wechsel befragt.

Phase II: Im zweiten Teil sollen Sie zusammen mit einem/einer anderen Kandidaten/Kandidatin ein Rollenspiel durchführen. Dazu erhalten Sie vom Prüfer / von der Prüferin Rollenkarten, auf denen eine Situation beschrieben ist, die Sie vorspielen sollen.

Hilfsmittel: allgemeines zweisprachiges Wörterbuch

Interaktion 30 Punkte

Ihre Aufgaben für Phase I könnten wie folgt lauten:

Geben Sie Auskünfte über sich anhand folgender Stichworte:

Ihr beruflicher Werdegang:	– Ausbildung, Abschlüsse, Praktika usw. – Gründe für diese Berufswahl
Ihre Ausbildungsfirma:	– allgemeines Geschäftsfeld / Spezialisierungsbereiche – Anzahl der Beschäftigten, Arbeitsbedingungen usw.
Ihr Arbeitsalltag in der Firma:	– Verwaltungsaufgaben (Beispiele) – Vorlieben/Abneigungen
Ihre Pläne für die Zukunft:	– wo Sie beruflich gerne in fünf Jahren wären

Ihre Aufgaben für Phase II könnten wie folgt lauten:

Rollenkarte A

Sie besuchen eine europäische Berufsmesse in Belgien, da Sie sich für ein Praktikum in einem englischsprachigen Land interessieren. Ihre Ausbildung als Industriekauffrau/mann endet in einem halben Jahr. Sie sind noch nicht sicher, ob Sie in einer internationalen Firma arbeiten möchten oder ob Sie ein Studium der Logistik anschließen möchten. In jedem Fall erhoffen Sie sich aber eine Verbesserung Ihrer sprachlichen und beruflichen Kenntnisse.

Die Firma GloboTyre aus England hat einen interessanten Stand. Sie nehmen Kontakt zu einem Repräsentanten auf, um Fragen bezüglich eines Praktikums zu klären.
Vorab haben Sie sich einen Notizzettel mit den für Sie wichtigsten Aspekten gemacht:

- Leistungsspektrum der Firma?
- Praktikum für sechs Monate möglich?
- Tätigkeit in verschiedenen Abteilungen möglich?
- Logistikabteilung vorhanden?
- Erfahrung mit Praktikanten/Praktikantinnen?
- Bezahlung?
- Unterbringung?

Rollenkarte B

Sie arbeiten für die Firma GloboTyre aus Birmingham, England und vertreten diese heute auf einer europäischen Berufsmesse in Belgien.
GloboTyre ist ein großes Industrieunternehmen, das sich auf die Herstellung von Autoreifen (*car tyres*) spezialisiert hat. Diese werden europaweit per Bahn, per Schiff oder mit einer eigenen Lastwagenflotte vertrieben. Im Unternehmen arbeiten zurzeit 145 Angestellte, verteilt auf mehrere Abteilungen.
Für Ihre Firma ist das Rekrutieren von Angestellten für die vielen verschiedenen Abteilungen wichtig, da dringend Leute mit Sprachkenntnissen gebraucht werden. Im letzten Jahr haben Sie erfolgreich Praktikanten und Praktikantinnen aus Frankreich und Polen anwerben können, die nun fest angestellt sind.
Ihre Firma tut einiges dafür passende Bewerber/innen zu finden, zwar gibt es keine Bezahlung bei einem Praktikum, aber die Unterbringung in der Nähe der Firma und das Essen in der Kantine sind kostenlos.
Darüber hinaus können Interessenten *evening courses* an der nahe gelegenen Berufsschule besuchen.
Ihnen ist es wichtig etwas über die Motivation, die Zukunftspläne und den bisherigen beruflichen/schulischen Werdegang eines Bewerbers / einer Bewerberin zu erfahren.

G Grammar

Simple present

1 I **work** in the Export department of a manufacturing company. I **arrange** for goods to be shipped abroad.
2 The company **produces** components for the automobile industry.
3 The company **doesn't ship** its goods to Asia.

- Das *simple present* wird für wiederholte, oft regelmäßige Handlungen in der Gegenwart verwendet.
- Signalwörter: *regularly, sometimes, often, always, normally* usw.
- Manche Verben, die keine Handlung, sondern einen Zustand ausdrücken (*need, like, want, hate, love, know, believe*), stehen (fast) ausschließlich im *simple present*.
- In der 3. Person (*he, she, it, Peter, the firm* usw.) wird ein -s angefügt (2).
- Verneinungen werden mit *doesn't/don't* gebildet (3).

Present progressive

1 Our department **is** currently **trying** to find a new supplier.
2 The managers **are negotiating** with a company from Poland right now.

- Das *present progressive* wird gebraucht, wenn man gerade ablaufende oder noch nicht abgeschlossene Handlungen beschreibt.
- Signalwörter: *at the moment, (right) now, just, currently* usw.

Questions and short answers

1 **Do** you **write** a lot of enquiries? – Yes, I **do**. / No, I **don't**.
2 **Did** you **reply** to her email? – Yes, I **did**. / No, I **didn't**.
3 **Can** you **book** the hotel online? – Yes, you **can**. / No, you **can't**.
4 **Is** it easy to use? – Yes, it **is**. / No, it **isn't**.
5 **When/Why/How did** you **find** a new supplier?

- Fragen im *simple present* werden mit *do/does* gebildet (1).
- Fragen im *simple past* werden mit *did* gebildet (2).
- In Sätzen mit Hilfsverben (*is/have/can/will/should/...*) bildet man Fragen, indem man das Hilfsverb des Aussagesatzes vor das Subjekt stellt (3, 4).
- Kurzantworten bestehen aus *yes/no* + Personalpronomen + Hilfsverb (+ *n't*) (1–4).
- Fragewörter stehen immer am Anfang des Fragesatzes (5).

Simple past

1 I **talked** to my line manager about the complaint last week.
2 I **ordered** the new office supplies we need yesterday.
3 What time **did** you **start** work?
4 My first day at work **was** a disaster.

Eine Liste der unregelmäßigen Verben befindet sich auf S. 264.

- Das *simple past* verwendet man, um zu sagen, wann etwas geschehen ist (1, 2), oder um über Vergangenes zu berichten (4).
- Signalwörter: *yesterday, last week, two days ago, in 1998, When ...?* usw.
- Bei den regelmäßigen Verben wird im *simple past* in allen Personen meist *-ed* angehängt.
- Verneinungen und Fragen werden in allen Personen mit *did/didn't* gebildet.

Past progressive

1 I **was working** in the Marketing department last week.
2 I **was talking** to a customer when a colleague **bumped** into me and I **dropped** the phone.

- Mit dem *past progressive* drückt man aus, dass eine Handlung oder ein Vorgang zu einer bestimmten Zeit in der Vergangenheit gerade im Verlauf war (1).
- Es beschreibt oft eine Handlung, die gerade im Verlauf war, als eine zweite Handlung einsetzte. Die zweite Handlung steht im *simple past* (2).

Present perfect

1 We**'ve** just **updated** the organigram on our website.
2 We**'ve** recently **reviewed** our terms and conditions.
3 We **haven't found** out why the delivery was late yet.
4 **Have** you **been able** to decide which marketing strategy is best?

Eine Liste der unregelmäßigen Verben befindet sich auf S. 264.

- Mit dem *present perfect* sagt man, dass (nicht: wann!) etwas geschehen ist.
- Signalwörter (Zeitadverbien): *this week, already, just, recently, yet* usw.
- Mit *for* (z. B. *for two years*) and *since* (z. B. *since 2015*) drückt man auch aus, wie lange oder seit wann ein Zustand schon andauert.

Future with *will* and *going to*

1 I think the meeting **will take** about two hours.
2 We've run out of stationery. – OK. **I'll (will) contact** the supplier.
3 We **won't (will not) need** the order until next week.
4 We**'re going to refurnish** all the offices next year.
5 This old computer **is going to break down** soon.

- *Will* wird verwendet, um Vorhersagen zu machen oder Vermutungen über die Zukunft auszudrücken (1).
- *Will* wird für spontane Entscheidungen, Angebote und Versprechen verwendet (2).
- Im gesprochenen Englisch lautet die Verneinung *won't*, ansonsten *will not* (3).
- *Be going to* (+ Infinitiv des Verbs) wird verwendet, um über Pläne oder Absichten zu sprechen (4), oder wenn die Gewissheit (oder ein Anzeichen dafür) besteht, dass etwas geschehen wird (5).

Passive forms

1 The goods **are stored** in our new modern warehouse.
2 The order **was delivered** on Tuesday morning.
3 The shipment **has** already **been dispatched**.
4 The new materials **could be bought** from a local supplier.
5 The equipment **will be installed by** them as part of their customer service.

- Das Passiv wird oft verwendet, wenn man auf eher unpersönliche Art und Weise über Fakten, Vorgänge und Zahlen berichtet.
- Das Passiv wird mit der entsprechenden Form von *be* + Partizip Perfekt (3. Verbform) gebildet. Es können alle Zeiten gebildet werden.
- Passivsätze mit modalen Hilfsverben werden mit einem modalen Hilfsverb + *be* + Partizip Perfekt (3. Verbform) gebildet (4).
- „Von" und „durch" werden in Passivsätzen durch *by* ausgedrückt (5).

Conditional sentences

1 Type 1: **If** you **order** over 200 items, you**'ll receive** a 5% discount.
2 Type 2: If there **was** a delay, we **would inform** you immediately.
3 Type 2: I **wouldn't do** that if I **was/were** you.
4 Type 3: If we **had advertised** the product in the right places, we **would have sold** more.

- Ein *if*-Satz des Typs 1 drückt eine Bedingung aus, die der Sprecher für durchaus möglich oder wahrscheinlich hält. Der damit verbundene Hauptsatz drückt eine Vorhersage aus, die je nach Situation als Warnung, Versprechen o. ä. zu verstehen ist (1).
- Durch einen *if*-Satz des Typs 2 gibt der Sprecher seinem Gesprächspartner einen Ratschlag oder teilt ihm mit, dass er die Erfüllung der Bedingung für unmöglich, unwahrscheinlich (2) oder nicht wünschenswert (3) hält.
- Ein *if*-Satz des Typs 3 drückt eine nicht mehr erfüllbare Bedingung aus. Die Bedinging bezieht sich auf die Vergangenheit (4).
- Steht der *if*-Nebensatz an erster Stelle, wird er durch ein Komma vom Hauptsatz abgetrennt (1, 2, 4).

Relative clauses

1 Our customer service agents are the people **who/that deal with customer complaints**.
2 The supplier **(which/that) our company uses** is based in Berlin.
3 ComTech Ltd**, which is our biggest competitor,** offers a similar product for a lower price.

- Relativpronomen leiten Relativsätze ein.
- Es gibt den notwendigen und den nicht notwendigen Relativsatz. Notwendige Relativsätze sind für das Verständnis des Satzes unbedingt erforderlich (1, 2) und stehen ohne Komma. Nicht notwendige geben lediglich Zusatzinformationen und werden durch Kommata getrennt (3).
- In notwendigen Relativsätzen kann das Relativpronomen wegfallen, wenn es Objekt ist, d. h. wenn im Relativsatz ein Subjekt steht (2).

Verb + infinitive or *-ing* form

1 I enjoy **working** in a team.
2 I expect **to qualify** as an industrial management assistant in June.
3 I began **working / to work** for the company last year.
4 I'd prefer **to work** from home more often.
5 I'm interested in **getting** some work experience abroad.

- Auf eine Gruppe von Verben folgt immer die *-ing*-Form (1). Zu diesen Verben gehören *dislike, enjoy, finish, give up, imagine, involve, keep, mind, miss, practise, recommend, risk, stop, suggest.*
- Auf eine zweite Gruppe von Verben folgt immer ein *to*-Infinitiv (2). Zu diesen Verben gehören *afford, agree, arrange, choose, decide, expect, hope, learn, manage, offer, plan, promise, want.*
- Auf eine dritte Gruppe von Verben kann sowohl die *-ing*-Form als auch ein *to*-Infinitiv folgen (3). Zu diesen Verben gehören *begin, continue, hate, like, love, prefer, start*
- Nach *would hate, would like, would love* and *would prefer* (Kurzform *'d like* usw.) steht nur der *to*-Infinitiv (4).
- Nach einer Präposition kommt immer die *-ing*-Form (5).

Gerunds

1 **Travelling** from place to place means there is a lot of variety in my job.
2 Do you like **working** in the office?
3 My work consists of **dealing** with orders and shipment.

- Das Gerundium (= *-ing*-Form des Verbs) kann die Rolle eines Nomens übernehmen.
- Das Gerundium kann als Subjekt (1), Objekt (2) oder nach Präpositionen (3) verwendet werden.

Comparatives and superlatives

1 The new system is **harder/easier** to use.
2 It's **more expensive than** shipping the goods by rail.
3 It's the **simplest** and **cheapest** offer, but not the **best**.
4 This type of trade fair stand is the **most flexible** solution.
5 The company spent **less** money on advertising last year.
6 The new system is**n't as easy** to update **as** the old one.

- Einsilbige Adjektive und zweisilbige Adjektive, die auf *-y* enden, steigert man mit *-er/-est* (1).
- Zweisilbige Adjektive, die nicht auf *-y* enden, und alle Adjektive mit mehr als zwei Silben steigert man mit *more/most* (2).
- Unregelmäßig sind: *good – better – best, bad – worse – worst, little* (wenig) *– less – least, far – farther/further – farthest/furthest* (3, 5).
- Vergleiche bildet man mit *than* und *(not) as ... as* (2, 6).

Reported speech

1 The Sales Manager **said** that sales **had risen** since last year.
2 The intern **asked** if she **could take part** in the meeting.
3 My line manager **told** me that the trade fair **is** always **held** in Frankfurt.

- Man verwendet die indirekte Rede, um zu berichten, was jemand gesagt hat.
- Steht das einleitende Verb (*ask, say* usw.) in der Vergangenheit, verschieben sich die Verben im Satz entsprechend (1, 2).
- Wenn das Berichtete immer oder immer noch gültig ist, muss keine Zeitverschiebung erfolgen (3).

direkte Rede	**indirekte Rede**
simple present	simple past
present progressive	past progressive
simple past	past perfect
present perfect	past perfect
will	would
can	could

Adverbs of frequency

1 The apprentices **sometimes** attend trade fairs during their training.
2 We have **often** attended sales meetings abroad.
3 The Sales Director is **frequently** away on business.
4 We deliver goods to China **weekly**.

- Häufigkeitsadverbien der unbestimmten Zeit stehen vor dem ersten Hauptverb (1), nach dem ersten Hilfsverb (2), und nach *to be* (3). Zu ihnen gehören: *already, always, ever, frequently, mostly, never, soon* usw.
- Häufigkeitsadverbien der bestimmten Zeit stehen meistens am Satzende, z. B. *annually, daily, monthly, once, twice, weekly, yearly* (4). Dies gilt auch für *a lot, before, very much, yet.*

Modals and their substitutes

1 I **can** work from home two days a week.
2 I **could** work longer hours if I lived closer to the office.
3 The manufacturing costs **must** be covered by the retail price.
4 You **will be able to** order the new product line from May onwards.
5 We **won't be allowed to** install the new software on our own.
6 We **should** compare the costs of the different methods of transport.
7 Some items in the consignment were broken and **had to** be replaced.
8 You **mustn't** accept an offer before talking to your line manager.
9 You **needn't** ring the supplier. I'll do it in a minute.
10 I **would** like to gain some work experience abroad.

- Modale Hilfsverben wie *can, could, may, would* usw. drücken eine Fähigkeit, eine Erlaubnis, eine Empfehlung, ein Verbot oder einen Wunsch aus.
- Modale Hilfsverben haben in allen Personen die gleiche Form; bei der Verneinung gibt es zusammengezogene Kurzformen.
- Modale Hilfsverben stehen normalerweise in der Gegenwartsform, manche auch in der Vergangenheit. Ersatzverben (*substitutes*) werden benutzt, um alle übrigen Zeiten zu bilden.

Hilfsverb	Ersatzverb
can	*be able to*
could	
may	*be allowed to*
might	
must	*have to*
need not	*don't have to*
shall	
should/ought to	
must not	*not be allowed to*

T Transcripts

Track 2: Unit 1, Foundation, exercise 1A

Hello. My name is Sophie, I'm 19 years old. I'm from Bremen. I left school last year with A levels in English, German and Mathematics. I work at ABC Manufacturing where I'm training to be an industrial management assistant. My apprenticeship lasts for three years. I'm doing a work-based apprenticeship. I work in the office from 9 to 5 and do block release at vocational school every three months. I get a small salary from the company. It's not much, but I still live with my parents, so I don't have expenses like rent or food. My colleagues are great and help me a lot. I'd like to work in one of the company's foreign branches one day.

Track 3: Unit 1, Foundation, exercise 1B

My name is Robert Köpke, I'm 18 years old and I come from Berlin. I left school with A levels in German and Computer Studies. I work at Import/Export GmbH where I'm training to be a management assistant in wholesale and foreign trade. My apprenticeship lasts for two and a half years. It's a work-based apprenticeship. I work in the office three days a week from eight a.m. till four p.m. and I have day-release at vocational college one and a half days a week. The company pays for my course and I also get a small salary. I hope they will offer me a permanent position in the company when I've finished my training

Track 4: Unit 1, Part A, exercise 2A

1 Lisa

Mirko Hi, I'm Mirko from Finland. Is it all right if I interview you?
Lisa Yes, go ahead. I'm Lisa from Germany.
Mirko Thanks. So, what size company do you work for?
Lisa I work for a large company. It's a consumer electronics retailer with branches all over Europe.
Mirko A consumer electronics retailer … and which department are you in?
Lisa I'm in Procurement. We buy goods from suppliers, but I'll soon be in a different department.
Mirko And you're in Procurement … OK, I've got that. How many other apprentices are there at your company?
Lisa I really can't say! It's so big. All I know is that Procurement has ten apprentices.
Mirko That's fine. Now I need to find out about the hours you work, your breaks and overtime.
Lisa I work seven hours a day, five days a week.
Mirko So that's 35 hours a week. And when do you start and finish each day?
Lisa I clock in just before 7 a.m. and clock out at 3 p.m.
Mirko And what about breaks?
Lisa I usually have an hour's lunch break in the canteen between 12 and 1 p.m.
Mirko Is that all? Don't you have a morning break?
Lisa Not officially. I just get a cup of coffee when I feel like it.
Mirko I see. And what about overtime?
Lisa There's no regular overtime, but if there's a big event like an open day, my boss expects everyone to stay late the night before and clear up when it's over. That usually means about 3 hours' overtime.
Mirko Ah yes, I see what you mean. Now what about a dress code? Do you have one at your company?
Lisa Oh, yes. We have it in writing and it's quite strict because we often visit our suppliers and customers all over Germany.
Mirko Ah yes, of course. You need to look smart for the customers. And your trips are all over Germany?
Lisa Yes, and next month I'm going to the Czech Republic to visit a supplier. I'm really looking forward to that.
Mirko So you also go on business trips abroad. We only have a few more questions now. The next one is: when can your boss contact you?
Lisa Only during working hours. We don't get phone calls or texts outside working hours.
Mirko Not even when you're on standby?
Lisa Well, apprentices don't have to be on standby in my department, so that never happens.
Mirko I see. Now I need to know about your office. How big is it?
Lisa I work in a large open-plan office with about 50 people in it, so it's never really quiet, but I like it. And we also hot-desk.
Mirko Hot-desk? What's that?
Lisa We don't have our own personal desks in the office. We just take a free desk anywhere and log in.
Mirko I see. And what facilities and benefits does your company give its employees?
Lisa Well, as I said, we have a canteen; there are free drinks from drinks machines on each floor; and we have a snack bar on the ground floor.
Mirko Any benefits?
Lisa Benefits … just let me think. Ah yes, they pay for my travel ticket, and we all have a tablet that we can keep after the apprenticeship … and we get discounts on some of the goods.
Mirko Well, that sounds like a very good employer, Lisa. My final questions are whether you want to stay on after your apprenticeship and what job offer you expect?
Lisa I very much want to stay on and I think I'll get at least a one-year contract when I finish.
Mirko That's it. Thanks for that, Lisa.
Lisa You're welcome.

2 Lukas

Fabienne Hi, I'm Fabienne from France. You're from Germany aren't you, Lukas?
Lukas Yes, that's right.
Fabienne Is it all right if I interview you?
Lukas No problem. What would you like to know?
Fabienne Well, first I want to know how big your company is?
Lukas It's a small company, a family business with about 20 employees. We make furniture and sell it all over the world.
Fabienne A small company … and what department are you in?
Lukas I'm in the Logistics department at the moment.
Fabienne And how many apprentices are there at your company?
Lukas I'm the only apprentice.
Fabienne I see. Now what about your working hours?
Lukas Well, officially I work 8 hours a day from Monday to Friday.
Fabienne So that's 40 hours per week.

Lukas Yes, we all start very early at 6.30 a.m. and we have a 30-minute break together at 9 o'clock. There's one hour for lunch at 1 o'clock and we all finish at 4 p.m.

Fabienne And do you clock in and out?

Lukas No, we don't have to. We all come and go at the same time.

Fabienne And what about overtime?

Lukas I do a lot of overtime! We have to meet our delivery deadlines, so I sometimes do up to 8 hours a week.

Fabienne That's a lot. My next question is about a dress code. Is there one at your company?

Lukas No, there's no dress code. We can wear what we want.

Fabienne So you don't go on business trips?

Lukas No, never. They need me in the office.

Fabienne I see. And when can your boss contact you?

Lukas Whenever he needs to, really. If there's a problem, he phones or texts me after work. I don't mind. That's what it's like in a small company.

Fabienne So he can contact you at any time?

Lukas Yes, that's right.

Fabienne Now please describe your office, the facilities at your company and any benefits you may get.

Lukas Office, facilities and benefits … OK, I work in a small office with one other person. We have a hot and cold drinks machine and that's about it.

Fabienne And do you have a company phone, tablet or laptop?

Lukas No, nothing like that.

Fabienne Any other benefits like discounts and so on?

Lukas Well, come to think of it, I could buy the furniture we make at cost price if I wanted, so that's a big discount.

Fabienne And now for my last two questions. Would you like to stay at the company after your apprenticeship and if so, what offer do you think your boss will make you?

Lukas I'm not sure about staying on because it's a very small company. My boss has already said I could get a permanent contract if I wanted to, but I need to think about it.

Fabienne And that completes the questionnaire. Thanks.

Lukas That was quick!

Track 5: Unit 1, Part B, exercise 1B/C

Trainer I'm so pleased to be working with an international group today and I think we'll all learn a lot from each other at this seminar. OK, now you've all had some time to guess the names of the countries and I think some of you will be surprised when you hear the answers. Now let's start with the only country in which employers don't have to pay their employees for national holidays and annual leave. Which one is it?

Apprentice 1 Japan?

Trainer I'm afraid not. We hear a lot about the Japanese never taking time off work, but they are second to last in our diagram with ten days' paid annual leave and no paid national holidays.

Apprentice 2 The US?

Trainer Exactly! That's why they call the US the "no vacation nation". OK, so we have Japan and the US. Now let's look at the country with most paid holiday and leave. Which one is it?

Apprentice 2 Germany?

Trainer Almost! Germany has the second highest number of paid days off work with 30 days in all, but the winner is Austria! It has the highest number of paid days off work with 38 in all. OK, so now we have Japan, the US, Germany and Austria, so let's look at the two remaining countries – Greece and the UK. Which of these two has to pay its employees for 28 days' annual leave but not for national holidays?

Apprentice 1 The UK?

Trainer Exactly! In the UK, national holidays may or may not be part of your paid annual leave. If your employer lets you have them as additional holiday days, you may or may not be paid for them. It all depends on your contract of employment. Now I want to look at productivity in these countries. Which, would you say, has the highest productivity per working hour?

Apprentice 2 Germany?

Trainer Almost! Once again it has the second highest. The highest is the US. Then comes Germany and then …?

Apprentice 1 Austria?

Trainer Very good! And after that?

Apprentice 2 Japan?

Trainer Sorry, it's the UK in fourth place followed by …?

Apprentice 1 Japan and Greece.

Trainer That's right. So to sum up the US has the highest productivity, followed by Germany, Austria, the UK, Japan and Greece, which has the lowest productivity. Let's take a break now and …

Track 6: Unit 1, Communication, exercise 1A

Martyna Hello. I'm Martyna Nowak. I'm 42. I was born in Poland. I'm a human resources manager.

Halil Good morning. My name is Halil Özdemir. I'm 29 years old. I was born in Germany. I'm a training supervisor.

Deema Good afternoon. My name is Deema Mansour. I'm 19. I was born in Syria. I'm an apprentice office management assistant.

Robert Hello. I'm Robert Klein. I'm 21. I was born in Austria. I'm an IT management assistant.

Canan Hello. I'm Canan Tolon. I'm 25 years old. I was born in Turkey. I'm a management assistant for office communication.

Alexei Good morning. My name is Alexei Melnyk. I'm 29 years old. I was born in Ukraine. I'm a management assistant in wholesale and foreign trade.

Track 7: Unit 2, Foundation, exercise 2A

Hello everybody. Thank you for being here. My name is Alisha Warner and I'm an office consultant. I plan offices in which people should be able to do their work efficiently and happily. For me, the main purpose of a good office environment is to support the people who work there. Whether it's writing, telephoning or computer work, every office should be a nice place to work in. So, today, I'd like to compare two very different types of offices: the small office and the open-plan office. Let's look first at the small office.
This is one of the oldest types of offices, a small room which is generally used by one or two people. We all know these offices from visits to public administration buildings. You walk down a long corridor and see one door after another. The doors are closed but you know that someone is in there, working. The benefit of this type

of office is that it lets people focus on their work. Most employees who work in a small office say they enjoy being able to concentrate on their work without being interrupted.
In contrast – and it's a big contrast – we have the open-plan office where everyone works together in one big room. There are two ways to set up an open-plan office. First, there's the cubicle set-up. Each desk is hidden by a low partition, and the employees sit in their cubicles and get on with the work. Some employees like this set-up, others say that their open-plan office is noisy and they can't concentrate on what they're doing.
The second set-up is the open-plan office in which there are no partitions at all. You'll often see this kind of thing in start-ups. The desks and workplaces are completely open and everyone can move about easily. Sometimes the employees share one large table. Two big advantages of working at one table are that it supports a sense of community in the workplace and, if employees are working on a team project, they're able to complete it quickly because they can communicate better.
Another idea is hot-desking, the employees don't have their own desk, they just work at any desk that's free. There are pros and cons attached to hot-desking. At the end of the day, each space must be cleared and ready for whoever uses it next, so the office is always neat and tidy. The downside of this is that employees can't put their personal mark on their section of the office. This may result in an office lacking warmth or personality, and feeling uninviting.
So, what's the answer? A small office or an open-plan office? An open-plan office with partitions and cubicles, or a totally open, shared working space? A lot depends on the type of business you do, but whatever your business, employees should always feel happy and comfortable in their place of work. That way, they'll do a better job.

Track 8: Unit 2, Part A, exercise 2A/B

1 The people in my department are responsible for a whole contract. We sometimes get very big orders, so we always have a lot to do. Our responsibilities include supervising work at customers' sites, checking that everything is on schedule, and sometimes also training the customers' staff to operate our machines.
2 Finding new customers, making offers to old customers and keeping the price down – that's what I do most of the time. My job also means going to trade fairs, talking to potential customers at our stand and making them offers.
3 I'm in charge of planning and supervising the budget – which is not always so easy. This entails analysing sales figures and profit margins every month and reporting them to the board of directors.
4 I really enjoy doing my job and I learn something new every day. The field I work in is very large, but I would say that, to put it simply, my work involves understanding what materials need to be bought and then finding the best supplier at the lowest possible price.

Track 9: Unit 2, Part B, exercise 2A/B

1 We travel all over the world in our department and I often go to Scandinavia. Most of our work involves negotiating the best possible terms with suppliers and then making sure they deliver on time.
2 Well, I'm basically responsible for finding the best person for the job. My department also sometimes organizes in-house training courses to help people with personal problems.
3 I'm in charge of public relations, so I manage the company's Facebook page and sometimes organize events.
4 Working in my department means understanding customs regulations. We have to obtain the right shipping documents and we also track freight movements, so we know where the goods are all the time.
5 As the manager of my department it's my responsibility to make sure that we sell as many of our products as possible, so each employee has to hand in a report every month. We use this information to analyse our sales figures.
6 In my department we oversee the whole manufacturing and delivery process from beginning to end. We agree standards with our customers and always make sure that they are kept to.

Track 10: Unit 2, Communication, exercise 2

Hi, this is Roger Dalton from Esher Engineering. Thanks for your message. I'm afraid we'll have to change the date of the maintenance technicians' visit to check the lathes. We have a Chinese delegation here on Tuesday, 7 June, so we can offer you Wednesday, 8 June, any time in the afternoon after 1 o'clock. If that doesn't work for you, the technicians can come on Friday, 10 June, but only in the morning from 7 to 12. Please confirm one of these dates with my secretary, Sandy. Her number is 0044 1372 464022. Bye for now.

Track 11: Unit 2, Communication, exercise 3B

Receptionist Esher Engineering, good morning. This is Duncan speaking. How can I help?
Niklas Good morning, it's Niklas Hartmann from Hamm Engineering UK. Could I speak to Mr Dalton, please?
Receptionist Just a moment, sir. I'll see if he's in. Please hold the line.
Niklas Thanks.
Receptionist I'm afraid his line is engaged. Would you like to call back later?
Niklas Well, it's pretty important.
Receptionist In that case, would you like to speak to someone else?
Niklas How about his personal assistant, Simon Smith?
Receptionist Simon Smith ... I'm trying to connect you ...
Niklas Thanks.
Receptionist I'm sorry, but Mr Smith is unavailable at the moment.
Niklas Oh dear ... looks like I'm out of luck today.
Receptionist I could put you through to Mr Dalton's secretary. Perhaps she can help you.
Niklas Yes, all right.
Receptionist I'll put you through.
Niklas Thanks.
Secretary Hello, Mr Dalton's office, Sandy speaking. How can I help?
Niklas Hello, I'm trying to get through to Mr Dalton. It's urgent and I hope you can help me. It's about our technicians' visit next week.
Secretary I see. Who's calling, please?
Niklas Oh, sorry. I forgot to introduce myself. It's Niklas Hartmann from Hamm Engineering.
Secretary Nicholas ... er ... Could you spell your name, please?
Niklas Yes, certainly. Niklas is my first name. That's N - i - k - l - a - s and my surname is Hartmann spelt H - a - r - t - m - a - n - n.
Secretary Thanks. I'm afraid Mr Dalton is out all day today. Would you like to leave a message?

Niklas	Yes, all right. Please tell him that our maintenance technicians are coming to check the lathes on Friday, 10 June, at 8 a.m.
Secretary	I'm sorry, I didn't catch that. Could you repeat that, please?
Niklas	Yes, our maintenance technicians are coming to check the lathes on Friday, 10 June, at 8 a.m. ...

Track 12: KMK Exam practice 1, exercise 2, Hörverstehen

1

Machine	Monday September 5, 8.30 p.m
Caller 1	Good evening, this is Carol Myers from Office Experts in Dublin. I'm returning a call from Michael Sullivan asking for more information about our new ergonomic swivel chairs. Can he please call me back tomorrow afternoon? I've already sent our brochure and price list by mail, but it makes much more sense to talk about it personally. My number is 003531-564229. Thank you, goodbye.

2

Machine	Wednesday February 13, 1.30 a.m.
Caller 2	Hello, my name is Carl Jefferson and I work for the website and blog "Worldwide Apprenticeships". I'm not sure whether I've reached the correct department, but we're looking for apprentices training to become an industrial management assistant. We'd like someone to write a personal report for our website. It would be great if the Human Resources Manager could return my call to talk about details. My number is 001-312-555421. I really appreciate it.

Track 13: Unit 3, Part A, exercise 2A/B

Tour 1

Geide	Good morning, gentlemen. My name is Rolf Geide. I'm the Managing Director of Cantec, and this morning I'm also your guide. Please come this way. Welcome to Cantec and to Germany. We are delighted to welcome you to our company. You've had a very long trip here from China Tomato in Xinjiang and we very much hope you enjoy your stay here in Germany.
Interpreter	Managing Director Wang Wei and his colleagues wish to thank you for your kind invitation to Cantec in Germany. He believes this is the beginning of a long friendship between our two companies. Cantec's canning technology will be an efficient way for Chinese farmers to keep their tomatoes fresh for over a year, so they can be sold all over China and abroad. At the moment, many rot in the fields because it takes too long to transport them to their destination. Canning technology will solve this problem.
Geide	We are glad we can help, Mr Wang. We are also sure that this is the beginning of a long friendship and look forward to visiting you at your company in China next month. Are there any questions before we begin? ... In that case, we'll start here in the conference room with a short presentation about Cantec, its products, services and history ... Well, that was a brief overview of the company. Are there any questions? No? In that case, I'll now take you down the corridor to the Design department.
Interpreter	Excuse me, Mr Geide.
Geide	Yes, Mr Chang?
Interpreter	What is the name of the Head of the Design department?
Geide	His name is Dr Lentz.
Interpreter	Thank you, Mr Geide.
Geide	You're welcome, Mr Chang. ... Now this is the Design department. The gentleman to the left of the window is Dr Lentz. He and his team will design whatever components we need. Now, we take quality very seriously at Cantec, so our next stop is the Quality Management department, where you will meet our head of Quality Management, Mr Sieke. He and his colleagues check all our processes all of the time ... Well, now you've met the Quality Management team, it's time to go downstairs to see how our machines are built, so let's just take the lift over here ... We're in the assembly hall now. Here you can see how our production lines are put together, which is what will happen at your canning plant in China next month. There's an END-O-MAT machine for the lids, and over there you can see a CAN-O-MAT for the bodies. Now please follow me to the showroom, which is the last stop of our tour ... Well, that concludes our tour. I hope you enjoyed it and if you have any questions, please feel free to ask them. After that we will take you on a tour of Essen, including the Gruga Exhibition Centre ...

Tour 2

Steinwender	Good morning, ladies and gentlemen and welcome to Cantec. My name is Mareike Steinwender, I work in the Human Resources department, and we very much hope you will enjoy your time here. There are also other work experience students being shown round the company at the moment. They all speak English or German, and you'll meet them when we finish the tour. I'm your guide for the next hour, so please feel free to ask any questions. We're starting our tour here in the showroom. You can see our two main products, the CAN-O-MAT and the END-O-MAT, and a very wide range of cans.
Student 1	May I ask a question?
Steinwender	Yes, certainly.
Student 1	How many cans can these machines produce?
Steinwender	The CAN-O-MAT produces up to 1,300 can bodies per minute and the END-O-MAT up to 4,000 can ends. Any more questions? ... In that case, let's spend a few more minutes here to look around and then I'll show you the production hall. ... We're now in the production hall where we make the parts for our equipment. Some of you will be working alongside our specialists here, and they will show you how the machines work. Any questions? ... Yes?
Student 1	How long does it take to ...
Steinwender	So let's now take the lift upstairs to the third floor ... OK, now we're on the third floor and I'm going to take you to meet Mr Keller, the head of the Project Management department, and his team. ... Good morning, Mr Keller!
Keller	Good morning!

Everyone Good morning.

Keller Welcome to the Project Management department. My name is Matthias Keller and here you will see how customers' orders are turned into projects. Each order has its own project manager who sees the project through from start to finish. Would you like to ask any questions?

Student 2 Yes, I would like to ask a question, please. Which countries do you export to?

Keller We export all over the world but a lot of our work is in Asia and Africa, and at the moment we're working on a big project for South Africa.

Student 2 Thank you.

Steinwender Thanks, Mr Keller. Let's now go on to the Purchasing department, which is just down the corridor ... This is where all the materials for our machines are ordered and also the tools needed to make them. I can see this department is very busy today, so let's now go to our last stop, which is Mr Geide's office. Mr Geide is our Managing Director, and he's going to tell you something about the history of the company. The Managing Director's office is just down here ...

Track 14: Unit 3, Part B, exercise 1C

Good morning, ladies and gentlemen and welcome to Cantec. We're delighted to have you here in Essen and we hope you will enjoy your visit. My name is Vanessa Koch and I work in the Sales department. The agenda for today's meeting is in the folder in front of you. Right, I'd like to begin by giving you a presentation about the company. I'll start with some background information and company statistics, and will then move on to our products and services. Then at the end, I'll be happy to answer any questions you may have.

Cantec in Germany is a high-tech company manufacturing high-end can-making machines. We have a workforce of 162 and last year our turnover was approximately 39 million euros. We export 98% of our products and have a global market share of about 40%.

As you can see from this slide, we belong to a group of companies. The parent company is Soudronic in Switzerland. The Soudronic Group has subsidiaries in Germany, France and Italy.

This next slide shows how our products are exported all over the world and in particular to Africa and Asia, where canning facilities are often used by farmers to overcome poor transport infrastructure.

Now, let's move on to our next point: the products and services that Cantec has to offer. Our speciality at Cantec is providing the customer with a whole production line. We transport all the components to our customers in containers and assemble them on site. Customers can design their cans themselves or choose one of our standard models. We also train the customers' employees to operate our machines.

The next thing I'd like to show you is our production hall. It has state-of-the-art machinery and ample space for a large number of orders to be handled at the same time.

That was a brief overview of Cantec, Germany. Many thanks for listening. Now if you'd like to ask any questions, I'd be delighted to answer them and then we can go to lunch ...

Track 15: Unit 3, Communication, exercise 4

Presentation 1

Nina Hello everyone. Vincent's given you all the handouts, so you know what the presentation's about.

Vincent I haven't given out the handouts! We said at the end.

Nina We said *before* the presentation, Vincent.

Vincent Sorry, I'll give them out now.

Nina Let's just wait for a moment while Vincent gives out the handouts ... Don't forget that lady over there by the door, Vincent.

Vincent Sorry, here you are.

Nina ... OK, so you now have the handouts. I'm Nina Schicktanz and I'm in Sales.

Vincent And my name's Hase.

Nina Say your department, Vincent.

Vincent Sales.

Nina Now before we start, do you have any questions about the presentation? No ...? In that case, Vincent will now start.

Vincent We said *you* were going to start!

Nina Vincent! Please start!

Vincent All right. I've prepared some examples of the work we do here. We had a big order from a Chinese company last year and here on the screen you can see a picture of the construction site. We're at the top but I can't quite reach it with my hand on this big screen ...

Nina Use the laser pointer!

Vincent What?

Nina Use the laser pointer! And face the audience!

Vincent Oh, sorry. I always forget to do that. Pipelines are very important nowadays. There are about three and a half million kilometres of them all over the word and we are going to build ten more in China. My other example is of a stainless-steel worktop made by our company for a kindergarten in Wanne-Eickel. Here's a picture.

Nina That's the wrong picture! Show the worktop not the children!

Vincent Oh sorry. Here's a picture of the worktop. Any questions? No? Well, in that case welcome to Muckermann Metals here in Gelsenkirchen. We export our products all over the world and now it's time to take a break before we show you the factory ...

Presentation 2

Nina Hello everyone. Vincent's given you all the handouts, so you have some background information on the company. I'm Nina Schicktanz and I'm in Sales.

Vincent And my name's Hase.

Nina Now before we start, do you have any questions about the handouts? No ...? So let me say that, All in all, our company not only manufactures high-quality products for both the domestic and international market and has many customers in the Far East and Asia. It also supports charities and contributes to good causes in the markets that it serves. Vincent will now start.

Vincent All right. I've prepared some examples of what we do here. At the moment we're working on a big order for a Chinese company and here on the screen you can see a picture of the construction site near Beijing. The pipeline we're installing is at the top. We're going to build ten more pipelines in China over the next five years including a big one at Shengli. My next example is very different. It's a stainless-steel worktop made by our company for use in kindergartens, canteens and so on. Any questions?

Visitor Yes, I have a question. What material are the pipelines made of?
Vincent Metal.
Visitor Only metal?
Vincent I think it's mainly metal, perhaps with some other materials but mainly metal.
Visitor What other materials are used?
Vincent Let's discuss this later, shall we? Any more questions? No? ... Well, let me say that we're very pleased that you have come to see Muckermann Metals here in Gelsenkirchen and we hope you enjoy your visit today. Now it's time to for lunch and then we'll show you around the factory.

Presentation 3

Nina Good morning ladies and gentlemen and welcome to Muckermann Metals. My name is Nina Schicktanz and this is my colleague, Vincent Hase.
Vincent Good morning.
Nina We work in the sales department and this morning we'd like to begin by giving you a presentation about our products and the markets we serve all over the world. We'll then show you some examples of our products and after that you'll have the opportunity to ask any questions before we break for lunch at 12.30. After lunch we'll be going on a tour of the factory. On the table in front of you there's a folder with an overview of the company, its products and its markets. Are there any questions before we start? ... In that case I'll hand over to Vincent,
Vincent Thanks. I'll start with some key facts about Muckermann Metals. As you can see from this slide, our turnover last year was just over a hundred million euros and 75% of that was for pipelines but we also make a wide range of other products. This next slide is a breakdown of the pipeline figures. As you can see, most of our work is in China and a small percentage is in Siberia. Our pipelines are made of high-quality carbon steel because it is both light and extremely strong. This next slide shows an oil pipeline in China at one of our largest sites near Shengli. Muckermann also has a plastics division – Muckermann Plastics – which makes plastic pipelines for drinking water, waste water and chemicals. Here's an example of a drinking water pipeline near Beijing. Nina will now tell you about some of our other products.
Nina Thanks. As Vincent said, Muckermann Metals doesn't only make pipelines. We also make high-quality stainless-steel products used, for example, for catering. Here's an example of a stainless-steel kitchen worktop at a kindergarten ... and another in a factory canteen. The folder in front of you has further examples of our products. To conclude our presentation this morning, I'd also like to mention some of the other work our company does. We support charities, in particular children's charities, both in Germany and abroad. This slide was taken at a children's home built by us in China. All in all, our company not only manufactures high-quality products for both the domestic and international market and has many customers in Asia and the Far East. It also supports charities and contributes to good causes in the markets that it serves. That was a brief overview of what we do at Muckermann. Now if you'd like to ask any questions, I'd be delighted to answer them.
Visitor Yes, I have a question. Do you also manufacture medical products?
Nina Yes sir, we do indeed. We manufacture equipment for hospitals and hospital operating theatres. The details are in the folder. Is there anything specific you're interested in?
Visitor Just a general question, that's all.
Nina All right. Any more questions? ... No? In that case, we can now go to lunch. Please follow me ...

Track 16: Unit 4, Part A, exercise 2BC

Claudia Good morning ladies and gentlemen. As you know Sharon Jackson from Industrial Solutions and her team have been observing our productions process for the last two weeks and have produced a report, so I'll hand over to Sharon Jackson straight away.
Sharon Thanks, Claudia. Let me begin by saying that this company has great potential. Your order books are full, so the future is rosy. Our problem is the present. You all have our problem-solving tool so let's start with step 1, clarify the problem. In your case, the problem is not that you have a bad product or bad marketing. It's that you can't produce enough goods fast enough. The next step, step 2, is to break down the problem and when we break it down, we see that factory space is being wasted and production is inefficient.
Thomas Can I come in on that please, Claudia?
Claudia Yes, but keep it short please, Thomas.
Thomas As Production Manager of this company for the last ten years, I wish to say that we use all our space. There are no empty spaces anywhere.
Claudia That's true, Thomas but it's how you're using the space that's the problem because you're using it for the wrong things.
Thomas I fail to see how you can say that because ...
Claudia Can we leave the discussion for later, Thomas! This isn't the time for comments. Please go ahead, Sharon.
Sharon Thanks, Claudia. Let's look at your production process. It's highly inefficient. There is no communication between manufacturing, painting and assembly and this leads to stop-and-go production.
Claudia Could you explain what you mean by communication?
Sharon By communication I don't mean talking or having meetings. I mean knowing when to give the next section work and when to wait.
Thomas Are you asking our workers to stop working?
Claudia Please let Sharon finish before you make any more comments, Thomas!
Thomas Asking them to wait indeed ...
Sharon Let's move on to step 3. Step 3 is set a target but set a target that you will achieve. The first goal is to establish communication between the manufacturing, painting and assembly sections, so I suggest we introduce the Japanese kanban system, also called the Toyota name plate system.
Thomas Toyota! They make cars not furniture!
Claudia Please continue, Sharon.
Sharon The kanban system prevents parts from building up at any point and stopping production. Each point requests more work when it is ready. At the moment, your production is using a *push* system, with the result that parts are pushed to work points and they are often flooded. Kanban uses a *pull* system,

meaning that no items are made or moved without a request. Our first target is therefore to introduce the kanban system, which will mean retraining the workers in three sections.

Claudia And the next step?

Sharon The next step, step 5, is to analyse the root cause.

Claudia So the root cause isn't the push-pull problem?

Sharon It's part of it but when you analyse the root cause you see that how you use your factory space is the real problem. You use 50% of your factory space to store things. You should be using it to make things.

Thomas So are you suggesting we store our wood outside in the wind and rain?

Sharon I suggest storing no wood at all. Have it delivered just in time. Store your bulky materials on trucks out on the road on their way to you.

Claudia These ideas are very radical, Sharon but I think we need a radical solution.

Sharon I very much agree, Claudia. Let's move on to step 5, develop countermeasures. Develop countermeasures means tackling the root cause, which is the use of space and in your case it's warehousing. You need to shrink warehousing to next to nothing. Look at your materials and decide which to store on site and which not. Only store smaller items needed for every order. Have the bigger items delivered just in time. If a supplier can't deliver just in time, change the supplier. You can then use the space saved on warehousing to produce more goods. It's win-win.

Claudia This is a job for Production and Human Resources together, I would say.

Sebastian We in HR will do our best to retrain the workforce.

Claudia Excellent! And Production?

Thomas We'll see.

Claudia Once you've developed the countermeasures in step 5, step 6 is to implement them. Here you need to focus on one countermeasure at a time, implement it as soon as possible and then get feedback on it. Communication is very important at this stage and it doesn't matter if you make mistakes. Step 7 is evaluate the results and process. Was it an effective countermeasure or was it just luck? If it was effective, you can move on to step 8, which is standardize success and learn from failures. And remember. This whole process never stops. Your overall goal must be continuous improvement.

Sharon Well, thanks for that, Claudia. You've certainly opened our eyes to a lot of issues. Now if there are any questions or comments ...

Track 17: Unit 4, Part B, exercise 3A

Walker Hello, and welcome to *Technology Trends*. My name's Jack Walker and in this edition, I'll be taking a look at Industry 4.0. Not everybody has noticed but a revolution is taking place. It's the Fourth Industrial Revolution. We've all heard of the first three stages – mechanization, electrification and automation – but what's the best way to describe the fourth stage? Let's ask our studio guest Professor Michael Benson from the University of Cambridge. Professor Benson, how would you describe Industry 4.0?

Benson I would call it cyber-physical, decentralized and intelligent.

Walker Cyber-physical, decentralized and intelligent. Could you help our listeners to understand these terms a little better?

Benson Yes, certainly. We're talking about manufacturing goods in a smart factory. Cyber-physical in manufacturing means that the digital and physical worlds come together. This means that every component has a digital identity and in real terms this is usually an RFID tag.

Walker RFID?

Benson Radio-frequency identification. The tag is about as big as a grain of rice. It identifies the component and lives with it for the rest of its life. And very importantly, it also has instructions about what is to be done with the component.

Walker Instructions? Could you explain that in more detail?

Benson The instructions are needed for decentralized production in a smart factory. Let's think of shoe-manufacturing. With conventional manufacturing we have centralized production, meaning that every stage of production is controlled by a control centre or a central brain that does all the thinking. So, for example, when the leather for the shoes arrives at the factory, the central brain says: "Take it to the assembly line". It then tells the assembly line: "Cut the leather into pieces for size 9 shoes". Next the brain says: "Stick the size 9 leather to the size 9 soles". It then says: "Label the shoes and pack them in size 9 boxes", and so on.

Walker But nowadays all this is already done by computers, isn't it?

Benson Yes, but the instructions still come from a central point or brain. The central brain can be a person, a team or a program, and each stage of production is separate. In a smart factory, on the other hand, there is decentralized production in an intelligent network, meaning that each stage has its own brain. The stages are linked and communicate with each other autonomously without needing instructions from a central brain. So when the leather and other shoe components arrive, they are scanned and the instructions on the RFID tags are carried out automatically. The transport robot scans the RFID tag on the leather, identifies the material, reads the instructions and feeds the leather into the cutting-machine. The cutting-machine cuts it to size and tells the transport robot to take the pieces to the sticking-machine. The sticking-machine sticks the pieces together and tells the labelling-machine to stick on the labels. The labelling-machine tells the packing-machine to get the right boxes and pack the shoes in them, and so on. And I might add that production can be programmed to make any type, colour or size of shoe in any quantity, meaning we have mass customization. So you can see ...

Track 18: Unit 4, Part B, exercise 3C

Walker Hello and welcome back to *Technology Trends*. We've just been hearing from Professor Benson how Industry 4.0 turns a conventional factory into a smart factory, but now we're going to hear about something very different – farming. Professor Benson, can farmers really change their production methods and turn their farms into smart farms?

Benson Well, at first sight it would seem rather difficult but it's not really that hard. Let's look at how a traditional dairy farmer can turn a dairy farm into a smart farm. Let's say the farmer has a cow called Daisy. First of all, Daisy gets a radio-frequency collar with GPS. When Daisy is milked in the morning, the milking-machine scans the collar and knows which cow the milk is from and when and where it was produced. When the milk tank is full, the smart system calls a milk tanker to take the milk to the dairy. When the milk is scanned on the farm, its quality is analysed using big data algorithms. So if, for example, the scan shows that Daisy's milk is low on potassium, an automated feeding system registers this and changes her feed. Big data also tells the system that Daisy has been grazing in a particular field, so using Daisy's GPS, an automated vehicle is sent to the field and adds fertilizer to raise the potassium level of the grass.

Walker This is truly amazing stuff, Professor Benson. But surely Industry 4.0 only affects production, doesn't it? I mean, it can't affect things like education, can it?

Benson Teachers are becoming less and less important nowadays because they can be replaced by smart systems ...

Track 19: Unit 4, Communication, exercise 1B

Manager I'll just give you my email address. It's m dot maffay at hoffmann underscore moebelbau dot de.

Customer Sorry, could you repeat that, please?

Mananger No problem. m dot maffay at hoffmann underscore moebelbau dot de. That's Hoffmann with double-f and double-n. And Möbelbau is spelt m-o-e-b-e-l-b-a-u.

Customer Thank you. Well, my email address is mary hyphen anne hyphen brown at five plus five services dot net. The fives are written as numbers. Oh, and my first name, Mary-Anne – Anne is written with an e.

Manager OK. I'll just read that back to you. Mary hyphen Anne hyphen brown at five plus five services dot net. Mary-Anne with a hyphen, the fives written as numbers and Mary-Anne written with an e at the end of Anne.

Customer Yes. That's correct.

Track 20: KMK Exam practice 2, exercise 1, Hörverstehen

Miller Car Plus Company, Purchasing Department. This is Chris Miller speaking. How can I help you?

Fielding Hello Mr Miller. This is Ellen Fielding of Spiritz Ltd.

Miller Ah, Ms Fielding. Thank you so much for calling back. It's about our opening party. We hope that you can help us with the drinks for the presentation and reception.

Fielding I'm sure we can help you, Mr Miller. What is it exactly that you need?

Miller Well, we're expecting about 1000 guests at our opening party and presentation next month, and we would like to offer a selection of wines and sparkling wine in addition to the usual soft drinks.

Fielding That doesn't sound like a problem. Do you know roughly how much you will need?

Miller: We think we'll need about 300 bottles of sparkling wine and maybe 500 bottles of different wines. But I'm not sure if that is enough, or what kind of wines we should offer. I'm not an expert on wine, I'm afraid.

Fielding That's not a problem. That's what we are here for. Look ... we can send one of our sales reps round to your premises with a selection of wines to have a wine-tasting. She can also answer your questions in detail. Or maybe you and a few colleagues would like to visit us and have a wine-tasting in our wine cellar.

Miller: Oh, that sounds interesting! I think I would prefer the second option. Could someone call my assistant to arrange that?

Fielding Don't worry. I'll see to it. For now we'll email you our catalogue to give you a first impression of our products.

Miller Great, thank you. Oh, I almost forgot the other reason why I needed to talk to you. We would like to offer our VIP guests a special give-away. We thought of something like little champagne bottles with our company logo and a special label. For the opening party on Thursday 3rd, we need 150 bottles, and then for the presentation of the premises two days later another 200. Do you still have the special offer with the additional labels I saw on your website last month?

Fielding: Yes, the special offer is still available. So as soon as I receive the design with your logo and the text for the label, we will order them immediately so that they arrive on time.

Miller: Thank you very much, I appreciate that. Yes, please go ahead and order the bottles, and I'll email you the design later today.

Fielding OK. Is there anything else I can assist you with?

Miller No, that's all for now. I look forward to the wine-tasting. Thank you for your help.

Fielding It's my pleasure. Goodbye and have a nice day.

Miller Goodbye.

Track 21: Unit 5, Part A, exercise 2

Ben Good morning everyone and welcome to today's meeting to discuss how to market our new line. I'm Ben Kaiser, the Managing Director of Textil-Manufaktur Mahler, and I'm delighted to welcome Mary Garcia from P&Q Marketing. Mary's put a lot of thought into this project and today she's going to outline her strategy. Over to you, Mary!

Mary Thanks Ben, and good morning to you all. I think you have a great new line! Now some of you may already know about the approach I'm going to use to get the right marketing mix for this line. It's called the four Ps. It's a well-established marketing strategy, and I'm going to outline how to use it.
The first of the four Ps is the product itself: What is the exact nature of the product? We have taken a very close look at your line, and I can see that your products are all about sustainability because that's what socially-responsible consumers expect nowadays. In your case, the bottom line here is not just profits. Your product has a *triple* bottom line – people, planet *and* profits! The *people* – these are the consumers – need to know how they are helping the *planet* and understand that your company also needs to make a *profit*. No tricks. Everything must be out in the open from beginning to end, and that's why I have a very special name for this line. I want to call it the *Honesty* line. What do you think?

Ben The *Honesty* line! That's a great idea, Mary! I really like it and I'm sure we all agree that that's what this company is all about.

Voice 1 Yes, I agree!
Voice 2 Good idea!
Voice 3 Exactly!
Mary I'm glad you all like it. Now the second P stands for promotion. This means *how* we tell the consumer about the line, so what I'm basically talking about is branding and advertising. Advertising is changing fast, and we're less interested in the traditional mass media for these new products. They need to be promoted through social media and internet search engines like Google and YouTube, but this is such a big field that I want to deal with this separately. Is that all right, Ben?
Ben Fine by me, Mary.
Mary Great! So let's move on to the third of our four Ps – place. By place we mean where and how the line will be sold, so what we're talking about is distribution. The question is what does the consumer have to do to get an article of clothing from this new line? Let's all think for a moment. How do you all buy your clothes? Think of the last thing you bought and how you bought it. Who'd like to start? ... Yes?
Markus My name's Markus Koch and I'm pretty lazy, so I get most of my clothes online.
Mary Online ... How about the rest of you?
Ben Well, I'm old-fashioned because I get mine from a shop.
Mary Well, I have news for both of you. You're neither lazy nor old-fashioned because you represent today's two big sales channels – online sales and bricks and mortar outlets.
Markus I'm sorry but I'm not sure what bricks and mortar means.
Mary No problem, Markus. It means a real shop, not a virtual, online shop. We call this the stationary trade.
Markus Thanks.
Mary You're welcome, Markus. Now let's move on to the last of the four Ps. The price ... and we're talking here about the recommended retail price. For this we need to look at the consumers. What sort of people are they and, above all, how much are they prepared to pay for this sort of product? Let's start with the *Honesty* jacket. We know it costs about 25 euros to make this jacket, but do we want the price to be as low as possible, let's say under 100 euros? Or can we go for a higher price? I'm thinking of 200 euros plus. Or is it somewhere in between – at about the 150 euro mark? I want you to talk to each other about the price now and then we can discuss it as a group ...

Track 22: Unit 5, Part B, exercise 2A/B

Jenny Hi, this is Jenny Andrews reporting today from Germany on a very unusual event. ... It's rush hour here at Dusseldorf Central Station, and I'm standing outside a pop-up shop with a long queue of people loaded up with plastic bottles. Let's talk to Ben Kaiser, the managing director of Textil-Manufaktur Mahler, to find out what's happening. What's going on, Ben?
Ben Well, there's a lot going on today because my company wants to do something about the huge problem of plastic water bottle pollution in the oceans. 20,000 bottles are bought all over the world every *second*, and last year billions of bottles were thrown away and ended up in the oceans. That's why each of our new *Honesty* jackets is made from 25 recycled plastic bottles.
Jenny A jacket made from recycled plastic bottles! That's a great idea, but why are the people all *carrying* empty plastic bottles themselves?
Ben That's because today is Day 1 of our *Save the Oceans* campaign and just for today, we're asking people to pay for the jacket not with cash but with plastic bottles, which we will recycle for them. The regular price is 150 euros but today it's 25 plastic bottles because that's how many are recycled in one jacket. We're not taking cash today, just bottles, so to all the people listening to this programme, come to the station with 25 plastic bottles, get an *Honesty* jacket and help save the oceans.
Jenny And if they can't make it to the station today?
Ben Our *Honesty* jackets will be on sale in sports shops and online via our mobile phone app and website as from next week, but for 150 euros not 25 bottles.
Jenny That's good to know, Ben, but let's just talk to one of the customers waiting in the queue. Excuse me, madam. I'm from the BBC. May I ask you a question?
woman Sure, go ahead.
Jenny Would you have recycled those 25 plastic bottles if you hadn't heard about this event?
woman Yes, I would have taken them to the recycling centre, but I know a lot of people who wouldn't.
Jenny Thanks ... Just a moment, Ben. Something's happening outside the shop!
Ben Yes, Germany's number 1 surfer, Timo von Struck, has just arrived. He's here with his new surfboard made entirely out of recycled plastic bottles and he's going to paddle down the Rhine and collect plastic litter all the way.
Jenny Wow! All the way down the Rhine on a surfboard! That's a long way!
Ben Yes, it's twelve hundred kilometres and he plans to do it in 28 days.
Jenny Can we get Timo over here, Ben? I'm sure our listeners would love to hear what he has to say about his trip.
Ben Yes, he's just finished his TV interview. Timo! Come over here for a moment, please! Here he comes ...
Jenny Great to have you here today, Timo! Everybody knows you as Germany's top surfer, but today you're here for a very different reason.
Timo Yes, I'm here to help stop the destruction of our oceans and waterways. I hope my trip down the Rhine will make people think again before they throw away a plastic bottle, and I'd also like to say that my trip wouldn't have been possible if Textil-Manufaktur Mahler hadn't offered to sponsor me and my team. We also hope that other surfers will join me along the way and help clean up the Rhine. This is going to be a big event and we need all the help we can get!
Jenny So if you hadn't had a sponsor, you couldn't have done it.
Timo Exactly.
Jenny Sounds like a great idea. Is there anything else you'd like to say to our listeners, Ben?
Ben Yes, I want to thank Timo von Struck for his support. If he hadn't been prepared to help, we wouldn't have recycled so many bottles today. You'll soon be able to watch Timo's progress down the Rhine on his YouTube vlog, which we're also sponsoring. He'll be giving you a day-by-day update, so you won't miss a thing and remember: recycle your plastic, cheer Timo on when he paddles past, and wear an *Honesty* jacket!

Track 23: Unit 5, Communication, exercise 2A

I'd like to move on now to this table. As you can see, this company's sales in the UK were at 10.3 million euros in the first quarter of the financial year and, in the second quarter, sales rose rapidly to 11.4 million euros. However, when we look at the third quarter, we can see that sales dropped drastically to 8.2 million euros. By the end of the year, things had recovered and sales rose to 10.3 million euros, reaching the same volume of sales as in the first quarter. Now, you can see at a glance that sales figures for Germany over the same period were much lower. We start off with ...

Track 24: Unit 6, Foundation, exercise 2

Penny I've made a list of all the things we have to do for the meeting next month. Shall we just go through it point by point to make sure I haven't forgotten anything?

Niklas Yes, that's a good idea. So what do we need to do before the meeting?

Penny My first point is to check the number of participants, so we know which room to reserve.

Niklas I checked with the CEO's PA and the number is still six, so we don't need a big room.

Penny In that case, they can use the small conference room. How about equipment in the room?

Niklas The CEO wants to give a presentation, so she'll need the data projector and perhaps a flipchart.

Penny OK, so the second point is to reserve the room and equipment.

Niklas And order refreshments. What do you think they'll want?

Penny I'm sure the Bolivians drink coffee, but I think we should also have tea and soft drinks.

Niklas So point three is to order refreshments. Can't we do that on the day?

Penny I think it's better to order them well in advance.

Niklas Yes, OK, that's safer. What's next on your list?

Penny Point four is to send out invitations to the participants by email.

Niklas Any attachments?

Penny Yes, they'll need the agenda and the documents they're going to discuss at the meeting.

Niklas So that's send invitations, agenda and documents. Anything else we should do before the day of the meeting?

Penny We'll need to make hard copies of the agenda, the minutes of the last meeting and the documents needed at the meeting a few days earlier.

Niklas Yes, we certainly can't leave that until the day of the meeting, even though it's at 9.30 a.m.

Penny So point five is to make hard copies of the agenda, minutes and documents.

Niklas Anything else before the meeting?

Penny Yes, name tags. We need to make a name tag for each participant well in advance.

Niklas So name tags are point six. How many points have you got, Penny?

Penny Twelve. We're halfway down my list.

Niklas I see. So let's have the next point.

Penny The next points are things to do on the day of the meeting. We have to check the room that day to make sure it's ready.

Niklas So what do we need to check?

Penny As it'll be January, we'll need to check the heating and also make sure that there are enough chairs. People sometimes take a chair and don't put it back.

Niklas Ah yes, of course. So point seven is to check the room, heating and chairs. How about directions to the room. Will they all be able to find it?

Penny I expect so, but if anyone arrives late or in a hurry we should remind reception to display the meeting on the info screen at the entrance to the building. They'll then see the name of the meeting, the time and the room.

Niklas Yes, good idea. So that was point eight, display the meeting on the info screen at the entrance. Point nine?

Penny Point nine is extremely important. We have to lay each place in the conference room with everything the participants need.

Niklas Meaning copies of the agenda and the documents to be discussed?

Penny Yes, but not only that. Each participant will also need writing materials and a cup and saucer for tea or coffee, and a glass for soft drinks.

Niklas So point nine is ... agenda, documents, writing materials, cup, saucer, glass. Right. I've got that. So what are the last three points?

Penny There are two more on the day of the meeting. Provide refreshments in the conference room and put out the name tags on a table by the door for people to pick up as they come in.

Niklas So ten is refreshments and eleven is name tags. After the meeting?

Penny I only have one point, and that is to circulate the minutes of the meeting to all the participants and any absentees.

Niklas So circulate minutes to participants and absentees is point twelve. Great! Let's get started ...

Track 25: Unit 6, Foundation, exercise 3

Mary ... Now, I've drafted the agenda for the meeting with the two representatives from Grano de Cacao next month and I'd like you to send it out to everyone by email with some other documents when we've finished this discussion.

Niklas Yes, fine.

Mary We're starting the meeting at 9.30. The CEO will be chairing it, so she'll welcome everyone and then go over the minutes of the last meeting and answer any questions.

Niklas And how long will that take?

Mary I think half an hour should be enough, so ten o'clock should be a good time for opening negotiations. I've planned two hours for that, so that'll be from 10 to 12. Have you reserved the small conference room?

Niklas Yes, it's reserved and we've also ordered refreshments and a data projector for the CEO's presentation.

Mary Excellent. Then Helen Clark is going to take everyone on a tour of the warehouse. She's aiming to finish at 12.30 so I've planned lunch from 12.45 to a quarter to two.

Niklas In that case, I'll tell the canteen to reserve a table for six.

Mary Yes, good idea. Now people will want to freshen up after lunch, so the second part of the meeting is scheduled for 2 o'clock. The CEO aims to finalize negotiations and sign the contract at around half-past four, and then there will be the usual things – any other business and the date of the next meeting.

Niklas So the meeting should be over by 5 p.m., right?

Mary Yes, I would say five. Here are the documents I'd like you to send out with the agenda and also copy for each participant on the day.
Niklas Thanks.
Mary Anything we've forgotten?
Niklas No, I think we have everything now.
Mary Good. So you can get started, and please let me know if there's anything else you need.
Niklas We will, thanks …

Track 26: Unit 6, Part A, exercise 2

Sarah Good morning everybody and welcome to today's meeting. I'm Sarah Bonrath, the Export Sales Director at B2B here in Germany, and since we don't all know each other, the first item on today's agenda is our new agent in Singapore. Would you like to introduce yourself, Wen Fang?
Wen Fang Sure. I'm Wen Fang from Singapore Trading. I came on board six weeks ago, so I'm the new girl.
Sarah Thanks for that, Wen Fang. Would the others like to introduce themselves to Wen Fang? Donald, would you go first, please?
Donald Hi. I'm Donald Masters at UK Wholesale Trading in London. I've been acting as an agent for B2B for about three years.
Sarah Thanks, Donald. Rajiv?
Rajiv Good morning. My name is Rajiv Mittal. My company is called India Trading Services Private Limited and I have had the pleasure of acting on behalf of B2B for ten years now.
Sarah Many thanks, Rajiv. Our next topic is Rajiv's presentation, so would you go ahead please, Rajiv?
Rajiv Certainly, Sarah. My presentation is called "Beer in Mumbai" …
…
Rajiv … To conclude, I would say the figures are very positive.
Sarah Many thanks, Rajiv. Would anyone like to comment or ask a question?
Donald I'd just like to say that Rajiv's done a great job!
Sarah Yes, I agree. Well done, Rajiv! Let's move on to the next topic, which is our current order situation. Can you all give us a brief update? Donald?
Donald As you can see from this graph, my orders are up 10% on last year.
Sarah Wen Fang?
Wen Fang It's too early to say much, but they're rising.
Sarah Rajiv?
Rajiv My orders are up 5% on last year.
Sarah Thanks, Rajiv. Let's move on to the next topic, which is deliveries. How are things going here? Are there any issues?
Donald Deliveries are now punctual 95% of the time, which is better than last year when only 85% of deliveries were punctual.
Sarah That's good to hear! Anything else on deliveries? No? In that case, the next point is complaints. Are there any complaints?
Wen Fang Well, it's only a small thing but could I just say that some of the equipment is arriving dirty.
Sarah Dirty! Well, we can't have that. Any idea why, Wen Fang?
Wen Fang I think it's poor packing, and I think it makes a bad impression when the equipment arrives dirty.
Donald Can I come in on that, Sarah?
Sarah Go ahead, Donald.
Donald I thoroughly agree with Wen Fang. We can't deliver dirty equipment. It's bad for our image.
Sarah Yes, I agree. I'll pass that on to our Logistics department. Any other complaints? No? All right, so we've covered point number 4, delivery, and point number 5, complaints, and we've decided to postpone the topic of installing and operating equipment, so we've covered all five items on today's agenda. Let's wrap up the meeting with AOB, shall we? I just have the one final point here from Rajiv – travel expenses. I've checked with Finance and they'll get back to you next week, Rajiv. Is that all right?
Rajiv That's fine, Sarah.
Sarah Well, that would seem to be it. You'll be getting the minutes by email tomorrow. Many thanks for coming to the meeting …

Track 27: Unit 6, Part B, exercise 1B/C

Wenzel Good morning, Mr Popescu. Please take a seat.
Popescu Good morning, Ms Wenzel. I'm very pleased to be here. Munich is such a beautiful city and the weather is so good today!
Wenzel Let's get down to business, shall we, Mr Popescu? I wrote in my email that we are reviewing all contracts because of the stiff competition in the denim market, so are you prepared to reduce your prices?
Popescu Well, it's not so easy at the moment.
Wenzel I need a straight answer, Mr Popescu.
Popescu I think we can … a little.
Wenzel We need a 10% reduction. Can you reduce your prices by 10%?
Popescu 10%! That's a big reduction for a small company like mine. Can I think about it?
Wenzel I have a lot of meetings today, Mr Popescu, and I also want to talk about quantity and delivery. The market for low-priced denim is expanding fast, so we need to increase our sales by 20%. Will your company be able to increase production by 20%?
Popescu 20% is a lot. We would need more machines and more workers …
Wenzel And we also need guaranteed delivery within 30 days. Too many shipments have been late. Will you give us a guaranteed delivery period of 30 days?
Popescu The freight forwarder we are using has old lorries that break down a lot …
Wenzel Do you accept these terms, Mr Popescu? I need an answer now and the next supplier is waiting.
Popescu This is very hard for me, Ms Wenzel, very hard …

Track 28: Unit 6, Part B, exercise 2A

Wenzel Good morning, Mr Popescu. How nice to see you again! I hope you're well.
Popescu Good morning, Ms Wenzel. I'm very well thank you and I hope you are, too.
Wenzel Yes, I'm fine thanks. Did you have a good trip?
Popescu Yes, thank you. I flew straight here from Bucharest yesterday.

Wenzel	Excellent! Now, let's take a look at our business arrangements, shall we? We need to review a few points.
Popescu	Yes, fine.
Wenzel	As I said in my email, competition is very stiff and our competitors are 10% cheaper than us. Do you see what I mean?
Popescu	Yes, I understand. A 10% reduction … just let me think for a moment …
Wenzel	Please take your time, Mr Popescu, and I have something for you because we are thinking of ordering 20% more from your company.
Popescu	20% more! That's great, but I would need more workers and machines, and I can't afford new machines.
Wenzel	We can help you with that, Mr Popescu. We can provide you with more machines if you can find more workers.
Popescu	Well, I can certainly find the workers.
Wenzel	And we need to talk about the delivery period, as well.
Popescu	The delivery period? Is 30 days too long?
Wenzel	30 days is fine, but it's sometimes a week longer and that is a problem for us. We need a *maximum* delivery period of 30 days.
Popescu	I understand, but the problem is the freight forwarder. His lorries break down a lot.
Wenzel	And I have the name of another company for you, Mr Popescu. I suggest that you use Road Train GmbH. Here's their card.
Popescu	Thank you!
Wenzel	Would you like some time to think about the new terms? Shall we take a break for coffee?
Popescu	Yes, fine.
…	
Wenzel	Have you had enough time to think about the new terms?
Popescu	Yes, and we are happy to accept them. I've phoned my boss and we can reduce the price by 5% as from next month and 10% as soon as we get the new machines. I've also phoned Road Train and they can start working for us next month.
Wenzel	That's good news, Mr Popescu! Now let's …

Track 29: Unit 6, Communication, exercise 2

Paul	Guten Morgen. Top Mode GmbH, Paul Schmidt am Apparat
Mary	Good morning. This is Mary Doyle calling from Dublin. I'd like to speak to Paul Schmidt, please.
Paul	Good morning, Ms Doyle. Paul Schmidt speaking. How can I help you?
Mary	Oh, hello, Mr Schmidt. I'm sorry to call at such short notice, but I'm afraid I have to reschedule our meeting on Thursday morning. I'm sorry, but something has come up and, unfortunately, I can't get out of it.
Paul	Oh. That's a pity. Do you have another time in mind?
Mary	Well, could we postpone the meeting until Friday at the same time? Would that suit you?
Paul	Hmm. I'll just check my diary … . Yes. That would be fine.
Mary	Oh. Thank you so much. I apologize for the trouble.
Paul	Don't worry. These things happen. OK, then. I'm looking forward to meeting you on Friday the twenty-seventh at 9.30.
Mary	Thank you. I look forward to meeting you, too. Bye.

Track 30: KMK exam practice 3, exercise 3, Hörverstehen

Mr Warden	OK, thanks for coming along this morning. Erm … as I said in my email of 4 September, the purpose of the meeting this morning is for us to brainstorm some ideas. We're looking for promotional activities, basically, that we can use to make sure that the launch of BeFair Ltd is a success right from the start. I'm very open to any ideas … and we've got no limitation in our budget … at the moment, anyway … so fire away!
Stephanie	Fantastic, no budget constraints!
Claudine	That's great! I'm thinking television … and radio!
Stephanie	Well, that really sounds big and exciting.
Mr Warden	Go ahead, Claudine.
Claudine	Well, if we have no limitation on the budget, we could reach a wide audience with something like that, and we could focus on some of the big business network television channels. If we want to reach a global market, I mean, if that's what we're aiming at …
Stephanie	Yeah, TV and radio have been quite successful for some of our other projects, haven't they?
Mr Warden	That's right, it is definitely a focused way of advertising. But is it too focused and therefore a bit limited?
Stephanie	Well, I've been working on some cheaper solutions, just in case there are budget problems. I thought we could do some effective online promotion, which is actually quite cheap. We should definitely do direct mailing, but we should also register the site effectively with the big search engines. That way, anybody who surfs the net looking for business solutions comes up with our website.
Mr Warden	Well, yes, we should definitely do some of that.
Claudine	What about press advertising? Traditional news-papers, business magazines, journals?
Mr Warden	Yes, good idea. We've done that effectively in the past. We've had some good response rates to the ads we've placed before.
Claudine	Yes, and that would be something we could do more often, not just once, but in a kind of campaign, over a period of time.
Stephanie	And then, going back to cheaper solutions, we could use the database we've got, you know, all the market research we've been doing for this website. We've got some very good contacts from that. I think we could send out glossy brochures, maybe a demonstration CD …
Mr Warden	That sounds like a good idea. What do you think …

Track 31: Unit 7, Foundation, exercise 2A

1: Row stands
Row stands open onto the aisle. They have two neighbouring stands, one on each side. The benefit of row stands is that visitors walk past each stand as they go along the aisle. These are the cheapest stands to rent.

2: Corner stands
Corner stands are located at the end of a row and open onto two aisles which meet at the corner. These two aisles lead more visitors to this type of stand. Rental fees for a corner stand are higher than

for a row stand.

3: End of block stands
End of block stands open onto three aisles. This openness makes this stand appear more welcoming than a row stand or a corner stand. End of block stands are more expensive than corner stands.

4: Island stands
Island stands are surrounded by aisles on all sides. The fact that they stand alone makes them very welcoming to visitors. These are the most expensive type of stand.

5: Outdoor stands
These stands are outside the exhibition hall. They are best for showing very large products like construction equipment. The rent for outdoor stands varies, depending on the product being shown.

Track 32: Unit 7, Part A, exercise 2

Dermot Good morning and thank you for calling Booth-Tech. You're through to Dermot. How can I help?
Lena Good morning, it's Lena Richter from Ökobau Müller in Germany. I'm calling about a stand for the Architecture and Building Expo in Dublin next year.
Dermot And we'll be delighted to help you! Let me take down some details about what you need. First of all, what is the purpose of your stand? Is your company launching a new product, for example?
Lena Well, no actually. We make eco-friendly house-building materials and we want to show our products to architects from all over Europe at the exhibition.
Dermot So your purpose is brand awareness.
Lena Yes, brand awareness. That sounds right.
Dermot And what size should the stand be?
Lena We want to show samples of our products – building materials for walls, floors, roofs and so on.
Dermot Walls, floors and roofs ... In that case, I would suggest having a larger stand, so you have enough room for all your products. I would say about ten by five metres,
Lena Yes, that sounds about right and it also needs to be high.
Dermot We can go up to four metres.
Lena Four metres should be enough.
Dermot So that's ten by five and four metres high. Now what features should it have?
Lena Well, we'd like a counter at the front and a big screen for video loops.
Dermot Counter and screen ... And how about seating? Tables and chairs, or bar tables and stools?
Lena Just let me think ... I think a table, or perhaps even two tables, with three or four chairs each would be best.
Dermot So let's say two tables and chairs ... And I would also recommend having some literature racks for your sales literature.
Lena Yes, that's a good idea. I think we'll need two literature racks for brochures and so on.
Dermot OK, fine. Anything else on the stand?
Lena We'd like some storage space.
Dermot Shall we include a lockable cupboard? I would strongly recommend including one, so you can store your valuables.
Lena Ah yes, that's a good idea.
Dermot And how is the space on the stand to be divided up? How much space will you need for your building materials?
Lena ... I'd say about twenty-five square metres.
Dermot So that means 50% of the space will be for building materials in the product demonstration area. Now what about the other 25 square metres? How do you want to divide it up?
Lena Well, we'll need some space for the tables and chairs and some in front of the screen, and then there's the counter ...
Dermot OK, I suggest that you split the other 25 square metres 50/50, and say half for the tables and chairs and the other half for the rest, the rest being the counter, the screen and the lockable cupboard. All right?
Lena Sounds good.
Dermot And how often do you want to use the stand?
Lena Well, we're also going to exhibit in the UK and Scandinavia after the trade fair in Dublin ... so if we can re-use the stand, that would be great.
Dermot So it's for multiple use. And have you thought about whether you want the stand to be one of a row of stands with access from the front only or do you want it to stand alone with access from all sides?
Lena I think access from all sides would be better.
Dermot In that case I would recommend that you have an island stand because that gives you access from all sides.
Lena Yes, I think that would be best.
Dermot OK, I've got that. Now what type of stand would suit you best – modular, shell scheme or bespoke?
Lena Well, as our products are building materials, we like the idea of a shell scheme stand because it can be made to look like the framework of a house.
Dermot Yes, that makes good sense, Lena. We always recommend using a shell scheme stand if you're exhibiting at different locations. Can I just have your details, so I can send you an offer?
Lena Yes, it's Ökobau Müller ... that's spelt ...

Track 33: Unit 7, Part B, exercise 2A

Dialogue 1: Japanese businessman
Alina Good morning, Mr Nakashima, and welcome back to our booth. I hope you are enjoying your visit to London.
Visitor 1 Good morning, Ms Adler. Yes, I love the culture in London and there is a lot to do here.
Alina Yes, I agree. Everybody finds something interesting to do in London. Would you like something to drink? A cup of coffee or tea or a mineral water?
Visitor 1 Mineral water, please.
Alina Still or sparkling?
Visitor 1 Still, please.
Alina Here you are.
Visitor 1 Thank you.
Alina You were interested in seeing the technical drawings of the adjustable table you looked at yesterday. Would you like to look at them now?
Visitor 1 Yes, please.
Alina Here you are.
Visitor 1 Thank you.
...
Visitor 1 Are the legs made of metal or wood?
Alina They're made of wood.
Visitor 1 Thank you. Can the length of the table be adjusted?
Alina Yes, it can be between 120 and 220 centimetres and the height is adjustable, too, so it can be a coffee or dining-room table. Would you like me to send you an offer

for this table, Mr Nakashima? It's one of our best-selling lines.

Visitor 1 Perhaps later, Ms Adler.

Alina No problem at all, Mr Nakashima. Would you like to call by again tomorrow? It's the last day of the fair, but we'll still have some time to talk and if you place your order before the end of the month, you'll get a 20% discount.

Visitor 1 Yes, we can think about that and perhaps talk again. I need to talk to my colleagues.

Alina Yes, of course, Mr Nakashima. Thank you for …

Dialogue 2: Italian businessman

Alina Good morning, Mr Lombardi. It's nice to see you again.

Visitor 2 Good morning, Ms Adler. I'm very pleased to be back, and the weather is very good for London at this time of year, don't you think?

Alina Yes, indeed. I was expecting rain but it's a beautiful sunny day again.

Visitor 2 And we both have a lot of work to do before we can go outside and enjoy London. Have you been to the new Botticelli exhibition at the Tate Gallery?

Alina Yes, I went last weekend and I really enjoyed it.

Visitor 2 So did I. Each time I see his work I discover something new.

Alina Exactly. Would you like something to drink? Tea, coffee or water perhaps?

Visitor 2 No, thanks. I'm fine.

Alina Would you like me to demonstrate the adjustable table for you now, Mr Lombardi?

Visitor 2 Well, as it's almost midday, I thought we could first have lunch somewhere quieter and talk about our two companies and also get to know each other a little better before we do business. Do you have a lunch appointment?

Alina No, not today.

Visitor 2 Good because there's a very nice little restaurant just a few minutes from here.

Alina That's a nice idea, Mr Lombardi. But I have to be back by …

Visitor 2 Excuse me, Ms Adler. Pronto! … Arrivederci. That was my boss on the phone. He wants me to report back about the trade fair this evening and he also wants to know about your company before he places an order, so shall we go for lunch now before the restaurant gets very full?

Alina Yes, let's do that.

Visitor 2 Benissimo!

Dialogue 3: American businesswoman

Alina Good afternoon, Ms Parker. It's nice to see you again.

Visitor 3 Yes, I'm glad I was able to make it back. I have so much to do at the moment.

Alina Yes, I understand. Would you like something to drink? Coffee, tea or water perhaps?

Visitor 3 Thanks, but I really don't have much time right now. Let's talk about that adjustable table, shall we? The one right here in front of us. You gave me a brochure about it.

Alina Yes, that's right. Shall I demonstrate it to you?

Visitor 3 No, thanks. I've seen what I need to know. Look, I want to make you an offer for that table right now.

Alina Well … yes, if you have all the information you need.

Visitor 3 I do and if you can supply it for … Excuse me while I switch off my cell. Sorry about that.

Alina No problem.

Visitor 3 Well, as I was saying, if you can supply these tables for €200 per unit, you have a deal. Now, as I was saying …

Track 34: Unit 7, Communication, exercise 1

Katy British Airways Booking Service. Katy Atkins speaking. How can I help you?

Maria Good morning, Katy. This is Maria Weber in Berlin.

Katy Hi, Maria. Lovely to hear you. I haven't heard from you for ages. How are things in Berlin?

Maria They're fine, Katy. And how are you?

Katy Everything's just great, Maria. Still working for British Airways … So, what can I do for you today?

Maria Well, I'm going to a conference in London, so I need two return flights, please. I'd like direct flights from Berlin to London on Thursday, April 19th, returning to Berlin on Monday, April 23rd.

Katy OK. Just a minute … Berlin to London, Thursday, April 19th, returning to Berlin on Monday, April 23rd. Business class or economy?

Maria I'm travelling with my assistant, so economy class, please.

Katy Right. What time do you want to leave Berlin?

Maria Sometime around nine in the morning would be good.

Katy I have a departure from Berlin, Tegel at 8.55 a.m., arriving in London, Heathrow at 9.50 a.m. That's BA flight 995. There are a few seats available in economy class on that flight. Only aisle seats left, I'm afraid; but I have two aisle seats in the same row, so you can talk across the aisle, if you want.

Maria I suppose that's OK. What about the return flight? That should be sometime in the late afternoon.

Katy Monday, 23rd, late afternoon. That looks more difficult. All the direct flights are booked till the early evening. Hang on, though … Here's flight BA 320. It's a direct flight, departure from London Heathrow at 19.40, arrival in Berlin at 22.35. Would that be OK? I have two seats next to each other, one of them is a window seat.

Maria Hmm. Listen. Can you reserve those seats on both flights for me, please? I'd like to check with my assistant if the later flight is OK with her.

Katy Of course. Just a moment, please … There you go. They're reserved till tomorrow at this time.

Maria Thanks, Katy. I'll get my assistant to call and confirm. Listen. When are you coming over to Berlin again?

Track 35: Unit 7, Communication, exercise 3A

1

Receptionist Good morning. Welcome to the International Hotel.

Guest 1 Good morning. My name is Rossi – Giovanni Rossi. I have a reservation.

Receptionist Here we are. Giovanni Rossi.

Guest 1 Yes. From Rossi Technology, Rome.

Receptionist Thank you. You're in room 303, on the third floor.

Guest 1 What time is breakfast served?

Receptionist We serve a buffet breakfast in the dining room between 8 and 10 a.m.

Guest 1 Eight till 10? Can I have a swim before breakfast?

Receptionist Yes, of course. The swimming pool is open from 6 a.m. till 10 p.m.

Guest 1 That's great. Thank you.

Receptionist You're welcome. Enjoy your stay, Mr Rossi.

2

Receptionist Good morning. Welcome to the International Hotel.

Guest 2 Good morning. I have a reservation under McGregor, McGregorRobotics.

Receptionist	Mary McGregor, from Glasgow.
Guest 2	Yes. That's right. I booked a room on the ground floor, with wheelchair access.
Receptionist	Yes, that's correct. You're in room 15, on this floor.
Guest 2	Does the dining room have wheelchair access?
Receptionist	Yes, it does. All of our rooms and facilities have wheelchair access.
Guest 2	Good. Thank you.
Receptionist	Let me know if you need any extra towels or pillows.
Guest 2	That's very kind of you.
Receptionist	My pleasure. Have a good stay, Ms McGregor.

3

Receptionist	Good morning. Welcome to the International Hotel.
Guest 3	Thank you. I would like to check in.
Receptionist	Of course. What name is the reservation under?
Guest 3	My name is Yusuf Zuabi.
Receptionist	Could you spell your surname, please?
Guest 3	Yes. It's Z U A B I, "Zuabi", with a Z. The reservation may be under the name of my company, Tech Solutions.
Receptionist	Thank you. Ah, yes, here it is, Tech Solutions, Berlin, Mr Yusuf Zuabi. You're in room 201, on the second floor. Here's your key. The buffet breakfast is served in the dining room between 8 and 10 a.m.
Guest 3	Thank you. I have a question. Where can I park my car?
Receptionist	There's a secure car park at the back of the hotel. The man at the gate will let you in.
Guest 3	Good. Thank you.
Receptionist	No problem. Enjoy your stay.

Track 36: Unit 8, Foundation, exercise 2B

Hello everybody, and welcome to today's *Business Matters* podcast. Today, I'm going to talk about what to look for in a supplier. We're all looking for a good deal, but the lowest price is not always the best value for money. Don't jump at an offer just because the price is inviting. Remember the saying, "You get what you pay for". Keeping this in mind, you should always check the whole package before you make a decision about a supplier. Here are five important things to take into consideration.

Firstly, the quality of the goods you buy needs to be consistent. Your customers will associate poor quality with you, not your suppliers, so it's important to find out if a new supplier can consistently provide high-quality goods. One way to judge this is to ask them how long they have been working with their other clients. It's a good sign if they have long-standing relationships with other buyers. References from other clients might be useful. Ask friends and business acquaintances. You're more likely to get an honest assessment of the strengths and weaknesses of a prospective supplier from someone who has used its services. Be careful with anonymous recommendations on the internet.

You should also take warranties into account. The most common warranty deals with the product being free from defects when it leaves a supplier. Usually, these are limited warranties, and a buyer has to make a claim within a specific time. Look into warranties very carefully before you finally decide on a supplier and make sure that they suit you.

Next, you should look at terms and conditions. It's important that you know your Incoterms. How are the responsibilities and obligations for the transport of the goods shared? Make sure that you are happy with the conditions a supplier is offering before you decide to go into business with them. You should also consider the terms of payment carefully. The best option for you would be open account terms, but a new supplier might ask for payment in advance until your relationship is established.

Last but not least, it's especially important to find out about the solvency of the supplier you're considering. If you don't do this, you might put your business at risk. Financial stability is important, especially if you are entering into a long-term contract or if the vendor is the only source of a particular item you need for your business. Search the internet for a company that will do a credit check for you before you make your final choice.

Well, I hope these ideas will help you when you are choosing a new supplier. Our next topic on *Business Matters* is ...

Track 37: Unit 8, Part A, exercise 3

Sauerwald	Cantec GmbH, Dirk Sauerwald am Apparat. Was kann ich für Sie tun?
Booysen	Good morning, Mr Sauerwald. It's Luke Booysen from AgriTrade on the line. How are things?
Sauerwald	I can't complain ... and how about you?
Booysen	It's another sunny day here in South Africa, so we can't complain, either.
Sauerwald	That's good to hear, Mr Booysen. How can I help you?
Booysen	The reason I'm calling is to ask a few questions about your company's initial proposal. Do you have a few moments?
Sauerwald	I most certainly do. What would you like to know?
Booysen	There are only a few points, so it won't take long. Let's start with the delivery period. How soon can you deliver?
Sauerwald	Well, after you have accepted our offer it normally takes about seven months.
Booysen	I see. Is there any chance of earlier delivery? Could you do three months?
Sauerwald	Well, that would be very difficult for us, Mr Booysen. We already have a number of orders. We can probably deliver in six months instead of seven, but I'm afraid we can't do three months. Sorry.
Booysen	All right, I've made a note of that. The next point is training. According to your proposal, you'll train our staff to operate the production line. Would that be here in South Africa?
Sauerwald	No, it's here in Germany. Your staff will be invited to our factory here in Essen, where your CAN-O-MAT production line will be up and running. We will then train them how to operate and maintain it, and we'll also show them how to troubleshoot if there are any problems.
Booysen	Very good. Now I see that the whole production line costs eight hundred thousand euros, but does this price include delivery to the port of Cape Town? That would be ideal for us because we are only 60 kilometres away.
Sauerwald	Delivery from Germany to the port of Cape Town would be CIF or CFR Cape Town and that would be a lot more expensive for you. Our price is an FOB price, meaning in this case that we will deliver the goods to a European North Sea port. The nearest ports to us are Rotterdam or Hamburg.
Booysen	So that means that we're responsible for shipping from Europe to South Africa. I see ... Will you be able to assist us with finding a suitable shipping company?

Sauerwald We most certainly will, Mr Booysen. And the good news is that our price includes seaworthy packing to make sure the goods arrive in Cape Town in perfect condition.

Booysen Great! Now what about payment? How much do you need in advance, 30%?

Sauerwald Well, 33% in fact, which is usual in this sector.

Booysen I see. And when would you require us to pay the remainder?

Sauerwald When the goods are shipped. We'll let you have all the details in our official offer. Anything else I can do for you?

Booysen Yes, I'd like to know a little more about after-sales service, but that's my last point. What does your after-sales service include?

Sauerwald Well, it includes spare parts, of course, but we also store details of all the machinery we supply on a database, so if there's a problem, we first try to diagnose it remotely. We then know what spare parts to send you or what to repair.

Booysen That's an excellent service, but what if remote diagnosis doesn't find the fault? Do you have a local representative or agent in South Africa?

Sauerwald No, not yet, but if remote diagnosis doesn't work, we send over a technician from Germany and any parts needed are delivered by express.

Booysen Good. I think I have all the information I need now. When can I expect your offer?

Track 38: Unit 8, Part B, exercise 2

1: Electricity generators

Majlen Hej, Energi AB, Majlen Lofquist.

Sven Hej, Sven Maier. Forstar du engelska?

Majlen Yes, I do. How can I help?

Sven Well I'm glad you speak English, because that's all the Swedish I know!

Majlen No problem at all, Mr Maier. How can I help you?

Sven I'm a buyer at MegaKauf in Dusseldorf, Germany. I'm phoning to enquire about your electricity generators. We're interested in buying fifteen of your Full Power 500 model.

Majlen Full Power 500 … just a moment … I have it here on the screen. It's a very popular generator.

Sven Exactly. We know what the basic price is, so now we'd like to talk about your terms of delivery.

Majlen I see. A lot of our German customers give us the name of a ship to load the goods onto at the port of Malmö and then pick them up at the port of Hamburg. Our factory is in Lund, which is close to the port of Malmö. Shall we do that for you?

Sven Thanks, but we'd prefer to pick them up at Dusseldorf Central Station. Can you send them to us to arrive in Dusseldorf by rail?

Majlen No problem. With or without insurance?

Sven With insurance, please. Could you send me a quotation?

Majlen Yes, certainly. By rail from our factory in Lund to Dusseldorf Central Station, with insurance …

2: Garden furniture

Ken Hello, Shenzhen Trading China. How can I help you?

Sven Hello, It's Sven Maier from MegaKauf in Dusseldorf, Germany. Can I speak to Mr Woo, please?

Ken Speaking, Mr Maier. How can I help you?

Sven Hello, Mr Woo. My company is interested in your garden furniture.

Ken We are very pleased to hear that you are interested in our products, Mr Maier. Would you like some more information?

Sven Yes, can I ask you some questions about shipment of your furniture?

Ken Certainly, Mr Maier. What would you like to know?

Sven Well, we're interested in a full container load, which we would like to collect at the port of Rotterdam.

Ken I see. Rotterdam in the Netherlands. Not Hamburg?

Sven We are, in fact, nearer Rotterdam than Hamburg here. Can you ship the container to Rotterdam, with insurance?

Ken With insurance to the port of Rotterdam … That is possible, but the Chinese shipping line we use is booked up for eight weeks.

Sven Eight weeks! Oh dear, that's a long time. Can *we* suggest a German shipping line to you? I'm thinking of the Hamburg Süd line.

Ken Yes, Mr Maier but then your shipping line must collect the container at the port of Shenzhen. This means that we will load the container onto a German ship at the port of Shenzhen and you will organize transport from there.

Sven That's fine, Mr Woo. I'll contact Hamburg Süd and get them to pick up the container at the port of Shenzhen …

3: LED displays

Lorna Dublin Electronics, you're through to Lorna. How can I help?

Sven Hello, it's Sven Maier from MegaKauf in Dusseldorf, Germany. Can I speak to someone about ordering a thousand LED displays, type SA15?

Lorna I can help you with that. Just let me check … Yes, we have them in stock. And you need – how many did you say, a thousand?

Sven Yes, that's right. How soon can you deliver?

Lorna Well, we can add them to our container on board a ship leaving Dublin port and docking in Rotterdam next Friday. That's the cheapest option but it's without insurance, Sven.

Sven From Dublin port to Rotterdam next Friday without insurance. Well, that's a bit too slow for us, Lorna. Is there a faster option?

Lorna What if we send them by air? They're pretty light.

Sven Yes, that's right and we're very near Dusseldorf airport. How soon would we get them?

Lorna 48 hours after receipt of order. Would that be soon enough?

Sven Yes, that would be fine. Could you send me an offer today?

Lorna Yes, no problem. With or without insurance to Dusseldorf airport?

Sven Well, they're not breakable and the displays aren't expensive. I'd say without insurance.

Lorna So that's delivery to Dusseldorf Airport without insurance …

Track 39: Unit 9, Part A, exercise 3

Booysen Good morning, AgriTrade, Luke Booysen speaking. How can I help you?

Sauerwald Good morning, Luke. It's Dirk Sauerwald from Cantec. How are you?

Booysen	Hi, Dirk. I'm fine, and thanks for getting back to me so quickly. How about you?
Sauerwald	Busy as always, but that's the way I like it.
Booysen	I'm glad to hear that, Dirk, and I'm sure you're phoning about my email about noise levels, right?
Sauerwald	Exactly. In it you say that you would like to reduce the noise level of the production line.
Booysen	Yes, that's right. The line's running perfectly but we're operating it almost round the clock and the constant noise level is over 80 decibels, so we'd like to do something about that.
Sauerwald	Well, I think we have the perfect solution, and I don't mean ear protectors!
Booysen	Well, we're already wearing them here but some operators forget and that's not good.
Sauerwald	I totally agree, Luke. What I'm talking about is a noise protection hood. It's placed around the machine and cuts noise emissions to well under 80 dB.
Booysen	Sounds great, Dirk, but it also sounds like a big job, and we don't want the line down for a couple of days. And what about servicing the machine? Surely that will be more difficult if it's in a hood.
Sauerwald	Well, the beauty of this solution is that it can be retrofitted in a matter of hours and all the existing installations, like electricity, water and air, are unaffected. It also doesn't get in the way when you service the machine because all you do is slide the hood to one side.
Booysen	Sounds like the perfect solution, but how easy is it to install?
Sauerwald	We can send over a technician and fit it in a day. Once you've taken delivery of the hood, we can arrange a date for installation.
Booysen	I see. Can you send me some sales literature on it?
Sauerwald	Yes, certainly. I'll email you our brochure.
Booysen	And what about the price?
Sauerwald	Our basic price is €5,000 FCA Essen and our terms of payment are 30 days net.
Booysen	FCA? Would you explain that for me, Dirk?
Sauerwald	Yes, of course. FCA or free carrier, Essen means you send a lorry to our factory in Essen and we load the hood onto it for you and you arrange the rest. And in addition to that there's the installation costs, meaning the cost of flying a technician to your site and back.
Booysen	I see. Well, ideally we'd like you to deliver the hood to us here.
Sauerwald	We can do that, Luke, but it will make the price more expensive. And what about risks in transit. Do you want coverage for that?
Booysen	Yes, we'll need that, I suppose.
Sauerwald	Air or sea freight?
Booysen	Sea freight.
Sauerwald	Well, let me just take a look at our forwarder's freight rates ... You have a number of options for sea freight. Do you want door-to-door delivery or do you want to pick up the load at the port of Cape Town yourself?
Booysen	Door-to-door delivery would be best.
Sauerwald	In that case ... DAP your premises in Paarl would be €3,150 and DAP covers all risks in transit.
Booysen	Oh, I see... Is there a cheaper option?
Sauerwald	How about CIF Cape Town? That includes insurance in transit and would cost you €1,750 but you would need to collect the goods at the port yourself.
Booysen	I think that sounds like the best option because we're only 60 km from Cape Town here. How long would it take?
Sauerwald	22 days and there's a ship from Rotterdam to Cape Town once a week.
Booysen	And the price of €5,000? Is there any flexibility?
Sauerwald	Our prices are already very competitive, Luke.
Booysen	Well at the moment, the whole deal will cost us about €6,750 plus installation costs. Could we somehow get that closer to €6,000?
Sauerwald	We can't change our prices, Luke but we can send over a technician to install the hood for free if you foot the hotel bill. A return flight from Dusseldorf to Cape Town will cost us about €1,000, but if you pay for our technician's hotel and look after him while he's there, we'll pay his air fare.
Booysen	We can do that, Dirk. We'll get him a nice hotel, pick him up at the airport and look after him. No problem at all.
Sauerwald	Good. Anything else I can do for you?
Booysen	Yes, what about the delivery period?
Sauerwald	30 days after receipt of order.
Booysen	And we have a deal, Dirk. Would you send me all this in writing?
Sauerwald	I most certainly will ...

Track 40: Unit 9, Part B, exercise 3

Dialogue 1

Maria	Pronto?
Emil	Pronto, buongiorno. Sono Emil Partmann in Germania. Do you speak English?
Maria	Yes, I do, Mr Partmann. How can I help you?
Emil	I work for Möbelbau Konrad, a furniture-manufacturing company in Germany. My boss saw your products at the EuroBlech trade fair in Hanover and now I'm calling about your expanded metal for outdoor furniture. We would like to know what your terms are.
Maria	With pleasure, Mr Partmann. What would you like to know?
Emil	My boss told me that the price was €700 per roll DAP Düsseldorf. Is that right and is there a minimum order quantity?
Maria	The price and Incoterm are correct. There is no minimum order quantity for an initial order but after that it's five rolls.
Emil	I see. How long does it take to deliver them?
Maria	Our delivery period is 13 days, door-to-door to you in Dusseldorf.
Emil	Door-to-door ... thanks. Could you tell me what your terms of payment are?
Maria	CWO or letter of credit. If you place regular orders our terms are 30 days net.
Emil	Good. What guarantee do you give?
Maria	Five years.
Emil	Do you grant a quantity discount?
Maria	How many rolls are you thinking of ordering?
Emil	20 rolls.

Maria Well, we could grant you a quantity discount of 2% but on 100 rolls.

Emil I see.

Maria Is there anything else you would like to know, Mr Partmann?

Emil That's it for the time being. I'll be in touch.

Maria Thanks for calling and have a nice day.

Emil You too. Bye.

Maria Bye.

Dialogue 2

Amélie Bonjour, merci d'appeler Tôlerie Industrielle. Je suis Amélie. Que puis-je faire pour vous?

Emil Bonjour. Ici Emil Partmann en Allemagne. Do you speak English?

Amélie Yes, I do, Monsieur Partmann. How can I help you?

Emil I'm calling you from Möbelbau Konrad, a furniture-manufacturing company in Germany. Our Purchasing Director saw your products at the EuroBlech trade fair in Hanover and we'd like to know what your terms are for expanded metal for outdoor furniture.

Amélie Of course, Monsieur Partmann. It's on special offer at the moment.

Emil Excellent!

Amélie One roll costs €700 and we also deliver DAT to your local terminal. Where is that for you, Monsieur Partmann?

Emil Düsseldorf Central Station. We're very near it, so we would only need to collect the load and take it to our premises. Is there a minimum order quantity?

Amélie Yes, it's five rolls.

Emil Thanks. How long would it take to deliver?

Amélie We have the metal in stock, so it would take one day from here to Dusseldorf.

Emil Yes, it isn't very far from Metz to Düsseldorf. Could you tell me what your terms of payment are?

Amélie They are CWO for an initial order, then 10 days 2%, 30 days net for regular orders.

Emil Thanks. How long is your guarantee?

Amélie Three years.

Emil What about discounts?

Amélie If 50 or more rolls are ordered, we grant a 3% discount.

Emil 3% ... thanks.

Amélie Is there anything else you'd like to know, Monsieur Partmann?

Emil That's all for the time being. I'll be in touch.

Amélie Thanks for calling Tôlerie Industrielle and have a nice day.

Emil You too. Bye.

Amélie Bye.

Track 41: Unit 9, Communication, exercise 1B/C

Mary Marx Kitchens, Sales Department. Mary Hamilton speaking. How can I help you?

John Ah. Good morning. This is John Jamieson speaking. I've just received an offer in reply to an enquiry I sent last week, but some of the details are missing.

Mary Oh. I'm sorry to hear that, Mr Jamieson. Just a moment, please. Is that J-A-M-I-E-S-O-N?

John Erm, yes.

Mary OK, I have a copy of the offer here. It appears to be complete. Shall we go through the details together?

John Yes. I think that would be the best idea. I need the goods urgently, so I really would like to have everything sorted out as soon as possible.

Mary Of course. If you could just tell me what you need to know.

John Well, first of all, I'd like to know your terms of delivery.

Mary We deliver within six weeks, cost, insurance, freight. I see you're in Liverpool, so that's CIF to Liverpool.

John CIF, Liverpool. Good. There's a note here about smaller numbers of items being delivered from stock. How many items would that be?

Mary Anything up to ten items.

John OK. Ten. And what about bulk orders? There's mention of a discount on bulk orders, but there's no mention of how many items that covers.

Mary We give a discount on orders of more than 50 items.

John And how much is the discount?

Mary The discount is three per cent.

John OK. Three per cent discount on bulk orders of more than 50 items. Erm. There's a note here about payment for first orders, but again, the most important information is missing.

Mary For new customers, we prefer cash with the first order.

John I understand that. That's no problem. Cash with first order. OK. So, the last thing is, the catalogue was enclosed with the offer, but I can't see any information on page 6 about the VAT. Do your prices include VAT or not?

Mary I'm afraid our prices do not include VAT.

John Ah. I thought that might be the case. Well, I think I have all the information I need now.

Mary Mr Jamieson, I really must apologize for the problems with the offer. I'm so sorry that you've had to go to all this trouble. Is there anything else I can help you with?

John No, I don't think so, Ms Hamilton. I'd like to discuss the offer with my partner before we go any further. Thank you. Goodbye.

Track 42: Unit 9, Communication, exercise 2A

John Jamieson and Walker, John Jamieson speaking.

Mary Good morning, Mr Jamieson. Mary Hamilton, Marx Kitchens here. Is this a good time to call?

John Yes, of course. Nice to hear from you. What can I do for you, Ms Hamilton?

Mary Well, it's about your order.

John Oh, dear. I hope there aren't any problems with the delivery.

Mary No. There aren't any problems with the delivery. It's just that there are a few mistakes in the order form which we should clear up.

John OK. Hang on a second. I'll just call it up on my screen. Here we are: "Microwave ovens and electric kettles".

Mary Yes. That's the first problem, I'm afraid. Do you have a copy of our catalogue handy?

John Yes. I do. Here we are.

Mary I need to know the item number of the ovens you'd like, and the item number of the kettles.

John Oh, sorry ... just a moment ... Here it is. The oven we'd like to order is MM 89 in white, and the number of the kettle is EK 39, blue.

Mary Aha. MM 89 white, and EK 39, the blue kettle.

John That's correct. The blue kettle.

Mary Now, the next thing is the final payment. If you remember, we discussed the discount on bulk orders. I'm afraid you have to buy 50 of each of the items before you get that discount.

John Oh dear. Sorry about that. I must have misunderstood.

Mary	No problem. The last thing is the VAT. I'm afraid we need to recalculate the total price.
John	Of course. Should I re-submit the order?
Mary	No, don't worry, Mr Jamieson. I'll ask my assistant to make the corrections and I'll email you a new copy of the order. All right?
John	Thank you, Ms Hamilton. I really appreciate that.

Track 43: Unit 10, Part A, exercise 2A

Nasir	A.P. Leather International. Good morning, Nasir Mahmood speaking. How can I help you?
Sven	Good morning, Mr Mahmood. It's Sven Maier from Brinkmeyer Lederwarenmanufaktur in Germany.
Nasir	Good morning Mr Maier! It's very nice to hear from you again. Is the quality of our leather to your satisfaction?
Sven	Indeed it is, Mr Mahmood and I would like to order some more.
Nasir	That is excellent news, Mr Maier. How much would you like?
Sven	Well, before we talk about that, I'd like to discuss your terms and prices.
Nasir	I see, Mr Maier. Our prices are already very competitive.
Sven	Yes, but so far we have only placed smaller orders but now we would like to place regular orders for much larger quantities.
Nasir	That sounds very good, Mr Maier.
Sven	And we require delivery CIF Bremen for the same price.
Nasir	The same price! We will go bankrupt, Mr Maier! That's impossible. I'm very sorry but we cannot afford that. Our ex works price is already very competitive.
Sven	Now we wish to order 3,000 hides and 10,000 square feet of nappa leather.
Nasir	3,000 hides and 10,000 square feet!
Sven	On a regular basis. I mean every three months. And for that we want open account terms with quarterly settlement.
Nasir	Every three months! So that's 12,000 hides and 40,0000 square feet of nappa leather a year. Let me think ...
Sven	Well, don't think for too long, Mr Mahmood because we have customers waiting over here.
Nasir	Look, can we offer you FCA Lahore. That is much better for your driver when he comes to collect the leather here in Lahore because we will load it onto his lorry for him.
Sven	I'm afraid that isn't enough, Mr Mahmood. We have other suppliers who offer much more.
Nasir	All right, Mr Maier. We will accept all risks and pay the transport costs of the leather from Lahore to the Port of Karachi including loading and export clearance.
Sven	So you're offering FOB Karachi ... And your terms of payment?
Nasir	Yes, FOB Karachi, and please understand that to finance production of such a large amount of leather we will still need part of the payment in advance.
Sven	We're already paying you 25% in advance, Mr Mahmood.
Nasir	But for such big orders we need to make a much bigger investment here... Look, I can offer you one-third with order, one-third on delivery and one-third 30 days after delivery.
Sven	All right, Mr Mahmood. To get you started we'll accept FOB Karachi, but then the terms of payment must be one-third with order, one-third on delivery and one-third *90* days after delivery.
Nasir	90 days ...
Sven	Yes, and we'll accept those terms for one year only starting today. After that we'll expect open account terms. And there's another thing, Mr Mahmood. So far, we've had groupage consignments and that's a security risk.
Nasir	But your orders have not filled a container, Mr Maier so that's why they were LCL.
Sven	Yes, but now we want FCL.
Nasir	No problem, Mr Maier because such large quantities will be full container loads, so we can change the terms from LCL to FCL.
Sven	But I want a guarantee in writing, Mr Mahmood. It must *always* be FCL and *never* LCL.
Nasir	All right, it's a deal, Mr Maier.
Sven	Good, but these new terms are only valid for one year, Mr Mahmood. After that we'll review everything again. Please send me an email confirming the new terms in writing and I'll email you our order straight away.
Nasir	You'll get my email in a few minutes, Mr Maier ...

Track 44: Unit 10, Part B, exercise 3A

Louisa	Guten Morgen, Brewery-2-Brewery, Sie sprechen mit Louisa Schneider. Was kann ich für Sie tun?
Kevin	Good morning. This is Kevin King from Harpoon Brew Supply in Bedford, Massachusetts. I hope you speak English, ma'am.
Louisa	No problem, Mr King. How can I help you?
Kevin	Well, I'm phoning about the microbrewery that we ordered. It's order no. MB721A. Have you shipped it yet?
Louisa	Just a moment, Mr King ... MB721A ... Ah yes, here it is. Yes, we shipped it yesterday. It's at the port of Hamburg now and will be loaded on MS Arcadia, which sails for the port of Boston tomorrow. The consigment is due to arrive in Boston at the end of next week.
Kevin	Well, thank goodness I phoned you in time!
Louisa	I don't understand, Mr King.
Kevin	Well, I have bad news for you. We've had a big fire in our warehouse here in Bedford, Massachusetts. The whole building has burned down, so we won't be able to pay for the microbrewery until the insurance company has paid us. I thought it best to warn you as soon as possbible. The good news is that we've found another customer in Philadelphia who will buy the microwbrewery. The customer is Lopez Catering Incorporated. They have agreed to buy the equipment if we deliver it to their door, so we would like you to ship it to them instead.
Louisa	Just a minute, Mr King. Let me check the terms of payment and delivery ... I see that payment is by letter of credit with delivery CFR Boston, Massachusetts ...
Kevin	And we'd like you to change that to CFR Philadelphia for the new customer, Lopez Catering.
Louisa	Well, I'm afraid we can't do that, Mr King. In fact we can't change anything at all because it's an irrevocable letter of credit.
Kevin	Oh no! We have nowhere to put the microbrewery and we can't pay for it either!
Louisa	But the good news is that as it's a *confirmed* letter of credit, we have already received payment from our bank. We presented the documents listed in the credit, they were in order and we received payment.
Kevin	So where are the documents? We haven't heard anything from our bank yet.

Louisa They're somewhere in the banking system, Mr King. Our bank will send them to your bank, and your bank will ask you to pay.
Kevin But we can't! That's the problem.
Louisa I understand that you're in a very difficult situation, Mr King, but as you already have a customer for the microbrewery, you now need to speak to your bank and ask them to release the documents to the new customer in Philadelphia instead of to you.
Kevin I see. So the consignment will arrive in Boston one way or another and then has to be shipped to Philadelphia.
Louisa Exactly. We can't change the destination now. I suggest you get onto your bank and transfer ownership of the consignment to Lopez Catering. Then you will have to arrange for shipment of the goods from Boston to Philadelphia. If you need help, you can always contact Nancy Kline, our agent in New York. I'll send you her contact details.
Kevin OK, I'll give it a try. Thanks for your help.
Louisa You're welcome, Mr King. Is there anything else I can do for you?
Kevin No thanks, Ms Schneider. Have a nice day,
Louisa You too, Mr King. Bye for now.
Kevin Bye.

Track 45: Unit 10, Part B, exercise 4A/B

Kevin Harpoon Brew, this is Kevin King speaking. How may I help you?
Nancy Good morning, Mr King. It's Nancy Kline from Brewery-2-Brewery in New York. I'm calling about the microbrewery.
Kevin Good morning, Ms Kline. Thanks for getting back to me. Have you spoken to Lopez Catering?
Nancy Yes, I've been in touch with them and I think we have a solution now, Mr King.
Kevin You mean you can reroute it?
Nancy Not exactly, but as good as. As you know, the equipment is still on board a ship in the Atlantic and the documents are in the banking system. You now need to get onto your bank and transfer ownership to Lopez Catering in Philadelphia. I've spoken to Lopez Catering myself and they will pay your bank for the equipment after it has been unloaded in Boston. We'll organize the rest for you.
Kevin That sounds good. Can I now leave it all to you and the bank?
Nancy Well, not exactly, Mr King. Remember that it's a CFR delivery, which means that the buyer pays for unloading at the port of destination, in this case the port of Boston.
Kevin And at this moment I'm still the buyer, right?
Nancy Exactly, so you'll have to pay for that. And then the goods will have to be collected at the port of Boston and transported to Lopez Catering in Philadelphia.
Kevin So I'll have to pay for that too …
Nancy Yes, but remember that you're lucky to have found a buyer so quickly, Mr King!
Kevin Yes, I suppose you're right. OK, so tell me about transporting the goods to Philadelphia. Would it not be easiest just to send the consignment from Boston to Philadelphia by ship? It could be loaded onto another ship in Boston and finally unloaded in Philadelphia.
Nancy I see what you mean, but according to the terms of the documentary credit, the goods need to be unloaded in Boston first and transshipment is not allowed.
Kevin I see. So what do you suggest?
Nancy Well, we can either send the equipment to Philadelphia by rail or road.
Kevin I see. What about the price? I want to keep it as low as possible.
Nancy I understand, Mr King. Six wooden crates packed in three containers delivered CPT Philadelphia train station would cost $1,590, but that's without insurance and you would still need to have the containers picked up and taken to Lopez Catering.
Kevin And by road?
Nancy DAP delivery by road to Lopez Catering would cost $1,600.
Kevin And insurance?
Nancy DAP includes insurance.
Kevin Well, as Lopez Catering wants door-to-door delivery, that sounds like the best option but, just out of interest, how much would it cost to ship the consignment to the port of Philadelphia by sea?
Nancy It would cost $2,160 for delivery port-to-port. In this case it would be CFR Philadelphia and it would take at least seven days.
Kevin That's a big difference.
Nancy And it wouldn't be door-to-door.
Kevin Ah yes, of course. What's the delivery time overland?
Nancy One day.
Kevin Well, I think you've found the best option, Ms Kline. What do I do next?
Nancy You will be contacted by Pennsylvania Logistics. That's the freight forwarder I recommend because they've worked for us in the past. They will send you a contract of carriage for you to sign and they'll do the rest.
Kevin Well, thanks for your help, Ms Kline. That's a load off my shoulders!
Nancy You're welcome, Mr King, and we'll make sure the load gets to Lopez Catering for you …

Track 46: KMK Exam practice 5, exercise 3, Hörverstehen

Hi, there, Tom here, sorry I was very busy this morning, and now you're away. Well, I guess the old answering machine will do …
I haven't finished all my research yet, but here's what I've found out so far. There are two options in the region. The first warehouse is only about 400 metres away, so it's actually in the direct neighbourhood of our warehouse. It's rather big, 600 square metres, and in good condition. It was renovated recently and is completely equipped with thermal insulation. It will be available next spring. My contact was a Mr Miller, a very friendly person, and he showed me the whole place. I'm no expert but it looks good. By the way, Mr Miller is in the picture, and you can call him directly for more information. That would be 0707 3294410.
The second warehouse I looked at was in Chester, about one mile away from the company. It consists of two parts that could be connected, so it would be either 200 square metres or 450 square metres. The good thing is that we could rent it straight away as there is no tenant at the moment. But frankly, the place looks rather shabby and it was dirty, perhaps we need to look somewhere else …

Anyway, I don't have a contact person for that warehouse yet, apart from the estate agent who gave me the address. The facility manager of the place didn't call me back, so I just went there on my own. That's why I'd suggest writing an official mail. You can find all the information on the website of Benson Warehousing, the email address is benson@spaceplace.com, that's B-E-N-S-O-N.
Oh, I nearly forgot: prices! Benson is £35 per square metre, per quarter. The agent had a list for me. The other one, you know, the one nearby, is £160 per square metre, per year.
OK, that's all for now. You said you needed the information quickly. If you have any questions, or if I've forgotten anything, just call me on my mobile. Have a nice day!

Track 47: Unit 11, Foundation, exercise 3

... We all know that mistakes happen every so often, and we have to complain to our suppliers too every now and then. In case you ever have to deal with a complaint, I'd just like to run through a few points with you. Let's start with telephone complaints. Before you make the call, have all the paperwork you need beside you. And have something you can make notes with.
At the start of the call, get the name of the person you're talking to. And, by the way, always be polite. The person you speak to on the phone is not responsible for the mistake. That person is simply an employee of a company, just like you are, so remember to stay calm and keep cool.
No matter what the problem is, follow up your telephone complaint with an email to the supplier so that everyone has a record of what has been agreed. Copy in your line manager so that everyone knows that the complaint is being dealt with.
When you make a complaint in writing, start with the details of the transaction, things like the order number and the date of delivery. In the body of the letter, describe the problem clearly and point out the inconvenience this is causing the company.
Make a suggestion how to resolve the problem, for example, the company could send a replacement or give you a discount.
In conclusion, ask for immediate action. OK. That's it. Any questions? No? Good. It's not too difficult to deal with a complaint as long as you ...

Track 48: Unit 11, Part A, exercise 3A/B

Hannah Guten Morgen, Kältetechnik Lohmann GmbH. Sie sprechen mit Hannah Schmidt. Was kann ich für Sie tun?
Gunner Good morning, it's Gunner Kristoffersen from Fixit DIY Stores in Copenhagen. I hope you speak English.
Hannah Yes, I do, Mr Kristoffersen. How can I help you?
Gunner The reason I'm calling is to tell you that we're extremely dissatisfied with the portable air conditioners we received from you last week. Some of them are faulty, meaning that they cut out after a short time. Others are noisy and several of them are discoloured.
Hannah Oh dear, faulty, noisy and discoloured! I'm very sorry to hear that, Mr Kristoffersen. Could I have the order number, please?
Gunner Yes, it's order number SA450 dated the twelfth of last month.
Hannah Let me just check. Yes, I've got it here. An order for 500 portable ACU2 air conditioners.
Gunner Yes, and let me point out that they are still under warranty and we sell them to our customers in Denmark with both the statutory 24-month warranty and an extra three years' guarantee on our part, meaning they must last at least five years. These air conditioners haven't lasted a week!
Hannah We're extremely sorry to hear that, Mr Kristoffersen. We take customers' complaints very seriously and I assure you we'll find a solution as soon as possible.
Gunner Well it had better be soon because our customers are complaining and we don't want to lose them. We have our company's good name to think of!
Hannah I fully understand, Mr Kristoffersen. I'll contact our Production department immediately and get back to you.
Gunner We expect you to replace the whole consignment free of charge. And we won't be paying for the air conditioners until we are perfectly satisfied.
Hannah I see ... Well, the terms of payment are 10 days 2%, 30 days net, so we still have some time.
Gunner If we don't get replacements we'll return the whole consignment carriage forward and cancel all future orders.
Hannah I'm sure that won't be necessary, Mr Kristoffersen.
Gunner We'll see. You have exactly one week to send us replacements and no longer.
Hannah Please let me apologize for the inconvenience this has caused you, Mr Kristoffersen. You'll be hearing from us again very soon and I'm sure we'll find a solution.
Gunner I hope so. Goodbye.
Hannah Thanks for calling, Mr Kristoffersen. Goodbye.

Track 49: Unit 11, Part B, exercise 4A/C

Rita Porzellanmanufaktur Querenburg GmbH, Ronstadt, guten Morgen. Was kann ich für Sie tun?
Rory Good morning, it's Rory Kelly from Sligo Supplies. Am I speaking to Rita Ronstadt?
Rita Yes, you are, Mr Kelly. Thanks for calling. Is it about the statement?
Rory Yes, that's right. I got your email yesterday. Sorry about the mix-up with the prices and so on, but I think I've got to the bottom of it now.
Rita Good. What went wrong? Did you just forget the credit note?
Rory Well, it's not as simple as that. Let me first explain why it wasn't included. The €498 was for goods returned to us last year and we sent you a credit note in the form of a code. That meant we would deduct €498 from your next order.
Rita Well, I understand but our next order on 9 January was only for €300 so we didn't include the code.
Rory That's no problem but you should have included it at some time during the quarter and you didn't, so that's why it was omitted from your statement.
Rita Oh, I see. Is it too late now?
Rory No, you can still include it, and we'll then update your account.
Rita Good. And what about the special offer for the moulds and the clay? What happened there?
Rory I've investigated that as well and I've found out what went wrong. You saw the offer on our website, didn't you?
Rita Yes, that's right. We were delighted because we use a lot of moulds and clay, so we ordered immediately.
Rory I'm glad to hear that, Ms Ronstadt but you didn't order through the website. I mean you didn't click the button on the website to place your order and get your special price discount.

Rita Didn't I click the button? … Just let me think … Ah yes, I remember. No, I didn't click the button and order through the website. I just ordered in the usual way by email.
Rory Well, that explains why you didn't get the special offer because our software was programmed to grant the reduction on all orders placed via the button on the website.
Rita I see. So what's going to happen now? We're talking about a difference of more than €600.
Rory I have the solution, Ms Ronstadt. I'll send you an email with a special link to your account. If you then type in the details of your order for the moulds and clay again and also include the code for the credit note we sent you for €498, our software will update your account with the right amounts and we'll send you a new statement. Is that all right?
Rita Yes, that's fine, Mr Kelly. When can I expect your email?
Rory I'll send it straight away. Is there anything else I can do for you?
Rita No, thanks very much.
Rory Well, I'm glad we were able to sort it all out. Please get in touch if you have any more queries.
Rita I'll do that, Mr Kelly. Thanks for calling. Bye.
Rory Bye.

Track 50: Unit 11, Communication, exercise 2A

Melissa Wolf.
Jerzy Oh. Hello. Erm. Do you speak English?
Melissa Yes.
Jerzy Oh. Good. This is Jerzy Adamczyk calling from the Anatol Kaminski Clinic in Warsaw. Is that MedEquip in Berlin … the Sales department?
Melissa Yes.
Jerzy And, erm, who am I speaking to, please?
Melissa Wolf.
Jerzy Ah. Ms Wolf. Erm. Is, erm, are you the correct person to take a complaint about a delivery?
Melissa What's the problem?
Jerzy It's about my order for operating theatre monitors. Both of the monitors were damaged. One of them – the screen on one of the monitors is scratched, and the other monitor is dented. I mean, the metal casing is dented. I think that …
Melissa What's the order number?
Jerzy 942761.
Melissa OK. I can't do anything at the moment. I'll get it sorted after lunch.
Jerzy So, will you phone me back? My phone number is …
Melissa It's here on the display.
Jerzy 0048 129 577 042?
Melissa Yes.
Jerzy And my name is Adamczyk. You will be sure to look into this? Well, thank you very much.

Track 51: Unit 11, Communication, exercise 2B

Melissa Guten Morgen. MedEquip GmbH, Verkaufsabteilung. Melissa Wolf am Apparat.
Jerzy Oh. Hello. Erm. Do you speak English?
Melissa Yes, of course. How can I help you?
Jerzy Oh. Good. This is Jerzy Adamczyk calling from the Anatol Kaminski Clinic in Warsaw. Is that the Sales department?
Melissa Yes, this is the Sales department. My name's Melissa Wolf.
Jerzy Ah. Mrs, erm, Ms Wolf. Hmm. Is, erm, are you the correct person to take a complaint about a delivery?
Melissa It depends on what it's about. Could you give me some details?
Jerzy It's about my order for operating theatre monitors. Both of the monitors were damaged. One of them – the screen on one of the monitors is scratched and the other monitor is dented. I mean, the metal casing is dented. I think that there was a problem during transport.
Melissa Oh, I'm sorry to hear that. Could you give me the order number, please?
Jerzy It's 942761.
Melissa Just a moment, please. Right. 942761. I have it here. Two X-ray machines. And you say that both of them are damaged?
Jerzy That is correct. I am sorry, but I have to say that I am disappointed about this business. This is a trial order, but I had to complain last week because the equipment didn't arrive on the date we agreed. Now the monitors are here and I can't use them.
Melissa Oh, dear. I'm extremely sorry to hear that you've had so much trouble. I'm sure my superior would like to discuss this with you. Can I ask her to phone you when she comes in to work tomorrow?
Jerzy Yes. All right. I'll be at home all day tomorrow, so she should call me there. The number is 0048 129 546 993.
Melissa 0048 129 546 993. Yes. You'll get a call from my superior tomorrow, Mr Adamczyk.
Jerzy Could you tell me her name, please?
Melissa It's Mia Richter.
Jerzy Mia Richter. Good. Thank you very much, Ms Wolf.
Melissa You're welcome, Mr Adamczyk. Thank you for calling.
Jerzy Goodbye.

Track 52: Unit 11, Communication, exercise 3C

Jeanette Good morning. Sheffield Metal, Sales Department, Jeannette Hogg speaking.
Max Good morning. This is Max Jahn from MedEquip in Germany.
Jeanette Good morning, Mr Jahn. How can I help you?
Max I'm calling to enquire about my order for containers for medical equipment. The order was sent almost one month ago, on 18 April, and delivery was promised by 3 May but, so far, nothing has arrived.
Jeanette Oh. I'm sorry to hear that. Could you give me the order number?
Max Yes. It's DF54736.
Jeanette DF54736. Just a moment, please. I'll check. I'm sorry, Mr Jahn. I don't seem to have any record of your order. Can I just check that I've understood everything? The order number is DF54736 and you ordered the containers on 18 April. Could you give me the exact details of the order, please?
Max Yes, it's an order for your aluminium containers for medical equipment.
Jeanette Aluminium containers for medical equipment. Mr Jahn, I'll have to speak to my colleague to find out what the problem is. Can I get back to you later?
Max Well, yes. But I hope it won't take long. We can't fulfil our orders until we have your containers.

Jeanette	Yes. I realize that, Mr Jahn. I'm very sorry about this and I will do my best to get back to you as soon as possible.
Max	Many thanks for your help, Ms Hogg.

Track 53: Unit 12, Foundation, exercise 1

1: Maren

Presenter	Hello, and welcome to this week's podcast. This week, we're talking to a group of people who have recently gained their business qualifications. Let's start with you, Maren. Would you like to introduce yourself?
Maren	OK. I'm Maren, and I've just completed my apprenticeship as a customer services specialist in the wholesale trade.
Presenter	What did you like best about your apprenticeship?
Maren	I liked the mixture of going to vocational college and doing practical work.
Presenter	What do you do at work?
Maren	I respond to customers' enquiries and guide them through the purchasing process.
Presenter	Right. Now, what about the future? What would you like to do in the future?
Maren	I'd like to become a customer services manager.
Presenter	Well, all the best Maren.

2: Garry

Garry	My name's Garry and I'm a marketing assistant.
Presenter	OK. What did you enjoy most about your apprenticeship, Garry?
Garry	I enjoyed going to meetings.
Presenter	Apart from going to meetings, what else do you do in your job?
Garry	Well, I usually work on my own. I analyse data and write reports. I also help with marketing projects.
Presenter	Sounds as if the work is quite varied. Now that you've finished your training, where do you go from here?
Garry	Oh, that's easy. I'd like to get another qualification and become an office manager.
Presenter	Oh. That's great!

3: Delon

Presenter	Hello. Can you tell us your name and something about your apprenticeship?
Delon	Yes. My name's Delon, and I've just qualified as an industrial management assistant.
Presenter	What did you like best about your apprenticeship?
Delon	I enjoyed learning from experienced people.
Presenter	So, what does an industrial management assistant do at work?
Delon	Basically, an industrial management assistant purchases goods or raw materials and makes sure that stocks are up to date. We also calculate costs for orders, but we can also be involved in sales and marketing.
Presenter	Hmm. Now that you've qualified, what about the future? Where would you like to work?
Delon	I'd like to find a job abroad where I can use my English.
Presenter	That sounds good.

Track 54: Unit 12, Part B, exercise 1A

Interview 1: Tobias Klein

Tobias	Hallo?
Jennifer	Good evening. Am I speaking to Tobias Klein?
Tobias	Wer ist das? Ich versteh' nichts. Bist du das Kati?
Jennifer	This is Jennifer Winters. I'm the Recruitment Manager at Energy International plc. Am I speaking to Mr Tobias Klein?
Tobias	Oh! Oh yes! Energy International plc. Yes, I understand. Yes, my name is Tobias Klein. Please wait a moment. I must go outside ...
Jennifer	Is this a good time to call you, Mr Klein?
Tobias	Yes! It's very good! No problem, Mrs Winter. We can talk in a moment. Just let me go outside with my mobile ...
Jennifer	I can't hear you very ...
Tobias	Thank you for calling me, Miss Winters! I am very happy to answer your questions!
Jennifer	Could you tell me what job you're doing at the moment, Mr Klein?
Tobias	Yes, I'm an Azubi – I mean a trainee, but I've finished now, so I'm not, but I was ... but I'm still at Atlas Machinery in Frankfurt!
Jennifer	I see ... I think we ... problem ... signal strength.
Tobias	Strength? Yes, I have strengths, Mrs Winter. I am very good at work and at school and at football because I am a team player.
Jennifer	I see ... And what about your weaknesses?
Tobias	Weaknesses? I sometimes forget important things ... but I now use the reminder function on my mobile. That helps.
Jennifer	And why do you want a job at Energy International, Mr Klein?
Tobias	I've always wanted to work in Manchester. It has a famous football team and very nice people.
Jennifer	We are in London, Mr Klein, but that doesn't really matter now. Could you tell me something about your plans for the future?
Tobias	Well, I want a well-paid job so I can be independent and free.
Jennifer	I see. Are there any questions you would like to ask about the job, Mr Klein?
Tobias	I'm sorry. I didn't hear what you said, Miss Winter. The signal is very bad and the battery of my mobile is almost ...

Interview 2: Bianca Tiemeyer

Bianca	Tiemeyer?
Jennifer	Good morning. Am I speaking to Bianca Tiemeyer?
Bianca	Yes, that's right.
Jennifer	This is Jennifer Winters. I'm the Recruitment Manager at Energy International plc. Is this a good time to talk to you for a few minutes about your application for the post of a German-speaking customer services specialist?
Bianca	Yes, I'm at work but I have permission to use the office phone because it's my father's company – Tiemeyer Import/Export in Dortmund.
Jennifer	Oh I see. Now I've studied your CV and would like to know a little more about you. Would you like to take me through your CV?
Bianca	Well, I think the CV says everything, really. I haven't got a copy in front of me now, but it lists my skills and abilities. I went to the States for a year, so my English is very good.
Jennifer	And what other strengths do you have?

Bianca Other strengths? That's a standard question isn't it? Anyway, I would say I have all the usual strengths – I'm punctual, so I'm reliable, honest, hard-working and so on.
Jennifer I see. And weaknesses?
Bianca That's a very good question. Weaknesses ... Well, perhaps I expect too much from other people. My own standards are very high, and I suppose it's unfair to want everyone to be perfect.
Jennifer And why do you want this job in particular?
Bianca Why this job? Well, I think I'm probably best qualified for it. My grades at school were very good and I'd like to work abroad for a few years.
Jennifer I see. What are your future plans, Miss Tiemeyer? Where do you see yourself in five years' time?
Bianca I really can't say. It depends whether I like the job or not. If I like it, I'll stay on for a few years. It depends on the people, really.
Jennifer Do you have any questions you wish to ask?
Bianca That's another standard question, isn't it? Actually, I do have one question. Would you help me to find a good flat? I want something comfortable and not too far from the company.
Jennifer I'll pass the question on, Miss Tiemeyer. Is there anything else you'd like to know?
Bianca No, that's all, thanks. When will I hear from you?
Jennifer Within the next 48 hours. Thanks for answering my questions. Goodbye.
Bianca Bye.

Interview 3: Sebastian Hartmann

Sebastian Hartmann?
Jennifer Good evening. Am I speaking to Sebastian Hartmann?
Sebastian Yes, that's right.
Jennifer This is Jennifer Winters. I'm the Recruitment Manager at Energy International plc. Is this a good time to talk to you for a few minutes about your application for the post of a German-speaking customer services specialist?
Sebastian Yes, evenings are fine.
Jennifer Good. Um I've studied your CV and would like to know a little more about you. Would you like to take me through it?
Sebastian Yes, certainly. I would say one of my skills is the ability to work in a team and get the best out of myself with the help of others. That's one of the reasons why my team won the Team Project Management Competition. I also organized a programme for some Norwegian visitors to the company last year. It was great fun, and they've invited me back to Norway next summer. And I learned a lot about living and working in the UK when I worked for Commercial Services in York. I saw very good customer services there and would like to offer the same standard myself.
Jennifer So, in a nutshell, what would you say your strengths are?
Sebastian Teamwork, taking the initiative, working independently and understanding what the customer wants.
Jennifer And what about your weaknesses?
Sebastian I'm sure I have many but I would say a lack of experience. That's why I want to start work now.
Jennifer What made you apply for this job?
Sebastian The skills listed are exactly what I have learned in my traineeship. There is also a link with Germany, so I feel I can make a special contribution. And I like working in the UK, so I see it as the perfect opportunity.
Jennifer What are your plans for the future?
Sebastian I hope to develop in the job. I want to gain experience and then perhaps study for higher qualifications in the evening. London is a good place for that.
Jennifer Would you like to ask any questions yourself?
Sebastian Yes, on your website it says you sometimes send employees to India or the Far East, for example. Would this be an option for me?
Jennifer Not in the first year, but if you stay longer, you can apply to be posted overseas. Many young people do this. Any other questions?
Sebastian That was the most important one, thanks.
Jennifer In that case we'll be in touch again within 48 hours and thank you for answering my questions.
Sebastian My pleasure. Goodbye.
Jennifer Goodbye, Mr Hartmann.

Track 55: Unit 12, Part B, exercise 3B

Sam Thanks for coming along to talk to us today, Pat.
Pat My pleasure. It's nice to be here.
Sam Good. Now, today you're going to give us advice about how to prepare for an interview.
Pat Correct. I'm going to go through each of the five stages of a job interview and talk about how candidates can prepare themselves. So, stage one, greetings and introductions. That's perhaps the easiest part of the interview but it still needs some preparation. First of all, you should find out where the interview location is and how to get there so that you arrive in good time. Try to give yourself enough time to relax and calm down. You should also make sure that you're wearing appropriate clothes.
Sam First impressions count. Would you advise people to buy new clothes specially for the interview?
Pat No, not particularly. Your clothes need to be appropriate for the job, clean and smart, that's all. They don't have to be new.
Sam Right. What about body language at the start of the interview?
Pat Body language is important. Walk into the room as confidently as possible, shake hands and make eye contact. Don't be shy. Look directly at the interviewer or interviewers. You'll be asked to take a seat, and there will be a bit of small talk.
Sam Talking about the weather, your journey, that kind of thing?
Pat That's right. There might also be a question about where you live or your hobbies.
Sam Some people find it difficult to make small talk, even in their own language. What advice can you give us there, Pat?
Pat I think the best thing to do is to simply get into the habit of making small talk in English with a colleague or a friend.
Sam That's a good idea. Practise making small talk whenever you can.
Pat That's it. Now, let's move on to the main part of the interview. You'll be asked questions by one or more interviewers.

Sam The interview might be conducted by more than one person?

Pat That's correct. Sometimes there's a panel of interviewers. Now, preparation for this part is extremely important. Think about the questions you might be asked and make a list. You'll definitely be asked to talk about yourself. Perhaps the interviewer will ask you about your strengths and weaknesses. Write down the questions – and think about how you're going to answer. And always remember to relate your answers to the job on offer.

Sam Yes, that's important. Keep focused on the job. What should a candidate do if he or she doesn't understand a question?

Pat If you don't understand a question, ask the interviewer to clarify. You can say: "Could you explain what you mean by … ?" – whatever it is. A good interviewer will ask the question again in a slightly different way.

Sam Hmm. I hope so. Now, earlier you mentioned questions from the candidate. I remember my very first interview. I had no idea what to ask.

Pat Oh, dear. Some preparation would have helped. It's important to do some background research into the company before you go for the interview. Find out about the company's most recent developments and the future prospects of the company you hope to work for. Go to the firm's home page on the internet, read the business section of your newspaper, or look through business magazines. As you're doing your research, note down any questions that occur to you concerning the company. You should also, of course, prepare some questions about the job itself. Then, when you're asked if you have any questions, this is your chance to show your interest in the company and the job.

Sam Right. Be prepared with questions about the company and the job! And that's the end of the interview and you can say goodbye.

Pat Well, not quite. Before the interview comes to an end, the interviewer usually says when the candidate can expect to hear from the company or if there's to be a further interview or a test – hmm – say, in the form of an assessment centre evaluation. So, only after these arrangements have been made, is your last task as a candidate to say thank you and goodbye. Again, a good, firm handshake and a smile, and that's it.

Sam Well, thank you, Pat, for these very helpful interviewing tips. I'm sure our listeners have learned a lot today and that they'll be able to put your tips to good use in their interviews. Now, next week's podcast is about …

Track 56: KMK Mock Exam, Rezeption I, Hörverstehen

Floyd GreatSpirits Ltd, Miranda Floyd speaking. How can I help you?

Graham Hello, Ms Floyd. This is Tim Graham from Richard Bond Ltd in York.

Floyd Oh, hello Mr Graham! Nice to hear from you again! How are you?

Graham I'm fine, thank you. How about you?

Floyd I'm OK. We have a lot of work right now, as we have lots of orders to deal with. Are you calling to place an order?

Graham No, that's not the reason for my call. Unfortunately, we have a few problems with your last delivery.

Floyd Oh, really? I'm sorry to hear that. What seems to be the problem?

Graham First of all, the sparkling wine didn't arrive on the date you promised. That's a big problem because we need it for our company anniversary party, which is the day after tomorrow.

Floyd Oh dear. I can see that that is a problem.

Graham That's right. But more to the point, when the delivery arrived this morning, it was not the correct brand and there were only 700 bottles instead of the 1000 bottles we ordered.

Floyd I'm very sorry about that, Mr Graham. One moment, please. Let me put my colleague Gavin Porter on the speakerphone as well. He's in charge of the North England sales area. Maybe he can explain what has happened and what we can do now.

Graham Thank you very much, I'd appreciate that.

Floyd Please hold the line for a second …

…

Porter Mr Graham? This is Gavin Porter.

Graham Yes, hello, Mr Porter.

Porter Ms Floyd has informed me about the reason for your call, and I think I know what has caused the problem. There was a mix-up at the transport company; they confused two deliveries and sent you the wrong container. Your sparkling wine was delivered to another customer's warehouse in Leeds this morning. They called 15 minutes ago to complain.

Graham Oh, no! What a mess! But what can you do about it? We really need the delivery as soon as possible. It's our anniversary party in two days' time!

Porter It's OK. I've already made arrangements to sort things out. SuperCarrier, a local transport company, will pick up the wrong containers and deliver them to the right company. They've promised to deliver your container this afternoon and pick up the wrong one.

Graham Oh, that would be great! I'll make sure that the container that was delivered to us is ready to be picked up. Thanks for your help!

Porter You're welcome! In addition, we would like to offer you a 20% discount on this order. We really appreciate our long-term business relationship, so I'll also send you a box of our best champagne for your company anniversary. Of course, we'll also make sure that wrong deliveries like this don't happen again.

Graham Yes, I hope so too. Anyway, thanks for your help … and the champagne! Goodbye!

Porter You're welcome. Goodbye.

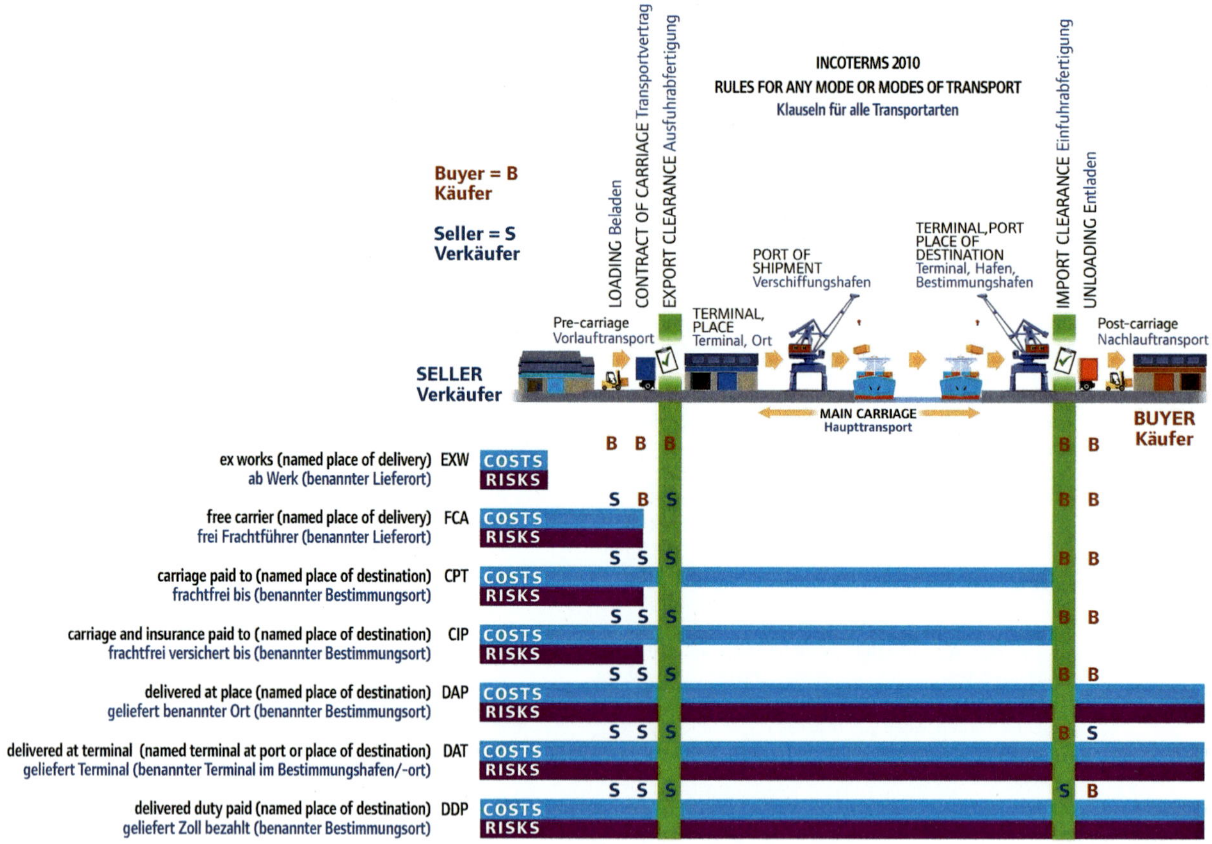
INCOTERMS 2010
RULES FOR ANY MODE OR MODES OF TRANSPORT
Klauseln für alle Transportarten
Buyer = B
Käufer
Seller = S
Verkäufer
LOADING Beladen
CONTRACT OF CARRIAGE Transportvertrag
EXPORT CLEARANCE Ausfuhrabfertigung
IMPORT CLEARANCE Einfuhrabfertigung
UNLOADING Entladen
Pre-carriage
Vorlauftransport
TERMINAL, PLACE
Terminal, Ort
PORT OF SHIPMENT
Verschiffungshafen
TERMINAL, PORT PLACE OF DESTINATION
Terminal, Hafen, Bestimmungshafen
Post-carriage
Nachlauftransport
SELLER
Verkäufer
MAIN CARRIAGE
Haupttransport
BUYER
Käufer
ex works (named place of delivery) EXW
ab Werk (benannter Lieferort)
free carrier (named place of delivery) FCA
frei Frachtführer (benannter Lieferort)
carriage paid to (named place of destination) CPT
frachtfrei bis (benannter Bestimmungsort)
carriage and insurance paid to (named place of destination) CIP
frachtfrei versichert bis (benannter Bestimmungsort)
delivered at place (named place of destination) DAP
geliefert benannter Ort (benannter Bestimmungsort)
delivered at terminal (named terminal at port or place of destination) DAT
geliefert Terminal (benannter Terminal im Bestimmungshafen/-ort)
delivered duty paid (named place of destination) DDP
geliefert Zoll bezahlt (benannter Bestimmungsort)
COSTS
RISKS
EXW: B B B … B B
FCA: S B S … B B
CPT: S S S … B B
CIP: S S S … B B
DAP: S S S … B B
DAT: S S S … B S
DDP: S S S … S B

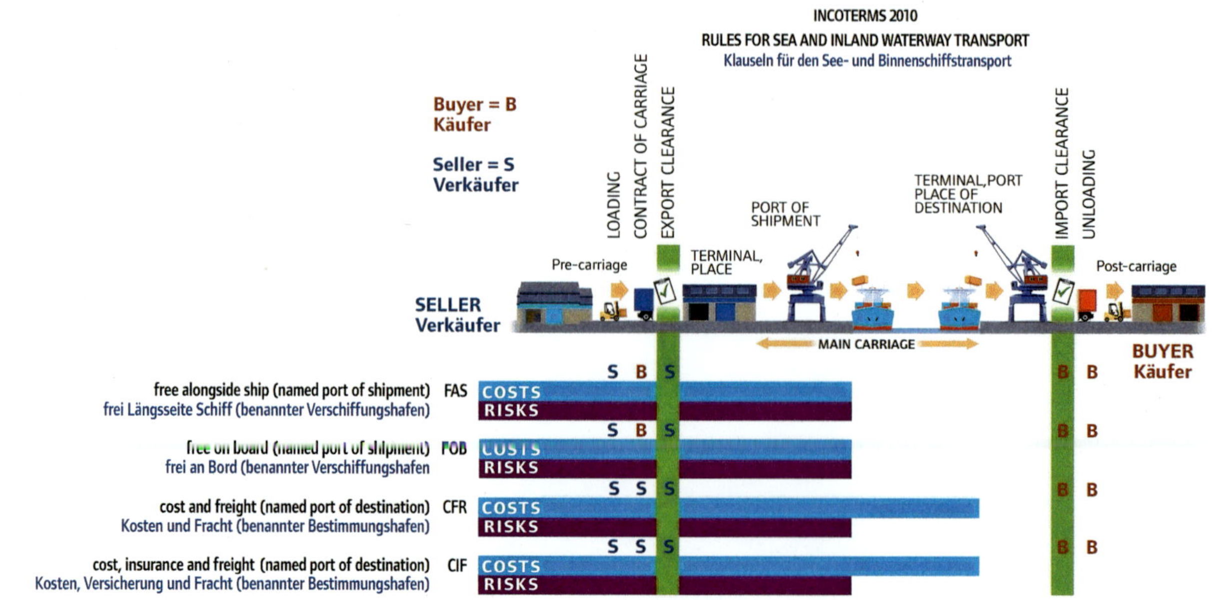
INCOTERMS 2010
RULES FOR SEA AND INLAND WATERWAY TRANSPORT
Klauseln für den See- und Binnenschiffstransport
Buyer = B
Käufer
Seller = S
Verkäufer
LOADING
CONTRACT OF CARRIAGE
EXPORT CLEARANCE
IMPORT CLEARANCE
UNLOADING
Pre-carriage
TERMINAL, PLACE
PORT OF SHIPMENT
TERMINAL, PORT PLACE OF DESTINATION
Post-carriage
SELLER
Verkäufer
MAIN CARRIAGE
BUYER
Käufer
free alongside ship (named port of shipment) FAS
frei Längsseite Schiff (benannter Verschiffungshafen)
free on board (named port of shipment) FOB
frei an Bord (benannter Verschiffungshafen
cost and freight (named port of destination) CFR
Kosten und Fracht (benannter Bestimmungshafen)
cost, insurance and freight (named port of destination) CIF
Kosten, Versicherung und Fracht (benannter Bestimmungshafen)
COSTS
RISKS
FAS: S B S … B B
FOB: S B S … B B
CFR: S S S … B B
CIF: S S S … B B

In international trade the eleven Incoterms® 2010 Rules (international commercial terms) are used in contracts of sale to define the rights and obligations of the buyer and seller as regards risk, transport, insurance, packing, customs duty and documentation. They are terms of delivery.

Rules for any mode or modes of transport

EXW – EX WORKS (... named place of delivery)
The seller makes the goods available at his premises in the customary packing. The seller assists the buyer in obtaining any documentation needed at the buyer's expense. The buyer is responsible for loading the goods, transporting them to their destination, customs clearance and insurance.

FCA – FREE CARRIER (... named place of delivery) Multimodal transport
The seller is not responsible for the main carriage of the goods. The seller delivers the goods at his own expense and risk, in the customary packing, cleared for export to the carrier nominated by the buyer. The seller provides the commercial invoice and, if requested, a certificate of origin at the buyer's expense. If the goods are collected at the seller's premises, the seller loads the goods. The seller bears the risks until the goods are in the custody of the first carrier. After that the buyer bears all the costs and risks of transporting the goods to their destination.

CPT – CARRIAGE PAID TO (... named place of destination) Multimodal transport
The seller pays for the main carriage of the goods. The seller delivers the goods, in the customary packing, cleared for export to the carrier which he nominates. The seller bears the risk until the goods have been delivered into the custody of the first carrier. The seller pays the transport costs for the goods, excluding transport insurance, up to the named destination. The buyer is responsible for insuring the goods for the main carriage and pays all import duties and taxes.

CIP – CARRIAGE AND INSURANCE PAID TO (... named place of destination) Multimodal transport
The seller pays for the main carriage of the goods. The seller delivers the goods in the customary packing, cleared for export to the carrier which he nominates. The seller bears the risk until the goods have been delivered into the custody of the first carrier. The seller pays the transport costs for the goods, including transport insurance, up to the named destination. The buyer pays all import duties and taxes.

DAP – DELIVERED AT PLACE (... named place of destination) Multimodal transport
The seller is responsible for the carriage of the goods in the customary packing, cleared for export to the named terminal at the destination by the carrier which he nominates. He bears the risk until the goods have been delivered to the named terminal. The buyer is responsible for unloading the goods at the place of destination and pays all import duties and taxes.

DAT – DELIVERED AT TERMINAL (... named terminal at port or place of destination) Multimodal transport
The seller is responsible for the carriage of the goods in the customary packing, cleared for export to the named terminal at the destination by the carrier which he nominates. He bears the risk until the goods have been delivered to the named terminal. The seller is responsible for unloading the goods at the place of destination. The buyer pays all import duties and taxes.

DDP – DELIVERED DUTY PAID (... named place of destination) Multimodal transport
The seller is responsible for the carriage of the goods in the customary packing, cleared for export to the named terminal at the destination by the carrier which he nominates. He bears the risk until the goods have been delivered to the named destination. The seller pays all import duties and taxes. The buyer is responsible for unloading the goods at the place of destination.

Rules for sea and inland waterway transport

FAS – FREE ALONGSIDE SHIP (... named port of shipment)
The seller is not responsible for the main carriage of the goods. The seller delivers the goods at his own expense and risk, in the customary packing, cleared for export, alongside the vessel selected by the buyer at the named port of shipment. Thereafter, the buyer bears all the costs and risks of transporting the goods to their destination.

FOB – FREE ON BOARD (... named port of shipment)
The seller is not responsible for the main carriage of the goods. The seller delivers the goods at his own expense and risk, in the customary packing, cleared for export, on board the vessel selected by the buyer unless otherwise agreed, at the named port of shipment. Thereafter, the buyer bears all the costs and risks of transporting the goods to their destination.

CFR – COST AND FREIGHT (... named port of destination)
The seller pays for the main carriage of the goods. The seller delivers the goods at his own expense and risk, in the customary packing, cleared for export, on board the vessel selected by the buyer, at the named port of shipment. The seller pays the transport costs for the goods, excluding transport insurance, up to the named port of destination. The buyer is responsible for insuring the goods for the main carriage and pays all import duties and taxes.

CIF – COST INSURANCE FREIGHT (... named port of destination)
The seller pays for the main carriage of the goods. The seller delivers the goods at his own expense and risk, in the customary packing, cleared for export, on board the vessel selected by the buyer, at the named port of shipment. The seller pays the transport costs for the goods, including transport insurance, up to the named port of destination. The buyer pays all import duties and taxes.

Terms of payment

payment in advance	Vorauszahlung/Vorkasse
cash with order (CWO)	Barzahlung bei Auftragserteilung
payment by irrevocable and confirmed documentary (letter of) credit	Zahlung durch unwiderrufliches und bestätigtes Dokumentenakkreditiv
documents against payment (D/P) / cash against documents (CAD)	Kasse gegen Dokumente
cash on delivery (COD)	gegen Nachnahme
1/3 with order, 1/3 on delivery, 1/3 within 30 days after delivery	1/3 bei Auftragserteilung, 1/3 bei Lieferung, 1/3 innerhalb von 30 Tagen nach Lieferung
payment within 60 days from date of invoice	Zahlung innerhalb von 60 Tagen nach Rechnungsdatum
10 days 2%, 30 days net	Zahlung innerhalb 10 Tagen abzüglich 2 % Skonto oder innerhalb 30 Tagen netto
payment on receipt of goods	Zahlung bei Erhalt der Waren
payment on receipt of invoice	Zahlung bei Rechnungserhalt
documents against (three months') acceptance (D/A)	Dokumente gegen (Dreimonats-)Akzept
open account terms with monthly/quarterly settlement	offenes Zahlungsziel mit monatlicher/vierteljährlicher Abrechnung

Useful phrases

Describing apprenticeships	Unit 1
– I work for … (name of employer) in … (place).	– *Ich arbeite für … (Name des Arbeitgebers) in … (Ort).*
– I'm in the first/second/third/last year of my apprenticeship.	– *Ich befinde mich im ersten/zweiten/dritten/letzten Jahr meiner Ausbildung.*
– I go to vocational training college on day release every … (e.g. Monday and Tuesday).	– *Ich gehe jeden … (z. B. Montag und Dienstag) in die Berufsschule zum berufsbegleitenden Unterricht.*
– … on block release for six weeks / three months twice/three times a year.	– *… habe Blockunterricht für sechs Wochen / drei Montate zwei-/dreimal im Jahr.*
– I decided to train as a management assistant in wholesale and foreign trade because I like working in commerce / buying and selling.	– *Ich entschied mich, eine Ausbildung zum/zur Groß- und Außenhandelskaufmann/-frau / Kaufmann/-frau im Groß- und Außenhandel zu machen, weil ich gerne im Handel arbeite / kaufe und verkaufe.*
– My apprenticeship lasts/takes three years / is three years long.	– *Meine Ausbildung dauert drei Jahre / geht drei Jahre lang.*

Making introductions	Unit 1
Greeting people you do not know	
– Good morning/afternoon/evening. I'm …	– *Guten Morgen/Tag/Abend. Ich bin …*
– How do you do? My name is …	– *Freut mich. Mein Name ist …*
– Nice/Pleased to meet you.	– *Es freut mich, Sie kennen zu lernen.*
– Nice to meet you, too.	– *Ganz meinerseits.*
– Excuse me. Are you …?	– *Entschuldigung. Sind Sie …?*
– Yes, I am. / No, I'm not. I'm …	– *Ja, das bin ich / Nein, das bin ich nicht … Ich heiße …*
– Welcome to …	– *Herzlich willkommen bei/in …*
– Thank you. It's nice to be here.	– *Dankeschön. Es ist schön, hier zu sein.*
Introducing people	
– This is … . / These are my colleagues, John and Mary.	– *Das ist … . / Das sind meine Kollegen, John und Mary.*
– I'd like to introduce … from the … department.	– *Darf ich Ihnen … aus der …-Abteilung vorstellen?*
Making small talk	
– I hope you're well.	– *Ich hoffe, es geht dir/Ihnen gut.*
– … is such a beautiful city!	– *… ist so eine schöne Stadt.*
– The weather is so good today!	– *Das Wetter ist heute so schön.*
– Did you have a good trip/flight?	– *Hattest du / Hatten Sie eine gute Reise / einen guten Flug?*

Describing jobs and responsibilities	Unit 2
– I work in a team of management assistants.	– *Ich arbeite in einem Team von Managementassistenten/-assistentinnen.*
– I make sure that we sell as many products as possible.	– *Ich stelle sicher, dass wir so viele Produkte wie möglich verkaufen.*
– I report directly to the Export Sales Manager.	– *Ich bin dem/der Vertriebsleiter/in direkt unterstellt.*
– I arrange for goods to be shipped abroad.	– *Ich organisiere den Güterversand ins Ausland.*
– I make sure our products get to our customers.	– *Ich stelle sicher, dass unsere Produkte zu unseren Kunden/Kundinnen geliefert werden.*
– It's my responsibility to obtain the necessary shipping documents.	– *Ich bin dafür verantwortlich, die Lieferpapiere zu besorgen.*

– I'm in charge of public relations, so my work involves managing our Facebook page and sometimes organizing events.	– *Ich bin für die Öffentlichkeitsarbeit zuständig/verantwortlich. Unter anderem betreue ich unsere Facebook-Seite und organisiere ab und an Veranstaltungen.*
– I am responsible for maintaining our customer database.	– *Ich bin dafür verantwortlich, die Kundendatenbank zu pflegen.*
– Working in my department means understanding customs regulations.	– *Für die Arbeit in meiner Abteilung ist es wichtig, die Zollvorschriften zu kennen.*
– I work fixed hours / a 39-hour week.	– *Ich habe feste Arbeitszeiten / eine 39-Stunden-Woche.*
– I do a lot of overtime.	– *Ich mache viele Überstunden.*

Telephoning **Unit 2**

Identifying yourself	
– Good morning. My name's …	– *Guten Morgen. Ich heiße …*
– Good afternoon. This is … from … (company).	– *Guten Tag. Hier spricht … von … (Firma).*
– Good evening. I work for …	– *Guten Abend. Ich arbeite bei …*
Explaining the reason for your call	
– I'm enquiring about …	– *Ich wollte mich nach … erkundigen.*
– I'd like some information on …	– *Ich hätte gern nähere Informationen zu …*
Asking for a person/department	
– I'd like to speak to Mr/Ms …	– *Ich würde gerne (mit) Herrn/Frau … sprechen.*
– Could you put me through to the … department, please?	– *Könnten Sie mich bitte zur …-Abteilung durchstellen/weiterleiten?*
Saying what you want to do	
– Can I leave a message?	– *Kann ich eine Nachricht hinterlassen?*
– I'll call again later.	– *Ich rufe später noch einmal an.*
– Could you ask Mr/Ms … to call me back?	– *Könnten Sie Herrn/Frau … bitten, mich zurückzurufen?*
Ending the call	
– Thank you for your help/assistance.	– *Vielen Dank für Ihre Hilfe/Unterstützung.*
– You're welcome.	– *Gern geschehen. / Bitte sehr.*
– Goodbye.	– *Auf Wiederhören.*
– Have a nice day/evening.	– *Einen schönen Tag/Abend noch.*

Taking telephone calls **Unit 2**

– Who's calling, please?	– *Wie ist Ihr Name bitte?*
– Could you spell your name, please?	– *Könnten Sie bitte Ihren Namen buchstabieren?*
– I'm sorry, I didn't understand. Could you repeat that, please?	– *Es tut mir leid, ich habe das nicht verstanden. Könnten Sie das bitte wiederholen?*
– I'll put you through.	– *Ich stelle Sie durch.*
– I'm trying to connect you.	– *Ich versuche, Sie zu verbinden.*
– Please hold the line.	– *Bleiben Sie bitte dran.*
– I'm afraid the line is engaged.	– *Der Anschluss ist leider besetzt.*
– I'm sorry, … (name) is unavailable at the moment.	– *Es tut mir leid, aber … (Name) ist im Moment nicht da.*
– Would you like to speak to someone else?	– *Möchten Sie mit jemand anderem sprechen?*
– Would you like to leave a message?	– *Möchten Sie eine Nachricht hinterlassen?*

Showing visitors around the company	Unit 3
Giving a tour of the company	
– Let's start by visiting …	– *Lassen Sie uns zuerst mit dem Besuch der/des … beginnen.*
– Here we have the … department.	– *Hier ist die …-Abteilung.*
– On the left/right, you can see …	– *Zu Ihrer Linken/Rechten sehen Sie …*
– This is where we make/dispatch …	– *Hier stellen wir … her / versenden wir …*
Asking for and giving directions	
– Could you tell me the way to …, please?	– *Könnten Sie mir bitte sagen, wie ich nach/zur/zum … komme?*
– Yes, certainly.	– *Ja, selbstverständlich.*
– Go down the corridor until you get to …	– *Gehen Sie den Flur entlang, bis Sie zur/zum … kommen.*
– Take the first/second/last door on your right.	– *Nehmen Sie die erste/zweite/letzte Tür rechts.*
– Turn right at the end of the corridor.	– *Biegen Sie am Ende des Flures rechts ab.*
Offering help/refreshments	
– Can I take your coat?	– *Möchten Sie Ihren Mantel ablegen?*
– Would you like something to drink?	– *Darf ich Ihnen etwas zu trinken anbieten?*
– Would you like some tea/coffee/water?	– *Möchten Sie Tee/Kaffee/Wasser?*

Describing companies	Unit 3
Describing your company	
– We are based/located in … (country/city).	– *Wir sind in … (Land/Stadt) ansässig.*
– Our headquarters is in … (country/city).	– *Unsere Hauptfiliale befindet sich in … (Land/Stadt).*
– The company was founded in … (year).	– *Das Unternehmen wurde im Jahr … gegründet.*
– We are in the … industry.	– *Wir sind in der …-Branche (tätig).*
– We are a multinational/local/small company/ business.	– *Wir sind ein internationales/regionales/kleines Unternehmen / ein kleiner Betrieb.*
– We are a start-up.	– *Wir sind ein Start-Up(-Unternehmen).*
– We have branches/subsidiaries/offices in … (country) / all over the world.	– *Wir haben Filialen/Tochterfirmen/Büros in … (Land) / überall auf der Welt.*
– We have … (number) employees.	– *Wir haben … (Anzahl) Angestellte.*
– We are a privately-owned company / corporation.	– *Wir sind ein Privatunternehmen.*
Talking about the company's products/services	
– We make/produce/manufacture …	– *Wir produzieren/erzeugen … / stellen … her.*
– We sell/distribute …	– *Wir verkaufen/vertreiben …*
– We offer/provide …	– *Wir liefern … / bieten … an.*
– We make sure the goods get from A to B.	– *Wir stellen sicher, dass die Güter von A nach B geliefert werden.*

Giving presentations	Unit 3
Introduction	
– My name is … and this is my partner, …	– *Mein Name ist … und das ist meine/e Partner/in, …*
– We are apprentices at … in Germany.	– *Wir sind Auszubildende bei … in Deutschland.*
– This morning, I'm / we're going to talk about …	– *Heute spreche ich / sprechen wir über …*
– Our topic today is …	– *Das heutige Thema lautet …*
Structure	
– I've divided my presentation into three main parts, as follows: …	– *Ich habe meine Präsentation in drei (Haupt-)Teile gegliedert, und zwar …*
– First/Firstly, … ; Second/Secondly, … ; After that / Then …	– *Erstens, … ; Zweitens, … ; Anschließend/Dann …*

Signposts

– To begin with, ...; Next, ...; Now ...	– *Zuerst, ...; Als Nächstes, ...; Jetzt ...*
– The next topic I'm going to talk about is ...	– *Das nächste Thema, das ich behandeln möchte, lautet ...*
– Now I'd like to move on to ...	– *Jetzt möchte ich zum Thema ... übergehen.*

Handouts

– I've prepared a few things/handouts for you to take away.	– *Ich habe etwas/Handouts für Sie zum Mitnehmen vorbereitet.*
– I hope you'll find these copies of the graphics useful.	– *Ich hoffe, dass Sie diese Kopien der Grafiken nützlich finden.*

Conclusion

– Before I finish my presentation, I'd just like to mention ...	– *Bevor ich meinen Vortrag beende, möchte ich ... kurz erwähnen.*
– I'd like to go over the main points again.	– *Ich möchte die Hauptpunkte/Hauptargumente nochmals kurz darlegen.*
– Finally, ...; In conclusion, ...; In summary, ...	– *Zum Schluss ...; Abschließend ...; Zusammenfassend ...*

Questions / Thanking the audience

– Are there any questions?	– *Gibt es / Haben Sie noch Fragen?*
– We have time for a few questions / one last question.	– *Wir haben noch Zeit für ein paar Fragen / eine letzte Frage.*
– Well, that's the end of my presentation.	– *Damit bin ich am Ende meiner Präsentation angelangt.*
– Thank you for your attention / for listening.	– *Vielen Dank für Ihre Aufmerksamkeit / fürs Zuhören.*

Writing emails — Unit 4

Salutation

– Dear Sir or Madam (*formal*)	– *Sehr geehrte Damen und Herren,*
– Dear Mr/Ms Smith (*formal*)	– *Sehr geehrter Herr / Sehr geehrte Frau Schmidt,*
– Dear Paul (und Paula)	– *Lieber Paul (, Liebe Paula),*
– Good morning, Paul (*less formal*)	– *Guten Morgen, Paul,*
– Hi/Hello Paula (*less formal*)	– *Hallo Paula,*

Complimentary close

– Yours faithfully (*formal*)	– *Mit freundlichen Grüßen*
– Regards / Best regards / Best wishes / Yours sincerely (*formal*)	– *Mit freundlichen Grüßen / Freundliche Grüße*
– Regards / Best regards / Best wishes	– *Viele Grüße / Mit freundlichen Grüßen*
– All the best (*less formal*)	– *Alles Gute / Herzliche Grüße*

Opening sentence

– I'm just writing to ... (*formal*)	– *Ich schreibe Ihnen, um zu / weil ...*
– Just a quick note/message to ... (*less formal*)	– *Nur eine kurze Mitteilung/Nachricht, um zu ...*

Conclusion

– I look forward to your reply / to hearing from you. (*formal*)	– *Ich freue mich auf Ihre Antwort.*
– Many thanks in advance. (*formal*)	– *Vielen Dank im Voraus.*
– I hope to hear from you soon. (*less formal*)	– *Ich freue mich, bald von Ihnen/dir zu hören.*

Describing graphs — Unit 5

– The graph/chart shows/presents ...	– *Die Grafik / Das Diagramm zeigt ... / stellt ... dar.*
– The horizontal/vertical axis has a scale from ... to ...	– *Die waagerechte/senkrechte Achse hat eine Skala von ... bis ...*
– The x axis / The y axis is divided into ... units/sections each representing ...	– *Die X-Achse / Die Y-Achse ist unterteilt in ... Einheiten/Abschnitte, die ... darstellen.*

– The number of export sales decreased slightly last month.	– *Die Zahl der Exportverkäufe ging im letzten Monat leicht zurück.*
– The number of orders jumped sharply in June.	– *Die Zahl der Bestellungen nahmen im Juni stark zu.*
– They reached their peak in August, then levelled off towards the end of the year.	– *Sie erreichten ihren Höhepunkt im August und blieben dann bis zum Ende des Jahres gleich.*
– New customers accounted for about/roughly/ approximately one third of all orders.	– *Neukunden machten etwa/annähernd/ungefähr ein Drittel aller Bestellungen aus.*
– Sales to China made up just over/under one tenth of export sales.	– *Exporte nach China machten etwas über/unter ein Zehntel der Exportverkäufe aus.*

Taking part in meetings	**Unit 6**
Starting the meeting	
– Good morning everybody and welcome to ...	– *Guten Tag alle zusammen und Willkommen zu ...*
– The first item on today's agenda is ...	– *Der erste Punkt der heutigen Tagesordnung lautet ...*
Asking someone to speak	
– Would you go ahead, please?	– *Würden Sie / Würdest du bitte fortfahren?*
– Can you give us a brief update?	– *Könnten Sie / Könntest du uns einen kurzen Zwischenstand geben?*
Asking for reactions	
– Would anyone like to comment or ask a question?	– *Möchte jemand einen Kommentar abgeben oder eine Frage stellen?*
– Are there any issues?	– *Gibt es Probleme?*
Asking for opinions	
– What do you think about ...?	– *Wie denken Sie / denkst du über ...?*
– What's your opinion of / view on ...?	– *Was ist Ihre/deine Meinung zu ...?*
Expressing a point of view	
– It seems to me (that) ...	– *Mir kommt es so vor, als ob ...*
– In my opinion, ...	– *Meiner Meinung nach ...*
– From what I can see, ...	– *Soweit ich sagen kann, ...*
Asking to speak	
– Could I just say that ...?	– *Darf ich (kurz) anmerken, dass ...?*
– Can I come in on that?	– *Darf ich dazu etwas sagen?*
Agreeing	
– Yes, I agree.	– *Ja, ich stimme zu / ich bin (damit) einverstanden.*
– I thoroughly agree with ... (name).	– *Ich stimme ... (Name) völlig zu.*
Disagreeing politely	
– (I'm afraid) I don't agree with ... (name).	– *Leider stimme ich ... (Name) nicht zu. / Ich kann ... (Name) leider nicht zustimmen.*
– I agree up to a point, but ...	– *Ich stimme bis zu einem gewissen Punk zu, aber ...*
– Actually, / In fact, I think (that) ...	– *Eigentlich/Vielmehr denke ich, dass ...*
Starting a new topic	
– Let's move on to the next topic, which is ...	– *Lassen Sie uns / Lass uns mit dem nächsten Thema fortfahren, es handelt sich um ...*
– The next point is ...	– *Der nächste Punkt lautet ...*
Promising action	
– I'll pass that on to ...	– *Ich werde das an ... weiterleiten.*
– We'll get back to you.	– *Wir werden auf Sie/dich zurückkommen.*
Finishing the meeting	
– Let's wrap up the meeting with ...	– *Lassen Sie uns / Lass uns das Treffen damit zum Abschluss bringen.*
– Well, that would seem to be it.	– *Gut, das scheint alles zu sein.*

Negotiating	Unit 6
Direct approach	
– Are you prepared to …?	– *Sind Sie bereit, …?*
– Can you reduce the price by … (e.g. €20)?	– *Können Sie den Preis um … (z. B. € 20) reduzieren?*
– Will you increase … (e.g. production) by …?	– *Werden Sie … (z. B. die Produktion) um … steigern?*
– Are you able to guarantee … (e.g. delivery)?	– *Können Sie … (z. B. die Auslieferung) garantieren?*
– Do you accept these terms?	– *Akzeptieren Sie diese Bedingungen?*
Indirect approach	
– We need to talk about …	– *Wir müssen über … sprechen.*
– … is a problem for us.	– *… ist ein Problem für uns.*
– … (e.g. our competitors) are …% cheaper.	– *… (z. B. unsere Konkurrenz) ist/sind … % günstiger.*
– We're thinking of ordering more/less …	– *Wir denken darüber nach, mehr/weniger … zu bestellen.*
– We need a maximum/minimum of …	– *Wir benötigen ein Maximum/Minimum von …*
– How much more … can you produce?	– *Wie viel mehr … können Sie produzieren?*
Offering help	
– We can help you with …	– *Wir können Ihnen helfen, indem wir …*
– We can give you … if you can …	– *Wir können Ihnen … geben, wenn Sie … (können).*
– I suggest that you …	– *Ich schlage vor, (dass) Sie …*
Accommodating changes to the offer	
– I have some room to move.	– *Ich habe etwas Spielraum.*
– OK. I'm prepared to offer you that.	– *In Ordnung. Das kann ich Ihnen gern anbieten.*
– Yes, I think we can do that for you.	– *Ja, ich denke, dass wir das für Sie tun können.*
Refusing what the client asks for	
– I'm sorry, but the price that I quoted you is the best I can do.	– *Es tut mir leid, aber dies ist der äußerste Preis. Mehr kann ich Ihnen nicht anbieten.*
– No. I'm afraid I can't do that.	– *Nein, das kann ich leider nicht tun.*
– Well, I can't offer you … . But what I can do is …	– *Ich kann Ihnen kein/e … anbieten. Ich kann Ihnen jedoch …*

Making arrangements	Unit 6
Inviting sb to a meeting	
– Ms Smith would like to invite you to a meeting on … (day) at … (time).	– *Frau Smith möchte Sie zu einem Treffen am … (Tag) um … (Zeit) Uhr einladen.*
– I would like to invite you to lunch/dinner.	– *Ich würde Sie gern zum Mittagessen/Abendessen einladen.*
– The meeting will take place at my office / our premises in … (place/city).	– *Das Treffen findet in meinem Büro / in unseren Räumlichkeiten in … (Ort/Stadt) statt.*
Accepting/Declining the invitation	
– Thank you for your invitation to meet you at … (place).	– *Vielen Dank für Ihre Einladung zum Treffen in … (Ort).*
– I am pleased / We are delighted to accept your invitation/offer.	– *Gern nehme(n) ich/wir Ihre Einladung / Ihr Angebot an.*
– I'm sorry, but I'm … (reason) on that date / at that time.	– *Es tut mir leid, aber ich kann an diesem Tag / zu dieser Zeit nicht, da … (Grund).*
Making an alternative suggestion	
– How about meeting on … (day) at … (time) instead?	– *Wie wäre es, wenn wir uns stattdessen am … (Tag) um … (Uhrzeit) treffen?*
Conclusion	
– I look forward to your reply. (*formal*)	– *Ich freue mich auf Ihre Antwort.*
– I hope to hear from you soon. Many thanks.	– *Ich hoffe, bald von Ihnen zu hören. Besten Dank.*

Advising customers	Unit 7
Greeting a potential customer	
– Good morning/afternoon/evening, Mr/Ms … / sir/ madam.	– *Guten Morgen/ Tag/Abend, Herr/Frau …*
– Is there anything (in particular) I can do for you, or would you like just to look around?	– *Kann ich etwas für Sie tun oder möchten Sie sich erstmal umschauen?*
– Just let me know if you need any help.	– *Lassen Sie mich wissen, wenn Sie Hilfe brauchen.*
Asking about the customer's needs	
– What sort of thing are you looking for?	– *Nach was / Wonach genau suchen Sie?*
– Is it for commercial/industrial or private use?	– *Ist es für den geschäftlichen/gewerblichen oder privaten Gebrauch gedacht?*
Suggesting suitable products/services	
– How about / What about … (product)?	– *Wie wäre es mit … (Produkt)?*
– Here's a(n) … . Is this the sort of thing you're looking for?	– *Hier ist ein/e … . Suchen Sie (nach) so etwas?*
Following up the discussion	
– Would you like me to send you an offer?	– *Soll/Darf ich Ihnen ein Angebot schicken / zukommen lassen?*
– You'll get our offer today/tomorrow / by the end of the week.	– *Sie erhalten unser Angebot heute/morgen / bis zum Ende der Woche.*

Writing business letters	Unit 8
Salutation	
– Dear Sir or Madam (*to a firm*)	– *Sehr geehrte Damen und Herren,*
– Dear Mr/Ms Brown	– *Sehr geehrte/r Herr/Frau Brown,*
– Dear Sharon	– *Liebe Sharon,*
Complimentary close	
– Yours faithfully (*BE: to a firm*)	– *Mit freundlichen Grüßen*
– Yours very truly / Cordially yours (*AE: to a firm*)	– *Mit freundlichen Grüßen*
– Yours sincerely (*BE*)	– *Mit freundlichen Grüßen*
– Sincerely yours / Best personal regards (*AE*)	– *Mit freundlichen Grüßen / Beste Grüße*

Writing enquiries	Unit 8
Source of address	
– I was most impressed by the … (product[s]) you showed me on your stand at the … (name of – trade fair / exhibition).	– *Ich war von den … (Produkten), die Sie mir an Ihrem Stand auf der … (Name der Handelsmesse/ Ausstellung) gezeigt haben, sehr beeindruckt.*
– We have seen your company's advertisement in the current edition of … (name of publication) and are most interested in your products.	– *Wir haben Ihre Anzeige in der aktuellen Ausgabe von … (Name der Veröffentlichung) gesehen und interessieren uns sehr für Ihre Produkte.*
– We note from your company's website that you sell a wide range of … (products).	– *Wir entnehmen der Homepage Ihres Unternehmens, dass Sie ein breites Sortiment an/von … (Produkten) anbieten.*
– You have been recommended to us by … (name of the person/company), who tells us that you have brought out … (product).	– *Sie wurden uns von … (Name der Person/Firma) empfohlen, der/die uns mitgeteilt hat, dass Sie … (Produkt) auf den Markt gebracht haben.*
Description of your company	
– We are a rapidly growing / leading producer/ importer/exporter/wholesaler of … with excellent business contacts all over … (region/country) and beyond.	– *Wir sind ein schnell wachsender / führender Produzent von … / Importeur/Exporteur/Großhändler für … mit hervorragenden Geschäftskontakten in ganz … (Region/Land) und darüber hinaus.*

– Our company is a major/well-established (German) wholesaler of … (goods) both at home and abroad.	– *Unser Unternehmen ist ein bedeutender / gut eingeführter (deutscher) Großhändler von (Waren/ Dienstleistungen) im In- und Ausland.*
– We have many long-standing customers all over Europe.	– *Wir haben viele langjährige Kunden in ganz Europa.*
Reason for your enquiry	
– At present we are particularly interested in … (goods/ services) at reasonable prices.	– *Gegenwärtig gilt unser besonderes Interesse … (Waren/Dienstleistungen) zu vernünftigen Preisen.*
– We are looking for a supplier of …	– *Wir suchen nach einem Lieferanten für …*
– … as goods of this nature are currently in great demand.	– *… da zurzeit eine große Nachfrage für Waren dieser Art besteht.*
Your requirements	
– Please send us a favourable quotation for these items / for … (products).	– *Bitte schicken Sie uns ein passendes (Preis)Angebot für diese Artikel / für … (Produkte).*
– We would welcome a quotation for …	– *Wir hätten gerne ein (Preis)Angebot für …*
– We would therefore/also be grateful if you would let us have details of your entire range.	– *Wir wären Ihnen deshalb/ebenso dankbar, wenn Sie uns Einzelheiten über Ihre gesamte Produktpalette schicken würden.*
– Please let us have your latest catalogue …	– *Bitte lassen Sie uns Ihren neuesten Katalog … zukommen.*
– … and export price list	– *… und Exportpreisliste*
– … including all discounts granted	– *… einschl. aller gewährten Rabatte*
– Please also let us know if you are able to provide samples.	– *Bitte teilen Sie uns auch mit, ob Sie Muster/Proben zur Verfügung stellen können.*
– … including details of your terms of delivery and payment.	– *… einschl. Einzelheiten über Ihre Liefer- und Zahlungsbedingungen.*
– Details of your terms of delivery and payment would also be appreciated.	– *Bitte lassen Sie uns Informationen zu Ihren Liefer- und Zahlungsbedingungen zukommen.*
– We would require delivery … (e.g. within 6 weeks / by the end of the month) at the latest.	– *Die Lieferung hätten wir gerne spätestens … (z. B. innerhalb 6 Wochen / bis Ende des Monats).*
– How soon can you deliver?	– *Wie schnell können Sie liefern?*
– We would be grateful if a representative could call on us.	– *Wir wären dankbar, wenn uns ein/e Außendienstmitarbeiter/in besuchen könnte.*
References	
– References are available on request.	– *Referenzen sind auf Wunsch erhältlich.*
Polite ending	
– If your products meet our requirements, we will place a substantial order.	– *Wenn Ihre Produkte unseren Anforderungen entsprechen, werden wir einen größeren Auftrag erteilen.*
– We look forward to hearing from you soon / in the near future.	– *Wir hoffen auf baldige Antwort. / Wir freuen uns auf Ihre Antwort.*
– We look forward to your early reply with interest.	– *Wir sehen Ihrer baldigen Antwort mit Interesse entgegen.*

Writing offers	Unit 9
Reference to enquiry	
– As agreed in our telephone conversation of this morning (of today) ...	– *Wie heute (Morgen) telefonisch vereinbart ...*
– We were delighted to receive your enquiry dated ... about our ... product(s).	– *Wir waren sehr erfreut, Ihre Anfrage vom ... über unser(e) ... Produkt(e) zu erhalten.*
– I am pleased to let you have details of our offer in writing.	– *Gerne lasse ich Ihnen ein schriftliches Angebot zukommen.*
– Many thanks for the above-mentioned enquiry / your enquiry dated ...	– *Wir danken für die oben genannte Anfrage / Ihre Anfrage vom ...*
Description of your company/goods/services	
– We are a major distributor of ... (product/s) ...	– *Wir sind ein bedeutender Großhändler für ... (Produkt/e) ...*
– ... with an excellent reputation throughout Europe.	– *... mit einem hervorragenden Ruf in ganz Europa.*
– Our company manufactures a wide range of high-quality (engineering) products ...	– *Unser Unternehmen stellt eine breite Palette von hochwertigen (Maschinenbau)Produkten her ...*
– ... and already has many satisfied customers throughout Western Europe and North America.	– *... und hat bereits viele zufriedene Kunden überall in Westeuropa und Nordamerika.*
Sales material	
– A brochure on ... / Our current catalogue and price list is/are attached/enclosed for your information.	– *Zu Ihrer Information ist/sind ein Prospekt über ... / unser aktueller Katalog und eine aktuelle Preisliste angehängt/beigefügt.*
– To download details of our entire range together with our export price list, please visit our website at www.cantec.com.	– *Um Einzelheiten über unsere gesamte Produktpalette sowie unsere Exportpreisliste herunterzuladen, besuchen Sie bitte Sie unsere Homepage unter www.cantec.com.*
– Samples are available on request.	– *Muster sind auf Wunsch erhältlich.*
Price	
– As regards the goods requested, we are pleased to submit the following quotation:	– *Was die gewünschten Waren betrifft, freuen wir uns, Ihnen folgendes Angebot zu unterbreiten:*
– ... and will be pleased to supply you with ... (product/s) at ... (price) each.	– *... und liefern Ihnen gerne ... (Produkt/e) zu je ... (Preis).*
– at ... (price, e.g. €10) per unit	– *zu ... (Preis, z. B. € 10) pro Stück*
Terms and discounts	
– Our prices are quoted FOB Hamburg.	– *Unsere Preise verstehen sich FOB Hamburg.*
– Delivery will be made CIP Frankfurt Airport / DDP your premises.	– *Die Lieferung erfolgt CIP Flughafen Frankfurt / DDP Ihren Geschäftsräumen.*
– Wholesalers are granted a trade discount of ...%.	– *Großhändlern wird ein Handelsrabatt von ... % eingeräumt.*
– A quantity discount of ...% is granted on orders for 10 or more ... (e.g. machines, items).	– *Bei Abnahme von 10 oder mehr ... (z. B. Geräten, Artikeln) wird ein Mengenrabatt von ... % gewährt.*
– Our terms of payment for an initial order are CWO.	– *Bei Erstauftrag kann lediglich bar bei Auftragserteilung gezahlt werden.*
– Our usual terms of payment are 1/3 with order and 2/3 by irrevocable and confirmed documentary letter of credit.	– *Unsere üblichen Zahlungsbedingungen sind 1/3 bei Auftragserteilung und 2/3 per unwiderrufliches und bestätigtes Doumentenakkreditiv.*
– ... or, with favourable references, 10 days 3%, 30 days net.	– *... oder bei günstigen Referenzen, 3 % Skonto bei Zahlung innerhalb von 10 Tagen, netto bei Zahlung innerhalb von 30 Tagen.*
– Regular customers may be granted preferential terms.	– *Stammkunden können wir ein Angebot zu günstigen (Zahlungs-)Konditionen machen.*
– If regular orders are placed with our company, open account terms may be granted.	– *Wenn unserer Firma regelmäßige Aufträge erteilt werden, kann ein offenes Zahlungziel gewährt werden.*

Delivery

– within … days after receipt of order	– *innerhalb von … Tagen nach Auftragseingang*
– Delivery is made within approx. 30 days after receipt of order.	– *Die Lieferung erfolgt innerhalb von ca. 30 Tagen nach Auftragseingang.*
– while stocks last	– *solange der Vorrat reicht*

Polite ending

– We look forward to receiving your order.	– *Wir freuen uns über Ihren Auftrag.*
– We feel sure that a trial order will convince you of the quality of our products.	– *Wir sind sicher, dass ein Probeauftrag Sie von der Qualität unserer Produkte überzeugen wird.*
– We hope our offer is to your liking …	– *Wir hoffen, dass unser Angebot Ihnen zusagt …*
– … and look forward to doing business with you.	– *… und freuen uns auf die Zusammenarbeit.*
– Please do not hesitate to contact us if you require further details.	– *Bitte zögern Sie nicht, mit uns Kontakt aufzunehmen, wenn Sie weitere Einzelheiten benötigen.*

Clarifying details on the phone — Unit 9

Repeating what somebody says

A: We can deliver everything by Thursday.	*A: Wir können alles am Donnerstag liefern.*
B: Thursday. Right.	*B: Donnerstag, in Ordnung.*

Asking for clarification

A: My address is 23 Fairfield Gardens.	*A: Meine Adresse lautet 23 Fairfield Gardens.*
B: Sorry. Did you say 23 or 33?	*B: Entschuldigung, sagten Sie 23 oder 33?*

Reading something back

A: My number is 0171 452869.	*A: Meine Nummer lautet 0171452869.*
B: I'll just read that back to you. 0171 452869.	*B: Ich wiederhole: 0171 452869.*
– Can you just read that back to me?	– *Könnten Sie das bitte wiederholen?*
– Can I just check that? It's …	– *Kann ich das kurz kontrollieren/überprüfen? Es ist die …*

Writing orders — Unit 10

Reference to offer

– Many thanks for your offer dated …	– *Vielen Dank für Ihr Angebot vom …*
– Having seen your offer on the internet and spoken to you on the telephone …	– *Nachdem wir Ihr Angebot im Internet gesehen und mit Ihnen gesprochen haben …*
– We have seen your offer for … on the internet.	– *Wir sind im Internet auf Ihr Angebot von … aufmerksam geworden.*

Details of goods/services ordered

– We now wish to place an order / a trial order for the following goods:	– *Wir möchten einen Auftrag/Probeauftrag über folgende Waren erteilen:*
– [*Headings*] Quantity / Description / Size / Article no.	– *[Überschriften] Menge / Beschreibung / Größe / Artikel-Nr.*

Price(s) and discount(s)

– [*Headings*] Unit price / List price / Catalogue price / Total	– *[Überschriften] Stückpreis / Listenpreis / Katalogpreis / Gesamt*
– Subtotal / Total price	– *Zwischensumme / Gesamtpreis*
– 19% VAT (value added tax)	– *19 % USt/MwSt (Umsatzsteuer/Mehrwertsteuer)*

Delivery

– delivery date/period	– Liefertermin/-zeit
– within 10 days after receipt of order	– innerhalb 10 Tagen nach Auftragserhalt
– by 30 June 20..	– bis zum 30. Juni 20..

Transport/Insurance

– Transport and insurance of the goods from … to … via …	– *Versand und Versicherung der Ware von … nach … über …*
– …will be arranged by us/you.	– *… wird von uns/Ihnen übernommen.*

Payment	
– 30% in advance, 70% after completion	– *30 % im Voraus, 70 % bei Fertigstellung*
– by transfer to our a/c at ... (bank)	– *per Überweisung auf unser Konto bei ... (Geldinstitut)*
Acknowledgement/Advice of dispatch	
– We look forward to receiving your advice of dispatch.	– *Wir freuen uns auf den Erhalt Ihrer Versandanzeige.*
– Please send us your confirmation of order and advice of dispatch in the near future.	– *Bitte schicken Sie uns Ihre Auftragsbestätigung und Versandanzeige in den nächsten Tagen zu.*
Polite ending	
– We trust the goods will arrive punctually and in good condition ...	– *Wir vertrauen darauf, dass die Ware pünktlich und in gutem Zustand ankommt ...*
– ... and will place further/regular orders if they sell well.	– *... und werden weitere/regelmäßige Aufträge erteilen, wenn sie sich gut verkauft.*

Making complaints	**Unit 11**
Reference to goods	
– The above-mentioned goods were delivered on ... and forwarded to our customers all over Germany/ Europe.	– *Die obengenannten Waren wurden am ... geliefert und unseren Kunden überall in Deutschland/Europa zugestellt.*
– We regret to inform you that they/we are dissatisfied with them.	– *Leider müssen wir Ihnen mitteilen, dass sie/wir damit unzufrieden sind.*
Description of problem	
– On examining the goods / When they opened the boxes ...	– *Bei Prüfung der Ware / Beim Öffnen der Kartons ...*
– ... we / our customers discovered that ...	– *... stellten wir / unsere Kunden fest, dass ...*
– ... some/all of the articles/appliances were dirty/ discoloured / (badly) damaged.	– *... einige/alle Artikel/Geräte verschmutzt/verfärbt / (stark) beschädigt waren.*
– The appliances have proved to be unreliable and (often) produce ... (e.g. poor results / half-cooked food).	– *Die Geräte haben sich als unzuverlässig* – *erwiesen und liefern (oft) ... (z. B. schlechte Ergebnisse / halbgare Lebensmittel).*
– We enclose/attach photographs of these items for your information.	– *Wir fügen Fotos dieser Artikel zu Ihrer Information bei.*
Request for explanation	
– Please explain why our order was so poorly executed / how this could happen.	– *Bitte erklären Sie, warum unser Auftrag so schlecht ausgeführt wurde / wie dies geschehen konnte.*
– We would welcome your explanation of the damage.	– *Wir würden eine Erklärung (von Ihnen) für den Schaden begrüßen.*
Consequences for the buyer and seller	
– Whatever the case may be, ...	– *Wie dem auch sei, ...*
– ... we are returning the damaged/faulty/defective goods to you carriage forward.	– *... wir schicken die beschädigten/fehlerhaften/ defekten Güter unfrei an Sie zurück.*
– You will appreciate that ...	– *Bitte haben Sie Verständnis, dass ...*
– ... we cannot sell these articles (at the normal price).	– *... wir diese Artikel nicht (zum normalen Preis) verkaufen können.*
Request for action	
– We must therefore insist that you ...	– *Wir müssen daher darauf bestehen, dass Sie ...*
– We must therefore ask you to ...	– *Wir müssen Sie deshalb bitten, ...*
– ... supply us with replacements free of charge by return.	– *... uns umgehend kostenlosen Ersatz liefern.*
– ... replace the entire consignment.	– *... die ganze Lieferung (zu) ersetzen.*
– ... as these goods are needed urgently / are still under warranty.	– *... da die Waren dringend benötigt werden / da es sich um einen Garantiefall handelt.*
– We must therefore ask you to reduce the price by ...%.	– *Wir bitten Sie daher, den Preis um ... % zu reduzieren.*

English	German
Polite ending	
– We feel sure you will appreciate that …	– *Sie werden sicherlich dafür Verständnis haben, dass …*
– … our future business relationship will depend on how this matter is dealt with.	– *… die Fortsetzung unserer Geschäftsbeziehung von der Regelung dieser Angelegenheit abhängig ist.*
– We trust you will deal with this matter without delay.	– *Wir vertrauen darauf, dass Sie sich unverzüglich mit dieser Angelegenheit befassen werden.*
– We expect to hear from you in the very near future.	– *Wir erwarten, von Ihnen recht bald zu hören.*
– We look forward to receiving your comments on this matter without delay.	– *Wir erwarten Ihre unverzügliche Stellungnahme zu dieser Angelegenheit.*

Responding to complaints	**Unit 11**
Acknowledgement of complaint	
– We have (just) received your email/letter regarding the above-mentioned consignment of …	– *Wir haben (soeben) Ihre E-Mail / Ihren Brief bezüglich der oben erwähnten Lieferung … erhalten.*
– Your complaint is now being investigated.	– *Ihre Beschwerde wird jetzt geprüft.*
First expression of regret	
– We are sorry to hear the consignment was delayed and that some of the good are below standard.	– *Es tut uns leid zu hören, dass die Sendung verzögert eintraf und dass einige der Waren nicht der Qualität entsprachen.*
– … and are dismayed to hear that the consignment is unsatisfactory.	– *… und es tut uns (sehr) leid zu hören, dass die Lieferung unzufriedenstellend ist.*
Action taken	
– Since hearing from you, / receiving your email, …	– *Nach Erhalt Ihrer Nachricht/E-Mail …*
– … we have investigated the matter and discovered / found out that …	– *… haben wir die Angelegenheit untersucht und herausgefunden, dass …*
– … the wrong component was used in (some of the) … (e.g. the machines / appliances).	– *… das falsche Bauteil in (einigen) … (z. B. Maschinen / Geräten) benutzt wurde .*
– … there was an error in our dispatch section / quality control department.	– *… es einen Fehler in unserer Versand- / Qualitätssicherungsabteilung gab.*
Solution	
– In the meantime, we are sending you replacements at no extra charge by return.	– *In der Zwischenzeit schicken wir Ihnen umgehend kostenlosen Ersatz.*
– The missing… (articles) / Replacements will be delivered to you carriage paid within 24/48 hours.	– *Die fehlenden … (Artikel) / Ersatzgeräte werden Ihnen innerhalb 24/48 Stunden frachtfrei geliefert.*
– If you are prepared to keep the … (goods), we will grant you a reduction in price of …%.	– *Wenn Sie bereit sind, die … (Waren) zu behalten, gewähren wir Ihnen einen Rabatt von … %.*
– Under the circumstances, we are willing to offer you a replacement consignment or a reduction in price of …% on the unsatisfactory items.	– *Unter diesen Umständen sind wir bereit, Ihnen eine Ersatzsendung oder eine Preisreduzierung von … % auf die nicht zufriedenstellenden Artikel anzubieten.*
Second apology	
– Please accept our apologies for this.	– *Wir entschuldigen uns vielmals.*
– In the meantime, please accept our apologies for the inconvenience caused (which was due to circumstances beyond our control).	– *Bitte entschuldigen Sie die Unannehmlichkeiten. Leider entzogen sich die Umstände in diesem Fall unserer Kontrolle.*
– We assure you it will not happen again.	– *Wir versichern Ihnen, dass es nicht wieder vorkommen wird.*
Polite ending	
– We hope this suggestion/solution will find your approval.	– *Wir hoffen, dass dieser Vorschlag / diese Lösung Ihre Zustimmung finden wird.*
– We look forward to doing further business with you.	– *Wir freuen uns darauf, weitere Geschäfte mit Ihnen zu tätigen.*

Querying invoices	**Unit 11**
Reference to invoice/statement	
– Thank you for the above-mentioned invoice/statement for … (details, e.g. skiing boots / goods received last quarter).	– *Danke für die obengenannte (Ab)Rechnung für … (Einzelheiten, z. B. Skischuhe / die im letzten Quartal erhaltenen Waren).*
– We refer to your/our statement / invoice no. … dated … for … (amount).	– *Wir beziehen uns auf Ihre/unsere (Ab)Rechnung Nr. … vom … über … (Betrag).*
Reference to payment of statement/invoice	
– Our statement/invoice no. … is enclosed/attached for settlement.	– *Unsere (Ab)Rechnung Nr. … ist zwecks Zahlung beigefügt.*
– On receipt of your remittance for €1,000 the goods will be shipped.	– *Nach Erhalt Ihrer Überweisung von € 1.000 werden die Waren versandt.*
– Please note that payment was due on … (date).	– *Bitte nehmen Sie zur Kenntnis, dass die Zahlung am … (Datum) fällig war.*
– We would appreciate settlement of the total amount due in the next few days.	– *Wir bitten Sie, den fälligen Gesamtbetrag in den nächsten Tagen zu begleichen.*
Reference to discrepancies/errors/amendments	
– Having checked your statement/invoice against our (own) records, …	– *Nachdem wir Ihre (Ab)Rechnung mit unseren (eigenen) Aufzeichnungen verglichen haben, …*
– … we must point out that …	– *… müssen wir darauf hinweisen, dass …*
– … it is incorrect in the following points:	– *… sie in folgenden Punkten nicht korrekt ist:*
– … you have not included our credit note no. XYZ123 for €200 dated 10 August.	– *… Sie unsere Gutschrift Nr. XYZ123 über € 200 vom 10. August … nicht berücksichtigt haben.*
– … items 1 and 2 of your statement have been incorrectly charged.	– *… die Posten 1 und 2 Ihres Kontoauszugs nicht richtig belastet worden sind.*
– … you have omitted to include the quantity/special discount of …% granted on orders for 100 units or more.	– *… Sie haben versäumt, den Mengen-/Sonderrabatt von … %, der für Aufträge über 100 Stück oder mehr gewährt wird, einzubeziehen.*
– … the (special) discount granted on items 1 and 2 for … (e.g. skiing boots) is only 15% instead of 50%, as promised.	– *… der auf den Posten … / die Posten … und … gewährte (Sonder)Rabatt für … (z. B. Skischuhe) nur 15 % beträgt statt wie versprochen 50 %.*
– … you have overcharged/undercharged us by (a total of) €200.	– *… Sie uns (insgesamt) € 200 zu viel / zu wenig berechnet haben.*
– We can confirm that the …% discount promised on … (goods) was not granted.	– *Wir können bestätigen, dass der versprochene Rabatt von … % auf … (Ware) nicht gewährt wurde.*
– We are returning your statement/invoice and would request you …	– *Wir schicken Ihnen Ihre (Ab)Rechnung zurück und bitten Sie, …*
– … to amend it.	– *… diese abzuändern.*
– … to send us an amended statement/invoice, which we will pay by transfer to your account.	– *… uns eine berichtigte (Ab)Rechnung zu schicken, die wir per Überweisung auf Ihr Konto begleichen werden.*
– As soon as we have received your amended statement/invoice we will remit the sum owing.	– *Sobald wir Ihre berichtigte (Ab)Rechnung erhalten haben, werden wir Ihnen den geschuldeten Betrag überweisen.*
– An amended statement/invoice for … (amount) is enclosed/attached.	– *Wir fügen eine berichtigte (Ab)Rechnung über … (Betrag) bei.*
Polite ending	
– Please do not hesitate to contact us should you have any queries.	– *Bitte zögern Sie nicht, mit uns Kontakt aufzunehmen, wenn Sie irgendwelche Fragen haben.*
– We apologize for the inaccuracy/inaccuracies in our statement/invoice and assure you there will be no recurrence of this in the future.	– *Wir entschuldigen uns für die Unstimmigkeit(en) in unserer (Ab)Rechnung und versichern Ihnen, dass sich dies in Zukunft nicht wiederholen wird.*
– We apologize for the inconvenience and look forward to doing further business with you.	– *Wir entschuldigen uns für die Unannehmlichkeiten und freuen uns darauf, weitere Geschäfte mit Ihnen zu tätigen.*

– We look forward to receiving your corrected statement/invoice.	– *Bitte schicken Sie uns die berichtigte (Ab)Rechnung zu.*
– We trust you will be remitting the amount in question in the next few days.	– *Wir vertrauen darauf, dass Sie den ausstehenden Betrag in den nächsten Tagen überweisen werden.*
– If payment has already been made please disregard this letter/email.	– *Wenn die Zahlung bereits erfolgt ist, betrachten Sie diesen Brief / diese E-Mail bitte als gegenstandslos.*

Writing reminders

– I am writing in connection with the attached unpaid invoice for …	– *Ich schreibe in Zusammenhang mit der angefügten unbezahlten Rechnung für …*
– I would like to draw your attention to invoice no. …	– *Bitte sehen Sie sich Rechnung Nr. … noch einmal an.*
– We are sure this must be an oversight and have included a copy of the invoice for your convenience.	– *Wir sind uns sicher, dass es sich hierbei um einen Irrtum handelt, und fügen zu Ihrer Information eine Kopie der Rechnung bei.*
– Would you please settle your account by the end of the month at the latest.	– *Bitte begleichen Sie die Rechnung bis spätestens zu Ende des Monats.*
– If your payment of our invoice has crossed with this letter, we kindly ask you to ignore this reminder.	– *Falls Sie die Rechnung schon beglichen haben sollten, betrachten Sie dieses Schreiben bitte als gegenstandslos.*
– Payment is now … (length of time) overdue.	– *Ihre Zahlung is nun … (Zeitspanne) überfällig.*
– If we have not received your payment within the next seven days, we will have to instruct our solicitors to take legal action.	– *Wenn wir Ihre Zahlung nicht innerhalb der nächsten sieben Tage erhalten, werden wir unseren Anwalt hinzuziehen, um rechtliche Schritte einzuleiten.*

Writing covering letters **Unit 12**

Opening phrases	
– With reference to your advertisement in … (newspaper) of … (date), …	– *Bezugnehmend auf Ihre Ausschreibung in … (Zeitung) vom … (Datum), …*
– I would like / wish to apply for the above-mentioned position/post of … (job).	– *Hiermit möchte ich mich für die oben genannte Stelle als … (Berufsbezeichnung) bewerben.*
Education, training, present employment	
– I attended … (school/college) for … (length of time).	– *Von … bis … (Jahr) besuchte ich … (Schule/ Hochschule).*
– I studied … (subjects) at vocational school in … (place) from … (date) to … (date).	– *An der Berufs(fach)schule in … (Ort) lernte/belegte ich … (Fächer) von … (Datum) bis … (Datum).*
– At present I am working for a/an … (type of company) as a/an … (job).	– *Zurzeit arbeite ich bei einem/einer … (Firmenbezeichnung) als … (Berufsbezeichnung).*
– I will complete my period of training on … (date).	– *Am … (Datum) werde ich meine Ausbildung abschließen.*
Closing paragraph	
– I enclose / Enclosed is my CV (*BE*) / résumé (*AE*) / a list of my qualifications and experience.	– *Anbei finden Sie meinen Lebenslauf / eine Übersicht meiner Qualifikationen und Erfahrungen.*
– I am available for interview at your earliest convenience.	– *Für ein Vorstellungsgespräch stehe ich Ihnen jederzeit gern zur Verfügung.*
– I hope you will consider my application favourably and …	– *Über eine positive Antwort freue ich mich sehr und …*
– … (I) look forward to hearing from you in the near future.	– *… (ich) freue mich darauf, bald von Ihnen zu hören.*

Thematic vocabulary

Training and apprenticeships — Unit 1

A levels *pl*	Abitur, Abiturfächer
apprentice	Auszubildende/r, Lehrling
apprenticeship	Lehre, Ausbildung
block release	Blockunterricht (an der Berufsschule)
certificate	Zeugnis, Diplom
course	Studiengang
coursework	schriftliche Arbeit(en)
day release	tagweise Freistellung zur beruflichen Weiterbildung
degree	Abschluss
diploma	Abschlusszeugnis
final grade	Abschlussnote
grade	Note
internship	Praktikum
job experience	Berufserfahrung, praktische Erfahrung
living expenses *pl*	Lebenshaltungskosten
part-time	Teilzeit
to qualify	einen/den Abschluss machen
qualification	Qualifikation, Abschluss
salary	Gehalt
school leaving certificate	Schulabschluss
school qualification	Schulabschluss
theoretical	theoretisch
to train (to be a ...)	eine Aubildung (zum/zur ...) machen
trainee	Auszubildende/r
training company	Ausbildungsbetrieb
training course	Ausbildung
training supervisor	Ausbildungsleiter/in
vocational college/school	Berufsschule, Berufsfachschule
vocational training	Berufsausbildung
work experience	Praktikum
workplace	Arbeitsplatz

Working conditions — Unit 1

availability	Verfügbarkeit
benefits *pl*	Zusatzleistungen, Sozialleistungen
business trip	Geschäftsreise
company car	Firmenwagen
condition	Bedingung
contract	Vertrag
dress code	Kleiderordnung
facilities *pl*	Einrichtungen, Anlagen
flexitime	Gleitzeit
hot-desking	Hotdesking
job prospects *pl*	berufliche Perspektiven
lunch break	Mittagspause
open-plan office	Großraumbüro
overtime	Überstunden
permanent	unbefristet
salary	Gehalt
shared desk	gemeinsamer Arbeits-/Schreibtisch
shift work	Schichtarbeit
working conditions *pl*	Arbeitsbedingungen
working hours *pl*	Arbeitszeit(en)

Job titles — Unit 2

accountant	Buchhalter/in
accounting manager	Buchhaltungsleiter/in
chief executive officer (CEO)	Vorstandsvorsitzende/r, Geschäftsführer/in
colleague	Kollege, Kollegin
commercial director	kaufmännische/r Leiter/in
employee	Arbeitnehmer/in, Beschäftigte/r
employer	Arbeitgeber/in, Unternehmer/in
factory manager	Betriebsleiter/in, Werksleiter/in
head of department	Abteilungsleiter/in
industrial management assistant	Industriekaufmann/-frau
IT management assistant	Informatikkaufmann/-frau
legal adviser	Justiziar/in
line manager	(direkte/r) Vorgesetzte/r
management assistant in wholesale and foreign trade	Kaufmann/-frau im Groß- und Außenhandel
manager	Manager/in
managing director	Geschäftsführer/in
office management assistant	Kaufmann/-frau für Büromanagement
personal assistant (PA)	Persönliche/r Assistent/in
production manager	Produktionsleiter/in
project manager	Projektleiter/in
purchasing director/manager	Einkaufsleiter/in
receptionist	Empfangsmitarbeiter/in
sales director	Vertriebsleiter/in
(sales) representative	(Handels-)Vertreter/in
secretary	Sekretär/in
specialist	Fachmann/-frau
staff	Personal
technician	Techniker/in
warehouse manager	Lagerleiter/in

Company departments — Unit 2

Accounting / Accounts (department)	Buchhaltung
Administration	Verwaltung
board (of directors)	Geschäftsführung, Vorstand
department	Abteilung
Distribution (department)	Vertrieb
Finance (department)	Rechnungswesen
Financial Controlling (department)	Controlling
head office/headquarters	Zentrale
Human Resources (HR) (department)	Personal(abteilung)
labelling	Bezeichnung, Etikettierung
Legal department	Rechtswesen
management	Geschäftsleitung, Geschäftsführung
manufacturing	Fertigung, Herstellung
Market Research (department)	Marktforschung(sabteilung)
material delivery	Materialanlieferung

press	Presse
Pricing (department)	Kalkulation
project management	Projektleitung
Purchasing (department)	Einkauf(sabteilung)
Quality Assurance/ Management (department)	Qualitätssicherung
reception	Rezeption, Empfang
Research and Development (R&D) (department)	Forschung(s-) und Entwicklung(sabteilung)
Sales (department)	Verkauf(sabteilung), Vertrieb
warehouse	Lager(halle)

Company organization — Unit 3

(general) partnership	Personengesellschaft, offene Handelsgesellschaft (OHG)
limited company (Ltd) *BE* / **closed corporation** *AE*	Gesellschaft mit beschränkter Haftung (GmbH)
limited partnership	Kommanditgesellschaft (KG)
public limited company (plc) *BE* / **open corporation** *AE*	Aktiengesellschaft (AG)
share	Aktie
shareholder	Aktionär/in, Teilhaber/in
sole proprietor/trader	Einzelunternehmer/in

The supply chain — Unit 4

buyer	Käufer/in
carrier	Spediteur, Spedition
client	Klient/in
competition	Konkurrenz
competitor	Konkurrent/in, Konkurrenz
consumer	(End)Verbraucher/in
customer, client	Kunde, Kundin
distribution	Vertrieb
exporter	Exporteur
forwarding agent	Spediteur, Spedition
freight forwarder	Spediteur, Spedition
importer	Importeur
manufacturer	Hersteller/in
retailer	Einzelhändler/in
seller	Verkäufer/in
supplier	Lieferant
wholesaler	Großhändler

Sales and marketing — Unit 5

to analyse	analysieren
cashier	Kassierer/in
check-out	Kasse
customer loyalty	Kundenbindung, Kundentreue
customer satisfaction	Kundenzufriedenheit
to customize sth	etw individuell anpassen
field research	Feldforschung
to gather data	Daten erfassen
to launch sth	etw auf den Markt bringen, etw starten
to market sth	etw vermarkten
market research	Marktforschung
marketing strategy	Vermarktungsstrategie
pricing strategy	Preisstrategie
primary research	Primärforschung
product brief	Produktbeschreibung
product launch	Produkteinführung
product line	Produktlinie
product range	Sortiment
to promote sth	für etw werben, etw promoten
to publish	veröffentlichen
purchasing history	Kaufhistorie, Einkaufsverhalten
questionnaire	Fragebogen
recommendation	Empfehlung
recommended retail price (RRP)	unverbindliche Preisempfehlung (UVP)
retail outlet	Einzelhandelsgeschäft
sales channel	Absatzweg, Vertriebskanal
secondary research	Sekundärforschung
specific	bestimmte/r/s
statistics	Statistik(en)
study	Untersuchung, Studie
survey	Umfrage
target group	Zielgruppe
to target sb	jdn ins Visier nehmen
unique selling proposition (USP)	Alleinstellungsmerkmal

Advertising strategies — Unit 5

to advertise sth	etw bewerben, für etw Werbung machen
advertising	Reklame, Werbung
brand	Marke
branding	Markenbildung
bricks and mortar outlet	stationäres Geschäft
campaign	(Werbe-)Kampagne
catalogue	Katalog
catchphrase	Schlagwort, Slogan
celebrity endorsement	Werbung mit Prominenten
consultant	Berater/in
customer discount	Kundenrabatt
discount	Rabatt, Skonto
giveaway	Werbegeschenk
to have sth on offer	etw im Angebot haben, etw anbieten
mass media *pl*	Massenmedien
niche	Nische
promotion	Werbung, Promotion
promotional	Werbe-
social media *pl*	soziale Medien
special deal	Sonderangebot
stealth advertising	heimliche Werbung, Schleichwerbung
targeted advertising	gezielte/zielgruppengenaue Werbung
testimonial	Erfahrungsbericht
traditional	traditionell, hergebracht
virtual	virtuell

Describing graphs — Unit 5

bar chart	Säulendiagramm
chart	Diagramm
decrease	Abnahme, Rückgang
to decrease	abnehmen, zurückgehen
drastic(ally)	drastisch
drop	Fall, Rückgang
to drop	fallen, zurückgehen
figures *pl*	Zahlen
financial year	Geschäftsjahr
to flatten out	auf gleichem Stand bleiben
graph	Diagramm, Kurve
to hit a maximum	einen Höchstwert/-stand erreichen
increase	Zunahme, Anstieg
to increase	zunehmen, ansteigen
to level off	sich einpendeln
line graph	Liniendiagramm
minimum	Tiefstwert, Tiefstand
output	Produktion
pie chart	Tortendiagramm
quarter	Quartal
quarterly	vierteljährlich, Quartals-
to recover	sich erholen
to remain constant	gleich bleiben
to rise	steigen, ansteien
sales figures *pl*	Umsatzzahlen, Verkaufszahlen
unit	Einheit, Stück
volume of sales	Umsatzvolumen
x-axis	X-Achse
y-axis	Y-Achse

Meetings and presentations — Unit 6

absence	Abwesenheit
absentee	Abwesende/r
agenda	Tagesordnung
any other business (AOB)	Verschiedenes
audience	Publikum
body language	Körpersprache
to call a meeting	eine Sitzung einberufen
to circulate sth	etw (an alle) verteilen
conference	Tagung, Konferenz
conference room	Besprechungsraum, Sitzungssaal
contact details *pl*	Kontaktdaten
to cover	(Thema) behandeln
date	Termin
eye contact	Blickkontakt
to face sb	sich jdm zuwenden, jdn anschauen
feedback	Reaktion(en), Rückmeldung(en)
gesture	Geste
to get a message across	eine Botschaft vermitteln
graphic	Grafik
handout	Arbeitsblatt, Broschüre
to highlight	hervorheben
index card	Karteikarte
invitation	Einladung
item on the agenda	Tagesordnungspunkt
minutes *pl*	Protokoll
to participate	teilnehmen
participant	Teilnehmer/in
to point to sth	auf etw deuten, auf etw zeigen
presenter	Redner/in, Vortragende/r, Moderator/in
prompt card	Moderationskarte
report	Bericht
to reserve	reservieren
screen	Leinwand, Bildschirm
slide	*(Präsentation:)* Folie
to take place	stattfinden
to take the chair / to be in the chair	die Sitzung leiten
talk/lecture	Vortrag
transparency	(Overhead-)Folie, Dia
to turn one's back on sb	jdm den Rücken zuwenden
visual aids *pl*	visuelle Hilfsmittel

Trade fairs — Unit 7

booth	(Messe-)Stand
brochure	Broschüre, Prospekt
corner stand	Eckstand
end of block stand	Kopfstand
event	Veranstaltung
exhibition hall	Messehalle, Ausstellungshalle
fair	Messe
flyer	Faltblatt
giveaway	Werbegeschenk
to hand sth out	etw austeilen, etw ausgeben
island stand	Inselstand
loyalty card	Kundenkarte
rental fee	Miete
sales literature	Verkaufsprospekte, Informationsmaterial
stand	(Messe-)Stand
trade fair	Fachmesse, Branchenmesse
venue	Veranstaltungsort

Business trips — Unit 7

accommodation	Unterkunft, Unterbringung
air-conditioned	klimatisiert
air conditioning	Klimaanlage, Klimatisierung
appointment	Termin
arrival	Ankunft
to attend sth	etw besuchen, an etw teilnehmen
to cancel	absagen, stornieren
to check in	sich anmelden, einchecken
to check out	sich abmelden, auschecken
conference centre	Tagungszentrum, Kongresszentrum
connecting flight	Anschlussflug
departure	Abreise, Abflug
dining room	*(Hotel:)* Speisesaal
excess *BE*	*(Versicherung:)* Selbstbehalt
front desk	Rezeption
insurance cover	Versicherungsschutz
meeting room	Sitzungszimmer, Konferenzraum
mileage	*(Mietwagen:)* (enthaltene) Kilometer

one-way flight	einfacher Flug
passenger	Passagier/in
to postpone	verschieben
reception	Empfang, Rezeption
receptionist	Empfangsmitarbeiter/in
request	Bitte, Anfrage
requirement	Anforderung
reservation	Reservierung, Buchung
return flight	Hin- und Rückflug
shuttle	Zubringer
smoke-free	rauchfrei
trade fair	Messe
travel expenses *pl*	Reisekosten, Reisespesen

Commercial correspondence — Units 8–10

address	Adresse
addressee	Empfänger/in
to attach sth	anhängen *(E-Mail)*
attachment	Anhang
attention (attn)	zu Händen
attention line	Zeile „zu Händen"
(Best) Regards	Viele Grüße, Mit freundlichen Grüßen
Best wishes	Mit freundlichen Grüßen
body	Haupttext
complimentary close	Schlussformel
date	Datum
Dear Sir or Madam	Sehr geehrte Damen und Herren,
to enclose	beifügen *(Brief)*
enclosure (enc)	Anlage
inside address	Innenadresse
letterhead	Briefkopf
paragraph	Absatz
reference (ref)	Zeichen
registered mail/post	Einschreiben
salutation	Anrede
sender	Absender
signature block	Signatur
signature	Unterschrift
subject (line)	Betreff(zeile)
Yours faithfully	Mit freundlichen Grüßen
Yours sincerely	Mit freundlichen Grüßen

Business transactions — Units 8–10

acknowledgement/ confirmation (of an order)	Auftragsbestätigung
to acknowledge an order	einen Auftrag bestätigen
to adjust a complaint	eine Reklamation bearbeiten/ regulieren
advice of dispatch	Versandanzeige, Versandmitteilung
advice of payment	Zahlungsanzeige
complaint	Reklamation, Beschwerde
consignment	Sendung
contract	Vertrag
to deliver	liefern
delivery	Lieferung
to dispatch	versenden, absenden
enquiry	Anfrage
to fill an order	einen Auftrag erledigen
to place an order	einen Auftrag erteilen
order	Auftrag, Bestellung
order form	Bestellformular
order number	Bestellnummer
quotation	Angebot, Kostenvoranschlag
receipt (of goods)	Erhalt, (Waren-)Eingang
repeat order	Folgeauftrag
sales *pl*	Verkäufe, Umsatz
sample	Muster
to ship	versenden
shipping documents *pl*	Versandpapiere
stock	Ware(n), (Lager-)Bestand
terms of delivery *pl*	Lieferbedingungen
terms of payment *pl*	Zahlungsbedingungen
trial order	Probeauftrag
turnover	Umsatz

Shipping documents — Units 8–10

advice of dispatch	Versandanzeige
airfreight	Luftfracht
air waybill (AWB)	Luftfrachtbrief
approval: on approval	zur Ansicht, auf Probe
bill of lading (B/L)	Seefrachtbrief, Konnossement
bonded warehouse	Zollverschlusslager
cargo	Ladung, Fracht
cargo liner	Frachtschiff
cargo space	Frachtraum
certificate of origin (C/O)	Ursprungszeugnis
chamber of (industry and) commerce	(Industrie- und) Handelskammer
combined transport waybill	kombinierter Warenbegleitschein
commercial invoice	Handelsrechnung
consignment note [road or rail]	Frachtbrief [Straßen- oder Bahn-]
consignee	Empfänger/in
consignor	Absender/in, Versender/in
consular invoice	Konsularrechnung, Konsultatsfaktura
contract of carriage	Beförderungsvertrag
customs clearance	Zollabfertigung
customs declaration	Zollinhaltserklärung
customs invoice	Zollrechnung, Zollfaktura
dangerous goods certificate	Gefahrgutbescheinigung
delivery note	Lieferschein
destination; port of destination	Bestimmungsort; Bestimmungshafen
export licence	Exportlizenz
forwarder's certificate of receipt (FCR)	Spediteurübernahmebescheinigung
freight	Fracht
freight rates	Frachttarife
import licence	Einfuhrgenehmigung
to take out insurance	eine Versicherung abschließen
insurance certificate (IC)	Versicherungsschein, -police

to insure goods against a risk	Ware gegen ein Risiko versichern
to issue	ausstellen, ausfertigen
loss; total or partial loss	Verlust; Gesamt- oder Teilverlust
packing list	Packliste
pro forma invoice (P/I)	Proforma-Rechnung
rail consignment note	Bahnfrachtbrief
receipt	Erhalt; Empfangsbescheinigung
ro-ro (roll on-roll off) ferry/vessel	von Straßenfahrzeugen befahrbare/s Fähre/Schiff
shipping note (S/N)	Schiffszettel, Warenbegleitschein
single administrative document	Einheitspapier
waybill (WB)	Frachtbrief

Packaging

bag	Tasche (groß); Beutel (klein)
bale	Ballen
barrel	Fass, Tonne
basket	Korb
bottle	Flasche
box	Kasten, Kiste, Schachtel
can, tin	Dose
carton	Karton
crate	Kiste
drum	Tonne
packet	Paket
pallet	Laderost, Pallette
pouch (small)	Tasche
roll	Rolle
sack	Sack
sea container	Seecontainer
tube	Tube

Complaints — Unit 11

apology	Entschuldigung
broken	zerbrochen
to cancel sth	etw stornieren
compensation	Entschädigung
credit note	Gutschrift
damaged	beschädigt
dented	verbeult
dirty	verschmutzt
discoloured	verfärbt
discrepancy	Unstimmigkeit, Diskrepanz
dissatisfied	unzufrieden
delayed	verspätet
faulty	mangelhaft, defekt
free of charge	unentgeltlich, kostenlos
inconvenience	Unannehmlichkeiten
late	verspätet
mix-up	Durcheinander, Verwechslung
to overcharge sb	jdm zu viel berechnen
to query sth	etw infrage stellen, etw anzweifeln
to rectify defects	Mängel beheben
to reimburse sb	jdm Geld zurückzahlen, jdn entschädigen
reimbursement	Rückerstattung
to remit	*(Geld:)* überweisen
to replace sth	etw ersetzen
replacement	Ersatz
to resolve sth	etw lösen
scratched	verkratzt
soiled	beschmutzt
statutory	gesetzlich vorgeschrieben
unsatisfactory	unzulänglich, unbefriedigend
warranty period	Gewährleistungszeit

Conversion tables

Distance

1 inch (in)	= 2.54 centimetres
1 foot (ft)	= 30.48 centimetres
1 yard (yd)	= 0.9144 metres
1 mile (mi)	= 1.609 kilometres
1 centimetre	= 0.3937 inches (3⁄8 inch)
1 metre	= 39.37 inches (3 feet, 3 3⁄8 inches)
1 kilometre	= 0.62137 miles

Area

1 square inch (in^2)	= 6.452 square centimetres
1 square foot (ft^2)	= 0.0929 square metres
1 square mile (m^2)	= 2.59 square kilometres
1 square centimetre	= 0.155 square inches
1 square metre	= 10.764 square feet
1 square kilometre	= 0.3861 square miles

Mass/Weight

1 ounce (oz)	= 28.35 grams
1 pound (lb)	= 0.453 kilograms
1 UK ton ('long ton')	= 1,016 kilograms
1 US ton ('short ton')	= 907 kilograms
1 gram	= 0.035 ounces
1 kilogram	= 2 pounds, 3.3 ounces

Volume

1 UK pint (pt)	= 0.568 litres
1 UK quart (qt)	= 1.137 litres
1 UK gallon (gal)	= 4.546 litres
1 US pint	= 0.473 litres
1 US quart	= 0.946 litres
1 US gallon	= 3.785 litres
1 cubic inch (in^3)	= 16 cubic centimetres
1 cubic foot (ft^3)	= 0.03 cubic metres

1–12 Unit word list

Dieses Wörterverzeichnis enthält alle neuen Wörter aus *Industry Matters 3rd edition* in der Reihenfolge ihres Erscheinens (Seitenzahlen sind angegeben). Nicht angeführt sind die Wörter aus dem Grundwortschatz (vgl. **Handreichungen für den Unterricht**). Wörter aus den Hörverständnisübungen sind mit einem T (Transkript) und Wörter aus den *Partner files* mit einem **P** gekennzeichnet. Die Zahl am linken Rand gibt die Seitenzahl an.

Abkürzungen	*AE* = amerikanisches Englisch	*jdm* = jemandem	*pl* = plural noun
	BE = britisches Englisch	*jdn* = jemanden	*sb* = somebody
	etw = etwas	*jds* = jemandes	*sth* = something

UNIT 1

6	**condition** [kən'dɪʃn]	Bedingung
	working conditions *pl* [ˌwɜːkɪŋ kən'dɪʃnz]	Arbeitsbedingungen
	apprenticeship [ə'prentɪʃɪp]	Lehre, Ausbildung
	apprentice [ə'prentɪs]	Auszubildende/r, Lehrling
	specialist company ['speʃəlɪst kʌmpəni]	Fachbetrieb, Spezialfirma
	steel [stiːl]	Stahl
	trainee [treɪ'niː]	Auszubildende/r, Lehrling
	section ['sekʃn]	Bereich, Abschnitt
	line manager [laɪn 'mænɪdʒə]	(direkte/r) Vorgesetzte/r
	A levels *pl* ['eɪ levlz]	Abitur, Abiturfächer
	to **train to be a ...** ['treɪn tə bi ə]	eine Aubildung zum/zur ... machen
	manufacturing [ˌmænju'fæktʃərɪŋ]	Fertigung, Herstellung, Produktion
	industrial management assistant [ɪnˌdʌstriəl ˌmænɪdʒmənt ə'sɪstənt]	Industriekaufmann/-frau
	block release [ˌblɒk rɪ'liːs]	Blockunterricht *(an der Berufsschule)*
	vocational school [vəʊˌkeɪʃənl 'skuːl]	Berufsschule
	salary ['sæləri]	Gehalt
	expenses *pl* [ɪk'spensɪz]	Kosten, Auslagen
	rent [rent]	Miete
	branch [brɑːntʃ]	Niederlassung, Filiale
	school qualification [ˌskuːl kwɒlɪfɪ'keɪʃn]	Schulabschluss
	training company ['treɪnɪŋ kʌmpəni]	Ausbildungsbetrieb
	living expenses *pl* ['lɪvɪŋ ɪkspensɪz]	Lebenshaltungskosten
	to **qualify** ['kwɒlɪfaɪ]	einen/den Abschluss machen
	training course ['treɪnɪŋ kɔːs]	Ausbildung
	to **divide sth** [dɪ'vaɪd]	etw aufteilen
T	**computer studies** *pl* [kəm'pjuːtə stʌdiz]	Informatik
	wholesale ['həʊlseɪl]	Großhandel
	foreign trade [ˌfɒrən 'treɪd]	Außenhandel
	management assistant in wholesale and foreign trade [mænɪdʒmənt əˌsɪstənt ɪn ˌhəʊlseɪl ənd ˌfɒrən 'treɪd]	Kaufmann/-frau im Groß- und Außenhandel
7	to **structure** ['strʌktʃə]	aufbauen, strukturieren
	vocational training [vəʊˌkeɪʃənl 'treɪnɪŋ]	Berufsausbildung
	to **enter a scheme** [ˌentər ə 'skiːm]	an einem Programm teilnehmen
	job experience [ˌdʒɒb ɪk'spɪəriəns]	Berufserfahrung, praktische Erfahrung
	theoretical [ˌθɪə'retɪkl]	theoretisch, Theorie-
	vocational college [vəʊˌkeɪʃənl 'kɒlɪdʒ]	Berufsschule, Berufsfachschule
	profession [prə'feʃn]	Beruf
	depending on ... [dɪ'pendɪŋ ɒn]	je nach
	contract ['kɒntrækt]	Vertrag
	to **fire sb** ['faɪə]	jdn entlassen
	programme ['prəʊgræm]	Programm
	to **gain sth** [geɪn]	etw erlangen, etw erwerben, etw gewinnen
	standard ['stændəd]	Maßstab, Norm
	throughout ... [θruː'aʊt]	in ganz ...
	recognized ['rekəgnaɪzd]	anerkannt
	even though ['iːvn ðəʊ]	auch wenn
	to **train** [treɪn]	eine Ausbildung machen
	commerce ['kɒmɜːs]	Handel, Wirtschaft
	to **split sth** [splɪt]	etw aufteilen
	in-company ['ɪn kʌmpəni]	betriebsintern
	explanation [ˌekspl ə'neɪʃn]	Erläuterung
8	to **encourage sb** [ɪn'kʌrɪdʒ]	jdn ermutigen, jdn ermuntern
	trainer ['treɪnə]	Ausbilder/in
	to **brainstorm** ['breɪnstɔːm]	Ideen sammeln
	medium-sized ['miːdiəm saɪzd]	mittelgroß, mittelständisch

	to **subsidize** ['sʌbsɪdaɪz]	subventionieren, bezuschussen
	smart [smɑːt]	*(Kleidung:)* schick
	open-plan office [ˌəʊpənplæn 'ɒfɪs]	Großraumbüro
	flexitime ['fleksitaɪm]	Gleitzeit
	shift work ['ʃɪft wɜːk]	Schichtarbeit
	company car ['kʌmpəni kɑː]	Firmenwagen
	dress code ['dres kəʊd]	Kleiderordnung
	to **give reasons for sth** [ˌgɪv 'riːznz fə]	etw begründen
	to **conduct sth** [kən'dʌkt]	etw durchführen
	survey ['sɜːveɪ]	Umfrage
	in my opinion [ɪn maɪ ə'pɪniən]	meiner Meinung nach
	participant [pɑː'tɪsɪpənt]	Teilnehmer/in
	department [dɪ'pɑːtmənt]	Abteilung
	working hours *pl* [ˌwɜːkɪŋ 'aʊəz]	Arbeitszeit(en)
	overtime ['əʊvətaɪm]	Überstunden
	business trip ['bɪznəs trɪp]	Geschäftsreise
	availability [əˌveɪlə'bɪləti]	Verfügbarkeit
	facilities *pl* [fə'sɪlətiz]	Einrichtungen, Anlage(n)
	benefits *pl* ['benɪfɪts]	Zusatzleistungen, Sozialleistungen
	job prospects *pl* ['dʒɒb prɒspekts]	berufliche Perspektiven
T	**Go ahead.** [ˌgəʊ ə'hed]	Nur zu! Na los!
	consumer electronics [kənˌsjuːmər ˌɪlek'trɒnɪks]	Unterhaltungselektronik
	retailer ['riːteɪlə]	Einzelhändler/in
	procurement [prə'kjʊəmənt]	Beschaffung
	goods *pl* [gʊdz]	Ware(n), Güter
	supplier [sə'plaɪə]	Zulieferer, Lieferant, Anbieter
	to **clock in/out** [ˌklɒk 'ɪn/'aʊt]	ein-/ausstempeln
	morning break ['mɔːnɪŋ breɪk]	Frühstückspause
	official(ly) [ə'fɪʃl]	offiziell
	to **feel like sth** ['fiːl laɪk]	Lust auf etw haben
	event [ɪ'vent]	Veranstaltung
	open day ['əʊpən deɪ]	Tag der Offenen Tür
	to **clear up** [ˌklɪər 'ʌp]	aufräumen
	in writing [ɪn 'raɪtɪŋ]	schriftlich, in Schriftform
	strict [strɪkt]	streng
	text (message) ['tekst mesɪdʒ]	SMS
	standby ['stændbaɪ]	Bereitschaft
	to **log in** [ˌlɒg 'ɪn]	sich einloggen
	drinks machine [ˌdrɪŋks mə'ʃiːn]	Getränkeautomat
	ground floor [ˌgraʊnd 'flɔː]	Erdgeschoss
	discount ['dɪskaʊnt]	Rabatt, Skonto
	to **stay on** [ˌsteɪ 'ɒn]	bleiben, dableiben
	job offer ['dʒɒb ɒfə]	Stellenangebot
	at least [ət 'liːst]	mindestens, zumindest
	That's it. [ðæts' ɪt]	Das war's.
	You're welcome. [jɔː 'welkəm]	Bitte (sehr). Gern geschehen.
	family business ['fæməli bɪznəs]	Familienunternehmen
	furniture ['fɜːnɪtʃə]	Möbel
	logistics [lə'dʒɜːstɪks]	Logistik
	deadline ['dedlaɪn]	Frist, Fertigstellungstermin
	to **meet a deadline** [ˌmiːt ə 'dedlaɪn]	eine Frist einhalten
	to **text sb** [tekst]	jdm eine SMS schicken
	I don't mind. [aɪ dəʊnt 'maɪnd]	Ich habe nichts dagegen.
	Come to think of it ... [kʌm tə 'θɪŋk əv ɪt]	Wenn ich es mir recht/genau überlege ...
	at cost price [ət ˌkɒst 'praɪs]	zum Selbstkostenpreis
	questionnaire [ˌkwestʃə'neə]	Fragebogen
9	to **look the part** [ˌlʊk ðə 'pɑːt]	entsprechend (rollengerecht) aussehen
	appearance [ə'pɪərəns]	Erscheinungsbild, Auftreten
	appropriate [ə'prəʊpriət]	angemessen, passend
	dress [dres]	Kleid
	earring ['ɪərɪŋ]	Ohrring
	flat [flæt]	flach
	loud [laʊd]	*(Farbe:)* grell, knallig, bunt
	low-cut [ˌləʊ 'kʌt]	tief ausgeschnitten
	top [tɒp]	Oberteil
	low-heeled [ˌləʊ 'hiːld]	mit niedrigem Absatz
	tie [taɪ]	Krawatte
	skirt [skɜːt]	Rock
	blouse [blaʊz]	Bluse
	suit [suːt]	Anzug; Kostüm
	trainers *pl* ['treɪnəz]	Turnschuhe, Sportschuhe
	trouser suit ['traʊzə suːt]	Hosenanzug
	visible ['vɪzəbl]	sichtbar
	tattoo [tə'tuː]	Tätowierung
	jewellery ['dʒuːəlri]	Schmuck
	dispute [dɪ'spjuːt]	Streit, Streitigkeiten, Debatte
	to **break a rule** [ˌbreɪk ə 'ruːl]	eine Regel brechen, eine Vorschrift missachten
	agency ['eɪdʒənsi]	Agentur
	receptionist [rɪ'sepʃənɪst]	Empfangsmitarbeiter/in
	management consultancy [ˌmænɪdʒmənt kən'sʌltənsi]	Unternehmensberatung
	supervisor ['suːpəvaɪzə]	Vorgesetzte/r
	to **point at sth** ['pɔɪnt ət]	auf etw zeigen, auf etw deuten
	heels *pl* [hiːlz]	Pumps, Schuhe mit hohen Absätzen
	reception [rɪ'sepʃn]	Empfang, Rezeption
	ridiculous [rɪ'dɪkjələs]	lächerlich, albern, absurd
	to **laugh at sth** ['lɑːf ət]	sich über etw lustig machen
	issue ['ɪʃuː]	Problem
	to **get one's head round sth** [ˌget wʌnz 'hed raʊnd]	etw begreifen
	to **refuse** [rɪ'fjuːz]	sich weigern

	guidelines *pl* [ˈɡaɪdlaɪnz]	Richtlinien
	to **be in line with sth** [bɪ ˌɪn ˈlaɪn wɪð]	einer Sache entsprechen
	standard practice [ˌstændəd ˈpræktɪs]	übliches Vorgehen, übliche Praxis
	incident [ˈɪnsɪdənt]	Vorfall
	petition [pəˈtɪʃn]	Petition, Eingabe
	account [əˈkaʊnt]	Konto
	support [səˈpɔːt]	Unterstützung
	to **be expected to do sth** [bi ɪkˈspektɪd tə]	etw tun sollen
	to **respond to sth** [rɪˈspɒnd tə]	auf etw reagieren
	legal situation [ˌliːɡl sɪtʒuˈeɪʃn]	Rechtslage, Gesetzeslage
	workplace [ˈwɜːkpleɪs]	Arbeitsplatz
	to **attract attention** [əˌtrækt əˈtenʃn]	Aufmerksamkeit erregen
	media *pl* [ˈmiːdiə]	Medien
	point of view [ˌpɔɪnt əv ˈvjuː]	Sicht, Perspektive
	customer-facing job [ˌkʌstəmə feɪsɪŋ ˈdʒɒb]	Tätigkeit mit Kundenkontakt
	uniform [ˈjuːnɪfɔːm]	Dienstkleidung, Uniform
10	**productivity** [ˌprɒdʌkˈtɪvəti]	Produktivität
T	to **be pleased to do sth** [bi ˈpliːzd tə]	etw gern tun; sich freuen, etw zu tun
	surprised [səˈpraɪzd]	überrascht, erstaunt
	national holiday [ˌnæʃnəl ˈhɒlədeɪ]	gesetzlicher Feiertag
	annual leave [ˌænjuəl ˈliːv]	Jahresurlaub
	off (work) [ɒf]	frei
	to take time off (work) [teɪk ˌtaɪm ˈɒf]	sich frei nehmen
	I'm afraid [aɪm əˈfreɪd]	leider
	second to last [ˌsekənd tə ˈlɑːst]	zweitletzte/r/s
	vacation *AE* [vəˈkeɪʃn]	Ferien, Urlaub
	winner [ˈwɪnə]	Sieger/in
	by the way [baɪ ðə ˈweɪ]	übrigens
	remaining [rɪˈmeɪnɪŋ]	übrige/r/s
	additional [əˈdɪʃənl]	zusätzlich
	to **depend on sth** [dɪˈpend ɒn]	von etw abhängen, auf etw ankommen
	contract of employment [ˌkɒntrækt əv ɪmˈplɔɪmənt]	Arbeitsvertrag
	to sum up [tə ˌsʌm ˈʌp]	zusammenfassend (gesagt)
	to **take a break** [ˌteɪk ə ˈbreɪk]	eine Pause machen
	obligation [ˌɒblɪˈɡeɪʃn]	Pflicht, Verpflichtung
11	**career** [kəˈrɪə]	(berufliche) Laufbahn, Karriere
	diploma [dɪˈpləʊmə]	Abschlusszeugnis
	course [kɔːs]	Studiengang
	business administration [ˈbɪznəs ədmɪnɪstreɪʃn]	Betriebswirtschaft
	grade [ɡreɪd]	Note
	final grade [ˌfaɪnl ˈɡreɪd]	Abschlussnote
	coursework [ˈkɔːswɜːk]	schriftliche Arbeit(en)
	internship [ˈɪntɜːnʃɪp]	Praktikum
	for free [fə ˈfriː]	umsonst
	folks *pl* [fəʊks]	Leute
	tuition fees *pl* [tjuˈɪʃn fiːz]	Studiengebühren
	part-time [ˌpɑːtˈtaɪm]	Teilzeit
	convenience store [kənˈviːniəns stɔː]	Gemischtwarenladen, Spätkauf
	to **be in debt** [bi ɪn ˈdet]	Schulden haben, verschuldet sein
	goal [ɡəʊl]	Ziel
	buyer [ˈbaɪə]	Einkäufer/in
	clothing industry [ˌkləʊðɪŋ ˈɪndəstri]	Kleidungsbranche
	to **get into debt** [ˌɡet ɪntə ˈdet]	sich verschulden
	to **earn sth** [ɜːn]	etw verdienen
	intermediate [ˌɪntəˈmiːdiət]	mittlere/r/s
	assessor [əˈsesə]	Betreuer/in, Gutachter/in
	to **upload** [ˌʌpˈləʊd]	hochladen
	portfolio [pɔːtˈfəʊliəʊ]	Arbeitsmappe
	fees *pl* [fiːz]	Gebühren
	limit [ˈlɪmɪt]	Beschränkung, Begrenzung
	final examination [ˌfaɪnl ɪɡzæmɪˈneɪʃn]	Abschlussprüfung
	advanced [ədˈvɑːnst]	fortgeschritten, weiterführend
	long-term [ˌlɒŋˈtɜːm]	langfristig
	to **role-play** [ˈrəʊl pleɪ]	mit verteilten Rollen spielen
	introductions *pl* [ˌɪntrəˈdʌkʃnz]	Bekanntmachen, Vorstellen
	academic [ˌækəˈdemɪk]	akademisch, Universitäts-, universitär
	qualification [ˌkwɒlɪfɪˈkeɪʃn]	Abschluss, Qualifikation
	finance [ˈfaɪnæns]	Finanz(en)
	assessment [əˈsesmənt]	Beurteilung, Bewertung, Einschätzung, Urteil
	industrialized country [ɪnˌdʌstriəlaɪzd ˈkʌntri]	Industrieland, -staat
	to **vary** [ˈveəri]	variieren, sich unterscheiden
	pros and cons *pl* [ˌprəʊz ənd ˈkɒnz]	Argumente dafür und dagegen, Vor- und Nachteile
	practical [ˈpræktɪkl]	praktisch, Praxis-
	e.g. [ˌiː ˈdʒiː]	z. B.
12	**Human Resources (HR)** [ˌhjuːmən rɪˈsɔːsɪz]	Personal(abteilung)
	computerized [kəmˈpjuːtəraɪzd]	Computer-
	personnel [ˌpɜːsəˈnel]	Personal, Mitabeiter/innen
	personnel file [ˌpɜːsəˈnel faɪl]	Personalakte
	place of birth [ˌpleɪs əv ˈbɜːθ]	Geburtsort
	job description [ˈdʒɒb dɪskrɪpʃn]	Stellenbeschreibung
	training supervisor [ˌtreɪnɪŋ ˈsuːpəvaɪzə]	Ausbildungsleiter/in

T	**office management assistant** [ˌɒfɪs mænɪdʒmənt əˈsɪstənt]	Bürokaufmann/-frau, Kaufmann/-frau für Büromanagement
	IT management assistant [aɪ ˌtiː mænɪdʒmənt əˈsɪstənt]	Informatikkaufmann/-frau
13	**formal(ly)** [ˈfɔːml]	formell, förmlich
	suitable [ˈsuːtəbl]	geeignet, passend
	to **avoid** [əˈvɔɪd]	vermeiden
	illness [ˈɪlnəs]	Krankheit
	politics [ˈpɒlətɪks]	Politik
	journey [ˈdʒɜːni]	Fahrt, Anreise
	meeting place [ˈmiːtɪŋ pleɪs]	Treffpunkt
	pay [peɪ]	Bezahlung, Gehalt
	response [rɪˈspɒns]	Antwort, Reaktion
	to **be based in ...** [bi ˈbeɪst ɪn]	seinen Sitz in ... haben, in ... sein
	fantastic [fænˈtæstɪk]	phantastisch, toll
	view [vjuː]	Aussicht, Blick
	in fact [ɪn ˈfækt]	genau genommen, tatsächlich, eigentlich
	Excuse me. [ɪkˈskjuːz miː]	Verzeihung. Entschuldigung.
	to **hold up sb** [ˌhəʊld ˈʌp]	jdn aufhalten
	coat [kəʊt]	Jacke, Mantel
	to **keep sb waiting** [kiːp ˈweɪtɪŋ]	jdn warten lassen
	refreshment [rɪˈfreʃmənt]	Erfrischung

UNIT 2

14	**work placement** *BE* [ˈwɜːk pleɪsmənt]	Praktikum
	administration [ədˌmɪnɪˈstreɪʃn]	Verwaltung
	cybersecurity [ˌsaɪbəsɪˈkjʊərəti]	Internetsicherheit
	aspect [ˈæspekt]	Gesichtspunkt, Seite, Aspekt
	procedure [prəˈsiːdʒə]	Verfahren, Vorgehen
	inventory [ˈɪnvəntri]	Bestandsliste, -aufnahme, Inventar
	to **key sth in** [ˌkiː ˈɪn]	etw *(am Computer)* eingeben
	data *pl* [ˈdeɪtə]	Daten
	likes and dislikes *pl* [ˌlaɪks ən ˈdɪslaɪks]	Vorlieben und Abneigungen
	photocopy [ˈfəʊtəʊkɒpi]	Fotokopie
15	**consultant** [kənˈsʌltənt]	Berater/in
T	**efficient(ly)** [ɪˈfɪʃnt]	effizient
	purpose [ˈpɜːpəs]	Zweck
	to **support** [səˈpɔːt]	unterstützen
	benefit [ˈbenɪfɪt]	Vorteil, Nutzen
	to **focus on sth** [ˈfəʊkəs ɒn]	sich auf etw konzentrieren
	to **concentrate (on sth)** [ˈkɒnsntreɪt]	sich (auf etw) konzentrieren
	to **interrupt** [ˌɪntəˈrʌpt]	unterbrechen, stören
	in contrast [ɪn ˈkɒntrɑːst]	im Gegensatz (dazu)
	to **set sth up** [ˌset ˈʌp]	etw einrichten, etw aufbauen

cubicle [ˈkjuːbɪkl]	Arbeitsplatz *(im Großraumbüro)*
set-up [ˈsetʌp]	Anordnung, Einrichtung, System
to **hide sth** [haɪd]	etw verbergen
partition [pɑːˈtɪʃn]	Trennwand
to **get on with one's work** [get ˌɒn wɪð wʌnz ˈwɜːk]	seine Arbeit machen
noisy [ˈnɔɪzi]	laut
sense of community [ˌsens əf kəˈmjuːnəti]	Gemeinschaftssinn
to **communicate** [kəˈmjuːnɪkeɪt]	kommunizieren
to **be attached to sth** [bi əˈtætʃt tə]	mit etw verbunden sein
to **clear a space** [klɪər ə ˈspeɪs]	einen Platz räumen
neat and tidy [niːt ən ˈtaɪdi]	sauber und ordentlich
downside [ˈdaʊnsaɪd]	Nachteil, Schattenseite
to **put your personal mark on sth** [pʊt jɔː ˌpɜːsnl ˈmɑːk ɒn]	einer Sache seinen persönlichen Stempel aufdrücken
to **result in sth** [rɪˈzʌlt ɪn]	zu etw führen, etw ergeben
to **lack sth** [læk]	etw nicht haben
warmth [wɔːmθ]	Wärme
personality [ˌpɜːsəˈnæləti]	Persönlichkeit
uninviting [ˌʌnɪnˈvaɪtɪŋ]	wenig einladend
to **be up to date with sth** [bi ˌʌp tə ˈdeɪt wɪð]	bei etw auf dem neuesten Stand sein
Trojan [ˈtrəʊdʒn]	Trojaner
social engineering [ˌsəʊʃl ˌendʒɪˈnɪərɪŋ]	soziale Manipulation
to **block sth** [blɒk]	etw versperren, etw blockieren
access [ˈækses]	Zugang, Zutritt
sum of money [ˌsʌm əv ˈmʌni]	Geldbetrag
to **flood sth** [flʌd]	etw überschwemmen
request [rɪˈkwest]	Anfrage
to **operate** [ˈɒpəreɪt]	arbeiten, funktionieren
to **crash** [kræʃ]	abstürzen
network [ˈnetwɜːk]	Netz, Netzwerk
compromised [ˈkɒmprəmaɪzd]	(von Schadsoftware) befallen
psychological [ˌsaɪkəˈlɒdʒɪkl]	psychologisch
to **give sth away** [ˌgɪv əˈweɪ]	etw preisgeben
sensitive information [ˌsensətɪv ɪnfəˈmeɪʃn]	vertrauliche Informationen
to **re-direct** [ˌriː dəˈrekt]	umleiten
identical [aɪˈdentɪkl]	identisch
fake [feɪk]	gefälscht, falsch
to **appear to do sth** [əˈpɪə tə]	etw anscheinend tun
infamous [ˈɪnfəməs]	berüchtigt
cyberattack [ˈsaɪbərətæk]	Cyberangriff
on average [ɒn ˈævərɪdʒ]	im Durchschnitt

	attack [əˈtæk]	Angriff
	to **infect** [ɪnˈfekt]	infizieren, befallen
	to **hit** [hɪt]	treffen
	National Health Service *BE* [ˌnæʃnəl ˈhelθ sɜːvɪs]	*Nationaler Gesundheitsdienst in Großbritannien*
	device [dɪˈvaɪs]	Gerät
	MRI scanner [ˌem ɑːr ˈai skænə]	Kernspintomograph
	blood [blʌd]	Blut
	storage [ˈstɔːrɪdʒ]	Lagerung, Speicherung
	to **affect sth** [əˈfekt]	etw betreffen
	ransom [ˈrænsəm]	Lösegeld
	target [ˈtɑːgɪt]	Ziel
	outdated [ˌaʊtˈdeɪtɪd]	veraltet
	to **advise sb to do sth** [ədˈvaɪz]	jdm empfehlen, etw zu tun; jdm raten, etw zu tun
	principle [ˈprɪnsəpl]	Grundsatz, Prinzip
	to **install** [ɪnˈstɔːl]	installieren
	locally [ˈləʊkəli]	dezentral, vor Ort
	to **target sb** [ˈtɑːgɪt]	jdn ins Visier nehmen
	to **have sth in common** [həv ɪn ˈkɒmən]	etw gemeinsam haben
	regarding [rɪˈgɑːdɪŋ]	betreffend
	attachment [əˈtætʃmənt]	*(E-Mail:)* Anhang
16	**organization chart** [ˌɔːgənaɪˈzeɪʃn tʃɑːt]	Organigramm
	canning [ˈkænɪŋ]	Konservenherstellung
	machinery [məˈʃiːnəri]	Maschinen, Geräte
	manufacturer [ˌmænjuˈfæktʃərə]	Hersteller/in
	management [ˈmænɪdʒmənt]	Geschäftsleitung, Geschäftsführung
	head of department [ˌhed əv dɪˈpɑːtmənt]	Abteilungsleiter/in
	commercial director [kəˌmɜːʃl dəˈrektə]	kaufmännische/r Leiter/in
	managing director [ˌmænɪdʒɪŋ dəˈrektə]	Geschäftsführer/in
	quality management [ˈkwɒləti mænɪdʒmənt]	Qualitätssicherung
	press [pres]	Presse
	pricing [ˈpraɪsɪŋ]	Kalkulation, Preisgestaltung
	Research & Development (R & D) [rɪˌsɜːtʃ ən dɪˈveləpmənt]	Forschung und Entwicklung
	purchasing [ˈpɜːtʃəsɪŋ]	Einkauf
	financial controlling [faɪˌnænʃl kənˈtrəʊlɪŋ]	Controlling
	project management [ˌprɒdʒekt ˈmænɪdʒmənt]	Projektleitung
	assembly [əˈsembli]	Montage
	accounts [əˈkaʊnts]	Buchhaltung
	to **work sth out** [ˌwɜːk ˈaʊt]	etw berechnen, etw ausrechnen
	to **monitor** [ˈmɒnɪtə]	überwachen
	component [kəmˈpəʊnənt]	Bestandteil, Bauteil
	existing [ɪgˈzɪstɪŋ]	bestehend, existierend
17	to **be in charge of sth** [bi ɪn ˈtʃɑːdʒ əv]	für etw zuständig/verantwortlich sein
	to **coordinate** [kəʊˈɔːdɪneɪt]	miteinander abstimmen, koordinieren
	material [məˈtɪəriəl]	Baustoff, Rohmaterial, Material
	to **deal with sth** [ˈdiːl wɪð]	sich um etw kümmern, sich mit etw befassen
	invoice [ˈɪnvɔɪs]	Rechnung
	potential [pəˈtenʃl]	möglich, potenziell
	to **report to sb** [rɪˈpɔːt tə]	jdm unterstehen
T	**responsibility** [rɪˌspɒnsəˈbɪləti]	Aufgabe, Zuständigkeit, Verantwortlichkeit
	to **supervise sth** [ˈsuːpəvaɪz]	etw beaufsichtigen, etw betreuen, etw überwachen
	site [saɪt]	Standort, Gelände
	schedule [ˈʃedjuːl]	Zeitplan
	on schedule [ɒn ˈʃedjuːl]	planmäßig, termingerecht
	to **operate sth** [ˈɒpəreɪt]	etw bedienen
	trade fair [ˈtreɪd feə]	Fachmesse, Branchenmesse
	budget [ˈbʌdʒɪt]	Etat, Budget
	to **entail sth** [ɪnˈteɪl]	etw mit sich bringen
	to **analyse** [ˈænəlaɪz]	analysieren
	sales figures *pl* [ˈseɪlz fɪgəz]	Umsatzzahlen, Verkaufszahlen
	profit margin [ˈprɒfɪt mɑːdʒɪn]	Gewinnspanne
	to **report sth to sb** [rɪˈpɔːt tə]	jdm etw melden
	board of directors [ˌbɔːd əv dəˈrektəz]	Vorstand
	field [fiːld]	Gebiet, Bereich, Feld
	to **put** [pʊt]	formulieren, sagen
	to put it simply [tə ˌpʊt ɪt ˈsɪmpli]	vereinfacht gesagt
	to **involve sth** [ɪnˈvɒlv]	etw beinhalten, etw umfassen
	to **run sth** [rʌn]	etw leiten
	shipment [ˈʃɪpmənt]	Sendung
18	**job profile** [ˈdʒɒb prəʊfaɪl]	Stellenprofil
	work experience [ˈwɜːk ɪkspɪəriəns]	Praktikum
	assignment [əˈsaɪnmənt]	Auftrag, Aufgabe
	accounting [əˈkaʊntɪŋ]	Buchhaltung
	quality assurance [ˈkwɒləti əʃʊərəns]	Qualitätssicherung
	to **determine sth** [dɪˈtɜːmɪn]	etw festlegen, etw bestimmen
	to **handle sth** [ˈhændl]	etw bearbeiten
	payment [ˈpeɪmənt]	Zahlung
	receipt [rɪˈsiːt]	Beleg, Quittung
	norm [nɔːm]	Norm
	to **maintain sth** [meɪnˈteɪn]	etw warten, etw instandhalten
	performance [pəˈfɔːməns]	Leistung
	manpower [ˈmænpaʊə]	Arbeitskräfte
	financial report [faɪˌnænʃl rɪˈpɔːt]	Finanzbericht
	to **obtain sth** [əbˈteɪn]	etw erhalten, sich etw verschaffen
	shipping documents *pl* [ˈʃɪpɪŋ dɒkjumənts]	Transportpapiere, Versanddokumente
	to **recruit** [rɪˈkruːt]	*(Personal)* einstellen

	to **promote sb** [prəˈməʊt]	jdn befördern
	to **ship** [ʃɪp]	versenden, verschicken
	plant [plɑːnt]	Werk, Fabrik
19	**recording** [rɪˈkɔːdɪŋ]	Aufzeichnung, Aufnahme
	to **negotiate** [nɪˈgəʊʃieɪt]	verhandeln, (etw) aushandeln
	terms *pl* [tɜːmz]	(Vertrags-)Bedingungen
	customs regulations *pl* [ˈkʌstəmz regjuleɪʃnz]	Zollvorschriften
	to **make sure** [ˌmeɪk ˈʃʊə]	sicherstellen, gewährleisten, dafür sorgen
	process [ˈprəʊses]	Verfahren, Prozess
T	**on time** [ɒn ˈtaɪm]	pünktlich
	in-house [ˌɪn ˈhaʊs]	betriebsintern
	to **track** [træk]	verfolgen
	freight [freɪt]	Fracht
	to **hand sth in** [ˌhænd ˈɪn]	etw einreichen, etw abgeben
	to **oversee sth** [ˌəʊvəˈsiː]	etw überwachen, etw beaufsichtigen
	to **agree sth** [əˈgriː]	etw vereinbaren
	to **keep to sth** [ˈkiːp tə]	sich nach etw richten, sich an etw halten
	to **expand sth** [ɪkˈspænd]	etw ausweiten, etw erweitern
	to **miss sth** [mɪs]	etw übersehen
	project manager [ˌprɒdʒekt ˈmænɪdʒə]	Projektleiter/in
	to **take responsibility** [teɪk rɪˌspɒnsəˈbɪləti]	Verantwortung übernehmen
	project [ˈprɒdʒekt]	Projekt
	chain [tʃeɪn]	Kette
	to **supply sth** [səˈplaɪ]	etw liefern, etw bereitstellen
	specifications *pl* [ˌspesɪfɪˈkeɪʃnz]	Technische Daten, Spezifikationen
	production manager [prəˈdʌkʃn mænɪdʒə]	Produktionsleiter/in
	accounting manager [əˈkaʊntɪŋ mænɪdʒə]	Buchhaltungsleiter/in
	daily operations *pl* [ˌdeɪli ɒpəˈreɪʃnz]	Tagesgeschäft
	overall [ˌəʊvərˈɔːl]	Gesamt-
	in good time [ɪn ˌgʊd ˈtaɪm]	rechtzeitig
	to **be one's turn** [bi wʌnz ˈtɜːn]	an der Reihe sein
	flow chart [ˈfləʊ tʃɑːt]	Flussdiagramm
	blackboard [ˈblækbɔːd]	Wandtafel
20	**subsidiary** [səbˈsɪdiəri]	Niederlassung
	to **leave a message** [ˌliːv ə ˈmesɪdʒ]	eine Nachricht hinterlassen
	voicemail [ˈvɔɪsmeɪl]	Mailbox
	engineering [ˌendʒɪˈnɪərɪŋ]	Technik, Maschinenbau
	to **call back** [ˌkɔːl ˈbæk]	zurückrufen
	on behalf of sb [ɒn bɪˈhɑːf əv]	für jdn, in jds Namen
	as follows [əz ˈfɒləʊz]	wie folgt
	to **confirm** [kənˈfɜːm]	bestätigen
	lathe [leɪð]	Drehbank, Drehmaschine
	factory manager [ˈfæktəri mænɪdʒə]	Betriebsleiter/in, Werksleiter/in
	maintenance [ˈmeɪntənəns]	Wartung, Instandhaltung, Pflege
	technician [tekˈnɪʃn]	Techniker/in
	at the latest [ət ðə ˈleɪtɪst]	spätestens
	mobile [ˈməʊbaɪl]	Handy, Mobiltelefon
	to **pass sth on** [ˌpɑːs ˈɒn]	etw weiterleiten
	to **take a (phone) call** [ˌteɪk ə ˈkɔːl]	ein Gespräch entgegennehmen
	frequent(ly) [ˈfriːkwənt]	häufig
	expression [ɪkˈspreʃn]	Ausdruck
T	**Speaking.** [ˈspiːkɪŋ]	*(Telefon:)* Am Apparat.
	to **hold the line** [ˌhəʊld ðə ˈlaɪn]	*(Telefon:)* am Apparat bleiben
	engaged [ɪnˈgeɪdʒd]	*(Telefon:)* besetzt
	in that case [ɪn ˈðæt keɪs]	in diesem Fall
	to **connect (to/with sth)** [kəˈnekt]	(mit etw) verbinden, (an etw) anschließen
	to **be unavailable** [bi ˌʌnəˈveɪləbl]	*(Telefon:)* nicht zu sprechen sein
	to **put sb through** [ˌpʊt ˈθruː]	*(Telefon:)* jdn durchstellen
	urgent(ly) [ˈɜːdʒənt]	dringend
	to **catch sth** [kætʃ]	etw verstehen, etw mitbekommen
	to **be missing** [bi ˈmɪsɪŋ]	fehlen
21	**digit** [ˈdɪdʒɪt]	Ziffer
	separate(ly) [ˈseprət]	einzeln
	except for [ɪkˈsept fə]	außer
	instruction [ɪnˈstrʌkʃn]	Anweisung
	to **improvise** [ˈɪmprəvaɪz]	improvisieren

KMK Exam practice 1

22 T	to **return a call** [rɪˌtɜːn ə ˈkɔːl]	zurückrufen
	ergonomic [ˌɜːgəˈnɒmɪk]	ergonomisch
	swivel chair [ˈswɪvl tʃeə]	Drehstuhl
	brochure [ˈbrəʊʃə]	Broschüre, Prospekt
	to **make sense** [meɪk ˈsens]	sinnvoll sein
	to **appreciate sth** [əˈpriːʃieɪt]	etw zu schätzen wissen
	including sth [ɪnˈkluːdɪŋ]	mit etw, einschließlich einer Sache
	contact details *pl* [ˈkɒntækt diːteɪlz]	Kontaktdaten
23	**CEO (Chief Executive Officer)** [ˌtʃiːf ɪgˈzekjətɪv ɒfɪsə]	Vorstandsvorsitzende/r, Geschäftsführer/in
	internal [ɪnˈtɜːnl]	intern
	external [ɪkˈstɜːnl]	extern
	cooperation [kəʊˌɒpəˈreɪʃn]	Zusammenarbeit
	to **establish sth** [ɪˈstæblɪʃ]	etw schaffen, etw festlegen
	framework [ˈfreɪmwɜːk]	Rahmen
	director [dəˈrektə]	Vorstandsmitglied
	supervision [ˌsuːpəˈvɪʒn]	Aufsicht, Kontrolle
	monitoring [ˈmɒnɪtərɪŋ]	Überwachung
	necessity [nəˈsesəti]	Notwendigkeit

to **meet standards** [miːt ˈstændədz]	Normen erfüllen
obligatory [əˈblɪɡətri]	obligatorisch, zwingend vorgeschrieben
safety regulations *pl* [ˈseɪfti reɡjuleɪʃnz]	Sicherheitsvorschriften
thorough [ˈθʌrə]	gründlich
to **develop** [dɪˈveləp]	(sich) entwickeln
extensive [ɪkˈstensɪv]	umfangreich, ausführlich
market research [ˌmɑːkɪt rɪˈsɜːtʃ]	Marktforschung
to **evaluate sth** [ɪˈvæljueɪt]	etw auswerten, etw einschätzen, etw beurteilen
specifications *pl* [ˌspesɪfɪˈkeɪʃnz]	Vorgaben, Spezifikationen
to **ensure sth** [ɪnˈʃʊə]	für etw sorgen
to **fulfil requirements** [fʊlˌfɪl rɪˈkwaɪəmənts]	Anforderungen erfüllen
update [ˈʌpdeɪt]	Aktualisierung, Änderung
malfunction [ˌmælˈfʌŋkʃn]	Störung, Defekt, Ausfall
financial director [faɪˌnænʃl dəˈrektə]	Finanzvorstand
to **be licensed to do sth** [bi ˈlaɪsnst tə]	etw (mit offizieller Genehmigung) tun
transaction [trænˈzækʃn]	Geschäft, Vorgang, Transaktion
overseas transactions *pl* [əʊvəˌsiːz trænˈzækʃnz]	Auslandsgeschäft
tax [tæks]	Steuer(n)
revenue [ˈrevənjuː]	Einkünfte, Einnahmen
section [ˈsekʃn]	Abteilung
written correspondence [ˌrɪtn ˌkɒrɪˈspɒndəns]	Schriftverkehr
concerning sth [kənˈsɜːnɪŋ]	etw betreffend
to **deal with sb** [ˈdiːl wɪð]	mit jdm umgehen
recruitment [rɪˈkruːtmənt]	Einstellung, Anwerbung *(von Personal)*
redundancy [rɪˈdʌndənsi]	(betriebsbedingte) Kündigung
pension scheme [ˈpenʃn skiːm]	Altersversorgung
to **initiate sth** [ɪˈnɪʃieɪt]	etw veranlassen
annual [ˈænjuəl]	jährlich
evaluation [ɪˌvæljuˈeɪʃn]	Beurteilung, Evaluierung
member of staff [ˌmembər əf ˈstɑːf]	Mitarbeiter/in

UNIT 3

24 **business partner** [ˈbɪznəs pɑːtnə]	Geschäftspartner/in
timeline [ˈtaɪmlaɪn]	Zeitachse, Zeitschiene
to **surf the internet** [ˌsɜːf ði ˈɪntənet]	im Internet surfen
businessman [ˈbɪznəsmən]	Geschäftsmann
inventor [ɪnˈventə]	Erfinder/in
brand [brænd]	Marke
worth [wɜːθ]	wert
billion [ˈbɪliən]	Milliarde
empire [ˈempaɪə]	Reich, Imperium
business venture [ˈbɪznəs ventʃə]	Unternehmen, Geschäftsvorhaben
to **plant sth** [plɑːnt]	etw pflanzen
Christmas tree [ˈkrɪsməs triː]	Weihnachtsbaum
profit [ˈprɒfɪt]	Gewinn, Profit
technically speaking [ˈteknɪkli spiːkɪŋ]	genaugenommen
sole trader [ˌsəʊl ˈtreɪdə]	Einzelunternehmer/in
to **intend to do sth** [ɪnˈtend tə duː]	beabsichtigen, etw zu tun
unlimited [ʌnˈlɪmɪtɪd]	unbeschränkt, unbegrenzt
liability [ˌlaɪəˈbɪləti]	Haftung
rabbit [ˈræbɪt]	Kaninchen
record [ˈrekɔːd]	Schallplatte
mail order [ˌmeɪl ˈɔːdə]	Versandhandel
brand name [ˈbrænd neɪm]	Markenname
to **take business away from sb** [teɪk ˌbɪznəs əˈweɪ frəm]	jdm das Wasser abgraben
conventional [kənˈvenʃənl]	herkömmlich, konventionell
to **set up** [ˌset ˈʌp]	*(Unternehmen usw.)* gründen
unknown [ˌʌnˈnəʊn]	unbekannt
artist [ˈɑːtɪst]	Künstler/in
private limited company (Ltd) [ˌpraɪvət ˌlɪmɪtɪd ˈkʌmpəni]	Gesellschaft mit beschränkter Haftung (GmbH)
member [ˈmembə]	Mitglied
liable [ˈlaɪəbl]	haftbar
to the extent of sth [tə ði ɪkˈstent əv]	bis zu etw
investment [ɪnˈvestmənt]	Beteiligung, Einlage
personal wealth [ˌpɜːsnl ˈwelθ]	Privatvermögen
to **break out** [ˌbreɪk ˈaʊt]	ausbrechen
to **found sth** [faʊnd]	etw gründen
airline [ˈeəlaɪn]	Fluggesellschaft
to **finance** [ˈfaɪnæns]	finanzieren
public limited company (plc) [ˌpʌblɪk ˌlɪmɪtɪd ˈkʌmpəni]	Aktiengesellschaft (AG)
share [ʃeə]	Aktie
stock exchange [ˈstɒk ɪkstʃeɪndʒ]	Börse
chairman [ˈtʃeəmən]	Vorstandsvorsitzende/r
shareholder [ˈʃeəhəʊldə]	Aktionär/in
short-term [ˌʃɔːtˈtɜːm]	kurzfristig
to **enter the railway business** [ˌentə ðə ˈreɪlweɪ bɪznəs]	ins Bahngeschäft einsteigen
franchise [ˈfræntʃaɪz]	Konzession, Lizenz
route [ruːt]	Strecke
to **undercut sb** [ˌʌndəˈkʌt]	jdn unterbieten
financial services *pl* [faɪˌnænʃl ˈsɜːvɪsɪz]	Finanzdienstleistungen
to **launch sth** [lɔːntʃ]	etw starten, etw *(Unternehmen usw.)* gründen
to **operate** [ˈɒpəreɪt]	geschäftlich tätig sein

spectacular [spek'tækjələ] spektakulär
adventure [əd'ventʃə] Abenteuer
space travel ['speɪs trævl] Raumfahrt
voyage ['vɔɪɪdʒ] Reise, Fahrt
barrier ['bæriə] Hindernis
to **overcome sth** [ˌəʊvə'kʌm] etw bewältigen, etw überwinden
spacecraft ['speɪskrɑ:ft] Raumschiff
test flight ['test flaɪt] Testflug
to **kill sb** [kɪl] jdn töten
healthcare clinic ['helθkeə klɪnɪk] Klinik
to **hit the headlines** [hɪt ðə 'hedlaɪnz] Schlagzeilen machen
motor racing ['məʊtə reɪsɪŋ] Autorennen
gas balloon [gæs bə'lu:n] Gasballon
drone [drəʊn] Drohne
robotics [rəʊ'bɒtɪks] Robotertechnik
25 **recording studio** [rɪ'kɔ:dɪŋ stju:diəʊ] Tonstudio
train service ['treɪn sɜ:vɪs] Zugbetrieb
healthcare ['helθkeə] Gesundheitswesen
to **research sth** [rɪ'sɜ:tʃ] etw recherchieren
to **take a decision** [ˌteɪk ə dɪ'sɪʒn] eine Entscheidung treffen
closed [kləʊzd] geschlossen
circle ['sɜ:kl] Kreis
to **invest** [ɪn'vest] investieren
public ['pʌblɪk] Öffentlichkeit
bankruptcy ['bæŋkrʌpsi] Konkurs
to **sketch sth out** [ˌsketʃ 'aʊt] etw (vor)zeichnen
graphic ['græfɪk] Grafik
visual(ly) ['vɪʒuəl] visuell
appealing [ə'pi:lɪŋ] ansprechend
gallery walk ['gæləri wɔ:k] Galerierundgang
clarity ['klærəti] Klarheit, Deutlichkeit
to **get a message across** [get ə ˌmesɪdʒ ə'krɒs] eine Botschaft vermitteln
26 to **show sb around** [ˌʃəʊ ə'raʊnd] jdn herumführen
to **export** [ɪk'spɔ:t] exportieren, ausführen
guided tour [ˌgaɪdɪd 'tʊə] Führung
layout ['leɪaʊt] Grundriss, Anordnung, Plan
labelling ['leɪblɪŋ] Bezeichnung, Etikettierung
material delivery [mə'tɪəriəl dɪlɪvəri] Materialanlieferung
showroom ['ʃəʊru:m] Ausstellungsraum, Verkaufsraum
spare part [ˌspeə 'pɑ:t] Ersatzteil
entrance ['entrəns] Eingang
works council [ˌwɜ:ks 'kaʊnsl] Betriebsrat
stairs *pl* [steəz] Treppe, Treppenhaus
starting point ['stɑ:tɪŋ pɔɪnt] Ausgangspunkt
finishing point ['fɪnɪʃɪŋ pɔɪnt] Endpunkt

T **guide** [gaɪd] Führer/in
this way ['ðɪs weɪ] hier entlang
friendship ['frendʃɪp] Freundschaft
fresh [freʃ] frisch
to **rot** [rɒt] verfaulen, verrotten
destination [ˌdestɪ'neɪʃn] (Reise-, Fahrt-)Ziel, Zielort
to **solve** [sɒlv] lösen
conference room ['kɒnfərəns ru:m] Besprechungsraum, Sitzungssaal
brief [bri:f] kurz, knapp
overview ['əʊvəvju:] Überblick, Übersicht
corridor ['kɒrɪdɔ:] Flur, Gang
gentleman ['dʒentlmən] Herr
to **take sth seriously** [teɪk 'sɪəriəsli] etw ernst nehmen
stop [stɒp] Station, Halt
downstairs [ˌdaʊn'steəz] (nach) unten
lift *BE* [lɪft] Aufzug, Fahrstuhl
assembly hall [ə'sembli hɔ:l] Montagehalle
lid [lɪd] Deckel
body (of a can) ['bɒdi] Dosenrumpf, Dosenkörper
to **conclude sth** [kən'klu:d] etw beschließen, etw beenden
exhibition centre [ˌeksɪ'bɪʃn sentə] Messezentrum
lady ['leɪdi] Dame
to **feel free to do sth** [fi:l 'fri: tə] etw ruhig tun, gern etw tun können
wide range [waɪd 'reɪndʒ] großes Angebot, breite Palette
can [kæn] (Konserven-)Dose
can end ['kæn end] Dosendeckel
production hall [prə'dʌkʃn hɔ:l] Fertigungshalle, Produktionshalle
to **work alongside sb** [ˌwɜ:k ə'lɒŋsaɪd] mit jdm arbeiten
specialist ['speʃəlɪst] Fachmann/-frau, Experte/-in, Spezialist/in
to **turn sth into sth** ['tɜ:n ɪntə] etw zu etw machen, etw in etw umwandeln
to **see sth through** [ˌsi: 'θru:] etw *(Projekt)* durchgehend betreuen
tool [tu:l] Werkzeug, Instrument

27 to **give directions** [ˌgɪv də'rekʃnz] den Weg beschreiben
opposite ['ɒpəzɪt] gegenüber
upstairs [ˌʌp'steəz] (nach) oben
elevator *AE* ['elɪveɪtə] Aufzug, Fahrstuhl
polite(ly) [pə'laɪt] höflich
article ['ɑ:tɪkl] Artikel
including sth [ɪn'klu:dɪŋ] mit etw, einschließlich einer Sache
representative [ˌreprɪ'zentətɪv] Vertreter/in
importance [ɪm'pɔ:tns] Bedeutung, Wichtigkeit
first of all [ˌfɜ:st əv 'ɔ:l] zuerst, zunächst
tour [tʊə] Rundgang
to **be delighted** [bi dɪ'laɪtɪd] (hoch)erfreut sein, sich sehr freuen

	to **label** [ˈleɪbl]	bezeichnen, etikettieren
	to **cover** [ˈkʌvə]	*(Thema)* behandeln
28	**slide** [slaɪd]	*(Präsentation:)* Folie
	heading [ˈhedɪŋ]	Überschrift, Rubrik
	interior [ɪnˈtɪəriə]	Innenbereich, das Innere
	parent company [ˌpeərənt ˈkʌmpəni]	Muttergesellschaft
	market [ˈmɑːkɪt]	Markt
	turnover [ˈtɜːnəʊvə]	Umsatz
	approximately [əˈprɒksɪmətli]	ungefähr, zirka
	percentage [pəˈsentɪdʒ]	Anteil, Prozentsatz
	market share [ˌmɑːkɪt ˈʃeə]	Marktanteil
	production line [prəˈdʌkʃn laɪn]	Fertigungslinie, Produktionslinie
	slitter [ˈslɪtə]	Schneidemaschine, Schlitzer
	welding machine [ˈweldɪŋ məʃiːn]	Schweißmaschine
	seam covering [ˈsiːm kʌvərɪŋ]	Falzabdeckung, Bördeln
	curing oven [ˈkjʊərɪŋ ʌvn]	Einbrennofen
T	**agenda** [əˈdʒendə]	Programm, Tagesordnung
	folder [ˈfəʊldə]	Mappe, Ordner
	background [ˈbækgraʊnd]	Hintergrund
	statistics [stəˈtɪstɪks]	Statistik(en)
	to **be happy to do sth** [bi ˈhæpi tə duː]	etw gern tun
	to **manufacture** [ˌmænjuˈfæktʃə]	fertigen, herstellen
	workforce [ˈwɜːkfɔːs]	Belegschaft, Arbeitskräfte
	global market share [ˌgləʊbl ˈmɑːkɪt ʃeə]	Weltmarktanteil
	in particular [ɪn pəˈtɪkjələ]	insbesondere
	transport infrastructure [ˌtrænspɔːt ˈɪnfrəstrʌktʃə]	Verkehrsnetz
	speciality [ˌspeʃiˈæləti]	Spezialität
	to **assemble** [əˈsembl]	montieren, zusammenbauen
	on site [ɒn ˈsaɪt]	vor Ort
	state-of-the-art [ˌsteɪt əv ði ˈɑːt]	auf dem neuesten Stand der Technik, hochmodern
	ample space [ˌæmpl ˈspeɪs]	genügend Platz

29	**handout** [ˈhændaʊt]	Arbeitsblatt, Broschüre
	audience [ˈɔːdiəns]	Publikum
	visuals *pl* [ˈvɪʒuəlz]	visuelle Hilfsmittel
	conclusion [kənˈkluːʒn]	Schluss
	to **optimize** [ˈɒptɪmaɪz]	optimieren
	to **face sb** [feɪs]	sich jdm zuwenden, jdn anschauen
	aid [eɪd]	Hilfsmittel
	visual aids *pl* [ˈvɪʒuəl eɪdz]	visuelle Hilfsmittel
	transparency [trænsˈpærənsi]	(Overhead-)Folie, Dia
	to **overload** [ˌəʊvəˈləʊd]	überladen
	to **hand over to sb** [ˌhænd ˈəʊvə tə]	an jdn übergeben
	attire [əˈtaɪə]	Kleidung
	gesture [ˈdʒestʃə]	Geste

	body language [ˈbɒdi læŋgwɪdʒ]	Körpersprache
	contact details *pl* [ˈkɒntækt diːteɪlz]	Kontaktdaten
	business card [ˈbɪznəs kɑːd]	Visitenkarte
	eye contact [ˈaɪ kɒntækt]	Blickkontakt
	to **turn one's back on sb** [ˌtɜːn wʌnz ˈbæk ɒn]	jdm den Rücken zuwenden
	to **point to sth** [ˈpɔɪnt tə]	auf etw deuten, auf etw zeigen
	prompt card [ˈprɒmt kɑːd]	Moderationskarte
	keyword [ˈkiːwɜːd]	Stichwort
30	**structure** [ˈstrʌktʃə]	Aufbau, Struktur
	signpost [ˈsaɪnpəʊst]	Wegweiser
	to **invite sth** [ɪnˈvaɪt]	zu etw auffordern, um etw bitten
	correctness [kəˈrektnəs]	Richtigkeit
	spelling [ˈspelɪŋ]	Rechtschreibung
	to **come across** [ˌkʌm əˈkrɒs]	wirken
	presenter [prɪˈzentə]	Redner/in, Vortragende/r, Moderator/in
	either [ˈaɪðə]	jedes *(von zweien)*
	to **highlight** [ˈhaɪlaɪt]	hervorheben
	index card [ˈɪndeks kɑːd]	Karteikarte
	workshop [ˈwɜːkʃɒp]	Werkstatt
31	**feedback** [ˈfiːdbæk]	Reaktion(en), Rückmeldung(en)
	title [ˈtaɪtl]	Titel, Überschrift
	to **support** [səˈpɔːt]	*(Argumentation)* untermauern
	delivery [dɪˈlɪvəri]	Vortrag, Vortragsweise
	confident(ly) [ˈkɒnfɪdənt]	selbstbewusst
	to **take equal turns with sb** [teɪk ˌiːkwəl ˈtɜːnz wɪð]	sich mit jdm ausgewogen abwechseln
	manner [ˈmænə]	Art (und Weise)
	overall score [əʊvərˌɔːl ˈskɔː]	Gesamtpunktzahl

T	**construction site** [kənˈstrʌkʃn saɪt]	Baustelle
	to **reach** [riːtʃ]	herankommen, heranreichen
	pipeline [ˈpaɪplaɪn]	Leitung, Rohrleitung
	stainless steel [ˌsteɪnləs ˈstiːl]	Edelstahl
	worktop [ˈwɜːktɒp]	Arbeitsplatte
	domestic [dəˈmestɪk]	im Inland, heimisch
	charity [ˈtʃærəti]	Wohltätigkeitsorganisation
	to **contribute to sth** [kənˈtrɪbjuːt tə]	etw finanziell unterstützen
	good cause [gʊd ˈkɔːz]	gute Sache, guter Zweck
	to **serve a market** [ˌsɜːv ə ˈmɑːkɪt]	einen Markt bedienen
	including [ɪnˈkluːdɪŋ]	einschließlich, darunter
	canteen [kænˈtiːn]	Kantine
	to **break for lunch** [ˌbreɪd fə ˈlʌntʃ]	Mittagspause machen
	breakdown [ˈbreɪkdaʊn]	Aufstellung, Aufschlüsselung
	figures *pl* [ˈfɪgəz]	Zahlen

carbon steel [ˌkɑːbən ˈstiːl]	Kohlenstoffstahl
light [laɪt]	leicht
plastics *pl* [ˈplæstɪks]	Kunststoff(e)
division [dɪˈvɪʒn]	(Unternehmens-)Sparte
waste water [ˌweɪst ˈwɔːtə]	Abwasser
chemicals *pl* [ˈkemɪklz]	Chemikalien
catering [ˈkeɪtərɪŋ]	Gastronomie
to **mention sth** [ˈmenʃn]	etw erwähnen
children's home [ˌtʃɪldrənz ˈhəʊm]	Waisenhaus, Kinderheim
medical products *pl* [ˈmedɪkl prɒdʌkts]	Medizinprodukte
indeed [ɪnˈdiːd]	in der Tat, wirklich, allerdings
operating theatre [ˈɒpəreɪtɪŋ θɪətə]	Operationssaal
specific [spəˈsɪfɪk]	bestimmte/r/s, speziell
to **take it in turns to do sth** [ˌteɪk ɪt ɪn ˈtɜːnz tə]	etw abwechselnd tun
to **evaluate sth** [ɪˈvæljueɪt]	etw auswerten, etw einschätzen, etw beurteilen
to **make sure** [ˌmeɪk ˈʃʊə]	dafür sorgen, darauf achten
constructive [kənˈstrʌktɪv]	konstruktiv

UNIT 4

32 **value** [ˈvæljuː] — Wert
to **add value (to sth)** [ˌæd ˈvæljuː] — Wert schöpfen, den Wert (von etw) steigern
supply chain [səˈplaɪ tʃeɪn] — Lieferkette, Versorgungskette
to **import** [ɪmˈpɔːt] — einführen, importieren
raw materials *pl* [ˌrɔː məˈtɪəriəlz] — Rohstoffe, Rohmaterialien
to **review sth** [rɪˈvjuː] — etw überprüfen, etw überdenken

sourcing [ˈsɔːsɪŋ] — Beschaffung, Einkauf
policy [ˈpɒləsi] — Politik, Vorgehen, Richtlinien, Grundsätze

fact sheet [ˈfækt ʃiːt] — Informationsblatt, Datenblatt
retail price [ˌriːteɪl ˈpraɪs] — Einzelhandelspreis, Endverkaufspreis

stage [steɪdʒ] — Phase, Abschnitt
to **make the most of sth** [ˌmeɪk ðə ˈməʊst əv] — etw ausnutzen, möglichst viel aus etw herausschlagen

consumer [kənˈsjuːmə] — Verbraucher/in, Konsument/in

to **assume** [əˈsjuːm] — davon ausgehen, voraussetzen

to **make a profit** [meɪk ə ˈprɒfɪt] — einen Gewinn erzielen
low-wage country [ˌləʊ weɪdʒ ˈkʌntri] — Niedriglohnland
along the way [əˌlɒŋ ðə ˈweɪ] — unterwegs
to **retail at £14** [ˌriːteɪl ət ˌfɔːtiːn ˈpaʊndz] — (im Einzelhandel) für £14 verkauft werden

cotton [ˈkɒtn] — Baumwolle
to **grow** [grəʊ] — *(Pflanze)* anbauen
to **spin** [spɪn] — spinnen
middleman [ˈmɪdlmən] — Zwischenhändler
denim [ˈdenɪm] — Jeansstoff
button [ˈbʌtn] — Knopf
stud [stʌd] — Niete, Knopf
zip [zɪp] — Reißverschluss
wash [wɒʃ] — Wäsche, Waschgang
to **amount to sth** [əˈmaʊnt tə] — *(Kosten:)* sich auf etw belaufen
garment [ˈgɑːmənt] — Kleidungsstück
shock [ʃɒk] — Schock
massive [ˈmæsɪv] — riesig, gewaltig, saftig
times [taɪmz] — mal
distribution [ˌdɪstrɪˈbjuːʃn] — Vertrieb, Transport
to **make up sth** [ˌmeɪk ˈʌp] — *(Anteil usw.:)* etw ausmachen

price tag [ˈpraɪs tæg] — Preisschild, Preisetikett
VAT (value added tax) [ˌvæljuː ˈædɪd tæks] — MwSt (Mehrwertsteuer)

33 to **calculate sth** [ˈkælkjuleɪt] — etw berechnen
budget [ˈbʌdʒɪt] — Billig-
consumer goods *pl* [kənˈsjuːmə gʊdz] — Konsumgüter
processing plant [ˈprəʊsesɪŋ plɑːnt] — Verarbeitungsbetrieb, Aufbereitungsanlage
car manufacturer [ˌkɑː ˌmænjuˈfæktʃərə] — Autohersteller, Autobauer
car showroom [ˌkɑː ˈʃəʊəuːm] — Autohaus
crude oil [ˌkruːd ˈɔɪl] — Rohöl
dairy [ˈdeəri] — Molkereiprodukte
driver [ˈdraɪvə] — Fahrer/in
forest [ˈfɒrɪst] — Wald
furniture store [ˈfɜːnɪtʃə stɔː] — Möbelhaus
furniture-maker [ˈfɜːnɪtʃə meɪkə] — Möbelhersteller
home-owner [ˈhəʊm əʊnə] — Hausbesitzer/in, Wohnungseigentümer/in
oil refinery [ˌɔɪl rɪˈfaɪnəri] — Ölraffinerie
pasteurization plant [pæstʃərʌɪˈzeɪʃn plɑːnt] — Pasteurisationsanlage
toy [tɔɪ] — Spielzeug
shopper [ˈʃɒpə] — (Laden-)Kunde/Kundin
conflict zone [ˈkɒnflɪkt zəʊn] — Konfliktzone
minerals *pl* [ˈmɪnərəlz] — Mineralien
processing [ˈprəʊsesɪŋ] — Verarbeitung, Aufbereitung
refining [rɪˈfaɪnɪŋ] — Raffinieren
to **take place** [ˌteɪk ˈpleɪs] — stattfinden
channel [ˈtʃænl] — Kanal
distribution channel [ˌdɪstrɪˈbjuːʃn tʃænl] — Vertriebsweg, Vertriebskanal
rail [reɪl] — Schiene
warehousing [ˈweəhaʊzɪŋ] — Lagerhaltung, Lagerung
CO_2 footprint [siː əʊ ˌtuː ˈfʊtprɪnt] — CO_2-Fußabdruck

	retail outlet [ˈri:teɪl aʊtlet]	Verkaufsstelle, Einzelhandelsgeschäft
	caption [ˈkæpʃn]	Bildunterschrift
34	**line** [laɪn]	Linie, Produktlinie
	compact furniture [ˌkɒmpækt ˈfɜ:nɪtʃə]	Kleinmöbel
	to **keep up with sth** [ˌki:p ˈʌp wɪð]	mit etw Schritt halten
	demand [dɪˈmɑ:nd]	Nachfrage
	business consultant [ˈbɪznəs kənsʌltənt]	Unternehmensberater/in
	to **call sb in** [ˌkɔ:l ˈɪn]	jdn hinzuziehen, jdn einschalten
	improvement [ɪmˈpru:vmənt]	Verbesserung
	to **observe** [əbˈzɜ:v]	beobachten
	warehouse [ˈweəhaʊs]	Lager
	paint [peɪnt]	Lack, Farbe
	adhesive [ədˈhi:sɪv]	Klebstoff
	fittings *pl* [ˈfɪtɪŋz]	Beschläge, Armaturen
	packing [ˈpækɪŋ]	Verpackung
	finished product [ˌfɪnɪʃt ˈprɒdʌkt]	Endprodukt
	drilling [ˈdrɪlɪŋ]	Bohren
	to **paint** [peɪnt]	lackieren, bemalen
	to **spray** [spreɪ]	sprühen, spritzen, spritzlackieren
	to **dry** [draɪ]	trocknen
	screw [skru:]	Schraube
	nut [nʌt]	Mutter, Schraubenmutter
	bolt [bəʊlt]	Schraube, Schraubbolzen
	dispatch [dɪˈspætʃ]	Versand
	unloading [ˌʌnˈləʊdɪŋ]	Entladung, Löschen
	to **pack** [pæk]	verpacken
	available [əˈveɪləbl]	erhältlich, verfügbar
	quantity [ˈkwɒntəti]	Menge, Anzahl
	floor [flɔ:]	Fläche
	overhead [ˌəʊvəˈhed]	hoch (oben)
	high bay [ˌhaɪ ˈbeɪ]	Hochregal
	accessible [əkˈsesəbl]	zugänglich, erreichbar
	ladder [ˈlædə]	Leiter
	paint shop [ˈpeɪnt ʃɒp]	Lackiererei
	to **handle sth** [ˈhændl]	etw bewältigen
	section [ˈsekʃn]	Abteilung, Sparte
	to **stand idle** [ˌstænd ˈaɪdl]	stillstehen, untätig sein
	output [ˈaʊtpʊt]	Produktion
	to **exceed sth** [ɪkˈsi:d]	etw übersteigen
	capacity [kəˈpæsəti]	Kapazität, Fassungsvermögen
	to **waste** [weɪst]	verschwenden, vergeuden
	to **account for sth** [əˈkaʊnt fə]	etw ausmachen, für etw verantwortlich sein
	to **overload** [ˌəʊvəˈləʊd]	überlasten
	to **access sth** [ˈækses]	auf etw zugreifen
	inefficient [ˌɪnɪˈfɪʃnt]	ineffizient, unrationell, unwirtschaftlich
	emergency [ɪˈmɜ:dʒənsi]	Notfall, Not-
	to **call a meeting** [ˌkɔ:l ə ˈmi:tɪŋ]	eine Sitzung einberufen
	to **standardize** [ˈstændədaɪz]	normen, standardisieren
	to **implement sth** [ˈɪmplɪmənt]	*(Maßnahme usw:)* etw umsetzen, etw einführen
	to **develop** [dɪˈveləp]	(sich) entwickeln
	to **clarify** [ˈklærəfaɪ]	klären, abklären
	to **break sth down** [ˌbreɪk ˈdaʊn]	etw aufschlüsseln, etw aufgliedern
	to **achieve** [əˈtʃi:v]	*(Ziel)* erreichen
	root cause [ˈru:t kɔ:z]	Grundursache
	countermeasure [ˈkaʊntəmeʒə]	Gegenmaßnahme
	failure [ˈfeɪljə]	Misserfolg, Versagen, Scheitern
35	**solution** [səˈlu:ʃn]	Lösung
T	**straight away** [ˌstreɪt əˈweɪ]	sogleich, sofort
	potential [pəˈtenʃl]	Potenzial
	order book [ˈɔ:də bʊk]	Auftragsbuch
	rosy [ˈrəʊzi]	rosig
	to **come in on sth** [ˌkʌm ˈɪn ɒn]	zu etw etw sagen
	I fail to see … [aɪ ˌfeɪl tə ˈsi:]	Ich kann nicht sehen, …
	comment [ˈkɒment]	Bemerkung, Kommentar
	to **go ahead** [ˌgəʊ əˈhed]	weitermachen, fortfahren
	highly [ˈhaɪli]	sehr, höchst, in hohem Maße
	stop-and-go [ˌstɒp ən ˈgəʊ]	stockend
	to **establish sth** [ɪˈstæblɪʃ]	etw schaffen, etw aufbauen
	name plate [ˈneɪm pleɪt]	Typenschild, Namensschild
	to **continue** [kənˈtɪnju:]	fortfahren, weitermachen
	to **prevent sb/sth from doing sth** [prɪˈvent]	jdn/etw daran hindern, etw zu tun; verhindern, dass jd/etw etw tut
	to **build up** [ˌbɪld ˈʌp]	sich aufstauen, sich auftürmen
	to **request sth** [rɪˈkwest]	etw anfordern
	push system [ˈpʊʃ sɪstəm]	Push-System
	to **push** [pʊʃ]	schieben, stoßen
	pull system [ˈpʊl sɪstəm]	Pull-System
	item [ˈaɪtəm]	Artikel
	request [rɪˈkwest]	Anforderung
	to **retrain** [ˌri:ˈtreɪn]	umschulen
	just in time [ˌdʒʌst ɪn ˈtaɪm]	gerade rechtzeitig
	bulky [ˈbʌlki]	sperrig, voluminös
	truck [trʌk]	Lastwagen
	radical [ˈrædɪkl]	radikal
	to **tackle sth** [ˈtækl]	etw angehen, etw in Angriff nehmen
	to **shrink** [ʃrɪŋk]	schrumpfen, verkleinern
	next to nothing [ˌnekst tə ˈnʌθɪŋ]	fast nichts, so gut wie nichts
	to **save sth on sth** [ˈseɪv ɒn]	etw bei etw einsparen
	excellent [ˈeksələnt]	ausgezeichnet, hervorragend
	one at a time [ˌwʌn ət ə ˈtaɪm]	eins nach dem anderen
	to **matter** [ˈmætə]	wichtig sein, von Belang sein
	continuous [kənˈtɪnjuəs]	stetig, kontinuierlich
	issue [ˈɪʃu:]	Frage

	according to [əˈkɔːdɪŋ tə]	gemäß, entsprechend, zufolge
	lack (of sth) [læk]	Mangel (an etw), Fehlen (von etw)
	as regards [əz rɪˈgɑːdz]	was ... betrifft, in puncto
	lean [liːn]	schlank
	literature [ˈlɪtrətʃə]	Literatur, Lesestoff, Informationsmaterial
	corporation [ˌkɔːpəˈreɪʃn]	Unternehmen, Gesellschaft
	demand [dɪˈmɑːnd]	Bedarf
	to **forecast** [ˈfɔːkɑːst]	vorhersagen, schätzen
	seasonal [ˈsiːzənl]	jahreszeitlich, saisonal
	fluctuation [ˌflʌktʃuˈeɪʃn]	Schwankung(en)
	guesswork [ˈgeswɜːk]	Mutmaßung(en)
	in bulk [ɪn ˈbʌlk]	en gros, in großen Mengen
	to **take advantage of sth** [ˌteɪk ədˈvɑːntɪdʒ əv]	etw nutzen
	quantity discount [ˈkwɒntəti dɪskaʊnt]	Mengenrabatt
	to **mass-produce sth** [ˌmæs ˈprɒdjuːs]	etw in großen Mengen produzieren
	in anticipation of sth [ɪn ænˌtɪsɪˈpeɪʃn əv]	in Erwartung von etw, im Vorgriff auf etw
	to **tie up sth** [ˌtaɪ ˈʌp]	etw binden
	capital [ˈkæpɪtl]	Kapital, Mittel
	work in progress [ˌwɜːk ɪn ˈprəʊgres]	unfertige Erzeugnisse
	inventory [ˈɪnvəntri]	Lagerbestand
	inexact [ˌɪnɪgˈzækt]	ungenau
	unreliable [ˌʌnrɪˈlaɪəbl]	unzuverlässig
	wasteful [ˈweɪstfl]	verschwenderisch, unwirtschaftlich
	to **liken sth to sth** [ˈlaɪkən]	etw mit etw vergleichen
	uneven [ʌnˈiːvn]	ungleichmäßig
	loose [luːs]	(zu) locker
	unmanageable [ʌnˈmænɪdʒəbl]	unkontrollierbar
	to **re-organize** [riˈɔːgənaɪz]	neu ordnen, umorganisieren
	to **inspire** [ɪnˈspaɪə]	anregen, inspirieren
	to **transform sth** [trænsˈfɔːm]	etw grundlegend verändern
	signboard [ˌsaɪnbɔːd]	Schild
	visual [ˈvɪʒuəl]	optisch, visuell
	instruction [ɪnˈstrʌkʃn]	Anweisung
	bin [bɪn]	Tonne
	to **refill** [ˌriːˈfɪl]	nachfüllen
	to **pull** [pʊl]	ziehen
	storeroom [ˈstɔːruːm]	Lagerraum
	error [ˈerə]	Fehler, Irrtum
	hexagonal nut [heksˌægənl ˈnʌt]	Sechskantmutter
	unit weight [ˈjuːnɪt weɪt]	Stückgewicht
	gross weight [ˌgrəʊs ˈweɪt]	Bruttogewicht
36	**board** [bɔːd]	Tafel
	to **visualize sth** [ˈvɪʒuəlaɪz]	etw veranschaulichen, etw visualisieren
	to **pass through sth** [ˈpɑːs θruː]	etw durchlaufen
	to **track sth** [træk]	etw (nach)verfolgen
	to **identify** [aɪˈdentɪfaɪ]	identifzieren, bestimmen
	overload [ˈəʊvələʊd]	Überlastung
	shipment [ˈʃɪpmənt]	Versand
	backlog [ˈbæklɒg]	Rückstand
	to **be based on sth** [bi ˈbeɪst ɒn]	auf etw basieren
	waste [weɪst]	Verschwendung
	overproduction [ˌəʊvəprəˈdʌkʃn]	Überproduktion
	excess [ˈekses]	übermäßig, überschüssig
	unnecessary [ʌnˈnesəsəri]	unnötig
	physical [ˈfɪzɪkl]	physisch
	transportation [ˌtrænspɔːˈteɪʃn]	Beförderung, Transport
	defect [dɪˈfekt]	Mangel, Fehler
	to a standard [tu ə ˈstændəd]	einer Norm entsprechend
	unevenness [ʌnˈiːvnnəs]	Ungleichmäßigkeit
	to **overburden sb/sth** [ˌəʊvəˈbɜːdn]	jdn/etw überlasten
	to **break down** [ˌbreɪk ˈdaʊn]	zusammenbrechen, kaputtgehen
	to **empower sb to do sth** [ɪmˈpaʊə]	jdn ermächtigen/autorisieren, etw zu tun
	permission [pəˈmɪʃn]	Erlaubnis, Genehmigung
	tight [taɪt]	gespannt, angespannt
	to **handle sth** [ˈhændl]	etw handhaben, etw bedienen
	shelf, shelves [ʃelf, ʃelfvz]	Regal, Regale
	machine operator [məˌʃiːn ˈɒpəreɪtə]	Maschinenführer/in
	faulty [ˈfɔːlti]	schadhaft, mangelhaft, defekt
	to **rework sth** [ˌriːˈwɜːk]	etw überarbeiten, etw nachbessern
	experienced [ɪkˈspɪəriənst]	erfahren
	lorry *BE* [ˈlɒri]	Lastwagen
	metal-cutting machine [ˌmetlkʌtɪŋ məˈʃiːn]	Zerspanungsmaschine
37	**smart** [smɑːt]	intelligent
	changeover [ˈtʃeɪndʒəʊvə]	Umstellung
	chronological [ˌkrɒnəˈlɒdʒɪkl]	chronologisch, zeitlich
	automated [ˈɔːtəmeɪtɪd]	automatisch, automatisiert
	digitization [dɪdʒɪtaɪˈzeɪʃn]	Digitalisierung
	electronic [ˌɪlekˈtrɒnɪk]	elektronisch
	robot [ˈrəʊbɒt]	Roboter
	mass production [ˌmæs prəˈdʌkʃn]	Massenfertigung
	assembly line [əˈsembli laɪn]	Fertigungsstraße
	manual labour [ˌmænjuəl ˈleɪbə]	Handarbeit, körperliche Arbeit
	mechanical [mɪˈkænɪkl]	mechanisch
	equipment [ɪˈkwɪpmənt]	Geräte, Ausstattung, Ausrüstung

	to power [ˈpaʊə]	antreiben, mit Energie versorgen
	steam [stiːm]	Dampf
	cyber-physical system [ˌsaɪbəfɪsɪkl ˈsɪstəm]	cyber-physisches System
	technology [tekˈnɒlədʒi]	Technik, Technologie
	artificial intelligence (AI) [ɑːtɪˌfɪʃl ɪnˈtelɪdʒəns]	Künstliche Intelligenz (KI)
	Internet of Things (IoT) [ˌɪntənet əv ˈθɪŋz]	Internet der Dinge (IdD)
	big data [ˌbɪg ˈdeɪtə]	große Datenmengen
38	**blog entry** [ˈblɒg entri]	Blogeintrag
	mass customization [ˌmæs kʌstəmaɪˈzeɪʃn]	individualisierte/flexibilisierte Massenproduktion
	talk [tɔːk]	Vortrag
	sth is here to stay [ɪz ˌhɪə tə ˈsteɪ]	etw hat Einzug gehalten
	speaker [ˈspiːkə]	Vortragende/r, Redner/in
	wooden [ˈwʊdn]	Holz-, aus Holz
	fence [fens]	Zaun
	batch [bætʃ]	Charge, Los
	to reflect on sth [rɪˈflekt ɒn]	über etw nachdenken
	arrival [əˈraɪvl]	Einführung, Aufkommen *(einer Technologie)*
	steam-driven [ˈstiːm drɪvən]	dampfgetrieben
	standardized [ˈstændədaɪzd]	einheitlich, genormt
	electric motor [ɪˌlektrɪk ˈməʊtə]	Elektromotor
	oven [ˈʌvn]	Ofen
	to speed sth up [ˌspiːd ˈʌp]	etw beschleunigen
	inspector [ɪnˈspektə]	Kontrolleur/in, Prüfer/in
	unskilled worker [ˌʌnskɪld ˈwɜːkə]	Hilfsarbeiter/in, ungelernte Arbeitskraft
	computer-operated [kəmˈpjuːtər ˈɒpəreɪtɪd]	computergesteuert
	inspection tool [ɪnˈspekʃn tuːl]	Prüfwerkzeug
	brush [brʌʃ]	Bürste
	computing power [kəmˈpjuːtɪŋ paʊə]	Rechenleistung
	to link sth up [ˌlɪŋk ˈʌp]	etw (miteinander) verknüpfen
	by trial and error [baɪ ˌtraɪəl ənd ˈerə]	durch Ausprobieren
	not at all [ˌnɒt ət ˈɔːl]	überhaupt nicht, gar nicht
	tiny [ˈtaɪni]	winzig
	tag [tæg]	Etikett
	to process sth [ˈprəʊses]	etw verarbeiten, etw bearbeiten
	actuator [ˈæktʃʊeɪtə]	Aktor
	autonomous(ly) [ɔːˈtɒnəməs]	autonom, eigenständig, unabhängig
	without human intervention [wɪðaʊt ˌhjuːmən ɪntəˈvenʃn]	ohne menschliches Eingreifen
	to programme *BE* [ˈprəʊgræm]	programmieren
	shape [ʃeɪp]	Form, Gestalt
	to detect sth [dɪˈtekt]	etw aufspüren, etw feststellen
	to compensate for sth [ˈkɒmpənseɪt fə]	etw ausgleichen, etw wettmachen, etw kompensieren
	downtime [ˈdaʊntaɪm]	Ausfall, Ausfallzeit
	customized [ˈkʌstəmaɪzd]	individuell gefertigt, nach Kundenwunsch gefertigt
	energy source [ˈenədʒi sɔːs]	Energiequelle
	century [ˈsentʃəri]	Jahrhundert
	context [ˈkɒntekst]	Zusammenhang
	findings *pl* [ˈfaɪndɪŋz]	(Untersuchungs-)Ergebnisse
	clothing [ˈkləʊðɪŋ]	Kleidung
39	**leather** [ˈleðə]	Leder
	cutting machine [ˈkʌtɪŋ məʃiːn]	Schneidemaschine, Zuschneidemaschine
	sticking machine [ˈstɪkɪŋ məʃiːn]	Klebemaschine
	labelling machine [ˈleɪblɪŋ məʃiːn]	Etikettiermaschine
T	**edition** [ɪˈdɪʃn]	Ausgabe
	mechanization [ˌmekənaɪˈzeɪʃn]	Mechanisierung
	electrification [ɪlektrɪfɪˈkeɪʃn]	Elektrifizierung
	automation [ˌɔːtəˈmeɪʃn]	Automatisierung
	decentralized [ˌdiːˈsentrəlaɪzd]	dezentral
	term [tɜːm]	Begriff
	identity [aɪˈdentəti]	Identität
	radio frequency [ˌreɪdiəʊ ˈfriːkwənsi]	Funkfrequenz, Radiofrequenz
	grain [greɪn]	(Getreide-)Korn
	centralized [ˈsentrəlaɪzd]	zentral, zentralisiert
	control centre [kənˈtrəʊl sentə]	Steuerzentrale
	brain [breɪn]	Hirn, Gehirn
	to stick sth to sth [ˈstɪk tə]	etw an etw kleben, etw mit etw verkleben
	separate [ˈseprət]	eigenständig
	on the other hand [ɒn ði ˈʌðə hænd]	dagegen, andererseits
	to link [lɪŋk]	(miteinander) verknüpfen
	to scan [skæn]	erfassen, scannen
	to carry out sth [ˌkæri ˈaʊt]	etw ausführen
	to feed sth into sth [ˈfiːd ɪntə]	etw in etw (ein)führen
	to stick sth on [ˌstɪk ˈɒn]	etw aufkleben
	dairy farming [ˈdeəri fɑːmɪŋ]	Milchwirtschaft
	to adapt to sth [əˈdæpt tə]	sich an etw anpassen
T	**farming** [ˈfɑːmɪŋ]	Landwirtschaft
	farmer [ˈfɑːmə]	Landwirt/in
	farm [fɑːm]	Bauernhof, Hof

	at first sight [ət fɜːst ˈsaɪt]	auf den ersten Blick
	traditional [trəˈdɪʃənl]	traditionell, herkömmlich
	cow [kaʊ]	Kuh
	collar [ˈkɒlə]	Halsband
	to milk [mɪlk]	melken
	milking machine [ˈmɪlkɪŋ məʃiːn]	Melkmaschine
	tanker [ˈtæŋkə]	Tankwagen
	algorithm [ˈælgərɪðm]	Algorithmus
	to be low on sth [bi ˈləʊ ɒn]	(zu) wenig von etw *(Substanz usw.)* haben
	potassium [pəˈtæsiəm]	Kalium
	feeding system [ˈfiːdɪŋ sɪstəm]	Fütterungssystem
	to register sth [ˈredʒɪstə]	etw registrieren
	feed [fiːd]	Futter
	to graze [greɪz]	weiden, grasen
	particular [pəˈtɪkjələ]	bestimmt, speziell
	vehicle [ˈviːəkl]	Fahrzeug
	fertilizer [ˈfɜːtəlaɪzə]	Dünger
	to raise sth [reɪz]	etw erhöhen, etw steigern
	potassium level [pəˈtæsiəm levl]	Kaliumgehalt
	grass [grɑːs]	Gras, Rasen
	amazing [əˈmeɪzɪŋ]	erstaunlich, verblüffend, toll
	to change over to sth [ˈtʃeɪndʒ əʊvə tə]	auf etw umstellen
40	**to reply (to sth)** [rɪˈplaɪ]	(auf etw) antworten, (etw) beantworten
	enquiry [ɪnˈkwaɪəri]	Anfrage
	reply (to sth) [rɪˈplaɪ]	Antwort (auf etw)
	to appear [əˈpɪə]	vorkommen, auftauchen
	dot [dɒt]	Punkt
	hyphen [ˈhaɪfn]	Bindestrich, Minus
	underscore [ˈʌndəskɔː]	Unterstrich
	to dictate [dɪkˈteɪt]	diktieren
	to spell [spel]	buchstabieren
	subject line [ˈsʌbdʒɪkt laɪn]	Betreffzeile
	indication [ˌɪndɪˈkeɪʃn]	Hinweis, Anzeichen
	to state [steɪt]	angeben, erklären, sagen, darlegen, sagen
	request (for sth) [rɪˈkwest]	Bitte (um etw)
	assistance [əˈsɪstəns]	Hilfe, Unterstützung
	to announce [əˈnaʊns]	ankündigen
	change of plan [ˌtʃeindʒ əf ˈplæn]	Planänderung
	covering letter [ˈkʌvərɪŋ letə]	Anschreiben, Begleitschreiben
	brochure [ˈbrəʊʃə]	Broschüre, Prospekt
	venue [ˈvenjuː]	Veranstaltungsort
	flyer [ˈflaɪə]	Faltblatt
	to attach [əˈtætʃ]	*(E-Mail:)* anhängen
	update (on sth) [ˈʌpdeɪt]	aktuelle Informationen (zu etw), aktueller Überblick (über etw)
	inclusive [ɪnˈkluːsɪv]	einschließlich
	application [ˌæplɪˈkeɪʃn]	Antrag, Bewerbung
	stand [stænd]	(Messe-)Stand
	trade [treɪd]	Gewerbe, Branche
	fair [feə]	Messe
	to let sb know sth [ˌlet ˈnəʊ]	jdm etw mitteilen, jdm Bescheid sagen
	to interview sb [ˈɪntəvjuː]	mit jdm ein Vorstellungsgespräch führen
	export clerk [ˈekspɔːt klɑːk]	Außenhandelskaufmann/-frau
41	**chamber of commerce** [ˌtʃeɪmbər əv ˈkɒmɜːs]	Handelskammer
	to equip sth with sth [ɪˈkwɪp wɪð]	etw mit etw ausstatten
	to furnish sth [ˈfɜːnɪʃ]	etw einrichten
	fitted furniture [ˌfɪtɪd ˈfɜːnɪtʃə]	Einbaumöbel
	specifications *pl* [ˌspesɪfɪˈkeɪʃnz]	Vorgaben, Spezifikationen
	variety (of) [vəˈraɪəti]	Vielzahl, Vielfalt, verschiedene
	at short notice [ət ˌʃɔːt ˈnəʊtɪs]	kurzfristig
	Yours sincerely [ˌjɔːz sɪnˈsɪəli]	*(Brief:)* Mit freundlichen Grüßen
	purchasing director [ˈpɜːtʃəsɪŋ dərektə]	Einkaufsleiter/in
	initial [ɪˈnɪʃl]	erste/r/s
	consultation [ˌkɒnslˈteɪʃn]	Beratung
	to digitize [ˈdɪdʒɪtaɪz]	digitalisieren
	salutation [ˌsæljuˈteɪʃn]	*(Brief:)* Anrede
	complimentary close [ˌkɒmplɪˌmentri ˈkləʊz]	*(Brief:)* Schlussformel
	Dear Sir or Madam [ˌdɪə sɜː ɔː ˈmædəm]	*(Brief:)* Sehr geehrte Damen und Herren,
	Yours faithfully [ˌjɔːz ˈfeɪθfəli]	(Brief:) ... und verbleiben mit freundlichen Grüßen
	(Best) Regards [rɪˈgɑːdz]	*(Brief:)* Viele Grüße, Mit freundlichen Grüßen
	Best wishes [best ˈwɪʃɪz]	*(Brief:)* Mit freundlichen Grüßen
	Regards [rɪˈgɑːdz]	*(Brief:)* Mit freundlichen Grüßen

KMK Exam practice 2

42	**sparkling wine** [ˌspɑːklɪŋ ˈwaɪn]	Schaumwein
	spirits *pl* [ˈspɪrɪts]	Spirituosen
T	**opening** [ˈəʊpnɪŋ]	Eröffnung
	selection [sɪˈlekʃn]	Auswahl
	in addition to sth [ɪn əˈdɪʃn tə]	zusätzlich zu etw
	sales rep(resentative) [ˈseɪlz rep(rɪzentətɪv)]	(Handels-)Vertreter/in
	premises *pl* [ˈpremɪsɪz]	Räumlichkeiten, Firmengelände
	wine-tasting [ˈwaɪn teɪstɪŋ]	Weinprobe
	in detail [ɪn ˈdiːteɪl]	ausführlich, detailliert
	wine cellar [ˈwaɪn selə]	Weinkeller
	to see to sth [ˈsiː tə]	sich um etw kümmern

	catalogue [ˈkætəlɒg]	Katalog
	giveaway [ˈgɪvəweɪ]	Werbegeschenk
	champagne [ʃæmˈpeɪn]	Champagner
	label [ˈleɪbl]	Etikett
	special offer [ˌspeʃl ˈɒfə]	Sonderangebot
	immediately [ɪˈmiːdiətli]	sofort, unverzüglich
	to **appreciate sth** [əˈpriːʃieɪt]	etw zu schätzen wissen
	to **assist sb with sth** [əˈsɪst]	jdm bei etw helfen
	privately-owned [ˈpraɪvətli əʊnd]	in Privatbesitz
	trading company [ˈtreɪdɪŋ kʌmpəni]	Handelsunternehmen
	to **source sth** [sɔːs]	etw *(Waren usw.)* beschaffen
	to **distribute sth** [dɪˈstrɪbjuːt]	etw vertreiben
	fashion [ˈfæʃn]	Mode
	overseas [ˌəʊvəˈsiːz]	im Ausland, in Übersee
	core business [ˈkɔː bɪznəs]	Kerngeschäft
	head office [ˌhed ˈɒfɪs]	Zentrale, Hauptsitz
	to **be situated** [bi ˈsɪtʃueɪtɪd]	sich befinden
	motorway *BE* [ˈməʊtəweɪ]	Autobahn
	nearby [ˈnɪəbaɪ]	in der Nähe, nahegelegen
	established [ɪˈstæblɪʃt]	etabliert
	highly-professional [ˌhaɪli prəˈfeʃənl]	hochprofessionell
	operation [ˌɒpəˈreɪʃn]	Betrieb
	consequently [ˈkɒnsɪkwəntli]	dementsprechend, folgerichtig
	retail [ˈriːteɪl]	Einzelhandel
	to **range from … to …** [ˈreɪndʒ frəm tə]	von … bis … reichen
	department store [dɪˈpɑːtmənt stɔː]	Kaufhaus
	to **be due to do sth** [bi ˈdjuː tə]	etw tun (in der Zukunft) sollen
	milestone [ˈmaɪlstəʊn]	Meilenstein
	purchase [ˈpɜːtʃəs]	Kauf
	freight forwarding company [ˈfreɪt fɔːwədɪŋ kʌmpəni]	Spedition
	impressive [ɪmˈpresɪv]	beeindruckend
	fleet [fliːt]	Fuhrpark, Flotte
	to **ensure sth** [ɪnˈʃʊə]	etw sicherstellen
43	**trader** [ˈtreɪdə]	Händler/in
	marketing channel [ˈmɑːkɪtɪŋ tʃænl]	Absatzweg, Vertriebskanal
	durable goods *pl* [ˌdjʊərəbl ˈgʊdz]	Gebrauchsgüter
	to **feature sth** [ˈfiːtʃə]	etw *(Merkmal usw.)* aufweisen
	link [lɪŋk]	Glied *(in einer Kette)*
	distributor [dɪˈstrɪbjətə]	Vertragshändler
	wholesaler [ˈhəʊlseɪlə]	Großhändler
	to **represent** [ˌreprɪˈzent]	vertreten, repräsentieren
	to **maintain sth** [meɪnˈteɪn]	etw unterhalten
	exclusive agreement [ɪkˌskluːsɪv əˈgriːmənt]	Exklusivvertrag
	to **limit** [ˈlɪmɪt]	begrenzen, beschränken
	to **enable sb to do sth** [ɪˈneɪbl]	jdm ermöglichen, etw zu tun
	to **cover sth** [ˈkʌvə]	etw abdecken
	territory [ˈterətri]	Gebiet, Territorium
	point of contact [ˌpɔɪnt əf ˈkɒntækt]	Ansprechpartner, Anlaufstelle
	prospective [prəˈspektɪv]	potenziell
	rarely [ˈreəli]	selten
	due to [ˈdjuː tə]	aufgrund von, wegen
	to **have sth on hand** [həv ˌɒn ˈhænd]	etw zur Verfügung haben
	to **acquire sth** [əˈkwaɪə]	etw erwerben, etw kaufen
	to **tend to do sth** [ˈtend tə]	dazu neigen, etw zu tun
	after-sales service [ˈɑːftəseɪlz sɜːvɪs]	Kundendienst
	high-volume [haɪˈvɒljuːm]	großvolumig, Groß-
	purchase order [ˈpɜːtʃəs ɔːdə]	Auftrag, Bestellung
	typically [ˈtɪpɪkli]	normalerweise
	to **improve** [ɪmˈpruːv]	verbessern
	buying power [ˈbaɪɪŋ paʊə]	Kaufkraft
	to **purchase** [ˈpɜːtʃəs]	kaufen
	merchandise [ˈmɜːtʃəndaɪs]	Ware
	ranging from … to … [ˈreɪndʒɪŋ frəm tə]	von … bis …
	storage space [ˈstɔːrɪdʒ speɪs]	Lagerfläche
	costly [ˈkɒstli]	kostspielig, teuer
	to **consist of sth** [kənˈsɪst əv]	aus etw bestehen
	to **realize a profit** [ˌrɪəlaɪz ə ˈprɒfɪt]	einen Gewinn erzielen
	to **coincide with sth** [ˌkəʊɪnˈsaɪd wɪð]	mit etw übereinstimmen, mit etw zusammenfallen
	business objective [ˈbɪznəs əbdʒektɪv]	Unternehmensziel
	competitive [kəmˈpetətɪv]	*(Preis:)* günstig
	pricing [ˈpraɪsɪŋ]	Preise, Preisgestaltung
	store rental [ˈstɔː rentl]	Ladenmiete
	obviously [ˈɒbviəsli]	natürlich
	to **be affected by sth** [bi əˈfektɪd baɪ]	von etw betroffen sein

UNIT 5

44	**marketing strategy** [ˈmɑːkɪtɪŋ strætədʒi]	Vermarktungsstrategie
	market research [ˌmɑːkɪt rɪˈsɜːtʃ]	Marktforschung
	gear [gɪə]	Ausrüstung, Klamotten
	sports equipment [ˈspɔːts ɪkwɪpmənt]	Sportartikel
	accessories *pl* [əkˈsesəriz]	Zubehör, Accessoires
	to **specialize in sth** [ˈspeʃəlaɪz ɪn]	sich auf etw spezialisieren

	exercise equipment ['eksəsaɪz ɪkwɪpmənt]	Trainingsgeräte
	sportswear ['spɔːtsweə]	Sportbekleidung
	option ['ɒpʃn]	Möglichkeit
	loyalty card ['lɔɪəlti kɑːd]	Kundenkarte
	specialist ['speʃəlɪst]	Fachgeschäft
	department store [dɪ'pɑːtmənt stɔː]	Kaufhaus
	prize draw ['praɪz drɔː]	Verlosung
	stamp [stæmp]	Briefmarke
	to **report back** [rɪˌpɔːt 'bæk]	Bericht erstatten
	to **disclose sth** [dɪs'kləʊz]	etw preisgeben
	privilege ['prɪvəlɪdʒ]	Vergünstigung
45	**recommendation** [ˌrekəmen'deɪʃn]	Empfehlung
	customer satisfaction [ˌkʌstəmə ˌsætɪs'fækʃn]	Kundenzufriedenheit
	to **predict** [prɪ'dɪkt]	vorhersagen
	to **react** [ri'ækt]	reagieren
	field research ['fiːld rɪsɜːtʃ]	Feldforschung
	to **gather data** [ˌgæðə 'deɪtə]	Daten erfassen
	to **publish** ['pʌblɪʃ]	veröffentlichen
	study ['stʌdi]	Untersuchung, Studie
	cashier [kæ'ʃɪə]	Kassierer/in
	to **swipe a card** [ˌswaɪp ə 'kɑːd]	eine Karte durchziehen
	check-out ['tʃekaʊt]	Kasse
	purchasing history ['pɜːtʃəsɪŋ hɪstri]	Kaufhistorie, Einkaufsverhalten
	strategy ['strætədʒi]	Strategie
	relationship [rɪ'leɪʃnʃɪp]	Beziehung
	to **manage sth** ['mænɪdʒ]	etw verwalten
	interaction [ˌɪntər'ækʃn]	Austausch, Kommunikation
	database ['deɪtəbeɪs]	Datenbank
	to **update** [ˌʌp'deɪt]	aktualisieren
	instantly ['ɪnstəntli]	sofort
	to **boost sth** [buːst]	etw ankurbeln, etw erhöhen
	to **improve** [ɪm'pruːv]	verbessern
	customer loyalty [ˌkʌstəmə 'lɔɪəlti]	Kundenbindung, Kundentreue
	to **customize sth** ['kʌstəmaɪz]	etw individuell anpassen
	advertising ['ædvətaɪzɪŋ]	Werbung
	one-size-fits-all [wʌn ˌsaɪz fɪts' ɔːl]	Einheits-, Standard-, 08/15-
	advertising campaign ['ædvətaɪzɪŋ kæmpeɪn]	Werbekampagne
	social media *pl* [ˌsəʊʃl 'miːdiə]	soziale Medien
	digital signage [ˌdɪdʒɪtl 'saɪnɪdʒ]	digitale Außenwerbung
	memo ['meməʊ]	Notiz
	method ['meθəd]	Verfahren, Methode
	firm [fɜːm]	Firma
	target group ['tɑːgɪt gruːp]	Zielgruppe
46	**product line** ['prɒdʌkt laɪn]	Produktlinie

	environmentally-friendly [ɪnˌvaɪrənˌmentəli 'frendli]	umweltfreundlich
	product range ['prɒdʌkt reɪndʒ]	Sortiment
	product brief ['prɒdʌkt briːf]	Produktbeschreibung
	unique selling proposition (USP) [juˌniːk 'selɪŋ prɒpəzɪʃn]	Alleinstellungsmerkmal
	organic cotton [ɔːˌgænɪk 'kɒtn]	Bio-Baumwolle
	socially-responsible [ˌsəʊʃəli rɪ'spɒnsəbl]	sozial verantwortlich
	and beyond [ənd bɪ'jɒnd]	und darüber hinaus
	stationary ['steɪʃənri]	ortsgebunden, ortsfest, stationär
	trade [treɪd]	Handel
	factor ['fæktə]	Faktor
	to **consider sth** [kən'sɪdə]	etw in Betracht ziehen, über etw nachdenken, etw berücksichtigen
	to **launch sth** [lɔːntʃ]	etw auf den Markt bringen
T	to **market sth** ['mɑːkɪt]	etw vermarkten
	thought [θɔːt]	Gedanke(n)
	to **put a lot of thought into sth** [pʊt ə ˌlɒt əf 'θɔːt ɪntə]	intensiv über etw nachdenken
	to **outline** ['aʊtlaɪn]	skizzieren, darstellen
	approach [ə'prəʊtʃ]	Ansatz, Herangehensweise, Vorgehen
	well-established [ˌwel ɪ'stæblɪʃt]	bewährt, fest etabliert
	nature (of sth) ['neɪtʃə]	Wesen (einer Sache)
	sth is about sth [ɪz ə'baʊt]	bei einer Sache geht es um etw
	sustainability [səˌsteɪnə'bɪləti]	Nachhaltigkeit
	bottom line [ˌbɒtəm 'laɪn]	das, worauf es ankommt
	triple ['trɪpl]	dreifach
	honesty ['ɒnəsti]	Ehrlichkeit, Aufrichtigkeit
	promotion [prə'məʊʃn]	Werbung, Promotion
	branding ['brændɪŋ]	Markenbildung
	traditional [trə'dɪʃənl]	traditionell, hergebracht
	mass media *pl* [ˌmæs 'miːdiə]	Massenmedien
	to **promote sth** [prə'məʊt]	für etw werben, etw promoten
	search engine ['sɜːtʃ endʒɪn]	Suchmaschine
	to **deal with sth** ['diːl wɪð]	etw *(Thema usw.)* behandeln
	separately ['seprətli]	separat, eigens
	Fine by me. [ˌfaɪn baɪ 'miː]	Von mir aus gern.
	lazy ['leɪzi]	faul, träge
	old-fashioned [ˌəʊld'fæʃənd]	altmodisch
	to **represent** [ˌreprɪ'zent]	repräsentieren, vertreten, darstellen
	sales channel ['seɪlz tʃænl]	Absatzweg, Vertriebskanal

	bricks and mortar outlet [ˌbrɪks ən ˈmɔːtər aʊtlet]	stationäres Geschäft
	virtual [ˈvɜːtʃuəl]	virtuell
	recommended retail price (RRP) [rekəˌmend ˈriːteɪl praɪs]	unverbindliche Preisempfehlung (UVP)
	to **be prepared to do sth** [bi prɪˈpeəd tə duː]	bereit sein, etw zu tun
	mark [mɑːk]	Marke
47	**optimization** [ˌɒptɪmaɪˈzeɪʃn]	Optimierung
	keyword [ˈkiːwɜːd]	Schlagwort
	traffic [ˈtræfɪk]	Verkehr
	to **increase sth** [ɪnˈkriːs]	etw steigern, etw erhöhen
	viewer [ˈvjuːə]	Zuschauer/in, Betrachter/in
	conversion rate [kənˈvɜːʃn reɪt]	Umwandlungsquote
	wooden furniture [ˌwʊdn ˈfɜːnɪtʃə]	Holzmöbel
	generic [dʒəˈnerɪk]	allgemein
	specific [spəˈsɪfɪk]	genau, bestimmt, spezifisch
	fitted kitchen [ˌfɪtɪd ˈkɪtʃɪn]	Einbauküche
	pine [paɪn]	Kiefer
	to **guide** [gaɪd]	leiten, führen
	search result [ˈsɜːtʃ rɪzʌlt]	Suchergebnis
	relevant (to sth) [ˈreləvənt]	wichtig (für etw), relevant (für etw)
	character [ˈkærəktə]	Zeichen
	to **direct** [dəˈrekt]	leiten, lenken
	to **rank higher** [ˌræŋk ˈhaɪə]	eine höhere Position einnehmen
	linked to sth [ˈlɪŋkt tə]	in direktem Zusammenhang mit etw
	compound [ˈkɒmpaʊnd]	zusammengesetzt
	custom-made [ˈkʌstəm meɪd]	individuell gefertigt
	category [ˈkætəgəri]	Kategorie, Klasse
	entertainment [ˌentəˈteɪnmənt]	Unterhaltung
	housing [ˈhaʊzɪŋ]	Wohnen, Wohnungsbau, Wohnverhältnisse
	item [ˈaɪtəm]	Punkt, Gegenstand
48	**product launch** [ˈprɒdʌkt lɔːntʃ]	Produkteinführung
	limit [ˈlɪmɪt]	(Ober-/Unter-)Grenze
	to **last** [lɑːst]	halten
	slave labour [ˈsleɪv leɪbə]	Sklavenarbeit
	You must be kidding! [juː ˌmʌst bi ˈkɪdɪŋ]	Das ist doch nicht dein/euer Ernst?
	reasonable [ˈriːznəbl]	vernünftig, angemessen
	consequence [ˈkɒnsɪkwəns]	Folge, Konsequenz
	pricing strategy [ˈpraɪsɪŋ strætədʒi]	Preisstrategie
	perfume [ˈpɜːfjuːm]	Parfüm
	production costs *pl* [prəˈdʌkʃn kɒsts]	Herstellungskosten
	penetration [penɪˈtreɪʃn]	*(Markt:)* Eindringen, Durchdringung
	to **break into sth** [ˈbreɪk ɪntə]	in etw einbrechen
	to **attract sb** [əˈtrækt]	jdn anlocken, jdn ansprechen, jdn anziehen
	to **establish oneself** [ɪˈstæblɪʃ]	sich etablieren
	to **raise prices** [ˌreɪz ˈpraɪsɪz]	die Preise anheben
	provider [prəˈvaɪdə]	Anbieter
	premium [ˈpriːmiəm]	Premium-, Hochpreis-
	artificial(ly) [ˌɑːtɪˈfɪʃl]	künstlich
	luxury [ˈlʌkʃəri]	Luxus
	therefore [ˈðeəfɔː]	daher, folglich
	to **disregard sth** [ˌdɪsrɪˈgɑːd]	etw vernachlässigen, etw übersehen
	to **perceive** [pəˈsiːv]	wahrnehmen
	to **be willing to do sth** [bi ˈwɪlɪŋ tə]	bereit sein, etw zu tun
	fashionwear [ˈfæʃnweə]	Modekleidung
	pharmaceutical [ˌfɑːməˈsuːtɪkl]	pharmazeutisch, Pharma-
	shortage [ˈʃɔːtɪdʒ]	Knappheit, Mangel
	break-even point [ˌbreɪk ˈiːvn pɔɪnt]	Gewinnschwelle
	competition [ˌkɒmpəˈtɪʃn]	Wettbewerb
	discounter [dɪsˈkaʊntə]	Billiganbieter, Discounter
	government contract [ˈgʌvənmənt kɒntrækt]	öffentlicher Auftrag
	utility [juːˈtɪləti]	Versorgungsbetrieb
49	**final consumer** [ˌfaɪnl kənˈsjuːmə]	Endverbraucher/in
	intermediary [ˌɪntəˈmiːdiəri]	Zwischenhändler, Mittelsmann
	production site [prəˈdʌkʃn saɪt]	Produktionsstätte
	aircraft [ˈeəkrɑːft]	Flugzeug
	vessel [ˈvesl]	Schiff
	to **pick** [pɪk]	*(Obst)* pflücken
	vegetable [ˈvedʒtəbl]	Gemüse
	high-volume [haɪˈvɒljuːm]	Massen-, großvolumig
	toothpaste [ˈtuːθpeɪst]	Zahncreme
	washing powder [ˈwɒʃɪŋ paʊdə]	Waschpulver
	label [ˈleɪbl]	Etikett
	wholesaler [ˈhəʊlseɪlə]	Großhändler
	multiple [ˈmʌltɪpl]	mehrere
	party [ˈpɑːti]	Partei
	agent [ˈeɪdʒənt]	Vermittler/in, Zwischenhändler/in
	broker [ˈbrəʊkə]	Makler/in
	to **arrange for sth** [əˈreɪndʒ fə]	etw vermitteln, etw organisieren
	commission [kəˈmɪʃn]	Kommission, Provision
	non competing [ˌnɒn kəmˈpiːtɪŋ]	nicht miteinander konkurrierend
	related [rɪˈleɪtɪd]	verwandt, ähnlich
	distributor [dɪˈstrɪbjətə]	Vertragshändler
	to **stock** [stɒk]	*(Ware)* führen
	point of sale [ˌpɔɪnt əf ˈseɪl]	Verkaufsstelle

50	**eco-friendly** ['i:kəʊ frendli]	umweltfreundlich
	to **devise sth** [dɪ'vaɪz]	etw entwickeln, etw ausarbeiten
	celebrity endorsement [səˌlebrəti ɪn'dɔ:smnt]	Werbung mit Prominenten
	niche [nɪtʃ]	Nische
	stealth advertising ['stelθ ædvətaɪzɪŋ]	heimliche Werbung, Schleichwerbung
	testimonial [ˌtestɪ'məʊnɪəl]	Erfahrungsbericht
	unique [ju'ni:k]	einzigartig
	satisfied ['sætɪsfaɪd]	zufrieden
	targeted advertising [ˌtɑ:gɪtɪd 'ædvətaɪzɪŋ]	gezielte/zielgruppengenaue Werbung
	temporary ['temprəri]	vorübergehend, vorläufig
	unconventional [ˌʌnkən'venʃənl]	unkonventionell
	to **advertise sth** ['ædvətaɪz]	etw bewerben, für etw Werbung machen
51	**campaign** [kæm'peɪn]	(Werbe-)Kampagne
	to **agree sth** [ə'gri:]	sich auf etw einigen, etw beschließen
	to **cover sth** ['kʌvə]	*(Medien:)* über etw berichten
	broadcast ['brɔ:dkɑ:st]	(Radio-)Sendung
T	**unusual** [ʌn'ju:ʒʊəl]	ungewöhnlich
	central station ['sentrəl steɪʃn]	Hauptbahnhof
	queue [kju:]	Warteschlange
	loaded up with sth [ˌləʊdɪd 'ʌp wɪð]	mit etw beladen, voll mit etw
	pollution [pə'lu:ʃn]	Verschmutzung
	ocean ['əʊʃn]	Ozean, Weltmeer
	to **throw sth away** [ˌθrəʊ ə'weɪ]	etw wegwerfen
	to **end up** [ˌend 'ʌp]	(irgendwo) landen
	cash [kæʃ]	Bargeld
	programme ['prəʊgræm]	(TV-, Radio-)Sendung
	station ['steɪʃn]	Bahnhof
	recycling centre [ˌri:'saɪklɪŋ sentə]	Wertstoffhof
	surfboard ['sɜ:fbɔ:d]	Surfbrett
	entirely [ɪn'taɪəli]	völlig, ganz
	to **paddle** ['pædl]	paddeln
	litter ['lɪtə]	Müll, Abfall
	listener ['lɪsnə]	Hörer/in
	destruction [dɪ'strʌkʃn]	Zerstörung
	to **sponsor sb** ['spɒnsə]	jdn sponsern
	to **clean sth up** [ˌkli:n 'ʌp]	etw säubern
	progress ['prəʊgres]	Fortkommen, Fahrt
	day-to-day update [deɪ tə ˌdeɪ 'ʌpdeɪt]	täglicher aktueller Bericht
	to **cheer sb on** [ˌtʃɪər 'ɒn]	jdn anfeuern, jdm zujubeln
	to **realize sth** ['rɪəlaɪz]	sich über etw im Klaren sein, etw wissen
	to **form** [fɔ:m]	(sich) bilden
	waterway ['wɔ:təweɪ]	Wasserstraße
	to **correspond** [ˌkɒrɪ'spɒnd]	entsprechen, korrespondieren
	catchphrase ['kætʃfreɪz]	Schlagwort, Slogan
	to **suit sb/sth** [su:t]	(zu) jdm/etw passen
	to **come up with sth / an idea** [ˌkʌm 'ʌp wɪð]	sich etw einfallen lassen
	handshake ['hændʃeɪk]	Handschlag
	pale [peɪl]	blass, hell
	tone [təʊn]	Farbton
	conscience ['kɒnʃəns]	Gewissen
	priority [praɪ'ɒrəti]	Anliegen, Priorität
	clientele [kli:ɒn'tel]	Kundschaft, Klientel
	sense [sens]	Sinn
	responsibility [rɪˌspɒnsə'bɪləti]	Verantwortung
	environmentally conscious [ɪnvaɪrənˌmentəli 'kɒnʃəs]	umweltbewusst
52	**graph** [grɑ:f]	Diagramm, Kurve
	chart [tʃɑ:t]	Diagramm
	union ['ju:niən]	Gewerkschaft
	conference ['kɒnfərəns]	Tagung, Konferenz
	to **refresh** [rɪ'freʃ]	auffrischen
	bar chart ['bɑ: tʃɑ:t]	Säulendiagramm
	line graph ['laɪn grɑ:f]	Liniendiagramm
	pie chart ['paɪ tʃɑ:t]	Tortendiagramm
	to **remain constant** [rɪˌmeɪn 'kɒnstənt]	gleich bleiben
	to **increase** [ɪn'kri:s]	zunehmen, ansteigen
	increase ['ɪŋkri:s]	Zunahme, Anstieg
	to **hit a maximum** [ˌhɪt ə 'mæksɪməm]	einen Höchstwert/-stand erreichen
	minimum ['mɪnɪməm]	Tiefstwert, Tiefstand
	to **flatten out** [ˌflætn 'aʊt]	auf gleichem Stand bleiben
	to **level off** [ˌlevl 'ɒf]	sich einpendeln
	to **decrease** [dɪ'kri:s]	abnehmen, zurückgehen
	decrease ['di:kri:s]	Abnahme, Rückgang
	to **drop** [drɒp]	fallen, zurückgehen
	drop [drɒp]	Fall, Rückgang
	to **rise** [raɪz]	steigen, ansteigen, zunehmen
	rise [raɪz]	Anstieg
	to **fluctuate** ['flʌktʃueɪt]	schwanken
	to **climb** [klaɪm]	ansteigen
	climb [klaɪm]	Anstieg
	to **peak** [pi:k]	einen Höchstwert/-stand erreichen
	peak [pi:k]	Höchstwert, Höchststand
	traveller ['trævələ]	Passagier, Fahrgast
	time of day [taɪm əv 'deɪ]	Tageszeit
P	**unit** ['ju:nɪt]	Einheit, Stück
53	**quarterly** ['kwɔ:təli]	vierteljährlich, Quartals-
T	**financial year** [faɪˌnænʃl 'jɪə]	Geschäftsjahr
	drastic(ally) ['dræstɪkli]	drastisch
	to **recover** [rɪ'kʌvə]	sich erholen
	volume of sales [ˌvɒlju:m əf 'seɪlz]	Umsatzvolumen
	quarter ['kwɔ:tə]	Quartal
	at a glance [ət ə 'glɑ:ns]	auf einen Blick

	to contrast sth [kən'trɑ:st]	etw (einander) gegenüberstellen, etw (miteinander) vergleichen
	lunch break ['lʌntʃ breɪk]	Mittagspause
	blue-collar workers *pl* [ˌblu:'kɒlə wɜ:kəz]	Arbeiter/innen
	white-collar workers *pl* [ˌwaɪt kɒlə 'wɜ:kəz]	Angestellte

UNIT 6

54	**negotiation** [nɪˌgəʊʃi'eɪʃn]	Verhandlung
	cocoa bean ['kəʊkəʊ bi:n]	Kakaobohne
	co-operative [kəʊ'ɒpərətɪv]	Genossenschaft, Kooperative
	to come up [ˌkʌm 'ʌp]	bevorstehen
	minutes *pl* ['mɪnɪts]	Protokoll
	CEO (Chief Executive Officer) [ˌtʃi:f ɪg'zekjətɪv ɒfɪsə]	Vorstandsvorsitzende/r, Geschäftsführer/in
	ref. [ref]	Unser Zeichen
	to make arrangements [meɪk ə'reɪndʒmənts]	Vorbereitungen treffen
55 T	**to reserve** [rɪ'zɜ:v]	reservieren
	data projector [ˌdeɪtə prə'dʒektə]	Beamer
	in advance [ɪn əd'vɑ:ns]	im Voraus
	invitation [ˌɪnvɪ'teɪʃn]	Einladung
	hard copy [ˌhɑ:d 'kɒpi]	Papierexemplar, Ausdruck
	name tag ['neɪm tæg]	Namensschild
	heating ['hi:tɪŋ]	Heizung
	directions *pl* [də'rekʃnz]	Wegbeschreibung
	hurry ['hʌri]	Eile
	to remind sb (of sth) [rɪ'maɪnd]	jdn (an etw) erinnern
	to display [dɪ'spleɪ]	etw *(auf einem Bildschirm)* anzeigen
	to lay sth [leɪ]	etw herrichten, etw *(Tisch)* decken, etw *(Gedeck)* auflegen
	saucer ['sɔ:sə]	Untertasse
	to circulate sth ['sɜ:kjəleɪt]	etw (an alle) verteilen
	absentee [æbsn'ti:]	Abwesende/r
	to draft [drɑ:ft]	*(Text)* entwerfen, verfassen
	to chair a meeting [ˌtʃeər ə 'mi:tɪŋ]	eine Sitzung leiten
	to aim to do sth ['eɪm tə du:]	beabsichtigen, etw zu tun
	to freshen up [ˌfreʃn 'ʌp]	sich frisch machen
	to finalize sth ['faɪnəlaɪz]	etw abschließen
	to sign [saɪn]	unterzeichnen
	any other business (AOB) [eni ˌʌðə 'bɪznəs]	*(Tagesordnung:)* Verschiedenes
	warehouse manager [ˌweəhaʊs 'mænɪdʒə]	Lagerleiter/in
	purchasing manager ['pɜ:tʃəsɪŋ mænɪdʒə]	Einkaufsleiter/in
	legal adviser [ˌli:gl əd'vaɪzə]	Justiziar/in
56	**brewery** ['bru:əri]	Brauerei
	brewing equipment ['bru:ɪŋ ɪkwɪpmənt]	Brauanlage(n)
	to postpone [pə'spəʊn]	(nach hinten) verschieben
	to be unable to do sth [bi ʌn'eɪbl tə]	etw nicht tun können
	to schedule ['ʃedju:l]	*(Termin)* ansetzen
	item ['aɪtəm]	Tagesordnungspunkt
	order situation ['ɔ:də sɪtʒueɪʃn]	Auftragslage
T	**agent** ['eɪdʒənt]	Vertreter/in
	to come on board [ˌkʌm ɒn 'bɔ:d]	an Bord kommen
	to act as sth ['ækt əz]	als etw fungieren
	pleasure ['pleʒə]	Vergnügen
	to conclude [tə kən'klu:d]	abschließend
	to comment ['kɒment]	kommentieren, einen Kommentar abgeben
	punctual ['pʌŋktʃuəl]	pünktlich
	complaint [kəm'pleɪnt]	Reklamation, Beschwerde
	impression [ɪm'preʃn]	Eindruck
	to agree thoroughly with sb [əˌgri: 'θʌrəli wɪð]	voll und ganz einer Meinung mit jdm sein
	to wrap sth up [ˌræp 'ʌp]	etw abschließen, etw zum Abschluss bringen
	travel expenses *pl* ['trævl ɪkspensɪz]	Reisekosten, Reisespesen
	to get back to sb [ˌget 'bæk tə]	jdn zurückrufen, sich (wieder) bei jdm melden
57	**to check sth against sth** ['tʃek əgenst]	etw mit etw abgleichen
	to notice ['nəʊtɪs]	bemerken
	attendee [əˌten'di:]	Teilnehmer/in
	to complain [kəm'pleɪn]	sich beklagen, sich beschweren
	due to ['dju: tə]	aufgrund von, wegen
58	**to be in favour of sth** [bi ɪn 'feɪvər əv]	für etw sein, etw befürworten
	to consult with sb [kən'sʌlt wɪð]	mit jdm Rücksprache halten, sich mit jdm besprechen
	to load [ləʊd]	beladen, verladen
	to unload [ˌʌn'ləʊd]	entladen
	to guarantee [ˌgærən'ti:]	garantieren
	paperwork ['peɪpəwɜ:k]	Unterlagen
P	**core time** ['kɔ: taɪm]	Kernzeit
	to invent sth [ɪn'vent]	etw erfinden
	married ['mærid]	verheiratet
	early shift ['ɜ:li ʃɪft]	Frühschicht
	in a row [ɪn ə 'rəʊ]	nacheinander
59	**to host sb** [həʊst]	jdn *(als Gast)* empfangen
	fashion ['fæʃn]	Mode
	annual ['ænjuəl]	jährlich
	terms *pl* **of business** [ˌtɜ:mz əv 'bɪznəs]	Konditionen
	outcome ['aʊtkʌm]	Ergebnis, Resultat, Auswirkung(en)
	in view of sth [ɪn 'vju: əv]	angesichts von etw

	because of sth [bɪˈkɒz əv]	wegen etw
	stiff competition [ˌstɪf kɒmpəˈtɪʃn]	harter Wettbewerb
	supplier's contract [səˌplaɪəz ˈkɒntrækt]	Liefervertrag, Lieferantenvertrag
	competitive [kəmˈpetətɪv]	konkurrenzfähig
	therefore [ˈðeəfɔː]	daher, folglich
	significant(ly) [sɪgˈnɪfɪkənt]	deutlich
	low-priced [ˌləʊˈpraɪst]	preisgünstig
	to **expand rapidly** [ɪkˌspænd ˈræpɪdli]	schnell wachsen
	to **keep up with sth** [ˌkiːp ˈʌp wɪð]	mit etw Schritt halten
	worst-case scenario [wɜːst ˌkeɪs səˈnɑːriəʊ]	schlimmster anzunehmender Fall
T	to **take a seat** [ˌteɪk ə ˈsiːt]	Platz nehmen
	straight [streɪt]	direkt
	reduction [rɪˈdʌkʃn]	Nachlass, Preissenkung, Reduzierung
	to **expand** [ɪkˈspænd]	expandieren
	delivery period [dɪˈlɪvəri pɪəriəd]	Lieferzeit
	freight forwarder [ˈfreɪt fɔːwədə]	Spedition
	to **break down** [ˌbreɪk ˈdaʊn]	*(Auto:)* eine Panne haben, liegen bleiben
	wording [ˈwɜːdɪŋ]	Formulierung
60	**indirect** [ˌɪndəˈrekt]	indirekt
T	**business arrangements** *pl* [ˈbɪznəs əreɪndʒmənts]	Modalitäten
	competitor [kəmˈpetɪtə]	Wettbewerber/in, Konkurrent/in
	to **afford sth** [əˈfɔːd]	sich etw leisten (können)
	range [reɪndʒ]	Bereich, Spielraum
	packing charge [ˈpækɪŋ tʃɑːdʒ]	Verpackungskosten
	guarantee [ˌgærənˈtiː]	Garantie
	extra guarantee [ˌekstrə gærənˈtiː]	Garantieverlängerung
	return [rɪˈtɜːn]	Retoure
	agreement [əˈgriːmənt]	Vereinbarung
	prompt [prɒmpt]	Stichwort
61	**negotiator** [nɪˈgəʊʃieɪtə]	Verhandler/in
P	**initial order** [ɪˌnɪʃl ˈɔːdə]	Erstauftrag
	copper [ˈkɒpə]	Kupfer
	Euro-pallet [ˈjʊərəʊ pælət]	Euro-Palette
	plastic sheeting [ˌplæstɪk ˈʃiːtɪŋ]	Plastikfolie, Plastikplane
	square metre [ˈskweə miːtə]	Quadratmeter
	ton [tʌn]	Tonne
	timber [ˈtɪmbə]	(Bau-)Holz
	cubic metre [ˈkjuːbɪk miːtə]	Kubikmeter
	introductory discount [ɪntrəˌdʌktəri ˈdɪskaʊnt]	Einführungsrabett
	terms *pl* **of payment** [ˌtɜːmz əf ˈpeɪmənt]	Zahlungsbedingungen
	score sheet [ˈskɔː ʃiːt]	Punktzettel
	score [skɔː]	Punkte
	to **adapt sth** [əˈdæpt]	etw anpassen, etw abändern
	rice bowl [ˈraɪs bəʊl]	Reisschale
	saleswoman/-man [ˈseɪlzwʊmən, ˈseɪlzmən]	Verkäufer/in
	competitive [kəmˈpetətɪv]	*(Preis:)* günstig
	cash with order (CWO) [ˌkæʃ wɪð ˈɔːdə]	Vorkasse
	to **be in great demand** [bi ɪn ˌgreɪt dɪˈmɑːnd]	stark nachgefragt sein
	priority [praɪˈɒrəti]	Vorrang
62	to **exhibit** [ɪgˈzɪbɪt]	ausstellen
	to **rearrange sth** [ˌriːəˈreɪndʒ]	etw *(Termin usw.)* verschieben
	to **set sth up** [ˌset ˈʌp]	etw *(Termin usw.)* vereinbaren
	timetable [ˈtaɪmteɪbl]	Fahrplan
T	to **reschedule sth** [ˌriːˈʃedjuːl]	etw *(Termin usw.)* verschieben
	Something has come up. [sʌmθɪŋ həz ˌkʌm ˈʌp]	Es/Mir/Uns ist etwas dazwischen gekommen.
	to **get out of sth** [get ˈaʊt əv]	um etw herumkommen
	That's a pity. [ðæts ə ˈpɪti]	Das ist schade.
	to **have sth in mind** [həv ɪn ˈmaɪnd]	etw im Sinn haben, an etw denken
	to **suit sb** [suːt]	jdm passen
	to **inconvenience sb** [ˌɪnkənˈviːniəns]	jdm Umstände bereiten
	to **apologize** [əˈpɒlədʒaɪz]	sich entschuldigen
	to **worry** [ˈwʌri]	sich Sorgen machen
	Don't worry. [dəʊnt ˈwʌri]	Keine Sorge.
	equivalent [ɪˈkwɪvələnt]	Entsprechung, Übersetzung
	lunchtime [ˈlʌntʃtaɪm]	Mittagszeit
63	**business associate** [ˈbɪznəs əsəʊʃiət]	Geschäftspartner/in
	itinerary [aɪˈtɪnərəri]	Reiseplan
P	**buffet** [ˈbʊfeɪ]	Büfett
	association [əˌsəʊsiˈeɪʃn]	Verband

KMK Exam practice 3

64	**transformation** [ˌtrænzfəˈmeɪʃn]	(grundlegende) Veränderung, Wandel
	conference centre [ˈkɒnfərəns sentə]	Tagungszentrum, Kongresszentrum
	headquarters *pl* [ˌhedˈkwɔːtəz]	Zentrale, Hauptsitz
	convention centre [kənˈvenʃn sentə]	Tagungszentrum, Kongresszentrum
	accommodation [əˌkɒməˈdeɪʃn]	Unterkunft
	in addition [ɪn əˈdɪʃn]	außerdem
	to **request sth** [rɪˈkwest]	etw anfordern, um etw bitten
	evaluation [ɪˌvæljuˈeɪʃn]	Beurteilung, Evaluierung

	independent [ˌɪndɪˈpendənt]	unabhängig
	review [rɪˈvjuː]	Rezension, Kritik
	script [skrɪpt]	Manuskript, Drehbuch
	surroundings *pl* [səˈraʊndɪŋz]	Umgebung
	ranging from … to … [ˈreɪndʒɪŋ frəm tə]	von … bis …
	square foot [ˌskweə ˈfʊt]	Quadratfuß *(ca. 0,09 qm)*
	specialty [ˈspeʃəlti]	Besonderheit
	spa [spɑː]	Wellnessbereich
	gym [dʒɪm]	Fitness-Studio
	rating [ˈreɪtɪŋ]	Bewertung
	to **award sb sth** [əˈwɔːd]	jdm etw *(Preis usw.)* verleihen
	fair [feə]	mittelmäßig
	exceptional [ɪkˈsepʃənl]	außergewöhnlich
	registration [ˌredʒɪˈstreɪʃn]	Anmeldung
	beverage [ˈbevərɪdʒ]	Getränk
65 T	**promotional** [prəˈməʊʃənl]	Werbe-
	launch [lɔːntʃ]	Start
	limitation [ˌlɪmɪˈteɪʃn]	Begrenzung, Beschränkung
	to **fire away** [ˌfaɪər əˈweɪ]	losschießen
	constraint [kənˈstreɪnt]	Beschränkung
	television [ˈtelɪvɪʒn]	Fernsehen
	television channel [ˈtelɪvɪʒn tʃænl]	Fernsehsender
	to **aim at sth** [ˈeɪm ət]	etw zum Ziel haben
	focused [ˈfəʊkəst]	gebündelt, konzentriert
	limited [ˈlɪmɪtɪd]	beschränkt, begrenzt
	direct mailing [dəˌrekt ˈmeɪlɪŋ]	Direktwerbung *(per Post)*
	to **register sth with sth** [ˈredʒɪstə wɪð]	etw bei etw anmelden
	response rate [rɪˈspɒns reɪt]	Rücklaufquote
	to **place an ad** [pleɪs ən ˈæd]	eine Anzeige schalten
	glossy brochure [ˌglɒsi ˈbrəʊʃə]	Hochglanzbroschüre
	demonstration [ˌdemənˈstreɪʃn]	Vorführung

UNIT 7

66	**up-to-date** [ˌʌp tə ˈdeɪt]	aktuell, auf dem neuesten Stand
	exhibition hall [ˌeksɪˈbɪʃn hɔːl]	Messehalle, Ausstellungshalle
T	**row stand** [ˈrəʊ stænd]	Reihenstand
	aisle [aɪl]	(Mittel-)Gang
	neighbouring [ˈneɪbərɪŋ]	benachbart
	past sth [pɑːst]	an etw vorbei
	corner stand [ˈkɔːnə stænd]	Eckstand
	rental fee [ˈrentl fiː]	Miete
	end of block stand [ˌend əv ˈblɒk stænd]	Kopfstand
	openness [ˈəʊpənnəs]	Offenheit
	to **appear** [əˈpɪə]	wirken, scheinen
	welcoming [ˈwelkəmɪŋ]	einladend
	island stand [ˈaɪlənd stænd]	Blockstand, Inselstand
	to **surround sth** [səˈraʊnd]	etw umgeben
	construction equipment [kənˈstrʌkʃn ɪkwɪpmənt]	Baumaschinen
	to **rent** [rent]	mieten
67	**giveaway** [ˈgɪvəweɪ]	Werbegeschenk
	sales literature [ˈseɪlz ˌlɪtrətʃə]	Verkaufsprospekte, Informationsmaterial
	to **attract sb to sth** [əˈtrækt]	jdn zu etw locken
	corporate [ˈkɔːprət]	Unternehmens-
	to **hand sth out** [ˌhænd ˈaʊt]	etw austeilen, etw ausgeben
	immediately [ɪˈmiːdiətli]	sofort, unverzüglich
	tote bag [ˌtəʊt bæg]	Tragetasche
	hand sanitizer [ˈhænd sænɪtaɪzə]	Handdesinfektionsmittel
	reusable [ˌriːˈjuːzəbl]	wiederverwendbar
	beaker [ˈbiːkə]	Becher
	trade show [ˈtreɪd ʃəʊ]	Fachmesse
	keychain [ˈkiːtʃeɪn]	Schlüsselbund
	flashlight [ˈflæʃlaɪt]	Taschenlampe
	charger [ˈtʃɑːdʒə]	Ladegerät
	sticky notes *pl* [ˈstɪki nəʊts]	Haftnotizen
	to **link sth to sth** [ˈlɪŋk tə]	etw mit etw verknüpfen, etw mit etw verbinden
	memory stick [ˈmeməri stɪk]	Speicherstick
68	to **commission sth** [kəˈmɪʃn]	etw in Auftrag geben
	architecture [ˈɑːkɪtektʃə]	Architektur
	expo [ˈekspəʊ]	Messe, Ausstellung
	catering [ˈkeɪtərɪŋ]	Verpflegung
	booth [ˌdʒæki ˈbuːð]	(Messe-)Stand
	brand awareness [ˈbrænd əweənəs]	Bekanntheitsgrad einer Marke
	to **demonstrate sth** [ˈdemənstreɪt]	etw vorführen
	feature [ˈfiːtʃə]	Merkmal, Eigenschaft
	shell scheme stand [ˈʃel skiːm stænd]	Systemstand
	box-shaped [ˈbɒks ʃeɪpt]	kastenförmig
	framework [ˈfreɪmwɜːk]	Rahmen
	post [pəʊst]	Säule, Pfosten
	multiple [ˈmʌltɪpl]	mehrfach
	to **fit** [fɪt]	passen
	modular [ˈmɒdjələ]	modular, in Modulbauweise
	wall panel [ˈwɔːl pænl]	Wandplatte
	bespoke [bɪˈspəʊk]	maßgeschneidert
	visualization [ˌvɪʒuəlaɪˈzeɪʃn]	Visualisierung
	requirements *pl* [rɪˈkwaɪəmənts]	Anforderungen, Bedürfnisse, Wünsche
	division of space [dɪˌvɪʒn əf ˈspeɪs]	Raumaufteilung

T	**architect** ['ɑːkɪtekt]	Architekt/in
	sample ['sɑːmpl]	Probe, Muster, Probepackung
	roof [ruːf]	Dach
	counter ['kaʊntə]	Theke, Tresen
	seating ['siːtɪŋ]	Sitzgelegenheiten
	bar table ['bɑː teɪbl]	Stehtisch
	stool [stuːl]	Hocker
	literature rack ['lɪtrətʃə ræk]	Prospektständer
	storage space ['stɔːrɪdʒ speɪs]	Lagerfläche, Stauraum
	to **include sth** [ɪn'kluːd]	etw einplanen
	lockable ['lɒkəbl]	abschließbar, verschließbar
	valuables *pl* ['væljuəblz]	Wertsachen
	demonstration [ˌdemən'streɪʃn]	Vorführung
	to **divide sth up** [dɪ'vaɪd ʌp]	etw aufteilen
	row [rəʊ]	Reihe
	to **make sense** [meɪk 'sens]	einleuchten
69	**with reference to** [wɪð 'refrəns tə]	mit Bezug auf, bezugnehmend auf
	pleasant ['pleznt]	angenehm, nett
	display stand [dɪ'spleɪ stænd]	Präsentationsstand
	semi-closed ['semɪ kləʊzd]	halbgeschlossen
	infill panel ['ɪnfɪl pænl]	Ausfachung, Füllung
	backdrop ['bækdrɒp]	Messewand
	dimensions *pl* [dɪ'menʃnz]	Abmessungen
	depth [depθ]	Tiefe
	sketch [sketʃ]	Skizze
	firm offer [ˌfɜːm 'ɒfə]	verbindliches Angebot
	panel ['pænl]	Platte, Tafel
70	**menu** ['menjuː]	Menü
	to **cater for sth** ['keɪtə fə]	für etw *(Veranstaltung usw.)* Speisen und Getränke liefern
	to **sit back** [ˌsɪt 'bæk]	sich zurücklehnen
	selection [sɪ'lekʃn]	Auswahl
	hospitality [ˌhɒspɪ'tæləti]	Bewirtung
	pack [pæk]	Paket
	on request [ɒn rɪ'kwest]	auf Anfrage
	Please note: [ˌpliːz 'nəʊt]	Bitte beachten Sie:
	cover ['kʌvə]	Gedeck
	waiting staff ['weɪtɪŋ stɑːf]	Servierkräfte
	in addition to sth [ɪn ə'dɪʃn tə]	zusätzlich zu etw
	sth is chargeable at £20 [ɪz 'tʃɑːdʒəbl ət]	für etwas werden £ 20 berechnet
	beverage ['bevərɪdʒ]	Getränk
	to **brew** [bruː]	*(Tee, Kaffee:)* kochen
	herbal tea [ˌhɜːbl 'tiː]	Kräutertee
	decaffeinated [ˌdiː'kæfɪneɪtɪd]	koffeinfrei
	sparkling water [ˌspɑːklɪŋ 'wɔːtə]	Sprudelwasser
	litre ['liːtə]	Liter
	ale [eɪl]	*brit. Biersorte*
	wine list ['waɪn lɪst]	Weinkarte
	savoury ['seɪvəri]	herzhaft
	bites *pl* [baɪts]	Häppchen
	fork [fɔːk]	Gabel
T	**charge** [tʃɑːdʒ]	Gebühr
	labour price ['leɪbə praɪs]	Lohnkosten
71	**space-saving** ['speɪs seɪvɪŋ]	raumsparend
	cultural ['kʌltʃərəl]	kulturell
	background ['bækgraʊnd]	Herkunft
	to **do research into sth** [du rɪ'sɜːtʃ ɪntə]	etw recherchieren, Recherchen über etw anstellen
	etiquette ['etɪket]	Umgangsformen
	awareness [ə'weənəs]	Bewusstsein, Sensibilität
	humour ['hjuːmə]	Humor
	rude [ruːd]	unhöflich
	anger ['æŋgə]	Verärgerung
	to **stress sth** [stres]	etw betonen
	to **respect** [rɪ'spekt]	respektieren, achten
	modesty ['mɒdəsti]	Bescheidenheit
	patience ['peɪʃns]	Geduld
	intelligence [ɪn'telɪdʒəns]	Intelligenz
	plate [pleɪt]	Teller
	shoulder ['ʃəʊldə]	Schulter
	silence ['saɪləns]	Schweigen, Stille
72	**punctuality** [ˌpʌŋktʃu'æləti]	Pünktlichkeit
	superior [suː'pɪəriə]	Vorgesetzte/r
	view (of sb/sth) [vjuː]	Auffassung, Bild (von jdm/einer Sache)
	to **approach sth** [ə'prəʊtʃ]	an etw herangehen, etw angehen
	contrast ['kɒntrɑːst]	Gegensatz
	behaviour [bɪ'heɪvjə]	Verhalten, Benehmen
	trading partner ['treɪdɪŋ pɑːtnə]	Handelspartner/in
	to **adapt to sb/sth** [ə'dæpt tə]	sich an jdn/etw anpassen, sich an jdn/etw gewöhnen
	appointment [ə'pɔɪntmənt]	Termin
	folding table ['fəʊldɪŋ teɪbl]	Klapptisch
	focus ['fəʊkəs]	(inhaltlicher) Schwerpunkt
	interruption [ˌɪntə'rʌpʃn]	Störung, Unterbrechung
	to **reject sth** [rɪ'dʒekt]	etw ablehnen, etw abweisen
T	**adjustable** [ə'dʒʌstəbl]	verstellbar
	best-selling [ˌbest'selɪŋ]	meistverkauft
	to **place an order** [ˌpleɪs ən 'ɔːdə]	einen Auftrag erteilen, eine Bestellung aufgeben
	mid-day [ˌmɪd'deɪ]	Mittag
	to **switch sth off** [ˌswɪtʃ 'ɒf]	etw ausschalten, etw abschalten
	cell (phone) *AE* ['sel fəʊn]	Handy
	per unit [ˌpɜː 'juːnɪt]	pro Stück
	deal [diːl]	Geschäft, Abschluss
73	to **perform sth** [pə'fɔːm]	etw aufführen
74	**jar** [dʒɑː]	(Marmeladen-)Glas

	food industry ['fu:d ɪndəstri]	Nahrungsmittelbranche
	to **hire sth** ['haɪə]	etw mieten
T	**for ages** [fər 'eɪdʒɪz]	eine Ewigkeit
	departure [dɪ'pɑ:tʃə]	Abreise, Abflug
	to **suppose** [sə'pəʊz]	vermuten, annehmen, glauben
	Hang on. [ˌhæŋ 'ɒn]	Einen Moment. Warte mal.
	arrival [ə'raɪvl]	Ankunft
	accommodation [əˌkɒmə'deɪʃn]	Unterkunft, Unterbringung
	conference centre ['kɒnfərəns sentə]	Tagungszentrum, Kongresszentrum
	spacious ['speɪʃəs]	geräumig
	air-conditioned ['eəkəndɪʃənd]	klimatisiert
	to **feature sth** ['fi:tʃə]	etw *(Merkmal usw.)* aufweisen
	fitted with ['fɪtɪd wɪð]	ausgestattet mit
	gym [dʒɪm]	Fitness-Studio
	indoor pool [ˌɪndo: 'pu:l]	Hallenbad
	range [reɪndʒ]	Auswahl, Angebot
	stylish ['staɪlɪʃ]	elegant, stilvoll
	daily ['deɪli]	täglich
	well-stocked [ˌwel 'stɒkt]	gut sortiert
	lounge [laʊndʒ]	Gesellschaftsraum, Lounge
	to **serve** [sɜ:v]	servieren
	snack [snæk]	Imbiss
	front desk [ˌfrʌnt 'desk]	Rezeption
	smoke-free ['sməʊk fri:]	rauchfrei
	shuttle ['ʃʌtl]	Zubringer
	drive [draɪv]	Fahrt *(mit dem Auto)*
	nature reserve ['neɪtʃə rɪzɜ:v]	Naturschutzgebiet
75	to **check in** [ˌtʃek 'ɪn]	sich anmelden, einchecken
T	**reservation** [ˌrezə'veɪʃn]	Reservierung
	buffet breakfast ['bʌfeɪ brekfəst]	Frühstücksbüfett
	dining room ['daɪnɪŋ ru:m]	*(Hotel:)* Speisesaal
	wheelchair ['wi:ltʃeə]	Rollstuhl
	towel ['taʊəl]	Handtuch
	pillow ['pɪləʊ]	Kopfkissen
	secure [sɪ'kjuə]	sicher, bewacht
	gate [geɪt]	Tor, Einfahrt
	to **check out** [ˌtʃek 'aʊt]	sich abmelden, auschecken
	air conditioning ['eə kəndɪʃnɪŋ]	Klimaanlage, Klimatisierung
	meeting room ['mi:tɪŋ ru:m]	Sitzungszimmer, Konferenzraum
	countryside ['kʌntrisaɪd]	Landschaft, ländliche Gegend
	mileage ['maɪlɪdʒ]	*(Mietwagen:)* (enthaltene) Kilometer
	insurance cover [ɪn'ʃʊərəns kʌvə]	Versicherungsschutz
	excess *BE* ['ekses]	*(Versicherung:)* Selbstbehalt
	accident ['æksɪdənt]	Unfall
	to **pick sth up** [ˌpɪk 'ʌp]	etw abholen

UNIT 8

76	**terms** *pl* **of delivery** [ˌtɜ:mz əv dɪ'lɪvəri]	Lieferbedingungen
	range [reɪndʒ]	Sortiment
	prospective [prə'spektɪv]	potenziell
	to **exchange sth** [ɪks'tʃeɪndʒ]	etw austauschen
77 T	**value for money** [ˌvælju: fə 'mʌni]	(preis)günstig
	to **jump at sth** ['dʒʌmp ət]	sich auf etw stürzen
	inviting [ɪn'vaɪtɪŋ]	verlockend
	saying ['seɪɪŋ]	Sprichwort
	to **keep sth in mind** [ˌki:p ɪn 'maɪnd]	etw nicht vergessen
	package ['pækɪdʒ]	Paket
	to **take sth into consideration** [ˌteɪk ɪntə kənˌsɪdə'reɪʃn]	etw in Betracht ziehen, etw berücksichtigen
	consistent(ly) [kən'sɪstənt]	gleichbleibend, beständig, durchgehend
	to **associate sth with sth** [ə'səʊʃieɪt wɪð]	etw mit etw in Verbindung bringen
	to **judge sth** [dʒʌdʒ]	etw beurteilen
	client ['klaɪənt]	Kunde/Kundin
	long-standing [ˌlɒŋ 'stændɪŋ]	langjährig
	buyer ['baɪə]	Käufer/in
	reference ['refərəns]	Referenz
	business acquaintance ['bɪznəs əkweɪntəns]	Geschäftsfreund/in
	strength [streŋθ]	Stärke
	weakness ['wi:knəs]	Schwäche
	anonymous [ə'nɒnɪməs]	anonym
	warranty ['wɒrənti]	Gewährleistung
	limited ['lɪmɪtɪd]	beschränkt, begrenzt
	to **make a claim** [meɪk ə 'kleɪm]	einen Anspruch / eine Forderung geltend machen
	to **look into sth** [ˌlʊk 'ɪntə]	etw prüfen
	terms and conditions *pl* [ˌtɜ:mz ənd kən'dɪʃnz]	Allgemeine Geschäftsbedingungen
	open account [ˌəʊpən ə'kaʊnt]	offenes Zahlungsziel
	to **establish** [ɪ'stæblɪʃ]	festigen
	last but not least [ˌlɑ:st bʌt nɒt 'li:st]	zu guter Letzt
	solvency ['sɒlvənsi]	Zahlungsfähigkeit
	to **put sth at risk** [ˌpʊt ət 'rɪsk]	etw gefährden
	financial stability [faɪˌnænʃl stə'bɪləti]	Finanzstabilität
	to **enter into a contract** [ˌentər ɪntu ə 'kɒntrækt]	einen Vertrag (ab)schließen, in einen Vertrag eintreten
	vendor ['vendə]	Anbieter, Verkäufer
	source [sɔ:s]	Quelle
	credit check ['kredɪt tʃek]	Bonitätsprüfung
	reliability [rɪˌlaɪə'bɪləti]	Zuverlässigkeit

to rank [ræŋk] — einstufen, (in einer Rangliste) bewerten
ranking [ˈræŋkɪŋ] — Einstufung, Bewertung
ethical [ˈeθɪkl] — ethisch, moralisch vertretbar
to treat sb [triːt] — jdn behandeln
attitude (to sth) [ˈætɪtjuːd] — Einstellung (zu etw)
health and safety [ˌhelθ ənd ˈseɪfti] — Arbeitsschutz
regulations *pl* [ˌregjuˈleɪʃnz] — Vorschriften
to meet sth [miːt] — etw *(Vorschriften usw.)* einhalten
to be free to do sth [bi ˈfriː tə duː] — etw tun dürfen
trade union [ˌtreɪd ˈjuːniən] — Gewerkschaft
collective wage bargaining [kəˌlektɪv ˈweɪdʒ bɑːgɪnɪŋ] — Tarifverhandlungen
reputation [ˌrepjuˈteɪʃn] — Ruf
country of origin [ˌkʌntri əv ˈɒrɪdʒɪn] — Ursprungsland
human rights *pl* [ˌhjuːmən ˈraɪts] — Menschenrechte
sexual [ˈsekʃuəl] — sexuell
discrimination [dɪˌskrɪmɪˈneɪʃn] — Diskrimierung
suspicion [səˈspɪʃn] — Verdacht
forced labour [ˌfɔːst ˈleɪbə] — Zwangsarbeit
child labour [ˈtʃaɪld leɪbə] — Kinderarbeit
sustainable [səˈsteɪnəbl] — nachhaltig
to comply with sth [kəmˈplaɪ wɪð] — etw *(Norm usw.)* erfüllen, etw *(Vorschrift usw.)* einhalten
to do one's bit [du wʌnz ˈbɪt] — seinen Beitrag leisten
shipping [ˈʃɪpɪŋ] — Versand
distance [ˈdɪstəns] — Entfernung
carbon footprint [ˌkɑːbən ˈfʊtprɪnt] — CO_2-Fußabdruck

78 **sweet corn** [ˈswiːt kɔːn] — Zuckermais, Süßmais
to go rotten [gəʊ ˈrɒtn] — verfaulen
to note sth [nəʊt] — etw zur Kenntnis nehmen
fully-integrated [ˌfʊli ˈɪntɪgreɪtɪd] — vollintegriert
three-piece [ˈθriː piːs] — dreiteilig
producer [prəˈdjuːsə] — Produzent/in, Hersteller/in
exporter [ɪkˈspɔːtə] — Exporteur, Ausführer
to cut costs [kʌt ˈkɒsts] — Kosten senken
can-making [ˈkæn meɪkɪŋ] — Dosenherstellung
initially [ɪˈnɪʃəli] — zu Anfang, zunächst
diameter [daɪˈæmɪtə] — Durchmesser
favourable [ˈfeɪvərəbl] — günstig
quotation [kwəʊˈteɪʃn] — Preisangebot, Angebot, Offerte

79 **sales material** [ˈseɪlz mətɪəriəl] — Werbematerial, Verkaufsunterlagen
grateful [ˈgreɪtfl] — dankbar
to call on sb [ˈkɔːl ɒn] — jdn besuchen, bei jdm vorbeischauen
to meet requirements [miːt rɪˈkwaɪəmənts] — Anforderungen erfüllen
substantial [səbˈstænʃl] — erheblich, beträchtlich
to grant sth [grɑːnt] — etw gewähren, etw einräumen
proposal [prəˈpəʊzl] — Vorschlag
initial proposal [ɪˌnɪʃl prəˈpəʊzl] — Erstvorschlag

T **to be up and running** [bi ˌʌp ən ˈrʌnɪŋ] — in (laufendem) Betrieb sein
to troubleshoot [ˈtrʌblʃuːt] — Fehler suchen, Fehler beheben
to assist sb [əˈsɪst] — jdm helfen, jdn unterstützen
shipping company [ˈʃɪpɪŋ kʌmpəni] — Reederei
seaworthy [ˈsiːwɜːði] — seetüchtig
condition [kənˈdɪʃn] — Zustand
sector [ˈsektə] — Branche
to require sb to do sth [rɪˈkwaɪə] — von jdm verlangen, etw zu tun
remainder [rɪˈmeɪndə] — Rest
official offer [əˌfɪʃl ˈɒfə] — offizielles Angebot
after-sales service [ˈɑːftəseɪlz sɜːvɪs] — Kundendienst
to diagnose [ˈdaɪəgnəʊz] — diagnostizieren
remotely [rɪˈməʊtli] — aus der Ferne
remote diagnosis [rɪˌməʊt daɪəgˈnəʊsɪs] — Ferndiagnose

80 **to wholesale** [ˈhəʊlseɪl] — en gros handeln
terms *pl* **of insurance** [ˌtɜːmz əv ɪnˈʃʊərəns] — Versicherungsbedinungen
insurance in transit [ɪnˌʃʊərəns ɪn ˈtrænzɪt] — Transportversicherung
seller [ˈselə] — Verkäufer/in
mode of transport [ˌməʊd əv ˈtrænspɔːt] — Beförderungsart, Verkehrsmittel
loading [ˈləʊdɪŋ] — Verladen, Verladung
port of shipment [ˌpɔːt əf ˈʃɪpmənt] — Verschiffungshafen
carriage [ˈkærɪdʒ] — Transport, Beförderung, Fracht
main carriage [ˈmeɪn kærɪdʒ] — Hauptlauf
pre-carriage [ˈpriː kærɪdʒ] — Vorlauf
post-carriage [ˈpəʊst kærɪdʒ] — Nachlauf
contract of carriage [ˌkɒntrækt əv ˈkærɪdʒ] — Beförderungsvertrag, Frachtvertrag
terminal [ˈtɜːmɪnl] — Terminal
export clearance [ˈekspɔːt klɪərəns] — Ausfuhrabfertigung
import clearance [ˈɪmpɔːt klɪərəns] — Einfuhrabfertigung
place of destination [ˌpleɪs əv destɪˈneɪʃn] — Bestimmungsort
insurance [ɪnˈʃʊərəns] — Versicherung
duty [ˈdjuːti] — Zoll

	consignment [kən'saɪnmənt]	Sendung, Warensendung
	importer [ɪm'pɔ:tə]	Importeur, Einführer
81	**floor tiles** *pl* ['flɔ: taɪlz]	Bodenfliesen
	seafood ['si:fu:d]	Meeresfrüchte
	premises *pl* ['premɪsɪz]	Räumlichkeiten, Firmengelände
	convenient [kən'vi:niənt]	geeignet, zweckmäßig
	to **cover** ['kʌvə]	*(Kosten)* decken
	to **bear sth** [beə]	etw *(Risiko, Kosten)* tragen
	to **hand sth over** [ˌhænd 'əuvə]	etw übergeben
	carrier ['kæriə]	Spediteur, Reederei, Transportunternehmen
	to **pass to sb** ['pɑ:s tə]	auf jdn übergehen
	to **collect sth** [kə'lekt]	etw abholen
	to **insure** [ɪn'ʃuə]	versichern
	export licence ['ekspɔ:t laɪsns]	Ausführgenehmigung
	documentation [ˌdɒkjumen'teɪʃn]	Papiere
	exception [ɪk'sepʃn]	Ausnahme
	customs duty [ˌkʌstəmz 'dju:ti]	Zollgebühr(en)
	to **refer to sth** [rɪ'fɜ: tə]	auf etw zurückgreifen, etw zu Hilfe nehmen
	unpaid [ˌʌn'peɪd]	unbezahlt
	electricity generator [ɪˌlek'trɪsəti 'dʒenəreɪtə]	Generator
T	to **enquire about sth** [ɪn'kwaɪər əbaut]	sich nach etw erkundigen
	by rail [baɪ 'reɪl]	mit der Bahn
	booked up [ˌbukt 'ʌp]	ausgebucht
	to **dock** [dɒk]	festmachen
	receipt of order [rɪˌsi:t əv 'ɔ:də]	Auftragseingang
	breakable ['breɪkəbl]	zerbrechlich
82	**transaction** [træn'zækʃn]	Geschäft, Vorgang, Transaktion
	irrevocable and confirmed documentary letter of credit [ɪˌrevəkəbl ən kənˌfɜ:md dɒkjuˌmentri letər əf 'kredɪt]	unwiderrufliches und bestätigtes Dokumentenakkreditiv
	simplified ['sɪmplɪfaɪd]	vereinfacht
	holder ['həuldə]	Inhaber/in
	to **take possession of sth** [teɪk pə'zeʃn əv]	etw in Besitz nehmen
	commercial invoice [kəˌmɜ:ʃl 'ɪnvɔɪs]	Handelsrechnung
	insurance certificate [ɪnˌʃuərəns sə'tɪfɪkət]	Versicherungsschein
	bill of lading (B/L) [ˌbɪl əv 'leɪdɪŋ]	Konnossement
	air waybill [ˌeə 'weɪbɪl]	Luftfrachtbrief
	consignment note [kən'saɪnmənt nəut]	Frachtbrief
	letter of credit (L/C) [ˌletər əf 'kredɪt]	Akkreditiv
83	**document of title** [ˌdɒkjumənt əv 'taɪtl]	Dispositionspapier, Traditionspapier
	ownership ['əunəʃɪp]	Eigentum, Eigentumsrecht
	title to the goods [ˌtaɪtl tə ðə 'gudz]	Eigentum(srecht) an den Waren
	to **inspect sth** [ɪn'spekt]	etw prüfen
	to **be in order** [bi ɪn 'ɔ:də]	in Ordnung sein
	to **charge a fee** [ˌtʃɑ:dʒ ə 'fi:]	eine Gebür verlangen
	case study ['keɪs stʌdi]	Fallstudie
	road construction ['rəud kənstrʌkʃn]	Straßenbau
	heavy machinery [ˌhevi mə'ʃi:nəri]	Schwermaschinen
	beef [bi:f]	Rindfleisch
	meat [mi:t]	Fleisch
	reliable [rɪ'laɪəbl]	zuverlässig
84	**layout** ['leɪaut]	Gestaltung, Aufbau, Layout
	medical supplies *pl* [ˌmedɪkl sə'plaɪz]	Sanitätsartikel
	clinic ['klɪnɪk]	Klinik
	body ['bɒdi]	*(Brief:)* Haupttext
	enclosure [ɪn'kləuʒə]	*(Brief:)* Anlage
	inside address [ˌɪnsaɪd ə'dres]	Innenadresse
	reference initials *pl* ['refərəns ɪnɪʃlz]	*(Brief:)* Zeichen
	signature ['sɪgnətʃə]	Unterschrift
	signature block ['sɪgnətʃə blɒk]	Signatur
	attention line [ə'tenʃn laɪn]	Zeile „zu Händen“
85	**for the attention of** [fə ði ə'tenʃn əv]	zu Händen
	trade magazine ['treɪd mægəzi:n]	Fachzeitschrift
	hardware ['hɑ:dweə]	Geräte
	outpatient clinic ['autpeɪʃnt klɪnɪk]	Ambulanz
	high-definition [ˌhaɪ ˌdefɪ'nɪʃn]	hochauflösend
	trial order [ˌtraɪəl 'ɔ:də]	Probebestellung
	packaging ['pækɪdʒɪŋ]	Verpackung
	attention [ə'tenʃn]	Beachtung, Aufmerksamkeit

KMK Exam practice 4

86	**from the beginning** [frəm ðə bɪ'gɪnɪŋ]	von Anfang an
	stationery ['steɪʃənri]	Schreibwaren
	office supplies *pl* ['ɒfɪs səplaɪz]	Bürobedarf
	launch [lɔ:ntʃ]	Eröffnung
	to **deal in sth** ['di:l ɪn]	mit etw handeln
	to **stimulate sth** ['stɪmjuleɪt]	etw beleben, etw ankurbeln
	opportunity [ˌɒpə'tju:nəti]	Gelegenheit, Möglichkeit
	exhibitor [ɪg'zɪbɪtə]	Aussteller
	array of products [əˌreɪ əf 'prɒdʌkts]	Produktangebot

	arts and crafts *pl* [ˌɑːts ənd ˈkrɑːfts]	Kunsthandwerk
	writing implement [ˈraɪtɪŋ ɪmplɪmənt]	Schreibgerät
	gift [gɪft]	Geschenk
	to **prove sth** [pruːv]	sich als etw erweisen
	increasingly [ɪnˈkriːsɪŋli]	zunehmend
	achievement [əˈtʃiːvmənt]	Leistung
	to **attribute sth to sb** [əˈtrɪbjuːt tə]	jdm etw zuschreiben
	to **be well received** [bi ˌwel rɪˈsiːvd]	(großen) Zuspruch finden
	to **access sth** [ˈækses]	etw erreichen
	emerging markets *pl* [ɪˌmɜːdʒɪŋ ˈmɑːkɪts]	Wachstumsmärkte, Schwellenmärkte
	nearby [ˈnɪəbaɪ]	in der Nähe, nahegelegen
	continued [kənˈtɪnjuːd]	anhaltend, kontinuierlich
	to **go a long way in sth** [gəʊ ə ˌlɒŋ ˈweɪ ɪn]	viel zu etw beitragen, viel für etw tun
	high-quality [ˌhaɪ ˈkwɒləti]	hochwertig
	stamp [stæmp]	Marke, Stempel
	customer base [ˈkʌstəmə beɪs]	Kundenstamm
	to **display sth** [dɪˈspleɪ]	etw ausstellen, etw zeigen
87	to **entertain sb** [ˌentəˈteɪn]	jdn bewirten
	to **occur** [əˈkɜː]	*(Problem usw.:)* auftreten
	imagination [ɪˌmædʒɪˈneɪʃn]	Phantasie
	to **make sth up** [ˌmeɪk ˈʌp]	sich etw ausdenken, sich etw einfallen lassen
	to **reassure sb** [ˌriːəˈʃʊə]	jdn beruhigen
	to **get annoyed about sth** [ˌget əˈnɔɪd əbaʊt]	sich über etw ärgern
	voucher [ˈvaʊtʃə]	Gutschein

UNIT 9

88	to **submit sth** [səbˈmɪt]	etw einreichen, etw abgeben
	hiking [ˈhaɪkɪŋ]	Wandern
	template [ˈtempleɪt]	Vorlage
89	**windproof** [ˈwɪndpruːf]	winddicht
	waterproof [ˈwɔːtəpruːf]	wasserdicht
	tent [tent]	Zelt
	canvas [ˈkænvəs]	Tuch
	to **refer to sth** [rɪˈfɜː tə]	auf etw Bezug nehmen, sich auf etw beziehen
	textiles *pl* [ˈtekstaɪlz]	Textilien
	manufacture [ˌmænjuˈfæktʃə]	Herstellung, Produktion, Fertigung
	as requested [əz rɪˈkwestɪd]	wie gewünscht
	to **enclose** [ɪnˈkləʊz]	*(Brief:)* beifügen
	catalogue [ˈkætəlɒg]	Katalog
	currently [ˈkʌrəntli]	momentan, augenblicklich
	in stock [ɪn ˈstɒk]	vorrätig, auf Lager, lieferbar
	immediate [ɪˈmiːdiət]	unverzüglich, sofortig
	to **draw sb's attention to sth** [ˌdrɔː əˈtenʃn tə]	jds Aufmerksamkeit auf etw lenken
	material [məˈtɪəriəl]	Stoff, Material
	" = inch [ɪntʃ]	Zoll
	roll [rəʊl]	Rolle
	beige [beɪʒ]	beige
	bulk discount [bʌlk ˈdɪskaʊnt]	Mengenrabatt
	to **quote a price** [ˌkwəʊt ə ˈpraɪs]	einen Preis angeben/nennen
	cash discount [ˈkæʃ dɪskaʊnt]	Skonto
	to **point sth out** [ˌpɔɪnt ˈaʊt]	auf etw hinweisen, auf etw aufmerksam machen
	to **convince sb of sth** [kənˈvɪns]	jdn von etw überzeugen
	to **be of assistance** [bi əv əˈsɪstəns]	behilflich sein
90	**logistics director** [ləˈdʒɪstɪks dərektə]	Logistikleiter/in
	sales director [ˈseɪlz dərektə]	Vertriebsleiter/in
	dated [ˈdeɪtɪd]	(mit Datum) vom
	above-mentioned [əˌbʌv ˈmenʃnd]	obengenannt
	entire [ɪnˈtaɪə]	gesamte/r/s, ganze/r/s
	to **supply sb with sth** [səˈplaɪ]	jdm etw liefern
	with order [wɪð ˈɔːdə]	bei Auftragserteilung
	on presentation of sth [ɒn ˌpreznˈteɪʃn əv]	bei Vorlage von etw
	to **hesitate** [ˈhezɪteɪt]	zögern
	to **require sth** [rɪˈkwaɪə]	etw benötigen, etw wünschen
91	**noise level** [ˈnɔɪz levl]	Geräuschpegel, Lärmpegel
	noise protection [ˈnɔɪz prəˈtekʃn]	Schallschutz, Lärmschutz
	hood [hʊd]	Haube, Abdeckung
	reference to sth [ˈrefərəns tə]	Verweis auf etw, Bezug auf etw
T	**decibel** [ˈdesɪbel]	Dezibel
	ear protectors *pl* [ɪə prˈtektəz]	Gehörschutz
	to **cut sth** [kʌt]	etw reduzieren
	noise emission [ˈnɔɪz ɪmɪʃn]	Schallemission, Lärmbelastung
	to **service sth** [ˈsɜːvɪs]	etw warten
	the beauty of it is ... [ðə ˈbjuːti əv ɪt ɪz]	Das Schöne daran ist, ...
	to **retrofit sth** [ˈretrəʊfɪt]	etw nachrüsten
	in a matter of hours [ɪn ə ˌmætər əv ˈaʊəz]	in nur wenigen Stunden
	to **be unaffected** [bi ˌʌnəˈfektɪd]	(von etw) nicht betroffen sein, (von etw) nicht beeinträchtigt werden
	to **slide sth to one side** [ˌslaɪd tə wʌn ˈsaɪd]	etw zur Seite schieben
	to **fit sth in** [ˌfɪt ˈɪn]	etw einbauen
	to **take delivery of sth** [ˌteɪk dɪˈlɪvəri əv]	etw *(Ware usw.)* in Empfang nehmen
	basic price [ˌbeɪsɪk ˈpreɪs]	Grundpreis
	net [net]	netto
	free carrier [ˌfriː ˈkæriə]	frei Frachtführer
	in transit [ɪn ˈtrænzɪt]	beim Transport

	coverage [ˈkʌvərɪdʒ]	Versicherungsschutz
	air freight [ˈeə freɪt]	Luftfracht
	sea freight [ˈsiː freɪt]	Seefracht
	freight rate [ˈfreɪt reɪt]	Frachtsatz, Frachtrate
	door-to-door delivery [dɔː tə ˌdɔː dɪˈlɪvəri]	Haus-zu-Haus-Lieferung
	flexibility [ˌfleksəˈbɪləti]	Flexibilität, Spielraum
	to **foot sth** [fʊt]	die Kosten für etw übernehmen
	We have a deal. [wiː ˌhæv ə ˈdiːl]	Abgemacht!
92	**via** [ˈvaɪə]	per, mittels, über
	expanded metal [ɪkˌspændɪd ˈmetl]	Streckmetall
	minimum order quantity [ˌmɪnɪməm ˈɔːdə kwɒntəti]	Mindestbestellmenge
	transit time [ˈtrænzɪt taɪm]	Laufzeit
	charge [tʃɑːdʒ]	Kosten
	shipping agent [ˈʃɪpɪŋ eɪdʒənt]	Spediteur
93	**import tax** [ˈɪmpɔːt tæks]	Einfuhrzoll
	shipping rate [ˈʃɪpɪŋ reɪt]	Frachtsatz, Versandkosten
	sea transport [ˈsiː trænspɔːt]	Seetransport
	to **handle sth** [ˈhændl]	etw erledigen
	on sb's behalf [ɒn bɪˈhɑːf]	für jdn
94	**unit price** [ˌjuːnɪt ˈpraɪs]	Stückpreis
	quote [kwəʊt]	(Preis-)Angebot
	closed wagon [ˌkləʊzd ˈwægən]	geschlossener Waggon
	in shared container [ɪn ˌʃeəd kənˈteɪnə]	in Sammelcontainer, als Beiladung
	applicable charges *pl* [əˌplɪkəbl ˈtʃɑːdʒɪz]	anfallende Gebühren
	My pleasure. [maɪ ˈpleʒə]	Ganz meinerseits! Gern geschehen!
95	**sub-total** [ˈsʌbtəʊtl]	Zwischensumme
T	**With pleasure.** [wɪð ˈpleʒə]	Aber gerne!
	for the time being [fə ðə ˌtaɪm ˈbiːɪŋ]	einstweilen, fürs Erste
	to **be/get in touch** [bi/get ɪn ˈtʌtʃ]	sich melden
	special offer [ˌspeʃl ˈɒfə]	Sonderangebot
	fleet [fliːt]	Fuhrpark, Flotte
	to **transfer sth** [trænsˈfɜː]	etw übertragen
96	to **sort sth out** [ˌsɔːt ˈaʊt]	etw klären, etw regeln
	misunderstanding [ˌmɪsʌndəˈstændɪŋ]	Missverständnis
T	**from stock** [frəm ˈstɒk]	ab Lager
	bulk order [ˌbʌlk ˈɔːdə]	Großauftrag, Großbestellung
	to **cover sth** [ˈkʌvə]	etw abdecken
	order form [ˈɔːdə fɔːm]	Bestellformular
	to **omit sth** [əˈmɪt]	etw weglassen
	calculation [ˌkælkjuˈleɪʃn]	Berechnung, Kalkulation
T	**microwave oven** [ˌmaɪkrəweɪv ˈʌvn]	Mikrowellenherd
	kettle [ˈketl]	Wasserkocher
	to **misunderstand sth** [ˌmɪsʌndəˈstænd]	etw missverstehen, etw falsch verstehen
	to **recalculate** [rɪˈkælkjuleɪt]	neu berechnen
	total price [ˌtəʊtl ˈpraɪs]	Gesamtpreis
	to **re-submit sth** [ˌrɪ səbˈmɪt]	etw *(Bestellung)* erneut aufgeben
	correction [kəˈrekʃn]	Korrektur
	to **appreciate sth** [əˈpriːʃieɪt]	etw zu schätzen wissen
97	to **re-write sth** [rɪˈraɪt]	etw neu schreiben
	extractor hood [ɪkˈstæktə hʊd]	Dunstabzugshaube
	customer discount [ˌkʌstəmə ˈdɪskaʊnt]	Kundenrabatt

UNIT 10

98	**contract of sale** [ˌkɒntrækt əv ˈseɪl]	Kaufvertrag
	duty [ˈdjuːti]	Aufgabe, Pflicht
99	**authority** [ɔːˈθɒrəti]	Befugnis, Vollmacht
	to **perform an obligation** [pəˌfɔːm ən ɒblɪˈgeɪʃn]	eine Verpflichtung erfüllen
	prior to sth [ˈpraɪə tə]	vor etw
	work and costs [ˌwɜːk ən ˈkɒsts]	Arbeit und Kosten
	to **incur** [ɪnˈkɜː]	*(Kosten:)* anfallen
	purchase price [ˈpɜːtʃəs praɪs]	Kaufpreis
	sb can be assumed to do sth [kən bi əˈsjuːmd tə duː]	es kann davon ausgegangen werden, dass jd etw tut
	unconditional(ly) [ˌʌnkənˈdɪʃənl]	vorbehaltlos, uneingeschränkt
	defective [dɪˈfektɪv]	mangelhaft
	date of delivery [ˌdeɪt əv dɪˈlɪvəri]	Lieferdatum
	performance (of a contract) [pəˈfɔːməns]	Erfüllung, Durchführung (eines Vertrags)
	circumstances *pl* [ˈsɜːkəmstənsɪz]	Umstände
	means [miːnz]	Mittel, Maßnahme
	promptly [ˈprɒmptli]	umgehend, unverzüglich, sofort
	to **assume responsibility** [əˌsjuːm rɪspɒnsəˈbɪləti]	die Verantwortung übernehmen
	loss [lɒs]	Verlust
	unless otherwise stated [ʌnles ˌʌðəwaɪz ˈsteɪtɪd]	sofern nicht anders angegeben
	due [djuː]	fällig
	to **swear** [sweə]	schwören
	to **cancel** [ˈkænsl]	*(Vertrag)* auflösen, annullieren
	cancellation [ˌkænsəˈleɪʃn]	*(Vertrag:)* Auflösung, Annullierung
	written [ˈrɪtn]	schriftlich

	statement [ˈsteɪtmənt]	Erklärung
	to **reject sth** [rɪˈdʒekt]	etw zurückweisen, etw beanstanden
	to **consent to sth** [kənˈsent tə]	einer Sache zustimmen
	alteration [ˌɔːltəˈreɪʃn]	Änderung
100	to **acknowledge an order** [əkˌnɒlɪdʒ ən ˈɔːdə]	einen Auftrag bestätigen
	hide [haɪd]	Haut, Leder
	buffalo [ˈbʌfələʊ]	Büffel
	a/c (= account) [əˈkaʊnt]	Konto
	palletized [ˈpælətaɪzd]	auf Paletten, palettiert
	confirmation of order [kɒnfəˌmeɪʃn əv ˈɔːdə]	Auftragsbestätigung
	advice of dispatch [ədˌvaɪs əv dɪˈspætʃ]	Versandanzeige
	to **trust** [trʌst]	hoffen(, dass)
	punctually [ˈpʌŋktʃuəli]	pünktlich
101	**general purpose** [ˌdʒenrəl ˈpɜːpəs]	Allzweck-
	payload [ˈpeɪləʊd]	Zuladung, Nutzlast
	lb = pound [paʊnd]	Pfund *(ca. 454 g)*
	groupage consignment [ˈgruːpɪdʒ kənsaɪnmənt]	Sammelladung
	abbreviation [əˌbriːviˈeɪʃn]	Abkürzung
	inch [ɪntʃ]	Zoll *(ca. 2,54 cm)*
	validity [vəˈlɪdəti]	Gültigkeit

T	to **go bankrupt** [gəʊ ˈbæŋkrʌpt]	Pleite gehen
	quarterly settlement [ˌkwɔːtəli ˈsetlmənt]	vierteljährliche Abrechnung
	investment [ɪnˈvestmənt]	Investition
	valid [ˈvælɪd]	gültig

102	**trade discount** [ˈtreɪd dɪskaʊnt]	Händlerrabatt
	sturdy [ˈstɜːdi]	stabil, robust
	carton [ˈkɑːtn]	Karton
	receipt of invoice [rɪˌsiːt əv ˈɪnvɔɪs]	Rechnungseingang
	currency sign [ˈkʌrənsi saɪn]	Währungssymbol
	sewing machine [ˈsəʊɪŋ məʃiːn]	Nähmaschine
103	**microbrewing equipment** [ˈmaɪkrəʊbruːɪŋ ɪkwɪpmənt]	Geräte für Klein(st)-brauereien
	application [ˌæplɪˈkeɪʃn]	*(Akkreditiv:)* Eröffnungsauftrag, Akkreditivauftrag
	documentary letter of credit (L/C) [dɒkjuˌmentri ˌletər əf ˈkredɪt]	Dokumentenakkreditiv
	negotiable [nɪˈgəʊʃiəbl]	begebbar
	transferable [trɑːnsˈfɜːrəbl]	übertragbar
	clean bill of lading [ˌkliːn ˌbɪl əv ˈleɪdɪŋ]	reines Konnossement
	foul bill of lading [ˌfaʊl ˌbɪl əv ˈleɪdɪŋ]	unreines Konnossement

	apparent [əˈpærənt]	anscheinend
	in good order and condition [ɪn gʊd ˌɔːdər ənd kənˈdɪʃn]	in einwandfreiem Zustand
	non-negotiable [ˌnɒn nɪˈgəʊʃiəbl]	nicht begebbar
	CMR document [ˌsiː em ˈɑː dɒkjumənt]	CMR-Frachtbrief
	truck waybill [ˈtrʌk weɪbɪl]	Lastwagenfrachtbrief
	multi-modal [ˌmʌlti ˈməʊdl]	multimodal
	to **prove sth** [pruːv]	etw nachweisen
	documentary credit transaction [dɒkjuˌmentri ˈkredɪt trænzækʃn]	Akkreditivgeschäft
	certificate of origin [səˌtɪfɪkət əv ˈɒrɪdʒɪn]	Ursprungszeugnis
	to **issue** [ˈɪʃuː]	*(Dokument)* ausstellen
	to **assess sth** [əˈses]	*(Zollgebühren usw.)* ansetzen, berechnen
	packing list [ˈpækɪŋ lɪst]	Packliste
	bill of exchange [ˌbɪl əv ɪksˈtʃeɪndʒ]	Wechsel
	draft [drɑːft]	Tratte
104	**sign (of sth)** [saɪn]	Anzeichen (von etw)
	to **present sb sth** [prɪˈzent]	jdm etw *(Dokument usw.)* vorlegen
	payable [ˈpeɪəbl]	zahlbar
	presentation [ˌpreznˈteɪʃn]	Vorlage *(eines Dokuments)*
	currency [ˈkʌrənsi]	Währung
	load [ləʊd]	Ladung
	to **split** [splɪt]	teilen
105	**file number** [ˈfaɪl nʌmbə]	Aktenzeichen
	applicant [ˈæplɪkənt]	*(Akkreditiv:)* Auftraggeber/in
	guarantor [ˌgærənˈtɔː]	Bürge/Bürgin
	advising bank [ədˌvaɪzɪŋ ˈbæŋk]	avisierende Bank
	blank [blæŋk]	leer
	for account of sb [fər əˈkaʊnt əv]	auf jds Rechnung
	in favor of sb *AE* [ɪn ˈfeɪvər əv]	zu jds Gunsten, zugunsten von jdm
	beneficiary [ˌbenɪˈfɪʃəri]	Begünstigte/r
	expiration date [ˌekspəˈreɪʃn deɪt]	Verfallsdatum
	to **draw a draft** [ˌdrɔː ə ˈdrɑːft]	eine Tratte/einen Wechsel ziehen
	figure [ˈfɪgə]	Ziffer
	covering [ˈkʌvərɪŋ]	Deckung
	to **specify sth** [ˈspesɪfaɪ]	etw (genau) angeben
	(at) sight [saɪt]	(bei) Vorlage
	partial shipment [ˌpɑːʃl ˈʃɪpmənt]	Teillieferung
	permitted [pəˈmɪtɪd]	erlaubt, gestattet
	transshipment [trænsˈʃɪpmənt]	Umladung
	taking in charge [ˌteɪkɪŋ ɪn ˈtʃɑːdʒ]	Übernahme

	merchandise [ˈmɜːtʃəndaɪs]	Ware
	microbrewery [ˈmaɪkrəʊbruːəri]	Klein(st)brauerei
	two-vessel brewhouse [tuː ˌvesl ˈbruːhaʊs]	Zweigerätesudhaus
	applicable [əˈplɪkəbl]	zutreffend
	insurance policy [ɪnˈʃʊərəns pɒləsi]	Versicherungspolice
	invoice value [ˈɪnvɔɪs væljuː]	Rechnungswert
	in duplicate [ɪn ˈdjuːplɪkət]	in zweifacher Ausfertigung
	to **effect sth** [ɪˈfekt]	etw ausführen, etw tätigen, etw erwirken
	war [wɔː]	Krieg
	full set [ˌfʊl ˈset]	vollständiger Satz *(von Dokumenten)*
	to **consign sth** [kənˈsaɪn]	etw übergeben
	to **notify sb** [ˈnəʊtɪfaɪ]	jdn in Kenntnis setzen, jdn benachrichtigen
	prepaid [priːˈpeɪd]	im Voraus bezahlt
	cover [ˈkʌvə]	Umschlag
	negotiating bank [nɪˌɡəʊʃieɪtɪŋ ˈbæŋk]	negoziierende Bank
	paying bank [ˌpeɪɪŋ ˈbæŋk]	ausführende Bank
	validation [ˌvælɪˈdeɪʃn]	Bestätigung
	to **authorize sb** [ˈɔːθəraɪz]	jdn ermächtigen, jdn bevollmächtigen
	by means of [baɪ ˈmiːnz əv]	mittels, durch
	to **debit** [ˈdebɪt]	*(Konto)* belasten, *(Geld)* abbuchen
	to **set forth** [ˌset ˈfɔːθ]	darlegen
	to **affect sth** [əˈfekt]	etw beeinflussen
	authorization [ˌɔːθəraɪˈzeɪʃn]	Ermächtigung, Vollmacht
	insufficient funds *pl* [ɪnsəˌfɪʃnt ˈfʌndz]	mangelnde Deckung, unzureichende Mittel
	setoff rights *pl* [ˈsetɒf raɪts]	Aufrechnungsrechte
	equity [ˈekwəti]	Billigkeit(srecht)
106	to **sail for ...** [ˈseɪl fə]	nach ... fahren
T	**Thank goodness!** [ˌθæŋk ˈɡʊdnəs]	Gott sei Dank!
	in time [ɪn ˈtaɪm]	rechtzeitig
	fire [ˈfaɪə]	Brand
	to **burn down** [ˌbɜːn ˈdaʊn]	niederbrennen
	to **warn sb** [wɔːn]	jdm (etw) sagen, jdn vorwarnen
	Incorporated (Inc.) [ɪnˈkɔːpəreɪtɪd]	GmbH
	instead [ɪnˈsted]	stattdessen
	to **release sth** [rɪˈliːs]	etw freigeben
	one way or another [ˌwʌn weɪ ɔːr əˈnʌðə]	so oder so
	to **give it a try** [ˌɡɪv ɪt ə ˈtraɪ]	es versuchen

	arrangements *pl* [əˈreɪndʒmənts]	Vereinbarungen, Abmachungen, Modalitäten
	formalities *pl* [fɔːˈmælətiz]	Formalitäten
	to **deal with sth** [ˈdiːl wɪð]	etw erledigen
T	to **reroute sth** [riːˈruːt]	etw umleiten
	wooden crate [ˌwʊdn ˈkreɪt]	Holzkiste
	out of interest [aʊt əv ˈɪntrəst]	interessehalber
107	to **apply for sth** [əˈplaɪ fə]	etw beantragen

KMK Exam practice 5

110	**individual training** [ɪndɪˌvɪdʒuəl ˈtreɪnɪŋ]	individuelle Weiterbildung, Einzelschulung
	no matter what ... [nəʊ ˌmætə ˈwɒt]	ganz gleich, was ...; egal, was ...
	expertise [ˌekspɜːˈtiːz]	Fachwissen, Fachkenntnisse
	competitive advantage [kəmˌpetətɪv ədˈvɑːntɪdʒ]	Wettbewerbsvorteil
	challenging [ˈtʃælɪndʒɪŋ]	anspruchsvoll, fordernd
	to **evaluate sth** [ɪˈvæljueɪt]	etw einstufen
	thus [ðʌs]	auf diese Weise, so
	introductory level [ɪntrəˌdʌktəri ˈlevl]	Einstiegsniveau
	operational [ˌɒpəˈreɪʃənl]	Betriebs-, Arbeits-
	one-to-one [ˌwʌn tə ˈwʌn]	Einzel-
	quality-assured experts *pl* [ˌkwɒləti əʃʊəd ˈekspɜːts]	qualifiziertes Fachpersonal
	subject matter [ˈsʌbdʒɪkt mætə]	Materie, Unterrichtsstoff
	work pace [ˈwɜːk peɪs]	Arbeitstempo
	session [ˈseʃn]	Unterrichtseinheit
	to **return costs** [rɪˈtɜːn kɒsts]	Kosten erstatten
	partial(ly) [ˈpɑːʃəli]	teilweise
	tax declaration [ˌtæks ˌdekləˈreɪʃn]	Steuererklärung
	increasingly [ɪnˈkriːsɪŋli]	zunehmend
	to **seek sth** [siːk]	etw suchen
	flexibility [ˌfleksəˈbɪləti]	Anpassungsfähigkeit, Flexibilität
	convenience [kənˈviːniəns]	Komfort
	cost-effectiveness [ˌkɒstɪˈfektɪvnəs]	Wirtschaftlichkeit
	return on investment [rɪˌtɜːn ɒn ɪnˈvestmənt]	Rendite, Ertrag
	to **time sth** [taɪm]	etw zeitlich abstimmen
	disruption (to sth) [dɪsˈrʌpʃn]	Störung (von etw)
	work schedule [ˈwɜːk ʃedjuːl]	Arbeitsablauf
	adaptable (to sth) [əˈdæptəbl]	anpassbar (an etw)
	shift [ʃɪft]	Schicht
	tailor-made (to sth) [ˌteɪləˈmeɪd]	individuell (auf etw) zugeschnitten

	tax-refundable [ˌtæks rɪˈfʌndəbl]	steuerlich absetzbar
	qualification offer [ˌkwɒlɪfɪˈkeɪʃn ɒfə]	Fortbildungsmaßnahme
	heterogeneous [ˌhetərəˈdʒiːnɪəs]	heterogen
	charges *pl* [ˈtʃɑːdʒɪz]	Gebühren, Kosten
	time savings *pl* [ˈtaɪm seɪvɪŋz]	Zeitersparnis
	comfort and relaxation [ˌkʌmfət ənd riːlækˈseɪʃn]	angenehme Atmosphäre
	to **strengthen** [ˈstreŋθn]	stärken
111 T	**answering machine** [ˈɑːnsərɪŋ məʃiːn]	Anrufbeantworter
	neighbourhood [ˈneɪbəhʊd]	Nachbarschaft
	thermal insulation [ˌθɜːml ɪnsjuˈleɪʃn]	Wärmedämmung
	contact (person) [ˈkɒntækt]	Ansprechpartner/in
	to **consist of sth** [kənˈsɪst əv]	aus etw bestehen
	tenant [ˈtenənt]	Mieter
	frankly [ˈfræŋkli]	offen gesagt
	shabby [ˈʃæbi]	heruntergekommen, schäbig
	estate agent [ɪˈsteɪt eɪdʒənt]	Immobilienmakler/in
	facility manager [fəˈsɪləti mænɪdʒə]	Objektleiter/in, Gebäudeverwalter/in

UNIT 11

112	**appliance** [əˈplaɪəns]	(Elektro-)Gerät
	on arrival [ɒn əˈraɪvl]	bei Ankunft, bei Eintreffen
	majority [məˈdʒɒrəti]	Mehrheit, Großteil
	to **relate to sth** [rɪˈleɪt tə]	sich auf etw beziehen
113 T	**every so often** [ˌevri səʊ ˈɒfn]	hin und wieder
	every now and then [evri ˌnaʊ ən ˈðen]	ab und an
	in case [ɪn ˈkeɪs]	für den Fall, dass; falls
	no matter what ... [nəʊ ˌmætə ˈwɒt]	ganz gleich, was ...; egal, was ...
	to **follow sth up** [ˌfɒləʊ ˈʌp]	etw nachbereiten, in einer Sache nachfassen
	record [ˈrekɔːd]	Aufzeichnung, Protokoll
	to **copy sb in** [ˌkɒpi ˈɪn]	*(E-Mail:)* jdn CC setzen
	order number [ˈɔːdə nʌmbə]	Bestellnummer, Auftragsnummer
	to **resolve sth** [rɪˈzɒlv]	etw lösen
	replacement [rɪˈpleɪsmənt]	Ersatz
	action [ˈækʃn]	Maßnahme(n)
	policy (on sth) [ˈpɒləsi]	Richtlinien (für etw)
	to **carry sth out** [ˌkæri ˈaʊt]	etw durchführen
	expectation [ˌekspekˈteɪʃn]	Erwartung
	interviewee [ˌɪntəvjuːˈiː]	Befragte/r
	acknowledgement [əkˈnɒlɪdʒmənt]	Eingeständnis, Würdigung
	as far as sth is concerned [əz fɑːr əz ɪz kənˈsɜːnd]	was etw betrifft
	apology [əˈpɒlədʒi]	Entschuldigung
	to **bring sth to the attention of sb** [brɪŋ tə ði əˈtenʃn əv]	jdn auf etw aufmerksam machen
	reimbursement [ˌriːɪmˈbɜːsmənt]	Rückerstattung
	compensation [ˌkɒmpənˈseɪʃn]	Entschädigung
	to **register sth** [ˈredʒɪstə]	etw melden, etw zum Ausdruck bringen
	satisfactory [ˌsætɪsˈfæktəri]	zufriedenstellend, befriedigend
	to **acknowledge sb** [əkˈnɒlɪdʒ]	jdn würdigen
	complainant [kəmˈpleɪnənt]	Beschwerdeführer/in
	to **reimburse sb** [ˌriːɪmˈbɜːs]	jdm Geld zurückzahlen, jdn entschädigen
	to **disappoint sb** [ˌdɪsəˈpɔɪnt]	jdn enttäuschen
	to **drive sb away** [ˌdraɪv əˈweɪ]	jdn vergraulen
114	**smoke alarm** [ˈsməʊk əlɑːm]	Rauchmelder
	safety [ˈseɪfti]	Sicherheit
	sub-standard [ˌsʌb ˈstændəd]	minderwertig
	to **forward sth** [ˈfɔːwəd]	etw weitersenden, etw verschicken
	various [ˈveəriəs]	mehrere
	to **discover sth** [dɪˈskʌvə]	etw feststellen
	battery [ˈbætəri]	Batterie
	mounting screw [ˈmaʊntɪŋ skruː]	Befestigungsschraube
	discoloured [dɪsˈkʌləd]	verfärbt
	to **execute** [ˈeksɪkjuːt]	ausführen
	whatever the case may be [wɒtevə ðə ˌkeɪs meɪ ˈbiː]	wie dem auch sei
	to **appreciate sth** [əˈpriːʃieɪt]	etw verstehen, etw einsehen
	to **replace sth** [rɪˈpleɪs]	etw ersetzen
115	**DIY chain** [ˌdiː aɪ ˈwaɪ tʃeɪn]	Baumarkt-Kette
	air conditioner [ˈeə kəndɪʃnə]	Klimaanlage
T	**portable** [ˈpɔːtəbl]	tragbar
	dissatisfied [dɪsˈsætɪsfaɪd]	unzufrieden
	to **cut out** [ˌkʌt ˈaʊt]	sich abschalten
	to **point out** [ˌpɔɪnt ˈaʊt]	darauf hinweisen(, dass ...)
	statutory [ˈstætʃətri]	gesetzlich vorgeschrieben
	on our part [ɒn ˈaʊə pɑːt]	auf/von unserer Seite
	meaning ... [ˈmiːnɪŋ]	das heißt ...
	I assure you ... [aɪ əˈʃʊə juː]	ich versichere Ihnen, ...

	free of charge [ˌfriː əf ˈtʃɑːdʒ]	unentgeltlich, kostenlos
	carriage forward [ˌkærɪdʒ ˈfɔːwəd]	unfrei
	to **cancel sth** [ˈkænsl]	etw stornieren
	inconvenience [ˌɪnkənˈviːniəns]	Unannehmlichkeiten

	to **distinguish** [dɪˈstɪŋgwɪʃ]	unterscheiden
	warranty period [ˈwɒrənti pɪəriəd]	Gewährleistungszeit
	to **rectify defects** [ˌrektɪfaɪ ˈdiːfekts]	Mängel beheben
	it is assumed that ... [ɪt ɪz əˈsjuːmd ðət]	es ist davon auszugehen, dass ...
	purchase [ˈpɜːtʃəs]	Kauf
	to **prove otherwise** [ˌpruːv ˈʌðəwaɪz]	das Gegenteil beweisen
	voluntary [ˈvɒləntri]	freiwillig
116	to **arrange sth** [əˈreɪndʒ]	etw anordnen, etw sortieren
	to **investigate sth** [ɪnˈvestɪgeɪt]	etw untersuchen
	carriage paid [ˌkærɪdʒ ˈpeɪd]	frachtfrei , franko
	approval [əˈpruːvl]	Zustimmung
	dismayed [dɪsˈmeɪd]	bestürzt
	unsatisfactory [ˌʌnˌsætɪsˈfæktəri]	unzulänglich
	chest freezer [ˈtʃest friːzə]	Tiefkühltruhe, Gefriertruhe
	butcher's shop [ˈbʊtʃəz ʃɒp]	Metzgerei
	electricity consumption [ɪˌlekˈtrɪsəti kənsʌmpʃn]	Stromverbrauch
117	**quarterly statement** [ˌkwɔːtəli ˈsteɪtmənt]	Quartalsabrechnung
	pottery [ˈpɒtəri]	Keramik, Töpferei
	discrepancy [dɪsˈkrepənsi]	Unstimmigkeit, Diskrepanz
	clearance sale [ˈklɪərəns seɪl]	Ausverkauf
	while stocks last [waɪl ˌstɒks ˈlɑːst]	solange der Vorrat reicht
	mould [məʊld]	Form, Gussform, Pressform
	porcelain [ˈpɔːsəlɪn]	Porzellan
	clay [kleɪ]	Ton
	statement [ˈsteɪtmənt]	Abrechnung
	teapot [ˈtiːpɒt]	Teekanne
	champagne [ʃæmˈpeɪn]	Champagner
	flute [fluːt]	Flöte
	to **overcharge sb** [ˌəʊvəˈtʃɑːdʒ]	jdm zu viel berechnen
	amendment [əˈmendmənt]	Änderung, Berichtigung
	as appropriate [əz əˈprəupriət]	je nachdem
118	to **query sth** [ˈkwɪəri]	etw infrage stellen, etw anzweifeln
	records *pl* [ˈrekɔːdz]	Unterlagen, Aufzeichnungen
	credit note [ˈkredɪt nəʊt]	Gutschrift
	in addition [ɪn əˈdɪʃn]	außerdem
	to **charge** [tʃɑːdʒ]	*(Preis:)* berechnen
	to **omit to do sth** [əˈmɪt tə]	es versäumen, etw zu tun
	special discount [ˌspeʃl ˈdɪskaʊnt]	Sonderrabatt
	to **amend sth** [əˈmend]	etw ändern, etw berichtigen
	to **remit** [rɪˈmɪt]	*(Geld)* überweisen
	sum owing [ˌsʌm ˈəʊɪŋ]	Forderung
	query [ˈkwɪəri]	Frage, Rückfrage
	to **owe sb sth** [əʊ]	jdm etw schulden
	to **qualify for sth** [ˈkwɒlɪfaɪ fə]	zu etw berechtigen, für etw infrage kommen

T	**mix-up** [ˈmɪks ʌp]	Durcheinander, Verwechslung
	to **get to the bottom of sth** [get tu ðə ˈbɒtəm əv]	etw herausfinden
	to **deduct** [dɪˈdʌkt]	abziehen
	to **type in sth** [ˌtaɪp ˈɪn]	etw eingeben, etw eintippen
	to **get in touch with sb** [get ɪn ˈtʌtʃ wɪð]	sich bei jdm melden, sich mit jdm in Verbindung setzen

119	**goose down** [ˈguːs daʊn]	Gänsedaunen
120	**X-ray machine** [ˈeks reɪ məʃiːn]	Röntgengerät

T	**dental clinic** [ˌdentl ˈklɪnɪk]	Zahnklinik
	scratched [skrætʃt]	verkratzt
	dented [ˈdentɪd]	verbeult
	casing [ˈkeɪsɪŋ]	Gehäuse
	to **get sth sorted** [ˌget ˈsɔːtɪd]	etw klären, sich um etw kümmern
	disappointed [ˌdɪsəˈpɔɪntɪd]	enttäuscht
	business [ˈbɪznəs]	Angelegenheit, Sache

	spelling [ˈspelɪŋ]	Schreibweise
	container [kənˈteɪnə]	Behälter
	to **fulfil an order** [fʊlˌfɪl ən ˈɔːdə]	einen Auftrag abwickeln, eine Bestellung ausführen
121	**transcript** [ˈtrænskrɪpt]	Mitschrift
	record [ˈrekɔːd]	Datensatz
	I realize that. [aɪ ˈrɪəlaɪz ðæt]	Das ist mir bewusst.

P	**express carrier** [ɪkˈspres kæriə]	Expressdienst
	rebate [ˈriːbeɪt]	Rabatt, Nachlass
	at no charge [ət ˌnəʊ ˈtʃɑːdʒ]	kostenfrei

UNIT 12

122	**(job) application** [ˌæplɪˈkeɪʃn]	Bewerbung
	to **apply for a job** [əˌplaɪ fər ə ˈdʒɒb]	sich um eine Stelle bewerben
	job agency [ˈdʒɒb eɪdʒənsi]	Arbeitsagentur, Arbeitsvermittlung

T	**mixture** [ˈmɪkstʃə]	Mischung
	on one's own [ɒn wʌnz ˈəʊn]	alleine

	varied ['veərid]	vielfältig
	to **be involved in sth** [bi ɪn'vɒlvd ɪn]	an etw beteiligt sein
123	**spreadsheet** ['spredʃi:t]	Tabellenkalkulation, Tabelle
	job opportunities *pl* [dʒɒb ˌɒpə'tju:nətiz]	Arbeitsmöglichkeiten
	career prospects *pl* [kə'rɪə prɒspekts]	berufliche Perspektiven
	sector ['sektə]	Bereich, Sektor
	to **pin sth to sth** [pɪn]	etw an etw heften
	CV (curriculum vitae) [ˌsi: 'vi:, kəˌrɪkjələm 'vi:taɪ]	Lebenslauf
	standardized ['stændədaɪzd]	genormt
	self-assessment [ˌself ə'sesmənt]	Selbsteinstufung
	mobility [məʊ'bɪləti]	Freizügigkeit
	to **acquire sth** [ə'kwaɪə]	etw erlangen, etw erwerben
	certificate [sə'tɪfɪkət]	Zeugnis, Diplom
	supplement ['sʌplɪmənt]	Zusatz, Ergänzung
	agent ['eɪdʒənt]	zuständige/r Mitarbeiter/in
124	**job advert(isement)** ['dʒɒb ædvɜ:t, ədvɜ:tɪsmənt]	Stellenanzeige
	recruitment agency [rɪ'kru:tmənt eɪdʒənsi]	Personalvermittlung
125	**job title** ['dʒɒb taɪtl]	Stellenbezeichnung
	freight forwarding company ['freɪt fɔ:wədɪŋ kʌmpəni]	Spedition
	export customs entry ['ekspɔ:t kʌstəmz entri]	Ausfuhranmeldung
	to **classify** ['klæsɪfaɪ]	klassifizieren
	administrative work [ədˌmɪnɪstrətɪv 'wɜ:k]	Verwaltungstätigkeiten
	invoicing ['ɪnvɔɪsɪŋ]	Fakturierung, Rechnungsstellung
	correspondence [ˌkɒrɪ'spɒndəns]	Schriftverkehr, Korrespondenz
	school leaving certificate [ˌsku:l li:vɪŋ sə'tɪfɪkət]	Schulabschluss
	fluent ['flu:ənt]	*(Sprache:)* fließend
	to **take sb on** [ˌteɪk 'ɒn]	jdn einstellen, jdn übernehmen
	reference number ['refərəns nʌmbə]	Aktenzeichen, Kennziffer
	to **advise sb** [əd'vaɪz]	jdn beraten
	exhibition [ˌeksɪ'bɪʃn]	Messe, Ausstellung
	accurate(ly) ['ækjərət]	exakt, genau
	continuous [kən'tɪnjuəs]	ständig, kontinuierlich
	support [sə'pɔ:t]	Betreuung
	opportunity [ˌɒpə'tju:nəti]	Gelegenheit, Möglichkeit
	follow-up education [ˌfɒləʊ ʌp edʒu'keɪʃn]	Weiterbildung
	promotion [prə'məʊʃn]	Beförderung, Aufstieg
	candidate ['kændɪdət]	Bewerber/in
126	**(job) interview** ['ɪntəvju:]	Vorstellungsgespräch
	to **be shortlisted** [bi 'ʃɔ:tlɪstɪd]	in die engere Auswahl kommen
	sales representative ['seɪlz reprɪzentətɪv]	(Handels-)Vertreter/in
	face-to-face [ˌfeɪs tə 'feɪs]	persönlich
T	**recruitment** [rɪ'kru:tmənt]	Einstellung, Anwerbung *(von Personal)*
	signal strength ['sɪgnəl streŋθ]	Signalstärke
	reminder function [rɪ'maɪndə fʌŋkʃn]	Erinnerungsfunktion
	independent(ly) [ˌɪndɪ'pendəntli]	unabhängig
	battery ['bætəri]	Akku
	post [pəʊst]	Posten, Stelle
	hard-working [ˌhɑ:d 'wɜ:kɪŋ]	fleißig
	in particular [ɪn pə'tɪkjələ]	ausgerechnet, gerade
	flat *BE* [flæt]	Wohnung
	in a nutshell [ɪn ə 'nʌtʃel]	kurz gesagt, mit einem Wort
	to **take the initiative** [ˌteɪk ði ɪ'nɪʃətɪv]	die Initative ergreifen
	traineeship [treɪ'ni:ʃɪp]	Ausbildung, Lehre
	link [lɪŋk]	Zusammenhang, Verbindung
	to **make a contribution** [ˌmeɪk ə ˌkɒntrɪ'bju:ʃn]	einen Beitrag leisten
	to **post sb to …** ['pəʊst tə]	jdn nach … versetzen
	role model ['rəʊl mɒdl]	Vorbild
	to **gather sth** ['gæðə]	etw zusammenstellen
	to **flick through sth** ['flɪk θru:]	etw durchblättern
	pile [paɪl]	Stapel, Haufen
	landline ['lændlaɪn]	Festnetz(telefon)
	to **charge** [tʃɑ:dʒ]	*(Akku)* aufladen
	to **dress** [dres]	sich kleiden
	appropriately [ə'prəʊpriətli]	angemessen
	professional [prə'feʃənl]	professionell
	to **meet sb's needs** [ˌmi:t 'ni:dz]	jds Bedürfnissen entsprechen, jds Anforderungen erfüllen
127	**clarification** [ˌklærɪfɪ'keɪʃn]	Klärung, Erläuterung
P	**(job) vacancy** ['veɪkənsi]	offene Stelle
	applicant ['æplɪkənt]	Bewerber/in
	to **justify** ['dʒʌstɪfaɪ]	rechtfertigen, begründen
	to **swap** [swɒp]	tauschen
T	to **calm down** [ˌkɑ:m 'daʊn]	sich beruhigen
	to **advise** [əd'vaɪz]	(jdm etw) raten
	Not particularly. [ˌnɒt pə'tɪkjələli]	Eigentlich nicht.
	to **shake hands with sb** [ˌʃeɪk 'hændz wɪð]	jdm die Hand geben
	shy [ʃaɪ]	schüchtern
	habit ['hæbɪt]	Gewohnheit
	to **get into the habit of doing sth** [ˌget ɪntə ðə 'hæbɪt əv]	sich daran gewöhnen, etw zu tun
	panel ['pænl]	Gremium

	to **relate sth to sth** [rɪˈleɪt tə]	etw auf etw beziehen
	to **clarify sth** [ˈklærəfaɪ]	etw erläutern
	slight(ly) [ˈslaɪtli]	geringfügig, etwas
	future prospects *pl* [ˌfjuːtʃə ˈprɒspekts]	Zukunftsperspektiven
	to **occur to sb** [əˈkɜː tə]	jdm einfallen
	concerning sth [kənˈsɜːnɪŋ]	etw betreffend
	firm handshake [ˌfɜːm ˈhændʃeɪk]	fester Händedruck
	to **put sth to good use** [ˌpʊt tə gʊd ˈjuːs]	etw sinnvoll nutzen
P	to **progress** [prəˈgres]	vorankommen
128	**mixed up** [ˌmɪkst ˈʌp]	durcheinander
	ability [əˈbɪləti]	Fähigkeit
	set [set]	vorgegeben, starr, fest
	to **grab sb's attention** [ˌgræb əˈtenʃn]	jds Aufmerksamkeit fesseln
	motivated [ˈməʊtɪveɪtɪd]	motiviert
	trade industry [ˈtreɪd ɪndəstri]	Handelsbranche
	reverse order [rɪˌvɜːs ˈɔːdə]	umgekehrte Reihenfolge
	employment [ɪmˈplɔɪmənt]	Beschäftigung, Anstellung
	achievement [əˈtʃiːvmənt]	Leistung
	driving licence [ˈdraɪvɪŋ laɪsns]	Führerschein
	socializing [ˈsəʊʃəlaɪzɪŋ]	Ausgehen
	data protection [ˈdeɪtə prətekʃn]	Datenschutz
	referee [ˌrefəˈriː]	Referenz(geber)
129	**mobile** [ˈməʊbaɪl]	mobil
	to **seek sth** [siːk]	etw suchen
	accountancy [əˈkaʊntənsi]	Buchführung
	economics [ˌiːkəˈnɒmɪks]	Wirtschaft
	native speaker [ˌneɪtɪv ˈspiːkə]	Muttersprachler/in
	tourist board [ˈtʊərɪst bɔːd]	Fremdenverkehrsamt
	to **interact with sb** [ˌɪntərˈækt wɪð]	mit jdm kommunizieren
	first aid [ˌfɜːst ˈeɪd]	Erste Hilfe
	athletics [æθˈletɪks]	Leichtathletik
130	**personable** [ˈpɜːsnəbl]	umgänglich, sympathisch
	flexible [ˈfleksəbl]	flexibel
	atmosphere [ˈætməsfɪə]	Atmosphäre
131	**particularly** [pəˈtɪkjələli]	insbesondere
	to **be keen to do sth** [bi ˈkiːn]	jdm liegt sehr daran, etw zu tun
	to **apply sth** [əˈplaɪ tə]	etw anwenden
	on a daily basis [ɒn ə ˌdeɪli ˈbeɪsɪs]	täglich, jeden Tag
	to **benefit sb** [ˈbenɪfɪt]	jdm nützen

KMK Exam practice 6

132	**workwear** [ˈwɜːkweə]	Arbeitskleidung
	order confirmation [ˈɔːdə kɒnfəmeɪʃn]	Auftragsbestätigung
	forwarding agent [ˈfɔːwədɪŋ eɪdʒənt]	Spedition
	parcel [ˈpɑːsl]	Paket
	accidentally [ˌæksɪˈdentəli]	versehentlich
	damages *pl* [ˈdæmɪdʒɪz]	Schadenersatz
	to **be up to standard** [bi ˌʌp tə ˈstændəd]	den Anforderungen entsprechen
	see below [ˌsiː bɪˈləʊ]	siehe unten
	crushed [krʌʃt]	eingedrückt
	stained [steɪnd]	fleckig
133	**pump** [pʌmp]	Pumpe
	visual inspection [ˌvɪʒuəl ɪnˈspekʃn]	Sichtprüfung
	rough handling [ˌrʌf ˈhændlɪŋ]	unsanfte Behandlung
	incorrect storage [ˌɪnkəˈrekt ˈstɔːrdʒ]	unsachgemäße Lagerung
	surplus [ˈsɜːpləs]	überschüssig
	to **unpack** [ʌnˈpæk]	auspacken
	scratch [skrætʃ]	Kratzer

A–Z word list

Dieses Wörterverzeichnis enthält alle neuen Wörter aus *Industry Matters 3rd edition* in alphabetischer Reihenfolge. Nicht angeführt sind Wörter, die zum Grundwortschatz (*Basic word list*) gehören. Die Zahl nach dem Stichwort bezieht sich auf die Seite, auf der das Wort zum ersten Mal erscheint. Wörter aus den Hörverständnisübungen sind zusätzlich mit einem **T** (Transkript) und Wörter aus den *Partner files* mit einem **P** gekennzeichnet.

A

abbreviation *101* Abkürzung
ability *128* Fähigkeit
about, sth is ~ sth *46T* bei einer Sache geht es um etw
above-mentioned *90* obengenannt
absentee *55T* Abwesende/r
academic *11* akademisch, Universitäts-, universitär
access *15* Zugang, Zutritt
to **access sth** *34* auf etw zugreifen; *86* etw erreichen
accessible *34* zugänglich, erreichbar
accessories *pl* *44* Zubehör, Accessoires
accident *75* Unfall
accidentally *132* versehentlich
accommodation *64* Unterkunft; *74* Unterbringung
according to *35* gemäß, entsprechend, zufolge
account *9* Konto; **~s** *16* Buchhaltung; **for ~ of sb** *105* auf jds Rechnung; **open ~** *77T* offenes Zahlungsziel
to **account for sth** *34* etw ausmachen, für etw verantwortlich sein
accountancy *129* Buchführung
accounting *18* Buchhaltung; **~ manager** *19* Buchhaltungsleiter/in
accurate(ly) *125* exakt, genau
to **achieve** *34* *(Ziel)* erreichen
achievement *86* Leistung
to **acknowledge: ~ sb** *113* jdn würdigen; **~ an order** *100* einen Auftrag bestätigen
acknowledgement *113* Eingeständnis, Würdigung
acquaintance, business ~ *77T* Geschäftsfreund/in
to **acquire sth** *43* etw erwerben, etw kaufen; *123* etw erlangen
to **act as sth** *56T* als etw fungieren
action *113T* Maßnahme(n)
actuator *38* Aktor
ad, to **place an ~** *65T* eine Anzeige schalten
to **adapt: ~ to sth** *39* sich an etw anpassen; **~ sth** *61P* etw anpassen, etw abändern; **~ to sb/sth** *72* sich an jdn/etw gewöhnen
adaptable (to sth) *110* anpassbar (an etw)
to **add value (to sth)** *32* Wert schöpfen, den Wert (von etw) steigern
addition, in ~ *64* außerdem; **in ~ to sth** *42T* zusätzlich zu etw
additional *10T* zusätzlich
address, inside ~ *84* Innenadresse
adhesive *34* Klebstoff
adjustable *72T* verstellbar
administration *14* Verwaltung; **business ~** *11* Betriebswirtschaft
administrative work *125* Verwaltungstätigkeiten
advance, in ~ *55T* im Voraus
advanced *11* fortgeschritten, weiterführend
advantage, competitive ~ *110* Wettbewerbsvorteil; to **take ~ of sth** *35* etw nutzen
adventure *24* Abenteuer
advert(isement), job ~ *124* Stellenanzeige
to **advertise sth** *50* etw bewerben, für etw Werbung machen
advertising *45* Werbung; **stealth ~** *50* heimliche Werbung, Schleichwerbung; **targeted ~** *50* gezielte/zielgruppengenaue Werbung; **~ campaign** *45* Werbekampagne
advice of dispatch *100* Versandanzeige
to **advise** *127T* (jdm etw) raten; **~ sb** *125* jdn beraten; **~ sb to do sth** *15* jdm empfehlen, etw zu tun; jdm raten, etw zu tun
adviser, legal ~ *55* Justiziar/in
advising bank *105* avisierende Bank
to **affect sth** *15* etw betreffen; *105* etw beeinflussen
affected, to **be ~ by sth** *43* von etw betroffen sein
to **afford sth** *60T* sich etw leisten (können)
afraid, I'm ~ *10T* leider
after-sales service *43* Kundendienst
age, for ~s *74T* eine Ewigkeit
agency *9* Agentur; **job ~** *122* Arbeitsagentur, Arbeitsvermittlung; **recruitment ~** *124* Personalvermittlung
agenda *28T* Programm, Tagesordnung
agent *49* Vermittler/in, Zwischenhändler/in; *56T* Vertreter/in; *123* zuständige/r Mitarbeiter/in; **estate ~** *111T* Immobilienmakler/in;
forwarding ~ *132* Spedition; **shipping ~** *92* Spediteur
to **agree: ~ sth** *19T* etw vereinbaren; *51* sich auf etw einigen, etw beschließen; **~ thoroughly with sb** *56T* voll und ganz einer Meinung mit jdm sein
agreement *60* Vereinbarung; **exclusive ~** *43* Exklusivvertrag
aid *29* Hilfsmittel; **first ~** *129* Erste Hilfe; **visual ~s** *pl* *29* visuelle Hilfsmittel
to **aim: ~ to do sth** *55T* beabsichtigen, etw zu tun; **~ at sth** *65T* etw zum Ziel haben
air conditioner *115* Klimaanlage
air conditioning *75* Klimaanlage, Klimatisierung
air-conditioned *74* klimatisiert
air freight *91T* Luftfracht
aircraft *49* Flugzeug
airline *24* Fluggesellschaft
air waybill *82* Luftfrachtbrief
aisle *66T* (Mittel-)Gang
ale *70* *brit. Biersorte*
A levels *pl* *6* Abitur, Abiturfächer
algorithm *39T* Algorithmus
all, not at ~ *38* überhaupt nicht, gar nicht
along the way *32* unterwegs
alongside, to **work ~ sb** *26T* mit jdm arbeiten
alteration *99* Änderung
amazing *39T* erstaunlich, verblüffend, toll
to **amend sth** *118* etw ändern, etw berichtigen
amendment *117* Änderung, Berichtigung
to **amount to sth** *32* *(Kosten:)* sich auf etw belaufen
ample space *28T* genügend Platz
to **analyse** *17T* analysieren
and beyond *46* und darüber hinaus
anger *71* Verärgerung
to **announce** *40* ankündigen
annoyed, to **get ~ about sth** *87* sich über etw ärgern
annual *23* jährlich; **~ leave** *10T* Jahresurlaub
anonymous *77T* anonym
answering machine *111T* Anrufbeantworter

anticipation, in ~ of sth *35* in Erwartung von etw, im Vorgriff auf etw
any other business (AOB) *55T* *(Tagesordnung:)* Verschiedenes
to **apologize** *62T* sich entschuldigen
apology *113* Entschuldigung
apparent *103* anscheinend
appealing *25* ansprechend
to **appear** *40* vorkommen, auftauchen; *66T* wirken, scheinen; **~ to do sth** *15* etw anscheinend tun
appearance *9* Erscheinungsbild, Auftreten
appliance *112* (Elektro-)Gerät
applicable *105* zutreffend; **~ charges** *pl* *94* anfallende Gebühren
applicant *105* *(Akkreditiv:)* Auftraggeber/in; *127P* Bewerber/in
application *40* Antrag, Bewerbung; *103* *(Akkreditiv:)* Eröffnungsauftrag, Akkreditivauftrag
to **apply: ~ sth** *131* etw anwenden; **~ for sth** *107* etw beantragen; **~ for a job** *122* sich um eine Stelle bewerben
appointment *72* Termin
to **appreciate sth** *22T* etw zu schätzen wissen; *114* etw verstehen, etw einsehen
apprentice *6* Auszubildende/r, Lehrling
apprenticeship *6* Lehre, Ausbildung
approach *46T* Ansatz, Herangehensweise, Vorgehen
to **approach sth** *72* an etw herangehen, etw angehen
appropriate *9* angemessen, passend; **as ~** *117* je nachdem
appropriately *126* angemessen
approval *116* Zustimmung
approximately *28* ungefähr, zirka
architect *68T* Architekt/in
architecture *68* Architektur
to **arrange: ~ sth** *116* etw anordnen, etw sortieren; **~ for sth** *49* etw vermitteln, etw organisieren
arrangements *pl* *106* Vereinbarungen, Abmachungen, Modalitäten; to **make ~** *54* Vorbereitungen treffen; **business ~** *60T* Modalitäten
array of products *86* Produktangebot
arrival *38* Einführung, Aufkommen *(einer Technologie)*; *74T* Ankunft; **on ~** *112* bei Ankunft, bei Eintreffen
art, state-of-the-~ *28T* auf dem neuesten Stand der Technik, hochmodern
article *27* Artikel
artificial *48* künstlich; **~ intelligence (AI)** *37* Künstliche Intelligenz (KI)
artist *24* Künstler/in
arts and crafts *pl* *86* Kunsthandwerk
as: ~ follows *20* wie folgt; **~ regards** *35* was ... betrifft, in puncto; **~ requested** *89* wie gewünscht
aspect *14* Gesichtspunkt, Seite, Aspekt
to **assemble** *28T* montieren, zusammenbauen
assembly *16* Montage; **~ hall** *26T* Montagehalle; **~ line** *37* Fertigungsstraße
to **assess sth** *103* *(Zollgebühren usw.)* ansetzen, berechnen
assessment *11* Beurteilung, Bewertung, Einschätzung, Urteil; **self-~** *123* Selbsteinstufung
assessor *11* Betreuer/in, Gutachter/in
assignment *18* Auftrag, Aufgabe
to **assist: ~ sb** *79T* jdm helfen, jdn unterstützen; **~ sb with sth** *42T* jdm bei etw helfen
assistance *40* Hilfe, Unterstützung; to **be of ~** *89* behilflich sein
assistant, industrial management ~ *6* Industriekaufmann/-frau; **IT management ~** *12T* Informatikkaufmann/-frau; **management ~ in wholesale and foreign trade** *6T* Kaufmann/-frau im Groß- und Außenhandel; **office management ~** *12T* Bürokaufmann/-frau, Kaufmann/-frau für Büromanagement
associate, business ~ *63* Geschäftspartner/in
to **associate sth with sth** *77T* etw mit etw in Verbindung bringen
association *63P* Verband
to **assume** *32* davon ausgehen, voraussetzen; **sb can be ~ed to do sth** *99* es kann davon ausgegangen werden, dass jd etw tut; **it is ~ed that ...** *115* es ist davon auszugehen, dass ...; **~ responsibility** *99* die Verantwortung übernehmen
assurance, quality ~ *18* Qualitätssicherung
to **assure, I ~ you ...** *115T* ich versichere Ihnen, ...
assured: quality-~ experts *pl* *110* qualifiziertes Fachpersonal
at all, not ~ *38* überhaupt nicht, gar nicht
athletics *129* Leichtathletik
atmosphere *130* Atmosphäre
to **attach** *40* *(E-Mail:)* anhängen
attached, to **be ~ to sth** *15T* mit etw verbunden sein
attachment *15* *(E-Mail:)* Anhang
attack *15* Angriff
attendee *57* Teilnehmer/in
attention *85* Beachtung, Aufmerksamkeit; **for the ~ of** *85* zu Händen; to **attract ~** *9* Aufmerksamkeit erregen; to **bring sth to the ~ of sb** *113* jdn auf etw aufmerksam machen; to **draw sb's ~ to sth** *89* jds Aufmerksamkeit auf etw lenken; to **grab sb's ~** *128* jds Aufmerksamkeit fesseln; **~ line** *84* Zeile „zu Händen"
attire *29* Kleidung
attitude (to sth) *77* Einstellung (zu etw)
to **attract: ~ sb** *48* jdn anlocken, jdn ansprechen, jdn anziehen; **~ sb to sth** *67* jdn zu etw locken; **~ attention** *9* Aufmerksamkeit erregen
to **attribute sth to sb** *86* jdm etw zuschreiben
audience *29* Publikum
authority *99* Befugnis, Vollmacht
authorization *105* Ermächtigung, Vollmacht
to **authorize sb** *105* jdn ermächtigen, jdn bevollmächtigen
automated *37* automatisch, automatisiert
automation *39T* Automatisierung
autonomous(ly) *38* autonom, eigenständig, unabhängig
availability *8* Verfügbarkeit
available *34* erhältlich, verfügbar
average, on ~ *15* im Durchschnitt
to **avoid** *13* vermeiden
to **award sb sth** *64* jdm etw *(Preis usw.)* verleihen
awareness *71* Bewusstsein, Sensibilität; **brand ~** *68* Bekanntheitsgrad einer Marke

B

back, to **turn one's ~ on sb** *29* jdm den Rücken zuwenden
backdrop *69* Messewand
background *28T* Hintergrund; *71* Herkunft
backlog *36* Rückstand
bag, tote ~ *67* Tragetasche
balloon, gas ~ *24* Gasballon
bank, advising ~ *105* avisierende Bank; **negotiating ~** *105* negoziierende Bank; **paying ~** *105* ausführende Bank
bankrupt, to **go ~** *101T* Pleite gehen
bankruptcy *25* Konkurs
bar: ~ chart *52* Säulendiagramm; **~ table** *68T* Stehtisch
bargaining, collective wage ~ *77* Tarifverhandlungen
barrier *24* Hindernis
base, customer ~ *86* Kundenstamm

based, to **be ~ in ...** *13* seinen Sitz in ... haben, in ... sein; to **be ~ on sth** *36* auf etw basieren
basic price *91T* Grundpreis
basis, on a daily ~ *131* täglich, jeden Tag
batch *38* Charge, Los
battery *114* Batterie; *126T* Akku
bay, high ~ *34* Hochregal
to **be: sth is about sth** *46T* bei einer Sache geht es um etw
beaker *67* Becher
bean, cocoa ~ *54* Kakaobohne
to **bear sth** *81* etw *(Risiko, Kosten)* tragen
beauty, the ~ of it is ... *91T* Das Schöne daran ist, ...
because of sth *59* wegen etw
beef *83* Rindfleisch
behalf, on ~ of sb *20* für jdn, in jds Namen; **on sb's ~** *93* für jdn
beginning, from the ~ *86* von Anfang an
behaviour *72* Verhalten, Benehmen
beige *89* beige
below, see ~ *132* siehe unten
beneficiary *105* Begünstigte/r
to **benefit sb** *131* jdm nützen
benefit *15T* Vorteil, Nutzen
benefits *pl* *8* Zusatzleistungen, Sozialleistungen
bespoke *68* maßgeschneidert
best: B~ regards *41* *(Brief:)* Viele Grüße, Mit freundlichen Grüßen; **B~ wishes** *41* *(Brief:)* Mit freundlichen Grüßen
best-selling *72T* meistverkauft
beverage *64* Getränk
big data *37* große Datenmengen
bill: ~ of exchange *103* Wechsel; **~ of lading (B/L)** *82* Konnossement; **clean/foul ~ of lading** *103* reines/unreines Konnossement
billion *24* Milliarde
bin *35* Tonne
birth, place of ~ *12* Geburtsort
bit, to **do one's ~** *77* seinen Beitrag leisten
bites *pl* *70* Häppchen
blackboard *19* Wandtafel
blank *105* leer
to **block sth** *15* etw versperren, etw blockieren
block release *6* Blockunterricht *(an der Berufsschule)*
blog entry *38* Blogeintrag
blood *15* Blut
blouse *9* Bluse
blue-collar workers *pl* *53* Arbeiter/innen
board *36* Tafel; to **come on ~** *56T* an Bord kommen; **tourist ~** *129* Fremdenverkehrsamt; **~ of directors** *17T* Vorstand
body *84* *(Brief:)* Haupttext; **~ (of a can)** *26T* Dosenrumpf, Dosenkörper; **~ language** *29* Körpersprache
bolt *34* Schraube, Schraubbolzen
book, order ~ *35T* Auftragsbuch
booked up *81T* ausgebucht
to **boost sth** *45* etw ankurbeln, etw erhöhen
booth *68* (Messe-)Stand
bottom, to **get to the ~ of sth** *118T* etw herausfinden; **~ line** *46T* das, worauf es ankommt
bowl, rice ~ *61P* Reisschale
box-shaped *68* kastenförmig
brain *39T* Hirn, Gehirn
to **brainstorm** *8* Ideen sammeln
branch *6* Niederlassung, Filiale
brand *24* Marke; **~ awareness** *68* Bekanntheitsgrad einer Marke; **~ name** *24* Markenname
branding *46T* Markenbildung
to **break: ~ down** *36* zusammenbrechen, kaputtgehen; *59T* *(Auto:)* eine Panne haben, liegen bleiben; **~ sth down** *34* etw aufschlüsseln, etw aufgliedern; **~ into sth** *48* in etw einbrechen; **~ out** *24* ausbrechen; **~ a rule** *9* eine Regel brechen, eine Vorschrift missachten; **~ for lunch** *31T* Mittagspause machen
break, lunch ~ *53* Mittagspause; **morning ~** *8T* Frühstückspause; to **take a ~** *10T* eine Pause machen
breakable *81T* zerbrechlich
breakdown *31T* Aufstellung, Aufschlüsselung
break-even point *48* Gewinnschwelle
breakfast, buffet ~ *75T* Frühstücksbüfett
to **brew** *70* *(Tee, Kaffee:)* kochen
brewery *56* Brauerei
brewhouse, two-vessel ~ *105* Zweigerätesudhaus
brewing equipment *56* Brauanlage(n)
bricks and mortar outlet *46T* stationäres Geschäft
brief *26T* kurz, knapp; **product ~** *46* Produktbeschreibung
to **bring sth to the attention of sb** *113* jdn auf etw aufmerksam machen
broadcast *51* (Radio-)Sendung
brochure *22T* Broschüre, Prospekt; **glossy ~** *65T* Hochglanzbroschüre
broker *49* Makler/in
brush *38* Bürste
budget *17T* Etat, Budget; *33* Billig-
buffalo *100* Büffel
buffet *63P* Büfett; **~ breakfast** *75T* Frühstücksbüfett
to **build up** *35T* sich aufstauen, sich auftürmen
bulk: in ~ *35* en gros, in großen Mengen; **~ discount** *89* Mengenrabatt; **~ order** *96T* Großauftrag, Großbestellung
bulky *35T* sperrig, voluminös
to **burn down** *106T* niederbrennen
business *120T* Angelegenheit, Sache;
business, to **take ~ away from sb** *24* jdm das Wasser abgraben; **core ~** *42* Kerngeschäft; **family ~** *8T* Familienunternehmen; **terms** *pl* of **~** *59* Konditionen; **any other ~ (AOB)** *55T* *(Tagesordnung:)* Verschiedenes; to **enter the railway ~** *24* ins Bahngeschäft einsteigen; **~ acquaintance** *77T* Geschäftsfreund/in; **~ administration** *11* Betriebswirtschaft; **~ arrangements** *pl* *60T* Modalitäten; **~ associate** *63* Geschäftspartner/in; **~ card** *29* Visitenkarte; **~ consultant** *34* Unternehmensberater/in; **objective** *43* Unternehmensziel; **~ partner** *24* Geschäftspartner/in; **~ trip** *8* Geschäftsreise; **~ venture** *24* Unternehmen, Geschäftsvorhaben
businessman *24* Geschäftsmann
butcher's shop *116* Metzgerei
button *32* Knopf
buyer *11* Einkäufer/in; *77T* Käufer/in
buying power *43* Kaufkraft
by the way *10T* übrigens

C

to **calculate sth** *33* etw berechnen
calculation *96* Berechnung, Kalkulation
to **call: ~ back** *20* zurückrufen; **~ sb in** *34* jdn hinzuziehen, jdn einschalten; **~ on sb** *79* jdn besuchen, bei jdm vorbeischauen; **~ a meeting** *34* eine Sitzung einberufen
call, to **return a ~** *22T* zurückrufen; to **take a (phone) ~** *20* ein Gespräch entgegennehmen
to **calm down** *127T* sich beruhigen
campaign *51* (Werbe-)Kampagne; **advertising ~** *45* Werbekampagne
can *26T* (Konserven-)Dose; **~ end** *26T* Dosendeckel; **~-making** *78* Dosenherstellung
to **cancel** *99* *(Vertrag)* auflösen, annullieren; **~ sth** *115T* etw stornieren
cancellation *99* *(Vertrag:)* Auflösung, Annullierung
candidate *125* Bewerber/in

canning 16 Konservenherstellung
canteen 31T Kantine
canvas 89 Tuch
capacity 34 Kapazität, Fassungsvermögen
capital 35 Kapital, Mittel
caption 33 Bildunterschrift
car: company ~ 8 Firmenwagen; **~ manufacturer** 33 Autohersteller, Autobauer; **~ showroom** 33 Autohaus
carbon: ~ footprint 77 CO_2-Fußabdruck; **~ steel** 31T Kohlenstoffstahl
card, business ~ 29 Visitenkarte; **index ~** 30 Karteikarte; **loyalty ~** 44 Kundenkarte; **prompt ~** 29 Moderationskarte
career 11 (berufliche) Laufbahn, Karriere; **~ prospects** *pl* 123 berufliche Perspektiven
carriage 80 Transport, Beförderung, Fracht; **contract of ~** 80 Beförderungsvertrag, Frachtvertrag; **main ~** 80 Hauptlauf; **post-~** 80 Nachlauf; **pre-~** 80 Vorlauf; **~ forward** 115T unfrei; **~ paid** 116 frachtfrei, franko
carrier 81 Spediteur, Reederei, Transportunternehmen; **express ~** 121P Expressdienst; **free ~** 91T frei Frachtführer
to **carry sth out** 39T etw ausführen; 113 etw durchführen
carton 102 Karton
case, in ~ 113T für den Fall, dass; falls; **in that ~** 20T in diesem Fall; **whatever the ~ may be** 114 wie dem auch sei; **worst-~ scenario** 59 schlimmster anzunehmender Fall
case study 83 Fallstudie
cash 51T Bargeld; **~ discount** 89 Skonto; **~ with order (CWO)** 61P Vorkasse
cashier 45 Kassierer/in
casing 120T Gehäuse
catalogue 42T Katalog
to **catch sth** 20T etw verstehen, etw mitbekommen
catchphrase 51 Schlagwort, Slogan
category 47 Kategorie, Klasse
to **cater for sth** 70 für etw *(Veranstaltung usw.)* Speisen und Getränke liefern
catering 31T Gastronomie; 68 Verpflegung
cause, root ~ 34 Grundursache
celebrity endorsement 50 Werbung mit Prominenten
cell (phone) *AE* 72T Handy
cellar, wine ~ 42T Weinkeller
central station 51T Hauptbahnhof
centralized 39T zentral, zentralisiert
century 38 Jahrhundert
CEO (Chief Executive Officer) 23 Vorstandsvorsitzende/r, Geschäftsführer/in
certificate 123 Zeugnis, Diplom; **~ of origin** 103 Ursprungszeugnis; **insurance ~** 82 Versicherungsschein; **school leaving ~** 125 Schulabschluss
chain 19 Kette; **DIY ~** 115 Baumarkt-Kette; **supply ~** 32 Lieferkette, Versorgungskette
chair, swivel ~ 22T Drehstuhl
to **chair a meeting** 55T eine Sitzung leiten
chairman 24 Vorstandsvorsitzende/r
challenging 110 anspruchsvoll, fordernd
chamber of commerce 41 Handelskammer
champagne 42T Champagner
change of plan 40 Planänderung
changeover 37 Umstellung
to **change over to sth** 39 auf etw umstellen
channel 33 Kanal; **distribution ~** 33 Vertriebsweg, Vertriebskanal; **marketing ~** 43 Absatzweg, Vertriebskanal; **sales ~** 46T Absatzweg, Vertriebskanal; **television ~** 65T Fernsehsender
character 47 Zeichen
charge 70P Gebühr; 92 Kosten; to **be in ~ of sth** 17 für etw zuständig/verantwortlich sein; **at no ~** 121P kostenfrei; **free of ~** 115T unentgeltlich, kostenlos; **packing ~** 60 Verpackungskosten; **taking in ~** 105 Übernahme
charges *pl* 110 Gebühren, Kosten; **applicable ~s** *pl* 94 anfallende Gebühren
to **charge** 118 *(Preis:)* berechnen; 126 *(Akku)* aufladen; **~ a fee** 83 eine Gebühr verlangen
chargeable, sth is ~ at £20 70 für etwas werden £ 20 berechnet
charger 67 Ladegerät
charity 31T Wohltätigkeitsorganisation
chart 52 Diagramm; **bar ~** 52 Säulendiagramm; **flow ~** 19 Flussdiagramm; **organization ~** 16 Organigramm; **pie ~** 52 Tortendiagramm
to **check: ~ sth against sth** 57 etw mit etw abgleichen; **~ in** 75 sich anmelden, einchecken; **~ out** 75 sich abmelden, auschecken
check, credit ~ 77T Bonitätsprüfung
check-out 45 Kasse
to **cheer sb on** 51T jdn anfeuern, jdm zujubeln
chemicals *pl* 31T Chemikalien
chest freezer 116 Tiefkühltruhe, Gefriertruhe
child labour 77 Kinderarbeit
children's home 31T Waisenhaus, Kinderheim
Christmas tree 24 Weihnachtsbaum
chronological 37 chronologisch, zeitlich
circle 25 Kreis
to **circulate sth** 55T etw (an alle) verteilen
circumstances *pl* 99 Umstände
claim, to **make a ~** 77T einen Anspruch / eine Forderung geltend machen
clarification 127 Klärung, Erläuterung
to **clarify** 34 klären, abklären; **~ sth** 127T etw erläutern
clarity 25 Klarheit, Deutlichkeit
to **classify** 125 klassifizieren
clay 117 Ton
clean bill of lading 103 reines Konnossement
to **clean sth up** 51T etw säubern
to **clear: ~ up** 8T aufräumen; **~ a space** 15T einen Platz räumen
clearance, export ~ 80 Ausfuhrabfertigung; **import ~** 80 Einfuhrabfertigung; **~ sale** 117 Ausverkauf
clerk, export ~ 40 Außenhandelskaufmann/-frau
client 77T Kunde/Kundin
clientele 51 Kundschaft, Klientel
climb 52 Anstieg
to **climb** 52 ansteigen
clinic 84 Klinik; **dental ~** 120T Zahnklinik; **healthcare ~** 24 Klinik; **outpatient ~** 85 Ambulanz
to **clock in/out** 8T ein-/ausstempeln
close, complimentary ~ 41 *(Brief:)* Schlussformel
closed 25 geschlossen; **~ wagon** 94 geschlossener Waggon
clothing 38 Kleidung; **~ industry** 11 Kleidungsbranche
CMR document 103 CMR-Frachtbrief
CO_2 footprint 33 CO_2-Fußabdruck
co-operative 54 Genossenschaft, Kooperative
coat 13 Jacke, Mantel
cocoa bean 54 Kakaobohne
code, dress ~ 8 Kleiderordnung
to **coincide with sth** 43 mit etw übereinstimmen, mit etw zusammenfallen
collar 39T Halsband; **blue-~ workers** *pl* 53 Arbeiter; **white-~ workers** *pl* 53 Angestellte
to **collect sth** 81 etw abholen
collective wage bargaining 77 Tarifverhandlungen

college, vocational ~ *7* Berufsschule, Berufsfachschule
to **come: ~ across** *30* wirken; **~ in on sth** *35T* zu etw etw sagen; **~ up** *54* bevorstehen; **~ up with sth / an idea** *51* sich etw einfallen lassen; **~ on board** *56T* an Bord kommen; **C~ to think of it ...** *8T* Wenn ich es mir recht/genau überlege ...; **Something has ~ up.** *62T* Es/Mir/Uns ist etwas dazwischen gekommen.
comfort and relaxation *110* angenehme Atmosphäre
comment *35T* Bemerkung, Kommentar
to **comment** *56T* kommentieren, einen Kommentar abgeben
commerce *7* Handel, Wirtschaft
commercial: ~ director *16* kaufmännische/r Leiter/in; **~ invoice** *82* Handelsrechnung
commission *49* Kommission, Provision
to **commission sth** *68* etw in Auftrag geben
common, to **have sth in ~** *15* etw gemeinsam haben
to **communicate** *15T* kommunizieren
community, sense of ~ *15T* Gemeinschaftssinn
compact furniture *34* Kleinmöbel
company, freight forwarding ~ *42* Spedition; **parent ~** *28* Muttergesellschaft; **private limited ~ (Ltd)** *24* Gesellschaft mit beschränkter Haftung (GmbH); **public limited ~ (plc)** *24* Aktiengesellschaft (AG); **shipping ~** *79T* Reederei; **specialist ~** *6* Fachbetrieb, Spezialfirma; **trading ~** *42* Handesunternehmen; **training ~** *6* Ausbildungsbetrieb; **~ car** *8* Firmenwagen
to **compensate for sth** *38* etw ausgleichen, etw wettmachen, etw kompensieren
compensation *113* Entschädigung
competition *48* Wettbewerb; **stiff ~** *59* harter Wettbewerb
competitive *43* *(Preis:)* günstig; *59* konkurrenzfähig; **~ advantage** *110* Wettbewerbsvorteil
competitor *60T* Wettbewerber/in, Konkurrent/in
to **complain** *57* sich beklagen, sich beschweren
complainant *113* Beschwerdeführer/in
complaint *56T* Reklamation, Beschwerde
complimentary close *41* *(Brief:)* Schlussformel

to **comply with sth** *77* etw *(Norm usw.)* erfüllen, etw *(Vorschrift usw.)* einhalten
component *16* Bestandteil, Bauteil
compound *47* zusammengesetzt
compromised *15* (von Schadsoftware) befallen
computer-operated *38* computergesteuert
computer studies *pl* *6T* Informatik
computerized *12* Computer-
computing power *38* Rechenleistung
to **concentrate (on sth)** *15T* sich (auf etw) konzentrieren
concerned, as far as sth is ~ *113* was etw betrifft
concerning sth *23* etw betreffend
to **conclude: ~ sth** *26T* etw beschließen, etw beenden; **to ~** *56T* abschließend
conclusion *29* Schluss
condition *6* Bedingung; *79T* Zustand; **in good order and ~** *103* in einwandfreiem Zustand
conditions *pl*, **working ~** *6* Arbeitsbedingungen; **terms and ~** *77T* Allgemeine Geschäftsbedingungen
to **conduct sth** *8* etw durchführen
conference *52* Tagung, Konferenz; **~ centre** *64* Tagungszentrum, Kongresszentrum; **~ room** *26T* Besprechungsraum, Sitzungssaal
confident(ly) *31* selbstbewusst
to **confirm** *20* bestätigen
confirmation, order ~ *132* Auftragsbestätigung; **~ of order** *100* Auftragsbestätigung
confirmed, irrevocable and ~ documentary letter of credit *82* unwiderrufliches und bestätigtes Dokumentenakkreditiv
conflict zone *33* Konfliktzone
to **connect (to/with sth)** *20T* (mit etw) verbinden, (an etw) anschließen
conscience *51* Gewissen
conscious, environmentally ~ *51* umweltbewusst
to **consent to sth** *99* einer Sache zustimmen
consequence *48* Folge, Konsequenz
consequently *42* dementsprechend, folgerichtig
to **consider sth** *46* etw in Betracht ziehen, über etw nachdenken, etw berücksichtigen
consideration, to **take sth into ~** *77T* etw in Betracht ziehen, etw berücksichtigen
to **consign sth** *105* etw übergeben
consignment *80* Sendung, Warensendung; **groupage ~** *101* Sammelladung; **~ note** *82* Frachtbrief

to **consist of sth** *43* aus etw bestehen
consistent(ly) *77T* gleichbleibend, beständig, durchgehend
constant, to **remain ~** *52* gleich bleiben
constraint *65T* Beschränkung
construction: road ~ *83* Straßenbau; **~ equipment** *66T* Baumaschinen; **~ site** *31T* Baustelle
constructive *31T* konstruktiv
to **consult with sb** *58* mit jdm Rücksprache halten, sich mit jdm besprechen
consultancy, management ~ *9* Unternehmensberatung
consultant *15* Berater/in; **business ~** *34* Unternehmensberater/in
consultation *41* Beratung
consumer *32* Verbraucher/in, Konsument/in; **final ~** *49* Endverbraucher/in; **~ electronics** *8T* Unterhaltungselektronik; **~ goods** *pl* *33* Konsumgüter
consumption, electricity ~ *116* Stromverbrauch
contact: ~ (person) *111T* Ansprechpartner/in; **point of ~** *43* Ansprechpartner, Anlaufstelle; **eye ~** *29* Blickkontakt; **~ details** *pl* *22* Kontaktdaten
container *120* Behälter; **in shared ~** *94* in Sammelcontainer, als Beiladung
context *38* Zusammenhang
to **continue** *35T* fortfahren, weitermachen
continued *86* anhaltend, kontinuierlich
continuous *35T* stetig, kontinuierlich; *125* ständig
contract *7* Vertrag; **government ~** *48* öffentlicher Auftrag; **supplier's ~** *59* Liefervertrag, Lieferantenvertrag; **~ of carriage** *80* Beförderungsvertrag, Frachtvertrag; **~ of employment** *10T* Arbeitsvertrag; **~ of sale** *98* Kaufvertrag; to **enter into a ~** *77T* einen Vertrag (ab)schließen, in einen Vertrag eintreten; **performance of a ~** *99* Erfüllung/Durchführung eines Vertrags
contrast *72* Gegensatz; **in ~** *15T* im Gegensatz (dazu)
to **contrast sth** *53* etw (einander) gegenüberstellen, etw (miteinander) vergleichen
to **contribute to sth** *31T* etw finanziell unterstützen
contribution, to **make a ~** *126T* einen Beitrag leisten
control centre *39T* Steuerzentrale
controlling, financial ~ *16* Controlling
convenience *110* Komfort; **~ store** *11* Gemischtwarenladen, Spätkauf
convenient *81* geeignet, zweckmäßig

convention centre 64 Tagungszentrum, Kongresszentrum
conventional 24 herkömmlich, konventionell
conversion rate 47 Umwandlungsquote
to convince sb of sth 89 jdn von etw überzeugen
cooperation 23 Zusammenarbeit
to coordinate 17 miteinander abstimmen, koordinieren
copper 61P Kupfer
to copy sb in 113T *(E-Mail:)* jdn CC setzen
copy, hard ~ 55T Papierexemplar, Ausdruck
core: ~ business 42 Kerngeschäft; ~ time 58P Kernzeit
corn, sweet ~ 78 Zuckermais, Süßmais
corner stand 66T Eckstand
corporate 67 Unternehmens-
corporation 35 Unternehmen, Gesellschaft
correction 96T Korrektur
correctness 30 Richtigkeit
to correspond 51 entsprechen, korrespondieren
correspondence 125 Schriftverkehr, Korrespondenz; written ~ 23 Schriftverkehr
corridor 26T Flur, Gang
cost, at ~ price 8T zum Selbstkostenpreis
costs *pl*, production ~s *pl* 48 Herstellungskosten; work and ~s 99 Arbeit und Kosten; to cut ~s 78 Kosten senken; to return ~ 110 Kosten erstatten
cost-effectiveness 110 Wirtschaftlichkeit
costly 43 kostspielig, teuer
cotton 32 Baumwolle; organic ~ 46 Bio-Baumwolle
council, works ~ 26 Betriebsrat
counter 68T Theke, Tresen
countermeasure 34 Gegenmaßnahme
country, industrialized ~ 11 Industrieland, -staat; low-wage ~ 32 Niedriglohnland; ~ of origin 77 Ursprungsland
countryside 75 Landschaft, ländliche Gegend
course 11 Studiengang; training ~ 6 Ausbildung
coursework 11 schriftliche Arbeit(en)
cover 70 Gedeck; 105 Umschlag; insurance ~ 75 Versicherungsschutz
to cover 27 *(Thema)* behandeln; 81 *(Kosten)* decken; ~ sth 43 etw abdecken; 51 *(Medien:)* über etw berichten; 96T etw abdecken

coverage 91T Versicherungsschutz
covering 105 Deckung; seam ~ 28 Falzabdeckung, Bördeln
covering letter 40 Anschreiben, Begleitschreiben
cow 39T Kuh
craft, arts and ~s *pl* 86 Kunsthandwerk
to crash 15 abstürzen
crate, wooden ~ 106T Holzkiste
credit: letter of ~ (L/C) 82 Akkreditiv; documentary letter of ~ (L/C) 103 Dokumentenakkreditiv; irrevocable and confirmed documentary letter of ~ 82 unwiderrufliches und bestätigtes Dokumentenakkreditiv; documentary ~ transaction 103 Akkreditivgeschäft; ~ check 77T Bonitätsprüfung; ~ note 118 Gutschrift
crude oil 33 Rohöl
crushed 132 eingedrückt
cubic metre 61P Kubikmeter
cubicle 15T Arbeitsplatz *(im Großraumbüro)*
cultural 71 kulturell
curing oven 28 Einbrennofen
currency 104 Währung; ~ sign 102 Währungssymbol
currently 89 momentan, augenblicklich
customer: ~ base 86 Kundenstamm; ~ discount 97 Kundenrabatt; ~ loyalty 45 Kundenbindung, Kundentreue; ~ satisfaction 45 Kundenzufriedenheit
customer-facing job 9 Tätigkeit mit Kundenkontakt
customization, mass ~ 38 individualisierte/flexibilisierte Massenproduktion
to customize sth 45 etw individuell anpassen
customized 38 individuell gefertigt, nach Kundenwunsch gefertigt
custom-made 47 individuell gefertigt
customs: export ~ entry 125 Ausfuhranmeldung; ~ duty 81 Zollgebühr(en); ~ regulations *pl* 19 Zollvorschriften
to cut: ~ sth 91T etw reduzieren; ~ out 115T sich abschalten; ~ costs 78 Kosten senken
cutting machine 39 Schneidemaschine, Zuschneidemaschine
CV (curriculum vitae) 123 Lebenslauf
cyberattack 15 Cyberangriff
cyber-physical system 37 cyberphysisches System
cybersecurity 14 Internetsicherheit

D

daily 74 täglich; on a ~ basis 131 täglich, jeden Tag; ~ operations *pl* 19 Tagesgeschäft
dairy 33 Molkereiprodukte; ~ farming 39 Milchwirtschaft
damages *pl* 132 Schadenersatz
data *pl* 14 Daten; big ~ 37 große Datenmengen; to gather ~ 45 Daten erfassen; ~ projector 55T Beamer; ~ protection 128 Datenschutz
database 45 Datenbank
date, expiration ~ 105 Verfallsdatum; to be up to ~ with sth 15 bei etw auf dem neuesten Stand sein; up-to-~ 66 aktuell, auf dem neuesten Stand; ~ of delivery 99 Lieferdatum
dated 90 (mit Datum) vom
day, open ~ 8T Tag der Offenen Tür; time of ~ 52 Tageszeit; ~-to-day update 51T täglicher aktueller Bericht
deadline 8T Frist, Fertigstellungstermin; to meet a ~ 8T eine Frist einhalten
deal 72T Geschäft, Abschluss; We have a ~. 91T Abgemacht!
to deal: ~ in sth 86 mit etw handeln; ~ with sb 23 mit jdm umgehen; ~ with sth 17 sich um etw kümmern, sich mit etw befassen; 46T etw *(Thema usw.)* behandeln; 106 etw erledigen
Dear Sir or Madam 41 *(Brief:)* Sehr geehrte Damen und Herren,
to debit 105 *(Konto)* belasten, *(Geld)* abbuchen
debt, to be in ~ 11 Schulden haben, verschuldet sein; to get into ~ 11 sich verschulden
decaffeinated 70 koffeinfrei
decentralized 39T dezentral
decibel 91T Dezibel
decision, to take a ~ 25 eine Entscheidung treffen
declaration, tax ~ 110 Steuererklärung
to decrease 52 abnehmen, zurückgehen
decrease 52 Abnahme, Rückgang
to deduct 118T abziehen
defect 36 Mangel, Fehler; to rectify ~s 115 Mängel beheben
defective 99 mangelhaft
delighted, to be ~ 27 (hoch)erfreut sein, sich sehr freuen
delivery 31 Vortrag, Vortragsweise; date of ~ 99 Lieferdatum; door-to-door ~ 91T Haus-zu-Haus-Lieferung; material ~ 26 Materialanlieferung; terms *pl* of ~ 76 Lieferbedingungen; to take ~ of sth 91T etw *(Ware usw.)* in Empfang nehmen; ~ period 59T Lieferzeit

demand *34* Nachfrage; *35* Bedarf; to **be in great ~** *61P* stark nachgefragt sein
to **demonstrate sth** *68* etw vorführen
demonstration *65T* Vorführung
denim *32* Jeansstoff
dental clinic *120T* Zahnklinik
dented *120T* verbeult
department *8* Abteilung; **head of ~** *16* Abteilungsleiter/in; **~ store** *42* Kaufhaus
departure *74T* Abreise, Abflug
to **depend on sth** *10T* von etw abhängen, auf etw ankommen
depending on … *7* je nach
depth *69* Tiefe
description, job ~ *12* Stellenbeschreibung
desk, front ~ *74* Rezeption
destination *26T* (Reise-, Fahrt-)Ziel, Zielort; **place of ~** *80* Bestimmungsort
destruction *51T* Zerstörung
detail, in ~ *42T* ausführlich, detailliert
to **detect sth** *38* etw aufspüren, etw feststellen
to **determine sth** *18* etw festlegen, etw bestimmen
to **develop** *23* (sich) entwickeln
development, Research & D~ (R & D) *16* Forschung und Entwicklung
device *15* Gerät
to **devise sth** *50* etw entwickeln, etw ausarbeiten
to **diagnose** *79T* diagnostizieren
diagnosis, remote ~ *79T* Ferndiagnose
diameter *78* Durchmesser
to **dictate** *40* diktieren
digit *21* Ziffer
digital signage *45* digitale Außenwerbung
digitization *37* Digitalisierung
to **digitize** *41* digitalisieren
dimensions *pl* *69* Abmessungen
dining room *75T* *(Hotel:)* Speisesaal
diploma *11* Abschlusszeugnis
to **direct** *47* leiten, lenken
direct mailing *65T* Direktwerbung *(per Post)*
directions *pl* *55T* Wegbeschreibung; to **give ~** *27* den Weg beschreiben
director *23* Vorstandsmitglied; **commercial ~** *16* kaufmännische/r Leiter/in; **financial ~** *23* Finanzvorstand; **logistics ~** *90* Logistikleiter/in; **managing ~** *16* Geschäftsführer/in; **purchasing ~** *41* Einkaufsleiter/in; **sales ~** *90* Vertriebsleiter/in; **board of ~s** *17T* Vorstand
to **disappoint sb** *113* jdn enttäuschen
disappointed *120T* enttäuscht
to **disclose sth** *44* etw preisgeben
discoloured *114* verfärbt
discount *8T* Rabatt, Skonto; **bulk ~** *89* Mengenrabatt; **cash ~** *89* Skonto; **customer ~** *97* Kundenrabatt; **introductory ~** *61P* Einführungsrabatt; **quantity ~** *35* Mengenrabatt; **special ~** *118* Sonderrabatt; **trade ~** *102* Händlerrabatt
discounter *48* Billiganbieter, Discounter
to **discover sth** *114* etw feststellen
discrepancy *117* Unstimmigkeit, Diskrepanz
discrimination *77* Diskrimierung
dislikes *pl*, **likes and ~** *14* Vorlieben und Abneigungen
dismayed *116* bestürzt
dispatch *34* Versand; **advice of ~** *100* Versandanzeige
to **display** *55T* etw *(auf einem Bildschirm)* anzeigen; **~ sth** *86* etw ausstellen, etw zeigen
display stand *69* Präsentationsstand
dispute *9* Streit, Streitigkeiten, Debatte
to **disregard sth** *48* etw vernachlässigen, etw übersehen
disruption (to sth) *110* Störung (von etw)
dissatisfied *115T* unzufrieden
distance *77* Entfernung
to **distinguish** *115* unterscheiden
to **distribute sth** *42* etw vertreiben
distribution *32* Vertrieb, Transport; **~ channel** *33* Vertriebsweg, Vertriebskanal
distributor *43* Vertragshändler
to **divide sth (up)** *6* etw aufteilen
division *31T* (Unternehmens-)Sparte; **~ of space** *68* Raumaufteilung
DIY chain *115* Baumarkt-Kette
to **dock** *81T* festmachen
document of title *83* Dispositionspapier, Traditionspapier
documentary: ~ credit transaction *103* Akkreditivgeschäft; **~ letter of credit (L/C)** *103* Dokumentenakkreditiv; **irrevocable and confirmed ~ letter of credit** *82* unwiderrufliches und bestätigtes Dokumentenakkreditiv
documentation *81* Papiere
documents *pl*, **shipping ~** *18* Transportpapiere, Versanddokumente
domestic *31T* im Inland, heimisch
door-to-door delivery *91T* Haus-zu-Haus-Lieferung
dot *40* Punkt
down, goose ~ *119* Gänsedaunen
downside *15T* Nachteil, Schattenseite
downstairs *26T* (nach) unten
downtime *38* Ausfall, Ausfallzeit
draft *103* Tratte; to **draw a ~** *105* eine Tratte/einen Wechsel ziehen
to **draft** *55T* *(Text)* entwerfen, verfassen
drastic(ally) *53T* drastisch
to **draw: ~ a draft** *105* eine Tratte/einen Wechsel ziehen; **~ sb's attention to sth** *89* jds Aufmerksamkeit auf etw lenken
draw, prize ~ *44* Verlosung
to **dress** *126* sich kleiden
dress *9* Kleid; **~ code** *8* Kleiderordnung
drilling *34* Bohren
drinks machine *8T* Getränkeautomat
drive *74* Fahrt *(mit dem Auto)*
to **drive sb away** *113* jdn vergraulen
driver *33* Fahrer/in
driving licence *128* Führerschein
drone *24* Drohne
drop *52* Fall, Rückgang
to **drop** *52* fallen, zurückgehen
to **dry** *34* trocknen
due *99* fällig; to **be ~ to do sth** *42* etw tun (in der Zukunft) sollen; **~ to** *43* aufgrund von, wegen
duplicate, in ~ *105* in zweifacher Ausfertigung
durable goods *pl* *43* Gebrauchsgüter
duty *80* Zoll; *98* Aufgabe, Pflicht; **customs ~** *81* Zollgebühr(en)

E

ear protectors *pl* *91T* Gehörschutz
early shift *58P* Frühschicht
to **earn sth** *11* etw verdienen
earring *9* Ohrring
eco-friendly *50* umweltfreundlich
economics *129* Wirtschaft
edition *39T* Ausgabe
education, follow-up ~ *125* Weiterbildung
to **effect sth** *105* etw ausführen, etw tätigen, etw erwirken
efficient(ly) *15T* effizient
e.g. *11* z. B.
either *30* jedes *(von zweien)*
electric motor *38* Elektromotor
electricity: ~ consumption *116* Stromverbrauch; **~ generator** *81* Generator
electrification *39T* Elektrifizierung
electronic *37* elektronisch
electronics, consumer ~ *8T* Unterhaltungselektronik
elevator *AE* *27* Aufzug, Fahrstuhl
emergency *34* Notfall, Not-
emerging markets *pl* *86* Wachstumsmärkte, Schwellenmärkte
empire *24* Reich, Imperium

employment *128* Beschäftigung, Anstellung; **contract of ~** *10T* Arbeitsvertrag
to **empower sb to do sth** *36* jdn ermächtigen/autorisieren, etw zu tun
to **enable sb to do sth** *43* jdm ermöglichen, etw zu tun
to **enclose** *89* *(Brief:)* beifügen
enclosure *84* *(Brief:)* Anlage
to **encourage sb** *8* jdn ermutigen, jdn ermuntern
end of block stand *66T* Kopfstand
to **end up** *51T* (irgendwo) landen
endorsement, celebrity ~ *50* Werbung mit Prominenten
energy source *38* Energiequelle
engaged *20T* *(Telefon:)* besetzt
engine, search ~ *46T* Suchmaschine
engineering *20* Technik, Maschinenbau; **social ~** *15* soziale Manipulation
to **enquire about sth** *81T* sich nach etw erkundigen
enquiry *40* Anfrage
to **ensure sth** *23* für etw sorgen; *42* etw sicherstellen
to **entail sth** *17T* etw mit sich bringen
to **enter: ~ a scheme** *7* an einem Programm teilnehmen; **~ into a contract** *77T* einen Vertrag (ab)schließen, in einen Vertrag eintreten; **~ the railway business** *24* ins Bahngeschäft einsteigen
to **entertain sb** *87* jdn bewirten
entertainment *47* Unterhaltung
entire *90* gesamte/r/s, ganze/r/s
entirely *51T* völlig, ganz
entrance *26* Eingang
entry, blog ~ *38* Blogeintrag; **export customs ~** *125* Ausfuhranmeldung
environmentally: ~ conscious *51* umweltbewusst; **~-friendly** *46* umweltfreundlich
equal, to **take ~ turns with sb** *31* sich mit jdm ausgewogen abwechseln
to **equip sth with sth** *41* etw mit etw ausstatten
equipment *37* Geräte, Ausstattung, Ausrüstung; **construction ~** *66T* Baumaschinen; **exercise ~** *44* Trainingsgeräte; **microbrewing ~** *103* Geräte für Klein(st)brauereien; **sports ~** *44* Sportartikel
equity *105* Billigkeit(srecht)
equivalent *62* Entsprechung, Übersetzung
ergonomic *22T* ergonomisch
error *35* Fehler, Irrtum; **by trial and ~** *38* durch Ausprobieren

to **establish** *77T* festigen; **~ sth** *23* etw schaffen, etw festlegen; *35T* etw aufbauen; **~ oneself** *48* sich etablieren
established *42* etabliert; **well-~** *46T* bewährt, fest etabliert
estate agent *111T* Immobilienmakler/in
ethical *77* ethisch, moralisch vertretbar
etiquette *71* Umgangsformen
Euro-pallet *61P* Euro-Palette
to **evaluate sth** *23* etw auswerten, etw einschätzen, etw beurteilen; *110* etw einstufen
evaluation *23* Beurteilung, Evaluierung
even though *7* auch wenn
event *8T* Veranstaltung
every: ~ now and then *113T* ab und an; **~ so often** *113T* hin und wieder
examination, final ~ *11* Abschlussprüfung
to **exceed sth** *34* etw übersteigen
excellent *35T* ausgezeichnet, hervorragend
except for *21* außer
exception *81* Ausnahme
exceptional *64* außergewöhnlich
excess *36* übermäßig, überschüssig; *75* *(Versicherung:)* Selbstbehalt
exchange, bill of ~ *103* Wechsel; **stock ~** *24* Börse
to **exchange sth** *76* etw austauschen
exclusive agreement *43* Exklusivvertrag
to **excuse: E~ me.** *13* Verzeihung. Entschuldigung.
to **execute** *114* ausführen
exercise equipment *44* Trainingsgeräte
to **exhibit** *62* ausstellen
exhibition *125* Messe, Ausstellung; **~ centre** *26T* Messezentrum; **~ hall** *66* Messehalle, Ausstellungshalle
exhibitor *86* Aussteller
existing *16* bestehend, existierend
to **expand** *59T* expandieren; **~ sth** *19* etw ausweiten, etw erweitern; **~ rapidly** *59* schnell wachsen
expanded metal *92* Streckmetall
expectation *113* Erwartung
expected, to **be ~ to do sth** *9* etw tun sollen
expenses *pl* *6* Kosten, Auslagen; **living ~** *6* Lebenshaltungskosten; **travel ~** *56T* Reisekosten, Reisespesen
experience, job ~ *7* Berufserfahrung, praktische Erfahrung; **work ~** *18* Praktikum
experienced *36* erfahren
expert, quality-assured ~s *pl* *110* qualifiziertes Fachpersonal
expertise *110* Fachwissen, Fachkenntnisse

expiration date *105* Verfallsdatum
explanation *7* Erläuterung
expo *68* Messe, Ausstellung
to **export** *26* exportieren, ausführen
export: ~ clearance *80* Ausfuhrabfertigung; **~ clerk** *40* Außenhandelskaufmann/-frau; **~ customs entry** *125* Ausfuhranmeldung; **~ licence** *81* Ausführgenehmigung
exporter *78* Exporteur, Ausführer
express carrier *121P* Expressdienst
expression *20* Ausdruck
extensive *23* umfangreich, ausführlich
extent, to the ~ of sth *24* bis zu etw
external *23* extern
extra guarantee *60* Garantieverlängerung
extractor hood *97* Dunstabzugshaube
eye contact *29* Blickkontakt

F

to **face sb** *29* sich jdm zuwenden, jdn anschauen
face-to-face *126* persönlich
facilities *pl* *8* Einrichtungen, Anlage(n)
facility manager *111T* Objektleiter/in, Gebäudeverwalter/in
fact, in ~ *13* genau genommen, tatsächlich, eigentlich; **~ sheet** *32* Informationsblatt, Datenblatt
factor *46* Faktor
factory manager *20* Betriebsleiter/in, Werksleiter/in
to **fail: I ~ to see ...** *35T* Ich kann nicht sehen, ...
failure *34* Misserfolg, Versagen, Scheitern
fair *40* Messe; *64* mittelmäßig; **trade ~** *17T* Fachmesse, Branchenmesse
faithfully, Yours ~ *41* *(Brief:)* ... und verbleiben mit freundlichen Grüßen
fake *15* gefälscht, falsch
family business *8T* Familienunternehmen
fantastic *13* phantastisch, toll
far, as ~ as sth is concerned *113* was etw betrifft
farm *39T* Bauernhof, Hof
farmer *39T* Landwirt/in
farming *39T* Landwirtschaft; **dairy ~** *39* Milchwirtschaft
fashion *42* Mode
fashionwear *48* Modekleidung
faulty *36* schadhaft, mangelhaft, defekt
favor *AE*, **in ~ of sb** *105* zu jds Gunsten, zugunsten von jdm
favour, to **be in ~ of sth** *58* für etw sein, etw befürworten
favourable *78* günstig

feature *68* Merkmal, Eigenschaft
to **feature sth** *43* etw *(Merkmal usw.)* aufweisen
fee, to **charge a ~** *83* eine Gebür verlangen; **rental ~** *66T* Miete; **tuition ~s** *pl* *11* Studiengebühren
feed *39T* Futter
to **feed sth into sth** *39T* etw in etw (ein)führen
feedback *31* Reaktion(en), Rückmeldung(en)
feeding system *39T* Fütterungssystem
to **feel: ~ like sth** *8T* Lust auf etw haben; **~ free to do sth** *26T* etw ruhig tun, gern etw tun können
fees *pl* *11* Gebühren
fence *38* Zaun
fertilizer *39T* Dünger
field *17T* Gebiet, Bereich, Feld
field research *45* Feldforschung
figure *105* Ziffer
figures *pl* *31T* Zahlen; **sales ~** *17T* Umsatzzahlen, Verkaufszahlen
file, personnel ~ *12* Personalakte; **~ number** *105* Aktenzeichen
final: ~ consumer *49* Endverbraucher/in; **~ examination** *11* Abschlussprüfung; **~ grade** *11* Abschlussnote
to **finalize sth** *55T* etw abschließen
to **finance** *24* finanzieren
finance *11* Finanz(en)
financial: ~ controlling *16* Controlling; **~ director** *23* Finanzvorstand; **~ report** *18* Finanzbericht; **~ services** *pl* *24* Finanzdienstleistungen; **~ stability** *77T* Finanzstabilität; **~ year** *53T* Geschäftsjahr
findings *pl* *38* (Untersuchungs-) Ergebnisse
fine: F~ by me. *46T* Von mir aus gern.
finished product *34* Endprodukt
finishing point *26* Endpunkt
fire *106T* Brand
to **fire: ~ sb** *7* jdn entlassen; **~ away** *65T* losschießen
firm *45* Firma; **~ handshake** *127T* fester Händedruck; **~ offer** *69* verbindliches Angebot
first: ~ aid *129* Erste Hilfe; **~ of all** *27* zuerst, zunächst
to **fit** *68* passen; **~ sth in** *91T* etw einbauen; **one-size-~s-all** *45* Einheits-, Standard-, 08/15-
fitted: ~ with *74* ausgestattet mit; **~ furniture** *41* Einbaumöbel; **~ kitchen** *47* Einbauküche
fittings *pl* *34* Beschläge, Armaturen
flashlight *67* Taschenlampe
flat *9* flach; *BE* *126T* Wohnung
to **flatten out** *52* auf gleichem Stand bleiben
fleet *42* Fuhrpark, Flotte
flexibility *91T* Flexibilität, Spielraum; *110* Anpassungsfähigkeit
flexible *130* flexibel
flexitime *8* Gleitzeit
to **flick through sth** *126* etw durchblättern
flight, test ~ *24* Testflug
to **flood sth** *15* etw überschwemmen
floor *34* Fläche; **ground ~** *8T* Erdgeschoss; **~ tiles** *pl* *81* Bodenfliesen
flow chart *19* Flussdiagramm
to **fluctuate** *52* schwanken
fluctuation *35* Schwankung(en)
fluent *125* *(Sprache:)* fließend
flute *117* Flöte
flyer *40* Faltblatt
focus *72* (inhaltlicher) Schwerpunkt
to **focus on sth** *15T* sich auf etw konzentrieren
focused *65T* gebündelt, konzentriert
folder *28T* Mappe, Ordner
folding table *72* Klapptisch
folks *pl* *11* Leute
to **follow: ~ sth up** *113T* etw nachbereiten, in einer Sache nachfassen; **as ~s** *20* wie folgt
follow-up education *125* Weiterbildung
food industry *74* Nahrungsmittelbranche
to **foot sth** *91T* die Kosten für etw übernehmen
footprint, carbon ~ *77* CO_2-Fußabdruck; **CO_2 ~** *33* CO_2-Fußabdruck
for the time being *95T* einstweilen, fürs Erste
forced labour *77* Zwangsarbeit
to **forecast** *35* vorhersagen, schätzen
foreign trade *6T* Außenhandel; **management assistant in wholesale and ~** *6T* Kaufmann/-frau im Groß- und Außenhandel
forest *33* Wald; **Black F~** *64* Schwarzwald
fork *70* Gabel
to **form** *51* (sich) bilden
form, order ~ *96* Bestellformular
formal(ly) *13* formell, förmlich
formalities *pl* *106* Formalitäten
forth, to **set ~** *105* darlegen
to **forward sth** *114* etw weitersenden, etw verschicken
forwarder, freight ~ *59T* Spedition
forwarding: ~ agent *132* Spedition; **freight ~ company** *42* Spedition
foul bill of lading *103* unreines Konnossement
to **found sth** *24* etw gründen
framework *23* Rahmen
franchise *24* Konzession, Lizenz
frankly *111T* offen gesagt
free: for ~ *11* umsonst; to **be ~ to do sth** *77* etw tun dürfen; to **feel ~ to do sth** *26T* etw ruhig tun, gern etw tun können; **~ carrier** *91T* frei Frachtführer; **~ of charge** *115T* unentgeltlich, kostenlos
freezer, chest ~ *116* Tiefkühltruhe, Gefriertruhe
freight *19T* Fracht; **air ~** *91T* Luftfracht; **sea ~** *91T* Seefracht; **~ forwarder** *59T* Spedition; **~ forwarding company** *42* Spedition; **~ rate** *91T* Frachtsatz, Frachtrate
frequency, radio ~ *39T* Funkfrequenz, Radiofrequenz
frequent(ly) *20* häufig
fresh *26T* frisch
to **freshen up** *55T* sich frisch machen
friendship *26T* Freundschaft
front desk *74* Rezeption
to **fulfil: ~ an order** *120* einen Auftrag abwickeln, eine Bestellung ausführen; **~ requirements** *23* Anforderungen erfüllen
full set *105* vollständiger Satz *(von Dokumenten)*
fully-integrated *78* vollintegriert
funds *pl*, **insufficient ~** *105* mangelnde Deckung, unzureichende Mittel
to **furnish sth** *41* etw einrichten
furniture *8T* Möbel; **compact ~** *34* Kleinmöbel; **fitted ~** *41* Einbaumöbel; **wooden ~** *47* Holzmöbel; **~-maker** *33* Möbelhersteller; **~ store** *33* Möbelhaus
future prospects *pl* *127T* Zukunftsperspektiven

G

to **gain sth** *7* etw erlangen, etw erwerben, etw gewinnen
gallery walk *25* Galerierundgang
garment *32* Kleidungsstück
gas balloon *24* Gasballon
gate *75T* Tor, Einfahrt
to **gather: ~ sth** *126* etw zusammenstellen; **~ data** *45* Daten erfassen
gear *44* Ausrüstung, Klamotten
general purpose *101* Allzweck-
generator, electricity ~ *81* Generator
generic *47* allgemein
gentleman *26T* Herr
gesture *29* Geste
to **get: ~ back to sb** *56T* jdn zurückrufen, sich (wieder) bei jdm melden;

~ out of sth 62T um etw herumkommen; **~ sth sorted** 120T etw klären, sich um etw kümmern; **~ on with one's work** 15T seine Arbeit machen; **~ one's head round sth** 9 etw begreifen; **~ to the bottom of sth** 118T etw herausfinden; **~ a message across** 25 eine Botschaft vermitteln
gift 86 Geschenk
to **give: ~ sth away** 15 etw preisgeben; **~ reasons for sth** 8 etw begründen
giveaway 42T Werbegeschenk
glance, at a ~ 53T auf einen Blick
global market share 28T Weltmarktanteil
glossy brochure 65T Hochglanzbroschüre
to **go: ~ ahead** 35T weitermachen, fortfahren; **Go ahead.** 8T Nur zu! Na los!; **~ a long way in sth** 86 viel zu etw beitragen, viel für etw tun
goal 11 Ziel
good cause 31T gute Sache, guter Zweck
goodness, Thank ~! 106T Gott sei Dank!
goods *pl* 8T Ware(n), Güter; **consumer ~** 33 Konsumgüter; **durable ~** 43 Gebrauchsgüter; **title to the ~** 83 Eigentum(srecht) an den Waren
goose down 119 Gänsedaunen
government contract 48 öffentlicher Auftrag
to **grab sb's attention** 128 jds Aufmerksamkeit fesseln
grade 11 Note; **final ~** 11 Abschlussnote
grain 39T (Getreide-)Korn
to **grant sth** 79 etw gewähren, etw einräumen
graph 52 Diagramm, Kurve; **line ~** 52 Liniendiagramm
graphic 25 Grafik
grass 39T Gras, Rasen
grateful 79 dankbar
to **graze** 39T weiden, grasen
gross weight 35 Bruttogewicht
ground floor 8T Erdgeschoss
groupage consignment 101 Sammelladung
to **grow** 32 *(Pflanze)* anbauen
to **guarantee** 58 garantieren
guarantee 60 Garantie; **extra ~** 60 Garantieverlängerung
guarantor 105 Bürge/Bürgin
guesswork 35 Mutmaßung(en)
to **guide** 47 leiten, führen
guide 26T Führer/in
guided tour 26 Führung
guidelines *pl* 9 Richtlinien
gym 64 Fitness-Studio

H
habit 127T Gewohnheit; to **get into the ~ of doing sth** 127T sich daran gewöhnen, etw zu tun
hall, exhibition ~ 66 Messehalle, Ausstellungshalle; **production ~** 26T Fertigungshalle, Produktionshalle
to **hand: ~ sth in** 19T etw einreichen, etw abgeben; **~ over to sb** 29 an jdn übergeben; **~ sth out** 67 etw austeilen, etw ausgeben; **~ sth over** 81 etw übergeben
hand, on the other ~ 39T dagegen, andererseits; to **have sth on ~** 43 etw zur Verfügung haben; to **shake ~s with sb** 127T jdm die Hand geben
to **handle sth** 18 etw bearbeiten; 34 etw bewältigen; 36 etw handhaben, etw bedienen; 93 etw erledigen
handling, rough ~ 133 unsanfte Behandlung
handout 29 Arbeitsblatt, Broschüre
hand sanitizer 67 Handdesinfektionsmittel
handshake 51 Handschlag; **firm ~** 127T fester Händedruck
to **hang: H~ on.** 74T Einen Moment. Warte mal.
happy, to **be ~ to do sth** 28T etw gern tun
hard copy 55T Papierexemplar, Ausdruck
hard-working 126T fleißig
hardware 85 Geräte
head: to **get one's ~ round sth** 9 etw begreifen; **~ of department** 16 Abteilungsleiter/in; **~ office** 42 Zentrale, Hauptsitz
heading 28 Überschrift, Rubrik
headline, to **hit the ~s** 24 Schlagzeilen machen
headquarters *pl* 64 Zentrale, Hauptsitz
health, National H~ Service *BE* 15 *Nationaler Gesundheitsdienst in Großbritannien;* **~ and safety** 77 Arbeitsschutz
healthcare 25 Gesundheitswesen; **~ clinic** 24 Klinik
heating 55T Heizung
heavy machinery 83 Schwermaschinen
heels *pl* 9 Pumps, Schuhe mit hohen Absätzen
herbal tea 70 Kräutertee
here to stay, sth is ~ 38 etw hat Einzug gehalten
to **hesitate** 90 zögern
heterogeneous 110 heterogen
hexagonal nut 35 Sechskantmutter
hide 100 Haut, Leder
to **hide sth** 15T etw verbergen
high bay 34 Hochregal
high-definition 85 hochauflösend
high-quality 86 hochwertig
high-volume 43 großvolumig, Groß-; 49 Massen-
to **highlight** 30 hervorheben
highly 35T sehr, höchst, in hohem Maße; **~-professional** 42 hochprofessionell
hiking 88 Wandern
to **hire sth** 74 etw mieten
history, purchasing ~ 45 Kaufhistorie, Einkaufsverhalten
to **hit** 15 treffen; **~ a maximum** 52 einen Höchstwert/-stand erreichen; **~ the headlines** 24 Schlagzeilen machen
to **hold: ~ up sb** 13 jdn aufhalten; **~ the line** 20T *(Telefon:)* am Apparat bleiben
holder 82 Inhaber/in
holiday, national ~ 10T gesetzlicher Feiertag
home-owner 33 Hausbesitzer/in, Wohnungseigentümer/in
honesty 46T Ehrlichkeit, Aufrichtigkeit
hood 91 Haube, Abdeckung; **extractor ~** 97 Dunstabzugshaube
hospitality 70 Bewirtung
to **host sb** 59 jdn *(als Gast)* empfangen
hours *pl*, **in a matter of ~** 91T in nur wenigen Stunden; **working ~** 8 Arbeitszeit(en)
housing 47 Wohnen, Wohnungsbau, Wohnverhältnisse
human: H~ Resources (HR) 12 Personal(abteilung); **~ rights** *pl* 77 Menschenrechte; **without ~ intervention** 38 ohne menschliches Eingreifen
humour 71 Humor
hurry 55T Eile
hyphen 40 Bindestrich, Minus

I
identical 15 identisch
to **identify** 36 identifzieren, bestimmen
identity 39T Identität
idle, to **stand ~** 34 stillstehen, untätig sein
illness 13 Krankheit
imagination 87 Phantasie
immediate 89 unverzüglich, sofortig
immediately 42T sofort, unverzüglich
implement, writing ~ 86 Schreibgerät

to implement sth *34* *(Maßnahme usw:)* etw umsetzen, etw einführen
to import *32* einführen, importieren
import: ~ clearance *80* Einfuhrabfertigung; **~ tax** *93* Einfuhrzoll
importance *27* Bedeutung, Wichtigkeit
importer *80* Importeur, Einführer
impression *56T* Eindruck
impressive *42* beeindruckend
to improve *43* verbessern
improvement *34* Verbesserung
to improvise *21* improvisieren
inch *101* Zoll *(ca. 2,54 cm)*
incident *9* Vorfall
to include sth *68T* etw einplanen
including *31T* einschließlich, darunter; **~ sth** *22* mit etw, einschließlich einer Sache
inclusive *40* einschließlich
in-company *7* betriebsintern
inconvenience *115T* Unannehmlichkeiten
to inconvenience sb *62T* jdm Umstände bereiten
Incorporated (Inc.) *106T* GmbH
increase *52* Zunahme, Anstieg
to increase *52* zunehmen, ansteigen; **~ sth** *47* etw steigern, etw erhöhen
increasingly *86* zunehmend
to incur *99* *(Kosten:)* anfallen
indeed *31T* in der Tat, wirklich, allerdings
independent(ly) *64* unabhängig
index card *30* Karteikarte
indication *40* Hinweis, Anzeichen
indirect *60* indirekt
individual training *110* individuelle Weiterbildung, Einzelschulung
indoor pool *74* Hallenbad
industrial management assistant *6* Industriekaufmann/-frau
industrialized country *11* Industrieland, -staat
industry, clothing ~ *11* Kleidungsbranche; **food ~** *74* Nahrungsmittelbranche; **trade ~** *128* Handelsbranche
inefficient *34* ineffizient, unrationell, unwirtschaftlich
inexact *35* ungenau
infamous *15* berüchtigt
to infect *15* infizieren, befallen
infill panel *69* Ausfachung, Füllung
information, sensitive ~ *15* vertrauliche Informationen
infrastructure, transport ~ *28T* Verkehrsnetz
in-house *19T* betriebsintern
initial *41* erste/r/s; **~ order** *61P* Erstauftrag; **~ proposal** *79* Erstvorschlag

initially *78* zu Anfang, zunächst
initials *pl*, **reference ~** *84* *(Brief:)* Zeichen
to initiate sth *23* etw veranlassen
initiative, to take the ~ *126T* die Initiative ergreifen
inside address *84* Innenadresse
to inspect sth *83* etw prüfen
inspection, visual ~ *133* Sichtprüfung; **~ tool** *38* Prüfwerkzeug
inspector *38* Kontrolleur/in, Prüfer/in
to inspire *35* anregen, inspirieren
to install *15* installieren
instantly *45* sofort
instead *106T* stattdessen
instruction *21* Anweisung
instruction *35* Anweisung
insufficient funds *pl* *105* mangelnde Deckung, unzureichende Mittel
insulation, thermal ~ *111T* Wärmedämmung
insurance *80* Versicherung; **~ in transit** *80* Transportversicherung; **terms** *pl* **of ~** *80* Versicherungsbedinungen; **~ certificate** *82* Versicherungsschein; **~ cover** *75* Versicherungsschutz; **~ policy** *105* Versicherungspolice
to insure *81* versichern
intelligence *71* Intelligenz; **artificial ~ (AI)** *37* Künstliche Intelligenz (KI)
to intend to do sth *24* beabsichtigen, etw zu tun
to interact with sb *129* mit jdm kommunizieren
interaction *45* Austausch, Kommunikation
interest, out of ~ *106T* interessehalber
interior *28* Innenbereich, das Innere
intermediary *49* Zwischenhändler, Mittelsmann
intermediate *11* mittlere/r/s
internal *23* intern
Internet of Things (IoT) *37* Internet der Dinge (IdD)
internship *11* Praktikum
to interrupt *15T* unterbrechen, stören
interruption *72* Störung, Unterbrechung
intervention, without human ~ *38* ohne menschliches Eingreifen
interview *126* Vorstellungsgespräch
to interview sb *40* mit jdm ein Vorstellungsgespräch führen
interviewee *113* Befragte/r
introductions *pl* *11* Bekanntmachen, Vorstellen
introductory: ~ discount *61P* Einführungsrabett; **~ level** *110* Einstiegsniveau
to invent sth *58P* etw erfinden
inventor *24* Erfinder/in

inventory *14* Bestandsliste, -aufnahme, Inventar
inventory *35* Lagerbestand
to invest *25* investieren
to investigate sth *116* etw untersuchen
investment *24* Beteiligung, Einlage; *101T* Investition; **return on ~** *110* Rendite, Ertrag
invitation *55T* Einladung
to invite sth *30* zu etw auffordern, um etw bitten
inviting *77T* verlockend
invoice *17* Rechnung; **commercial ~** *82* Handelsrechnung; **receipt of ~** *102* Rechnungseingang; **~ value** *105* Rechnungswert
invoicing *125* Fakturierung, Rechnungsstellung
to involve sth *17T* etw beinhalten, etw umfassen
involved, to be ~ in sth *122T* an etw beteiligt sein
irrevocable and confirmed documentary letter of credit *82* unwiderrufliches und bestätigtes Dokumentenakkreditiv
island stand *66T* Blockstand, Inselstand
issue *9* Problem; *35T* Frage
to issue *103* *(Dokument)* ausstellen
it, That's ~. *8T* Das war's.
IT management assistant *12T* Informatikkaufmann/-frau
item *35T* Artikel; *47* Punkt, Gegenstand; *56* Tagesordnungspunkt
itinerary *63* Reiseplan

J

jar *74* (Marmeladen-)Glas
jewellery *9* Schmuck
job: to apply for a ~ *122* sich um eine Stelle bewerben; **customer-facing ~** *9* Tätigkeit mit Kundenkontakt; **~ advert(isement)** *124* Stellenanzeige; **~ agency** *122* Arbeitsagentur, Arbeitsvermittlung; **~ application** *122* Bewerbung; **~ description** *12* Stellenbeschreibung; **~ experience** *7* Berufserfahrung, praktische Erfahrung; **~ interview** *126* Vorstellungsgespräch; **~ offer** *8T* Stellenangebot; **~ opportunities** *pl* *123* Arbeitsmöglichkeiten; **~ profile** *18* Stellenprofil; **~ prospects** *pl* *8* berufliche Perspektiven; **~ title** *125* Stellenbezeichnung; **~ vacancy** *127P* offene Stelle
journey *13* Fahrt, Anreise
to judge sth *77T* etw beurteilen
to jump at sth *77T* sich auf etw stürzen
just in time *35T* gerade rechtzeitig
to justify *127P* rechtfertigen, begründen

K

keen, to be ~ to do sth 131 jdm liegt sehr daran, etw zu tun
to keep: ~ to sth 19T sich nach etw richten, sich an etw halten; ~ up with sth 34 mit etw Schritt halten, ~ sb waiting 13 jdn warten lassen; ~ sth in mind 77T etw nicht vergessen
kettle 96T Wasserkocher
to key sth in 14 etw *(am Computer)* eingeben
keychain 67 Schlüsselbund
keyword 29 Stichwort; 47 Schlagwort
to kid: You must be ~ding! 48 Das ist doch nicht dein/euer Ernst?
to kill sb 24 jdn töten
kitchen, fitted ~ 47 Einbauküche
to know: to let sb ~ sth 40 jdm etw mitteilen, jdm Bescheid sagen

L

to label 27 bezeichnen, etikettieren
label 42T Etikett
labelling 26 Bezeichnung, Etikettierung; ~ machine 39 Etikettiermaschine
labour, child ~ 77 Kinderarbeit; forced ~ 77 Zwangsarbeit; manual ~ 37 Handarbeit, körperliche Arbeit; slave ~ 48 Sklavenarbeit; ~ price 70P Lohnkosten
lack (of sth) 35 Mangel (an etw), Fehlen (von etw)
to lack sth 15T etw nicht haben
ladder 34 Leiter
lading, bill of ~ (B/L) 82 Konnossement; clean/foul bill of ~ 103 reines/unreines Konnossement
lady 26T Dame
landline 126 Festnetz(telefon)
to last 48 halten; while stocks ~ 117 solange der Vorrat reicht
last, second to ~ 10T zweitletzte/r/s; ~ but not least 77T zu guter Letzt
latest, at the ~ 20 spätestens
lathe 20 Drehbank, Drehmaschine
to laugh at sth 9 sich über etw lustig machen
launch 65T Start; 86 Eröffnung; product ~ 48 Produkteinführung
to launch sth 24 etw starten, etw *(Unternehmen usw.)* gründen; 46 etw auf den Markt bringen
to lay sth 55T etw herrichten, etw *(Tisch)* decken, etw *(Gedeck)* auflegen
layout 26 Grundriss, Anordnung, Plan; 84 Gestaltung, Aufbau, Layout
lazy 46T faul, träge
lb = pound 101 Pfund *(ca. 454 g)*
lean 35 schlank
least, at ~ 8T mindestens, zumindest
leather 39 Leder
leave, annual ~ 10T Jahresurlaub
to leave a message 20 eine Nachricht hinterlassen
legal: ~ adviser 55 Justiziar/in; ~ situation 9 Rechtslage, Gesetzeslage
to let sb know sth 40 jdm etw mitteilen, jdm Bescheid sagen
letter, covering ~ 40 Anschreiben, Begleitschreiben; ~ of credit (L/C) 82 Akkreditiv; documentary ~ of credit (L/C) 103 Dokumentenakkreditiv; irrevocable and confirmed documentary ~ of credit 82 unwiderrufliches und bestätigtes Dokumentenakkreditiv
level, introductory ~ 110 Einstiegsniveau; potassium ~ 39T Kaliumgehalt
to level off 52 sich einpendeln
liability 24 Haftung
liable 24 haftbar
licence, driving ~ 128 Führerschein; export ~ 81 Ausfuhrgenehmigung
licensed, to be ~ to do sth 23 etw (mit offizieller Genehmigung) tun
lid 26T Deckel
lift *BE* 26T Aufzug, Fahrstuhl
light 31T leicht
to liken sth to sth 35 etw mit etw vergleichen
likes and dislikes *pl* 14 Vorlieben und Abneigungen
limit 11 Beschränkung, Begrenzung; 48 (Ober-/Unter-)Grenze
to limit 43 begrenzen, beschränken
limitation 65T Begrenzung, Beschränkung
limited 65T beschränkt, begrenzt; private ~ company (Ltd) 24 Gesellschaft mit beschränkter Haftung (GmbH); public ~ company (plc) 24 Aktiengesellschaft (AG)
line 34 Linie, Produktlinie; to be in ~ with sth 9 einer Sache entsprechen; to hold the ~ 20T *(Telefon:)* am Apparat bleiben; attention ~ 84 Zeile „zu Händen"; bottom ~ 46T das, worauf es ankommt; product ~ 46 Produktlinie; production ~ 28 Fertigungslinie, Produktionslinie; subject ~ 40 Betreffzeile; ~ graph 52 Liniendiagramm; ~ manager 6 (direkte/r) Vorgesetzte/r
link 43 Glied *(in einer Kette)*; 126T Zusammenhang, Verbindung
to link 39T (miteinander) verknüpfen; ~ sth to sth 67 etw mit etw verknüpfen, etw mit etw verbinden; ~ sth up 38 etw (miteinander) verknüpfen
linked to sth 47 in direktem Zusammenhang mit etw
Lisbon 81 Lissabon
list, packing ~ 103 Packliste; wine ~ 70 Weinkarte
listener 51T Hörer/in
literature 35 Literatur, Lesestoff, Informationsmaterial; sales ~ 67 Verkaufsprospekte, Informationsmaterial; ~ rack 68T Prospektständer
litre 70 Liter
litter 51T Müll, Abfall
living expenses *pl* 6 Lebenshaltungskosten
load 104 Ladung
to load 58 beladen, verladen
loaded up with sth 51T mit etw beladen, voll mit etw
loading 80 Verladen, Verladung
locally 15 dezentral, vor Ort
lockable 68T abschließbar, verschließbar
to log in 8T sich einloggen
logistics 8T Logistik
logistics director 90 Logistikleiter/in
long-standing 77T langjährig
long-term 11 langfristig
to look: ~ into sth 77T etw prüfen; ~ the part 9 entsprechend (rollengerecht) aussehen
loose 35 (zu) locker
lorry *BE* 36 Lastwagen
loss 99 Verlust
loud 9 *(Farbe:)* grell, knallig, bunt
lounge 74 Gesellschaftsraum, Lounge
low, to be ~ on sth 39T (zu) wenig von etw *(Substanz usw.)* haben; ~-cut 9 tief ausgeschnitten; ~-heeled 9 mit niedrigem Absatz; ~-priced 59 preisgünstig; ~-wage country 32 Niedriglohnland
loyalty, customer ~ 45 Kundenbindung, Kundentreue; ~ card 44 Kundenkarte
lunch, to break for ~ 31T Mittagspause machen; ~ break 53 Mittagspause
lunchtime 62 Mittagszeit
luxury 48 Luxus

M

machine, answering ~ 111T Anrufbeantworter; drinks ~ 8T Getränkeautomat; labelling ~ 39 Etikettiermaschine; metal-cutting ~ 36 Zerspanungsmaschine; milking ~ 39T Melkmaschine; sewing ~ 102 Nähmaschine; sticking ~ 39 Klebemaschine; welding ~ 28 Schweißmaschine; X-ray ~ 120 Röntgengerät; ~ operator 36 Maschinenführer/in
machinery 16 Maschinen, Geräte; heavy ~ 83 Schwermaschinen

madam, Dear Sir or M~ *41* *(Brief:)* Sehr geehrte Damen und Herren,
magazine, trade ~ *85* Fachzeitschrift
mail order *24* Versandhandel
mailing, direct ~ *65T* Direktwerbung *(per Post)*
main carriage *80* Hauptlauf
to **maintain sth** *18* etw warten, etw instandhalten; *43* etw unterhalten
maintenance *20* Wartung, Instandhaltung, Pflege
majority *112* Mehrheit, Großteil
to **make: ~ sth up** *32* *(Anteil usw.:)* etw ausmachen; *87* sich etw ausdenken, sich etw einfallen lassen; **~ sure** *19* sicherstellen, gewährleisten, dafür sorgen; *31T* dafür sorgen, darauf achten; **~ the most of sth** *32* etw ausnutzen, möglichst viel aus etw herausschlagen; **~ sense** *22T* sinnvoll sein; *68T* einleuchten
malfunction *23* Störung, Defekt, Ausfall
to **manage sth** *45* etw verwalten
management *16* Geschäftsleitung, Geschäftsführung; **project ~** *16* Projektleitung; **quality ~** *16* Qualitätssicherung; **industrial ~ assistant** *6* Industriekaufmann/-frau; **IT ~ assistant** *12T* Informatikkaufmann/-frau; **office ~ assistant** *12T* Bürokaufmann/-frau, Kaufmann/-frau für Büromanagement; **~ assistant in wholesale and foreign trade** *6T* Kaufmann/-frau im Groß- und Außenhandel; **~ consultancy** *9* Unternehmensberatung;
manager, accounting ~ *19* Buchhaltungsleiter/in; **facility ~** *111T* Objektleiter/in, Gebäudeverwalter/in; **factory ~** *20* Betriebsleiter/in, Werksleiter/in; **line ~** *6* (direkte/r) Vorgesetzte/r; **production ~** *19* Produktionsleiter/in; **project ~** *19* Projektleiter/in; **purchasing ~** *55* Einkaufsleiter/in; **warehouse ~** *55* Lagerleiter/in
managing director *16* Geschäftsführer/in
manner *31* Art (und Weise)
manpower *18* Arbeitskräfte
manual labour *37* Handarbeit, körperliche Arbeit
to **manufacture** *28T* fertigen, herstellen
manufacture *89* Herstellung, Produktion, Fertigung
manufacturer *16* Hersteller/in; **car ~** *33* Autohersteller, Autobauer
manufacturing *6* Fertigung, Herstellung, Produktion
margin, profit ~ *17T* Gewinnspanne
mark *46T* Marke; to **put your personal ~ on sth** *15T* einer Sache seinen persönlichen Stempel aufdrücken
market *28* Markt; to **serve a ~** *31T* einen Markt bedienen; **emerging ~s** *pl 86* Wachstumsmärkte, Schwellenmärkte; **global ~ share** *28T* Weltmarktanteil; **~ research** *23* Marktforschung; **~ share** *28* Marktanteil
to **market sth** *46T* etw vermarkten
marketing: ~ channel *43* Absatzweg, Vertriebskanal; **~ strategy** *44* Vermarktungsstrategie
married *58P* verheiratet
mass: ~ customization *38* individualisierte/flexibilisierte Massenproduktion; **~ media** *pl 46T* Massenmedien; **~ production** *37* Massenfertigung
to **mass-produce sth** *35* etw in großen Mengen produzieren
massive *32* riesig, gewaltig, saftig
material *17* Baustoff, Rohmaterial, Material; *89* Stoff; **raw ~s** *pl 32* Rohstoffe, Rohmaterialien; **sales ~** *79* Werbematerial, Verkaufsunterlagen; **~ delivery** *26* Materialanlieferung
to **matter** *35T* wichtig sein, von Belang sein
matter, in a ~ of hours *91T* in nur wenigen Stunden; **no ~ what …** *110* ganz gleich, was …; egal, was …; **subject ~** *110* Materie, Unterrichtsstoff
maximum, to **hit a ~** *52* einen Höchstwert/-stand erreichen
meaning … *115T* das heißt …
means *99* Mittel, Maßnahme; **by ~ of** *105* mittels, durch
meat *83* Fleisch
mechanical *37* mechanisch
mechanization *39T* Mechanisierung
media *pl 9* Medien; **mass ~** *46T* Massenmedien; **social ~** *45* soziale Medien
medical: ~ products *pl 31T* Medizinprodukte; **~ supplies** *pl 84* Sanitätsartikel
medium-sized *8* mittelgroß, mittelständisch
to **meet: ~ sth** *77* etw *(Vorschriften usw.)* einhalten; **~ a deadline** *8T* eine Frist einhalten; **~ requirements** *79* Anforderungen erfüllen
to **meet sb's needs** *126* jds Bedürfnissen entsprechen, jds Anforderungen erfüllen; **~ standards** *23* Normen erfüllen
meeting: to **call a ~** *34* eine Sitzung einberufen; to **chair a ~** *55T* eine Sitzung leiten; **~ place** *13* Treffpunkt; **~ room** *75* Sitzungszimmer, Konferenzraum
member *24* Mitglied; **~ of staff** *23* Mitarbeiter/in
memo *45* Notiz
memory stick *67* Speicherstick
to **mention: ~ sth** *31T* etw erwähnen; **above-~ed** *90* obengenannt
menu *70* Menü
merchandise *43* Ware
message, to **get a ~ across** *25* eine Botschaft vermitteln; to **leave a ~** *20* eine Nachricht hinterlassen; **text ~** *8T* SMS
metal, expanded ~ *92* Streckmetall; **~-cutting machine** *36* Zerspanungsmaschine
method *45* Verfahren, Methode
microbrewery *105* Klein(st)brauerei
microbrewing equipment *103* Geräte für Klein(st)brauereien
microwave oven *96T* Mikrowellenherd
mid-day *72T* Mittag
middleman *32* Zwischenhändler
mileage *75* *(Mietwagen:)* (enthaltene) Kilometer
milestone *42* Meilenstein
to **milk** *39T* melken
milking machine *39T* Melkmaschine
to **mind: I don't ~.** *8T* Ich habe nichts dagegen.
mind, to **have sth in ~** *62T* etw im Sinn haben, an etw denken; to **keep sth in ~** *77T* etw nicht vergessen
minerals *pl 33* Mineralien
minimum *52* Tiefstwert, Tiefstand; **~ order quantity** *92* Mindestbestellmenge
minutes *pl 54* Protokoll
to **miss sth** *19* etw übersehen
missing, to **be ~** *20* fehlen
to **misunderstand sth** *96T* etw missverstehen, etw falsch verstehen
misunderstanding *96* Missverständnis
mixed up *128* durcheinander
mixture *122T* Mischung
mix-up *118T* Durcheinander, Verwechslung
mobile *20* Handy, Mobiltelefon; *129* mobil
mobility *123* Freizügigkeit
mode of transport *80* Beförderungsart, Verkehrsmittel
model, role ~ *126* Vorbild
modesty *71* Bescheidenheit
modular *68* modular, in Modulbauweise
money, sum of ~ *15* Geldbetrag; **value for ~** *77T* (preis)günstig
to **monitor** *16* überwachen
monitoring *23* Überwachung
morning break *8T* Frühstückspause

mortar, bricks and ~ outlet 46T stationäres Geschäft
most, to **make the ~ of sth** 32 etw ausnutzen, möglichst viel aus etw herausschlagen
motivated 128 motiviert
motor racing 24 Autorennen
motorway *BE* 42 Autobahn
mould 117 Form, Gussform, Pressform
mounting screw 114 Befestigungsschraube
MRI scanner 15 Kernspintomograph
multi-modal 103 multimodal
multiple 49 mehrere; 68 mehrfach

N

name: ~ plate 35T Typenschild, Namensschild; **~ tag** 55T Namensschild
national: N~ Health Service *BE* 15 *Nationaler Gesundheitsdienst in Großbritannien;* **~ holiday** 10T gesetzlicher Feiertag
native speaker 129 Muttersprachler/in
nature: ~ (of sth) 46T Wesen (einer Sache); **~ reserve** 74 Naturschutzgebiet
nearby 42 in der Nähe, nahegelegen
neat and tidy 15T sauber und ordentlich
necessity 23 Notwendigkeit
needs *pl*, to **meet sb's ~** 126 jds Bedürfnissen entsprechen, jds Anforderungen erfüllen
negotiable 103 begebbar
to **negotiate** 19 verhandeln, (etw) aushandeln
negotiating bank 105 negoziierende Bank
negotiation 54 Verhandlung
negotiator 61 Verhandler/in
neighbourhood 111T Nachbarschaft
neighbouring 66T benachbart
net 91T netto
Netherlands 81T Niederlande
network 15 Netz, Netzwerk
New Zealand 81 Neuseeland, neuseeländisch
niche 50 Nische
noise emission 91T Schallemission, Lärmbelastung
noise level 91 Geräuschpegel, Lärmpegel
noise protection 91 Schallschutz, Lärmschutz
noisy 15T laut
non-competing 49 nicht miteinander konkurrierend
non-negotiable 103 nicht begebbar
norm 18 Norm
not at all 38 überhaupt nicht, gar nicht
note, consignment ~ 82 Frachtbrief; **credit ~** 118 Gutschrift; **sticky ~s** *pl* 67 Haftnotizen
to **note: ~ sth** 78 etw zur Kenntnis nehmen; **Please ~:** 70 Bitte beachten Sie:
nothing, next to ~ 35T fast nichts, so gut wie nichts
to **notice** 57 bemerken
notice, at short ~ 41 kurzfristig
to **notify sb** 105 jdn in Kenntnis setzen, jdn benachrichtigen
now, every ~ and then 113T ab und an
number, file ~ 105 Aktenzeichen; **order ~** 113T Bestellnummer, Auftragsnummer; **reference ~** 125 Aktenzeichen, Kennziffer
nut 34 Mutter, Schraubenmutter; **hexagonal ~** 35 Sechskantmutter
nutshell, in a ~ 126T kurz gesagt, mit einem Wort

O

objective, business ~ 43 Unternehmensziel
obligation 10 Pflicht, Verpflichtung; to **perform an ~** 99 eine Verpflichtung erfüllen
obligatory 23 obligatorisch, zwingend vorgeschrieben
to **observe** 34 beobachten
to **obtain sth** 18 etw erhalten, sich etw verschaffen
obviously 43 natürlich
to **occur** 87 *(Problem usw.:)* auftreten; **~ to sb** 127T jdm einfallen
ocean 51T Ozean, Weltmeer
off (work) 10T frei; to **take time ~ (work)** 10T sich frei nehmen
offer, firm ~ 69 verbindliches Angebot; **job ~** 8T Stellenangebot; **official ~** 79T offizielles Angebot; **qualification ~** 110 Fortbildungsmaßnahme; **special ~** 42T Sonderangebot
office, head ~ 42 Zentrale, Hauptsitz; **open-plan ~** 8 Großraumbüro; **~ management assistant** 12T Bürokaufmann/-frau, Kaufmann/-frau für Büromanagement; **~ supplies** *pl* 86 Bürobedarf
official 8T offiziell; **~ offer** 79T offizielles Angebot
often, every so ~ 113T hin und wieder
oil refinery 33 Ölraffinerie
old-fashioned 46T altmodisch
to **omit: ~ sth** 96 etw weglassen; **~ to do sth** 118 es versäumen, etw zu tun
one: ~-to-one 110 Einzel-; **~ at a time** 35T eins nach dem anderen; **~ way or another** 106T so oder so; **~-size-fits-all** 45 Einheits-, Standard-, 08/15-
open: ~ account 77T offenes Zahlungsziel; **~ day** 8T Tag der Offenen Tür; **~-plan office** 8 Großraumbüro
opening 42T Eröffnung
openness 66T Offenheit
to **operate** 15 arbeiten, funktionieren; 24 geschäftlich tätig sein; **~ sth** 17T etw bedienen
operating theatre 31T Operationssaal
operation 42 Betrieb; **daily ~s** *pl* 19 Tagesgeschäft
operational 110 Betriebs-, Arbeits-
operator, machine ~ 36 Maschinenführer/in
opinion, in my ~ 8 meiner Meinung nach
opportunity 86 Gelegenheit, Möglichkeit; **job ~ies** *pl* 123 Arbeitsmöglichkeiten
opposite 27 gegenüber
optimization 47 Optimierung
to **optimize** 29 optimieren
option 44 Möglichkeit
order, with ~ 90 bei Auftragserteilung; **in good ~ and condition** 103 in einwandfreiem Zustand; to **acknowledge an ~** 100 einen Auftrag bestätigen; to **be in ~** 83 in Ordnung sein; to **fulfil an ~** 120 einen Auftrag abwickeln, eine Bestellung ausführen; to **place an ~** 72T einen Auftrag erteilen, eine Bestellung aufgeben; **bulk ~** 96T Großauftrag, Großbestellung; **initial ~** 61P Erstauftrag; **mail ~** 24 Versandhandel; **purchase ~** 43 Auftrag, Bestellung; **reverse ~** 128 umgekehrte Reihenfolge; **trial ~** 85 Probebestellung; **order, receipt of ~** 81T Auftragseingang: **cash with ~ (CWO)** 61P Vorkasse; **confirmation of ~** 100 Auftragsbestätigung; **minimum ~ quantity** 92 Mindestbestellmenge; **~ book** 35T Auftragsbuch; **~ confirmation** 132 Auftragsbestätigung; **~ form** 96 Bestellformular; **~ number** 113T Bestellnummer, Auftragsnummer; **~ situation** 56 Auftragslage
organic cotton 46 Bio-Baumwolle
organization chart 16 Organigramm
origin, certificate of ~ 103 Ursprungszeugnis; **country of ~** 77 Ursprungsland
otherwise, unless ~ stated 99 sofern nicht anders angegeben; to **prove ~** 115 das Gegenteil beweisen

outcome 59 Ergebnis, Resultat, Auswirkung(en)
outdated 15 veraltet
outlet, bricks and mortar ~ 46T stationäres Geschäft; retail ~ 33 Verkaufsstelle, Einzelhandelsgeschäft
to outline 46T skizzieren, darstellen
outpatient clinic 85 Ambulanz
output 34 Produktion
oven 38 Ofen; curing ~ 28 Einbrennofen; microwave ~ 96T Mikrowellenherd
overall 19 Gesamt-; ~ score 31 Gesamtpunktzahl
to overburden sb/sth 36 jdn/etw überlasten
to overcharge sb 117 jdm zu viel berechnen
to overcome sth 24 etw bewältigen, etw überwinden
overhead 34 hoch (oben)
to overload 29 überladen; 34 überlasten
overload 36 Überlastung
overproduction 36 Überproduktion
overseas 42 im Ausland, in Übersee; ~ transactions *pl* 23 Auslandsgeschäft
to oversee sth 19T etw überwachen, etw beaufsichtigen
overtime 8 Überstunden
overview 26T Überblick, Übersicht
to owe: ~ sb sth 118 jdm etw schulden; sum owing 118 Forderung
to own: privately-owned 42 in Privatbesitz
own, on one's ~ 122T alleine
ownership 83 Eigentum, Eigentumsrecht

P

to pack 34 verpacken
pack 70 Paket
package 77T Paket
packaging 85 Verpackung
packing 34 Verpackung; ~ charge 60 Verpackungskosten; ~ list 103 Packliste
pace, work ~ 110 Arbeitstempo
to paddle 51T paddeln
paint 34 Lack, Farbe
to paint 34 lackieren, bemalen
paint shop 34 Lackiererei
pale 51 blass, hell
pallet, Euro-~ 61P Euro-Palette
palletized 100 auf Paletten, palettiert
panel 69 Platte, Tafel; 127T Gremium; infill ~ 69 Ausfachung, Füllung
panel, wall ~ 68 Wandplatte
paperwork 58 Unterlagen
parcel 132 Paket
parent company 28 Muttergesellschaft
part, on our ~ 115T auf/von unserer Seite; to look the ~ 9 entsprechend (rollengerecht) aussehen; spare ~ 26 Ersatzteil
partial 110 teilweise; ~ shipment 105 Teillieferung
participant 8 Teilnehmer/in
particular 39T bestimmt, speziell; in ~ 28T insbesondere; 126T ausgerechnet, gerade
particularly 131 insbesondere; Not ~. 127T Eigentlich nicht.
partition 15T Trennwand
partner, business ~ 24 Geschäftspartner/in; trading ~ 72 Handelspartner/in
part-time 11 Teilzeit
party 49 Partei
to pass: ~ sth on 20 etw weiterleiten; ~ through sth 36 etw durchlaufen; ~ to sb 81 auf jdn übergehen
past sth 66T an etw vorbei
pasteurization plant 33 Pasteurisationsanlage
patience 71 Geduld
pay 13 Bezahlung, Gehalt
payable 104 zahlbar
paying bank 105 ausführende Bank
payload 101 Zuladung, Nutzlast
payment 18 Zahlung; terms *pl* of ~ 61P Zahlungsbedingungen
peak 52 Höchstwert, Höchststand
to peak 52 einen Höchstwert/-stand erreichen
penetration 48 *(Markt:)* Eindringen, Durchdringung
pension scheme 23 Altersversorgung
per unit 72T pro Stück
to perceive 48 wahrnehmen
percentage 28 Anteil, Prozentsatz
to perform an obligation 99 eine Verpflichtung erfüllen
to perform sth 73 etw aufführen
performance 18 Leistung; ~ (of a contract) 99 Erfüllung, Durchführung (eines Vertrags)
perfume 48 Parfüm
period, delivery ~ 59T Lieferzeit; warranty ~ 115 Gewährleistungszeit
permission 36 Erlaubnis, Genehmigung
permitted 105 erlaubt, gestattet
personable 130 umgänglich, sympathisch
personal, to put your ~ mark on sth 15T einer Sache seinen persönlichen Stempel aufdrücken; ~ wealth 24 Privatvermögen
personality 15T Persönlichkeit
personnel 12 Personal, Mitabeiter/innen; ~ file 12 Personalakte
petition 9 Petition, Eingabe
pharmaceutical 48 pharmazeutisch, Pharma-
photocopy 14 Fotokopie
physical 36 physisch
to pick 49 *(Obst)* pflücken; ~ sth up 75 etw abholen
pie chart 52 Tortendiagramm
piece, three-~ 78 dreiteilig
pile 126 Stapel, Haufen
pillow 75T Kopfkissen
to pin sth to sth 123 etw an etw heften
pine 47 Kiefer
pipeline 31T Leitung, Rohrleitung
pity, That's a ~. 62T Das ist schade.
to place: ~ an ad 65T eine Anzeige schalten; ~ an order 72T einen Auftrag erteilen, eine Bestellung aufgeben
place, to take ~ 33 stattfinden; meeting ~ 13 Treffpunkt; ~ of birth 12 Geburtsort; ~ of destination 80 Bestimmungsort
placement, work ~ *BE* 14 Praktikum
plan, change of ~ 40 Planänderung
plant 18 Werk, Fabrik; pasteurization ~ 33 Pasteurisationsanlage; processing ~ 33 Verarbeitungsbetrieb, Aufbereitungsanlage
to plant sth 24 etw pflanzen
plastic sheeting 61P Plastikfolie, Plastikplane
plastics *pl* 31T Kunststoff(e)
plate 71 Teller; name ~ 35T Typenschild, Namensschild
pleasant 69 angenehm, nett
pleased, to be ~ to do sth 10T etw gern tun; sich freuen, etw zu tun
pleasure 56T Vergnügen; My ~. 94 Ganz meinerseits! Gern geschehen!; With ~. 95T Aber gerne!
point, break-even ~ 48 Gewinnschwelle; finishing ~ 26 Endpunkt; starting ~ 26 Ausgangspunkt; ~ of contact 43 Ansprechpartner, Anlaufstelle; ~ of sale 49 Verkaufsstelle; ~ of view 9 Sicht, Perspektive
to point: ~ at sth 9 auf etw zeigen, auf etw deuten; ~ to sth 29 auf etw deuten, auf etw zeigen; ~ out 115T darauf hinweisen(, dass ...); 89 auf etw hinweisen, auf etw aufmerksam machen
policy 32 Politik, Vorgehen, Grundsätze; ~ (on sth) 113 Richtlinien (für etw); insurance ~ 105 Versicherungspolice
polite(ly) 27 höflich
politics 13 Politik

pollution 51T Verschmutzung
pool, indoor ~ 74 Hallenbad
porcelain 117 Porzellan
port of shipment 80 Verschiffungshafen
portable 115T tragbar
portfolio 11 Arbeitsmappe
possession, to take ~ of sth 82 etw in Besitz nehmen
post 68 Säule, Pfosten; 126T Posten, Stelle
to post sb to ... 126T jdn nach ... versetzen
post-carriage 80 Nachlauf
to postpone 56 (nach hinten) verschieben
potassium 39T Kalium; ~ level 39T Kaliumgehalt
potential 17 möglich, potenziell; 35T Potenzial
pottery 117 Keramik, Töpferei
pound 101 Pfund *(ca. 454 g)*
powder, washing ~ 49 Waschpulver
power, computing ~ 38 Rechenleistung
to power 37 antreiben, mit Energie versorgen
practical 11 praktisch, Praxis-
practice, standard ~ 9 übliches Vorgehen, übliche Praxis
pre-carriage 80 Vorlauf
to predict 45 vorhersagen
premises *pl* 42T Räumlichkeiten, Firmengelände
premium 48 Premium-, Hochpreis-
prepaid 105 im Voraus bezahlt
prepared, to be ~ to do sth 46T bereit sein, etw zu tun
to present sb sth 104 jdm etw *(Dokument usw.)* vorlegen
presentation 104 Vorlage *(eines Dokuments)*; on ~ of sth 90 bei Vorlage von etw
presenter 30 Redner/in, Vortragende/r, Moderator/in
press 16 Presse
to prevent sb/sth from doing sth 35T jdn/etw daran hindern, etw zu tun; verhindern, dass jd/etw etw tut
price, basic ~ 91T Grundpreis; labour ~ 70P Lohnkosten; purchase ~ 99 Kaufpreis; recommended retail ~ (RRP) 46T unverbindliche Preisempfehlung (UVP); retail ~ 32 Einzelhandelspreis, Endverkaufspreis; total ~ 96T Gesamtpreis; unit ~ 94 Stückpreis; to quote a ~ 89 einen Preis angeben/nennen; to raise ~s 48 die Preise anheben; ~ tag 32 Preisschild, Preisetikett
priced, low-~ 59 preisgünstig
pricing 16 Kalkulation, Preisgestaltung, Preise; ~ strategy 48 Preisstrategie
principle 15 Grundsatz, Prinzip
prior to sth 99 vor etw
priority 51 Anliegen, Priorität; 61P Vorrang
private limited company (Ltd) 24 Gesellschaft mit beschränkter Haftung (GmbH)
privately-owned 42 in Privatbesitz
privilege 44 Vergünstigung
prize draw 44 Verlosung
procedure 14 Verfahren, Vorgehen
process 19 Verfahren, Prozess
to process sth 38 etw verarbeiten, etw bearbeiten
processing 33 Verarbeitung, Aufbereitung; ~ plant 33 Verarbeitungsbetrieb, Aufbereitungsanlage
procurement 8T Beschaffung
producer 78 Produzent/in, Hersteller/in
product, array of ~s 86 Produktangebot; finished ~ 34 Endprodukt; medical ~s *pl* 31T Medizinprodukte; ~ brief 46 Produktbeschreibung; ~ launch 48 Produkteinführung; ~ line 46 Produktlinie; ~ range 46 Sortiment
production, mass ~ 37 Massenfertigung; ~ costs *pl* 48 Herstellungskosten; ~ hall 26T Fertigungshalle, Produktionshalle; ~ line 28 Fertigungslinie, Produktionslinie; ~ manager 19 Produktionsleiter/in; ~ site 49 Produktionsstätte
productivity 10 Produktivität
profession 7 Beruf
professional 126 professionell; highly-~ 42 hochprofessionell
profile, job ~ 18 Stellenprofil
profit 24 Gewinn, Profit; to make a ~ 32 einen Gewinn erzielen; to realize a ~ 43 einen Gewinn erzielen; ~ margin 17T Gewinspanne
programme 7 Programm; 51T (TV-, Radio-)Sendung
to programme *BE* 38 programmieren
progress 51T Fortkommen, Fahrt; work in ~ 35 unfertige Erzeugnisse
to progress 127P vorankommen
project 19 Projekt; ~ management 16 Projektleitung; ~ manager 19 Projektleiter/in
projector, data ~ 55T Beamer
to promote: ~ sb 18 jdn befördern; ~ sth 46T für etw werben, etw promoten
promotion 46T Werbung, Promotion; 125 Beförderung, Aufstieg
promotional 65T Werbe-
prompt 60 Stichwort; ~ card 29 Moderationskarte
promptly 99 umgehend, unverzüglich, sofort
proposal 79 Vorschlag; initial ~ 79 Erstvorschlag
proposition, unique selling ~ (USP) 46 Alleinstellungsmerkmal
pros and cons *pl* 11 Argumente dafür und dagegen, Vor- und Nachteile
prospective 43 potenziell
prospects *pl*, career ~ 123 berufliche Perspektiven; future ~ 127T Zukunftsperspektiven; job ~ 8 berufliche Perspektiven
protection, data ~ 128 Datenschutz
protector, ear ~s *pl* 91T Gehörschutz
to prove: ~ sth 86 sich als etw erweisen; 103 etw nachweisen; ~ otherwise 115 das Gegenteil beweisen
provider 48 Anbieter
psychological 15 psychologisch
public 25 Öffentlichkeit; ~ limited company (plc) 24 Aktiengesellschaft (AG)
to publish 45 veröffentlichen
to pull 35 ziehen
pull system 35T Pull-System
pump 133 Pumpe
punctual(ly) 56T pünktlich
punctuality 72 Pünktlichkeit
to purchase 43 kaufen
purchase 42 Kauf; ~ order 43 Auftrag, Bestellung; ~ price 99 Kaufpreis
purchasing 16 Einkauf; ~ director 41 Einkaufsleiter/in; ~ history 45 Kaufhistorie, Einkaufsverhalten; ~ manager 55 Einkaufsleiter/in
purpose 15T Zweck; general ~ 101 Allzweck-
to push 35T schieben, stoßen
push system 35T Push-System
to put 17T formulieren, sagen; ~ sb through 20T *(Telefon:)* jdn durchstellen; ~ sth at risk 77T etw gefährden; ~ sth to good use 127T etw sinnvoll nutzen; to ~ it simply 17T vereinfacht gesagt

Q

qualification 11 Abschluss, Qualifikation; school ~ 6 Schulabschluss; ~ offer 110 Fortbildungsmaßnahme
to qualify 6 einen/den Abschluss machen; ~ for sth 118 zu etw berechtigen, für etw infrage kommen
quality: ~ assurance 18 Qualitätssicherung; ~ management 16 Qualitäts-

sicherung; **~-assured experts** *pl* *110* qualifiziertes Fachpersonal
quantity *34* Menge, Anzahl; **minimum order ~** *92* Mindestbestellmenge; **~ discount** *35* Mengenrabatt
quarter *53T* Quartal
quarterly *53* vierteljährlich, Quartals-; **~ settlement** *101T* vierteljährliche Abrechnung; **~ statement** *117* Quartalsabrechnung
query *118* Frage, Rückfrage
to **query sth** *118* etw infrage stellen, etw anzweifeln
questionnaire *8T* Fragebogen
queue *51T* Warteschlange
quotation *78* Preisangebot, Angebot, Offerte
quote *94* (Preis-)Angebot
to **quote a price** *89* einen Preis angeben/nennen

R

rabbit *24* Kaninchen
racing, motor ~ *24* Autorennen
rack, literature ~ *68T* Prospektständer
radical *35T* radikal
radio frequency *39T* Funkfrequenz, Radiofrequenz
rail *33* Schiene; **by ~** *81T* mit der Bahn
to **raise: ~ sth** *39T* etw erhöhen, etw steigern; **~ prices** *48* die Preise anheben
range *60* Bereich, Spielraum; *74* Auswahl, Angebot; *76* Sortiment; **product ~** *46* Sortiment; **wide ~** *26T* großes Angebot, breite Palette
to **range: ~ from ... to ...** *42* von ... bis ... reichen; **~ing from ... to ...** *43* von ... bis ...
to **rank** *77* einstufen, (in einer Rangliste) bewerten; **~ higher** *47* eine höhere Position einnehmen
ranking *77* Einstufung, Bewertung
ransom *15* Lösegeld
rapidly, to **expand ~** *59* schnell wachsen
rarely *43* selten
rate, conversion ~ *47* Umwandlungsquote; **freight ~** *91T* Frachtsatz, Frachtrate; **response ~** *65T* Rücklaufquote; **shipping ~** *93* Frachtsatz, Versandkosten
rating *64* Bewertung
raw materials *pl* *32* Rohstoffe, Rohmaterialien
to **reach** *31T* herankommen, heranreichen
to **react** *45* reagieren
to **realize: ~ sth** *51* sich über etw im Klaren sein, etw wissen; **~ a profit** *43* einen Gewinn erzielen; **I ~ that.** *121* Das ist mir bewusst.
to **rearrange sth** *62* etw *(Termin usw.)* verschieben
reason, to **give ~s for sth** *8* etw begründen
reasonable *48* vernünftig, angemessen
to **reassure sb** *87* jdn beruhigen
rebate *121P* Rabatt, Nachlass
to **recalculate** *96T* neu berechnen
receipt *18* Beleg, Quittung; **~ of invoice** *102* Rechnungseingang; **~ of order** *81T* Auftragseingang
received, to **be well ~** *86* (großen) Zuspruch finden
reception *9* Empfang, Rezeption
receptionist *9* Empfangsmitarbeiter/in
recognized *7* anerkannt
recommendation *45* Empfehlung
recommended retail price (RRP) *46T* unverbindliche Preisempfehlung (UVP)
record *24* Schallplatte; *113T* Aufzeichnung, Protokoll; *121* Datensatz
recording *19* Aufzeichnung, Aufnahme; **~ studio** *25* Tonstudio
records *pl* *118* Unterlagen, Aufzeichnungen
to **recover** *53T* sich erholen
to **recruit** *18* *(Personal)* einstellen
recruitment *23* Einstellung, Anwerbung *(von Personal)*; **~ agency** *124* Personalvermittlung
to **rectify defects** *115* Mängel beheben
recycling centre *51T* Wertstoffhof
to **re-direct** *15* umleiten
reduction *59T* Nachlass, Preissenkung, Reduzierung
redundancy *23* (betriebsbedingte) Kündigung
ref. *54* Unser Zeichen
to **refer to sth** *81* auf etw zurückgreifen, etw zu Hilfe nehmen; *89* auf etw Bezug nehmen, sich auf etw beziehen
referee *128* Referenz(geber)
reference *77T* Referenz; **~ to sth** *91* Verweis auf etw, Bezug auf etw; **with ~ to** *69* mit Bezug auf, bezugnehmend auf; **~ initials** *pl* *84* *(Brief:)* Zeichen; **~ number** *125* Aktenzeichen, Kennziffer
to **refill** *35* nachfüllen
refinery, oil ~ *33* Ölraffinerie
refining *33* Raffinieren
to **reflect on sth** *38* über etw nachdenken
to **refresh** *52* auffrischen
refreshment *13* Erfrischung
refundable, tax-~ *110* steuerlich absetzbar
to **refuse** *9* sich weigern
regard, Best ~s/R~s *41* *(Brief:)* Viele Grüße, Mit freundlichen Grüßen
to **regard: as ~s** *35* was ... betrifft, in puncto
regarding *15* betreffend
to **register: ~ sth** *39T* etw registrieren; *113* etw melden, etw zum Ausdruck bringen; **~ sth with sth** *65T* etw bei etw anmelden
registration *64* Anmeldung
regulations *pl* *77* Vorschriften; **customs ~** *19* Zollvorschriften; **safety ~** *23* Sicherheitsvorschriften
to **reimburse sb** *113* jdm Geld zurückzahlen, jdn entschädigen
reimbursement *113* Rückerstattung
to **reject sth** *72* etw ablehnen, etw abweisen; *99* etw zurückweisen, etw beanstanden
to **relate: ~ to sth** *112* sich auf etw beziehen; **~ sth to sth** *127T* etw auf etw beziehen
related *49* verwandt, ähnlich
relationship *45* Beziehung
relaxation, comfort and ~ *110* angenehme Atmosphäre
release, block ~ *6* Blockunterricht *(an der Berufsschule)*
to **release sth** *106T* etw freigeben
relevant (to sth) *47* wichtig (für etw), relevant (für etw)
reliability *77* Zuverlässigkeit
reliable *83* zuverlässig
to **remain constant** *52* gleich bleiben
remainder *79T* Rest
remaining *10T* übrige/r/s
to **remind sb (of sth)** *55T* jdn (an etw) erinnern
reminder function *126T* Erinnerungsfunktion
to **remit** *118* *(Geld)* überweisen
remote diagnosis *79T* Ferndiagnose
remotely *79T* aus der Ferne
rent *6* Miete
to **rent** *66* mieten
rental, store ~ *43* Ladenmiete; **~ fee** *66T* Miete
to **re-organize** *35* neu ordnen, umorganisieren
rep *27* Vertreter/in; **sales ~** *42T* (Handels-)Vertreter/in
to **replace sth** *114* etw ersetzen
replacement *113T* Ersatz
to **reply (to sth)** *40* (auf etw) antworten, (etw) beantworten
reply (to sth) *40* Antwort (auf etw)

to **report: ~ to sb** 17 jdm unterstehen; **~ sth to sb** 17T jdm etw melden; **~ back** 44 Bericht erstatten
report, financial ~ 18 Finanzbericht
to **represent** 43 vertreten, repräsentieren; 46T darstellen
representative 27 Vertreter/in; **sales ~** 42T (Handels-)Vertreter/in
reputation 77 Ruf
request 15 Anfrage; 35T Anforderung; **~ (for sth)** 40 Bitte (um etw); **on ~** 70 auf Anfrage
to **request: ~ sth** 35T etw anfordern; 64 um etw bitten; **as ~ed** 89 wie gewünscht
requirements *pl* 68 Anforderungen, Bedürfnisse, Wünsche; to **fulfil ~** 23 Anforderungen erfüllen; to **meet ~** 79 Anforderungen erfüllen
to **reroute sth** 106T etw umleiten
to **reschedule sth** 62T etw *(Termin usw.)* verschieben
research, to **do ~ into sth** 71 etw recherchieren, Recherchen über etw anstellen; **R~ & Development (R & D)** 16 Forschung und Entwicklung; **field ~** 45 Feldforschung; **market ~** 23 Marktforschung
to **research sth** 25 etw recherchieren
reservation 75T Reservierung
to **reserve** 55T reservieren
reserve, nature ~ 74 Naturschutzgebiet
to **resolve sth** 113T etw lösen
resource, Human R~es (HR) 12 Personal(abteilung)
to **respect** 71 respektieren, achten
to **respond to sth** 9 auf etw reagieren
response 13 Antwort, Reaktion; **~ rate** 65T Rücklaufquote
responsibility 17T Aufgabe, Zuständigkeit, Verantwortlichkeit; 51 Verantwortung; to **assume ~** 99 die Verantwortung übernehmen; to **take ~** 19 Verantwortung übernehmen
responsible, socially-~ 46 sozial verantwortlich
to **re-submit sth** 96T etw *(Bestellung)* erneut aufgeben
to **result in sth** 15T zu etw führen, etw ergeben
retail 42 Einzelhandel; **~ outlet** 33 Verkaufsstelle, Einzelhandelsgeschäft; **~ outlet** 50 Einzelhandelsgeschäft; **~ price** 32 EInzelhandelspreis, Endverkaufspreis; **recommended ~ price (RRP)** 46T unverbindliche Preisempfehlung (UVP)
to **retail at £14** 32 (im Einzelhandel) für £14 verkauft werden
retailer 8T Einzelhändler/in
to **retrain** 35T umschulen
to **retrofit sth** 91T etw nachrüsten
return 60 Retoure; **~ on investment** 110 Rendite, Ertrag
to **return: ~ a call** 22T zurückrufen; **~ costs** 110 Kosten erstatten
reusable 67 wiederverwendbar
revenue 23 Einkünfte, Einnahmen
reverse order 128 umgekehrte Reihenfolge
review 64 Rezension, Kritik
to **review sth** 32 etw überprüfen, etw überdenken
to **rework sth** 36 etw überarbeiten, etw nachbessern
to **re-write sth** 97 etw neu schreiben
rice bowl 61P Reisschale
ridiculous 9 lächerlich, albern, absurd
rights *pl*, **human ~** 77 Menschenrechte; **setoff ~** 105 Aufrechnungsrechte
rise 52 Anstieg
to **rise** 52 steigen, ansteigen, zunehmen
risk, to **put sth at ~** 77T etw gefährden
road construction 83 Straßenbau
robot 37 Roboter
robotics 24 Robotertechnik
role model 126 Vorbild
to **role-play** 11 mit verteilten Rollen spielen
roll 89 Rolle
roof 68T Dach
room, conference ~ 26T Besprechungsraum, Sitzungssaal; **dining ~** 75T *(Hotel:)* Speisesaal; **meeting ~** 75 Sitzungszimmer, Konferenzraum
root cause 34 Grundursache
rosy 35T rosig
to **rot** 26T verfaulen, verrotten
rotten, to **go ~** 78 verfaulen
rough handling 133 unsanfte Behandlung
route 24 Strecke
row 68T Reihe; **in a ~** 58P nacheinander; **~ stand** 66T Reihenstand
rude 71 unhöflich
rule, to **break a ~** 9 eine Regel brechen, eine Vorschrift missachten
to **run sth** 17 etw leiten

S

safety 114 Sicherheit; **health and ~** 77 Arbeitsschutz; **~ regulations** *pl* 23 Sicherheitsvorschriften
to **sail for ...** 106T nach ... fahren
salary 6 Gehalt
sale, contract of ~ 98 Kaufvertrag; **clearance ~** 117 Ausverkauf; **point of ~** 49 Verkaufsstelle
sales, volume of ~ 53T Umsatzvolumen; **~ channel** 46T Absatzweg, Vertriebskanal; **~ director** 90 Vertriebsleiter/in; **~ figures** *pl* 17T Umsatzzahlen, Verkaufszahlen; **~ literature** 67 Verkaufsprospekte, Informationsmaterial; **~ material** 79 Werbematerial, Verkaufsunterlagen; **~ rep(resentative)** 42T (Handels-)Vertreter/in
saleswoman/-man 61P Verkäufer/in
salutation 41 *(Brief:)* Anrede
sample 68T Probe, Muster, Probepackung
satisfaction, customer ~ 45 Kundenzufriedenheit
satisfactory 113 zufriedenstellend, befriedigend
satisfied 50 zufrieden
saucer 55T Untertasse
to **save sth on sth** 35T etw bei etw einsparen
savings *pl*, **time ~** 110 Zeitersparnis
savoury 70 herzhaft
saying 77T Sprichwort
to **scan** 39T erfassen, scannen
scanner, MRI ~ 15 Kernspintomograph
scenario, worst-case ~ 59 schlimmster anzunehmender Fall
schedule 17T Zeitplan; **on ~** 17T planmäßig, termingerecht; **work ~** 110 Arbeitsablauf
to **schedule** 56 *(Termin)* ansetzen
scheme, to **enter a ~** 7 an einem Programm teilnehmen; **pension ~** 23 Altersversorgung; **shell ~ stand** 68 Systemstand
school, vocational ~ 6 Berufsschule; **~ leaving certificate** 125 Schulabschluss; **~ qualification** 6 Schulabschluss
score 61P Punkte; **overall ~** 31 Gesamtpunktzahl; **~ sheet** 61P Punktzettel
scratch 133 Kratzer
scratched 120T verkratzt
screw 34 Schraube; **mounting ~** 114 Befestigungsschraube
script 64 Manuskript, Drehbuch
sea: ~ freight 91T Seefracht; **~ transport** 93 Seetransport
seafood 81 Meeresfrüchte
seam covering 28 Falzabdeckung, Bördeln
search: ~ engine 46T Suchmaschine; **~ result** 47 Suchergebnis
seasonal 35 jahreszeitlich, saisonal
seat, to **take a ~** 59T Platz nehmen
seating 68T Sitzgelegenheiten
seaworthy 79T seetüchtig

second to last 10T zweitletzte/r/s
section 6 Bereich, Abschnitt; 23 Abteilung; 34 Sparte
sector 79T Branche; 123 Bereich, Sektor
secure 75T sicher, bewacht
to **see: ~ to sth** 42T sich um etw kümmern; **~ sth through** 26T etw *(Projekt)* durchgehend betreuen; **~ below** 132 siehe unten
to **seek sth** 110 etw suchen
selection 42T Auswahl
self-assessment 123 Selbsteinstufung
seller 80 Verkäufer/in
selling proposition, unique ~ (USP) 46 Alleinstellungsmerkmal
semi-closed 69 halbgeschlossen
sense 51 Sinn; to **make ~** 22T sinnvoll sein; 68T einleuchten; **~ of community** 15T Gemeinschaftssinn
sensitive information 15 vertrauliche Informationen
separate(ly) 21 einzeln; 39T eigenständig; 46T separat, eigens
seriously, to **take sth ~** 26T etw ernst nehmen
to **serve** 74 servieren; **~ a market** 31T einen Markt bedienen
service, financial ~s *pl* 24 Finanzdienstleistungen; **train ~** 25 Zugbetrieb
to **service sth** 91T etw warten
session 110 Unterrichtseinheit
set 128 vorgegeben, starr, fest; **full ~** 105 vollständiger Satz *(von Dokumenten)*
to **set: ~ up** 15T einrichten, aufbauen; 24 *(Unternehmen usw.)* gründen; 62 *(Termin usw.)* vereinbaren; **~ forth** 105 darlegen
setoff rights *pl* 105 Aufrechnungsrechte
settlement, quarterly ~ 101T vierteljährliche Abrechnung
set-up 15T Anordnung, Einrichtung, System
sewing machine 102 Nähmaschine
sexual 77 sexuell
shabby 111T heruntergekommen, schäbig
to **shake hands with sb** 127T jdm die Hand geben
shape 38 Form, Gestalt
shaped, box-~ 68 kastenförmig
share 24 Aktie; **market ~** 28 Marktanteil; **global market ~** 28T Weltmarktanteil
shared container, in ~ 94 in Sammelcontainer, als Beiladung
shareholder 24 Aktionär/in
sheet, fact ~ 32 Informationsblatt, Datenblatt; **score ~** 61P Punktzettel
sheeting, plastic ~ 61P Plastikfolie, Plastikplane
shelf, shelves 36 Regal, Regale
shell scheme stand 68 Systemstand
shift 110 Schicht; **early ~** 58P Frühschicht; **~ work** 8 Schichtarbeit
to **ship** 18 versenden, verschicken
shipment 17 Sendung; 36 Versand; **partial ~** 105 Teillieferung; **port of ~** 80 Verschiffungshafen
shipping 77 Versand; **~ agent** 92 Spediteur; **~ company** 79T Reederei; **~ documents** *pl* 18 Transportpapiere, Versanddokumente; **~ rate** 93 Frachtsatz, Versandkosten
shock 32 Schock
shop, paint ~ 34 Lackiererei
shopper 33 (Laden-)Kunde/Kundin
shortage 48 Knappheit, Mangel
shortlisted, to **be ~** 126 in die engere Auswahl kommen
short-term 24 kurzfristig
shoulder 71 Schulter
show, trade ~ 67 Fachmesse
to **show sb around** 26 jdn herumführen
showroom 26 Ausstellungsraum, Verkaufsraum; **car ~** 33 Autohaus
to **shrink** 35T schrumpfen, verkleinern
shuttle 74 Zubringer
shy 127T schüchtern
sight, (at) ~ 105 (bei) Vorlage; **at first ~** 39T auf den ersten Blick
to **sign** 55T unterzeichnen
sign: ~ (of sth) 104 Anzeichen (von etw); **currency ~** 102 Währungssymbol
signage, digital ~ 45 digitale Außenwerbung
signal strength 126T Signalstärke
signature 84 Unterschrift; **~ block** 84 Signatur
signboard 35 Schild
significant(ly) 59 deutlich
signpost 30 Wegweiser
silence 71 Schweigen, Stille
simplified 82 vereinfacht
simply, to put it ~ 17T vereinfacht gesagt
sincerely, Yours ~ 41 *(Brief:)* Mit freundlichen Grüßen
sir, Dear S~ or Madam 41 *(Brief:)* Sehr geehrte Damen und Herren,
to **sit back** 70 sich zurücklehnen
site 17T Standort, Gelände; **on ~** 28T vor Ort; **construction ~** 31T Baustelle; **production ~** 49 Produktionsstätte
situated, to **be ~** 42 sich befinden
situation, legal ~ 9 Rechtslage, Gesetzeslage; **order ~** 56 Auftragslage
size, one-~-fits-all 45 Einheits-, Standard-, 08/15-
sketch 69 Skizze
to **sketch sth out** 25 etw (vor)zeichnen
skirt 9 Rock
slave labour 48 Sklavenarbeit
slide 28 *(Präsentation:)* Folie
to **slide sth to one side** 91T etw zur Seite schieben
slight(ly) 127T geringfügig, etwas
slitter 28 Schneidemaschine, Schlitzer
smart 8 *(Kleidung:)* schick; 37 intelligent
smoke: ~ alarm 114 Rauchmelder; **~-free** 74 rauchfrei
snack 74 Imbiss
social: ~ engineering 15 soziale Manipulation; **~ media** *pl* 45 soziale Medien
socializing 128 Ausgehen
socially-responsible 46 sozial verantwortlich
sole trader 24 Einzelunternehmer/in
solution 35T Lösung
to **solve** 26T lösen
solvency 77T Zahlungsfähigkeit
to **sort sth out** 96 etw klären, etw regeln
sorted, to **get sth ~** 120T etw klären, sich um etw kümmern
source 77T Quelle; **energy ~** 38 Energiequelle
to **source sth** 42 etw *(Waren usw.)* beschaffen
sourcing 32 Beschaffung, Einkauf
spa 64 Wellnessbereich
space, ample ~ 28T genügend Platz; **division of ~** 68 Raumaufteilung; **storage ~** 43 Lagerfläche; 68T Stauraum; to **clear a ~** 15T einen Platz räumen; **~ travel** 24 Raumfahrt; **~-saving** 71 raumsparend
spacecraft 24 Raumschiff
spacious 74 geräumig
spare part 26 Ersatzteil
sparkling: ~ water 70 Sprudelwasser; **~ wine** 42 Schaumwein
speaker 38 Vortragende/r, Redner/in; **native ~** 129 Muttersprachler/in
to **speak: S~ing.** 20T *(Telefon:)* Am Apparat.; **technically ~ing** 24 genau genommen
special: ~ discount 118 Sonderrabatt; **~ offer** 42T Sonderangebot
specialist 26T Fachmann/-frau, Experte/-in, Spezialist/in; 44 Fachgeschäft; **~ company** 6 Fachbetrieb, Spezialfirma

speciality *28T* Spezialität
to **specialize in sth** *44* sich auf etw spezialisieren
specialty *64* Besonderheit
specific *31T* bestimmte/r/s, speziell; *47* genau, spezifisch
specifications *pl* *19* Technische Daten, Spezifikationen; *23* Vorgaben
to **specify sth** *105* etw (genau) angeben
spectacular *24* spektakulär
to **speed sth up** *38* etw beschleunigen
to **spell** *40* buchstabieren
spelling *30* Rechtschreibung; *120* Schreibweise
to **spin** *32* spinnen
spirits *pl* *42* Spirituosen
to **split** *7* aufteilen; *104* teilen
to **sponsor sb** *51T* jdn sponsern
sports equipment *44* Sportartikel
sportswear *44* Sportbekleidung
to **spray** *34* sprühen, spritzen, spritzlackieren
spreadsheet *123* Tabellenkalkulation, Tabelle
square: ~ foot *64* Quadratfuß *(ca. 0,09 qm)*; **~ metre** *61P* Quadratmeter
stability, financial ~ *77T* Finanzstabilität
staff, waiting ~ *70* Servierkräfte; **member of ~** *23* Mitarbeiter/in
stage *32* Phase, Abschnitt
stained *132* fleckig
stainless steel *31T* Edelstahl
stairs *pl* *26* Treppe, Treppenhaus
stamp *44* Briefmarke; *86* Marke, Stempel
stand *35* (Messe-)Stand; **corner ~** *66T* Eckstand; **display ~** *69* Präsentationsstand; **end of block ~** *66T* Kopfstand; **island ~** *66T* Blockstand, Inselstand; **row ~** *66T* Reihenstand; **shell scheme ~** *68* Systemstand
to **stand idle** *34* stillstehen, untätig sein
standard *7* Maßstab, Norm; **to a ~** *36* einer Norm entsprechend; to **be up to ~** *132* den Anforderungen entsprechen; to **meet ~s** *23* Normen erfüllen; **~ practice** *9* übliches Vorgehen, übliche Praxis
to **standardize** *34* normen, standardisieren
standardized *38* einheitlich, genormt
standardized *123* genormt
standby *8T* Bereitschaft
starting point *26* Ausgangspunkt
to **state** *40* angeben, erklären, sagen, darlegen, sagen; **unless otherwise ~ed** *99* sofern nicht anders angegeben
state-of-the-art *28T* auf dem neuesten Stand der Technik, hochmodern
statement *99* Erklärung; *117* Abrechnung; **quarterly ~** *117* Quartalsabrechnung
station *51T* Bahnhof
stationary *46* ortsgebunden, ortsfest, stationär
stationery *86* Schreibwaren
statistics *28T* Statistik(en)
statutory *115T* gesetzlich vorgeschrieben
to **stay: ~ on** *8T* bleiben, dableiben; **sth is here to ~** *38* etw hat Einzug gehalten
stealth advertising *50* heimliche Werbung, Schleichwerbung
steam *37* Dampf; **~-driven** *38* dampfgetrieben
steel *6* Stahl; **carbon ~** *31T* Kohlenstoffstahl; **stainless ~** *31T* Edelstahl
to **stick: ~ sth on** *39T* etw aufkleben; **~ sth to sth** *39T* etw an etw kleben, etw mit etw verkleben
stick, memory ~ *67* Speicherstick
sticking machine *39* Klebemaschine
sticky notes *pl* *67* Haftnotizen
stiff competition *59* harter Wettbewerb
to **stimulate sth** *86* etw beleben, etw ankurbeln
to **stock** *49* *(Ware)* führen
stock, from ~ *96T* ab Lager; **in ~** *89* vorrätig, auf Lager, lieferbar; **while ~s last** *117* solange der Vorrat reicht; **~ exchange** *24* Börse
stocked, well-~ *74* gut sortiert
stool *68T* Hocker
stop *26T* Station, Halt; **~-and-go** *35T* stockend
storage *15* Lagerung, Speicherung; **~ space** *43* Lagerfläche; *68T* Stauraum; **incorrect ~** *133* unsachgemäße Lagerung
store, department ~ *42* Kaufhaus; **furniture ~** *33* Möbelhaus; **~ rental** *43* Ladenmiete
storeroom *35* Lagerraum
straight *59T* direkt; **~ away** *35T* sogleich, sofort
strategy *45* Strategie; **marketing ~** *44* Vermarktungsstrategie; **pricing ~** *48* Preisstrategie
strength *77T* Stärke; **signal ~** *126T* Signalstärke
to **strengthen** *110* stärken
to **stress sth** *71* etw betonen
strict *8T* streng
to **structure** *7* aufbauen, strukturieren
structure *30* Aufbau, Struktur
stud *32* Niete, Knopf
studio, recording ~ *25* Tonstudio
study *45* Untersuchung, Studie
sturdy *102* stabil, robust
stylish *74* elegant, stilvoll
subject: ~ line *40* Betreffzeile; **~ matter** *110* Materie, Unterrichtsstoff
to **submit sth** *88* etw einreichen, etw abgeben
subsidiary *20* Niederlassung
to **subsidize** *8* subventionieren, bezuschussen
sub-standard *114* minderwertig
substantial *79* erheblich, beträchtlich
sub-total *95* Zwischensumme
suit *9* Anzug; Kostüm; **trouser ~** *9* Hosenanzug
to **suit: ~ sb/sth** *51* (zu) jdm/etw passen; **~ sb** *62T* jdm passen
suitable *13* geeignet, passend
sum: ~ of money *15* Geldbetrag; **~ owing** *118* Forderung
to **sum up: to ~** *10T* zusammenfassend (gesagt)
superior *72* Vorgesetzte/r
to **supervise sth** *17T* etw beaufsichtigen, etw betreuen, etw überwachen
supervision *23* Aufsicht, Kontrolle
supervisor *9* Vorgesetzte/r; **training ~** *12* Ausbildungsleiter/in
supplement *123* Zusatz, Ergänzung
supplier *8T* Zulieferer, Lieferant, Anbieter; **~'s contract** *59* Liefervertrag, Lieferantenvertrag
supplies *pl*, **medical ~** *84* Sanitätsartikel; **office ~** *86* Bürobedarf
supply chain *32* Lieferkette, Versorgungskette
to **supply: ~ sth** *19* etw liefern, etw bereitstellen; **~ sb with sth** *90* jdm etw liefern
support *9* Unterstützung; *125* Betreuung
to **support** *15T* unterstützen; *31* *(Argumentation)* untermauern; *74T* vermuten, annehmen, glauben
sure, to **make ~** *19* sicherstellen, gewährleisten, dafür sorgen; *31T* darauf achten
to **surf the internet** *24* im Internet surfen
surfboard *51T* Surfbrett
surplus *133* überschüssig
surprised *10T* überrascht, erstaunt
to **surround sth** *66T* etw umgeben
surroundings *pl* *64* Umgebung
survey *8* Umfrage
suspicion *77* Verdacht
sustainability *46T* Nachhaltigkeit

sustainable *77* nachhaltig
to **swap** *127P* tauschen
to **swear** *99* schwören
sweet corn *78* Zuckermais, Süßmais
to **swipe a card** *45* eine Karte durchziehen
to **switch sth off** *72T* etw ausschalten, etw abschalten
swivel chair *22T* Drehstuhl

T
table, bar ~ *68T* Stehtisch; **folding ~** *72* Klapptisch
to **tackle sth** *35T* etw angehen, etw in Angriff nehmen
tag *38* Etikett; **name ~** *55T* Namensschild; **price ~** *32* Preisschild, Preisetikett
tailor-made (to sth) *110* individuell (auf etw) zugeschnitten
to **take: ~ sb on** *125* jdn einstellen, jdn übernehmen; **~ place** *33* stattfinden; **~ sth seriously** *26T* etw ernst nehmen
taking in charge *105* Übernahme
talk *38* Vortrag
tanker *39T* Tankwagen
target *15* Ziel; **~ group** *45* Zielgruppe
to **target sb** *15* jdn ins Visier nehmen
targeted advertising *50* gezielte/zielgruppengenaue Werbung
tasting, wine-~ *42T* Weinprobe
tattoo *9* Tätowierung
tax *23* Steuer(n); **import ~** *93* Einfuhrzoll; **VAT (value added ~)** *32* MwSt (Mehrwertsteuer); **~ declaration** *110* Steuererklärung; **~-refundable** *110* steuerlich absetzbar
teapot *117* Teekanne
technically speaking *24* genau genommen
technician *20* Techniker/in
technology *37* Technik, Technologie
television *65T* Fernsehen; **~ channel** *65T* Fernsehsender
template *88* Vorlage
temporary *50* vorübergehend, vorläufig
tenant *111T* Mieter
to **tend to do sth** *43* dazu neigen, etw zu tun
tent *89* Zelt
term *39T* Begriff; **long-~** *11* langfristig; **short-~** *24* kurzfristig
terminal *80* Terminal
terms *pl* *19* (Vertrags-)Bedingungen; **~ and conditions** *pl* *77T* Allgemeine Geschäftsbedingungen; **~ of business** *59* Konditionen; **~ of delivery** *76* Lieferbedingungen; **~ of insurance** *80* Versicherungsbedinungen; **~ of payment** *61P* Zahlungsbedingungen
territory *43* Gebiet, Territorium
test flight *24* Testflug
testimonial *50* Erfahrungsbericht
text (message) *8T* SMS
to **text sb** *8T* jdm eine SMS schicken
textiles *pl* *89* Textilien
theoretical *7* theoretisch, Theorie-
therefore *48* daher, folglich
therefore *59* daher, folglich
thermal insulation *111T* Wärmedämmung
to **think: Come to ~ of it ...** *8T* Wenn ich es mir recht/genau überlege ...
thorough *23* gründlich
thoroughly, to **agree ~ with sb** *56T* voll und ganz einer Meinung mit jdm sein
though, even ~ *7* auch wenn
thought *46T* Gedanke(n); to **put a lot of ~ into sth** *46T* intensiv über etw nachdenken
three-piece *78* dreiteilig
throughout ... *7* in ganz ...
to **throw sth away** *51T* etw wegwerfen
thus *110* auf diese Weise, so
tidy, neat and ~ *15T* sauber und ordentlich
tie *9* Krawatte
to **tie up sth** *35* etw binden
tight *36* gespannt, angespannt
tile, floor ~s *pl* *81* Bodenfliesen
timber *61P* (Bau-)Holz
time, in (good) ~ *19* rechtzeitig; **just in ~** *35T* gerade rechtzeitig; **on ~** *19T* pünktlich; **for the ~ being** *95T* einstweilen, fürs Erste; **one at a ~** *35T* eins nach dem anderen; **part-~** *11* Teilzeit; to **take ~ off (work)** *10T* sich frei nehmen; **~ of day** *52* Tageszeit; **core ~** *58P* Kernzeit; **transit ~** *92* Laufzeit; **~ savings** *pl* *110* Zeitersparnis
to **time sth** *110* etw zeitlich abstimmen
timeline *24* Zeitachse, Zeitschiene
times *32* mal
timetable *62* Fahrplan
tiny *38* winzig
title *31* Titel, Überschrift; **document of ~** *83* Dispositionspapier, Traditionspapier; **job ~** *125* Stellenbezeichnung; **~ to the goods** *83* Eigentum(srecht) an den Waren
ton *61P* Tonne
tone *51* Farbton
tool *26T* Werkzeug, Instrument; **inspection ~** *38* Prüfwerkzeug
toothpaste *49* Zahncreme
top *9* Oberteil
total, sub-~ *95* Zwischensumme; **~ price** *96T* Gesamtpreis
tote bag *67* Tragetasche
touch, to **be/get in ~** *95T* sich melden; to **get in ~ with sb** *118T* sich bei jdm melden, sich mit jdm in Verbindung setzen
tour *27* Rundgang; **guided ~** *26* Führung
tourist board *129* Fremdenverkehrsamt
towel *75T* Handtuch
toy *33* Spielzeug
to **track** *19T* verfolgen; **~ sth** *36* etw nachverfolgen
trade *40* Gewerbe, Branche; *42* Handel; **foreign ~** *6T* Außenhandel; **~ discount** *102* Händlerrabatt; **~ fair** *17T* Fachmesse, Branchenmesse; **~ industry** *128* Handelsbranche; **~ magazine** *85* Fachzeitschrift; **~ show** *67* Fachmesse; **~ union** *77* Gewerkschaft
trader *43* Händler/in; **sole ~** *24* Einzelunternehmer/in
trading: ~ company *42* Handelsunternehmen; **~ partner** *72* Handelspartner/in
traditional *39T* traditionell, herkömmlich; *46T* hergebracht
traffic *47* Verkehr
to **train** *7* eine Ausbildung machen; **~ to be a ...** *6* eine Aubildung zum/zur ... machen
train service *25* Zugbetrieb
trainee *6* Auszubildende/r, Lehrling
traineeship *126T* Ausbildung, Lehre
trainer *8* Ausbilder/in
trainers *pl* *9* Turnschuhe, Sportschuhe
training, individual ~ *110* individuelle Weiterbildung, Einzelschulung; **vocational ~** *7* Berufsausbildung; **~ company** *6* Ausbildungsbetrieb; **~ course** *6* Ausbildung; **~ supervisor** *12* Ausbildungsleiter/in
transaction *23* Geschäft, Vorgang, Transaktion; **documentary credit ~** *103* Akkreditivgeschäft; **overseas ~s** *pl* *23* Auslandsgeschäft
transcript *121* Mitschrift
to **transfer sth** *95* etw übertragen
transferable *103* übertragbar
to **transform sth** *35* etw grundlegend verändern
transformation *64* (grundlegende) Veränderung, Wandel
transit, in ~ *91T* beim Transport; **insurance in ~** *80* Transportversicherung; **~ time** *92* Laufzeit
transparency *29* (Overhead-)Folie, Dia

transport, mode of ~ *80* Beförderungsart, Verkehrsmittel; **sea ~** *93* Seetransport; **~ infrastructure** *28T* Verkehrsnetz
transportation *36* Beförderung, Transport
transshipment *105* Umladung
travel expenses *pl* *56T* Reisekosten, Reisespesen
traveller *52* Passagier, Fahrgast
to **treat sb** *77* jdn behandeln
trial, by ~ and error *38* durch Ausprobieren; **~ order** *85* Probebestellung
trip, business ~ *8* Geschäftsreise
triple *46T* dreifach
Trojan *15* Trojaner
to **troubleshoot** *79T* Fehler suchen, Fehler beheben
trouser suit *9* Hosenanzug
truck *35T* Lastwagen; **~ waybill** *103* Lastwagenfrachtbrief
to **trust** *100* hoffen(, dass)
try, to **give it a ~** *106T* es versuchen
tuition fees *pl* *11* Studiengebühren
to **turn: ~ sth into sth** *26T* etw zu etw machen, etw in etw umwandeln; **~ one's back on sb** *29* jdm den Rücken zuwenden
turn, to **be one's ~** *19* an der Reihe sein; to **take it in ~s to do sth** *31T* etw abwechselnd tun; to **take equal ~s with sb** *31* sich mit jdm ausgewogen abwechseln
turnover *28* Umsatz
two-vessel brewhouse *105* Zweigerätesudhaus
to **type in sth** *118T* etw eingeben, etw eintippen
typically *43* normalerweise

U

unable, to **be ~ to do sth** *56* etw nicht tun können
unaffected, to **be ~** *91T* (von etw) nicht betroffen sein, (von etw) nicht beeinträchtigt werden
unavailable, to **be ~** *20T* *(Telefon:)* nicht zu sprechen sein
unconditional(ly) *99* vorbehaltlos, uneingeschränkt
unconventional *50* unkonventionell
to **undercut sb** *24* jdn unterbieten
underscore *40* Unterstrich
uneven *35* ungleichmäßig
unevenness *36* Ungleichmäßigkeit
uniform *9* Dienstkleidung, Uniform
uninviting *15T* wenig einladend
union *52* Gewerkschaft; **trade ~** *77* Gewerkschaft
unique *50* einzigartig; **~ selling proposition (USP)** *46* Alleinstellungsmerkmal
unit *52P* Einheit, Stück; **per ~** *72T* pro Stück; **~ price** *94* Stückpreis; **~ weight** *35* Stückgewicht
unknown *24* unbekannt
unless otherwise stated *99* sofern nicht anders angegeben
unlimited *24* unbeschränkt, unbegrenzt
to **unload** *58* entladen
unloading *34* Entladung, Löschen
unmanageable *35* unkontrollierbar
unnecessary *36* unnötig
to **unpack** *133* auspacken
unpaid *81* unbezahlt
unreliable *35* unzuverlässig
unsatisfactory *116* unzulänglich
unskilled worker *38* Hilfsarbeiter/in, ungelernte Arbeitskraft
unusual *51T* ungewöhnlich
up, to **be ~ and running** *79T* in (laufendem) Betrieb sein
up to date, to **be ~ with sth** *15* bei etw auf dem neuesten Stand sein
up-to-date *66* aktuell, auf dem neuesten Stand
update *23* Aktualisierung, Änderung; **~ (on sth)** *40* aktuelle Informationen (zu etw), aktueller Überblick (über etw); **day-to-day ~** *51T* täglicher aktueller Bericht
to **update** *45* aktualisieren
to **upload** *11* hochladen
upstairs *27* (nach) oben
urgent(ly) *20T* dringend
use, to **put sth to good ~** *127T* etw sinnvoll nutzen
utility *48* Versorgungsbetrieb

V

vacancy *127P* offene Stelle
vacation *AE* *10T* Ferien, Urlaub
valid *101T* gültig
validation *105* Bestätigung
validity *101* Gültigkeit
valuables *pl* *68T* Wertsachen
value *32* Wert; **~ for money** *77T* (preis)günstig; **invoice ~** *105* Rechnungswert; to **add ~ (to sth)** *32* Wert schöpfen, den Wert (von etw) steigern; **VAT (~ added tax)** *32* MwSt (Mehrwertsteuer)
varied *122T* vielfältig
variety (of) *41* Vielzahl, Vielfalt, verschiedene
various *114* mehrere
to **vary** *11* variieren, sich unterscheiden
VAT (value added tax) *32* MwSt (Mehrwertsteuer)
vegetable *49* Gemüse
vehicle *39T* Fahrzeug
vendor *77T* Anbieter, Verkäufer
venture, business ~ *24* Unternehmen, Geschäftsvorhaben
venue *40* Veranstaltungsort
vessel *49* Schiff; **two-~ brewhouse** *105* Zweigerätesudhaus
via *92* per, mittels, über
view *13* Aussicht, Blick; **~ (of sb/sth)** *72* Auffassung, Bild (von jdm/einer Sache); **in ~ of sth** *59* angesichts von etw; **point of ~** *9* Sicht, Perspektive
viewer *47* Zuschauer/in, Betrachter/in
virtual *46T* virtuell
visible *9* sichtbar
visual *25* visuell; *35* optisch; **~ aids** *pl* *29* visuelle Hilfsmittel; **~ inspection** *133* Sichtprüfung
visualization *68* Visualisierung
to **visualize sth** *36* etw veranschaulichen, etw visualisieren
visuals *pl* *29* visuelle Hilfsmittel
vocational: ~ college *7* Berufsschule, Berufsfachschule; **~ school** *6* Berufsschule; **~ training** *7* Berufsausbildung
voicemail *20* Mailbox
volume of sales *53T* Umsatzvolumen
voluntary *115* freiwillig
voucher *87* Gutschein
voyage *24* Reise, Fahrt

W

wage, low-~ country *32* Niedriglohnland; **collective ~ bargaining** *77* Tarifverhandlungen
wagon, closed ~ *94* geschlossener Waggon
to **wait:** to **keep sb ~ing** *13* jdn warten lassen
waiting staff *70* Servierkräfte
wall panel *68* Wandplatte
war *105* Krieg
warehouse *34* Lager; **~ manager** *55* Lagerleiter/in
warehousing *33* Lagerhaltung, Lagerung
warmth *15T* Wärme
to **warn sb** *106T* jdm (etw) sagen, jdn vorwarnen
warranty *77T* Gewährleistung; **~ period** *115* Gewährleistungszeit
wash *32* Wäsche, Waschgang
washing powder *49* Waschpulver
to **waste** *34* verschwenden, vergeuden
waste *36* Verschwendung; **~ water** *31T* Abwasser

wasteful *35* verschwenderisch, unwirtschaftlich
water, sparkling ~ *70* Sprudelwasser; **waste ~** *31T* Abwasser
waterproof *89* wasserdicht
waterway *51* Wasserstraße
way, along the ~ *32* unterwegs; **by the ~** *10T* übrigens; **one ~ or another** *106T* so oder so; **this ~** *26T* hier entlang; to **go a long ~ in sth** *86* viel zu etw beitragen, viel für etw tun
waybill, air ~ *82* Luftfrachtbrief; **truck ~** *103* Lastwagenfrachtbrief
weakness *77T* Schwäche
wealth, personal ~ *24* Privatvermögen
weight, gross ~ *35* Bruttogewicht; **unit ~** *35* Stückgewicht
welcome, You're ~. *8T* Bitte (sehr). Gern geschehen.
welcoming *66T* einladend
welding machine *28* Schweißmaschine
well-established *46T* bewährt, fest etabliert
well-stocked *74* gut sortiert
whatever the case may be *114* wie dem auch sei
wheelchair *75T* Rollstuhl
while stocks last *117* solange der Vorrat reicht
white-collar workers *pl* *53* Angestellte
to **wholesale** *80* en gros handeln
wholesale *6T* Großhandel; **management assistant in ~ and foreign trade** *6T* Kaufmann/-frau im Groß- und Außenhandel
wholesaler *43* Großhändler
wide range *26T* großes Angebot, breite Palette
willing, to **be ~ to do sth** *48* bereit sein, etw zu tun
windproof *89* winddicht
wine, sparkling ~ *42* Schaumwein; **~ cellar** *42T* Weinkeller; **~ list** *70* Weinkarte; **~-tasting** *42T* Weinprobe
winner *10T* Sieger/in
wish, Best ~es *41* *(Brief:)* Mit freundlichen Grüßen
wooden *38* Holz-, aus Holz; **~ crate** *106T* Holzkiste; **~ furniture** *47* Holzmöbel
wording *59* Formulierung
work, shift ~ *8* Schichtarbeit; **~ in progress** *35* unfertige Erzeugnisse; **~ and costs** *99* Arbeit und Kosten; to **get on with one's ~** *15T* seine Arbeit machen; **~ experience** *18* Praktikum; **~ pace** *110* Arbeitstempo; **~ placement** *BE* *14* Praktikum; **~ schedule** *110* Arbeitsablauf
to **work: ~ alongside sb** *26T* mit jdm arbeiten; **~ sth out** *16* etw berechnen, etw ausrechnen
worker, blue-collar ~s *pl* *53* Arbeiter/innen; **unskilled ~** *38* Hilfsarbeiter/in, ungelernte Arbeitskraft; **white-collar ~s** *pl* *53* Angestellte
workforce *28T* Belegschaft, Arbeitskräfte
working: ~ conditions *pl* *6* Arbeitsbedingungen; **~ hours** *pl* *8* Arbeitszeit(en)
workplace *9* Arbeitsplatz
works council *26* Betriebsrat
workshop *30* Werkstatt
worktop *31T* Arbeitsplatte
workwear *132* Arbeitskleidung
to **worry** *62T* sich Sorgen machen; **Don't ~.** *62T* Keine Sorge.
worst-case scenario *59* schlimmster anzunehmender Fall
worth *24* wert
to **wrap sth up** *56T* etw abschließen, etw zum Abschluss bringen
writing, in ~ *8T* schriftlich, in Schriftform; **~ implement** *86* Schreibgerät
written *99* schriftlich; **~ correspondence** *23* Schriftverkehr

XYZ
X-ray machine *120* Röntgengerät
year, financial ~ *53T* Geschäftsjahr
You're welcome. *8T* Bitte (sehr). Gern geschehen.
Yours faithfully *41* *(Brief:)* ... und verbleiben mit freundlichen Grüßen
Yours sincerely *41* *(Brief:)* Mit freundlichen Grüßen
zip *32* Reißverschluss

Basic industry vocabulary (German–English)

Firmenorganisation – Company organization

Aktiengesellschaft (AG)	public limited company (plc) *BE*; open corporation *AE*
Aktie	share
Aktionär/in, Teilhaber/in	shareholder
Einzelunternehmer/in	sole proprietor/trader
Gesellschaft mit beschränkter Haftung (GmbH)	limited company (Ltd) *BE*; closed corporation *AE*
Kommanditgesellschaft (KG)	limited partnership
Personengesellschaft, offene Handelsgesellschaft (OHG)	(general) partnership

Firmenabteilungen – Company departments

Buchhaltung	Accounts (department)
Einkauf(sabteilung)	Purchasing (department)
Forschung(s-) und Entwicklung(sabteilung)	Research and Development (department, R&D)
Geschäftsführung, Vorstand	board (of directors)
Lager(halle)	warehouse
Marktforschung(sabteilung)	Market Research (department)
Personal(abteilung)	Human Resources (department, HR)
Rechnungswesen	Finance (department)
Rechtswesen	Legal department
Rezeption, Empfang	reception
Verkauf(sabteilung), Vertrieb	Sales (department)
Vertrieb	Distribution (department)
Verwaltung	administration
Zentrale	head office, headquarters

Mitarbeiter/innen – Members of staff

Abteilungsleiter/in	head of department
Arbeitgeber/in, Unternehmer/in	employer
Arbeitnehmer/in, Beschäftigte/r	employee
Arbeitsplatz	workplace
Ausbildung	training
Buchhalter/in	accountant
Empfangsmitarbeiter/in	receptionist
Gehalt	salary
Geschäftsführer/in	managing director (MD), chief executive officer (CEO)
Groß- und Außenhandelskaufmann/-frau	management assistant in wholesale and foreign trade
Handelsvertreter/in	sales representative
Industriekaufmann/-frau	industrial management assistant
Kollege, Kollegin	colleague
Lehre	apprenticeship
Manager/in	manager
Personal	staff
Persönliche/r Assistent/in	personal assistant (PA)
Qualifikation, Abschluss	qualification
Sekretär/in	secretary

Bürotätigkeiten – Office activities

etw ausrichten	to take a message
Berichte schreiben	to write reports
Briefe beantworten	to reply to letters
Mitteilungen, Vermerke, Notizen	to write memos
ein Telefongespräch annehmen	to answer the telephone
Textverarbeitung	word processing
Überstunden machen	to work overtime
Unterlagen, Schriftstücke	paperwork
etw weiterleiten	to forward sth

Geschäftsbriefe – Commercial correspondence

Absatz	paragraph
Absender	sender
Adresse	address
anhängen (*E-Mail*)	to attach sth
Anhang (*E-Mail*)	attachment
Anlage(n)	enclosure (enc)
Anrede	salutation
Antwort	reply
beifügen (*Brief*)	to enclose
Betreff(zeile)	subject (line)
Briefkopf	letterhead
Datum	date
Einschreiben	registered mail/post
Empfänger/in	addressee
Entschuldigungsschreiben	letter of apology
Mit den besten Wünschen	Best wishes
Mit freundlichen Grüßen	Yours faithfully
Mit freundlichen Grüßen	Yours sincerely
Mit freundlichen Grüßen, Viele Grüße	Best wishes, Regards
Mit herzlichen Grüßen	Best wishes, Cordially *AE*
Schlussformel	complimentary close
Unterschrift	signature
Zeichen	reference (ref)
zu Händen	attention (attn)

Besprechungen/Präsentationen – Meetings/ presentations

Abwesenheit	absence
Bericht	report
Einladung	invitation
Liniendiagramm	line chart
Protokoll	minutes *pl*
eine Rede halten	to make a speech
Säulendiagramm	bar chart
die Sitzung leiten	to take the chair / to be in the chair
stattfinden	take place
Tagesordnung	agenda
Tagesordnungspunkt	item on the agenda
teilnehmen	to participate
Teilnehmer/in	participant
Termin	date
Tortendiagramm	pie chart
Verschiedenes	any other business (AOB)
Vortrag	talk; lecture
vortragen	to report; to state
X-Achse	x-axis
Y-Achse	y-axis

Dienstreisen – Business trips

absagen	to cancel
Anforderung	requirement
Anschlussflug	connecting flight
Ausstellung	exhibition
etw besuchen, an etw teilnehmen	to attend sth
Bitte, Anfrage	request
einfacher Flug	one-way flight
Hin- und Rückflug	return flight
Messe	(trade) fair
Passagier/in	passenger
Reservierung, Buchung	reservation
stornieren	to cancel
Termin	appointment
Unterkunft	accommodation
verschieben	to postpone

Geschäftspartner und Händler – Business partners and traders

Einzelhändler/in	retailer
Exporteur	exporter
Großhändler	wholesaler
Importeur	importer
Käufer/in	buyer
Klient/in	client
Konkurrent/in, Konkurrenz	competitor
Konkurrenz	competition
Kunde, Kundin	customer, client
Lieferant	supplier
Spediteur	carrier; forwarding agent; freight forwarder
Verkäufer/in	seller

Geschäftsvorgänge – Business transactions

Anfrage	enquiry
Angebot, Kostenvoranschlag	quotation
Auftrag, Bestellung	order
einen Auftrag erteilen	to place an order
einen Auftrag erledigen	to fill an order
Auftragsbestätigung	acknowledgement/ confirmation (of an order)
einen Auftrag bestätigen	to acknowledge an order
Bestellformular	order form
Bestellnummer	order number
Erhalt, (Waren-)Eingang	receipt (of goods)
Folgeauftrag	repeat order
Lieferbedingungen	terms of delivery *pl*
liefern	to deliver
Lieferung	delivery
Muster	sample
Probeauftrag	trial order
Reklamation, Beschwerde	complaint
eine Reklamation bearbeiten/regulieren	to adjust a complaint
Sendung	consignment
Umsatz	turnover
Verkäufe, Umsatz	sales *pl*
Versandanzeige, Versandmitteilung	advice of dispatch
Versandpapiere	shipping documents *pl*
versenden	to ship
versenden, absenden	to dispatch
Vertrag	contract
Ware(n), (Lager-)Bestand	stock
Zahlungsanzeige	advice of payment
Zahlungsbedingungen	terms of payment *pl*

Zahlung – Payment

Dokumente gegen Akzept	documents against acceptance
Dokumente gegen Zahlung	documents against payment
Dokumentenakkreditiv	documentary letter of credit
fällig, ausstehend	overdue
Konto, Kreditkonto	account
letzte Mahnung	final demand
Mahnung	reminder
MwSt = Mehrwertsteuer	VAT = value added tax
Nicht(be)zahlung	non-payment
Rabatt, Nachlass	discount
Rate	instalment
Rechnung	bill, invoice
Skonto, Barzahlungsrabatt	cash discount
überweisen	to remit, to transfer
Überweisung, Zahlung	bank transfer, remittance
Vorauszahlung, Vorkasse	cash in advance
Wechsel	bill of exchange
zahlbar bei Lieferung, per Nachnahme	cash on delivery (COD)

Irregular verbs

be – was/were – been	sein
become – became – become	werden
begin – began – begun	anfangen, beginnen
break – broke – broken	brechen
bring – brought – brought	bringen
build – built – built	bauen
burn – burnt/burned – burnt/burned	(ver)brennen
buy – bought – bought	kaufen
catch – caught – caught	fangen
choose – chose – chosen	wählen
come – came – come	kommen
cost – cost – cost	kosten
cut – cut – cut	schneiden
do – did – done	tun, machen, erledigen
draw – drew – drawn	zeichnen
dream – dreamt – dreamt	träumen
drink – drank – drunk	trinken
drive – drove – driven	fahren
eat – ate – eaten	essen
fall – fell – fallen	fallen
feed – fed – fed	füttern, ernähren
feel – felt – felt	(sich) fühlen, empfinden
fight – fought – fought	kämpfen
find – found – found	finden
fit – fit/fitted – fit/fitted	passen
fly – flew – flown	fliegen
forget – forgot – forgotten	vergessen
get – got – got (*AE* gotten)	bekommen, erhalten
give – gave – given	geben
go – went – gone	gehen, fahren
grow – grew – grown	wachsen
hang – hung – hung	hängen
have – had – had	haben
hear – heard – heard	hören
hide – hid – hidden	(sich) verstecken
hit – hit – hit	schlagen, aufprallen auf
hold – held – held	halten, festhalten
keep – kept – kept	behalten
know – knew – known	kennen, wissen
lay – laid – laid	legen
lead – led – led	führen, leiten
learn – learnt/learned – learnt/learned	lernen
leave – left – left	abfahren, verlassen, weggehen
let – let – let	lassen
lose – lost – lost	verlieren
make – made – made	machen
mean – meant – meant	meinen, bedeuten
meet – met – met	treffen
pay – paid – paid	bezahlen
put – put – put	setzen, stellen, legen
read – read – read	lesen
ride – rode – ridden	reiten, fahren
ring – rang – rung	klingeln, anrufen
rise – rose – risen	(an)steigen
run – ran – run	laufen, rennen
say – said – said	sagen
see – saw – seen	sehen
sell – sold – sold	verkaufen
send – sent – sent	senden, schicken
shake – shook – shaken	schütteln
set – set – set	setzen, stellen
show – showed – shown	zeigen
shut – shut – shut	schließen
sing – sang – sung	singen
sit – sat – sat	sitzen
sleep – slept – slept	schlafen
smell – smelt/smelled – smelt/smelled	riechen
speak – spoke – spoken	sprechen
spell – spelt/spelled – spelt/spelled	buchstabieren
spend – spent – spent	ausgeben, verbringen
stand – stood – stood	stehen
steal – stole – stolen	stehlen
swim – swam – swum	schwimmen
take – took – taken	nehmen
teach – taught – taught	unterrichten, beibringen
tear – tore – torn	(zer)reißen
tell – told – told	sagen, erzählen
think – thought – thought	denken
throw – threw – thrown	werfen
understand – understood – understood	verstehen
wake – woke – woken	wecken
wear – wore – worn	tragen (Kleidung)
win – won – won	gewinnen
write – wrote – written	schreiben